UMI ANNUAL COMMENTARY

PRECEPTS FOR LIVING®

MISSION STATEMENT

*W*e are called
of God to create, produce, and distribute
quality Christian education products;
to deliver exemplary customer service;
and to provide quality Christian
educational services, which will empower
God's people, especially within the Black
community, to evangelize, disciple,
and equip people for serving Christ,
His kingdom, and church.

Urban Ministries, Inc.
*The African American Christian Publishing
& Communications Co.*

UMI ANNUAL SUNDAY SCHOOL LESSON COMMENTARY
PRECEPTS FOR LIVING® 2016–2017
INTERNATIONAL SUNDAY SCHOOL LESSONS
VOLUME 19
UMI (URBAN MINISTRIES, INC.)

Melvin Banks Sr., Litt.D., Founder and Chairman

C. Jeffrey Wright, J.D., CEO

La Verne Tolbert, Ph.D., Vice President of Editorial

Bible art: Fred Carter

Cover art: Copyright © Edwin Lester 2016 All Rights Reserved.

Item No.: 1-2012. ISBN-13: 978-1-60997-438-1. ISBN-10: 1-60997-438-7.

PFL Large Print Item No.:1-2612. ISBN-13: 978-1-60997-352-0, ISBN-10: 1-60997-352-6

Publisher: UMI (Urban Ministries, Inc.), Chicago, IL 60643. To place an order, call us at 1-800-860-8642, or visit our website at www.urbanministries.com.

Get the Precepts for Living® eBook!

Are you among those joining the digital revolution by reading books using a Kindle, iPad, NOOK, or other electronic readers? If so, there's good news for you! UMI is keeping up with the latest technology by publishing its annual Sunday School commentary, *Precepts for Living*®, in the leading eBook formats: Kindle (Amazon), NOOK (Barnes & Noble), and iBooks (Apple).

To buy an eBook copy of *Precepts for Living*®, visit our website at preceptsforlivingonline.com to find download links and step-by-step instructions.

If you've purchased *Precepts for Living*® for your e-reader, be sure to leave a rating and a review at the iTunes, B&N, or Amazon store sites to tell others what you think. Also, spread the word on your favorite social networking sites, and follow *Precepts for Living*® on Facebook and Twitter (with the handle @precepts4living).

CONTRIBUTORS

Editor

A. Okechukwu Ogbonnaya, Ph.D.

Developmental Editor

Ramon Mayo, M.A.

Copy Editors

Beth Potterveld, M.A.
Benton Sartore
William McGee

Cover Art

Edwin Lester

Design Layout

Kimberly Applewhite, B.A.

Bible Illustrations

Fred Carter

Contributing Writers

Essays/In Focus Stories
Darryl Aaron, D.Min.
Evangeline Carey, M.A.
Darryl Hairston, D.Min.
Jennifer King, M.A.
Michael Roussell, D.Min.
Virginia Stiths, M.Div.
Frederick Thomas, B.S.
Ricky Woods, D.Min.

Bible Study Guide Writers
John Burton, M.Div.
Connie Calloway, Ph.D.
Verna Cole, Ph.D.
Jean V. Garrison, M.A.
Kimberly Gillespie, M.Div.
Alisha Gordon, M.Div.
Charlesetta Watson Holmes, M.Div.
Wayne Hopkins, M.Div.
Victoria Saunders Johnson
Constance Jones, M.A.
Angela Lampkin, M.S.
Erwin Lee, M.Div.
Avril Logan M.A.
Beverly Moore M.A.
CaResse Rials M.Div.
Amy Rognlie
Suzanne Sang M.Div.
Elizabeth Simington
Wan Smith M.Div.
Maisie Sparks
Faith Waters M.Div.
Karen Wolfe M.A.

More Light on the Text
J. Adewuya Ph.D.
Judy Hull Ph.D.
Kevin Hrebik Ph.D.
Vanessa Lovelace Ph.D.
Harvey Kwiyani Ph.D.
Kelly Whitcomb Ph.D.

Dear Precepts Customer,

It is our privilege to present the 2016–2017 *Precepts For Living®* commentary. As you encounter God's Word through these lessons, we anticipate that you will find this resource to be indispensable.

Precepts For Living® comes to you in three versions: the Personal Study Guide (the workbook), the online version, and a large print edition. You will also notice that the biblical text for each lesson includes the New Living Translation in addition to the King James Version. This contemporary translation will enhance your textual understanding when you compare it side by side to the classic English translation. It is very helpful in illuminating your understanding of the text.

Precepts For Living® is designed to be a witness through our learning and sharing more of the Bible. Our intent is to facilitate innovative ways for pursuing a deeper understanding and practice of God's Word. One of the ways we strive to do this is by highlighting the larger narrative of God's work in salvation as a key part of understanding each biblical passage. We believe it is important to help you understand not only the particulars of the text but also the broad extent of God's revelation to us as well. This panoramic approach enhances our ability to witness to others about the saving power of Jesus Christ.

This year we explore the themes of God's sovereignty, creation, love, and call. Each year of Bible study offers great potential for a more intimate and transformative walk with God.

We want to continually refine *Precepts For Living®* as we endeavor to meet our customers' needs. We are always looking for ways to enhance your study of the Bible, and your comments and feedback are vital in helping us. If you have questions or suggestions, we encourage you to please e-mail us at precepts@urbanministries.com or mail your comments to UMI, *Precepts For Living®*, PO Box 436987, Chicago, IL 60643-6987.

May God draw you closer to the fullness of life with Him through this book.

God's blessings to you,

A. Okechukwu Ogbonnaya, Ph.D.

A. Okechukwu Ogbonnaya, Ph.D.
Editor

Uncovering the Benefits of Precepts

It is a great privilege to participate in Christian education and play a significant role in the spiritual formation of fellow Christians in our churches. *Precepts for Living®* is a resource that is designed to help you lead others toward greater knowledge and practice of following Jesus Christ. To that end, please take full advantage of the substantive offerings provided to you in this year's commentary. From the standpoint of your vocation as a teacher, it is very important to be aware of the great responsibility that goes along with your position. James 3:1 reminds us that we have such an important opportunity in front of us that we run the risk of greater judgment if we are derelict in our duties. This is a strong word that helps us understand the great influence we have when we help our students learn about God's Word.

Being a teacher means participating in one of the church's greatest tasks, one that the ancient church called "catechesis." While this word is often associated with particular denominations and with a form of teaching that relies upon a systematic question-and-answer format, the central meaning of the word is teaching. It carries with it the idea of imparting the entirety of the faith to Christians. While many might not be familiar with this word, the truth is that every time we help others learn about God's Word and ways, we are participating in this great task of the church that has been with us from the beginning. Our participation in catechesis is central to the life of the church. As a teacher, you have an opportunity to energize or revitalize this aspect of your church's ministry. Reflect on how you have prepared for the challenge.

What is the goal when you use *Precepts for Living®* to open up the riches of the Bible to your students? It is beyond the mere acquisition of "spiritual data." Certainly we want our students to grow in knowledge, but the knowledge we seek to pass on does not solely comprise Bible facts but includes a larger sense of transformation where the information and doctrine conveyed is oriented toward a faithful life of discipleship. It is very important that we enable our students to deepen their devotion to God and encourage them to better embody that devotion in a way that makes their lives a living witness to the world. Our hope from every lesson should be to inspire students to become the best living examples of the Scriptures with the understanding that their lives may be the only Bible some people ever read.

To best take advantage of this commentary and enhance the classroom experience, utilize the essays highlighting notable African Americans to emphasize quarterly themes.

The People, Places, and Times; Background; In Depth; and More Light on the Text sections are there to help you provide insight and understanding of the text. But the sections include more than a simple compilation of information. In each lesson, you will also see In Focus stories and Lesson in Our Society and Make It Happen sections serving as catalysts for applying the biblical text to life situations.

We believe this commentary is a great tool to help form fully devoted followers of Christ, and we invite you to wholeheartedly partake in all of the resources provided here. May God be glorified as you play your part in this great task of the church!

Creative Teaching

- **Energizing the Class.** Teacher enthusiasm energizes every classroom. The instructor who is excited about the lesson and who is well-prepared inspires students to learn. Engage the class with media such as videos and music. Also, allow students time to meet and greet one another. Invite them to share a brief testimony about their week.

- **Two Teachers in One Class— Team-teaching is fun! As teachers study and prepare together, iron sharpens iron for creative lessons that never bore.** Encourage teachers to study together, and then divide the segments of the lesson. Perhaps one will teach the introduction while the other teaches a section of the text. Encourage them to also become a true team with each contributing throughout the lesson.

- **Remember.** Everyone cannot read or write on the same level. Use different teaching techniques and styles when teaching. How you learn affects how you teach, so be open and willing to learn and teach through various media.

- **Avoid Study in Isolation.** People often "get it" when they are involved with more than talking about the lesson. Why not allow the class to see the connections themselves? Try using a chart to have adult students work in pairs or groups to compare and contrast Bible persons such as David and Solomon or Ruth and Orpah, Naomi's daughters-in-law. To help the students get started, suggest specific categories for comparisons such as lifestyles, families, or public ministry. As class members search the Scriptures, they will learn and remember much more than if you told them about either person.

- **Group Studies.** Have the class form groups, and have each group read the Scripture lesson and a section of the Background for the text. Have each group create a two-minute skit about the Scripture to share with the class. Encourage the groups to use their imaginations and energy. You may want to have at least one "leader" in a group if you have more than two or three reserved people in your class.

- **Volunteers.** Many classes begin with reading the lesson. When class members have studied, this activity is more "bringing minds" together than about the actual lesson. Still, some classes can benefit from dramatic and creative reading of Bible passages at any point in the lesson. When the passage under study lends itself, assign parts to volunteers. This need not be formal—standing up isn't even critical. This strategy works best in passages that have a story such as the conversation between Moses and his father-in-law, Jethro, or Paul confronting the merchants in Thessalonica. Assign one person to each speaking character in the Bible text. Feel free to be creative with giving the class roles as "the crowd." Make sure to assign a narrator who will read the nonspeaking parts. It is fun, it is fast, and it makes for memorable Bible reading.

- **Alternatives.** Select one or two persons from the class to read the Scripture lesson with enthusiasm and drama. Ask a few persons to develop a newspaper or magazine headline with a brief story that explains the headlines. Have another group write the headlines and a story that will be used in a cell phone video. (Let the class know that they should bring their cell phones—with video recording—so that most people can share in this activity.)

- **Materials.** You may want to have large sheets of paper, markers, glue or tape, newspapers, and magazines available on a weekly basis for the various activities.

• **Additional Methods.** Write the theme on a large poster board or sheet of paper, and ask each person to write a word or draw a picture that best describes the theme. Read the themes aloud, and discuss any of the pictures before you begin your class discussion or activities. If you have a very large class or time is limited, only select a few words and/or pictures for discussion. You can either lead the discussion or invite members of the class to do so.

• **Web sites.** Connect with us by logging on to urbanministries.com. E-mail us at precepts @urbanministries.com, and send us some of your favorite Teaching Tips for ages 18 and older that you want to share with others. If yours is selected, we will post them under our Teaching Tips sections for Precepts. If you have icebreaker activities, please submit them as well. Your submissions should be no longer than 125 words.

• **Closing.** At the end of the lesson, give your class the assignment of looking for scenes from films or television, advertisements, or parts of songs that either demonstrate the coming week's In Focus story, Lesson in Our Society section, or Make It Happen section. Encourage them to be creative and to come up with an explanation of how their contribution helps make the truth of the lesson come to life.

• **Prayer.** Have a Prayer Request Board for people to write their prayer requests on each Sunday. You may want to make this a weekly activity. Have someone read the prayer requests and let the class decide which prayer requests they will pray for during the week. One Sunday School teacher has his class write their prayer requests on sheets of paper and place them in the middle of the floor once a year. He then shares with the class that he will write them all down in a prayer journal that he keeps and prays over them at least once a week. Be creative and create your own prayer journal or prayer tradition(s) within your class.

Questions Related to the Heritage Profiles:

1. Why are some people chosen over others to be recognized for their achievements?

2. When reading the Heritage Profiles, what contemporary person comes to mind? A family member or friend can be a part of your decision.

3. Have you ever been recognized for a special achievement? How did you feel, and who have you lifted up to receive a special award in your church, community, or family? Why?

4. List three things you believe are important that someone else knows.

5. What similarities do you see between the historical figure and your life? If there are none, share ways the person's life may have made an impact on your life and on future generations.

6. List three characteristics that stand out about the Heritage Profiles that you think are either positive or negative. List three characteristics about your life that you believe are either positive or negative. Compare the lists and write a short paragraph about the similarities and/or differences.

Remember that creative teaching can maximize your students' learning experience.

TABLE OF CONTENTS

Fall Quarter 2016

THE SOVEREIGNTY OF GOD

LESSONS
Unit 1 • The Sovereignty of God
SEPTEMBER

Unit 2 • The Sovereignty of Jesus
OCTOBER

Unit 3 • Alpha and Omega
NOVEMBER

Winter Quarter 2016-2017

CREATION: A DIVINE CYCLE

LESSONS
Unit 1 • The Savior is Born
DECEMBER

Unit 2 • All Creation Praises God
JANUARY

Unit 3 • The Church is Born
FEBRUARY

2016–2019 Scope and Sequence—Cycle Spread

	FALL	WINTER	SPRING	SUMMER
YEAR ONE 2016–17	**GOD SOVEREIGNTY** Sovereignty of God Isaiah Matthew Hebrews Revelation	**CREATION** Creation: A Divine Cycle Psalms Luke Galatians	**LOVE** God Loves Us Psalms Joel Jonah John Romans Ephesians 1 John	**CALL** God's Urgent Call Exodus Judges Isaiah Jeremiah Ezekiel Amos Acts
YEAR TWO 2017–18	**COVENANT** Covenant with God Genesis Exodus Numbers 1 Samuel 2 Samuel Nehemiah Jeremiah Ezekiel 1 Corinthians Titus Hebrews	**FAITH** Faith in Action Daniel Matthew Acts Ephesians Colossians 1 Timothy James	**WORSHIP** Acknowledging God Genesis Exodus Leviticus 2 Chronicles Psalms Luke John 2 Corinthians Hebrews Revelation	**JUSTICE** Justice in the New Testament Matthew Luke Romans 2 Corinthians Colossians
YEAR THREE 2018–19	**CREATION** God's World and God's People Genesis	**LOVE** Our Love For God Exodus Deuteronomy Joshua Psalms Matthew Mark Luke Philippians 2 Thessalonians James 2 John	**CALL** Discipleship and Mission Matthew Luke Romans	**COVENANT** Covenant in God Ruth 1 Samuel Matthew Luke John Ephesians Hebrews Romans

The Anatomy of God's Call

Have you been "called into the ministry?" If so, the God of the universe has given you the unique privilege of being His hands and heart extended to serve the people He loves. To partner with Jesus Christ in winning a lost world is the most challenging, rewarding, substantial call in anyone's life.

It's important to note that all believers have been called. Peter says we are called "out of darkness into His marvelous light" (I Peter 2:9, KJV). We're called to a royal priesthood, which means that we function as priests who serve God and His people. There's also a specific call. It may be a call to the marketplace, or a call to the pulpit. It may be a call to the mission field overseas or to the mission field in the public schools. The call isn't confined to working in the church. We respond to the assignment that He has ordained for us no matter who we are or where we are.

How are we called? While some people attest to actually hearing an audible voice, most experience an inner tug of the spirit, a "knowing" in their heart that God is redirecting their lives. The way God's calls men and women into Christian service is as varied as the people whom He calls. Let's examine the anatomy of God's call in the life of Moses—a call centered on passion, purpose, plan, presence, and promotion.

As a Hebrew baby, Moses was spared the fate of infanticide by the Egyptian king when he was placed in a basket and sent down the river. Rescued by Pharaoh's daughter, he was raised in the king's palace as an Egyptian. However, it's apparent that Moses may have learned of his true ethnic identity from his mother who was summoned to be his nurse (Exodus 2:8).

As Moses grew and matured, so did his passion to pursue justice for his people.

And it came to pass in those days, when Moses was grown, that he went out unto his brethren, and looked on their burdens: and he spied an Egyptian smiting an Hebrew, one of his brethren. (Exodus 2:11, KJV)

Moses took justice into his own hands, killed the Egyptian, and escaped into the desert. While his response may seem to us to have been extreme, later on Moses' passion for justice and freedom helped him persist through a seemingly endless series of negotiations with Pharaoh.

In the anatomy of the call, God's purpose for Moses is revealed. When the cries and groans of the people "came up unto God by reason of the bondage" (Exodus 2:23), Moses would be God's instrument to free His people from Egyptian oppression. He sent Moses as His ambassador to tell Pharaoh, "Let my people go" (Exodus 5:1).

Purpose is probably best expressed by these lines from the movie *Chariots of Fire*. The character based on Olympic runner Eric Liddell says, "I believe God made me for a purpose, but he also made me fast. And when I run I feel His pleasure." Joy is the reward for doing what God has called us to do, whether it's sports, public speaking, writing, mentoring, gardening, drawing, singing, or managing a small business. God may also motivate us into His purpose through our own frustration with the injustice in our community. Dr. Martin Luther King, Jr. serves as a prime example.

With passion and purpose, Moses' desire would soon be fulfilled. But he had to wait for God's plan. Waiting is perhaps the most difficult part of responding to God's call. Moses was on the backside of the desert tending sheep for four decades. Likewise, it may take years for the vision that God placed in our hearts to fully manifest. Why does it take so long, we might ask? Why not sooner? The answer may be that time is God's ingredient for character formation. So "let us not be weary in well doing: for in due season we shall reap, if we faint not" (Galatians 6:9).

Even if we are passionate and realize God's purpose and plan for our lives, the call is incomplete without God's presence. Moses saw the burning bush and was amazed that the "bush was not consumed" (Exodus 3:2) so he drew near. The burning bush is symbolic of the on-going presence of the Holy Spirit in our lives inspiring us, encouraging us, propelling us forward. We have to be on the lookout for burning bushes and draw near to God.

Moses was commanded to take off his shoes. He was on holy ground. Humility and reverence are prerequisites for a listening ear that hears the call. Through his obedience, Moses acknowledged God and worshiped Him. Although God told Moses not to come any closer, Moses was, in fact, brought closer to God through this experience. God's call always brings us closer to Him and ushers us into sacred space. If the task doesn't draw us nearer, perhaps it's not a genuine call because ultimately, God's call is a call to Himself. The task is secondary. God calls us to worship and love Him first and foremost. And we will be guided in the task if we stay close to the Guide. Daily communion with God means listening to His voice as He speaks to us through His Word.

Finally, God's call involves promotion. Moses, once the prince in the palace, escaped to the desert and became a shepherd on the plains. This seemed to be a demotion but at the same time it was a promotion. It was there that God chose Moses to be His spokesperson, His hands extended, and He sent Moses back to the palace to speak to Pharaoh on His behalf. Moses' promotion was the culmination of all that he had learned and experienced. In the process of maturing, Moses cultivated a humble, listening heart that tempered—but did not diminish—his passion.

Of his humility the Bible says, "Now the man Moses was very meek, above all the men which were upon the face of the earth" (Numbers 12:3). Meekness or humility is not weakness. Like the powerful horse that is led about by the tiny bit in its mouth, meekness is strength under control. It's a willingness to go where God says "Go!" and do what God says do. Moses disregarded his position in Egypt to become a servant of the true King and his legacy is noted in the Hebrews Hall of Faith.

By faith Moses, when he was come to years, refused to be called the son of Pharaoh's daughter, choosing to suffer affliction with the people of God rather than enjoy the pleasures of sin for a season (Hebrews 11:24-25, KJV) .

Be careful not to view God's promotion through the world's lens. The value of the call is not measured by title or position. It's doing God's will, whether its parenting children in foster care, teaching Sunday School, helping the aged, visiting those who are in prison, or praying for the pastor.

Have you been called into ministry? As you evaluate your life, you may answer, "Yes," as you realize that the anatomy of the call is the very same process that you have experienced. Your life is a witness that working for the King—no matter the task to which you are called—is the greatest promotion of all.

The Sovereignty of God

The study of this quarter examines the sovereignty of God and of Jesus Christ, culminating with a close look at the vision of God's plan at the end of the age. The material from Isaiah and Hebrews highlights the sovereign position of the Father and the Son over the universe and how that affects the lives of the believer, while the material from Revelation unveils God's sovereignty over final events and the end results of His eternal plan.

UNIT 1 • The Sovereignty of God

The four lessons in this unit explore how the prophet Isaiah views the reign of God over the whole world through discussing a peaceful kingdom, a mountain of God, the foundations of the earth, and a new and everlasting covenant.

Lesson 1: September 4, 2016
The Peaceful Kingdom
Isaiah 11:1–9

We live in a world full of divisions, hatred, trouble, and chaos. Will we ever experience harmony? Isaiah's prophecy reveals that the sovereign God will bring about a world of peace.

Lesson 2: September 11, 2016
The Mountain of God
Isaiah 25:6–10a

Oppressed people seek relief from their injustices. Who will deliver them? Isaiah's prophecy reveals that the sovereign God will bring deliverance from oppression.

Lesson 3: September 18, 2016
Foundations of the Earth
Isaiah 40:21–31

We often trust in people or systems to sustain and guide our lives. Are these systems able to sustain us? Isaiah declares that God is the absolute power on whom we should depend.

Lesson 4: September 25, 2016
Everlasting Covenant
Isaiah 61:1–4, 8–11

People make agreements they hope will last, but are too often broken, causing stress and dismay. Can anyone make an agreement that will not be broken? God promises an everlasting covenant, which can never be broken.

UNIT 2 • The Sovereignty of Jesus

The five lessons in this unit study the images of the reign of the resurrected Christ from the letter to the Hebrews. In these lessons, Jesus is described as the imprint of God, the owner of a household, the great High Priest, Priest forever, and the Pioneer and Perfecter of our faith.

Lesson 5: October 2, 2016
The Imprint of God
Hebrews 1:1–9

People seek guidance for their lives, but might question who is the best person to give direction. Whom should they trust to provide direction and guidance? Christ, the reflection of God's glory, addresses life's questions with a powerful and sustaining Word.

Lesson 6: October 9, 2016
Builder of the House
Hebrews 3:1–6, Matthew 7:24–29

People often give credit for accomplishments to those who carry out the work rather than to the one who created the plan. Who is really responsible? The Scripture affirms that Jesus was faithful while accomplishing God's plan.

Lesson 7: October 16, 2016
Our Great High Priest
Hebrews 4:14–5:10

Gifted leaders work to carry out specific responsibilities on behalf of the communities they serve. How are such leaders chosen? Jesus was appointed by God to serve as High Priest for the people.

Lesson 8: October 23, 2016
The High Priest Forever
Hebrews 7:1–3, 19b–28

Practices, traditions, and institutions created in the past are expected to continue into the future. Who will sustain them? Jesus was chosen to give the practices, traditions, and institutions their ultimate meaning and role for the people for all generations.

Lesson 9: October 30, 2016
Pioneer and Perfecter of Our Faith
Hebrews 12:1–13

People seek guidance to help them endure the trials and temptations life brings their way. Is there anyone who can show them how to endure? Because Jesus endured suffering and death, He is the model for disciples who choose to follow Him faithfully.

UNIT 3 • Alpha and Omega

The four lessons in this unit are based on the last two chapters of the book of Revelation. In these lessons, John uses metaphors of one who makes all things new, a vision of a New Jerusalem, a river of life, and the beginning and the end of all things to explore how God reigns.

Lesson 10: November 6, 2016
Everything's Brand New
Revelation 21:1–8

People look for a place and time when life's stresses will not exist. Is such a refuge possible? John, the writer of the book of Revelation, suggests that God will create a new heaven and earth where life's challenges and stresses will be banished forever.

Lesson 11: November 13, 2016
I See A New Jerusalem
Revelation 21:9–14, 22–27

Leaving one's home and relocating to a new place can be a scary thought, even if that place seems beneficial. What will the new place be like? John uses figurative language to describe the new place that God will create.

Lesson 12: November 20, 2016
Living Waters
Revelation 22:1–7

Rivers give life and nourishment to the people, places, and creatures that exist around them. How do rivers nourish our lives? According to John, in the new world, God's power will be in the river and will nourish and heal everything in the city.

Lesson 13: November 27, 2016
Alpha and Omega
Revelation 22:12–21

People recognize that all things have a beginning and an end. What is the source and final purpose of human life? The book of Revelation affirms that God, who is the Alpha and Omega, controls all things.

The Sovereignty of God

The sovereignty of God—the doctrine that He is in control of everything in the universe—is the great comfort of the Christian life. Nothing is outside of His sway. All the molecules and atoms conform to His will. He governs time and space.

The sovereignty of God produces a great freedom for believers. Because of His sovereignty, we can trust Him in all our circumstances, no matter how unfavorable. Through His sovereignty, we find our place in the universe. We are servants, and He is the master.

We know intuitively that God is sovereign, but it is through the resurrection of Christ that we truly understand this fact. Not only is He in command of the living, but even death itself could not conquer Him. The forces of darkness gathered against Christ and believed they could prevail, but the sovereign God raised Him from the dead. In fact, even the evil forces working through the Jewish leaders and Pontius Pilate were governed and predetermined by the hand of God.

God's sovereignty informs us that we can overcome dire circumstances, even death. This truth has empowered and emboldened the followers of Jesus for millennia. When suffering or persecution threaten the preaching of the Gospel, men and women of God stand firmly, boldly knowing that their future is in His hands. If He has ordained for them to die, then they will be in the care of the One who knows what is best for them.

In Isaiah, we see God as sovereign through His judgment and subsequent restoration of Israel. God ordered the Assyrians and Babylonians to conquer and oppress them. If He ordered it, then He could also reverse it, which He did during the return from exile.

This return from exile was not a human plan, but God's plan for His people. God guided the course of history to work in favor of His people. He gave Isaiah a glimpse of the work He would do on their behalf. He was in control; the Assyrians and Babylonians were only tools in the hands of the One with a master plan.

In Revelation, God's sovereignty is apparent as believers who have been persecuted and killed for their faith see the glorious future awaiting them. Revelation shows us that God is in charge not only in the beginning of the story, but the middle and the end as well. Wickedness will also not be tolerated. God will punish those who oppose His people.

We as believers can find comfort and hope in these Scriptures. No matter what we see in the news, we can be assured that God is in control. Nothing surprises Him. In fact, the things that we deem evil and purposeless, God has ordained for His glory.

We can go forward knowing that God is sovereign. We do not have to be hesitant or fearful. Nothing can hinder God's work on earth. His purpose reigns supreme. He is sovereign over the entire universe, meaning He has control over the joys and trials of our lives as well.

The Sovereignty of God in Christian Education

by Rev. Michael K. Roussell

The story of Saul's conversion to the Apostle Paul was a story of the power of God changing a life through the Lord Jesus Christ. Saul was stopped in his tracks and completely turned his life around when he truly understood the sovereignty of God in the Person of Christ. We should try to share this kind of understanding every week in Sunday School and from the pulpit. A true revelation of the sovereignty of God is life-changing.

The Apostle Paul, known as Saul before his conversion, was born a Jew of the tribe of Benjamin in the city of Tarsus. Saul's father was a Pharisee who earned his family Roman citizenship. As a young man, Saul studied at the feet of the leading rabbi Gamaliel and became a Pharisee himself. The Bible says that he upheld the Jewish Law in every way, and that meant persecuting Christians. He was present at the stoning of Stephen. Paul himself says he was the tormentor of the church, taking every opportunity to purge Judaism of those who claimed Jesus was the sovereign God, a claim he saw as heresy.

However, we know that Jesus really is God, sovereign over all creation. Being sovereign means that the God we serve is an omnipotent God; He is all-powerful. Secondly, the God we serve is an omniscient God; He is all-knowing. Thirdly, the God we serve is an omnipresent God; He is everywhere at the same time. What a mighty God we serve!

When we speak of God being sovereign, we mean that He has supreme authority over the universe and absolute control of all things in heaven and earth. Nothing happens outside of God's knowing or by mistake. Only a God of this magnitude could turn someone's life around as He did Saul's.

While on the way to Damascus, where he planned to persecute more Christians, Saul had a life-changing experience. Suddenly, a light came down around him from heaven. Jesus Christ spoke to Saul and asked, "Why are you persecuting Me?" Saul, falling down to the ground, asked, "Who are You, Lord?" In the instant that Saul saw the glory of this vision, he knew that the Person he was seeing was the sovereign God, but he still needed to know who this Lord of all was. The Lord, who was bringing Saul out of darkness into His marvelous light, answered Saul saying, "I am Jesus, the one you are persecuting" (Acts 9:5, NLT).

Finally, old things passed away and all things became new. Saul continued to Damascus a changed man. The Lord used Ananias to restore Saul's physical sight and to be his first instructor in the way of Jesus. Saul became friends with the disciples, and learned from them for many years. After receiving this education, Paul preached in Damascus, visited Jerusalem, and worked in Antioch where he prepared to go on his first of three missionary trips. The seasons had changed in Paul's life.

Time has brought about a change of seasons in our lives today too. And while we abide with joy and peace in our knowledge of Christ, the world outside the church is crying out for change socially, economically, and politically. **The social climate has changed**; Christianity is no longer the default religion in the United States. Teenagers are now familiar with the threat and sting of violence, suicide, and abortion. Imprisonment has increased, especially for young Black men. Lawlessness and wickedness persist, sometimes even among those who are sworn to protect and defend. Society is clamoring for a change in its season.

Politically, the world has seen and continues to see upheaval. Take a look at the civil war in Syria, the apartheid in South Africa, the Perestroika in Russia, the Solidarity in Poland, and the fall of Mao in China. Dictatorships, monarchies, theocracies, and democracies have all failed to bring about a peaceful political season. There is political conflict, disenfranchisement, and misrepresentation in America.

Economically, setbacks have decimated our trust in the American dream. We can hardly keep up with knowing if the market is going through inflation, deflation, stagnation, recession, or depression. This causes oppression in the everyday situations and circumstances of our lives. Budget cuts affecting wages, Medicaid, Medicare, and welfare impact the lives of every American. Political promises of change have not solved as many problems as we had all hoped.

In the midst of all this uncertainty and surface change, we as believers have surety in our hope for the future because we have experienced true change. We have seen and understood the sovereignty of God over all of these social, political, and economic situations. We know He will protect us and strengthen our cause as we continue to fight for liberty and justice for all. We know King Jesus is the only ruler who will bring ultimate peace. We know He will provide everything we need day to day, just as He provides for every sparrow and lily in His creation. We know these things because we were diligently taught in Sunday School and dutifully listened to preaching from the pulpit.

Even though our culture's situation today is dire, it is no worse than what was in Saul's heart when he started out toward Damascus. Saul was set on the murder of the saints, but changed to become the apostle to the Gentiles. Saul's proud heart saw himself as perfectly upholding the Law, but changed to recognize himself as the worst of sinners. This is the kind of total change that knowing and acknowledging the sovereignty of God will bring about.

All educators in the Christian faith—teachers, pastors, and evangelists alike—hold the key to great change for their students' lives. By leading them to a deeper understanding of the fullness of God's control of the world, you can reach your students with new levels of trust in, peace from, and service to our one true God.

—————

Rev. Michael K. Roussell, D.Min., is the Senior Pastor of Friendship Assembly of God in Chicago, IL, and an Adjunct Professor at Trinity International University in Deerfield, IL. He is also the Presiding Bishop of the Chicagoland Ministerial Alliance.

I Will Be Your God and You Will Be My People: A Central Theme in Scripture

by Evangeline Carey

Scholars tell us that "it took some 40 men a period of approximately 1,600 years to produce the 66 books that constitute the Bible" (Thiessen 67). God inspired these men to record His inerrant Word in their original documents for several purposes: "for doctrine, for reproof, for correction, for instruction in righteousness" (2 Timothy 3:16). A central theme or thread running throughout the Scriptures is God's desire for the people He created to be in relationship with Him. God's heartbeat is for humanity to look to Him, be saved, and fulfill the purpose for which He created them in the first place.

Five Historical Books Called the "Pentateuch" (Genesis, Exodus, Leviticus, Numbers, and Deuteronomy)—the Books of the Law

In the Pentateuch, God's great love for mankind and His desire for relationship can be readily seen through (1) His creation of man and woman, (2) His hands-on involvement with Adam and Eve in the Garden of Eden, and (3) the binding agreements He made with His people in covenant relationship.

God desired to have a people who would love, honor, respect, and worship Him. He wanted a people who would walk with Him in obedience. When we explore the 66 books of the canon, we find God reaching out to humanity in unconditional love, salvation, and fellowship.

Genesis 1:27 (KJV), reads, "So God created man in his own image, in the image of God created he him; male and female created he them." God created man and woman to have fellowship with Him—to worship Him in spirit and in truth. He desired to be their God and for them to be His special people. However, their willful disobedience in the Garden of Eden caused sin to come upon all humanity. Adam and Eve's actions marred their fellowship with Almighty God, and evil staked its claim in humanity's life and then snaked its way from generation to generation. The cycle of sin began, and only the Lamb without blemish, Jesus Christ, could bridge the gap left between sinful man and a holy God.

After the Flood, God entered into a covenant relationship with Noah and his sons. He told them, "I do set my bow in the cloud, and it shall be for a token of a covenant between me and the earth...and the waters shall no more become a flood to destroy all flesh" (from Genesis 9:13–15, KJV). Through the saga of Noah, we see that God is indeed faithful to those who obey His commands. We also see that our obedience is a long-term commitment to God.

Then God continued His plan to set a people apart to worship Him—a people He would call His own. God promised to make Abraham's descendants into a great nation, but He also expected Abraham to obey and walk with Him in faith and obedience (Genesis 12:1–25:18). God's chosen people (the Israelites) were to be the channel through which the world would come to know Him. He became the Israelites' God, but the Israelites were a hardheaded, rebellious, stiff-necked people who disobeyed God at every turn.

The 12 Historical Books (Joshua, Judges, Ruth, 1 and 2 Samuel, 1 and 2 Kings, 1 and 2 Chronicles, Ezra, Nehemiah, and Esther)

From these historical books, we also come to appreciate God's character and know Him more intimately as we look at how He dealt with the Israelites. These books further explain how God tried to help His chosen people understand and obey His commands and remain in relationship with Him. He raised up priests, judges, and kings to help them stay on His path, but they still broke their covenant relationship with Him. They perpetuated a cycle of sin or disobedience, captivity (God's punishment for their sins), remorse, repentance, and deliverance.

The Five Poetry Books (Job, Psalms, Proverbs, Ecclesiastes, and Song of Solomon)

These books extol God's unconditional love for His people. They also share how He punishes sin. These accounts express the whole range of human emotion. We learn how to walk with a holy God in confession. We also learn how to focus on Him and lift our hearts in praise and worship to our God, who is more than enough in our times of need. Job, the central character of the book of Job, is a model of trust in and obedience to God. From his life, we learn that God is completely and eternally good, in spite of our suffering in a fallen world. We also learn that Almighty God is awesome, that the covenant-relationship with Him still

exists, and that Satan cannot do anything to God's children that God does not allow. We learn that Satan had to ask God for permission to afflict Job (1:12).

Psalms, Proverbs, Ecclesiastes, and Song of Solomon also help us picture the unconditional love of God for His sheep. These books show us that if we are going to let God be our God and if we are going to be His people, we should honor our daily commitment to Him by applying godly morals and wisdom, praising Him in good times and bad, and rejoicing in godly relationships.

The 17 Prophetic Books (Isaiah, Jeremiah, Lamentations, Ezekiel, Daniel, Hosea, Joel, Amos, Obadiah, Jonah, Micah, Nahum, Habakkuk, Zephaniah, Haggai, Zechariah, and Malachi)

These books continue to illustrate how God takes His covenant relationship with His people very seriously. God raised up spokesmen to warn His chosen people to turn from their sinful ways and turn back to Him. He wanted them to honor their agreement with Him. The prophets then called the people back to God and proclaimed His future provision of salvation through the coming Messiah, Jesus. They taught that God is love, God is merciful, but God is also Judge.

The Four Gospels (Matthew, Mark, Luke, and John

Whereas the 39 books of the Old Testament foretold the coming of the Messiah—Jesus Christ, who is the eternal King—the four Gospels declare that Jesus has come and He is the Word of God to man, the Word made flesh, and dwelling among us (John 1:14). Jesus has revealed Himself to a lost and dying world as the only way back to a holy God. The gap or gulf between sinful man and a holy God is closed when sinners believe on the Lord Jesus Christ. With true belief and repentance, Jesus becomes our Lord and Savior.

The Acts of the Apostles

The book of Acts, a sequel to the Gospel of Luke, covers the 30 years after Jesus' ascension into heaven. From the book of Acts, again we see God stressing His message to believers, "I will be your God and you will be My people," as He uses His promised Holy Spirit (the Comforter, Counselor, and Guide) to advance and direct His church outward "in Jerusalem, and in all Judaea, and in Samaria, and unto the uttermost part of the earth" (Acts 1:8, KJV). Using His disciples, "the Lord added to the church daily such as should be saved" (Acts 2:47), and the church's roll grew from 11 to 12 to 120 to 3,000 to 5,000 (Acts 2–4). God invited sinners to become His people, and He became their God.

The 21 Epistles or Letters (Romans, 1 and 2 Corinthians, Galatians, Ephesians, Philippians, Colossians, 1 and 2 Thessalonians, 1 and 2 Timothy, Titus, Philemon, Hebrews, James, 1 and 2 Peter, 1, 2, and 3 John, and Jude)

The epistles, or letters, definitely demonstrate a loving, merciful Father's desire for relationship with His people and His concern for their well-being. Under the anointing of the Holy Spirit, Paul, Peter, James, John, and Jude wrote letters to the infant churches, which Paul helped establish on three missionary journeys.

Paul presented his case for the Good News of the Gospel of Jesus Christ. Often, these letters were written from prison, in chains, after beatings with wooden rods, and in the midst of other perils. In them, Paul explained that Christ's death provided a way for all humanity to be reconciled to God the Father. The letters explained further that an omniscient (all-knowing), omnipotent (all-powerful), and omnipresent (present everywhere) God was and is saying to His followers, "I will be to them a God, and they shall be to me a people" (Hebrews 8:10, KJV).

Revelation—The Book of Hope

God used the Apostle John, while he was exiled on the island of Patmos in the Aegean Sea, to spell out the hope that believers have of a life beyond the grave in God's kingdom. John had a vision or revelation from Jesus Christ, which unveiled the victorious Lord Jesus' Second Coming. Jesus is coming back to rule the earth! He will no longer be a suffering Servant, but a Judge who vindicates the righteous and punishes the wicked.

God, who is Creator, Redeemer, Sustainer, and Judge, gave His revelation to the Apostle John nearly 2,000 years ago. This unveiling agrees with what the other 65 books of the Bible proclaim to all believers: that God says and means, "I will be your God and you will be My people forever and ever and ever!"

Sources
Boer, Harry R. *Pentecost and Missions.* Grand Rapids, Michigan: Eerdmans, 1961, 161.
Thiessen, Henry C. *Lectures in Systematic Theology.* Grand Rapids, Michigan: Eerdmans, 2000, 67–255.

In Loving Memory of Evangeline Carey 1949-2011

Evangeline Carey was a staff writer for UMI and had been an adult Sunday School teacher and Bible scholar for more than 25 years.

Frederick Douglass

by UMI Staff

(February 1818–February 20, 1895)

Frederick Douglass was born a slave but rose to become one of the great African American leaders of the 19th century as an impassioned abolitionist, social reformer, politician, writer, editor, and presidential advisor.

For 50 years (1845 to 1895), Douglass wrote and spoke against slavery and for a range of causes including women's rights, Irish freedom, federal aid to education, and the right of oppressed people everywhere to equal protection under the law, earning him the title "Father of the Protest Movement." Those years spanned the Abolitionist movement, the Civil War, Reconstruction, and the post-Reconstruction period.

He was born Frederick Washington Bailey in 1818 in Talbot County on Maryland's Eastern Shore. After early separation from his mother, Harriet Bailey, young Frederick lived with his maternal grandmother, Betty Bailey. At age 7, he was separated from his grandmother and taken to another plantation. After that plantation owner died, he was given to the wife of a plantation owner in Baltimore. His mother died when he was about 10.

Sophia Auld in Baltimore started teaching the young slave the alphabet, but the slavemaster prohibited it. Douglass then secretly taught himself to read, hiding papers in his pockets and spelling out words when no one was watching. Reading from newspapers, pamphlets, political material, and books led him to denounce the institution of slavery. He would later often say, "Knowledge is the pathway from slavery to freedom."

He taught several slaves to read the New Testament at weekly Sunday School sessions that sometimes drew more than 40 slaves. Eventually slave owners burst in on the gathering with clubs and stones to disperse to the congregation permanently. Douglass conducted Sunday School in the woods until he was warned that he would be killed if he did not stop.

Dressed as a sailor, with identification papers borrowed from a freed Black seaman, Douglass successfully escaped in 1838 at age 20. He boarded a train and eventually made it to New York. His wife-to-be, a free Black woman from Baltimore, met him there, and they were married. From there, an abolitionist directed them to Massachusetts where Douglass was able to work and support his family.

When leaders in the abolitionist movement became aware of Douglass, they asked him to tell his story so that people could learn about the horrors of slavery. Three years later, the fugitive slave was quickly gaining prominence as an agitator for racial justice with a new name: Frederick Douglass, a name adopted from the hero of Sir Walter Scott's *The Lady of the Lake*.

With a tall, imposing presence, deep-set eyes, rich baritone voice, and impressive crown of hair that complemented his eloquence and persuasiveness, Douglass grew into a celebrated social reformer and one of the best-known orators in the United States. He was active in Black conventions, the abolitionist movement, the Underground Railroad, and many other efforts to improve the conditions of his race.

His friends and mentors, fearing the publicity would draw the attention of his ex-owner, persuaded him to tour Ireland, as many former slaves had done. Douglas took a boat to Liverpool on August 16, 1845. He spent two years in England and Ireland, where he gave many lectures in churches and chapels, winning friends and influencing people for the antislavery cause. He toured Ireland just as the Irish Potato Famine was beginning.

After returning to the United States, Douglass started publishing his first abolitionist paper, the *North Star*, from the basement of the Memorial AME Zion Church in Rochester, New York. The *North Star*'s motto was "Right is of no Sex—Truth is of no Color—God is the Father of us all, and we are all brethren." His editorials demanded the end of capital punishment, mistreatment of Chinese immigrants and American Indians, and neglect of education for the poor. That newspaper and the papers that Douglass later published were primarily funded by English supporters.

Douglass wrote several biographies, including his best-known work, *Narrative of The Life of Frederick Douglass, An American Slave*, which was published in 1845. Douglass published three versions of his autobiography during his lifetime and revised the third one, each time expanding on the previous one.

By the time of the Civil War, Douglass was one of the most famous Black men in the country, known for his orations on the condition of the Black race and issues such as women's rights. During the war, he urged President Abraham Lincoln to free the slaves and arm all Negro men. When Lincoln finally adopted these policies, he asked Douglass to serve as his adviser. Douglass raised troops for the Union Army, and his two sons were among the first to enlist.

After the war, he continued to push for reforms, urging Congress to enact a national system of aid to education and a series of laws that would protect the rights of the liberated Negroes. He served in several high governmental posts in Washington and as U.S. minister in Haiti.

The gospel of struggle he preached is illustrated by a well-known quotation from his great speech of August 4, 1857: "The whole history of the progress of human liberty shows that all concessions yet made to her august claims, have been born of earnest struggle. … If there is no struggle, there is no progress. Those who profess to favor freedom yet deprecate agitation, are men who want crops without plowing up the ground, they want rain without thunder and lightning. They want the ocean without the mighty roar of its many waters. … This struggle may be a moral one, or it may be a physical one, and it may be both moral and physical, but it must be a struggle. Power concedes nothing without a demand. It never did and it never will."

On January 1, 1863, Douglass, William Lloyd Garrison, Harriet Beecher Stowe, Charles Brady, and other freedom fighters gathered at Tremont Temple in Boston to hear Lincoln speak the words that declared the freedom of all slaves in Confederate-held territory. (Slaves in Union-held territory would be freed with the adoption of the 13th Amendment on December 6, 1865.)

Douglass died on February 20, 1895, in Washington, D.C., at age 78 of a massive heart attack or stroke shortly after delivering a speech on behalf of women's rights.

Teaching Tips

Words You Should Know
A. Rod (Isaiah 11:1) *khoter*—Branch, twig, rod.

B. Rest (v. 2) *nuakh*—To settle down, and remain.

Teacher Preparation
Unifying Principle—God Brings Harmony. We live in a world full of divisions, hatred, trouble, and chaos. Will we ever experience harmony? Isaiah's prophecy reveals that the sovereign God will bring about a world of peace.

A. Read the Focal Verses in multiple translations.

B. Read about multiple peace treaties and why some were broken.

O—Open the Lesson
A. Open with prayer, including the Aim to Change.

B. Introduce today's lesson title: "The Peaceful Kingdom."

C. Have your students read the Aim for Change and the Keep in Mind verse together. Discuss the importance of peace and what it looks like to them.

P—Present the Scriptures
A. Ask for volunteers to read the Focal Verses.

B. Use the People, Places, and Times; Background; Search the Scriptures; At-A-Glance Outline; In Depth; and More Light on the Text to clarify the verses.

E—Explore the Meaning
A. Divide the class into three groups of those for, against, and ambivalent on some trivial matter (e.g., hamburgers vs. hot dogs). The first two groups will try to create a peace treaty. The third group will be the mediator to aid in the process of drafting a successful peace treaty.

B. Divide the class into groups to read the Discuss the Meaning, Lesson in Our Society, and Make It Happen sections. Let a chosen representative share their highlights.

N—Next Steps for Application
A. Summarize the lesson.

B. Ask the students if they have any takeaways they would like to share.

C. Close with prayer.

Worship Guide

Theme: The Peaceful Kingdom
Song: "It is Well With My Soul"
Devotional Reading: Psalm 72:1–7

The Peaceful Kingdom

Bible Background • ISAIAH 11:1–9
Printed Text • ISAIAH 11:1–9 | Devotional Reading • PSALM 72:1–7

Aim for Change

By the end of the lesson we will: ANALYZE the key descriptors of God's peaceful kingdom; LOOK forward to the day when Christian communities will be known for their godly life of peace; and IDENTIFY an area of church or community life that does not meet God's intention for peace and develop a strategy to address it.

In Focus

Gerald walked the streets of his old neighborhood at night. He couldn't believe what had happened since he had been gone. Where vibrant stores had once attracted customers, there were now abandoned buildings. Where beautiful homes had once stood, there were now just empty lots. Just this past weekend there had been three shootings. Gerald couldn't help but think of how many churches were in his community. Every Sunday they spoke of miracles and the God who could do the impossible. Somehow that didn't translate into changing things in the very communities where they worshiped. Thinking about this only drove him to be angry. Soon anger turned to sadness. As he rounded the corner to go home, he found himself crying.

Gerald reasoned within himself, *I can't complain about what churches are not doing. I'm a Christian. I'm a follower of Christ. If change is going to come, then I have to be changed myself. I left this neighborhood searching for greener pastures and now it's falling apart. I have to own my responsibility for how things are in this community.* Just then Gerald came across some young men whom he recognized as the grandsons of some of his parents' friends. They looked as if they were up to no good. He walked up to them and began to ask them questions about life and what they could do to rebuild the community. It wasn't the total solution, but it was a start.

In today's lesson, we will discuss the ways that God's people can help meet the needs of communities and live out His intentions for peace. What are some things that keep us from meeting those needs in our communities?

Keep in Mind

"They shall not hurt nor destroy in all my holy mountain: for the earth shall be full of the knowledge of the LORD, as the waters cover the sea"
(Isaiah 11:9).

"They shall not hurt nor destroy in all my holy mountain: for the earth shall be full of the knowledge of the LORD, as the waters cover the sea" (Isaiah 11:9).

Focal Verses

KJV Isaiah 11:1 And there shall come forth a rod out of the stem of Jesse, and a Branch shall grow out of his roots:

2 And the spirit of the LORD shall rest upon him, the spirit of wisdom and understanding, the spirit of counsel and might, the spirit of knowledge and of the fear of the LORD;

3 And shall make him of quick understanding in the fear of the LORD: and he shall not judge after the sight of his eyes, neither reprove after the hearing of his ears:

4 But with righteousness shall he judge the poor, and reprove with equity for the meek of the earth: and he shall smite the earth: with the rod of his mouth, and with the breath of his lips shall he slay the wicked.

5 And righteousness shall be the girdle of his loins, and faithfulness the girdle of his reins.

6 The wolf also shall dwell with the lamb, and the leopard shall lie down with the kid; and the calf and the young lion and the fatling together; and a little child shall lead them.

7 And the cow and the bear shall feed; their young ones shall lie down together: and the lion shall eat straw like the ox.

8 And the suckling child shall play on the hole of the asp, and the weaned child shall put his hand on the cockatrice' den.

9 They shall not hurt or destroy in all my holy mountain: for the earth shall be full of the knowledge of the LORD, as the waters cover the sea.

NLT Isaiah 11:1 Out of the stump of David's family will grow a shoot— yes, a new Branch bearing fruit from the old root.

2 And the Spirit of the LORD will rest on him – the Spirit of wisdom and understanding, the Spirit of counsel and might, the Spirit of knowledge and the fear of the LORD.

3 He will delight in obeying the LORD. He will not judge by appearance nor make a decision based on hearsay.

4 He will give justice to the poor and make fair decisions for the exploited. The earth will shake at the force of his word, and one breath from his mouth will destroy the wicked.

5 He will wear righteousness like a belt and truth like an undergarment.

6 In that day the wolf and the lamb will live together; the leopard will lie down with the baby goat. The calf and the yearling will be safe with the lion, and a little child will lead them all.

7 The cow will graze near the bear. The cub and the calf will lie down together. The lion will eat hay like a cow.

8 The baby will play safely near the hole of a cobra. Yes, a little child will put its hand in a nest of deadly snakes without harm.

9 Nothing will hurt or destroy in all my holy mountain, for as the waters fill the sea, so the earth will be filled with people who know the LORD.

The People, Places, and Times

Jesse. Jesse was the grandson of Ruth and Boaz. He was a shepherd and raised his sons in that occupation. Jesse was the father to eight sons. The youngest of these sons was David who eventually became King of Israel. Not much is said about Jesse after David takes him and his wife to live in Moab (1 Samuel 22:3–4), because David became a fugitive hunted by Saul.

The Branch. The Branch is a term that symbolized the Davidic Messiah. The term can be found in the prophets (Jeremiah 23:5, Zechariah 3:8), but its origins may have stemmed from other uses of the word "branch" in reference to rulers. In Daniel 11:7, the word is used to reference political strife that will occur between a ruler and her offspring. Elsewhere, Isaiah speaks of God's people collectively being a branch planted by God that will grow (60:21).

Background

As in much of Isaiah's prophecies, the present and future can be intermingled. In chapter 10, Isaiah speaks of the Assyrian oppression and captivity. This speaks to the situation of Israel at the time of Assyrian world dominance. The Assyrians were used by God to discipline the Children of Israel. Isaiah then speaks of this dominance fading away and the Assyrian yoke destroyed.

At the same time, intermingled with verses of liberation from Assyrian oppression, Isaiah speaks of a time when the remnant of Israel and Judah will return, the time of the consummated kingdom of God. Isaiah fully describes this period of time in chapter 11—a time of peace and prosperity, security and safety. This is not because of any inherent goodness in the time itself, but the glory and greatness of the King who will reign: Jesus Christ.

At-A-Glance

1. The Messiah Gives Real Hope
(Isaiah 11:1–5)
2. The Messiah Gives Real Peace (vv. 6–9)

In Depth

1. The Messiah Gives Real Hope (Isaiah 11:1–5)

These Scriptures in Isaiah speak about hope. This kind of hope cannot be in man. God promised David that he would have someone from his family to reign over his throne forever (1 Chronicles 22:10). Verse 1 says in part, "there shall come forth a rod out of the stem of Jesse." David came from Jesse's lineage. During Isaiah's time, Judah experienced fluctuation in their kings, despite all of them being from the lineage of Jesse and David. Whether the ruler at the time of the prophecy here was generally godly like Hezekiah or corrupt like Manasseh, all were human and made mistakes. But the ruler and judge Isaiah here refers to is not an ordinary man—He is the Messiah.

He is the One who would help God's people to trust and believe in Him again. This new King will be different from all the other kings. He will be the Savior of the world, the King who will sit on the throne forever. He is equipped to handle the monumental task of giving hope and bringing peace.

Isaiah wanted God's people to know that the Messiah came fully equipped with the wisdom/understanding, counsel/might, knowledge, and the fear of the Lord. He came to introduce the kingdom of God. His role is to implement God's righteousness on earth, not self-glorification. The words and images of this passage originated during Israel's captivity and exile, and therefore spoke to a future hope radically different from present circumstances.

2. The Messiah Gives Real Peace (vv. 6–9)

Isaiah's readers and hearers know that the prophet is referring to the Messiah here, because He is so different from earthly rulers. They were all temporary, but He is everlasting; He will reign forever. His kingdom should be totally different than any other kingdom, especially our present earthly kingdom. Verse 6 says the wolf and the lamb will dwell together, even though the lamb is food for the wolf.

The Scripture continues: "The leopard shall lie down with the kid; and the calf and the young lion and the fatling together; and a little child shall lead them." This is so different from our present world. A child could not lead a lion and fatling; the lion would devour them both. Yet Isaiah speaks of a time when the Messiah will bring peace to all of creation. He alone can bring peace for every aspect of our lives. All things that cause destruction—fire, tsunamis, frigid temperatures—will no longer exist. In this kingdom, everyone will get along, even predators and prey.

Search the Scriptures

1. Isaiah speaks of Jesus when he says "there shall come forth a rod out of the stem of Jesse, and a Branch shall grow out of his roots" (Isaiah 11:1). Draw a genealogical chart that outlines Jesse's family tree all the way to Jesus (Matthew 1:1–17).

2. How do we reconcile Christians being soldiers or police officers with Isaiah's words that "they shall not hurt or destroy in all my holy mountain" (v. 9)?

Discuss the Meaning

The believer is called to live a life that characterizes the peace of God's kingdom. How would you evaluate a person who lives a life filled with internal and external peace?

Lesson in Our Society

Peaceful is not a word that describes our current times. Nations are in uproar and wars are fought on many fronts. Unrest persists even in our national government and politics. Our young people are being slain in the streets. One day the Lord will bring peace to this world. For now, we must access the peace that He offers those who trust in Christ, and strive to work for peace in our neighborhoods and in our nation.

Make It Happen

List five things that give you peace as a believer in Christ. Volunteer for a "stop the violence" movement in your city. Practice meditating on Scripture as a way to tap into God's peace for your inner life.

Follow the Spirit

What God wants me to do:

_____

_____

_____

_____

Remember Your Thoughts

Special insights I have learned:

_____

_____

_____

_____

More Light on the Text
Isaiah 11:1–9

A popular TV show in the late 1980s called *The Equalizer* featured a mysterious figure who always appeared at the right time to help people in trouble and stop the bad guys. Who has not longed for such a lifesaver when problems threaten to overwhelm us? Isaiah writes about the coming righteous "equalizer" who will finally bring much-needed justice to a world overrun with evil.

The previous chapter focuses on God using Assyria to judge and destroy Israel and Jerusalem, before then turning His judgment on Assyria (Isaiah 10:33–34). Israel's hope-lessness and blight are then contrasted with a glimmer of hope that comes from the fallen Davidic kingdom, metaphorically expressed as a stump (v. 1, KJV: stem; a theme which is further developed in vv. 10 ff.). Just as many stumps with viable roots will send up new shoots, new life is possible (cf. Isaiah 6:13, which could also refer to the faithful remnant). A master of metaphors, Isaiah uses this and two other images (spirit and future utopia) to communicate the new plan that God is in the process of unfolding.

1 And there shall come forth a rod out of the stem of Jesse, and a Branch shall grow out of his roots:

Jesse was King David's father, placing him in the lineage of Jesus (1 Samuel 17:12; Matthew 1:6). Referring to the Messiah as a Branch (Heb. *netser*, **NEH-tser**) from the felled Davidic tree is not unique to this verse (see Isaiah 4:2; Jeremiah 23:5, 33:15; Zechariah 3:8, 6:12), but note that in each instance the word is capital-ized. These other verses use a different Hebrew word for branch than Isaiah 11:1, but the idea is the same. Cutting off dead branches allows the tree to grow back healthier than before.

2 And the spirit of the LORD shall rest upon him, the spirit of wisdom and under-standing, the spirit of counsel and might, the spirit of knowledge and of the fear of the LORD.

The spirit of the Lord is more than just our understanding of an existence outside bodily form. In Hebrew it means one's very breath (*ruakh*, **ROO-akh**). Isaiah promises that the Messiah will be filled with God's breath, and as a result, with God's wisdom, understand-ing, counsel, might, knowledge and reverence. These are all characteristics of a righteous ruler, characteristics not always exhibited by human

rulers, even those who seek God's guidance and the good of the people in all things.

The word "rest" (Heb. *nuakh*, **NU-akh**) is deeper than the idea of a bird landing, resting, and then flying away, but has a much more set-tled and profound sense. Whenever the Holy Spirit rested on an Old Testament figure, it was in the sense of an anointing and filling, and always for a purpose (cf. Numbers 11:25). Essentially, the Messianic King is completely equipped by God with everything He will need to rule righteously and effectively over Israel and the whole earth (cf. Isaiah 9:6–7, 11:10–12).

3 And shall make him of quick under-standing in the fear of the LORD: and he shall not judge after the sight of his eyes, neither reprove after the hearing of his ears.

Most scholars recognize that whenever a term or phrase is repeated in Scripture, the emphasis is significant. In this case, the aspect of the fear of the Lord could be seen to be inte-gral to the sum of the qualities of the Messiah King, especially when combined with the rest of the passage. This Messiah would not use His own understanding or personal judgment, but the standard of God's righteousness when weighing matters of grave importance—such as the fate of oppressors or the worthiness of the oppressed for salvation. In the end, even the strongest and wisest are subject to God, who directs the minds of kings even when they are unaware of it (Proverbs 21:1). Jesus made it clear throughout His ministry that He was there not to do His will, but His Father's (John 6:38).

4 But with righteousness shall he judge the poor, and reprove with equity for the meek of the earth: and he shall smite the earth with the rod of his mouth, and with the breath of his lips shall he slay the wicked.

5 And righteousness shall be the girdle of his loins, and faithfulness the girdle of his reins.

The poor have experienced far too much corruption and injustice, and waited far too long, so they very much need a righteous judge. For these afflicted souls, just judgment is synonymous with salvation. Fulfilling His righteous role, the Messiah King judges as the embodied, all-powerful Word of God (Revelation 19:11–13).

Scholars concur that the girdle, belt, or sash was a critical item in Middle Eastern clothing, holding the rest of the garments together—and also earning a New Testament mention in Paul's description of the well-armed believer girding his waist with truth (Ephesians 6:14).

6 The wolf also shall dwell with the lamb, and the leopard shall lie down with the kid; and the calf and the young lion and the fatling together; and a little child shall lead them. 7 And the cow and the bear shall feed; their young ones shall lie down together: and the lion shall eat straw like the ox. 8 And the sucking child shall play on the hole of the asp, and the weaned child shall put his hand on the cockatrice' den.

This idyllic, utopian scene has been the subject of countless paintings, songs, and literature; indeed, the peaceful co-existence of natural enemies and human babies, a world restored to an Eden-like state in the Messiah's reign, has sparked the imagination and dreams of humanity ever since the prophet penned the words.

An asp (Heb. *pethen*, **PEH-then**) means a snake or venomous serpent, which is synonymous with cockatrice (Heb. *tsepha'*, **TSEH-fah**), perhaps a cobra, adder, or viper (cf. Isaiah 59:5, "viper's brood"). The serpent has a unique role in human history dating from the garden temptation (Genesis 3) and has been symbolic of evil ever since. Clearly, if children and infants can play with poisonous snakes, the curse or enmity (Genesis 3:15) pronounced on Adam and Eve has been removed—and more than that, kingdom peace reigns over all.

9 They shall not hurt nor destroy in all my holy mountain: for the earth shall be full of the knowledge of the LORD, as the waters cover the sea.

These verses are similar to Isaiah 65:25 and Habakkuk 2:14. The reference to the holy mountain, or Mt. Zion, is a recurring theme throughout Isaiah, that also will be explored in next week's lesson (25:6, 10; cf. 10:32). Nature is restored, peace envelops the world, and God's glory fills the earth. Just as the first Adam was given dominion over creation (Genesis 1:26–28), so the second Adam, the Messianic King, will be given the same (Zechariah 14:9). With man ruling the first earth, peace was never possible, but with God, nothing is impossible (Luke 1:37). In the new creation, all will have new hearts and minds, and all of creation will be made new (2 Corinthians 5:17). This will make true peace an everlasting, perfect reality for all of God's people.

Meanwhile, the peace process has started in the hearts of believers, but it is not by any means a complete transformation. Indeed, Paul calls for these very characteristics among believers who are to "put on the new man" in Colossians 3:8–11. As we wait for that great day, in the spirit of hope for perfection in the messianic rule, each of us can surely touch someone else, be an example, and make a difference for them.

Say It Correctly

Cockatrice. **KA**-ka-treese.
Reprove. ree-**PROOV**.

Daily Bible Readings

MONDAY
God's Offer to Solomon
(1 Kings 3:3–9)

TUESDAY
God is Pleased with Solomon's Requests
(1 Kings 3:10–15)

WEDNESDAY
Live Together in Harmony
(1 Peter 3:8–13)

THURSDAY
Build a Peaceful Lifestyle
(2 Peter 1:3–11)

FRIDAY
Support the Interests of Others
(Philippians 2:1–11)

SATURDAY
Build a Just and Righteous Community
(Psalm 72:1–7)

SUNDAY
Presiding Over a Peaceful Community
(Isaiah 11:1–9)

Notes

Teaching Tips

Words You Should Know
A. Mountain (Isaiah 25:6–7) *har* (Heb)—Hill, mountain, hill country.

B. Victory (v. 8) *netsakh* (Heb)—Eminence, perpetuity, strength, enduring, everlastingness.

Teacher Preparation
Unifying Principle—The End of Oppression. Oppressed people always seek relief from their injustices. Who will deliver them? Isaiah's prophecy reveals that the sovereign God will give deliverance from oppression.

A. Pray for your students to understand that God is moving among nations and peoples.

B. Read the passage in multiple translations.

O—Open the Lesson
A. Open with prayer and praise, including the Aim to Change.

B. Introduce today's lesson title: "The Mountain of God."

C. Have your students read the Aim for Change and the Keep in Mind verse together.

D. Discuss the importance of the Mountain of God. Exactly what does it mean to each student?

E. Have them tell a brief story of what it means to be oppressed and then set free by God.

F. Tell the class to read the In Focus Story silently, and then discuss it.

G. Ask the students to tell of an occasion when they were delivered from a challenge; praise God for bringing them out.

P—Present the Scriptures
A. Have volunteers read the Focal Verses.

B. Use the People, Places, and Times; Background; Search the Scriptures; At-A-Glance Outline; In Depth; and More Light on the Text to clarify the verses.

E—Explore the Meaning
A. Divide the class into groups to complete the Discuss the Meaning, Lesson in Our Society, and Make It Happen sections. Ask students to choose a representative to report their responses.

B. Connect these sections to the Aim for Change and the Keep in Mind verse.

N—Next Steps for Application
A. Summarize the lesson.

B. Close with prayer.

Worship Guide

For the Superintendent or Teacher
Theme: The Mountain of God
Song: "I Will Praise the Lord at All Times"
Devotional Reading: 1 Corinthians 15:1–11

The Mountain of God

Bible Background • ISAIAH 25
Printed Text • ISAIAH 25:6–10a | Devotional Reading • 1 CORINTHIANS 15:1–11

—— Aim for Change ——

By the end of the lesson we will: DECIDE that God acts in the best interest of all peoples and nations; APPRECIATE that God removes barriers that cause people to feel separated from Him and one another; and REJOICE that God gives hope to all oppressed peoples.

In Focus

Some new neighbors had just recently moved into Sharon's neighborhood. The family was very large and did not appear to be native to the United States. It soon became obvious that their culture was different from the other families in the community. One thing everyone noticed was that their yard was not maintained and they kept chickens that wandered into other people's yards. The husband worked late into the night and their lights were on way past dinnertime. Additionally, they played loud music on Saturdays and disturbed people's sleep on Sunday. Many of the other families began to talk about the family. They predicted that if more people like them moved in, they would cause the property values of the homes to go down. Sharon began to wonder if they were right.

One day, she was on her way to work when her car wouldn't start. Sharon sat in the driveway, knowing that her husband had left with the jumper cables. Just then her new neighbor stopped by and asked if she needed help. He helped to start her car and she invited him to church. He couldn't make it to Sunday morning service because of his night schedule, but he was willing to come to Bible study on Wednesday nights.

In today's lesson, we learn how God breaks down barriers that separate us from Him and from one another. What are some barriers that keep people from God and from one another?

—— Keep in Mind ——

"He will swallow up death in victory; and the Lord GOD will wipe away tears from off all faces; and the rebuke of his people shall he take away from off all the earth: for the LORD hath spoken" (Isaiah 25:8).

"He will swallow up death in victory; and the Lord GOD will wipe away tears from off all faces; and the rebuke of his people shall he take away from off all the earth: for the LORD hath spoken" (Isaiah 25:8).

Focal Verses

KJV Isaiah 25:6 And in this mountain shall the LORD of hosts make unto all people a feast of fat things, a feast of wines on the lees, of fat things full of marrow, of wines on the lees well refined.

7 And he will destroy in this mountain the face of the covering cast over all people, and the vail that is spread over all nations.

8 He will swallow up death in victory; and the Lord GOD will wipe away tears from off all faces; and the rebuke of his people shall he take away from off all the earth: for the LORD hath spoken it.

9 And it shall be said in that day, Lo, this is our God; we have waited for him, and he will save us: this is the LORD; we have waited for him, we will be glad and rejoice in his salvation.

10a For in this mountain shall the hand of the LORD rest.

NLT Isaiah 25:6 In Jerusalem, the LORD of Heaven's Armies will spread a wonderful feast for all the people of the world. It will be a delicious banquet with clear, well-aged wine and choice meat.

7 There he will remove the cloud of gloom, the shadow of death that hangs over the earth.

8 He will swallow up death forever! The Sovereign LORD will wipe away all tears. He will remove forever all insults and mockery against his land and people. The LORD has spoken!

9 In that day the people will proclaim, "This is our God! We trusted in him, and he saved us! This is the LORD, in whom we trusted. Let us rejoice in the salvation he brings!"

10a For the LORD's hand of blessing will rest on Jerusalem.

The People, Places, and Times

Feast. In biblical times, weddings, harvest periods, and peace treaties were among the many occasions for feasting. These occasions symbolize everything that will take place in the future: Christ's marriage to His bride the church will be consummated, the harvest of His people will be gathered, and the peace between Him and His people will be celebrated. Feasts were always joyous occasions accompanied by rich food and wine.

This mountain. The references in the prophetic books to "this mountain" and "my holy mountain" are references to Jerusalem and the New Jerusalem. The reference to Jerusalem includes not only the Israelites who will return from exile, but all peoples (v. 7). This is an eschatological promise similar to the promise of the New Jerusalem that speaks of the city God's people will dwell in, in the age to come. There in the New Jerusalem, instead of an earthly temple, God will be the temple. This New Jerusalem will be a place of total peace and prosperity absent of war, suffering, and death (Revelation 21).

Background

Isaiah chapter 25 is in the midst of a section of the book that paints the picture of God's judgment on the nations and establishment of His kingdom. These chapters are especially focused on the end of the world; they speak of what will happen in the last days and what has already begun to happen, as the kingdom of God has been inaugurated with the coming of Christ.

Specifically, in chapter 24, Isaiah prophesies cosmic judgment and God's reign over all the earth. The very earth is pictured as reeling to and fro like a drunkard. Isaiah speaks of it being dissolved clean. Although this may sound discouraging, God will not leave the earth desolate. He will bring restoration through His coming reign, which is then described in full, rich detail in chapter 25. The joy of God's people and the blessings that will accompany His reign will be the result of His abolishing sin and death.

At-A-Glance

1. God Hosts a Party (Isaiah 25:6–7)
2. Death Will Be Destroyed (v. 8)
3. God's Hand of Protection (vv. 9–10)

In Depth

1. God Hosts a Party (Isaiah 25:6–7)

Verses 1–5 comprise a hymn, including a confession of faith (v. 1), praising God for delivering His people from oppression (Isaiah 24). Only God can break oppression and end bondages imposed by the evil one. Isaiah 25:6 talks about God throwing a feast that will end oppression. This feast will be for all people, and will be full of wine and the richest foods. This feast would have stirred the imagination of the Hebrew mind at the time. The imagery is one of plenteous food and joy.

Next Isaiah alludes to the Lord destroying a shroud or covering that is over all people. This shroud, which connects all people, no matter what ethnicity or culture, is death. The feast is for all people because this shroud will one day be destroyed.

2. Death Will Be Destroyed (v. 8)

Isaiah 25:8 talks about God removing the shadow of death. With this cloud of gloom removed from over His people, they can see the bigger picture: God is Sovereign and in control, and He can do whatever He chooses. We as believers look forward to the celebration that marks the end of all oppression. We wait for death to be done away with, for the New Heaven, the New Earth, and the New Jerusalem.

The strength and fear of death will be destroyed so that it no longer exists. Oppression will be completely severed. Our God says to all people who put their trust in Him that He will wipe away all tears. Not only will He swallow death and wipe away all tears, but the sting of insults and mockery will be removed against His land and people as well. The reputation of His people would be restored.

3. God's Hand of Protection (vv. 9–10)

God's people will proclaim, "He is our God!" Here, they will basically be saying, "We trusted in Him and He saved us. This is the Lord, in whom we have trusted." The people of God will come back and declare that Yahweh is their God because He has delivered them to freedom. This declaration points to salvation in Jesus Christ. Believers can exclaim the same truth: He is our God.

Next Isaiah speaks of God's hand of protection and blessings, which will rest on Jerusalem, the city where His people dwell. God's hand on His people will be seen. It will be evident and clear to all that God's people are His people. This is the hope and expectation of those who trust in Him. They will be vindicated in the age to come.

Search the Scriptures

1. What did Isaiah mean when he said, "And the Lord God will wipe away tears from off all faces; and the rebuke of his people shall he take away from off all the earth: for the Lord hath spoken it" (Isaiah 25:8)?

2. How can we discern if God's hand of blessing is on our lives (v. 10)?

Discuss the Meaning

Injustice and oppression are all around us. Is it better to accept it and wait until Jesus returns or to get involved in an opportunity to fight injustice and oppression?

Lesson in Our Society

If you turn on the evening news or surf the Internet, you can find out what people put their trust in. Many hope and trust in the government. Some put their trust in the economy, others in their health. All of these things will ultimately fail. Today's lesson tells people to put their hope in the Lord and His kingdom, where all of their aspirations will come true. The violence, oppression, and death that plagues us will one day be destroyed.

Make It Happen

The lesson tells us about a future feast day in God's kingdom. As you anticipate the feast you will share with the Lord in the age to come, plan a practice feast and invite your family, friends, and neighbors to a dinner that represents what you believe God wants us to enjoy in the future with Him.

Follow the Spirit

What God wants me to do:

_____

_____

_____

_____

Remember Your Thoughts

Special insights I have learned:

_____

More Light on the Text

Isaiah 25:6–10a

Fifteen years after the attacks on New York City's World Trade Towers on September 11, 2001, the world seems to be an even more dangerous place with terrorists seemingly coming out of the woodwork and multiplying like cockroaches. The news is regularly filled with new attacks, both in America and other nations; sometimes, the attacks target Christians in the most incomprehensibly inhumane ways. When and how will it all come to an end? Believers through the centuries have placed their hope in God, especially in times of great darkness and oppression. In these precious verses from Isaiah, we are granted a glimpse of the coming reward for faithfully trusting and hoping in God.

In a strongly worded contrast in the verses introducing the lesson, not only will justice arrive for the "poor and needy," but judgment also will visit the "terrible ones" (v. 4; "ruthless people," NIV). Isaiah's psalm of praise (25:1–5) describes that glorious day. Depending on one's perspective, the event is either good or bad news—for those who suffered and were oppressed but trusted God, He now responds to the cries of the centuries. Those who opposed Him and were "ruthless" (other versions, "powerful" or "oppressors," cf Isaiah 1:17, 21; see also "exalting thrones," 14:13; "haughty people," 24:4), who lifted themselves up, are now "brought low" (v. 5). In distinct contrast to the faithful Lord who will be exalted, the unrighteous oppressors will be humbled.

6 And in this mountain shall the LORD of hosts make unto all people a feast of fat things, a feast of wines on the lees, of fat things full of marrow, of wines on the lees well refined.

"In this mountain" refers again to Mt. Zion, which Isaiah establishes early on (2:1–5; cf. 24:23), and "unto all people" refers to the gathering of Israel and all other nations (cf. Zechariah 14:16) for the momentous occasion of a great feast. Indeed, it bears an undeniable resemblance to the "great supper," the wedding feast of the Lamb described in Luke 14:15–24. Just as in the parable, the guest list is open to all, although not all will attend—even among the first invitees. As can be imagined, this is the ultimate feast, and God spares no good thing, even for former enemies. In this sense, it is perhaps intentionally reminiscent of the prodigal son, whose father threw a lavish feast to welcome home his lost son, which speaks directly to the father's character. There is an interesting reiteration with dual usage of "a feast of fat things" (Heb. *shemen*, **SHEH-men**) and dual usage of "a feast of wines on the lees" (Heb. *shemer*, **SHEH-mer**), which might be similar to someone today extravagantly describing a "no expense spared, fully appointed, everything under the sun, fit for a king" feast. Lees is the name of the residual yeast that settles to the bottom during the fermentation process for wine and beer; it is stirred back into some expensive wines to enhance the flavor.

7 And he will destroy in this mountain the face of the covering cast over all people, and the vail that is spread over all nations.

The covering and veil have many potential meanings, including spiritual blindness, in the context of having the veil of blindness removed so one can perceive the truth (cf. 2 Corinthians 3:13–16, which leads to a New Testament salvation theme in v. 18, "unveiled face," NKJV).

Yet another view is that it refers to a burial cloth, similar to the one that encased Jesus' body (Matthew 27:59). The preponderance of scholars seem to agree, however, that this usage refers to the "mourning veil," and that what will be destroyed is the grieving associated with death, which has been part of mankind's curse since the fall of Adam and Eve (Genesis 3:19). Because everybody dies, mourning on earth has never ended, but with God death is not the end. Just as death once was introduced as a result of sin, so now at the end of human reign on earth, death and all its associated sadness will come to an end—not just for Israel, but for all nations, all humankind. In the reversal that only He could effect, God is saying is that the curse of death will have run its course.

8 He will swallow up death in victory; and the Lord GOD will wipe away tears from off all faces; and the rebuke of his people shall he take away from off all the earth: for the LORD hath spoken it.

Paul quotes from this verse in 1 Corinthians 15:54: "So when this corruptible shall have put on incorruption, and this mortal shall have put on immortality, then shall be brought to pass the saying that is written, death is swallowed up in victory," rendered "forever" in NLT. The Hebrew word (*netsakh*, **NET-sakh**) can mean glory or success as well as eternity. Isaiah takes advantage of the dual meaning in order to make his point. It will be an eternal victory when God destroys death. The process of its demise is called the end times, with the end of death being just one of the climaxes prior to the inauguration of God's kingdom.

Directly related to other aspects of the curse, all suffering, pain, and crying will end as well, along with all oppression and its associated disgrace, reproach, and shame (see Zephaniah 3:18; Joel 2:19). As with much of the Old Testament, the Scripture emphasizes the unique plight of Israel's persecutions, repeated in waves of anti-Semitism through history, which continue to the present day. In the KJV, Isaiah promises God will take away his people's rebuke. The NLT renders this word "disgrace" (Heb. *kherpah*, **kher-PAH**), which is more accurate for contemporary English because what Isaiah is promising is that the disgrace that God's people have faced through centuries of oppression will be done away with. Oppressors removed God's people from their home and devastated God's land, and now God uses Israel as the gathering place for righting the wrongs other nations have committed against her, focused on humanity generally as well as Israel specifically. Because of this view, Ambrose, an ancient church father, called Isaiah not only a prophet but also "the first apostle and evangelist" (Ibid., 192). God is committed to Israel but cares for all people of all nations; within this concern, however, is their need to respond to Him and turn toward Him, no longer rejecting Him. God's concern for the world is universal, but the world's response certainly hasn't been nor ever will be as universal; thus the distinction even in this grandest of promises of "His people" from all others.

Many similar verses, such as Revelation 21:4 ("And God shall wipe away all tears from their eyes; and there shall be no more death, neither sorrow, nor crying, neither shall there be any more pain"), have been quoted at many funerals, as they speak to the core of the abiding faith of believers through the centuries: No matter how great or painful the loss, all will be made right through God in the end, all loved ones will be reunited, and all tears of sorrow will give way to eternal gladness and rejoicing (cf. Psalm 126:5; Isaiah 35:10). God's sovereignty will make right the wrongs caused by the unfathomable suffering that has been ever present on the earth.

9 And it shall be said in that day, Lo, this is our God; we have waited for him, and he will save us: this is the LORD; we have waited for him, we will be glad and rejoice in his salvation. 10 For in this mountain shall the hand of the LORD rest.

Once again, continuing the psalm of praise he used to start the chapter, Isaiah breaks into song. Indeed, such celebration is found throughout the prophet's writings (among numerous examples, see the closely associated 24:14–16; cf 12:1–6, et al.). Those who hope in God will not be let down; He has heard every prayer ever uttered, He will save us, and then we will rejoice greatly as all our suffering finally, mercifully, and permanently ends. This is God's final answer to every evil known to man from the Fall, the fulfillment of every promise in every prophecy. "The hand of God" is a phrase found throughout both testaments, from recognizing God's hand at work in both trials (e.g., Job 19:21) and victories (e.g., Exodus 32:11), to Jesus Himself being exalted to the place of God's right hand (Acts 2:33), to a context for discipleship ("humble yourselves therefore under the mighty hand of God," 1 Peter 5:6). God's hand is a symbol of power, used for judgment, destruction and creation. In this oracle of salvation, Isaiah promises that after the power of God's judgment will come the power of God's rest.

Say It Correctly

Lees. **LEES**.
Vail. **VAY**-il.

Daily Bible Readings

MONDAY
Praise for Deliverance From Oppression
(Isaiah 25:1–5)

TUESDAY
Healing Can't Wait
(Luke 14:1–6)

WEDNESDAY
Wait to Be Seated
(Luke 14:7–11)

THURSDAY
Invite the Needy to Your Table
(Luke 14:12–14)

FRIDAY
Dinner Will Be Served
(Luke 14:15–23)

SATURDAY
Christ Died for Our Sins
(1 Corinthians 15:1–11)

SUNDAY
The Mountain of God
(Isaiah 25:6–10)

Notes

_____

_____

_____

_____

Teaching Tips

Words You Should Know

A. Known (Isaiah 40:21, 28) *yada* (Heb.)—learned, perceived, or acknowledged.

B. Wait (v. 31) *qavah* (Heb.)—To look for, hope for, expect.

Teacher Preparation

Unifying Principle—Ultimate Power. We often place loyalty in people or systems to sustain and guide our lives. Are these systems able to sustain us? Isaiah declares that God is the absolute power in whom we should depend.

A. Read Focal Verses in multiple translations.

B. Study the companion lesson in the *Precepts for Living®* Personal Study Guide.

O—Open the Lesson

A. Ask for a volunteer to pray.

B. Share one or more of the articles that question God's authority.

C. Open a brief Q&A to sense the class' general opinions and observations.

P—Present the Scriptures

A. Read the Focal Verses together as a class.

B. Read The People, Places, and Times and Background to better understand the lesson.

C. Read In Depth and discuss the Search the Scriptures questions.

E—Explore the Meaning

A. Use Discuss the Meaning to contrast the believer's view of God's power versus that of non-Christians.

B. Continue the discussion with Lesson in Our Society to determine evangelistic opportunities within this lesson.

N—Next Steps for Application

A. Ask students to name something they might wait for. Is there a difference between waiting on God and waiting on others?

B. Have the class share some impossible situations and agree to pray over them.

Worship Guide

For the Superintendent or Teacher
Theme: Foundations of the Earth
Song: "Blessed Assurance"
Devotional Reading: Isaiah 40:1–8

Foundations of the Earth

Bible Background • ISAIAH 40
Printed Text • ISAIAH 40:21–31 | Devotional Reading • ISAIAH 40:1–8

Aim for Change

By the end of this lesson we will: CONTRAST God's power to control and effect change with human inability to do the same; REFLECT on the poetic imagery the writer uses to witness to God's sovereign power and personal presence with the people; and EMBRACE God's sovereignty and ability to address people's situations and needs.

In Focus

Deborah didn't know if she could go on anymore. This was the fifth night that she had to do overtime. The graveyard shift was definitely not her thing. Being a mother of five made it that much harder. Deborah didn't want to work so much, but she had no other option. She had to put food on the table for her children and make sure they had a roof over their heads. On top of all that, she didn't like her job. Her co-workers were pretty mean to her and always seemed to find a way to tell her dirty jokes.

This last night she was exhausted. She curled up on the bed and cried. She thought about all the mistakes that she had made in life and how she ended up in this situation. She looked for love in the arms of men who didn't care about her at all and faced multiple pregnancies on her own. She wondered whether she deserved whatever consequences came from her past mistakes. She wondered why God didn't send a good man or a better job her way? As she knelt down on the side of the bed to pray, the phone rang. It was a company calling about a job a friend had encouraged her to apply for. She didn't think she was qualified for such a nice position, but believed that if God wanted it to happen, then it would. After she had previously gone in for an interview, she felt certain she wouldn't get the job, but now they were calling to tell her it was hers. She could start Monday morning.

In today's lesson, we learn about God's ability to change the circumstances of His people. Have you ever experienced God doing the impossible in your own personal life?

Keep in Mind

"Hast thou not known? hast thou not heard, that the everlasting God, the LORD, the Creator of the ends of the earth, fainteth not, neither is weary? there is no searching of his understanding" (Isaiah 40:28).

"Hast thou not known? hast thou not heard, that the everlasting God, the LORD, the Creator of the ends of the earth, fainteth not, neither is weary? there is no searching of his understanding" (Isaiah 40:28).

Focal Verses

KJV

Isaiah 40:21 Have ye not known? have ye not heard? hath it not been told you from the beginning? have ye not understood from the foundations of the earth?

22 It is he that sitteth upon the circle of the earth, and the inhabitants thereof are as grasshoppers; that stretcheth out the heavens as a curtain, and spreadeth them out as a tent to dwell in:

23 That bringeth the princes to nothing; he maketh the judges of the earth as vanity.

24 Yea, they shall not be planted; yea, they shall not be sown: yea, their stock shall not take root in the earth: and he shall also blow upon them, and they shall wither, and the whirlwind shall take them away as stubble.

25 To whom then will ye liken me, or shall I be equal? saith the Holy One.

26 Lift up your eyes on high, and behold who hath created these things, that bringeth out their host by number: he calleth them all by names by the greatness of his might, for that he is strong in power; not one faileth.

27 Why sayest thou, O Jacob, and speakest, O Israel, My way is hid from the LORD, and my judgment is passed over from my God?

28 Hast thou not known? hast thou not heard, that the everlasting God, the LORD, the Creator of the ends of the earth, fainteth not, neither is weary? there is no searching of his understanding.

29 He giveth power to the faint; and to them that have no might he increaseth strength.

30 Even the youths shall faint and be weary, and the young men shall utterly fall:

31 But they that wait upon the LORD shall renew their strength; they shall mount up with wings as eagles; they shall run, and not be weary; and they shall walk, and not faint.

NLT

Isaiah 40:21 Haven't you heard? Don't you understand? Are you deaf to the words of God—the words he gave before the world began? Are you so ignorant?

22 God sits above the circle of the earth. The people below seem like grasshoppers to him! He spreads out the heavens like a curtain and makes his tent from them.

23 He judges the great people of the world and brings them all to nothing.

24 They hardly get started, barely taking root, when he blows on them and they wither. The wind carries them off like chaff.

25 "To whom will you compare me? Who is my equal?" asks the Holy One.

26 Look up into the heavens. Who created all the stars? He brings them out like an army, one after another, calling each by its name. Because of his great power and incomparable strength, not a single one is missing.

27 O Jacob, how can you say the LORD does not see your troubles? O Israel, how can you say God ignores your rights?

28 Have you never heard? Have you never understood? The LORD is the everlasting God, the Creator of all the earth. He never grows weak or weary. No one can measure the depths of his understanding.

29 He gives power to the weak and strength to the powerless.

30 Even youths will become weak and tired, and young men will fall in exhaustion.

31 But those who trust in the LORD will find new strength. They will soar high on wings like eagles. They will run and not grow weary. They will walk and not faint.

The People, Places, and Times

Chaff/Stubble. The loose shells that were separated from grain. The husks were then blown away with the wind and the edible grain would remain. These became a metaphor for the wicked who would be judged by God. They would be driven away by the wrath of His judgment, and only the righteous would remain.

Eagles. In biblical times, eagles were known for their speed and power and came to represent the speed and power of deliverance, but also disaster. The eagle, along with the lion, the ox, and mankind, is one of four faces of the cherubim (Ezekiel 1:10). The book of Leviticus forbade the Israelites to eat certain birds, including eagles, probably because they ate carrion, which made them unclean animals unsuitable for consumption or sacrifice (Leviticus 11:13–19). Palestine is home to four varieties of eagles.

Background

Isaiah 40 is a significant turning point in the book of Isaiah. Up until now, the prophetic oracles have largely been about impending judgment on Judah and the other nations of the world. Judah worshiped idols and committed oppression; as a result, they will be judged with other nations. This judgment will result in exile, and the people of God will be scattered to the ends of the earth. The talk of judgment is interspersed with talk of the joy and peace of God's coming kingdom.

Now in Isaiah 40, God brings the people back from exile and into their promised land. Their suffering will be over, and their punishment will be complete. Those who had been led into captivity will return. Isaiah 40 focuses on the God who has the power to rescue His people from exile and return them to their home with mercy and compassion.

At-A-Glance

1. God's Power Over Creation (Isaiah 40:21–22)
2. God's Power Over Human Authority (vv. 23–27)
3. God's Power Over Our Lives (Isaiah 40:28–31)

In Depth

1. God's Power Over Creation (Isaiah 40:21–22)

Any discussion of God's sovereignty must acknowledge the fullness of His identity. In Isaiah 40, the prophet reminds Israel that God's primary identity is that of Creator. Genesis 1 details God's initial activities that created our world, and notes the up-close and personal nature with which He engaged creation from the start. In creating the earth, God's Spirit moved. He spoke things into existence and then looked at His work with eyes of approval (Genesis 1:2–5). He then provided the literal ground on which we stand as He made the dry land in contrast to the waters. As Isaiah reflects on the truths of Genesis, he reminds the people that God is not simply in power or in control. He is indeed involved. Isaiah 40:22 says, "he sitteth upon the circle of the earth..." This image of God overseeing the actions of the earth's inhabitants is interesting. The circle of the earth invokes the revolving nature of human behavior, and also places God just outside our horizon. While He is involved and engaged with us, He is still apart from creation, primarily because He created it. Nevertheless, God chooses to dwell with us. Even if we are comparatively as insignificant as grasshoppers, our Sovereign God still provides a tent of protection over us, and has made the entirety of this planet for our use.

A further look at Isaiah 40:1–3 reveals Messianic messages that acknowledge God the Creator and herald the coming of Christ the Comforter. While the forces of nature do not necessarily require a messiah, comforter, or savior, it is still relevant that God's creation power is at work in the midst of all things. The prophet would later be echoed by the Apostle Paul, as he notes in Colossians 1:15–16 that "by him all things were created ... whether they be thrones, or dominions, or principalities, or powers: all things were created by him, and for him." This helps to explain that God's power over creation was not simply to make things, but also order them, give them purpose and reason, and ultimately give Him glory by their existence. Anyone seeking a foundation must understand that no part of our lives is accidental. God has made everything intentionally, including us, and He has made everything we need to survive and thrive.

2. God's Power Over Human Authority (vv. 23–27)

Many people seek stability and foundation in conventional human authority. True enough, God has ordained order and instructs everyone to be obedient to the chain of responsibility within their immediate realm (Hebrews 13:7, 17). Yet God has also made clear that He is not in competition with mankind for ultimate authority. Isaiah 40:23 says, "[He] bringeth the princes to nothing: he maketh the judges of the earth as vanity." God's judgment is a fascinating concept, because He alone embodies righteousness, and only He can evaluate the entire world down to its elements. God's judgment is not limited to weighing sins and crimes against a sinner's intentions or heart. He does not merely engage in conflict resolution, nor operate solely to place some people high and keep others low. God's judgment is simply an aspect of His being. As Creator, He can evaluate

His creation—remarking on it, instructing it, and re-purposing it all at His discretion. Isaiah 40:26–27 likens God to a mighty general, commanding the march of the stars, each with an identity and purpose. The author also notes the irony of our desire to fit into the scheme of God's will through our works and ambitions. While the conventions of human authority have a place and purpose in structuring our lives, it is a great relief to know that God can re-issue commands that can protect us while we are imprisoned, and restore joy in the midst of our mourning. Isaiah is prophesying the period of Babylonian captivity, which imposed new human authority over God's people who relish their unique identity in the known world of their time. Isaiah reminds the people that while they are at times subject to human authority, they should not worship or put trust in it. Even as God has allowed a change in designation, He still retains control of their destiny, and must continue to be worshiped and praised for deliverance before, until, and after it has come.

3. God's Power Over Our Lives (vv. 28–31)

This oft-quoted Scripture is at once poetic, provocative, and powerful. The hypothetical "have you not known, have you not heard" are rhetorical questions that seek to comfort the believer who expresses doubt or exasperation at God's timing and motivations. The very heartfelt encouragements within these verses acknowledge both God's power and His concern over our lives. He is not distant, if He created and dwells in the ends of the earth. He knows when we are faint and re-energizes us. He increases the physical, mental, and moral strength of those helpless to fend off opponents. Essentially, the foundation that we enjoy in God is not based on our place in society, our obedience to government, or even our diligence toward His works. He alone is our foundation, meaning He provides and protects us completely on His own!

To wait on God (v. 31) must then mean that we actively and excitedly seek and see God's involvement at all times. If there is no searching of His understanding, this means there is no limit to what He can do to remedy our situations. Paul expresses this idea in Philippians 4:19: "My God shall supply all your need according to his riches in glory by Christ Jesus." Waiting on God means that we surrender to His authority personally. Our individual yielding to God allows us to intimately benefit from the strength and supply that He provides.

The primary difference between God's sovereignty and human authority is motivation. In most cases, the powers of humankind could very easily end poverty, war, and brutality. Even the advances in science technology and medicine could sharply reduce disease and suffering for millions, if not billions of people. Sadly, however, human authority erects barriers to access and thus, progress, because of our greed and quest for power while neglecting the needs of others. God's model, by contrast, is to renew strength. Waiting on God is not waiting in a bureaucratic line, but rather waiting with hope and expectation for the miraculous to happen among the mundane. As the prophet Isaiah issues this song of expectation, he elicits worship out of worry and converts panic into praise. The end result is not just deliverance for personal gain, but deliverance of all who witness the victory that comes after the wait.

Search the Scriptures

1. When looking at the size of humanity in comparison to the Lord, what is one humble action you can choose to acknowledge God's greatness (Isaiah 40:22)?

2. If God reduces princes to nothing and judges to vanity, what attitude should we as believers have when engaging in politics (v. 24)?

Discuss the Meaning

1. Isaiah speaks of God renewing our strength. In what way does God renew your strength when you are tired and discouraged?

2. Isaiah encouraged God's people to wait on Him. Why should we wait on the Lord?

Lesson in Our Society

Today's political seasons seem to last longer than the actual term of office. Often politicians wage campaigns built on the promise of change and reform, yet once in office, they continue to support archaic systems that continue to leave the least powerful people impoverished and hungry. In America, citizens enjoy not only a vote, but also the right to pray and worship freely. Despite political parties' claims of morality and righteousness, it is the citizens who have the ultimate ability to invoke God's presence and obey His will even while serving under an unjust or ungodly administration.

Make It Happen

Isaiah 40 speaks peace in the midst of turmoil. While our lives may not be rife with grave injustice on a daily basis, it is still good to know that hope in God and trust in His foundation will guarantee eventual good. "They that wait upon the Lord" cannot simply be a platitude or a comforting saying. Waiting is an action word, meaning that faith is put to work, resulting in a closer relationship with God and a deeper respect for our place within His creation.

Follow the Spirit

What God wants me to do:

_____

_____

_____

_____

Remember Your Thoughts

Special insights I have learned:

_____

_____

_____

_____

More Light on the Text

Isaiah 40:21–31

Isaiah has just written to the Israelites about the absurdity of worshiping idols. People are worshiping something they made out of the materials that our Creator-God made. We may think that we would not do something as crazy as worshiping idols, but anytime we elevate material things above the spiritual, we are guilty of this very sin. Isaiah had an amazing vision of God (Isaiah 6:1–4), and now he is sharing with the Hebrew people a little bit of how big God is. This should be nothing new to His people. From their beginning as a nation, God has been revealing Himself to them. Even before then, God was making Himself known to those with eyes to see and hearts to receive.

21 Have ye not known? have ye not heard? hath it not been told you from the beginning? have ye not understood from the foundations of the earth? 22 It is he that sitteth upon the circle of the earth, and the inhabitants thereof are as grasshoppers; that stretcheth out the heavens as a curtain, and spreadeth them out as a tent to dwell in:

Isaiah begins by asking his audience if they really understand who God is. The greatness of God, the Creator, should be evident to anyone whether they are familiar with the Bible or not. Paul echoes this thought in Romans 1:20: "For the invisible things of him from the creation of the world are clearly seen, being understood by the things that are made, even his eternal power and Godhead; so that they are without excuse." Genesis 1–2 gives us a creation theology that informs our understanding of God's nature. He is not a part of His creation, but distinct from it. There is God, and everything else is not God, including us, His created beings. Any belief that calls us gods is wrong.

The phrase "circle of the earth" fits into the ancient Near Eastern world view of the structure of the universe. In ancient cosmology, the sky was a dome over the earth, partly because stars and other celestial bodies were thought to move from horizon to horizon in a half circle. The earth in turn sat on primordial waters, and underneath lay a netherworld or underworld. In the ancient world, the earth was seen as a circle rather than a sphere, more than likely due to the disk-shaped curvature of the horizon. Isaiah is both declaring that God dwells on the horizon—just in sight—and playing on the sound of the words for horizon (Heb. *khug*, **KHOOG**) and grasshopper (Heb. *khagab*, **KHAH-gahv**), which begin with similar sounds that represent the expanse of God's creation from the vast horizon to the multitude of small insects.

Isaiah compares our significance to grasshoppers. These insects were so prolific and familiar to the Israelites that the Old Testament contains about a dozen different words for them. This passage emphasizes the smallness of the grasshopper. Isaiah pictures the heavens above the earth as a great vault. If we go outside in an open field on a starry night, we can look up at the stars above as well as the horizon, which appears as a great circle. Imagine God sitting up in the star-filled sky and looking down upon the earth at us. We appear as small to God as a tiny grasshopper would appear to us. Just as we can stomp on a grasshopper and end it, so God has the destiny of every human life in His hands. This thought should cause us to tremble in awe before our almighty God!

23 That bringeth the princes to nothing; he maketh the judges of the earth as vanity. 24 Yea, they shall not be planted; yea, they shall not be sown: yea, their stock shall not take root in the earth: and he shall also blow upon them, and they shall wither, and the whirlwind shall take them away as stubble.

The Hebrew word for "vanity" is *tohu* (**TOE-hoo**). Among the synonyms for this word are desolation, desert, worthless thing, confusion, nothingness, waste, or wilderness. Great civilizations such as the great African empires, the Aztec and Incan empires, and the Roman empire have come and gone. All people are capable of great civilizations, but these are very fragile. The study of history helps us to see the bigger picture, but all of this is known to God. He sees the beginning and end of all the kingdoms and empires of the world. He is the God of both history and creation.

The Israelites were looking at the mighty Babylonian empire and trembling. But we worship the God of the long view. God dwells in eternal time; He can simultaneously see seconds, years, and even millions of years—past, present, and future. Individual rulers may be in charge almost their entire lifetimes and empires may last hundreds of years, but this is just a little blip in God's eternal plans. Earlier in this chapter (40:7–8), we read that people are just like grass—transitory. None of us will last forever. Even kingdoms of great cultures have come and gone. So we should not idolize or fear a mighty ruler, the head of the corporation we work for, or even our middle-level manager. Just like the summer dandelion whose seeds can be blown away with one little puff, so are the political power structures and even superpowers that will be blown away in time.

25 To whom then will ye liken me, or shall I be equal? saith the Holy One. 26 Lift up your eyes on high, and behold who hath created these things, that bringeth out their host by number: he calleth them all by names by the greatness of his might, for that he is strong in power; not one faileth. 27 Why sayest thou, O Jacob, and speakest, O Israel, My way is hid from the Lord, and my judgment is passed over from my God?

The Hebrew word for equal is *shavah* (**shah-VAH**), a word that invites comparison as to whether something is of equal value or quality. The answer is that no one, no god, nothing can compare to God, the Holy One; nothing is equal to Him.

Just as many people do today, the Babylonians consulted their horoscopes to see what was in their future. Isaiah points out that the stars are all under God's command. Why consult the stars, when we know the God who created and controls them? He has a name for each star. The Milky Way alone contains 100 billion stars. To count them all would take about 3,000 years, to say nothing of the task of naming them. This causes us to remember that God knows each one of us by name and even knows how many hairs there are on our heads (Matthew 10:30).

We may think that no one sees the things we do in secret or knows the things we think about, but God does. Not only does He know everything about us, but He is the one who judges us. Judgment (Heb. *mishpat*, **mish-POT**) means a judicial verdict (whether favorable or unfavorable). So this is a paradox. God loves us far more than we could imagine, but He is completely holy and cannot let sin into His presence. This is why each of us needs the Cross. On the Cross our sins were judged, and through the resurrection, we are assured that God has accepted the sacrifice of Jesus for our sins.

28 Hast thou not known? hast thou not heard, that the everlasting God, the Lord, the Creator of the ends of the earth, fainteth not, neither is weary? there is no searching of his understanding. 29 He giveth power to the faint; and to them that have no might he increaseth strength. 30 Even the youths shall faint and be weary, and the young men shall utterly fall: 31 But they that wait upon the Lord shall renew their strength; they shall mount up with wings as eagles; they shall run, and not be weary; and they shall walk, and not faint.

"Everlasting" (Heb. *'olam*, **oh-LOM**) means existing beyond time, before time began, and without any end. As humans, we understand history in terms of a timeline, but the everlasting God sees everything at all times. This is why we can trust our futures to Him. He knows the things that have happened and brought us to this point. He also sees what lies beyond today, and controls all the ages; certainly He has our futures in His hands.

In this section, Isaiah shows us that although God is greater than we can ever imagine, He cares for us as individuals far more than we can conceive. Whether we are emotionally drained, burnt out, hurt, or just physically exhausted, God is there to pick us up and carry us on His wings. Jesus reaffirms this promise in Matthew 11:28: "Come unto me, all ye that labour and are heavy laden, and I will give you rest." In fact, this is when He most desires to help us—when we realize our own helplessness.

Think of the young parents who are totally exhausted after being up all night with crying babies, or the elderly couple who are becoming unable to care for one another. Those we love and care for cannot be depended upon forever to pick us when we fall down, because often they are too tired themselves. But not our God. He never wearies. Even at night, He never shuts His eyes (Psalm 121:4).

Even more exciting is to think on the mind of our God. Isaiah tells us there is no searching of His understanding. We read in Psalm 139:17–18: "How precious also are thy thoughts unto me, O God! how great is the sum of them! If I should count them, they are more in number than the sand." We can never understand the mind of God, but it's delightful to think that He shares so many of His thoughts with us in His Word.

The Hebrew for "wait" is *qavah* (**kah-VAH**), meaning to wait expectantly and to look for patiently. Waiting on the Lord is not merely marking time; it is living in confident expectation of His action on our behalf. He has both strength and understanding to help us.

Say It Correctly

Orthoptera. Or-**THOP**-ter-a.
Liken. **LIE**-kin.

Daily Bible Readings

MONDAY
See God's Saving Power
(Luke 3:2–6)

TUESDAY
Power to Overcome Illness
(Isaiah 38:9–20)

WEDNESDAY
God's Word Stands Forever
(Isaiah 40:1–8)

THURSDAY
God Leads Like a Shepherd
(Isaiah 40:9–11)

FRIDAY
God's Wisdom is Unmatched
(Isaiah 40:12–14)

SATURDAY
God Unlike the Nations and Idols
(Isaiah 40:15–20)

SUNDAY
Our Powerful and Everlasting God
(Isaiah 40:21–31)

Notes

_____

_____

_____

_____

Teaching Tips

Words You Should Know

A. Judgment (Isaiah 61:8) *mishpat* (Heb.)—Justice, ordinance, propriety.

B. Covenant (v. 8) *berith* (Heb.)—Alliance, treaty, divine ordinance.

Teacher Preparation

Unifying Principle—Reliable Promises. People make agreements they intend to keep but too often break, causing stress and dismay. Can anyone make an agreement that will not be broken? In Isaiah, God promises an everlasting covenant, which can never be broken.

A. Pray for clarity and application, for you and your students.

B. Study the companion lesson in the *Precepts For Living®* Study Guide thoroughly, in advance.

O—Open the Lesson

A. Open with song and prayer.

B. Introduce the lesson title: "Everlasting Covenant."

C. Read the In Focus story and discuss the accompanying question.

P—Present the Scriptures

A. Read the Focal Verses together as a class.

B. Read The People, Places, and Times and Background to better understand the lesson.

C. Read In Depth and discuss the Search the Scriptures questions.

E—Explore the Meaning

A. Review the Discuss the Meaning section.

B. Discuss the Lesson in Our Society.

N—Next Steps for Application

A. Allow the class to share their experiences with covenant building and covenant keeping.

B. Close with prayer specifically for those who are in need of God's justice and grace.

Worship Guide

For the Superintendent or Teacher
Theme: Everlasting Covenant
Song: "I Will Trust in the Lord"
Devotional Reading: Isaiah 42:5–9

Everlasting Covenant

Bible Background • ISAIAH 61
Printed Text • ISAIAH 61:1–4, 8–11 | Devotional Reading • ISAIAH 42:5–9

Aim for Change

By the end of the lesson, we will: ACKNOWLEDGE that God has high ethical standards and enters into secure and enduring covenants with people; APPRECIATE what it means to live justly and faithfully according to God's covenant expectations; and PREPARE a statement of human response to God's covenant that reflects life today.

In Focus

The congregation at First AME Church of Macedonia had endured years and years of talk about building a community center that would meet the needs of the surrounding neighborhood. Many had donated sacrificially. Those who couldn't give large amounts had helped to raise the funds through selling barbecue dinners and candy bars. It was a vision that rallied the congregation together. They knew that God wanted to do something special in their community. Looking at all the needs of the many people in the neighborhood, they had seen where the church could provide the resources and care that would lead to transformation.

The problem was that it seemed like it was just all talk. The pastor would mention it every now and then, but there seemed to be no progress with the building. Some members began to murmur and gossip about where the money was spent. Construction had stalled, and people began to wonder if it was ever going to happen.

But one Sunday, Pastor Jones let everyone know that there would be a final unveiling in the coming months. An exuberant praise rang through the congregation. They finally began to see that their pastor and, most importantly, God, had not let them down. They had done their part, and God had done even more to show them He is faithful.

In today's lesson, we will learn what it means to live justly and faithfully according to God's covenant. What does it mean for you to live justly and faithfully to God's covenant?

Keep in Mind

"For I the LORD love judgment, I hate robbery for burnt offering; and I will direct their work in truth, and I will make an everlasting covenant with them" (Isaiah 61:8).

"For I the LORD love judgment, I hate robbery for burnt offering; and I will direct their work in truth, and I will make an everlasting covenant with them" (Isaiah 61:8).

Focal Verses

KJV **Isaiah 61:1** The Spirit of the Lord GOD is upon me; because the LORD hath anointed me to preach good tidings unto the meek; he hath sent me to bind up the brokenhearted, to proclaim liberty to the captives, and the opening of the prison to them that are bound;

2 To proclaim the acceptable year of the LORD, and the day of vengeance of our God; to comfort all that mourn;

3 To appoint unto them that mourn in Zion, to give unto them beauty for ashes, the oil of joy for mourning, the garment of praise for the spirit of heaviness; that they might be called trees of righteousness, the planting of the LORD, that he might be glorified.

4 And they shall build the old wastes, they shall raise up the former desolations, and they shall repair the waste cities, the desolations of many generations.

8 For I the LORD love judgment, I hate robbery for burnt offering; and I will direct their work in truth, and I will make an everlasting covenant with them.

9 And their seed shall be known among the Gentiles, and their offspring among the people: all that see them shall acknowledge them, that they are the seed which the LORD hath blessed.

10 I will greatly rejoice in the LORD, my soul shall be joyful in my God; for he hath clothed me with the garments of salvation, he hath covered me with the robe of righteousness, as a bridegroom decketh himself with ornaments, and as a bride adorneth herself with her jewels.

11 For as the earth bringeth forth her bud, and as the garden causeth the things that are sown in it to spring forth; so the Lord GOD will cause righteousness and praise to spring forth before all the nations.

NLT **Isaiah 61:1** The Spirit of the Sovereign LORD is upon me, for the LORD has anointed me to bring good news to the poor. He has sent me to comfort the brokenhearted and to proclaim that captives will be released and prisoners will be freed.

2 He has sent me to tell those who mourn that the time of the LORD's favor has come, and with it, the day of God's anger against their enemies.

3 To all who mourn in Israel, he will give a crown of beauty for ashes, a joyous blessing instead of mourning, festive praise instead of despair. In their righteousness, they will be like great oaks that the LORD has planted for his own glory.

4 They will rebuild the ancient ruins, repairing cities destroyed long ago. They will revive them, though they have been deserted for many generations.

8 "For I, the LORD, love justice. I hate robbery and wrongdoing. I will faithfully reward my people for their suffering and make an everlasting covenant with them.

9 Their descendants will be recognized and honored among the nations. Everyone will realize that they are a people the LORD has blessed."

10 I am overwhelmed with joy in the LORD my God! For he has dressed me with the clothing of salvation and draped me in a robe of righteousness. I am like a bridegroom dressed for his wedding or a bride with her jewels.

11 The Sovereign LORD will show his justice to the nations of the world. Everyone will praise him! His righteousness will be like a garden in early spring, with plants springing up everywhere.

The People, Places, and Times

Acceptable Year of the Lord. The acceptable year of the Lord is an allusion to the year of Jubilee (Leviticus 25), a time in Israel's calendar when all debts were forgiven and all the slaves were set free. Isaiah points toward the new age of the Messiah as a time characterized by the same blessings as the year of Jubilee.

Oil. In ancient times, oil was commonly derived from olives (and sometimes myrrh). Oil was utilized for various purposes, including anointing people in office such as priests and kings. More commonly, it was used as a cosmetic to moisturize the body. It could also be used for medicinal purposes to soothe wounds and as a fuel for lamps.

Background

The book of Isaiah provides a wealth of commentary, history, and of course prophecy that documents important acts in the life of Israel and informs the confirmation of Jesus as the Christ, or Messiah, in the New Testament. The prophet observes a broad scope of events that are verified via the other prophets as well as non-biblical texts. Isaiah also speaks God's messages of warning, instruction, and promise to His people. As the prophet prophesies deliverance from Babylonian captivity, he maintains a conversation with the chosen of Israel that reiterates God's demand for justice, balanced by His promise of hope. As Isaiah is quoted and referenced throughout the New Testament, it is clear that God's Word is timeless and eternal, and those who inherit His promise can continue to expect results even after the present generations have perished.

At-A-Glance

1. Eternal Promise (Isaiah 61:1–2)
2. Eternal Salvation (vv. 3–4)
3. Eternal Covenant (vv. 8–11)

In Depth

1. Eternal Promise (Isaiah 61:1–2)

Isaiah's proclamation of good tidings reflects the essence of God's interaction with humankind. The "good tidings" he mentions here are reflected much later by Jesus as He invokes this entire passage (Luke 4:18). Surely any word from God should be considered good news, although the prophets had the difficult task of issuing both pleasant and fearful messages from above. Contrary to the normal practices of those in political or social power, here God directs the prophet to share a message of hope to those who lack influence.

First, anointing is required for such a message. The anointing brings to mind the physical anointing of Aaron in Leviticus 8:12 or Saul in 1 Samuel 9:14–17. This is more than a physical anointing, though, because even with Isaiah's influence, wisdom of age, and other credentials, he could not simply proclaim healing and deliverance on his own, beyond a charitable compassion. Unlike people, God is able to anoint, appoint, and engage every necessary resource in order to execute His promises. Isaiah speaks here under God's spiritual anointing. The anointing here verifies the eternal nature of God's promises.

Not only is the messenger anointed and therefore consecrated for duty, but also the promise itself is consecrated for the particular blessings and the people for whom they are designed. Following Jesus' initial recitation of this passage from Isaiah, He demonstrated the beginning of the fulfillment of God's eternal promise to encourage the meek, free captives, and comfort the hurting (Matthew 5:3–12). While Isaiah refers to deliverance from Babylon, God's promise of deliverance is not limited to specific events or circumstances. His full promise is more comprehensive, and the method for fulfilling His promises is the ultimate sacrifice. God reveals Himself as personally and intimately engaged with our well-being. He anoints the prophet and provides for the people without reservation or limitation.

2. Eternal Salvation (vv. 3–4)

As surely as God is sovereign, and therefore singular in His authority to judge, He is also the author of love, and He is generous with favor to those He chooses to bless. The symbols of salvation are consistent with God's desire to bless, even if at times He has to warn or punish. The crown of beauty symbolizes the reign in which the redeemed will share, once they have passed their sinful states. As weeping is exchanged for rejoicing, it becomes clear that God's promises and His salvation will not be revoked. Human interaction is inconsistent compared to God's stability. Even before entering God's heavenly presence, we are afforded the opportunity to experience the benefits of His great joy via our salvation. If humans had the power to withhold salvation for a ransom or force certain behavior, most likely we would. Yet God uses the great oaks as a mighty and sturdy example of what it means to be rooted in His favor, and the permanence of the gift of salvation. Psalm 1:1–3 heralds the person who delights in God's law, and he or she will be like a tree planted by a river. Security in God's law includes security in His promises, especially those that will save and preserve His people for eternity.

The imagery of rebuilding ancient ruins is a compelling vision of restoration after the Babylonian captivity. It also is a hint at the finite nature of humankind. While we build grand tributes to ourselves in the form of large buildings and great cities, any of them could come to ruin at any time for a number of reasons, and all of them will decay over time. Our bodies in a similar way can become great specimens of physical prowess, but age will eventually render us helpless, if death does not snatch us away first. Ultimately we must accept that God's salvation allows our souls to have a more permanent security than our physical bodies can provide. Through God's salvation, we are granted restoration beyond a simple renovation, given without restriction.

3. Eternal Covenant (vv. 8–11)

Judgment, justice, righteousness, rightness—these not only describe what God loves, but embody who He is! If our God loves judgment, then He conversely must hate injustice and dishonesty, particularly when they victimize His people. As Isaiah elaborated in verse 2 (and would later reiterate), and as Paul recalled in his letter to the Romans, God's vengeance is not a threat; it is indeed among His promises (Isaiah 63:4; Romans 12:19). God issued warnings and advisories through the prophets for the people's benefit. He also exacted acts of vengeance for correction. The entire Babylonian captivity is proof of God's long-suffering when it comes to sin.

While the wages of sin is death (Romans 6:23), and the Law is filled with lists of crimes and their appropriate punishments, God is no common murderer. He does not kill for sport or pleasure, but He allows us to become our own best examples for why not to thwart His will. Judgment comes because of our own disobedience and unjust practices.

Isaiah continues (61:9–10) to elaborate on the results of God's eternal covenant. Those who are called, saved, and covered by His promises will be granted prosperity for their future generations. They will be established with prominence and visible, tangible increase. If this blessing had come at their own hands, by their own doing, that would be unjust. Yet because God decides to bless His children despite their circumstances, these blessings are generous and just. The key to remaining prosperous is staying aware of God's active work on our behalf. While our worship and works may give evidence that we are under covenant, we fall short of being perfect covenant-keepers.

The final portion of the passage (verse 11) gives a full view of God's plan for how the covenant can and will be maintained. The prophet likens salvation to the cyclical growth of plants and vegetation. Seasons of growth and increase are guaranteed, just as the seasons of restoration and regeneration come at alternate times. Once the seed is planted, the bud will continue to bloom and the garden will grow. The seeds of our faith must be planted by preaching and teaching in order to develop into faith. Once our faith is in place, God is able to continually fulfill His promises, and through us He will demonstrate His power for all to see.

Search the Scriptures

1. What is the source of empowerment for preaching good tidings (Isaiah 61:1)?

2. Are we sure we know what the Lord loves and what the Lord hates (v. 8)? Create a list of what the Lord loves and what the Lord hates. Here are a few examples to get you started: Psalm 33:5, Deuteronomy 7:9, Proverbs 6:17-19, Malachi 2:16.

Discuss the Meaning

1. Are challenges to covenant keeping today different from Isaiah's day?

2. How can we express and share the principles of God's everlasting covenant with those who are not yet Christians?

Lesson in Our Society

Today's world and culture is rife with evidence that we need stronger covenant relationships. Parents lament when their children land in jail or fail to complete their education but often embrace a philosophy that "you're on your own" after a certain age. Similarly, interpersonal relationships can struggle with intimacy because of distrust and previous hurt. An "every person for him/herself" mentality is not about survival but fear. Instead of fearing what others can take from us or do to us, we are instructed to fear God. That fear is not cowering to prevent abuse or harm; instead it's a great respect and love for a sovereign God who acts out of love and keeps His covenant to bless us despite our shortcomings.

Make It Happen

Evaluate your personal relationships. Are these casual or covenant-level connections? Are there people whom you should treat more like God treats us?

Follow the Spirit

What God wants me to do:

_____

_____

_____

Remember Your Thoughts

Special insights I have learned:

_____

_____

_____

More Light on the Text
Isaiah 61:1–4, 8–11

Chapter 61 can be viewed as a stage play. First comes the Anointed One's soliloquy, or speech to the audience (vv. 1–4). In verses 8 and 9 we hear from God Himself, who addresses the Israelites in the audience. He proclaims that the blessings mentioned in the previous verses are a gift from Him. Finally, in the last two verses, the audience responds in thanksgiving for all that God has done.

1 The Spirit of the Lord GOD is upon me; because the Lord hath anointed me to preach good tidings unto the meek; he hath sent me to bind up the brokenhearted, to proclaim liberty to the captives, and the opening of the prison to them that are bound; 2 To proclaim the acceptable year of the LORD, and the day of vengeance of our God; to comfort all that mourn.

The speaker in these verses is the Anointed One. Anointing in the Old Testament usually announced a new kingly dynasty, prophet, or high priest. In this case, the anointing with oil is closely associated with the Holy Spirit, so the speaker is filled with God's presence. The Hebrew for anointed is *mashach* (**maw-SHAKH**), where our word "Messiah" comes from; when Jesus read these words, He said that they were fulfilled in Him (Luke 4:17–21). Some have called the words in Luke 4:18–19 the ordination speech of our Savior and Messiah. When we look at what Jesus read and applied to Himself, we can have a greater understanding of this prophecy from Isaiah.

We also see the Trinity in these verses: the Spirit, the Lord God, and the Anointed One (the Messiah Jesus). The Hebrew for Lord is 'Adonay (**ah-doe-NYE**), used as the proper name for God only. Its essential meaning is "my master." When applied to God, it presents Him as the owner and governor of the whole earth.

Yahweh (Hebrew for God) is the Jewish personal name for God, the eternal, self-existent One. Jews were so careful not to blaspheme the name of God that they never pronounced His name, instead reading aloud 'Adonay when YHWH (Yahweh) was written in the Scripture. Meditating on the names for God gives us greater insight into who He is; thinking of the Jewish reverence for His name reminds us not to use His name casually in our conversations.

We can apply the words of Isaiah 61:1–2 to our own communities as we carry out the mission of our Lord. The Hebrew word for meek (Heb. 'anav, **ah-NAHV**) can also be translated as poor, the meaning Jesus relates when He quotes these verses. There in Luke, also, many translations use the word "gospel" instead of "good tidings," because the words have the same meaning, although "gospel" also connotes salvation. If preaching to the poor is Jesus' mission, it should be ours as well. What better task for us than preaching the Gospel to the poor, whether economically or spiritually? Jesus continues that He also came to heal the brokenhearted, another task for us as His followers.

Next we see that our Messiah has come to "proclaim liberty to the captives, and the opening of the prison to them that are bound." God has always desired to set free slaves and all who are imprisoned. In fact, the Jews were given a special year to set captives free—the Year of Jubilee, which was scheduled for every 50 years (Leviticus 25). Unfortunately, there is no record of this event ever being observed. God designed His Law to create a society with no permanent underclass, and observing this would have helped lessen the effect of class distinctions. We know that God is pleased when we as individuals and churches involve ourselves in jail ministry, especially as work to keep our young men out of prison.

Jesus completed His quotation of these verses just before "and the day of vengeance of our God." Many biblical scholars believe that this indicates that the final day of judgment is in the future. We must remember that where abuse exists, judgment must eventually come to provide justice. For those of us who have been victims of injustice, these words of judgment come as a comfort. God will repay those who have hurt us (Romans 12:19).

3 To appoint unto them that mourn in Zion, to give unto them beauty for ashes, the oil of joy for mourning, the garment of praise for the spirit of heaviness; that they might be called trees of righteousness, the planting of the LORD, that he might be glorified. 4 And they shall build the old wastes, they shall raise up the former desolations, and they shall repair the waste cities, the desolations of many generations.

This prophecy points toward Judah's return from exile and its ultimate fulfillment as the kingdom being consummated at the end of the age. They will face a time when their beautiful temple and city will be burned to the ground, leaving only ashes and broken stones, but Isaiah prophesies a wonderful time of rebuilding. Many of our inner cities look almost the same, but we have the same God who can empower us to bring new life to our communities.

8 For I the LORD love judgment, I hate robbery for burnt offering; and I will direct their work in truth, and I will make an everlasting covenant with them. 9 And their seed shall be known among the Gentiles, and their offspring among the people: all that see them shall acknowledge them, that they are the seed which the LORD hath blessed.

The word "judgment" (Heb. *mishpat*, mish-POT) can also be translated as justice. The word can also mean a decision free from favoritism and bias. As such, the decision conforms to established rules and laws, and it is fair and right toward those it affects. Justice is one of the themes of the book of Isaiah; the prophet uses this word 42 times in the book.

We can see from this first phrase how closely our Lord identifies Himself with justice. We see that God is not pleased with what His people are doing. The solution is an everlasting covenant that can come only through His grace, not anything that the people deserved.

In verse 9, we realize that God's commitment to the Israelite/Jewish people did not end with the exile. God is still planning to bless them, and all people will acknowledge them as His people.

10 I will greatly rejoice in the LORD, my soul shall be joyful in my God; for he hath clothed me with the garments of salvation, he hath covered me with the robe of righteousness, as a bridegroom decketh himself with ornaments, and as a bride adorneth herself with her jewels. 11 For as the earth bringeth forth her bud, and as the garden causeth the things that are sown in it to spring forth; so the Lord GOD will cause righteousness and praise to spring forth before all the nations.

Now we switch from God speaking, to the people responding in thankful praise. Garments of salvation and a robe of righteousness are the cause of their rejoicing. People of God proudly display these as a "bridegroom decketh himself with ornaments" and a "bride adorneth herself with her jewels." The word "decketh" (Heb. *kahan*, ka-HAN) means to dress ornately, as in priestly garments. This is underscored by the word for ornaments, which actually means a headdress or turban, which is what the high priest wore as part of his ceremonial garments. The next image is of a bride who "adorneth herself with her jewels." The word for "adorneth" is *adah* (Heb. ah-DAH) and it conveys the idea of making something more attractive by adding ornament or color.

From this imagery, we see God's people as proudly rejoicing and displaying the joy that comes from being made righteous before Him.

Next Isaiah switches to a garden metaphor. Perhaps the nations had concluded that Yahweh was irrelevant, but the Jewish people are going to continue to be God's object lesson in His grace. The springtime garden is our example. Most of the plants seem to be dead all winter long, but in the spring, all the bulbs wake up with the warming temperatures and show their beauty. This is how our God views righteousness and justice and how He wants us to prepare for this same growth in our lives.

Say It Correctly

Soliloquy. So-**LIH**-lo-quee.

Daily Bible Readings

MONDAY
A Light to the Nations
(Isaiah 42:5–9)

TUESDAY
Anointed for Ministry
(Luke 4:16–21)

WEDNESDAY
No Ministry in Our Backyard
(Luke 4:22–30)

THURSDAY
The Exiles Will Return
(Isaiah 60:1–5)

FRIDAY
The Glory of the Nation Restored
(Isaiah 60:19–22)

SATURDAY
With Everlasting Love and Compassion
(Isaiah 54:4–8)

SUNDAY
Righteousness and Praise Will Always Rule
(Isaiah 61:1–4, 8–11)

Notes

_____

_____

_____

_____

Teaching Tips

Words You Should Know

A. Angel (Hebrews 1:4) *angelos* (Gk.)—Spiritual being, messenger; a part of the heavenly order.

B. Justice (v. 9) *dikaiosyne* (Gk.)—A practice of what is right; what is fair according to rules, laws, or codes; righteousness.

Teacher Preparation

Unifying Principle—Seeking Guidance. People seek guidance for their lives but do not know whom to turn to for direction. Whom should they trust to provide direction? Christ, the reflection of God's glory, addresses life's questions with a powerful and sustaining Word.

A. Pray for your class session for your students. Ask God to reveal a new truth or revelation to you or your students so the lesson might have a greater impact.

B. Read the Scripture lesson in different translations and make observations of subtle differences.

C. Review and complete the companion lesson in the *Precepts for Living*® Personal Study Guide.

O—Open the Lesson

A. Begin the class session by asking for a volunteer to pray.

B. Ask students to share insights or life experiences that correlated from last week's lesson.

C. Have students read Aim for Change and the Keep in Mind verse.

D. Read the In Focus story aloud and discuss.

P—Present the Scriptures

A. Ask students about their understanding of the word "reflection."

B. Review the Scripture text and analyze the key points from the In Depth session.

E—Explore the Meaning

A. Engage students in a discussion regarding the purpose and work of Christ.

B. Divide the class into pairs or small groups and discuss Lesson in Our Society and Make It Happen.

N—Next Steps for Application

A. Summarize the lesson.

B. Ask for questions or reflections regarding today's lesson.

C. Conclude with prayer.

Worship Guide

For the Superintendent or Teacher
Theme: The Imprint of God
Song: "Jesus, the Light of the World"
Devotional Reading: John 1:1–5, 10–14

The Imprint of God

Bible Background • HEBREWS 1
Printed Text • HEBREWS 1:1–9 | Devotional Reading • JOHN 1:1–5, 10–14

Aim for Change

By the end of the lesson, we will: DECIDE that Jesus expresses fully God's very being in the world; APPRECIATE that Jesus during His earthly life experienced the full range of human experience; and CREATE ways to seek Jesus' continued guidance in our lives.

In Focus

"Great, I'll be there next week," Mr. Atkins said. The Atkins Group was a full-service marketing firm. It was established in 1980, the same year Mr. Atkins' son, Rashad, was born. He always believed he received two great gifts in one year. As time passed, Rashad joined the family business a year after college. Having graduated with honors in Business Administration, he effortlessly assisted his father and the Atkins Group team in his first year at the firm.

Walking into the office one day, Rashad asked, "Did I just hear you were going somewhere next week, Dad?" "I sure am," the senior Atkins replied with a laugh. Puzzled at his father's response, Rashad inquired, "Who is going to hold down the fort while you're away?" Again his father chuckled. "You are!" Completely taken aback, Rashad replied, "Me?" "Yes, son, you are. Although I could put your brother or sister in charge, you know this business inside and out. You need to spread your wings a bit." Rashad nervously agreed. Two weeks later, Mr. Atkins returned and found everything running smoothly. "Rashad, I have heard nothing but great things about how you handled yourself in all of the meetings last week." Grinning from ear to ear, Rashad replied, "Thanks, Dad," proudly adding, "Like father, like son."

In today's lesson, we will look at how Jesus' human presence was God's presence in the world.

Keep in Mind

"Who [Jesus] being the brightness of his glory, and the express image of his person, and upholding all things by the word of his power" (Hebrews 1:3a).

"Who [Jesus] being the brightness of his glory, and the express image of his person, and upholding all things by the word of his power" (Hebrews 1:3a).

Focal Verses

KJV **Hebrews 1:1** God, who at sundry times and in divers manners spake in time past unto the fathers by the prophets,

2 Hath in these last days spoken unto us by his Son, whom he hath appointed heir of all things, by whom also he made the worlds;

3 Who being the brightness of his glory, and the express image of his person, and upholding all things by the word of his power, when he had by himself purged our sins, sat down on the right hand of the Majesty on high:

4 Being made so much better than the angels, as he hath by inheritance obtained a more excellent name than they.

5 For unto which of the angels said he at any time, Thou art my Son, this day have I begotten thee? And again, I will be to him a Father, and he shall be to me a Son?

6 And again, when he bringeth in the first begotten into the world, he saith, And let all the angels of God worship him.

7 And of the angels he saith, Who maketh his angels spirits, and his ministers a flame of fire.

8 But unto the Son he saith, Thy throne, O God, is for ever and ever: a sceptre of righteousness is the sceptre of thy kingdom.

9 Thou hast loved righteousness, and hated iniquity; therefore God, even thy God, hath anointed thee with the oil of gladness above thy fellows.

NLT **Hebrews 1:1** Long ago God spoke many times and in many ways to our ancestors through the prophets.

2 And now in these final days, he has spoken to us through his Son. God promised everything to the Son as an inheritance, and through the Son he created the universe.

3 The Son radiates God's own glory and expresses the very character of God, and he sustains everything by the mighty power of his command. When he had cleansed us from our sins, he sat down in the place of honor at the right hand of the majestic God in heaven.

4 This shows that the Son is far greater than the angels, just as the name God gave him is greater than their names.

5 For God never said to any angel what he said to Jesus: "You are my Son. Today I have become your Father." God also said, "I will be his Father, and he will be my Son."

6 And when he brought his supreme Son into the world, God said, "Let all of God's angels worship him."

7 Regarding the angels, he says, "He sends his angels like the winds, his servants like flames of fire."

8 But to the Son he says, "Your throne, O God, endures forever and ever. You rule with a scepter of justice.

9 You love justice and hate evil. Therefore, O God, your God has anointed you, pouring out the oil of joy on you more than on anyone else."

The People, Places, and Times

Prophet. A prophet is someone who speaks on God's behalf and communicates His message to the person or people He assigns. Prophets have no authority or power of their own; their authority is attained solely through the Holy Spirit. The call of a prophet also required that he or she not be intimidated by his or her designated audience, so that he or she was unmoved by public opinion or scrutiny. Although some were called to a lifetime of work, others were called for a specific time frame. Moses, Samuel, Elijah, and Isaiah were important prophets.

Angel. A member of the heavenly order of beings, an angel is superior to animals and human beings through power and intelligence. Angels possess superhuman power but do not have power equal with God. Created by God, they were present to exult in the Creation of the world (Job 38:4–7). Angels can be either holy or fallen. Satan is the primary example of a fallen angel. Holy angels can be visible to humans, and their rare appearances invoke amazement (e.g., Luke 2:9). They have been known to aid humans with personal and spiritual direction.

Background

Besides 1 John, Hebrews is the only letter in the New Testament without a greeting. Written in the style of an essay or sermon, the epistle contains references to the Old Testament. The language and quotations of the Old Testament suggests the intended audience may have been Jews who had converted to Christianity. However, several aspects of the epistle are unclear. Initially, the author is not identified. Although traditionally ascribed to the Apostle Paul, the book's language and vocabulary differ from his other known authored letters, and the biblical book itself does not claim to be written by Paul. The author may have known or been heavily associated with those who knew Paul. Secondly, the date of the epistle is also unclear. Since the author's believed goal was to showcase how Christianity replaced Judaism with the destruction of the Temple, one possibility is that the latter was written after 70 AD. However, there are no clear references to the Temple's destruction, so it may have been written as early as 65-70 AD. A reference to Italy (13:24) is the only hint of where it could have been written.

The author sought to persuade his audience that Jesus is superior to all that was valued in Jewish tradition. Consequently, this is why language familiarity and cultural awareness were important areas for the author; the letter sought to dissuade and inform converted Jews who were tempted to revert to Judaism because of their lack of biblical understanding about Jesus. The theme of Jesus as absolute and complete adequacy fuels this passage. Through the lens of the Old Testament, Christ is revealed as the most excellent of all previous prophets, such as Moses, Samuel, and Elijah. The person Jesus is even superior to angels. For that reason, the former prophesies are true, accomplished in and through Jesus.

At-A-Glance

1. The Eminence of Jesus (Hebrews 1:1–4)
2. The Divinity of Jesus (vv. 5–9)

In Depth

1. The Eminence of Jesus (Hebrews 1:1–4)

The author has divided the time between before and after Christ. These verses relate to God's previous revelation in the Old Testament and His presence through Jesus in the New Testament. In the Old Testament, God used prophets to tell His message to specific communities under the old covenant. With the presence of Jesus, He established a new covenant between Himself and people. The wording of "last" or "final" days describes a messianic era. Jews at that time believed the Messiah's presence would be the beginning of God's new kingdom: freedom of political oppression by the Romans, and global peace. Instead, Jesus founded a godly kingdom, brought spiritual peace, and showcased His godly uniqueness.

The author showcases seven facts to show Jesus' superior greatness. (1) He is deemed the heir of creation. (2) He is the creator of all things made. (3) His radiance reveals God's glory. (4) He is the exact character of God. (5) He is the personified Word of God. (6) He is the priest who provided sacrifice for our sins. (7) He sits on the throne at God's right hand.

2. The Divinity of Jesus (vv. 5–9)

The author continues by further explaining Jesus' eminence through His divinity. This was done to help readers to appreciate that Jesus fulfilled the prophecy of the Old Testament. In doing so, the author wanted the people to gain a larger respect for Jesus as divine, having a rank higher than angels. Angels were important in Judaism because they aided in important pronouncements (Genesis 16:9; Exodus 3:2) and helped at Mount Sinai with the Mosaic Law (Deuteronomy 33:2). The belief that a man was higher in rank over angels could have been an area of contention for many Jews.

To further reinforce Jesus' divinity, the author utilizes several quotes from the Old Testament. God addresses Jesus as "my Son" (2 Samuel 7:14; Psalm 2:7). Additionally, the writer states He is the "begotten" or firstborn Son to the world and that even angels must worship Him because He created them (Psalm 97:7, 104:4). Finally, He is on the throne where He rules with all righteousness (Psalm 45:6–7). Through these illustrations, the author hoped to persuade Jews that Jesus was the foretold Messiah and God's Son.

Search the Scriptures

1. Why is Jesus' superiority to prophets and angels important (Hebrews 1:3–4)?

2. What is the meaning of "first begotten" or "supreme Son" (v. 6)?

Discuss the Meaning

In the passage, we are informed that Jesus Christ is the direct reflection of God. Why is that important to remember? In what ways does God validate this?

Lesson in Our Society

In a society where long-suffering often overshadows hope, many Christians fail to see Jesus' greatness. For that reason, people have continually sought other means for personal fulfillment. Inspirational and empowerment teachings seem to be society's recipe for personal greatness. An understanding of who Jesus is to us trumps them all. The knowledge of Jesus' identity and the greatness of His ever-present power in our lives allows us to know God truly cares about His children.

Make It Happen

Frequently, believers tend to focus on Jesus' divinity, but He is also human and faced challenges similar to what we face today. Through His example, we can believe that also we can overcome. "These things I have I spoken unto you, that in me ye might have peace. In the world ye shall have tribulation: but be of good cheer; I have overcome the world" (John 16:33).

Follow the Spirit

What God wants me to do:

_____

_____

_____

_____

Remember Your Thoughts

Special insights I have learned:

_____

_____

_____

_____

More Light on the Text

Hebrews 1:1–9

1 God, who at sundry times and in divers manners spake in time past unto the fathers by the prophets, 2 Hath in these days spoken unto us by his Son, whom he hath appointed heir of all things, by whom also he made the worlds.

The first four verses of Hebrews are only a single sentence in the Greek text. Unlike modern translations that have three or four sentences, the King James Version of the Bible retains the sense of the original Greek text in one rich and complete sentence.

In this epistle, the writer begins with God, the initiator of revelation; therefore, the focus is on Him, not on people. The first and second verses compare God's methods of communication in the past and the present. The phrase "at sundry times and in divers manners" refers to the fact that God chose the times and methods to communicate. The Old Testament records the clouds, dreams, visions, and other methods that God used to communicate with His people. God also used the prophets to reveal what He was saying. The reference to "prophets" here is not limited to the traditional prophets but it includes men of God such as Moses, David, and Solomon.

The phrase "in these last days" refers to both the present and end times. There is a clear sense that God has reached the climax of His self-revelation. He has saved the best for last. The writer intends to show that this last revelation of God is superior to what He has done in the past. The fact that God has already "spoken unto us by his Son" suggests that at the time of the writing of this epistle, the revelation had been completed.

Even though most English translations say "his son" or "the Son," the Greek has no definite article; it simply says "a Son." The writer assumes that the readers know to whom he is referring. The use of the indefinite article "a" supports this statement. Instead of identifying whom God spoke through, the phrase emphasizes the nature of the person whom God spoke through. Unlike the prophets, the Son is more than a messenger. His divine nature makes Him the right and only capable bearer of God's complete revelation. The book of Hebrews explains this truth about the revelation of God though Jesus Christ.

The phrase "appointed heir of all things, by whom also he made the worlds" indicates that Christ embodies a dual motif of sonship and priesthood. When speaking of Jesus as God's heir, Psalm 2:7–8 says, "Thou art my Son; this day have I begotten thee. Ask of me, and I shall give thee the heathen for thine inheritance, and the uttermost parts of the earth for thy possession." Everything God has belongs to Jesus. The Bible also reveals that Jesus is co-Creator with God (Colossians 1:16–17).

The word translated as "worlds" or "universe" (Hebrews 1:2, NIV) is *aionas* (**eye-OWE-nas**) in Greek, which literally means "ages" or "times." The preferred interpretation is "ages," which suggests that Jesus not only created the world, but He also controls the events of history.

3 Who being the brightness of his glory, and the express image of his person, and upholding all things by the word of his

power, when he had by himself purged our sins, sat down on the right hand of the Majesty on high.

In verse 3, we get a complete Christology. The first part of the verse talks about the Son's relationship with God, the second part deals with Christ's work, and the third part refers to His exaltation—the pre-existence, incarnation, and exaltation of Christ. The phrase "brightness of his glory" could mean that Jesus is either the reflection or the radiance of the glory of God. The Bible tells us that God is inapproachable, but Jesus makes it possible to know Him truly and intimately. What a blessing! The "express image of his person" literally means "the imprint or seal of God's nature," and the word *hypostasis* (Gk. **hoo-POH-sta-sis**), translated as "person," means "the reality or actuality of His being." Thus, Jesus fully represents God (cf. Colossians 2:9). "The exaltation of Christ" is an allusion to Psalm 110; "the Majesty" is a euphemism for God.

4 Being made so much better than the angels, as he hath by inheritance obtained a more excellent name than they.

The phrase "better than" or "superior to" is used 13 times in the Christology presented in Hebrews. Verse 4 introduces the major subjects—Christ and the angels—of the discussion to follow. To counter the worship of angels, the writer shows the real position of the angels in relation to Christ.

5 For unto which of the angels said he at any time, Thou art my Son, this day have I begotten thee? And again, I will be to him a Father, and he shall be to me a Son?

Hebrews 1:5–14 continues the explanation of who Jesus Christ is, and 2:1–4 challenges the reader to respond appropriately. The author follows this pattern throughout the epistle. Beginning with verse 5, we find frequent references to or quotations from the Old Testament (30 or more), especially the Psalms. Verse 5 is a combination of two Old Testament verses: Psalm 2:7 and 2 Samuel 7:14. The truth from Psalm 2:7 ("Thou art my Son; this day have I begotten thee") concerning Jesus' relationship to God was very significant for the early church's understanding of Christ. This truth was announced from heaven at Jesus' baptism (Mark 1:10–11) and preached by Paul (Acts 13:33–34). The author of Hebrews also adapts a declaration the Lord made about David, whose kingship Jesus completes, from 2 Samuel 7:14. He reminds the audience of God's relationship to Christ.

6 And again, when he bringeth in the first begotten into the world, he saith, And let all the angels of God worship him.

The term "first begotten" is translated from the Greek word *prototokos* (**proe-TOE-toe-kos**). It does not mean the first to be created, but it indicates the privilege, authority, inheritance, and responsibility that come with being the first-born in a family. Christ has the highest authority. The phrase "all the angels of God worship him" emphasizes His exalted state as God because only God can be worshiped. This is not an exaltation of His human nature, but it's a recognition of His Divinity.

7 And of the angels he saith, Who maketh his angels spirits, and his ministers a flame of fire.

Verse 7 contains an Old Testament quotation from Psalm 104:4. The meaning of this verse is clear when it is read in conjunction with verses 8 and 9. This verse is not saying that angels are Christ's messengers, though this is true. Instead, it teaches that while Christ is eternal, angels are temporal and transient.

8 But unto the Son he saith, Thy throne, O God, is for ever and ever: a sceptre of righteousness is the scepter of thy kingdom. 9 Thou hast loved righteousness, and hated iniquity; therefore God, even thy God, hath anointed thee with the oil of gladness above thy fellows.

These verses are a direct quotation of Psalm 45:6–7. Psalm 45 is a royal marriage psalm calling a princess of Tyre (vv. 12–14) to heed the king's call and "forget also thine own people, and thy father's house" (v. 10) in order to enter the king's palace, where there is great joy. This king loves righteousness and hates sin. This psalm has many Messianic applications. Hebrews 1:8–9 refers to the Son as God and says that His throne is exalted forever. Christ is superior to the angels—"anointed with the oil of gladness above thy fellows."

Say It Correctly

Divers. **DY**-vers.
Sceptre. **SEP**-ter.

Daily Bible Readings

MONDAY
Becoming Children of God
(John 1:1–14)

TUESDAY
Receiving Grace Upon Grace
(John 1:15–18)

WEDNESDAY
From Death to Life
(John 5:24–27)

THURSDAY
Jesus, Superior to the Angels
(Hebrews 1:10–14)

FRIDAY
Jesus Reconciles All Things
(Colossians 1:15–20)

SATURDAY
Jesus, Author of All Spiritual Blessings
(Ephesians 1:3–8a)

SUNDAY
Jesus, Imprint of God's Very Being
(Hebrews 1:1–9)

Notes

_____

_____

_____

_____

_____

_____

Teaching Tips

Words You Should Know

A. Apostle (Hebrews 3:1) *apostolos* (Gk.)—A unique messenger commissioned by God or Jesus.

B. Wise (Matthew 7:24) *phronimos* (Gk.)—Able to judge rightly and pursue proper course of action based on information and understanding.

Teacher Preparation

Unifying Principle—Planning the Work and Working the Plan. People often give credit for accomplishments to those who carry out the work rather than to the one who created the plan. Who is really responsible? The Scripture affirms that Jesus is the one who was faithful while accomplishing God's plan.

A. Pray for your class session for your students.

B. Reread the Focal Verses in a modern translation to observe subtle differences.

C. Review and complete the companion lesson in the *Precepts for Living®* Personal Study Guide.

O—Open the Lesson

A. Begin the class session with prayer, asking for a volunteer.

B. Have students read Aim for Change and the Keep in Mind verse.

C. Read the In Focus story aloud and discuss.

P—Present the Scriptures

A. Use The People, Places and Times and Background to provide context.

B. Ask students to share their reflections on the word "house."

C. Review the Scripture text and analyze the key points from the In Depth section.

E—Explore the Meaning

A. Engage students in a discussion regarding Jesus as a High Priest.

B. Divide the class into pairs or small groups and discuss Lesson in Our Society and Make It Happen.

N—Next Steps for Application

A. Summarize the lesson.

B. Ask for questions or reflections regarding today's lesson.

C. Conclude with prayer.

Worship Guide

For the Superintendent or Teacher
Theme: Builder of the House
Song: "Jesus, the Light of the World"
Devotional Reading: Hebrews 10:19-25

Builder of the House

Bible Background • HEBREWS 3:1–6; MATTHEW 7:19–29
Printed Text • HEBREWS 3:1–6; MATTHEW 7:24–29 | Devotional Reading • HEBREWS 10:19–25

—————— Aim for Change ——————

By the end of the lesson, we will: AGREE that Jesus, with divine authority, carried out God's intentions; AFFIRM that Jesus is the model for a life of dedication and service to the will of God; and DEDICATE our lives to Jesus with a commitment to engage in Christ-centered speech and actions.

————— In Focus —————

Monica was a good writer. In fact, anyone who read her work told her so. She had always had a fascination with telling stories and putting her particular flair on them. Having caught the writing bug in high school while working on the school newspaper, she decided she would try her hand at writing freelance. If she had this talent, she figured she should at least get paid for it. Monica's second passion was cooking. An exceptional home cook, she figured she'd write about food. She submitted her work to a few publications and was able to write several cookbook and restaurant reviews.

Having read some of Monica's work, the food editor at the local newspaper asked if she would be interested in writing a feature story. Overjoyed, Monica leapt at the opportunity. After conducting the interview, she feverishly wrote the story and submitted it to her editor. Soon after, the editor phoned her. She excitedly believed it would be another favorable conversation. Instead, the editor thanked Monica for her enthusiasm and alerted her she would need to revise it. To assist her, she would need to have a senior editor work with her to get her work to the newspaper's style standards. Monica was glad for the opportunity to grow from a good writer into a great one.

In today's lesson, we will look at Jesus' greatness in correlation to Moses' goodness. Have you ever been in awe of someone who was great at what they did? What made them great as opposed to just "good"?

————— Keep in Mind —————

"For this man [Jesus] was counted worthy of more glory than Moses, inasmuch as he who hath builded the house hath more honour than the house" (Hebrews 3:3).

"For this man [Jesus] was counted worthy of more glory than Moses, inasmuch as he who hath builded the house hath more honour than the house" (Hebrews 3:3).

Focal Verses

KJV

Hebrews 3:1 Wherefore, holy brethren, partakers of the heavenly calling, consider the Apostle and High Priest of our profession, Christ Jesus;

2 Who was faithful to him that appointed him, as also Moses was faithful in all his house.

3 For this man was counted worthy of more glory than Moses, inasmuch as he who hath builded the house hath more honour than the house.

4 For every house is builded by some man; but he that built all things is God.

5 And Moses verily was faithful in all his house, as a servant, for a testimony of those things which were to be spoken after;

6 But Christ as a son over his own house; whose house are we, if we hold fast the confidence and the rejoicing of the hope firm unto the end.

Matthew 7:24 Therefore whosoever heareth these sayings of mine, and doeth them, I will liken him unto a wise man, which built his house upon a rock:

25 And the rain descended, and the floods came, and the winds blew, and beat upon that house; and it fell not: for it was founded upon a rock.

26 And every one that heareth these sayings of mine, and doeth them not, shall be likened unto a foolish man, which built his house upon the sand:

27 And the rain descended, and the floods came, and the winds blew, and beat upon that house; and it fell: and great was the fall of it.

28 And it came to pass, when Jesus had ended these sayings, the people were astonished at his doctrine:

29 For he taught them as one having authority, and not as the scribes.

NLT

Hebrews 3:1 And so, dear brothers and sisters who belong to God and are partners with those called to heaven, think carefully about this Jesus whom we declare to be God's messenger and High Priest.

2 For he was faithful to God, who appointed him, just as Moses served faithfully when he was entrusted with God's entire house.

3 But Jesus deserves far more glory than Moses, just as a person who builds a house deserves more praise than the house itself.

4 For every house has a builder, but the one who built everything is God.

5 Moses was certainly faithful in God's house as a servant. His work was an illustration of the truths God would reveal later.

6 But Christ, as the Son, is in charge of God's entire house. And we are God's house, if we keep our courage and remain confident in our hope in Christ.

Matthew 7:24 "Anyone who listens to my teaching and follows it is wise, like a person who builds a house on solid rock.

25 Though the rain comes in torrents and the floodwaters rise and the winds beat against that house, it won't collapse because it is built on bedrock.

26 But anyone who hears my teaching and doesn't obey it is foolish, like a person who builds a house on sand.

27 When the rains and floods come and the winds beat against that house, it will collapse with a mighty crash."

28 When Jesus had finished saying these things, the crowds were amazed at his teaching,

29 for he taught with real authority—quite unlike their teachers of religious law.

The People, Places, and Times

Moses. Moses was a Hebrew prophet who delivered the Israelites from Egyptian slavery under Pharaoh's rule in the Old Testament. His name derived from the root of a word meaning "to take out" since he was taken out of the river bank as a baby. Moses served as the primary leader and legislator during the Israelites' time in the wilderness. Led by God, Moses was able to establish the nation of Israel from former oppressed slaves. He communicated to the people the Ten Commandments, God's covenant with Israel, which God gave him directly at Mount Sinai. Moses also acted as interpreter of the Law, which established faith and civil traditions that still exist today.

House. While the literal meaning of "house" is a place where one resides, it has other figurative meanings as well. The Temple in Jerusalem was known as the house of God. "House" can refer to where one's family lives; by extension it can refer solely to the family itself. A house in this sense would be an ancestral family or dynasty and its descendants. The people of God were also referred to as the house of God by the Apostle Paul.

Background

There is some question about the author of the book of Hebrews; while it is commonly attributed to the Apostle Paul, the lack of concrete evidence leaves the authorship uncertain. The author of Hebrews focuses his attention on Jesus' humanity, emphasizing His being both the Son of God and the Son of Man. Moreover, the author wanted to use this as a platform to assist the Jews in warning them about the risk of drifting away from the Gospel. He wanted to persuade them to continue in the faith and be active participants in their faith life. Although the first believers believed because they saw signs and wonders, this audience had the privilege of having the Word of God authenticated

through the presence of the Holy Spirit. During the time of Jesus' presence on earth, He was momentarily lower than the angels (Heb. 2:9). Frequently using the Psalms as a reference, the author lets his audience see how God and His glory fill all creation, like Jesus does. It distinguishes God from creation but also shows how He could equally dwell inside it. Additionally, God's creation is at the mercy of God, which made all things subject to Jesus also. The author also denotes that because of Jesus' death for the sake of humanity and obedience to the Father, God crowned Him with all glory and honor.

The book of Hebrews shows that it was necessary for Jesus to take on the form of humanity and die. First, His presence and suffering displayed His identification with human suffering. Secondly, Jesus' death signified the ultimate defeat of Satan and the power of death. For that reason, humanity should never fear death. Finally, His death permits Jesus to be the merciful and faithful High Priest on behalf of God. As an intermediary, Jesus has the authority to go to the Father on behalf of humanity.

At-A-Glance

1. The Greatness of Jesus (Hebrews 3:1–6)
2. The Teachings of Jesus (Matthew 7:24–29)

In Depth

1. The Greatness of Jesus (Hebrews 3:1–6)

In this passage, the author turns the focus on Jesus' eminence. The two attributes highlighted are faithfulness and mercy, which have been gleaned from verse 17 of the previous chapter. To show some degree of camaraderie, the author chooses to call his fellow Christians "brothers," indicating a family relationship that includes brothers and sisters. This name suggests their mutual relationship with Jesus (Hebrews 2:11). Jesus is also given the title of Apostle, the only time He gets this designation in the New Testament. Here, "apostle" suggests that Jesus is an official messenger of God.

The author also begins to make the comparison between Jesus and Moses. As Moses was the bearer of the old covenant, Jesus is the bearer of the new covenant. However, this is where the similarities end. Jesus goes on to act as the ultimate sacrifice for humanity, whereas Moses did not. Although Moses was faithful to the household of God, his faithfulness was to show devotion to God. Jesus' faithfulness is more esteemed because He is the Son "over" the household. The household is the personification of the body of believers, both in the Old Testament and New Testament.

2. The Teachings of Jesus (Matthew 7:24–29)

These verses contain a serious spiritual warning. The wise person hears the words of Jesus and puts them into practice (7:24). The result of such obedience is stability and security—the house does not fall in the midst of the storms and trials of life. The foolish person hears the words of Jesus and does not put them into practice (7:26). The result of such disobedience is destruction, as verse 27 so picturesquely portrays. The first meaning of Jesus' parable here refers to His Sermon on the Mount. Heeding the lessons of the sermon will bring security; disobedience will result in destruction.

The parable invites us to a life of obedience. Words are not a substitute for obedience. Preaching, casting out demons, and performing miracles can be divinely inspired, but they give no assurance of salvation. We should hear God's words and do them (see James 1:22–25). We must not stop with simply hearing (or studying) His words; our hearing must lead to

doing. This is what it means to build "upon a rock."

Search the Scriptures

1. Remaining confident in our faith in Christ is the evidence that we are a part of Christ's house (Hebrews 3:6). Create a plan that will assist you in maintaining your faith in Christ.

2. Why is not only hearing but obeying God so important (Matthew 7:24)?

Discuss the Meaning

In the passage, we are informed that although people hear the same message, they can respond differently. Why do you think this is important to remember? Does that mean the person who did the opposite does not love God?

Lesson in Our Society

People can hear the same information and still respond differently. This happens with siblings in the same house, as well as co-workers in the same business and people in the same church. Some people automatically put what they hear into practice while others resist change and drag their feet. For some, the information just goes in one ear and out the other, with no benefit. The difference is true belief.

Make It Happen

Jesus' presence and example on earth alert us to God's love for His creation. Through His guidance via His Word, devotional time, worship, and prayer, we are given the opportunity to appreciate His greatness and learn from it. Ask the Holy Spirit to guide you into all truth so you can accomplish His will for your life.

Follow the Spirit

What God wants me to do:

_____

_____

_____

_____

Remember Your Thoughts

Special insights I have learned:

_____

_____

_____

_____

More Light on the Text
Hebrews 3:1–6; Matthew 7:24–29

One of the important themes of the book of Hebrews is Jesus' superiority. His position over Moses particularly stands out because of Moses' unique role in the history of Israel. Moses could be regarded as the founder of Israel. He led Israel out of Egypt, and at Sinai formed them into the people of God with the covenant and laws central to their life as God's people and a nation under Him. Regarded as a national hero and architect of Israel's corporate life, Moses stood above all comparison for a Jew. In Hebrews 3:1–6, the author of Hebrews therefore carefully and skillfully sets up the comparison between Moses and Jesus not by disparaging Moses, but by endorsing the verdict of Numbers 12:7 that Moses was "faithful in all [God's] house." This emphasizes similarity rather than contrast in that Jesus, like Moses, was "faithful" (v. 2), but the mention

of the "house" prompts the further argument (vv. 3–6) that, while in that house Moses was merely a "servant" (Numbers 12:7). Jesus as the Son "has greater honor" in His Father's house.

1 Wherefore, holy brethren, partakers of the heavenly calling, consider the Apostle and High Priest of our profession, Christ Jesus; 2 Who was faithful to him that appointed him, as also Moses was faithful in all his house.

In verse 1, the author for the first time addresses his readers directly as "brethren," or "brothers and sisters," an important term previously used in 2:11–12, 17. To this designation he adds the word "holy" (Gk. *hagios*, **HA-gee-os**; sometimes translated "saints"), a term which here, as in 6:10 and 13:24 and often in the New Testament, distinguishes the people of God who are "made holy" by Christ (2:11) from mere earthly relationship. The author of Hebrews knows the community shares in the life of Christ together in the same manner that Christ has shared in their lives. Moreover, the author stresses that their calling is from heaven, implying that both the source and goal of their call is God Himself. Christians today are reminded that our calling is a heavenly calling. We are not simply members of a civic club, social organization, or academic and business community. The divine nature of our calling demands and challenges us to be serious about our response. The author then invites the community to "consider" or—as the Greek word *katanoeo* (**ka-ta-no-EH-oh**) implies here—"fix your mind intently on" Jesus, thereby alerting them that he is now about to explain another aspect of Jesus' special significance and superiority. He proceeds to introduce Him in a very unique manner—with a double title, "Apostle and High Priest." Interestingly, this is the only place Jesus is described as "Apostle" in the New Testament. This title denotes a representative sent by God, more often given to the men whom Jesus sent with His Gospel message. Since the word means "one who is sent," it is easy to see how this applies to Jesus, as He was sent by the Father. The term "High Priest" attributes to Jesus a role allocated not to Moses but to his brother Aaron. The author of Hebrews will go into Christ's role as High Priest as well as His superiority over other high priests later in the letter (Hebrews 4:14–16, 7:23–28). "Apostle" and "High Priest" are thus two different aspects of the special authority Christians confess or acknowledge.

Faithfulness is the overarching theme in this section, with the word "faithful" used for Moses (3:2, 5) and Christ (3:2) and implied in the treatment of the readers (3:6). Verse 2 recalls Numbers 12:1–8, where God rebukes Aaron and Miriam for their failure to respect Moses, and it describes him as "my servant Moses ... faithful in all mine house" (v. 7). Here the author of Hebrews starts to show that Jesus exceeds even Moses in authority, since the Son is more than a "servant." But first he discusses Moses' attribute of faithfulness or trustworthiness and points out that Jesus also deserves that accolade as the "faithful high priest" (Hebrews 2:17) who has undertaken the task His Father assigned and fulfilled it despite all opposition (12:2).

3 For this man was counted worthy of more glory than Moses, inasmuch as he who hath builded the house hath more honour than the house 4 For every house is builded by some man; but he that built all things is God.

Moses' status as "servant" will be discussed more directly in v. 5, but first Jesus' superiority is demonstrated by an argument that focuses not on Moses, but instead on the "house" in which his faithful service was performed. The Greek word translated "house" (*oikos*, **OY-kos**)

is open to different meanings (God's heavenly household, the people of Israel, the Davidic dynasty, Jewish and Christian communities). However, in Numbers 12:7, the "house" was probably understood as the people of Israel conceived as God's "household" or estate within which Moses acted as chief steward. If Moses was the servant in the "house," the house takes priority over the one who serves in it, whereas the householder, God, takes priority over the house He has founded.

5 And Moses verily was faithful in all his house, as a servant, for a testimony of those things which were to be spoken after, 6 But Christ as a son over his own house; whose house are we, if we hold fast the confidence and the rejoicing of the hope firm unto the end.

The author picks up from the quotation in v. 2 and draws the obvious conclusion that because Numbers 12:7 describes Moses as the "servant" in God's house, he is not on the same level as the Son, who, by His family status, has authority over the house. Both servant and son have tasks to perform faithfully for the householder. But while the former will always be looking after someone else's property, the latter will one day own it. Moses' ministry, no less than that of the prophets, was not complete in itself but looked forward to a coming time of fulfillment. He was looking after the house the Son would later inherit. What was the future for Moses was now a present reality. That "house" is now identified as "we"—the author, his readers, and all the people of faith whom they represent—the household over which the Son holds authority. But our status as that "household" is not automatic; it depends on our keeping a firm hold on our "confidence" and "hope." Note the similar conditional clause in 3:14 and the negative counterpart in 10:26. This note will be sounded repeatedly throughout the letter and leads the author directly into a lengthy warning on the danger of failing to keep that hope. He fears that for his readers, the Christian "confidence and hope," which should be their greatest boast, is in danger of becoming a matter of uncertainty and shame. The exhortation in Ephesians matches the warning of the author of Hebrews and is very much appropriate today—"to lead a life worthy of the vocation wherewith ye are called" (Ephesians 4:1).

The final section of the Sermon on the Mount (Matthew 7:13–29) consists of a series of warnings. Matthew 7:13–14 contrasts two ways of approaching life. Verses 15–23 warn against false prophets. Jesus then presents the parable of the wise and foolish builders in verses 24–27. The common theme in these passages is the importance of obedience. Heeding Christ's words and following His example is not optional for entry into the kingdom. Jesus impresses on the hearers the difference between real and merely nominal Christian discipleship.

Matthew 7:24 Therefore whosoever heareth these sayings of mine, and doeth them, I will liken him unto a wise man, which built his house upon a rock: 25 And the rain descended, and the floods came, and the winds blew, and beat upon that house; and it fell not: for it was founded upon a rock. 26 And every one that heareth these sayings of mine, and doeth them not, shall be likened unto a foolish man, which built his house upon the sand: 27 And the rain descended, and the floods came, and the winds blew, and beat upon that house; and it fell: and great was the fall of it.

Verses 24–27 present the parable of the wise and foolish builders. Told in a parable-style format, the passage encourages the audience to be not only hearers of the Word, but also doers. The imagery suggests people who build their lives according to God's Word are on a stable foundation, like a rock. When they live through the stormy seasons of life, they will not crumble. However, a hearer of the same Word who does not act on it will be as foolish as someone building on unstable sand. According to Jesus, the juxtaposition of wise and foolish is the choice each believer faces. The heart of a life devoted to God obeys His Words. Although both will be subject to judgment, the wise will avoid punishment, while the foolish will be held accountable.

28 And it came to pass, when Jesus had ended these sayings, the people were astonished at his doctrine: 29 For he taught them as one having authority, and not as the scribes.

The concluding thought surrounding this account was the fact that the people were astonished at Jesus' teaching prowess. His teachings were not like the scribes, which were handed down through tradition and Jewish teachers. Jesus taught with His own authority. He had the power to interpret the Law without the assistance of rabbis.

Following the conclusion of Jesus' teachings in the Sermon on the Mount, Matthew provides his own concluding comments in verses 28–29. The words "when Jesus had ended these sayings" (7:28) mark the end of the first block of teaching material in Matthew: the Sermon on the Mount. Similar words appear at the end of each block of teaching material in Matthew's Gospel (19:1, 26:1).

Say It Correctly

Accolade. **AH**-koe-laid.
Picturesquely. pik-chuh-**RESK**-lee.

Daily Bible Readings

MONDAY
Angels in God's Plan
(Hebrews 2:5–8b)

TUESDAY
Keep Your Commitment to Christ
(Hebrews 3:7–15)

WEDNESDAY
Hold Fast to Our Confession
(Hebrews 10:19–25)

THURSDAY
Jesus Christ, the Only Foundation
(1 Corinthians 3:10–12)

FRIDAY
Requesting Then Receiving Help
(Matthew 7:7–11)

SATURDAY
Obedient Actions Required of All Members
(Matthew 7:19–23)

SUNDAY
Working at Jesus' Behest
(Hebrews 3:1–6; Matthew 7:24–29)

Notes

Teaching Tips

Words You Should Know

A. High Priest (Hebrews 4:14) *archiereus* (Gk.)—Head or chief clergy, who offered sacrifices to God and appeared in in the Temple's inner sanctum (Holy of Holies) to make intercession for the people.

B. Order (5:6, 10) *taxis* (Gk.)—Arrangement, regularity, sequence.

Teacher Preparation

Unifying Principle—Gifted and Chosen Leaders. People often have someone who makes special efforts on their behalf. What qualifies and motivates a person to make that special effort? The writer of Hebrews informs us that God appointed Jesus, the High Priest, as an intercessor on behalf of His people.

A. Pray, interceding on behalf of your students for God to speak to them during their study time and to place you all on one accord.

B. Read The People, Places, and Times; Background; In Depth; and More Light on the Text.

C. Complete the companion lesson in the *Precepts for Living®* Personal Study Guide.

O—Open the Lesson

A. Open with prayer, asking students to make prayer requests on behalf of others' needs before their own.

B. Review the Aim for Change, asking students to keep in mind what they are to "do" in your time together.

C. Read and discuss the In Focus story and ask students to comment.

D. Ask students to recall and discuss a time when they needed someone to represent their interest personally.

P—Present the Scriptures

A. Read through the Focal Verses and have students discuss their thoughts as they read the text.

B. Highlight the salient points from the In Depth section along with what the Lord revealed to you during your own study. Have students also share.

E—Explore the Meaning

A. Have students break into groups to discuss Search the Scriptures and Discuss the Meaning.

B. Have students share their group consensus and points of difference.

N—Next Steps for Application

A. Ask students to partner up, take prayer requests that were spoken at the start of class and pray for one another.

B. End class with prayer and praise to God for the mercy and grace we receive through Jesus Christ our High Priest.

Worship Guide

For the Superintendent or Teacher
Theme: Our Great High Priest
Song: "Every Prayer"
Devotional Reading: Ephesians 4:7–13

Our Great High Priest

Bible Background • HEBREWS 4:14–5:10
Printed Text • HEBREWS 4:14–5:10 | Devotional Reading • EPHESIANS 4:7–13

―――――――――――― **Aim for Change** ――――――――――――

By the end of the lesson, we will: CONSIDER that God appointed Jesus as High Priest for the people; APPRECIATE that Jesus, in His humanity, fully understands and identifies with the daily life of all peoples; and IDENTIFY the kind of leaders who suffer, serve, and obey God's intentions in the spirit of Jesus.

――――――――――― **In Focus** ―――――――――――

Aiesha loved her big brother, Jay. They were eight years apart, and their parents had divorced when she was young. When her dad left them, she held tightly to Jay. Aiesha could always count on Jay to look out for her. While their mom was at work, he made sure she did her homework and chores, but he also took her out to do fun things like movies and ball games. Even when Jay started dating and eventually got married, he still looked out for his little sister. When Aiesha was a senior in high school, she wanted to stay out with her friends past her curfew. It was Jay who intervened and convinced their mom to trust Aiesha to make good decisions and allow her to stay out later. Jay was proven right. Even when she had the opportunity to make bad choices, Aiesha remembered Jay's defense of her to their mom, and rather than cave to peer pressure, she called her brother to come get her.

Have you ever had an older sibling or mentor advocate for you? In today's lesson, we will see that Jesus is our Elder Brother and High Priest, seated at the right hand of God with all power and majesty.

―――――――――――― **Keep in Mind** ――――――――――――

"Seeing then that we have a great high priest, that is passed into the heavens, Jesus the Son of God, let us hold fast our profession" (Hebrews 4:14).

"Seeing then that we have a great high priest, that is passed into the heavens, Jesus the Son of God, let us hold fast our profession" (Hebrews 4:14).

Focal Verses

KJV **Hebrews 4:14** Seeing then that we have a great high priest, that is passed into the heavens, Jesus the Son of God, let us hold fast our profession.

15 For we have not an high priest which cannot be touched with the feeling of our infirmities; but was in all points tempted like as we are, yet without sin.

16 Let us therefore come boldly unto the throne of grace, that we may obtain mercy, and find grace to help in time of need.

5:1 For every high priest taken from among men is ordained for men in things pertaining to God, that he may offer both gifts and sacrifices for sins:

2 Who can have compassion on the ignorant, and on them that are out of the way; for that he himself also is compassed with infirmity.

3 And by reason hereof he ought, as for the people, so also for himself, to offer for sins.

4 And no man taketh this honour unto himself, but he that is called of God, as was Aaron.

5 So also Christ glorified not himself to be made an high priest; but he that said unto him, Thou art my Son, to day have I begotten thee.

6 As he saith also in another place, Thou art a priest for ever after the order of Melchisedec.

7 Who in the days of his flesh, when he had offered up prayers and supplications with strong crying and tears unto him that was able to save him from death, and was heard in that he feared;

8 Though he were a Son, yet learned he obedience by the things which he suffered;

9 And being made perfect, he became the author of eternal salvation unto all them that obey him;

10 Called of God an high priest after the order of Melchisedec.

NLT **Hebrews 4:14** So then, since we have a great High Priest who has entered heaven, Jesus the Son of God, let us hold firmly to what we believe.

15 This High Priest of ours understands our weaknesses, for he faced all of the same testings we do, yet he did not sin.

16 So let us come boldly to the throne of our gracious God. There we will receive his mercy, and we will find grace to help us when we need it most.

5:1 Every high priest is a man chosen to represent other people in their dealings with God. He presents their gifts to God and offers sacrifices for their sins.

2 And he is able to deal gently with ignorant and wayward people because he himself is subject to the same weaknesses.

3 That is why he must offer sacrifices for his own sins as well as theirs.

4 And no one can become a high priest simply because he wants such an honor. He must be called by God for this work, just as Aaron was.

5 That is why Christ did not honor himself by assuming he could become High Priest. No, he was chosen by God, who said to him, "You are my Son. Today I have become your Father."

6 And in another passage God said to him, "You are a priest forever in the order of Melchizedek."

7 While Jesus was here on earth, he offered prayers and pleadings, with a loud cry and tears, to the one who could rescue him from death. And God heard his prayers because of his deep reverence for God.

8 Even though Jesus was God's Son, he learned obedience from the things he suffered.

9 In this way, God qualified him as a perfect High Priest, and he became the source of eternal salvation for all those who obey him.

10 And God designated him to be a High Priest in the order of Melchizedek.

The People, Places, and Times

Melchizedek or Melchisedec. A mysterious biblical character, Melchisedec is first referenced in Genesis as the king of Salem and "priest of the Most High God" (Genesis 14:17–20). Even though there is no biblical record of Melchisedec's ancestry, he is a real person. Since he lived in Canaan, an area occupied by descendants of Ham, it is quite possible his ancestry is Hamitic, from which Africans descended. His encounter with Abram (who would later be renamed Abraham) was after the defeat of Chedorlaomer and his allies, including the king of Sodom. Abraham's victory was not a single-handed success, but it was given by the hand of the Lord, who moved on his behalf. King Melchisedec, whose name means "My king is righteousness," brought out bread and wine to celebrate Abram and spoke a blessing over him. In response to God's goodness and honor, Abram gave King Melchisedec, the priest of the Most High God, one-tenth of the spoils of his victory. This is the first biblical instance of tithing.

Background

The book of Hebrews, one of the general epistles, was tailored and penned to reach a primarily Jewish Christian audience and is rich with displays that compare and contrast the Torah and the New Covenant. Its purpose is to exhort a second-generation church that had experienced persecution not to lose their faith. They were in danger of reverting to practices that neglected their faith in the power of Christ's life and death, so Hebrews often reminds the community of Christ's preeminent position of authority alongside God. Scholars' opinions vary on the authorship of Hebrews. Many believe Paul wrote it, even though it was not signed like his other letters. Nonetheless, it was counted as an inspired source and included in the Bible. A major theme of the book of Hebrews is showing Jesus as the Christ, the Son of God, in His position in the lives of believers as Savior, Priest, and King through His deity and humanity. It should also be noted that this audience of believers was the second generation of the church who were enduring persecution for their faith. Hebrews sought to provide sound doctrine for them to follow, to further root them in the faith by teaching Christ's superiority over angels and prophets, including Moses, and His position as the great High Priest.

At-A-Glance

1. Jesus the Great High Priest (Hebrews 4:14–16)
2. Jesus and Earthly High Priests (vv. 5:1–5)
3. Jesus and Melchisedec High Priest Forever (vv. 6–10)

In Depth

1. Jesus the Great High Priest (Hebrews 4:14–16)

Jesus in His role as our High Priest ends the need to petition anyone else for the forgiveness of sins. The writer reiterates to his audience that Jesus as the Son of God is the profession of the faith, and that because of Him, we are able to approach God's throne. Through this passage, Christians are invited to stand strong in this belief in the face of those who disagree. Throughout the opening of Hebrews, the writer makes the point that Jesus is the express image of God, just as in the world a child is the very reflection of his or her father in DNA, behavior, and character (Hebrews 1:3). Because of what Jesus accomplished through His death and resurrection, He is seated at the right hand of the Father with all power and majesty. This makes Him more than qualified to represent God to the people and the people to Him. Therefore, we are reminded that we do not have a High Priest who cannot empathize with our struggles. Instead we have a Savior who was at all points tempted or tried as we are but did not sin. As we stand in His righteousness, we are implored to come boldly to the throne of grace and receive what we need from God in the name of Jesus, just as He promised we could (John 14:13, 16:26–27).

2. Jesus and Earthly High Priests (vv. 5:1–5)

The writer goes on to draw comparisons to the office of high priest to show how Jesus perfects the custom. Under the Mosaic Law, God set apart the high priest to represent Himself to the people and the people to Him. God specifically established the priesthood to hail from the lineage of Aaron; he wore special clothing while functioning as priest. While before the people, he wore a uniform of great grandeur, and each piece represented a facet of his office on behalf of the people. However, when he went before the Lord in the Holy of Holies, he was stripped of that grandeur. The high priest entered the Holy of Holies once a year to make atonement of sins for himself and the people. The point the writer makes is that God the Father established His Son as the High Priest when He called Him out in His humanity

to represent the people by bearing our sins and glorifying His name (v. 5, John 12:28).

3. Jesus and Melchisedec High Priest Forever (vv. 6–10)

The writer closes this phase of his argument by introducing the order of Melchisedec and makes the link that Jesus is the High Priest forever. He draws this conclusion because in Old Testament Scripture, Melchisedec has no recorded father, his priesthood predates Aaron's, he is also a king, and he has no recorded end. Psalm 110:3–5 is a prophetic foreshadow of Christ saying: "The LORD hath sworn, and will not repent, Thou art a priest for ever after the order of Melchizedek" (v. 4, KJV). Melchisedec is a foreshadowing of Christ because he combined kingship and priesthood in his person; Jesus remains in the office of Priest and King forever, which is why we call Him Lord. Jesus remained faithful in the days of His humanity by staying in a posture of prayerful submission to God. Although He is the Son of God, He still suffered and knows the experience of what it takes to obey God, which again solidifies why He is the great High Priest who understands our infirmities in this earthly body. Later, the author of Hebrews writes that Christ entered into the heavenly Holy of Holies to apply His blood on the mercy seat on our behalf and now remains in the presence of God to make intercession for us (Hebrews 9:11–12).

Search the Scriptures

1. In what way was Christ "in all points tempted like as we are, yet without sin" (4:15)?

2. How does Christ as High Priest compare among the priests of the Old Testament (5:1–5)?

Discuss the Meaning

1. What does it mean for us today that Jesus "in the days of His flesh ... offered up prayers

and supplications" and "Though he were a Son, yet learned he obedience by the things which he suffered" (Hebrews 5:7,8)?

2. How does knowing Jesus as our High Priest add value to your relationship with Him?

Lesson in Our Society

If you ever need a lawyer, it is always good to have one who is able to best represent your interests. It is wonderful to know that in heaven, we have the best representation that money cannot buy, but purchased with the blood of Christ. Hebrews 7:25 says He lives forever to intercede with God on their behalf. Praise God that Jesus intercedes for us!

Make It Happen

Today and throughout the week, reflect on the fact that Jesus lives to intercede on your behalf. Live intentionally with the thought that no matter what you experience, there is grace to help in your time of need, and share this grace with others.

Follow the Spirit

What God wants me to do:

Remember Your Thoughts

Special insights I have learned:

More Light on the Text

Hebrews 4:14–5:10

14 Seeing then that we have a great high priest, that is passed into the heavens, Jesus the Son of God, let us hold fast our profession. 15 For we have not an high priest which cannot be touched with the feeling of our infirmities; but was in all points tempted like as we are, yet without sin. 16 Let us therefore come boldly unto the throne of grace, that we may obtain mercy, and find grace to help in time of need.

The author turns our attention to Jesus as the great High Priest. The adjective "great" (Gk. *megas*, **MEH-gahs**) places Him in a different category from any other high priest; He is the High Priest of all high priests. The phrase "passed into the heavens" is similar to what the high priest did on the Day of Atonement (Leviticus 16:2–3, 17–18). He "passed through" the curtain of the Temple and entered the Holy of Holies, where the Ark of the Covenant was placed. The Holy of Holies was where the Father resided.

This passage has two admonitions: to hold firmly to our faith and approach the throne of grace. Both are possible only through Jesus Christ, our great High Priest. Jesus was "touched with the feeling of our infirmities." This does not mean that He experienced every circumstance that we have experienced, but that He experienced and felt the same emotions and pain we feel in our own moments of weakness and suffering. As a human, Jesus experienced what we are going through, so we know that when we approach God in prayer, we will receive empathy and understanding. When we pray, we can also approach God with great hope and expectation because we know we will find forgiveness, mercy, and help to overcome our problems. The mention of the "throne of grace" alludes to the area of the Ark of the Covenant that was called the Mercy Seat, where the high priest sprinkled the blood of the sacrifice to make atonement with God for the people. The author is saying that unlike those other high priests who went into the Holy of Holies trembling because of their imperfection in light of God's perfect standard, we can come boldly to God because of the work of Jesus, our great High Priest.

5:1 For every high priest taken from among men is ordained for men in things pertaining to God, that he may offer both gifts and sacrifices for sins:

This section does not discuss all the features of this office, but it highlights those that correspond with what the author wants to say about Jesus as High Priest (vv. 1–4). A high priest must be one of the people in order to fulfill his role effectively. He is taken from among the people to mediate between them and God. These points are essential in understanding Jesus' priesthood. One of the high priest's functions is to "offer both gifts and sacrifices" or make atonement for sin. The high priest must be holy in all that he is and does, when representing a person or people before God. The high priest's life was governed by a particular set of rules regulating his behavior, even down to his apparel when offering sacrifices for the people. The high priest was a representative for the people in "things pertaining to God." Jesus is also holy, pure, and able to represent the people before God, not because of what He wears or by adhering to certain ritual regulations, but because He is holy in His very nature.

2 Who can have compassion on the ignorant, and on them that are out of the way;

for that he himself also is compassed with infirmity.

Another function of the priest is to empathize with the people. Even though this is not one of Aaron's specific requirements, it is implied to be his responsibility. The word translated "compassion" is *metriopatheo* (Gk. **meh-tree-oh-pah-THEH-oh**), used only here in the New Testament and meaning to act in moderation or control one's emotion. A high priest is expected to have compassion toward those who are ignorant and "on them that are out of the way" ("going astray," NIV; see also Leviticus 4; Numbers 15:22–29). The high priest should be compassionate toward those who have ignorantly sinned against the Lord. He should neither dismiss sin lightly nor severely condemn the sinner, but he should act in moderation. Jesus is able to have compassion because He was a human, and although He was without sin, He could identify with human weakness.

3 And by reason hereof he ought, as for the people, so also for himself, to offer for sins.

The high priest in the Old Testament also had to offer sacrifices for himself (Leviticus 16:11) because, like the people, he had sinned. His task, therefore, was not to condemn sinners, but to stand in solidarity with them. In doing so, he could offer a sacrifice for them. By recognizing his own weakness, he could be deeply compassionate toward and patient with those who were not walking in the truth. In contrast, Jesus is the High Priest without sin.

4 And no man taketh this honour unto himself, but he that is called of God, as was Aaron.

A high priest must be "called" (Gk. *kaloumenos*, **kah-LOO-men-ose**) or selected by God. One cannot just decide to enter into this high office and mediate between God and people. Since sinful humanity has violated God's righteous law, we cannot select the mediator. Only God can decide whom He wants as mediator. Aaron and his sons were appointed as priests by God Himself (Exodus 28:1).

5 So also Christ glorified not himself to be made an high priest; but he that said unto him, Thou art my Son, to day have I begotten thee. 6 As he saith also in another place, Thou art a priest for ever after the order of Melchisedec.

Although Christ is compared to the high priest and they are both called by God, Christ is superior. In verse 4, the word "called" indicates that the calling to the office of the high priest is an honor that God gives to whom He chooses. However, a stronger word, *doxazo* (**doke-SAHD-zo**), which means "to glorify, praise, or honor," is used to describe Jesus' becoming High Priest. Christ is glorified or exalted to this office. In verse 5, God's call is expressed in the words of Psalm 2:7 (which was also quoted in Hebrews 1:5).

Verse 6 is a quotation of Psalm 110. Unlike Aaron, Melchisedec was both king and priest. No king in Israel functioned as both king and priest. As priest and king, Melchisedec had no predecessor nor successor. Similarly, Christ is our High Priest forever. His perfect work of atonement is perpetual; He cannot be succeeded. Jesus Christ is the Son of God, our High Priest and King.

7 Who in the days of his flesh, when he had offered up prayers and supplications with strong crying and tears unto him that was able to save him from death, and was heard in that he feared.

Verse 7 emphasizes the humanity of Jesus, which was previously mentioned in Hebrews 2:9–18. The phrase "in the days of his flesh"

refers to His earthly ministry. The phrase "offered up prayers and supplications" is a reference to Jesus' "High Priestly" prayer in the Garden of Gethsemane (Matthew 26:36–46; Mark 14:32–42; Luke 22:40–46). The Gospel accounts clearly describe the fervency and intensity of this prayer. This shows that Jesus can completely empathize with our human condition of weakness.

Jesus prayed for deliverance from death, and was heard. God's answer was not that He would escape death, but that He would be resurrected. His prayer was heard because He "feared" God (or because of His "reverent submission," NIV). This does not mean that Jesus was afraid of the Father, but that He had the proper attitude of reverence in His duty.

8 Though he were a Son, yet learned he obedience by the things which he suffered.

Through His suffering, Jesus learned obedience. This does not mean that He was at any time disobedient, but He learned how to submit in obedience, laying down His will and rights. The writer engages in wordplay between the verb forms for "learned" (Gk. *emathen*, **EH-mah-thehn**) and "suffered" (Gk. *epathen*, **EH-pah-thehn**). In doing so, the writer suggests the falsity of the common understanding that obedience always results in peace and disobedience in suffering. Jesus' life and His death on the Cross prove that obedience can lead to suffering.

9 And being made perfect, he became the author of eternal salvation unto all them that obey him.

The phrase "being made perfect" (a single word in Greek; Gk. *teleiotheis*, **teh-lay-oh-THASE**) is not a reference to moral perfection, but the satisfactory completion of Christ's role as High Priest. The same word is used in the Greek translation of the Old Testament to refer to consecration and ordination (Leviticus 8:33; Numbers 3:3). Upon completion of this responsibility, Jesus became the "author" or source of eternal salvation for all who obey Him, just as He learned to obey God. The Greek word for "author" (*aitios*, **EYE-tee-ose**) could also be translated as "cause." The term "eternal salvation" is to be equated with eternal life, which Christ offers to those who believe in Him. Therefore, the reference to eternal salvation here is a description of Christ's work. His work of procuring salvation as our High Priest is eternally powerful—a perpetual priesthood.

10 Called of God an high priest after the order of Melchisedec.

Verse 10 ends this discussion of Jesus as our High Priest the way it began: with God's calling. It also introduces the new thought "after the order of Melchisedec," which points to His role as both Priest and King. He is a High Priest, but a different kind of high priest. As the Son of God, He is one with royal authority.

Say It Correctly

Melchisidec. mel-**KI**-si-dek.
Infirmity. in-**FER**-mi-tee.

Daily Bible Readings

MONDAY
Gifts for the Work of Ministry
(Ephesians 4:7–13)

TUESDAY
Grateful for God's Mercy
(1 Timothy 1:12–17)

WEDNESDAY
Maintain Faith and a Good Conscience
(1 Timothy 1:18–20)

THURSDAY
Guard Your Faith with Powerful Love
(2 Timothy 1:3–14)

FRIDAY
A Good Soldier of Jesus Christ
(2 Timothy 2:1–7)

SATURDAY
Jesus Carries Forward the Father's Will
(Matthew 26:36–39)

SUNDAY
Jesus the Great High Priest
(Hebrews 4:14–5:10)

Notes

_____

_____

_____

Teaching Tips

October 23
Bible Study Guide 8

Words You Should Know

A. Order of Melchisedec (Hebrews 7:21) *taxis Melchisedek* (Gk.)—The manner or likeness in official dignity of Melchisedec, the king whose priesthood superseded Aaron's.

B. Make intercession (v. 25) *entugchano* (Gk.)—To meet in order to converse or make a request for others; pleading in prayer or petition on behalf of another.

Teacher Preparation

Unifying Principle—Seeking Continuity and Permanence. Practices, traditions, and institutions are expected to continue into the future. Who will sustain them? Jesus gave the practices, traditions, and institutions established by God their ultimate meaning and role for all generations.

A. Pray that God will enlighten you with His Word.

B. Early in the week, start to conceptualize the Aim for Change, while studying the Focal Verses, Background, and In Depth sections.

C. Read The People, Places, and Times and More Light on the Text sections.

D. Study and complete lesson 8 in the *Precepts for Living®* Personal Study Guide.

O—Open the Lesson

A. Before the students arrive, write the lesson title, At-A-Glance outline, and the word "covenant" where the whole class can see them.

B. When the students arrive, open the class with prayer, including the Aim for Change objectives as a guide.

C. Ask students to define "covenant." Explain that today's lesson introduces Christ as our High Priest and intercessor who represents us before the Father.

D. Have a volunteer read the In Focus story.

P—Present the Scriptures

A. Have volunteers read the Focal Verses.

B. Use The People, Places, and Times; Background; Search the Scriptures; At-A-Glance; In Depth; and More Light on the Text to clarify the verses.

E—Explore the Meaning

A. Divide the class into groups to complete the Discuss the Meaning, Lesson in Our Society, and Make It Happen sections. Ask students to choose a representative to report their responses.

B. Connect these sections to the Aim for Change and the Keep in Mind verse.

N—Next Steps for Application

A. Summarize the lesson.

B. Close with prayer.

Worship Guide

For the Superintendent or Teacher
Theme: The High Priest Forever
Song: "I Will Trust in the Lord"
Devotional Reading: Psalm 110

The High Priest Forever

Bible Background • HEBREWS 7
Printed Text • HEBREWS 7:1–3, 19b–28 | Devotional Reading • PSALM 110

—————— Aim for Change ——————

By the end of the lesson, we will: COMPARE Melchisedec, "priest of the Most High God," with Jesus, the "priest forever"; APPRECIATE that people have someone who intercedes for them to God; and RESPOND to the realization that Jesus will always be our ultimate spiritual leader.

————— In Focus —————

Joseph couldn't believe it. He had just been chewed out by one of the elders at church. This was his mentor, one of the men that he looked up to. Not only did Rev. Jameson chew him out, but he defended his own unrepentant sin. The man he looked up to and patterned his life after was now having an affair with one of the sisters in the church.

When he confronted Rev. Jameson, Joseph didn't even believe the rumors, but now he knew that they were true. Rev. Jameson admitted to it him. He made excuses and rationalized his behavior as something God overlooked. It was nothing more than a weakness to the reverend. He scolded Joseph and told him to mind his own business and not be "holier than thou."

Now Joseph was devastated. To whom could he turn in this moment of crisis? A man he looked up to as his spiritual leader was now going astray. Then he remembered that He had never lost his true spiritual leader: Jesus. Joseph could turn to Him anytime. Jesus was perfect, compassionate, and sinless. Even though Rev. Jameson had let him down, Joseph knew that Jesus would never let him down. Right then and there he decided to pray for Rev. Jameson. He knew that Jesus was making intercession for the both of them.

Jesus is our ultimate spiritual leader and is always interceding for us. What are the qualities you look for in a spiritual leader?

————— Keep in Mind —————

"But this man, because he continueth ever, hath an unchangeable priesthood"
(Hebrews 7:24).

"But this man, because he continueth ever, hath an unchangeable priesthood"
(Hebrews 7:24).

Focal Verses

KJV **Hebrews 7:1** For this Melchisedec, king of Salem, priest of the most high God, who met Abraham returning from the slaughter of the kings, and blessed him;

2 To whom also Abraham gave a tenth part of all; first being by interpretation King of righteousness, and after that also King of Salem, which is, King of peace;

3 Without father, without mother, without descent, having neither beginning of days, nor end of life; but made like unto the Son of God; abideth a priest continually.

19b but the bringing in of a better hope did; by the which we draw nigh unto God.

20 And inasmuch as not without an oath he was made priest:

21 (For those priests were made without an oath; but this with an oath by him that said unto him, The Lord sware and will not repent, Thou art a priest for ever after the order of Melchisedec:)

22 By so much was Jesus made a surety of a better testament.

23 And they truly were many priests, because they were not suffered to continue by reason of death:

24 But this man, because he continueth ever, hath an unchangeable priesthood.

25 Wherefore he is able also to save them to the uttermost that come unto God by him, seeing he ever liveth to make intercession for them.

26 For such an high priest became us, who is holy, harmless, undefiled, separate from sinners, and made higher than the heavens;

27 Who needeth not daily, as those high priests, to offer up sacrifice, first for his own sins, and then for the people's: for this he did once, when he offered up himself.

NLT **Hebrews 7:1** This Melchizedek was king of the city of Salem and also a priest of God Most High. When Abraham was returning home after winning a great battle against the kings, Melchizedek met him and blessed him.

2 Then Abraham took a tenth of all he had captured in battle and gave it to Melchizedek. The name Melchizedek means "king of justice," and king of Salem means "king of peace."

3 There is no record of his father or mother or any of his ancestors—no beginning or end to his life. He remains a priest forever, resembling the Son of God.

19b But now we have confidence in a better hope, through which we draw near to God.

20 This new system was established with a solemn oath. Aaron's descendants became priests without such an oath,

21 but there was an oath regarding Jesus. For God said to him, "The LORD has taken an oath and will not break his vow: 'You are a priest forever.'"

22 Because of this oath, Jesus is the one who guarantees this better covenant with God.

23 There were many priests under the old system, for death prevented them from remaining in office.

24 But because Jesus lives forever, his priesthood lasts forever.

25 Therefore he is able, once and forever, to save those who come to God through him. He lives forever to intercede with God on their behalf.

26 He is the kind of high priest we need because he is holy and blameless, unstained by sin. He has been set apart from sinners and has been given the highest place of honor in heaven.

27 Unlike those other high priests, he does not need to offer sacrifices every day. They did

28 For the law maketh men high priests which have infirmity; but the word of the oath, which was since the law, maketh the Son, who is consecrated for evermore.

this for their own sins first and then for the sins of the people. But Jesus did this once for all when he offered himself as the sacrifice for the people's sins.

28 The law appointed high priests who were limited by human weakness. But after the law was given, God appointed his Son with an oath, and his Son has been made the perfect High Priest forever.

The People, Places, and Times

Levitical Priesthood. Synonymous with Aaronic priesthood and derived from the Law of Moses, this system restricted priestly duties to the tribe of Levi. Levitical priests were appointed by inheritance. They offered up animal sacrifices to the Lord daily for their own sins and for the people. This system was imperfect and impermanent because it relied on the existence of a tabernacle or temple and the ability of humans to carry out the tasks.

Melchisedec. He held the offices of both king and priest. He is characterized as a type of Christ in his priestly ministry. Greater than Levitical priests, Melchisedec blessed Abraham and received tithes from him. The Scriptures do not mention his ancestry, priestly pedigree, or birth and death, thereby echoing the eternal existence and unending priesthood of Christ. His name is also spelled Melchizedek, and it means "King of Righteousness." Salem, the name of his city, signified "peace." Thus, as king of peace, he typified Christ, the Prince of Peace, the One whose saving work reconciles God and humankind.

Background

In the first six chapters of Hebrews, the writer warms up the letter's recipients before making his point. Knowing that many of his readers were wavering in their faith, he began

the epistle with a message they could easily digest—that Jesus Christ is supreme over all. He then emphasized God's faithfulness to His Word and His promise of rest for believers. At the end of chapter 4, the writer introduced an unfamiliar concept, referring to Christ as "our great High Priest." He immediately moves into describing the credentials for the priesthood as they know it (chapter 5). Gently, he discusses the qualifications of a priest and contrasts them to qualify Jesus.

Although the writer mentions Melchisedec in chapter 5 and wants to discuss his priesthood in greater detail, he doesn't elaborate this point. Instead he writes that the readers are spiritually immature and "dull" and don't listen (5:11). He warns them of the danger of failing to grow in faith and tempers his rebuke with encouragement by saying, "But, beloved, we are persuaded better things of you ..." (6:9).

Finally, in chapter 7, the writer introduces this king who was also a priest: Melchisedec. As if anticipating their questions, he recounts how this king-priest met Abraham, blessed him, and received tithes from him. He also explains that the name Melchisedec means "king of righteousness" and "king of peace" and tells readers that his genealogy and dates of birth and death are not known. This description exalted Melchisedec above Abraham and portrayed the king-priest as a type of Christ, representing Jesus' eternal existence and unending priesthood.

Hebrews 7:11–14 reveals a transition of great significance: Anyone who turned to Christ and His priesthood must reject the Levitical priesthood and its law. The Levitical system disqualified Jesus from becoming a priest since He was not from the tribe of Levi, so a change in the order of the priesthood required a change in the priestly laws/instructions as well. However, Jesus' priesthood was of a higher order, not an earthly and imperfect one like the Levitical priesthood.

At-A-Glance

1. An Unending Life (Hebrews 7:1–3)
2. An Unbreakable Oath (vv. 19b–22)
3. An Unchangeable Priesthood (vv. 23–28)

In Depth

1. An Unending Life (Hebrews 7:1–3)

The writer of Hebrews highlights the character of Melchisedec in order to explain the kind of high priest we have in Christ. Melchisedec blessed Abraham after he came back from the battle of the five kings (Genesis 14:17–20). He also received a tithe from him. Melchisedec's two titles are unusual, as he is both a priest and a king in the same way that Christ is our High Priest and also the King of kings and Lord of lords.

Melchisedec's name means "king of righteousness," and as king of Salem, his title means "king of peace." These titles can both be applied to Christ. However, the most distinct similarity between Melchisedec and Christ is that there is no record in the Bible of the beginning or end to Melchisedec's life. He has no given genealogy, and no mention is made of his death. He is described as living forever and in this way he is similar to Christ.

2. An Unbreakable Oath (vv. 19b–22)

This new priesthood was marked by many changes. One such change was God's endorsement of the priest. God swore in Jesus with a solemn oath, "Thou art a priest for ever after the order of Melchisedec" (v. 21). Never had God done that in the Levitical priesthood. Jesus' priesthood, pledged in Psalm 110, was superior because it was divinely affirmed with an oath. Another change for the priesthood was that of its dispensation, or the way in which it was administered. The duties of the Levitical priesthood had to be carried out daily. Priests of the law were sinful and had to offer daily sacrifices for their own sins and those of the people. The important Day of Atonement, in which the high priest entered the Holy of Holies, came yearly. It was a "shadow of the real one in heaven," according to Hebrews 8:5 (NLT). But the Gospel dispensation was surer. With Christ as surety or a guarantee, humanity's reconciliation with God is guaranteed through an everlasting covenant. Christ, the Mediator, united the divine and human nature in His own Person. What animals' blood couldn't do, Jesus' blood did—once and for all.

3. An Unchangeable Priesthood (vv. 23–28)

According to verse 25, this Mediator of the new covenant "ever liveth to make intercession for them." This signified another change for the priesthood—Christ's priesthood was permanent and unchangeable. Whereas priests of the law died, leaving a vacancy in the priesthood until they were replaced, Jesus Christ as High Priest meant there will never be a vacancy in the priesthood. At all times, in all things, He will be available to negotiate our spiritual concerns in heaven by interceding with the Father on our behalf.

Another difference between these priesthoods was the moral qualifications of the priests. Verse 26 records that Jesus was "holy, harmless, undefiled, separate from sinners, and made higher than the heavens." Priests of the Law were mortal and sinful, so they had their share of physical infirmities and defects. No lawful priest could have qualified to make atonement for sin and intercession for sinners, without first atoning for his own sins and imperfections, except Christ, who was excellent Himself.

Search the Scriptures

1. What is the significance of Melchizidek being "Without father, without mother, without descent, having neither beginning of days, nor end of life" (Hebrews 7:3)?

2. What makes Jesus the kind of high priest we need (v. 26)? Create a list of the qualities of Jesus and the qualifications of the high priest from Leviticus 21. Note the similarities and differences.

Discuss the Meaning

Since Christ is always interceding for us, does this give us a license to sin? Why or why not?

Lesson in Our Society

We cannot do many things on our own. One of those things is to appear before a holy God. Only Jesus is equipped to do that. We can only go to God because Jesus is our High Priest. Without His ministry on our behalf, our prayers cannot be heard. It is one thing to pray, but it's another thing for God to hear our prayers and move on our behalf. This is what it means to have Jesus as our High Priest.

Make It Happen

List five benefits of having Jesus as our High Priest. Ask three friends for prayer requests. Pray for them knowing that Jesus is also interceding on your behalf and their behalf.

Follow the Spirit

What God wants me to do:

_____

_____

_____

_____

Remember Your Thoughts

Special insights I have learned:

_____

_____

_____

_____

More Light on the Text
Hebrews 7:1–3, 19b–28

7:1 For this Melchisedec, king of Salem, priest of the most high God, who met Abraham returning from the slaughter of the kings, and blessed him; 2 To whom also Abraham gave a tenth part of all; first being by interpretation King of righteousness, and after that also King of Salem, which is, King of peace; 3 Without father, without mother, without descent, having neither beginning of days, nor end of life; but made like unto the Son of God; abideth a priest continually.

Melchisedec is introduced as a king and priest of God Most High in Genesis 14:17–24.

This king and priest blessed Abraham and received tithes from him. His name and title allude to a connection to Christ. The writer points out the most distinguishing feature of Melchisedec—he has no record of ancestry or death. In this way, he is said to live forever, and through this distinction, Melchisedec is most like Christ. His eternal priesthood causes Melchisedec to resemble (Gk. *aphomoio*, **ah-fo-moy-OH-oh**) or be made analogous to the Son of God.

19b but the bringing in of a better hope did; by the which we draw nigh unto God.

The writer of Hebrews notes that with the coming of Jesus, the Levitical priesthood was set aside because it was weak and unprofitable (Hebrews 7:18). "A better hope" was introduced, "by the which we draw nigh unto God" (v. 19). The law could only remove our sins and bring us in relationship with God temporarily. Instead of being made right with God on an annual basis through sacrifices, now we can continually draw near to God through Jesus' intercession. Jesus did not sacrifice an animal, but He sacrificed Himself for our sins. Therefore, no other sacrifice is needed—ever. We now have (and will forever have) Jesus, who intercedes with the Father for us.

20 And inasmuch as not without an oath he was made priest.

This is the writer's way of saying Jesus' priesthood is of a higher order than Levitical succession. Jesus' priesthood was established by God with an oath, meaning God has sworn and will not change His mind. Just as God kept His covenant with Abraham, He will keep His promise regarding Jesus' priesthood. Jesus' priesthood is permanent, unlike the temporary Levitical priesthood.

21 (For those priests were made without an oath; but this with an oath by him that said unto him, The Lord sware and will not repent, Thou art a priest for ever after the order of Melchisedec:)

The Levitical priesthood established under Aaron (Exodus 28:1) was conditional. It was instituted without an oath and therefore lacked permanence. Christ's priesthood was confirmed by an oath, and He is therefore "a priest for ever." The fact that Jesus' priesthood is confirmed by divine oath leaves no room for Him to be disqualified because of any human weakness or sin.

The writer of Hebrews aims to show that Christ's priesthood is superior to the Levitical priesthood. To strengthen the argument, the writer references Psalm 110:4, which is understood to be God's comment to Christ. Hebrews is the only New Testament book that makes a direct reference to Melchisedec. This name appears in two passages in the Old Testament (Genesis 14:18–20; Psalm 110:4). In Genesis 14:18–20, he is referred to as "the king of Salem" and "the priest of the most high God." While several extra-biblical references to Melchisedec exist (2 Enoch, Philo, Josephus, Qumran documents), and it appears that some early Christian writers were aware of a Melchisedec tradition, he remains a mysterious figure. The lack of clarity regarding Melchisedec's role in biblical history, however, does not diminish the truth of the superiority and permanence of Christ's priesthood.

22 By so much was Jesus made a surety of a better testament.

Here the writer of Hebrews surprisingly moves his line of reasoning from the priesthood to a testament or covenant. The Greek word *diatheke* (**dee-ah-THAY-kay**, testament or covenant) is used in conjunction with the Greek word *egguos* (**EN-gue-oss**, surety; the guarantee that a promise will be fulfilled). These two words are meant to make perfectly clear the incontestability of God's oath whereby Jesus was made "a priest for ever." God made the promise, and Jesus is the guarantee that the promise will be fulfilled.

It is understood that a will or testament is final and absolute and therefore cannot be revised except by the person leaving it. God has laid the terms of Christ's priesthood down once and for all time. Jesus' life and God's oath make unnecessary a succession of priests after Christ.

23 And they truly were many priests, because they were not suffered to continue by reason of death:

The writer of Hebrews continues to contrast Jesus with the Levitical priests. Historians tell us that from the time of Aaron to the destruction of the Temple in AD 70, between 80 and 85 high priests served. Because they were all subject to death, numerous replacements were necessary.

24 But this man, because he continueth ever, hath an unchangeable priesthood.

Unlike the Levitical priests, Jesus' priesthood "continueth ever." He has "an unchangeable priesthood." The Greek word for unchangeable, *aparabatos* (**ahp-ar-AH-bah-toss**, something that cannot be transgressed or transferred to another), conveys the idea that Jesus' priesthood stays with Him through eternity. Since Jesus Himself "continueth ever," His priesthood can be "unchangeable." Jesus' priesthood cannot be transferred to another. Thus, He will be able to intercede for us and for all people in every generation yet unborn.

25 Wherefore he is able also to save them to the uttermost that come unto God by him,

seeing he ever liveth to make intercession for them.

The basic and most significant content of this verse is contained in the Greek verb *sozo* (**SOHD-zoh**, to save, deliver, make whole, or to preserve from danger, loss, and destruction). More specifically, in the context of Hebrews, it is salvation in its broadest and fullest meaning. It implies complete deliverance, no matter what our need, including deliverance from the punishment resulting from sin. In Jesus, we have a Savior able to bring complete salvation to all who "come unto God by him." Jesus lives to make intercession for us. Because He lives forever, His priestly concern for us never ends. Whatever our need, at any time or in any place, Jesus Christ stands ready to petition God the Father on our behalf. He is able and always available to speak for us.

26 For such an high priest became us, who is holy, harmless, undefiled, separate from sinners, and made higher than the heavens.

All priests who served in the Temple where God's presence dwelt were obliged to be holy, harmless, undefiled, and separate from sinners. In essence, they should be free of any impurity—actions or circumstances that would render them unclean according to the Mosaic Law. Any defilement rendered the priest incapable of interceding for the people.

The writer of Hebrews wants his readers to know that Jesus fulfills all of these requirements. He is holy, harmless, and undefiled, and although He is a friend of sinners, He has been "made higher than the heavens." While Jesus is apart from sinners, He nonetheless intercedes for sinners in ways that show His capacity to identify with even the outcasts of society. In fact, Hebrews 4:15 reminds us, "For we have not an high priest which cannot be touched with the feeling of our infirmities; but was in all points tempted like as we are, yet without sin." Christ's undefiled character attests to His capacity to go before God on our behalf. Unlike the Levitical priests, Jesus had no need to offer a sacrifice for Himself. By virtue of His deity and undefiled character, He was qualified to offer Himself as the atoning sacrifice for our sins. He was the "lamb without blemish and without spot" (from 1 Peter 1:19).

27 Who needeth not daily, as those high priests, to offer up sacrifice, first for his own sins, and then for the people's: for this he did once, when he offered up himself.

This verse presents meticulous students of the Scriptures with a problem. A careful reading of the relevant text will show that while sacrifices were offered daily, the high priest was not required to offer the daily sacrifices personally (Numbers 28:3). Those sacrifices requiring the high priest's attention were offered yearly, not daily (cf. Hebrews 9:7, 25, 10:1). However, the writer wishes to make the point that Jesus has no need to offer sacrifices daily or yearly for His own sins, because He was sinless (4:15). His perfect sacrifice was sufficient for all time.

The writer's use of the phrase translated as "for this he did once" is a critically important affirmation. It speaks not only of the eternal completeness and efficacy of Christ's sacrifice of Himself but it also nullifies every other sacrificial system because Jesus' sacrifice is complete and any other sacrifice is unnecessary. Christ's sacrifice of Himself is final and eternally adequate for our salvation.

28 For the law maketh men high priests which have infirmity; but the word of the oath, which was since the law, maketh the Son, who is consecrated for evermore.

Here the writer again compares the Levitical priests and Jesus. Under Levitical law, which was imperfect, priests were ordinary men appointed by ordinary men. Therefore priests,

even the high priest, are limited, just as all men are limited and weak. They are subject to death.

Standing in clear contrast to the Law is "the word of the oath," which came much later than the Law. One could ask: If the Law was perfect, making provision for the appointment of perfect priests, what need would there be for "the word of the oath"? The mere fact that "the word of the oath" came after the Law points to the inadequacies of the Aaronic priesthood.

This verse is really a summary of the preceding verses. It reiterates the thought that Jesus, the Son, is superior to all the priests appointed under the law. The continuous replacement of imperfect priests is contrasted with the permanent placement of the perfect Jesus "who is consecrated," or perfected (Gk. *teleioo*, **te-lay-oh-OH**). This word means to make perfect or full and specifically in this sense to be perfect in character and qualifications. This is the high priest who "always lives to make intercession for us."

Say It Correctly

Melchisedec. mel-**KIH**-zi-dek.
Consecrated. **KHAN**-se-kra-tid.

Daily Bible Readings

MONDAY
Victory of God's Priest King
(Psalm 110)

TUESDAY
Service by and Support of Priests
(Numbers 18:21–24)

WEDNESDAY
Believers' Inheritance in Christ
(Ephesians 1:11–16)

THURSDAY
Power of God Invested in Christ
(Ephesians 1:17–23)

FRIDAY
Jesus, Permanent Priest Forever
(Hebrews 1:1–3, 23–25)

SATURDAY
Power of an Indestructible Life
(Hebrews 7:15–17)

SUNDAY
The High Priest Forever
(Hebrews 7:1–3, 19b–28)

Notes

_____

_____

_____

_____

Teaching Tips

Words You Should Know

A. Author (Hebrews 12:2) *archegos* (Gk.)—One who takes the lead and sets the example; one who is first to use or apply something.

B. Perfecter (v. 2) *teleiotes* (Gk.)—One who executes or completes a task successfully.

Teacher Preparation

Unifying Principle—Embracing and Overcoming Trials. As adults, we face many struggles in life. As James 1:2–4 indicates, these trials can make us stronger, wiser, and increase our faith. However, it is difficult to weather these storms without the aid of others—people and, more importantly, God. Faith is what sustains us in difficult times.

A. Pray for clarity and application, for you and your students.

B. Study the companion lesson in the *Precepts for Living®* Personal Study Guide thoroughly in advance.

O—Open the Lesson

A. Begin by having students recall a childhood disciplinary action that resulted in an effective change or lesson learned. Recognize that some might have experienced abuse. Emphasize the difference between abuse and loving discipline.

B. Introduce today's lesson title and Aim for Change. Pray for students to develop a clear understanding of discipline and its presence and usefulness in our lives as adults.

C. Have students read the Keep in Mind verse and In Focus story.

P—Present the Scriptures

A. Have students read the Focal Verses; The People, Places, and Times; and Background.

C. Use In Depth content and Search the Scriptures to facilitate discussion of the Focal Verses.

E—Explore the Meaning

A. Have the class answer the questions in Discuss the Meaning.

B. Read Lesson in Our Society and have students make observations.

N—Next Steps for Application

A. Briefly review the lesson, highlighting the Keep in Mind verse.

B. Read Make It Happen and re-read the Aim for Change aloud.

C. Pray with students that they will be able to recognize God's discipline and help others through what they learn.

Worship Guide

For the Superintendent or Teacher
Theme: Pioneer and Perfecter of Our Faith
Song: "Take My Life"
Devotional Reading: Isaiah 53:1–6

Pioneer and Perfecter of Our Faith

Bible Background • HEBREWS 12:1–13
Printed Text • HEBREWS 12:1–13 | Devotional Reading • ISAIAH 53:1–6

Aim for Change

By the end of the lesson, we will: VALUE discipline in the family, in the congregation, and in other human settings; APPRECIATE the help provided by others who have experienced discipline; and SHARE personal struggles that resulted in a victorious and growing faith.

In Focus

Sara always accomplished her goals and became quite accustomed to success. She not only enjoyed it, but she also came to expect and worship her achievements. Sara lived to disprove naysayers, and developed an arrogance and intolerance for those she did not deem worthy of her time and attention. She knew better and had been raised differently, but she allowed the drive for competition and success to rule over her compassion. And one day, it all came crashing down. She lost everything. Her marriage, her career, and her house were all gone in the aftermath of nasty company politics and a bad economy.

Living in the basement of her mother's home, she came across a Bible. She recalled stories of her youth, long forgotten—David and Saul, the Hebrew boys and Nebuchadnezzar. She then recognized her own pride. She had elevated herself and her success above God, and she lived with faith only in her abilities. She recalled the people she cheated, ignored, and misused to get what she wanted. And now, she had nothing. Sara wept and remembered Proverbs 3:12: *For whom the Lord loveth he correcteth; even as a father the son in whom he delighteth.* She had memorized that verse in third grade. She could not explain it, but an overwhelming peace settled over her. At that moment, Sara knew that God's love and forgiveness were real. She would survive.

Love involves correction. In this lesson, we will learn how God uses trials for our growth. Have you ever experienced the discipline of God in your life?

Keep in Mind

"Let us run with patience the race that is set before us, looking unto Jesus the author and finisher of our faith" (from Hebrews 12:1–2).

"Let us run with patience the race that is set before us, looking unto Jesus the author and finisher of our faith" (from Hebrews 12:1–2).

Focal Verses

KJV **Hebrews 12:1** Wherefore seeing we also are compassed about with so great a cloud of witnesses, let us lay aside every weight, and the sin which doth so easily beset us, and let us run with patience the race that is set before us,

2 Looking unto Jesus the author and finisher of our faith; who for the joy that was set before him endured the cross, despising the shame, and is set down at the right hand of the throne of God.

3 For consider him that endured such contradiction of sinners against himself, lest ye be wearied and faint in your minds.

4 Ye have not yet resisted unto blood, striving against sin.

5 And ye have forgotten the exhortation which speaketh unto you as unto children, My son, despise not thou the chastening of the Lord, nor faint when thou art rebuked of him:

6 For whom the Lord loveth he chasteneth, and scourgeth every son whom he receiveth.

7 If ye endure chastening, God dealeth with you as with sons; for what son is he whom the father chasteneth not?

8 But if ye be without chastisement, whereof all are partakers, then are ye bastards, and not sons.

9 Furthermore we have had fathers of our flesh which corrected us, and we gave them reverence: shall we not much rather be in subjection unto the Father of spirits, and live?

10 For they verily for a few days chastened us after their own pleasure; but he for our profit, that we might be partakers of his holiness.

11 Now no chastening for the present seemeth to be joyous, but grievous: nevertheless afterward it yieldeth the peaceable fruit of righteousness unto them which are exercised thereby.

NLT **Hebrews 12:1** Therefore, since we are surrounded by such a huge crowd of witnesses to the life of faith, let us strip off every weight that slows us down, especially the sin that so easily trips us up. And let us run with endurance the race God has set before us.

2 We do this by keeping our eyes on Jesus, the champion who initiates and perfects our faith. Because of the joy awaiting him, he endured the cross, disregarding its shame. Now he is seated in the place of honor beside God's throne.

3 Think of all the hostility he endured from sinful people; then you won't become weary and give up.

4 After all, you have not yet given your lives in your struggle against sin.

5 And have you forgotten the encouraging words God spoke to you as his children? He said, "My child, don't make light of the LORD's discipline, and don't give up when he corrects you.

6 For the LORD disciplines those he loves, and he punishes each one he accepts as his child."

7 As you endure this divine discipline, remember that God is treating you as his own children. Who ever heard of a child who is never disciplined by its father?

8 If God doesn't discipline you as he does all of his children, it means that you are illegitimate and are not really his children at all.

9 Since we respected our earthly fathers who disciplined us, shouldn't we submit even more to the discipline of the Father of our spirits, and live forever?

10 For our earthly fathers disciplined us for a few years, doing the best they knew how. But God's discipline is always good for us, so that we might share in his holiness.

12 Wherefore lift up the hands which hang down, and the feeble knees;

13 And make straight paths for your feet, lest that which is lame be turned out of the way; but let it rather be healed.

11 No discipline is enjoyable while it is happening—it's painful! But afterward there will be a peaceful harvest of right living for those who are trained in this way.

12 So take a new grip with your tired hands and strengthen your weak knees.

13 Mark out a straight path for your feet so that those who are weak and lame will not fall but become strong.

The People, Places, and Times

Hebrews. In Genesis 14:13, Abram (Abraham) is the first person to be called a "Hebrew," and his descendants through Isaac would go on to be known as "Hebrews" (also called Israelites and Jews). The origin of the term is debated. Some scholars believe it is derived from the name Eber, one of Abram's ancestors (Genesis 11:14–17). Still others hold that it comes from the term *ha ibhri* from the Hebrew word *abar*, which means "to cross over." This phrase is used in Genesis to describe Abram "crossing over" the river Euphrates. It is believed that the book of Hebrews was written to a largely Jewish audience that had converted to Christianity some time prior to the writing of the epistle.

Cloud of Witnesses. In chapter 11, the writer of Hebrews provides a brief history of people who demonstrated great faith in God, beginning in Genesis with Abel, and continuing with those who "were tortured, refusing to turn from God in order to be set free" (Hebrews 11:35, NLT). These people of the faith make up this large multitude of witnesses, people who believed God and testified to His faithfulness and power. The Greek term used for "witnesses" is *martus* (from which we derive "martyr"), which can be translated as "a spectator, witness, or testifier."

Background

The book of Hebrews has a few unknowns. Origen, a Christian interpreter from the third century, engages in a debate regarding whether Paul wrote Hebrews. He determines that the style is different but that Paul's theology certainly influenced Hebrews strongly enough to include it in the tradition of Paul, even if only God knows whether or not Paul wrote the document. The first readers are unknown, although it is surmised from the epistle that they were persecuted Jewish Christians. The recipients appear to be familiar with the Old Testament, as it is quoted throughout the letter. They also were likely acquainted with Jewish teachings and rituals, perhaps tempted or coerced to elevate them above faith in Christ. The writer sets forth to establish the supremacy of Christ—speaking of His incarnation, death, priesthood, and His elevation above the angels, Moses, Joshua, and high priests. He then focuses on faith, providing its definition as "the substance of things hoped for, the evidence of things not seen" (Hebrews.11:1, KJV), and goes on to list those from Jewish history who are in the Great Hall of Faith. In so doing, he reminds readers of the necessity of faith in Christ, how "without faith it is impossible to please [God]" (11:6, NIV), and how faith supersedes rituals and sacrifices.

At-A-Glance

1. Be Faithful (Hebrews 12:1–4)
2. Be Disciplined (vv. 5–11)
3. Be Strong (vv. 12–13)

In Depth

1. Be Faithful (Hebrews 12:1–4)

The writer of Hebrews uses an illustration of a race, a common athletic event during Greco-Roman times. There are runners and witnesses. These "witnesses" are examples, though they were not "made perfect" (11:40). They trusted God and lived for Him to the end. Their testimonies encourage others to do the same. The writer exhorts his audience (runners) to "strip off" (i.e., take off excess clothing or weights while running) anything that hinders living faithfully, particularly sin (12:1). Instead of being sidetracked and encumbered, believers should run with endurance by focusing on Christ, the One who founded the Christian faith (v. 2) and created a path forward for those to come. He not only started it but He is the ultimate example—the One who demonstrates how perfect faith looks, and equips us. When the temptation arises to be overwhelmed in the face of trials, the writer encourages believers to not become weary and give up (v. 3), as one would be toward the end of a race. Instead, believers should be motivated by remembering how Christ endured a humiliating and excruciatingly painful death to overcome sin and restore our relationship with God. That was the joy set before Him (v. 2).

2. Be Disciplined (vv. 5–11)

The main focus of this passage is "discipline," from the Greek word *paideia*, which means "education, training, or correction." Winning a physical race involves disciplining one's body, abstaining from unhealthy practices, and intentionally engaging in healthy ones. The process is often painful, but necessary. The same is true of spiritual discipline. In this case, the writer reminds these persecuted believers that many trials that may tempt them to give up are actually tools in God's hand to lovingly correct. He quotes Proverbs 3:11–12 to remind them that while such discipline is unpleasant, it is a sign of God's love and indicative of a true relationship as His children. Only loving fathers take the time and effort to educate and train children. Training, correcting, educating, and rebuking are expected of earthly fathers, and they are respected for it. If earthly fathers discipline, how much more discipline should be expected from the heavenly Father whose desire is that we be wholly righteous (living as we ought to live) and experience peace.

3. Be Strong (vv. 12–13)

Because of the examples set forth by the "cloud of witnesses" and Christ, who not only began the faith but perfects it, and the realization that many trials are allowed to make believers more like God, readers are then encouraged to stand firm and be strengthened. Those who continue to believe and trust God in the midst of trials are approved by Him. Again, physical imagery is used of one overcoming weakness to get a firm grasp and footing. However, the purpose of gaining strength and marking out a straight path is not only for the individual's benefit, but also it eventually serves as an example for those who follow after.

Search the Scriptures

1. How can we determine the weights in our lives and the sin that so easily besets us (Hebrews 12:1)?

2. How do we develop an appropriate response to experiencing discipline from God (vv. 4–7)?

Discuss the Meaning

Very rarely is discipline viewed in the context of faith and growth. However Hebrews 12:10 says that God's discipline is "for our profit." Create a timeline of your own experiences of God's discipline. Share with the class how they affected your faith? Your character? Your growth? What lessons can others learn from your example?

Lesson in Our Society

Many people talk about needing to "exercise discipline" or "be disciplined." However, few people understand or appreciate the process. Discipline involves training, educating, and correcting, and it is accomplished in various ways. It requires effort, love, time, consistency, sacrifice, pain, and a degree of difficulty, but it is necessary in order to experience growth. Our society tends to think in terms of punishment and retaliation—not discipline and redemption. Suffering occurs for various reasons: sometimes it is punitive, sometimes simply because we live in a fallen world, and other times because God wants us to grow. This is good. His example should be followed with our children as well. How does this affect your view and approach to discipline?

Make It Happen

This lesson causes us to re-examine our view of suffering and discipline. Joseph's tumultuous journey ended with him being second-in-command in Egypt. The faith of Daniel's friends grew as they experienced God's deliverance in the furnace and Daniel's faith grew as he was delivered from the lion's den. Suffering is painful. But good can come from it. How are you challenged to change your view of suffering? What trials do you have now? Is there anything that needs to change in how you approach discipline in your life? Your children? Pray that God will give you the ability to see what He is doing and faith to endure.

Follow the Spirit

What God wants me to do:

_____

_____

_____

_____

Remember Your Thoughts

Special insights I have learned:

_____

_____

_____

_____

More Light on the Text

Hebrews 12:1–13

1 Wherefore seeing we also are compassed about with so great a cloud of witnesses, let us lay aside every weight, and the sin which doth so easily beset us, and let us run with patience the race that is set before us,

In this verse, "so great a cloud of witnesses" refers to the people mentioned in chapter 11. Here, the writer is saying that those who have gone before are examples to others of living the life of faith. God has confirmed their faithfulness, and they can be seen as examples of those who endured. Therefore, in light of our inspiring audience, we must rid ourselves of "every weight" and "run with patience." The Greek word for "patience" is *hupomone* (**hoo-po-mo-NAY**), which is derived from two Greek words: *hupo* (**hoo-PO**), meaning "under," and *meno* (**MEN-oh**), meaning "to remain." This paints the picture that by remaining under some trial, we may be molded to fit God's purposes.

2 Looking unto Jesus the author and finisher of our faith; who for the joy that was set before him endured the cross, despising the shame, and is set down at the right hand of the throne of God. 3 For consider him that endured such contradiction of sinners against himself, lest ye be wearied and faint in your minds.

To run the race, a person must stay focused on Jesus, as implied here by the use of the Greek word *aphorao* (**ah-foe-RAH-oh**), translated as "looking." *Aphorao* means "to focus attention, to see something clearly"—namely Jesus. We do so because Jesus is the "author" (Gk. *archegos*, **ar-khay-GOSS**), meaning chief leader. This term was used for heroes and founders of philosophical schools, as well as those who paved the way for others and were exalted for their efforts. So Jesus is the "pioneer" and the "finisher" (Gk. *teleiotes*, **teh-lay-oh-TACE**), which means "completer" of faith. In other words, His life and death make faith complete. The word "endured" comes from *hupomeno* (Gk. **hoo-poe-MEN-oh**), meaning "to remain or tarry." Jesus chose to remain on the Cross and bear the shame of crucifixion to save humanity. He focused on the future and finished the work of our redemption, bringing many to glory (Hebrews 2:10).

4 Ye have not yet resisted unto blood, striving against sin.

Here, the readers are reminded that although they may have suffered great persecution (Hebrews 10:32–34), none of them has shed blood and died like Jesus did. None had yet has become a martyr because of their confession of Jesus as their Messiah or Savior.

5 And ye have forgotten the exhortation that speaketh unto you as unto children, My son, despise not thou the chastening of the Lord, nor faint when thou art rebuked of him: 6 For whom the Lord loveth he chasteneth, and scourgeth every son he receiveth.

In verses 5 and 6, the author quotes Proverbs 3:11–12. In these verses, the reader is reminded of the parent-child relationship. Undisciplined children are unloved children. In this instance, the use of the Greek word *paideia* (**pie-DAY-ah**) means "nurturing" or "giving instruction." The writer is saying that one should not make light of God's instruction but welcome it as a means of spiritual growth.

7 If ye endure chastening, God dealeth with you as with sons; for what son is he whom the father chasteneth not? 8 But if ye be without chastisement, whereof all are partakers, then are ye bastards, and not sons.

Christians should view trials as a form of divine discipline. Just as a parent would discipline a child, God deals with the sinner. No wise father or mother would allow his or her children to continue bad behavior without correcting it. Therefore, receiving discipline can be viewed as a sign of God's fatherly love.

9 Furthermore we have had fathers of our flesh which corrected us, and we gave them reverence: shall we not much rather be in subjection unto the Father of spirits, and live?

Here, God is called "the Father of spirits" (an expression in the New Testament which occurs only here)—in contrast to the human "fathers of our flesh." The writer makes a comparison between an earthly father and the heavenly Father—the argument being, if earthly parents discipline us and we respect them for it in the long run, then we should respect our heavenly Father even more.

10 For they verily for a few days chastened us after their own pleasure; but he for our profit, that we might be partakers of his holiness.

Verse 10 points out the difference between human discipline and heaven's discipline. Our earthly parents discipline us "for a few days," whereas God's discipline gives us an eternal benefit. Human discipline is often inconsistent and usually provides a temporary benefit. However, the long-range goal in God's discipline is that we might be "partakers" of His holiness. Nothing pleases God more than children who grow to emulate Him.

11 Now no chastening for the present seemeth to be joyous, but grievous: nevertheless afterward it yieldeth the peaceable fruit of righteousness unto them which are exercised thereby.

Present discipline seems painful because it is! The purpose of our pain is to produce Christ-like behavior. Sometimes we have to endure painful discipline. The Greek word for "exercised" is *gumnazo* (**goom-NAHD-zoh**), and as used here, it implies exercise of the mind in order to endure persecution. The word is usually used for going to the gym to work out, much as we would today. This physical training was a key part of the *paideia* (**PIE-ee-dee-uh**) or education a young person was expected to undergo. Here, the author states it is also a key part of the discipline that God has His children undergo, exercising the mind in order to endure persecution so that they can later enjoy the "fruit of righteousness."

12 Wherefore lift up the hands which hang down, and the feeble knees; 13 And make straight paths for your feet, lest that which is lame be turned out of the way; but let it rather be healed.

These two verses encourage the Hebrew Christians to become strong, and by becoming stronger, they will be able to help even the weakest among them. In the race of faith, they are called to lift up their weak hands and knees. This is likely an allusion to Isaiah 35:3, a prophecy to Israel regarding the inaugurated kingdom of God. Through this, the writer implies that now Jesus' followers have experienced the inbreaking of the coming kingdom. This inbreaking, which is signified by the baptism of the Holy Spirit, is the basis for the believer's strengthened faith in the present as well as in the future.

The wording of verse 13 might have Proverbs 4:26 in mind. This verse is an exhortation to not stray away from the godly path. The writer of Hebrews says that by following the correct path, those who are already lame may become healed. They will avoid further suffering and spiritual disability.

Say It Correctly

Exhortation. eks-**ZOR**-tay-shun.
Chasteneth. **CHAY**-sen-ith

Daily Bible Readings

MONDAY
I Know Their Suffering
(Exodus 3:7–10)

TUESDAY
Cry for Help Answered
(Psalm 22:1–5)

WEDNESDAY
By His Bruises We Are Healed
(Isaiah 53:1–6)

THURSDAY
Run the Race to Win
(1 Corinthians 9:24–27)

FRIDAY
Endure Discipline, Share in God's Holiness
(Hebrews 10:35–39)

SATURDAY
You Are Blessed for Enduring Suffering
(James 1:12–16)

SUNDAY
Discipline Yields Peaceful Fruit
(Hebrews 12:1–13)

Notes

Teaching Tips

Words You Should Know

A. New (Revelation 21:1) *kainos* (Gk.)—Unused, unworn, fresh, not previously existing; beginning for the first time, or beginning again with improvements.

B. Dwell (v. 3) *skenoo* (Gk.)—To abide, live in a tent or tabernacle; to pitch a tent.

Teacher Preparation

Unifying Principle—Making Things New. People look for a place and time where life's stresses will not exist. Is such a time and place possible? John, the writer of the book of Revelation, suggests that God will create a new heaven and earth where life's challenges and stresses will be banished forever.

A. Read the Focal Verses in multiple translations.

B. Study the companion lesson in the *Precepts for Living*® Personal Study Guide.

O—Open the Lesson

A. Introduce today's lesson title and read aloud Revelation 21:1–8. A wonderful alternative is to read the final story in *The Jesus Storybook Bible* by Sally Lloyd-Jones.

B. Read the Aim for Change. Pray for students to have peace, hope, and joy in anticipation of God making all things new.

C. Have students read the Keep in Mind verse and In Focus story.

P—Present the Scriptures

A. Give students a few minutes to silently read The People, Places, and Times; and Background.

B. Have students read the Focal Verses silently, encouraging them to keep in mind the information presented in The People, Places, and Times and Background.

C. Use In Depth content and Search the Scriptures to facilitate discussion on the Focal Verses.

E—Explore the Meaning

A. Have the class discuss the questions in Discuss the Meaning.

B. Read the Lesson in Our Society and have students make observations.

N—Next Steps for Application

A. Briefly review the lesson, highlighting the Keep in Mind verse.

B. Read Make It Happen and re-read the Aim for Change aloud.

C. Pray with students that they will develop an eternal perspective and feel the urgency of coming to Christ or sharing their faith with others.

Worship Guide

For the Superintendent or Teacher
Theme: Everything is Brand New
Song: "Revelation Song"
Devotional Reading: Revelation 7:13–17

Everything's Brand New

Bible Background • REVELATION 21:1–8
Printed Text • REVELATION 21:1–8 | Devotional Reading • REVELATION 7:13–17

Aim for Change

By the end of the lesson, we will: EVALUATE the "apocalypse" genre that characterizes the book of Revelation to discern how to understand its message; CONTEMPLATE the coming of "a new heaven and a new earth" for the hope that this vision brings; and EMBRACE the peace of God that begins in this life with Jesus.

In Focus

Ms. Cattie knew growing old was a blessing. She had accumulated plenty of wisdom and experience throughout the years. However, it had its share of challenges too. Bones began to ache. Strength and speed diminished. Wrinkles and gray hair became her prominent features. One of the main problems with growing old, Ms. Cattie thought, was suffering a lot of loss. At 95 years old, Ms. Cattie had seen her share. She had buried both of her parents and two of her four children. The majority of her closest friends had passed, and those who remained struggled to remember the great times they had together.

Most recently, she had lost her husband of 70 years. However, as God would allow it, she was eagerly preparing to celebrate the arrival of her first two great-great-grandsons. Twins! It was a tangible reminder that one day God would wipe away all tears and erase sorrows, replacing them both with all things new. These days, Ms. Cattie thought a lot about heaven. As grateful as she was for the life she lived, the experiences she had, and the family she had raised, she yearned for the day when all of the pain and heartache of this life would be left behind. She knew it was coming sooner rather than later. And she was ready. One day all things would become new.

In this lesson, we will learn about God's redemptive plan for heaven and earth. What is the thing you most look forward to in God's new heaven and new earth?

Keep in Mind

"And God shall wipe away all tears from their eyes; and there shall be no more death, neither sorrow, nor crying, neither shall there be any more pain: for the former things are passed away" (Revelation 21:4).

"And God shall wipe away all tears from their eyes; and there shall be no more death, neither sorrow, nor crying, neither shall there be any more pain: for the former things are passed away" (Revelation 21:4).

Focal Verses

KJV **Revelation 21:1** And I saw a new heaven and a new earth: for the first heaven and the first earth were passed away ; and there was no more sea.

2 And I John saw the holy city, new Jerusalem, coming down from God out of heaven, prepared as a bride adorned for her husband.

3 And I heard a great voice out of heaven saying, Behold, the tabernacle of God is with men, and he will dwell with them, and they shall be his people, and God himself shall be with them, and be their God.

4 And God shall wipe away all tears from their eyes; and there shall be no more death, neither sorrow, nor crying, neither shall there be any more pain: for the former things are passed away.

5 And he that sat upon the throne said, Behold, I make all things new. And he said unto me, Write: for these words are true and faithful.

6 And he said unto me, It is done. I am Alpha and Omega, the beginning and the end. I will give unto him that is athirst of the fountain of the water of life freely.

7 He that overcometh shall inherit all things; and I will be his God, and he shall be my son.

8 But the fearful, and unbelieving, and the abominable, and murderers, and whoremongers, and sorcerers, and idolaters, and all liars, shall have their part in the lake which burneth with fire and brimstone: which is the second death.

NLT **Revelation 21:1** Then I saw a new heaven and a new earth, for the old heaven and the old earth had disappeared. And the sea was also gone.

2 And I saw the holy city, the new Jerusalem, coming down from God out of heaven like a beautiful bride prepared for her husband.

3 I heard a loud shout from the throne, saying, "Look, God's home is now among his people! He will live with them, and they will be his people. God himself will be with them.

4 "He will wipe every tear from their eyes, and there will be no more death or sorrow or crying or pain. All these things are gone forever."

5 And the one sitting on the throne said, "Look, I am making everything new!" And then he said to me, "Write this down, for what I tell you is trustworthy and true."

6 And he also said, "It is finished! I am the Alpha and the Omega—the Beginning and the End. To all who are thirsty I will give the springs of the water of life.

7 All who are victorious will inherit all these blessings, and I will be their God, and they will be my children.

8 But cowards, unbelievers, the corrupt, murderers, the immoral, those who practice witchcraft, idol worshipers, and all liars—their fate is in the fiery lake of burning sulfur. This is the second death."

The People, Places, and Times

John. John, whose name in Hebrew means "Jehovah is gracious," was one of Jesus' twelve disciples, and he is believed to be the author of the Gospel of John, three epistles, and the book of Revelation. The son of Zebedee and brother of James, he was one of the three in Jesus' inner circle (along with James and Peter) who witnessed the Transfiguration (Matthew 17:1), and he was present with Jesus in the Garden of Gethsemane right before His arrest (Mark 14:32–33). John is recorded as the only disciple present at the Crucifixion and was instructed by Jesus to care for His mother, Mary (John 19:25–27). Of the three, he was the only one not martyred (according to tradition). However, he was imprisoned on the isle of Patmos for his faith. It was there that he wrote the book of Revelation.

Jerusalem. Jerusalem is recorded as being founded by Canaanites (see Ezekiel 16:3) and either named after one of their gods (Shalim) or adapted from the Hebrew word "shalom," which means peace. It is purportedly one of the oldest continuously inhabited cities in the world, highly sought after—and fought over. Jerusalem has been besieged, attacked, and captured dozens of times, divided by Jews and Arabs (1948-1967), destroyed twice—and rebuilt. The city was captured by King David and became known as the "city of David" (2 Samuel 5:7). It is the place where Solomon's Temple (and subsequent temples) was built, and the place where events leading up to the Crucifixion, the Day of Pentecost, and much of the history of Acts occurred. It is claimed as the rightful possession of both Israeli and Palestinian nationals. Jerusalem is known as the "holy city" for three major world religions: Christianity, Judaism, and Islam.

Background

Although Revelation is the last book of the Bible, it is not necessarily the last book written. John's original visions may have occurred shortly before the destruction of the Temple (AD 70), but some aspects of the book suggest that the Apocalypse as we know it could also represent visions that occurred after the destruction of the Temple. Similar to portions of Ezekiel and Daniel, the book is apocalyptic literature filled with symbolism, poetry, and prophecy, specifically about the end times. Because of the symbolic language, it can be difficult to understand, and there are many interpretations of how or when particular events will occur (or whether they have occurred already). However, John makes it clear that this is a revelation of Christ, affirming God's sovereignty. This revelation serves as a warning to some, and it provides hope in the second coming of Christ and final victory over sin, Satan, and death for those who believe in Christ. With vivid imagery, he describes events that will occur, signs of end times, the awesome glory of God, and the beauty of a new heaven and new earth. Revelation 21 is one of the last two chapters of the book, and it grants a glimpse of eternity.

At-A-Glance

1. All New (Revelation 21:1–2)
2. God Dwells (vv. 3–4)
3. All Done (vv. 5–8)

In Depth

1. All New (Revelation 21:1–2)

John begins this chapter by sharing his vision of a new heaven and earth, a fulfillment of Isaiah 65:17–18. This could be a restored and wholly cleansed version of God's creation, or it could be an unused, fresh heaven and earth that replaces the one that was marred by sin and its effects—death, sorrow, and chaos. In the ancient Near East, the sea was a symbol of chaos (the Canaanites said the god Yam controlled the seas). John notes that the sea no longer exists, thus implying the establishment of complete order in the new creation.

Not only is there a new heaven and earth, but there's a new "holy city"—a New

Jerusalem—coming down from God Himself. Jerusalem has been at the center of Jewish and Christian tradition. While it is called the "holy city" because God's presence is said to dwell there, historically it has been marred by division, fighting, death, and chaos from its founding even into the present. In this vision, God presents Jerusalem as a bride—a virgin, untouched, untainted, pure, and presentable to a perfect Christ. He does not "fix" the current Jerusalem by going to it, but He presents a new true Holy City through His presence.

2. God Dwells (vv. 3–4)

Now that a new, holy, and perfect heaven, earth, and Jerusalem have been created, God is free to live among His people. The tabernacle was known as the place where God's glory resided temporarily (Exodus 25:8). When the cloud or pillar of fire (God's presence) moved, it indicated when the Israelites should pack up their tents and the Tabernacle, and move along with Him. In Revelation, God, from His throne, says He will set up His tent and live with the people. Human kings do not reside among the people, but God, reminiscent of the incarnation of Christ who "became flesh and made his dwelling among us" (John 1:14, NIV) chooses to do so. Because He is there, He wipes away every tear (Isaiah 25:8; 65:19; Revelation 7:17), removing death, sorrow, crying, and pain. The new earth will be as was the original one when God walked with Adam and Eve (Genesis 3:8), but this time without the influence or presence of Satan, who is now defeated (see Revelation 20). All things will be made new. It's a fresh start!

3. All Done (vv. 5–8)

"It is done!" While the events recorded by John have not yet occurred, this is a promise of completion from the all-powerful, all-knowing One—the Creator who is the beginning (Alpha, the first letter of the Greek alphabet) and the end (Omega, the final letter of the alphabet).

Throughout Scripture are references to living water (Jeremiah 2:13; Zechariah 14:8; John 7:38, Revelation 7:17), water that is not stagnant, like a pond, but free-flowing and fresh, as from a mountain stream. Stagnant water is often dirty, filled with harmful bacteria, and not recommended for drinking. Flowing streams and fountains, however, refresh and give life. No one can survive without physical water. Christ uses the "water of life" metaphor to demonstrate the need for us to quench our spiritual thirst through Him (John 4:10, 14). For those who thirst for Him, He offers this water—eternal life. Those who belong to Him will be children of God and inherit all the blessings already mentioned: new heaven and earth, eternal life free of pain, sorrow, and tears. In contrast, those who choose a sinful life apart from Him—fearful of a commitment to Him, rejecting Him, not believing, worshiping false gods, practicing sexual immorality—are destined for a place far worse, a place filled with pain and a second death.

Search the Scriptures

1. The location of the New Jerusalem is on earth (Revelation 21:3). How does this compare with popular perceptions of the afterlife?

2. In the New Heaven and New Earth everything will be made new (v. 5). If everything will be made new, is it okay to fail to take care of this present world?

Discuss the Meaning

Why is a new or restored heaven and earth necessary? Describe what it means to you when all things are made new and God dwells with us. How does this make you feel about those who do not yet know Jesus?

Lesson in Our Society

We are drawn to things that are new: new homes, new clothes, new jobs, new babies, and new cars (even a new car smell). There is something appealing about starting over; it provides hope, anticipation, a clearer outlook, and excitement. We appreciate newness. If such excitement exists in receiving new temporal things, which are here today and gone, broken, stolen, or old tomorrow, how much more excited should we be about the forthcoming new heaven and new earth?

Make It Happen

Life is full of suffering and difficulty, but this passage provides hope for a new, perfect world. We are often so focused on the present that we ignore that there is an eternity. When things are going well, we are content with the present. When we struggle, we strive to find a solution for the present. What challenges do you face now that viewing eternity helps you to put it into perspective? What decisions do you believe you need to make now in light of what is to come? Are you free from the sinful lifestyle described in these verses? Have you accepted Christ? If you have, are there people in your life that you need to tell about Jesus? Pray for courage to share your faith with others.

Follow the Spirit

What God wants me to do:

_____

_____

_____

_____

Remember Your Thoughts

Special insights I have learned:

_____

_____

_____

_____

More Light on the Text
Revelation 21:1–8

In the closing chapters of Isaiah, God promised that He would create a new heaven and a new earth that would endure before Him forever (Isaiah 66:22). The unfolding of the fulfillment of this prophecy is presented in John's vision of the New Jerusalem coming down out of heaven to take its place upon a renewed earth in Revelation 21:1–22:5. Chapter 21 begins with John's vision of the transformation of the new order. In verses 1–8, the first heaven and earth are replaced by a new heaven and earth. The vision shows an entirely new order of existence. It is new in that it is the redeemed order; it has taken place of the old. It is a creation that is renewed and brought to the glorious consummation for which it is intended. In verse 5, God speaks from His throne: "Behold, I make all things new."

1 And I saw new heaven and a new earth: for the first heaven had passed away; and there was no more sea.

John received a divine revelation from God concerning what He had purposed for the final stage of His created order, the final result of His creating activities. The adjectives "new" and "first" seem to describe a previous and latter cosmos standing in opposition to each other. The previous had "passed away" (Gk. *aperchomai*, **ap-AIR-kho-my**), which means to depart from a location. The sense is that the old heaven and earth have vanished and disappeared. The latter had come to take its place, and God intends that it stay forever without ever reversing into a negative direction again (Isaiah 65:17).

John also recognized that there was no more sea. The ancient mind feared the sea as a place of terror and chaos, and it was to be avoided. Evil beasts, such as Leviathan, who represented the enemies of God lurked in the sea. The fact that the sea was gone points toward a new creation that is orderly and absent of conflict and evil.

2 And I John saw the holy city, new Jerusalem, coming down from God out of heaven, prepared as a bride adorned for her husband.

The Apostle John saw the New Jerusalem, God's Holy City, descending from His presence from heaven. The city is God's place for renewing and refreshing His people after both their turbulence and success. It has no tears, sorrow, or pain; it is a place where we never die and wickedness is totally shut out. God Himself specially prepared it for His people.

John uses a metaphor of a good and promising marriage to describe the power and reality of what the new order brings to God's people. The city is personified as a bride adorned for a husband. The word "adorned" (Gk. *kosmeo*, **KAHS-meh-oh**) is appropriate and fitting for the city. It is also connected with the word for world in Greek, from which English gets the word cosmos (Gk. *kosmos*, **KOS-mos**; decoration; order; universe). The careful preparation and arrangement of a bride embodies the gift that God is giving to His people. This is no ordinary city; the new home for God's people is excellent beyond all our human imaginations or dreams. It has already been prepared for us and is waiting for us. It is the new and permanent place that Christ refers to (John 14:2–3).

3 And I heard a great voice out of heaven saying, Behold, the tabernacle of God is with men, and he will dwell with them, and they shall be his people, and God himself shall be with them, and be their God.

God's physical presence will be with His people in our new home. God has declared that He will never leave us nor forsake us (Hebrews 13:5). This is a reiteration of the covenant promise God gave to His people, which now at the consummation of the age is being fulfilled (Leviticus 26:11–12). In fact, the Tabernacle was a symbol of God's dwelling among His people (Exodus 25:8–9). However, in our new home, the content and context of God's abiding presence is totally different. The word "tabernacle" (Gk. *skene*, **ske-NAY**) used in this text does not literally mean the physical temple or sanctuary described in the Old Testament (Exodus 29:44; 1 Kings 6:12–13). Rather, it figuratively referred to a dwelling place of God. It includes the idea of God's kingdom, glory, and power tangibly filling up this "renewed" world that He created for His people.

The consequences and impact of a fallen human nature and society will be no more. God's presence in the new world becomes the light that dispels all forces of evil and destruction. The concept of "Emmanuel" (God with us) will once again become an everlasting reality in this new world.

4 And God shall wipe away all tears from their eyes; and there shall be no more death, neither sorrow, nor crying, neither shall there be any more pain: for the former things are passed away. 5 And he that sat upon the throne said, Behold, I make all things new. And he said unto me, Write: for these words are true and faithful.

The fall in Eden brought with it death, sickness, and poverty. The Bible teaches about three types of death: spiritual death is the result of the broken relationship between God and humankind (Ephesians 2:1 ff.); physical death occurs when our spirit is separated from the body (James 2:26); and eternal death occurs when sinners depart forever into condemnation by spending eternity in the lake of fire (Revelation 20:14–15, 21:8). But in our new home, the Scriptures reveal that all of these kinds of death shall be no more (Revelation 21:4).

Sickness is often the evidence of disease. Humankind is broken spiritually, psychologically, and physically. Poverty has stricken society on many levels, expressed spiritually as a lack of the knowledge of God; physically as poor health and malfunctioning of the body; materially as a lack of resources and money; and socially as political vulnerability and oppression. Poverty has produced misery and mourning in families and society. However, God has promised us that "neither shall there be any more pain" in the new world (Revelation 21:4).

When we go to our new home, "there shall there be no more death, neither sorrow, nor crying, neither shall there be any more pain" (Revelation 21:4). The "former things are passed away" because the fallen world system will be transformed into a new created order where God's entire creation is launched into an era of shalom. This is sealed by God's promising declaration: "Behold, I make all things new."

6 And he said unto me, It is done. I am Alpha and Omega, the beginning and the end. I will give unto him that is athirst of the fountain of the water of life freely.

The descent of the New Jerusalem from heaven and its attendant blessings is now considered accomplished as God tells John, "It is done." God further says, "I am Alpha and Omega, the beginning and the end." This claim was previously made by the risen Christ in 1:8. Again John hears the same voice that the great prophets had heard: "I am the first, and I am the last; and beside me there is no God" (Isaiah 44:6, KJV). This figure of speech, called a merism, states the opposite poles of something in order to emphasize the totality of all that lies between. Alpha is the first letter of the Greek alphabet, and omega is the last. God is the beginning and the end. The word for beginning is *arche* (**ar-KHAY**). It does not simply mean first in point of time, but it means the source of all things. The word for end is *telos* (**TEH-loce**). It does not simply mean the end as a point of time, but it means the end as the completed goal. John is saying that all life begins in God and ends in God. Paul expresses the same thing in Romans 11:36 and Ephesians 4:6.

To the announcement is added the promise of the living water or "the water of life," which may refer both to spiritual life now and eternal life in the new heaven and new earth. In the same manner as in the Gospel of John, this is an invitation to the spiritually thirsty to come and drink of the "water of life," but here and in 22:17 John adds "freely" (Gk. *dorean*, **do-reh-AN**); this word comes from the noun *doron* (**doh-RAHN**), which means gift. The water of life is a gift that can be taken freely. This may also reflect Isaiah 55:1, which adds to the invitation "come to the waters" and the further promise, "And you who have no money, come, buy and eat" (NASB).

7 He that overcometh shall inherit all things; and I will be his God, and he shall be my son.

The section concludes with a challenge to the readers to recognize the difference between those who are faithful and those who are not; that is, to decide whether to be an overcomer (v. 7) or a "coward" (v. 8, NLT). The opening, "he that overcometh," is drawn from the conclusion of each of the seven letters in Revelation 2–3, where it is followed by the promises given to all those who were victorious over the world with its temptations and suffering. The exalted Christ promises that the overcomers, who remain faithful in the face of opposition, will eat from the tree of life (2:7), escape the second death (2:11), receive a new name (2:17), receive authority over the nations (2:26), remain in the book of life (3:5), be eternally united with God in the heavenly city (3:12), and share the rule of Christ (3:21). The overcomers shall inherit these blessings of the eternal state. The language of overcoming or triumph in the messages to the seven churches seems to be echoed closely in the scene here. To these blessings of eternity is added the gift of life-giving water from a sovereign God (v. 6).

The last part of the verse sums up both the Abrahamic and Davidic covenants. In Genesis, God established a covenant with Abraham "to be your God and the God of your descendants after you" (from Genesis 17:7, NIV), and to David he made a promise concerning Solomon: "I will be his father, and he will be my son" (2 Samuel 7:14, NIV). The covenant is fulfilled for all who are Abraham's heirs by faith (Galatians 3:29). God now declares that the overcomers will be His children, and He will be their God. This expresses the intimate relationship between the saints and God.

8 But the fearful, and unbelieving, and the abominable, and murderers, and whoremongers, and sorcerers, and idolaters, and all liars, shall have their part in the lake which burneth with fire and brimstone: which is the second death.

In contrast to the overcomers in verse 7 are all those who cowered in the face of persecution and joined the company of sinners. Here we see the character of those who follow sin instead of the Lamb, and wish to exclude themselves from the presence of God in the New Jerusalem. The fact that the list begins with the fearful and ends with "all liars" suggests that the list is not a general statement about cowardice and falsehood, but instead it defines those who compromise with truth and righteousness.

The verse concludes with the eternal destiny of those who exclude themselves from the life of the new covenant. Those who only appeared to profess Christ but were not truly saved will go to "the lake which burneth with fire and brimstone: which is the second death." This is not a statement of the destiny of the wicked, who have already been cast into the lake of fire (**20:15**). It is a warning to those who continually, deliberately, habitually practice sin (**1 John 3:9**). True salvation is evidenced by a transformed lifestyle, and with it, the promise of eternal security. True salvation is more than just words. It is how we live day to day. To believe and not obey is not yet to believe. The Bible warns, "Be not deceived" (**1 Corinthians 6:9**).

The water images of this passage form a stark contrast. In the end, believers will drink from the water of life. Unbelievers will be thrown into the lake of fire (**21:6**).

Say It Correctly

Apocalyptic. ah-pah-ka-**LIP**-tik.
Whoremongers. **HOR**-mun-gers.
Abominable. uh-**BAH**-mi-nuh-buhl.

Daily Bible Readings

MONDAY
God Will Dwell Among Them
(Exodus 29:42–46)

TUESDAY
Who May Live With God?
(Psalm 15)

WEDNESDAY
Life in the New Heaven and Earth
(Isaiah 65:20–25)

THURSDAY
Those Who Believe Have Eternal Life
(John 6:35–40)

FRIDAY
Mercy of Jesus Leads to Eternal Life
(Jude 20–25)

SATURDAY
God Will Wipe Away All Tears
(Revelation 7:13–17)

SUNDAY
Mortals in God's Presence
(Revelation 21:1–8)

Notes

_____

_____

_____

_____

Teaching Tips

Words You Should Know

A. Glory (Revelation 21:23, 26) *doxa* (Gk.)—An especially divine quality; the manifestation of God's presence.

B. Defile (v. 27) *koinoo* (Gk.)—To make unclean, to pollute, to make common.

Teacher Preparation

Unifying Principle—Eternal Beauty. People have a hard time imagining living somewhere other than their home. What will the new creation be like? John uses figurative language to describe the new place that God will create.

A. Pray for your students and for lesson clarity.

B. Complete the companion lesson in the *Precepts for Living®* Personal Study Guide.

O—Open the Lesson

A. Open with prayer, including the Aim for Change.

B. Introduce the lesson's title.

C. Have students read the Aim for Change and Keep in Mind verse together and discuss.

D. Ask students to read the In Focus Story silently and then discuss it.

P—Present the Scriptures

A. Ask volunteers to read the Focal Verses

B. Use The People, Places, and Times; Background; Search the Scriptures; At-A-Glance outline; In Depth; and More Light on the Text to clarify the verses.

E—Explore the Meaning

A. Divide the class into groups to discuss the Discuss the Meaning, Lesson in Our Society and Make It Happen sections, and ask the students to select a representative to share the highlights of their discussion with the larger group.

B. Connect the group discussions with the Aim for Change and the Keep in Mind verse.

N—Next Steps for Application

A. Summarize the lesson.

B. Close in prayer.

Worship Guide

For the Superintendent or Teacher
Theme: I See a New Jerusalem
Song: "Soon and Very Soon"
Devotional Reading: Genesis 1:28–2:3

I See a New Jerusalem

Bible Background • REVELATION 21:9–27
Printed Text • REVELATION 21:9–14, 22–27 | Devotional Reading • GENESIS 1:28–2:3

—————— Aim for Change ——————

By the end of the lesson, we will: EXPLORE the possibility of living in a new place, even in another dimension of life; IMAGINE the richness and serenity of living in the New Jerusalem; and CELEBRATE God's provision of a new place for believers at the end of all things temporal and throughout eternity.

⟨ In Focus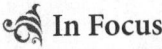

Keisha sat at the table and cried. She was completely overwhelmed and had no idea what her next step should be. Recent staffing cuts resulted in her being laid off from a job that she held for 6 years. She was positive that she would secure another position soon. Unfortunately, the job market had changed drastically since she was last looking for work, and it seemed like no one was hiring for the skill set that she had.

Keisha desperately tried everything to find full-time work. If she did not find something soon, she feared that she would lose her home. She wept as she thought about what would happen to her and her children. It all seemed too much. She looked back on how life had been when she had steady employment and wondered if she would ever have that same stability again. Bill collectors called daily, and Keisha barely had enough money to cover her family's day-to-day expenses. While sitting at the table, Keisha began to think about a recent Bible study at her church. The Bible study focused on how our troubles are temporary and encouraged the congregation to know that in the midst of trouble, brighter days are ahead. Keisha decided to encourage herself and anchor her hope in the fact that there was a bright future ahead of her despite her current situation.

In today's lesson, we will see that while we may sometimes feel like there is no hope, God is always acting to deliver and guide us to a happier life.

—————— Keep in Mind ——————

"And I saw no temple therein: for the Lord God Almighty and the Lamb are the temple of it. And the city had no need of the sun, neither of the moon, to shine in it: for the glory of God did lighten it, and the Lamb is the light thereof" (Revelation 21:22–23).

"And I saw no temple therein: for the Lord God Almighty and the Lamb are the temple of it. And the city had no need of the sun, neither of the moon, to shine in it: for the glory of God did lighten it, and the Lamb is the light thereof" (Revelation 21:22–23).

Focal Verses

KJV Revelation 21:9 And there came unto me one of the seven angels which had the seven vials full of the seven last plagues, and talked with me, saying, Come hither, I will shew thee the bride, the Lamb's wife.

10 And he carried me away in the spirit to a great and high mountain, and shewed me that great city, the holy Jerusalem, descending out of heaven from God,

11 Having the glory of God: and her light was like unto a stone most precious, even like a jasper stone, clear as crystal;

12 And had a wall great and high, and had twelve gates, and at the gates twelve angels, and names written thereon, which are the names of the twelve tribes of the children of Israel:

13 On the east three gates; on the north three gates; on the south three gates; and on the west three gates.

14 And the wall of the city had twelve foundations, and in them the names of the twelve apostles of the Lamb.

22 And I saw no temple therein: for the Lord God Almighty and the Lamb are the temple of it.

23 And the city had no need of the sun, neither of the moon, to shine in it: for the glory of God did lighten it, and the Lamb is the light thereof.

24 And the nations of them which are saved shall walk in the light of it: and the kings of the earth do bring their glory and honour into it.

25 And the gates of it shall not be shut at all by day: for there shall be no night there.

26 And they shall bring the glory and honour of the nations into it.

27 And there shall in no wise enter into it any thing that defileth, neither whatsoever worketh abomination, or maketh a lie: but they which are written in the Lamb's book of life.

NLT Revelation 21:9 Then one of the seven angels who held the seven bowls containing the seven last plagues came and said to me, "Come with me! I will show you the bride, the wife of the Lamb."

10 So he took me in the Spirit to a great, high mountain, and he showed me the holy city, Jerusalem, descending out of heaven from God.

11 It shone with the glory of God and sparkled like a precious stone—like jasper as clear as crystal.

12 The city wall was broad and high, with twelve gates guarded by twelve angels. And the names of the twelve tribes of Israel were written on the gates.

13 There were three gates on each side—east, north, south, and west.

14 The wall of the city had twelve foundation stones, and on them were written the names of the twelve apostles of the Lamb.

22 I saw no temple in the city, for the Lord God Almighty and the Lamb are its temple.

23 And the city has no need of sun or moon, for the glory of God illuminates the city, and the Lamb is its light.

24 The nations will walk in its light, and the kings of the world will enter the city in all their glory.

25 Its gates will never be closed at the end of day because there is no night there.

26 And all the nations will bring their glory and honor into the city.

27 Nothing evil will be allowed to enter, nor anyone who practices shameful idolatry and dishonesty—but only those whose names are written in the Lamb's Book of Life.

The People, Places, and Times

John the Apostle. John is identified in the Gospels as the son of Zebedee. He is attributed with writing the Gospel of John, the book of Revelation, and the epistles that now bear his name. He is identified as one of the twelve apostles and a firsthand witness of Jesus' ministry.

Patmos. Patmos is a small mountainous island off the coast of modern-day Turkey. The Romans banished people to this island as a punishment. The Christian church has identified Patmos as the place where the Apostle John received his revelation during his time of exile.

Background

Rome was a society that practiced cultic worship of the emperor. They believed that this loyalty to the emperor assured Roman prosperity. The Christian proclamation that Jesus is Lord was viewed as a threat to Roman society and led to the persecution of Christians as a result of the Great Fire of Rome in AD 64. Rome was becoming more intolerant of other religions, leading to rebellion against Rome in Jerusalem.

Jesus foretold the destruction of the Temple in Matthew 24:2. The Jewish historian Josephus provides us with a firsthand account of what happened. In response to the Jews' revolt, Rome laid siege to the city and captured the Fortress of Antonia just north of the Temple Mount in AD 70. Shortly thereafter they attacked the Temple and set fire to the gates. The Jews lost hope, and soon Jerusalem was in flames. After this time of civil unrest, persecution, and loss, John the apostle received a revelation from God. This revelation is of God being ultimately triumphant over the enemies of His people, and of the New Jerusalem, which will make the other one pale in comparison.

At-A-Glance

1. The Right Foundation (Revelation 21:9–14)
2. Living in God's Light (vv. 22–27)

In Depth

1. The Right Foundation (Revelation 21:9–14)

The heavenly city that John saw is a picture of perfection. It has perfect dimensions, beautifully adorned with precious gems and gold. The angel that spoke to John referred to the city as "the bride." In our lesson, we see the bride clothed in splendor and adorned in precious jewels. The heavenly city is protected with high, fortified walls. The twelve gates to the city are covered by twelve angels in order to ensure the city remains pure and unspoiled. The twelve gates echo the twelve gates in Ezekiel's new city, which represent the twelve tribes of Israel and the complete inclusion of God's people (Ezekiel 48:30–35).

However, one of the most interesting facts about the city is that it is built on twelve foundations, each one bearing the name of one of the twelve apostles, the first bearers of the Gospel. This is because only through the Gospel can one become a citizen of this heavenly city. Revelation identifies the heavenly city as a place free from tears and heartaches, and ultimately free from sin. In the heavenly city, we can experience God's presence and glory without constraints. This can only happen through our belief in the Good News of Jesus Christ.

2. Living in God's Light (vv. 22–27)

Our passage begins with the observation that the heavenly city has no temple. Initially, this seems odd. One would assume that the city that God created where He would dwell forever with humanity would have a temple dedicated for worship. However, the heavenly city is the place where God's presence is continually experienced fully and equally; no place in the Holy City will be more sacred or holy than any other. When we experience God's presence on earth, worship flows naturally. The only thing restricting this experience wherever we are is our own tendency to get distracted by earthly concerns. If we seek out opportunities to focus on God and His goodness in our lives, we can gradually transform worship from a weekly experience to a daily lifestyle.

Our passage also mentions that in the heavenly city, the glory of God gives light and that the Lamb, the Word of God, is the lamp for the city. This glory and light provide guidance to the nations. The Word of God provides illumination and guidance in all situations. Psalm 119:105 reminds us that the Word of God is a lamp for our feet and a light for our path. Some of the daily stress that we experience in life can be avoided by seeking God and trusting His Word to guide us. We must always remember that God's peace is built on His principles. It is important to know that the stability and security that we seek can be experienced by learning to trust God in every situation we face.

Search the Scriptures

1. Why is the New Jerusalem identified as the "bride" (Revelation 21:9)?

2. John lists those who will be excluded from the heavenly city (v. 27). How do we evaluate whether we will be included in the heavenly city?

Discuss the Meaning

It is very easy for us to lose hope when our faith is tested or shaken. How does belief in the coming heavenly city help to strengthen our faith?

Lesson in Our Society

Many of us seek to provide a good life for our families and loved ones. During times of economic and political uncertainty, that goal can seem far out of reach. We must understand that prosperity and peace are not the same thing. True stability and peace are found by relying on God for guidance. The Word of God is a solid foundation that will allow us to find peace and build a good life both now and for eternity.

Make It Happen

The heavenly city had 12 gates that were always open. This image serves as a reminder of God's desire for everyone to come into His presence and have a relationship with Him. As we strive to build our lives on a solid foundation, let us not forget to reach out to someone else and let him or her know that God is welcoming them to also come into His presence with open arms.

Follow the Spirit

What God wants me to do:

_____

_____

_____

Remember Your Thoughts

Special insights I have learned:

_____

_____

_____

More Light on the Text

Revelation 21:9–14, 22–27

9 And there came unto me one of the seven angels which had the seven vials full of the seven last plagues, and talked with me, saying, Come hither, I will show thee the bride, the Lamb's wife.

John's vision of heaven is told from two points of view: from heaven and from earth. Revelation 21:9 tells the narrative from the earthly viewpoint. Here John is approached by one of the seven angels who had the seven vials (or bowls) full of the seven last plagues. We are first introduced to these angels in Revelation 15, where one of the four beasts in heaven gave them the seven golden vials full of the seven last plagues, which are also called the wrath of God.

The pouring out of the last plagues from these vials signifies the final series of God's judgment, the conclusion of His wrath. After these, John told us of the fall of Babylon (Revelation 17–18), the triumph of the heavenly army led by Christ (Revelation 19), the binding, incarceration, and final judgment of Satan (Revelation 20), and then the passing away (the transformation) of the first heaven and earth, which were replaced by a new heaven and earth (Revelation 21:1). After this renewal, John beholds the Holy City, the New Jerusalem (v. 2).

In verse 9, the angel invites John to come, and shows him the Lamb's wife, the bride (Gk. *numphe*, **NOOM-fay**, a betrothed or newly married young woman). In the New Testament, the "bride" refers to the Church, showing the close relationship between the church and Christ (the "bridegroom)." Marriage imagery is used in the Old Testament to show a similar relationship between God and Israel; the word "bride" is one of the most important words used to refer to the Church. It normally signifies the relationship between Christ and the Church; here, however, we will see that "bride" is the Holy City of the New Jerusalem.

10 And he carried me away in the Spirit to a great and high mountain, and showed me that great city, the holy Jerusalem, descending out of heaven from God.

This verse runs parallel with verse 2, where John described this city using a personifying marital analogy, saying the city was "prepared as a bride adorned for her husband." This city is called "the bride" and "the Lamb's wife" (21:2, 9), just as the Church is also referred to as the Lamb's wife in Revelation 19:7. The fact that the same word is used for both the Church and the city is significant.

The earthly Jerusalem has been called to be the City of God (Psalm 48:1–2), the Holy City (Isaiah 52:1; Matthew 4:5), and the city where God has chosen to put His name (2 Chronicles 6:6). Today, it is the most famous holy city in the world and considered by most the spiritual capital of the world. The earthly Jerusalem is a prefiguration of the New Jerusalem from heaven.

11 Having the glory of God: and her light was like unto a stone most precious, even like a jasper stone, clear as crystal; 12 And had a wall great and high, and had twelve gates, and at the gates twelve angels, and names written thereon, which are the names of the twelve tribes of the children of Israel: 13 On the east three gates; on the north three gates; on the south three gates; and on the west three gates. 14 And the wall of the city had twelve foundations, and in them the names of the twelve apostles of the Lamb.

The holy Jerusalem is a city out of heaven. It is not heaven, but it possesses the features of heaven. It is the dwelling place of the resurrected bodies of the church (the redeemed bride), God, and Christ (Revelation 21:3, 22:3). In the Upper Room, Jesus promised to go prepare a place for His followers (John 14:2–3). This city is undoubtedly the promised prepared place for the redeemed bride. Our bodies are our temporary habitations for our spirits and souls (2 Corinthians 5:1–8). Our earthly homes are also temporary, but we have a final dwelling place: the Holy City, a wonderful place Jesus has prepared for us in heaven.

When God called Abraham to leave his country, God promised him he would possess a foreign country. Although he never saw this promise fulfilled, the author in Hebrews 11:10 infers that Abraham had a preview of the heavenly city, which sustained his faith. The heavenly city has been the destination of all those who live by faith.

22 And I saw no temple therein: for the Lord God Almighty and the Lamb are the temple of it.

John tells us that the city lacks a temple. What is translated as "temple" here is the Greek word *naos* (**nah-OS**). This refers to the inner sanctuary where only the priest could lawfully enter, and it is contrasted with *hieron* (**hee-er-ON**), which also means temple but denotes the entire temple complex with all its courts and auxiliary buildings. *Naos*, the inner sanctuary or Holy of Holies, is the location of the Ark of the Covenant in the Mosaic tabernacle and Solomon's temple. This is the place where God manifested His presence.

This city does not need a temple because God's manifest presence would be experienced by all. There would be no need for a house, because the entire new creation would be His household. The Lord and the Lamb would be eternally worshiped in the heavenly city. There would be no need for rituals or sacrifices. It will be a place where everyone will experience the unmediated presence of God.

23 And the city had no need of the sun, neither of the moon, to shine in it: for the glory of God did lighten it, and the Lamb is

the light thereof. **24 And the nations of them which are saved shall walk in the light of it: and the kings of the earth do bring their glory and honor into it.**

John further tells us that the city has no need of the natural light of the sun and moon. While these two agents of light are the main illuminators of planet Earth, they can also cause some discomfort to the people below. God's desire to shield His people from the effects of the light of the sun and moon is expressed by David: "the sun shall not smite thee by day, nor the moon by night. The LORD shall preserve thee from all evil: he shall preserve thy soul" (Psalm 121:6–7). This desire is ultimately fulfilled in the New Jerusalem.

These two heavenly bodies are also worshiped by various people because their light is necessary for life on earth. But the sun's light and heat will not be needed in the Holy City. In the New Jerusalem, the glory of God and the Lamb is declared to be greater and more enduring and blissful than sunlight and moonlight. Sun and moon are features of the heaven and earth that will pass away (Revelation 21:1).

The Greek word translated "glory" is *doxa* (**DOX-ah**), used here to denote the supernatural brightness or splendor emanating from God; this is the brightness manifested in Christ when He was transfigured (Matthew 17:1–2). This glory will illuminate the city, and cause it to shine on the entire face of the earth; the saved nations shall "walk in the light of it." The nations will not need any light from heavenly bodies but only light from one source—God and the Lamb.

It is very important to note that most of the activities, features, or manifestations in the book of Revelation run parallel to other books of the Bible, particularly those of the Old Testament. Some of the features and activities John saw in his vision are end-time fulfillments of some prophecies of Scripture. For instance, Isaiah and Micah prophesied about the coming glory and the exalted status of the house of God (Isaiah 2:2–3; Micah 4:1–2). This prophecy pictures a situation similar to what John describes: peoples of all nations flowing to the house of God to be taught His ways and "walk" in His paths in the last days (Revelation 21:24). In addition to the figurative meaning "to live," the word "walk" is also applied to the observance of religious ordinances. One of the main attractions to the City of God is the law, which is the Word of God (Isaiah 2:3). The saved nations will live by the light of the Word as they observe His statutes from the Holy City.

Jesus is the light of God—our light now and eternally, and our hope of glory. As we walk in His light, He will guide us to the realization of this great, glorious experience in the Holy City. God promised that the Children of Israel would possess the wealth of kings and nations (Isaiah 60:11). That promise is ultimately fulfilled in the times of the New Jerusalem. Although the original promise implied that the wealth would come from Gentile kings and nations, here it indicates that the wealth will come from a homage paid by saved nations and kings to the New Jerusalem because of its powerful and overwhelming presence on earth.

25 And the gates of it shall not be shut at all by day: for there shall be no night there. 26 And they shall bring the glory and honor of the nations into it.

The promise (actually a prophecy) in Isaiah 60:11 continues here with the description of the city's gates. Open gates indicate admittance and readiness; here they mean constant coming and going, with no need to close.

The sun and moon will no longer impose a set time to shut the gates of the Holy City. Thus, the absence of these heavenly bodies means the absence of day and night. Here again is a reference to the nations, presumably through the agency of kings (v. 24), bringing glory and honor to the Holy City. The word "glory" here is the same word used to refer to God in vv. 23–24. Glory and honor here are associated with the nations, or the various peoples who are not from the tribes of Israel. What is most precious and esteemed from the peoples of the earth is now being brought into the holy city to join with the glory of God.

27 And there shall in no wise enter into it any thing that defileth, neither whatsoever worketh abomination, or maketh a lie: but they which are written in the Lamb's book of life.

By designation, the New Jerusalem is called "the Holy City," and in accordance to this name, there is a divine restriction against anything that defiles or causes abomination and lies. The Greek word translated "defileth," *koinoo* (**koy-NO-o**), means to render unholy, to make common, pollute, or make unclean. This refers to things and practices that would defile the city by rendering it common or ordinary. The Holy City assumes the status of the Holy of Holies; it is a place of great beauty, lavishly built with precious stones, so nothing unclean would enter it.

The word translated "abomination" is *bdelugma* (**BDEL-oog-mah**), and it denotes an object of disgust or an idolatrous object. This term is used for idols. God and the Lord Jesus are the only objects of worship in the Holy City. No idol will be there. In Ezekiel's vision, he was made to see "where the idol that provokes to jealousy stood" at the entrance of the temple's inner court facing the north (Ezekiel 8:3, NIV). The image of the beast is also called "the abomination that causes desolation." There will be no abomination in the Holy City.

The word translated "lie" is *pseudos* (**PSYOO-dos**), simply meaning falsehood or something not true. Jesus is the Truth; anything contrary to Him is a lie and will not enter the Holy City.

Any creature or act that is described as something that "defileth" or an "abomination" or a "lie" is forbidden entry into the Holy City. This divine restriction brings about an ultimate realization of a city devoid of evil. It is an end-times fulfillment of God's prescribed course of conduct for human life. This prescribed course, prophesied in Isaiah 35:8, is laid down in its entirety in the faith we profess as Christians and will be perfectly realized in the Holy City.

No impure or unholy creature will enter His glorious presence, which fills the entire city. The only qualified entrants and occupants of this New Jerusalem are those whose names are written in the Lamb's Book of Life. Although we are not given the requirements needed for one's name to be written in this book, we can infer that it is comprised of those who are faithful to the Lamb, because the only reason for being blotted out is unfaithfulness (Revelation 3:5). The Greek word translated "life" is *zoe* (**dzo-AY**). This is the life of God and the life of Christ in the believer; it is eternal life.

Say It Correctly

Jasper. jas-**PUR**.
Defileth. di-**FY**-lith.

Daily Bible Readings

MONDAY
The First Heaven and Earth
(Genesis 1:28–2:3)

TUESDAY
The Glory of God Will Return
(Ezekiel 43:1–9)

WEDNESDAY
Dwellers in the New Jerusalem
(Revelation 3:10–12)

THURSDAY
Missing from the Holy City
(Revelation 21:1–4)

FRIDAY
City of the Alpha and Omega
(Revelation 21:5–8)

SATURDAY
The Architectural Splendor
of the New Jerusalem
(Revelation 21:15–21)

SUNDAY
Vision of the New Jerusalem
(Revelation 22:9–14, 22–27)

Notes

Teaching Tips

Words You Should Know

A. Fruit (Revelation 22:2) *karpos* (Gk.)— A product of plants or trees; figuratively, a product of work or effort, such as offspring, wages or moral attributes.

B. Quickly (v. 7.) *tachu* (Gk.)—An adverb that may refer to imminence ("soon") or suddenness ("quickly").

Teacher Preparation

Unifying Principle—Life and Healing. People are aware that rivers give life and nourishment to the things that exist around them. How do rivers nourish our lives? According to John, in the new creation, God's power will be in the river and will nourish and heal everything in the city.

A. Read the Bible Background and the Focal Verses.

B. Read Genesis 2:4–17 for background on the description of the New Jerusalem; read also Revelation 21:1–8, 11, 21 for a more complete picture of John's vision.

C. Consider how you and those you teach might struggle to believe the promises of God regarding the Christian's future hope, and why people might fail to long earnestly for that hope to be fulfilled.

O—Open the Lesson

A. Begin the class with prayer, thanking God for His kindness in storing up a secure and imperishable inheritance for His people, and revealing the wonder of that inheritance through His holy Word.

B. Ask a volunteer to read the In Focus story.

C. Share honestly your struggles to "seek those things which are above" and some of the things that keep you from doing so.

P—Present the Scriptures

A. Ask volunteers to read the Focal Verses.

B. Read and discuss The People, Places, and Times; Background; In Depth; and Search the Scriptures.

E—Explore the Meaning

A. Answer the Discuss the Meaning questions.

B. Read the Lesson in Our Society and discuss.

N—Next Steps for Application

A. Read the Make It Happen section and commit to applying the lesson during the week.

B. Pray for your class, thanking God for the life and healing found in the heavenly city.

Worship Guide

For the Superintendent or Teacher
Theme: Living Waters
Song: "I Shall Wear a Crown"
Devotional Reading: Psalm 46

Living Waters

Bible Background • Revelation 22:1–7
Printed Text •Revelation 22:1–7 | Devotional Reading • Psalm 46

—————— Aim for Change ——————

By the end of the lesson, we will: EVALUATE the biblical references to the "river of life" to learn its spiritual and symbolic meaning; APPRECIATE that in the "river of life" is God's continual provision; and RESPOND to the "river of life" through acceptance, faith, and entrance into the fullness of the kingdom.

———— 🐚 In Focus ————

Chris laughed along with the television audience as he watched his friend Jason, a popular comedian, deliver his punch lines with ease. His laughter was interrupted by a phone call from Jason. "Are you watching the show I taped last week?" Jason asked. "Yeah, I told you I would. Pretty funny stuff. I can never figure out where you're headed." "That's the secret of a good punchline." He chuckled. "Now I got a good one for you. I told you I would start reading the Bible. Today I have just finished the last chapter," Jason said. "You started with the last chapter?" Chris asked nervously. It wasn't that unusual. Jason always read the ending before considering any book.

"Jason, why would you do that?" Chris asked, thinking the end-of-the-world horrors might be too much for a new Christian. "Nobody told me where to start, so I figured I'd find out how everything was going to come out, you know, to see if the ending was worth it," Jason replied. Chris tried to explain, "But Genesis and the walk of Christ..." Before he could finish, he heard Jason howling in laughter. "Don't worry, the ending told me what I needed to know. We win in the end! Now I want to know more about how and why."

In the book of Revelation, Christians are assured of the ultimate happy ending—a triumphal procession in Christ!

—————— Keep in Mind ——————

"And he shewed me a pure river of water of life, clear as crystal, proceeding out of the throne of God and of the Lamb" (Revelation 22:1).

"And he shewed me a pure river of water of life, clear as crystal, proceeding out of the throne of God and of the Lamb" (Revelation 22:1).

Focal Verses

KJV Revelation 22:1 And he shewed me a pure river of water of life, clear as crystal, proceeding out of the throne of God and of the Lamb.

2 In the midst of the street of it, and on either side of the river, was there the tree of life, which bare twelve manner of fruits, and yielded her fruit every month: and the leaves of the tree were for the healing of the nations.

3 And there shall be no more curse: but the throne of God and of the Lamb shall be in it; and his servants shall serve him:

4 And they shall see his face; and his name shall be in their foreheads.

5 And there shall be no night there; and they need no candle, neither light of the sun; for the Lord God giveth them light: and they shall reign for ever and ever.

6 And he said unto me, These sayings are faithful and true: and the Lord God of the holy prophets sent his angel to shew unto his servants the things which must shortly be done.

7 Behold, I come quickly: blessed is he that keepeth the sayings of the prophecy of this book.

NLT Revelation 22:1 Then the angel showed me a river with the water of life, clear as crystal, flowing from the throne of God and of the Lamb.

2 It flowed down the center of the main street. On each side of the river grew a tree of life, bearing twelve crops of fruit, with a fresh crop each month. The leaves were used for medicine to heal the nations.

3 No longer will there be a curse upon anything. For the throne of God and of the Lamb will be there, and his servants will worship him.

4 And they will see his face, and his name will be written on their foreheads.

5 And there will be no night there—no need for lamps or sun—for the Lord God will shine on them. And they will reign forever and ever.

6 Then the angel said to me, "Everything you have heard and seen is trustworthy and true. The Lord God, who inspires his prophets, has sent his angel to tell his servants what will happen soon."

7 "Look, I am coming soon! Blessed are those who obey the words of prophecy written in this book."

The People, Places, and Times

Bride. The imagery of the bride is used widely in the Bible as a description of the people of God. In the Old Testament, the prophets presented Israel as a bride who had committed repeated adulteries (Jeremiah 3; Ezekiel 16; Hosea 3). The prophets also proclaimed that God was faithful to His unfaithful bride and would restore her (Isaiah 61:10). In the book of Revelation, bride imagery is used for the Church and her relationship to Christ. The bride belongs to Christ, who is the Bridegroom (Matthew 9:15). In Revelation, the Church, as the bride of the Lamb, has prepared herself for marriage by performing righteous deeds (19:7–8). In Revelation 21, the great wedding is portrayed with the Church prepared for her Bridegroom (21:2, 9). The bride pictured here has not earned her status through righteous deeds. These acts were the Church's obedient response to God's saving grace. The garments of righteousness were given to her.

New Jerusalem. Since Jerusalem was a significant focus of God's activity in the Old

Testament and the place where the Church was founded at Pentecost, the New Testament writers fittingly used the city in a figurative sense to speak of the Christian's salvation and future hope. In Galatians 4:26, Paul refers to the "Jerusalem which is above" when pointing out the Christian's spiritual status of freedom from the Law's curse. The author of Hebrews speaks of a "heavenly Jerusalem" (Hebrews 12:22) to denote the beauty and security of the New Covenant. The book of Revelation refers to "the holy city new Jerusalem" (21:2) and "that great city, the holy Jerusalem, descending out of heaven from God" (v. 10). Here the angel identifies the city with the bride, the Church. The following description, in which Jerusalem is massive and radiant with jewels and perfect in symmetry, shows the wonderful destiny of God's people, when He will dwell among them forever.

Background

The first part of Revelation 22 portrays, in visions and images, the wonderful future awaiting God's people in the new heaven and the new earth. Drawing heavily on the book of Isaiah, John's vision concludes by showing the certainty of the promise. Just as the prophecies of the Old Testament have been fulfilled in Christ's first coming, so the prophecy of Revelation will be ultimately fulfilled through Christ's Second Coming. And just as Christ's first coming was great news for some (the poor in spirit, who believed in Him) and bad news for others (the proud of heart, who rejected Him), so also His unstoppable Second Coming will be wonderful news for those who belong to Christ, and woeful news for those who spurn the message of His Gospel. Revelation, like the Bible as a whole, is a book of both promise and warning. John's remarkable vision calls the Church to take comfort in the incomparable

power and mercy of Christ, who comes for the redemption of His own.

At-A-Glance

1. The Glorious Abundance of God's People (Revelation 22:1–5)
2. The Glorious Promise of God (vv. 6–7)

In Depth

1. The Glorious Abundance of God's People (Revelation 22:1–5)

To paint a picture of the greatest possible abundance and blessing, John's vision returns to the place of God's original purpose: the Garden of Eden. Just as is true in Eden (Genesis 2:10), a life-giving river flows in the New Jerusalem; This "water of life" symbolizes the everlasting life given by Jesus through the Spirit (see John 7:37–39) and the "abundant life" He promises in John 10:10. Just as the tree of life stood in Eden (Genesis 2:9) as a sign of perfect fruitfulness and the provision of every human need, it will also stand in the New Jerusalem amidst the river, represented by twelve trees (a number symbolizing divine government and completeness). Humankind was not commanded to leave the earth as an untilled garden, but to work the ground and produce good things, thereby mirroring the creativity and benevolent reign of God over His creation. And though humankind fails miserably at the task God calls us to (this is the story of Genesis 3 to Revelation 20!), God brings about His purpose nonetheless, redeeming not only His chosen remnant, but also all the earth! And so the new heavens and new earth are a place of perfect abundance, a world fit for God and His people to reign. This is true, redeemed urban living!

What will life be like in this gloriously abundant dwelling place? As we saw in Revelation 21:3–4, God will heal and bind up all wounds—especially sin and spiritual brokenness, washed away as the nations partake of the tree of life (22:2). Although the divine Judge had frequently cursed the stubborn rebelliousness of humankind and set them apart for destruction (see Joshua 7:12), here no curse is possible, because God now dwells in perfect purity with a pure people. In the mystery of God's trinitarian being, Father and Son are shown to dwell on one "throne" (22:3).

Even as God exists in loving fellowship with Himself in three persons, so now all His people will be enfolded in that perfect triune love and communion. The sublime happiness promised to the saints might be summed up by showing that the great blessing of Numbers 6:24–27 is now perfectly fulfilled: "The LORD bless thee, and keep thee: The LORD make his face shine upon thee, and be gracious unto thee: The LORD lift up his countenance upon thee, and give thee peace. And they shall put my name upon the children of Israel; and I will bless them" (KJV).

2. The Glorious Promise of God (vv. 6–7)

God in His mercy frequently gives added testimony to the certainty of what He reveals. To call the Lord the "God of the holy prophets" (v. 6) is to show that these words, just like the prophets' words, are breathed out by God and cannot be false. Just as the prophets were able to say, "Thus says the LORD," so also the angel, with the same authority, promises that these words are "faithful and true," and that these things "must shortly be done" (v. 6). Likewise, when John is commanded not to seal up the prophecy, but write it down, God shows us that the vision is true. The record of that vision is also inspired by Him, and utterly reliable.

The promise is also given a specific urgency. Christ promises to come quickly, signaling to the believer that the words of the book should be not only read but immediately obeyed. This admonishes all believers to expect Christ's return and the glorious fulfillment of God's promises.

Search the Scriptures

1. How will we benefit from the curse being removed from everything (Revelation 22:3)?

2. How would you evaluate your awareness and expectancy that Jesus is coming soon (v. 7)?

Discuss the Meaning

1. What did John mean by saying "the time is at hand (v. 10)?

2. Why is it often hard to have a true longing for heaven?

Lesson in Our Society

The human race continues to encounter injustice, oppression, and misery. In particular, the African American community possesses a history of oppression—one that continues today through racism and economic injustice. God provides opportunity to redress wrong and injustice through political or social means. However, social justice can become an idol, and bitterness may ensue when cruelty and oppression continue. This passage reminds us that hope for a paradise on this earth is a misguided hope. The Christian's hope is set immeasurably higher. In the new heavens and new earth, God's bride, the Church, becomes as perfectly radiant as the New Jerusalem; only there will true healing take place. And so the Holy Spirit reminds us, through John's vision, that even as we seek to see the Gospel transform our society in the here and now, we are always to "seek those things which are above" (Colossians 3:1).

Make It Happen

Think about circumstances or relationships in your life that leave you feeling bitter or resentful because of the way you've been treated. How do you respond when you feel slighted? Does a focus on making things right in this world keep you from longing for the next? Take this opportunity to repent of your misplaced hope and turn to Christ for forgiveness. In light of the incredible promises of God about your identity and your abundant inheritance, take time each day to intentionally rejoice and give thanks for the glory that awaits you in God's presence.

Follow the Spirit

What God wants me to do:

_____

_____

_____

Remember Your Thoughts

Special insights I have learned:

_____

_____

_____

More Light on the Text
Revelation 22:1–7

1 And he showed me a pure river of water of life, clear as crystal, proceeding out of the throne of God and of the Lamb.

John's vision in the Spirit continues (cf. Revelation 21:10). He is given a panoramic view of the Holy City. He is shown a pure river containing the water of life. The Sons of Korah spoke prophetically of this river: "There is a river, the streams whereof shall make glad the city of God, the holy place of the tabernacles of the most High" (Psalm 46:4). The Greek word translated "river" is *potamos* (**pot-am-OS**), which means running water, like a stream, flood, or river. The Sons of Korah reveal to us in that passage that the river makes glad the city of God. It is the water of life that brings the life of God.

This river had been foreshadowed by the river in the Garden of Eden (Genesis 2:10). The river from the millennial temple (Ezekiel 47:1–12) also foreshadows this river; it brings life to all creatures wherever it flows. Zechariah also prophesied the issuing out of "living waters" from Jerusalem (Zechariah 14:8). A figurative reference to this river that Jesus makes describes one of the greatest spiritual realities of the Christian faith: the outpouring, deposit, and flow of the Holy Spirit in the life of the believer (John 7:38).

2 In the midst of the street of it, and on either side of the river, was there the tree of life, which bare twelve manner of fruits, and yielded her fruit every month: and the leaves of the tree were for the healing of the nations.

The New Jerusalem is naturally prefigured by the Garden of Eden, the first place where humans lived in their innocence. Both have rivers, and Eden is the first place where the tree of life was mentioned.

Everything in the Holy City is of the greatest proportion, being the most perfect reality compared to other references or similarities in the Bible, which are mere foreshadowings. For instance, the Bible talks about one tree of life in the middle of the Garden of Eden, but here numerous trees abound on both sides of the river.

The tree of life conferred immortality on anyone who ate its fruit, hence its name (Genesis 3:22). In Ezekiel's vision, he revealed that the fruit of the tree of life was meant for food and healing (Ezekiel 47:12). Here John tells us the same thing: The fruit and leaves are for the healing of the nations. This tree is said to bear twelve kinds of fruit every month. As a tree of life, it bears fruit to confer immortality on its eater and maintain life in the Holy City.

The Bible metaphorically calls four things the tree of life: wisdom (Proverbs 3:18), the fruit of righteousness (Proverbs 11:30), fulfilled desire (Proverbs 13:12), and a wholesome tongue (Proverbs 15:4). These things are all described as giving life to those who partake of them. The same can be said of this tree in Revelation, except that the life that this tree gives is eternal.

3 And there shall be no more curse: but the throne of God and the Lamb shall be in it: and his servants shall serve him: 4 And they shall see his face; and his name shall be in their foreheads.

The worst thing a person can say to someone else is a curse. The Greek word translated "curse" here is *katanathema* (**kah-tah-NAH-theh-mah**), meaning a wish that evil may befall a person. Curses served as protective and punitive measures against violating the terms of a treaty; they were intended to doom a person to calamity or destruction. The Curse in the Garden of Eden was a divine judgment against humankind's disobedience. But in the Holy City, curses have no place. The occupants of this city are not objects of divine wrath and punishment, so no disaster can come upon them. They are the redeemed who have qualified as occupants of the New Jerusalem by their faith in Christ and have distinguished themselves with lives above sin, curse, and calamity.

The New Jerusalem will offer ultimate bliss to the believer, the greatest rewards and privileges that are not available in our present world. The throne of God and Christ will be there, bringing the habitation, presence, and direct government of God to the redeemed.

Most blessedly of all, the "divine prohibition" will end. God's order that forbids humanity from seeing His face will no longer exist. This Old Testament order, communicated by God to Moses, stated: "Thou canst not see my face: for there shall no man see me, and live" (from Exodus 33:20). Over the ages, the physical sight of God had been denied to humans, because the consequence was death. But in the New Jerusalem, there will be a new order: God's servants will serve Him, and they will see His face and behold Him physically. This is because those who live in the Holy City will be completely transformed to be like God (1 John 3:2). They will be absent of sin, and their bodies will be changed (1 Corinthians 15:51–53). His name (seal of ownership) will be on their foreheads.

5 And there shall be no night there; and they need no candle, neither light of the sun; for the Lord God giveth them light: and they shall reign forever and ever.

In the beginning, God created light. This light came from the two main heavenly bodies (sun and moon), and came about on day four. One of their functions was to bring about day and night (Genesis 1:14). Here the passage says there shall be no night. Figuratively, the night stands for various periods and conditions in human life: a time of ignorance and helplessness (Micah 3:6), the depraved condition of humankind (1 Thessalonians 5:5–7), and also a time of inactivity or death (John 9:4). In the Holy City, there will be no ignorance, the depraved conditions of humankind will not exist, and death will be no more.

6 And he said unto me, These sayings are faithful and true: and the Lord God of the holy prophets sent his angel to show unto his servants the things which must shortly be done.

This is the second time the angel used the words "faithful" and "true" (21:5, 22:6), which also are applied directly to Christ (Revelation 3:14, 19:11). As Christ is faithful and true, so are His words sent via prophets or angels also faithful and true. The apparent redundancy here must indicate the special importance to the church of these particular words—even while underscoring that God always has, in the same trustworthy manner, revealed the future through His prophets. The phrase translated as "the Lord God, who inspires his prophets" in the NLT (cf. NIV) literally means that God is the prophets' very breath and spirit (Gk. *pneuma*, **puh-NEW-mah**; breath, spirit). This points to the authority of John's vision, connecting it to the prophets of the past as originating from God.

The hinge phrase "must shortly be done" (v. 6) has been translated many ways, yet all clearly concur that the Greek word *tachos* (**TAH-khos**) means quickness or speed. The original Greek did not intend "quickly" as commonly understood. Few would say 2,000 years is "quickly," but "suddenly" could happen at any time, even the distant future. This rendering also agrees with other verses that describe His coming as a thief in the night, taking a self-indulgent, self-absorbed world by surprise (Matthew 24:38–41; 1 Thessalonians 5:4).

Ever since John penned his vision, these words of imminent hope have been available for all to see and react to as they choose. When Christ finally does return, no one will be able to claim total surprise, and they also will have no one to blame if His coming isn't welcome.

7 Behold, I come quickly: blessed is he that keepeth the sayings of the prophecy of this book.

After reinforcing this element of surprise, the angel encourages believers, but subtly implies that those who don't "keep the true sayings in this book" won't be "blessed" at Jesus' sudden appearance. In this Revelation beatitude, believers will be blessed, more likely ecstatic, as our time of vindication and the completion of our redemption will have come at long last. In stark contrast, the unbelieving world will be judged and condemned. Here translated "sayings" but generally translated "words," John uses the Greek word *logos* (**LOG-os**), a word he used multiple times in thirty-six verses of his Gospel, to refer to the entire Word of God (see especially John 1).

Each succeeding generation must anticipate, prepare, watch, and be ready for Jesus' return. Nothing in our present world can give us enduring comfort and eternal joy; we must place all our hopes on Jesus Christ, serving Him wholeheartedly. He has prepared a wonderful and glorious future for those who put their trust in Him.

Say It Correctly

Shewed. **SHOOD.**
Redundancy. **REE**-dun-din-cee.

Daily Bible Readings

MONDAY
Wash and Be Healed
(2 Kings 5:10–14)

TUESDAY
Healing River Flows from the Temple
(Ezekiel 47:1–2, 12)

WEDNESDAY
God is Present and the City is Secure
(Psalm 46)

THURSDAY
The Sustaining Healing Water of Life
(Isaiah 41:17–20)

FRIDAY
The Lord Acts With Passion
(Isaiah 42:10–17)

SATURDAY
The Paralytic Walks Again
(Matthew 9:2–8)

SUNDAY
Ready for the Lord's Return
(Revelation 22:1–7)

Notes

Teaching Tips

Words You Should Know

A. Idolaters (Revelation 22:15) *eidololatres* (Gk.)—Image servants or worshipers.

B. Testify (v. 16) *martureo* (Gk.)—To be a witness, bear record, provide evidence.

Teacher Preparation

Unifying Principle—From Beginning to End. People are aware that things have a beginning and an end. What is the source and final purpose of human life? Revelation affirms that God, who is the Alpha and Omega, controls all things.

A. Think of a time when you were excited to be invited to join a group or attend an event.

B. Pray and ask God to help you facilitate a lesson that conveys the excitement of receiving the auspicious invitation to join God's kingdom.

C. Complete the companion lesson in the *Precepts for Living*® Personal Study Guide.

O—Open the Lesson

A. Ask the class to think of an instance when they were excited to be invited to join a group or attend an event. Once everyone has briefly shared the first memory, ask them to also recall something they pursued but had to wait a long time to obtain.

B. Pray and introduce the lesson.

C. Ask for a volunteer to read the Aim for Change and a different volunteer to read Keep in Mind.

D. Have participants read the In Focus story silently.

P—Present the Scriptures

A. Have a volunteer read the Focal Verses.

B. Use The People, Places, and Times; Background; Search the Scriptures; At-A-Glance Outline; In Depth; and More Light on the Text to clarify the verses.

E—Explore the Meaning

A. Answer the Search the Scripture questions together as a class.

B. Discuss the correlations between the In Focus story, the opening exercise, and the Scripture.

C. Read the Lesson in Our Society to the class.

N—Next Steps for Application

A. Allow participants to read and reflect individually on the Make It Happen sections.

B. Ask for a volunteer to summarize the lesson (assist if necessary).

C. Close with prayer.

Worship Guide

For the Superintendent or Teacher
Theme: Alpha and Omega
Song: "The Lily of the Valley"
Devotional Reading: Revelation 1:4b–8

Alpha and Omega

Bible Background • REVELATION 22:8–21
Printed Text • REVELATION 22:12–21 | Devotional Reading • REVELATION 1:4b–8

―――――――――― **Aim for Change** ――――――――――

By the end of this lesson, we will: SURVEY the biblical references to the Second Coming to see the importance of this hoped-for reality; REJOICE that the invitation from Jesus to join the new community continues through the end of all things; and EMBRACE the call to become part of God's kingdom.

―――――――――― **In Focus** ――――――――――

All throughout her life, Leslie had struggled in school. She had faced developmental issues as a child, and early on, she was found to have a learning disability. Now, however, her moment was finally here. Leslie remembered the day her parents dropped her off on campus. Almost four years had passed, but she vividly remembered how they reaffirmed her intelligence, encouraged her to be fearless in her pursuits, and cautioned her to make wise decisions. She distinctly remembered how her journey began—the first day of class, what her roommate said when they first met, even her feelings of anxiety. A lot had taken place between then and now. She had faced financial aid issues, the stress of maintaining her sports scholarship while working, and academic struggles.

After her parents dropped her off there four years ago, this was the day they had always waited for: Leslie was graduating with honors. In spite of all that Leslie faced as a child, her parents hoped and believed that she would excel. Over the last twenty-two years, sometimes setbacks made this day seem unlikely, but their faith never faltered. They instilled the same level of expectation, perseverance, and desire in Leslie, and finally it was a reality.

Walking in faith is necessary to prepare for Jesus' return. What are you doing to prepare for His return?

―――――――――― **Keep in Mind** ――――――――――

"I am Alpha and Omega, the beginning and the end, the first and the last"
(Revelation 22:13).

"I am Alpha and Omega, the beginning and the end, the first and the last" (Revelation 22:13).

Focal Verses

KJV **Revelation 22:12** And, behold, I come quickly; and my reward is with me, to give every man according as his work shall be.

13 I am Alpha and Omega, the beginning and the end, the first and the last.

14 Blessed are they that do his commandments, that they may have right to the tree of life, and may enter in through the gates into the city.

15 For without are dogs, and sorcerers, and whoremongers, and murderers, and idolaters, and whosoever loveth and maketh a lie.

16 I Jesus have sent mine angel to testify unto you these things in the churches. I am the root and the offspring of David, and the bright and morning star.

17 And the Spirit and the bride say, Come. And let him that heareth say, Come. And let him that is athirst come. And whosoever will, let him take the water of life freely.

18 For I testify unto every man that heareth the words of the prophecy of this book, If any man shall add unto these things, God shall add unto him the plagues that are written in this book:

19 And if any man shall take away from the words of the book of this prophecy, God shall take away his part out of the book of life, and out of the holy city, and from the things which are written in this book.

20 He which testifieth these things saith, Surely I come quickly. Amen. Even so, come, Lord Jesus.

21 The grace of our Lord Jesus Christ be with you all. Amen.

NLT **Revelation 22:12** "Look, I am coming soon, bringing my reward with me to repay all people according to their deeds.

13 I am the Alpha and the Omega, the First and the Last, the Beginning and the End."

14 Blessed are those who wash their robes. They will be permitted to enter through the gates of the city and eat the fruit from the tree of life.

15 Outside the city are the dogs—the sorcerers, the sexually immoral, the murderers, the idol worshipers, and all who love to live a lie.

16 "I, Jesus, have sent my angel to give you this message for the churches. I am both the source of David and the heir to his throne. I am the bright morning star."

17 The Spirit and the bride say, "Come." Let anyone who hears this say, "Come." Let anyone who is thirsty come. Let anyone who desires drink freely from the water of life.

18 And I solemnly declare to everyone who hears the words of prophecy written in this book: If anyone adds anything to what is written here, God will add to that person the plagues described in this book.

19 And if anyone removes any of the words from this book of prophecy, God will remove that person's share in the tree of life and in the holy city that are described in this book.

20 He who is the faithful witness to all these things says, "Yes, I am coming soon!" Amen! Come, Lord Jesus!

21 May the grace of the Lord Jesus be with God's holy people.

The People, Places, and Times

Book of Revelation. John, who lived in a time of Roman persecution, oppression, and idolatry, began by penning his message as "things which must shortly come to pass" (1:1). Whether the text is interpreted as literal events to take place in the future or as allegorical principles of the kingdom of God, it is clear that initially the text was a prophecy (1:3, 22:18) and a letter (1:4) to the seven churches in Asia Minor, the region we know today as Turkey. John writes from the island of Patmos, where he said his visions occurred.

John. Specifically naming himself as the author of Revelation, John writes with authority to the church as a whole. From reading these Scriptures, it is apparent the son of Zebedee was a visionary and a prophet. He and his brother James were nicknamed by Jesus as the "Sons of Thunder." John had a seemingly special relationship with Jesus. In at least three instances, John accompanied Jesus apart from the majority of the twelve disciples (Luke 8:51; Matthew 17:1; Mark 14:33).

Background

The book of Revelation is considered apocalypse writing. The term "apocalypse" refers to Jewish and Christian literature that uncovers or unveils future events or unseen realms of heaven and hell; conversationally, the word is applied to religious events surrounding the anticipated destruction of the world. Apocalyptic writing is notorious for mysterious language and imagery that could be perceived and interpreted in many different ways. In the Old and New Testaments, there are two full apocalypses (Daniel and Revelation), both of which speak cryptically of corrupt, human political realms in contrast to God's heavenly and eternal realm.

Eschatology, the study of end times and more specifically death, judgment, and heaven and hell, has been closely associated with apocalyptic literature. Both Revelation and Daniel (chapter 9) prophesy that the end is on the horizon. Daniel also introduces the Jewish (and then also Christian) concept of being raised from the dead (12:1–2), and the Book of Life mentioned throughout Revelation is first mentioned in Daniel (12:1).

Another heavily discussed or avoided topic is the second coming of Jesus. This phenomena has drawn a lot of thoughts that vary widely throughout the faith. In the most literal context, it is the belief that Jesus will literally return to earth and satisfy unfulfilled prophecies.

At-A-Glance

1. Alpha and Omega (Revelation 22:12–13)
2. City Gates (v. 14–15)
3. The Son of David is Coming (vv. 16–21)

In Depth

1. Alpha and Omega (Revelation 22:12–13)

The significance of the "I am" statement stems from the book of Exodus (3:13–15), when God instructs Moses to tell the people of Israel that God sent him. Moses asks God for a specific name, and God's response is, "I AM THAT I AM," that is, "I am everything and whatever is required at any given moment." The term is all-encompassing. God further explains that this will be His name forever.

Jesus employs the "I am" statement as an assertion of His divinity and connection to God. He quotes God's declaration of being the first and the last who is the one true God (Isaiah 44:6, 48:12). Jesus utilizes the first and last letters of the Greek alphabet (alpha and omega) to further stress the point. The phrase occurs four times throughout Revelation (1:8, 11; 21:6; 22:13).

2. City Gates (v. 14–15)

Revelation was written to churches in large cities. Thus John intentionally describes a particular place that contrasts with the metropolitan life the recipients are used to. Chapter 3 introduces this city of God as the New Jerusalem (3:12), while chapter 21 provides the description. The dimensions, ethos, foundation, building materials and jewels, walls, and character of its inhabitants are all detailed.

John writes that those who have the right to the tree of life will enter the city by the gatess; there are twelve of them. Three gates face each compass direction, and there is an angel and inscription of the twelve tribes at all the gates. The people outside the gates are those who are disobedient to God's commands. They would corrupt the city with their sin.

3. Root and Descendant of David (v. 16–21)

Throughout the messianic prophecies is a motif that connects the expectant Savior to the lineage and legacy of King David. The Gospels continue the motif by casting Jesus as the fulfillment of the prophecies, and whatever remains void, the New Testament asserts will be accomplished once Jesus returns. Based on Scripture and because of their plight as a people, the initial followers of Christ longed for a Davidic king who would conquer the enemies of God in the same way that David did.

Even in the apocalyptic text that was canonized last in sequence, Jesus identifies Himself with the legacy and lineage of David. An interpretation of Isaiah 11:1, 10 is that there is still a constant connection between what was and what will come.

Search the Scriptures

1. What is the severe punishment for anyone who adds or takes away from this book of prophecy (Revelation 22:18–19)?

2. Jesus calls those who follow His commandments blessed (v. 14). Write out a mission statement that details how you are going to live a blessed life.

Discuss the Meaning

1. How relevant is the Second Coming to the way you live your life?

2. What does it mean to you personally that Jesus is the beginning and the end?

Lesson in Our Society

Although Jesus graciously extends the invitation for us to enter the kingdom and offers "waters of life," we cannot receive these gifts without obligation and investment. Sometimes we can be so preoccupied with the daily routine of life that we have no interest in questions of ultimate significance. These are the things that need to occupy our minds and influence our lives on a daily basis.

Make It Happen

Verse 15 gives a few examples of actions and character flaws that can separate us from Jesus. Aside from what was mentioned, can you think of anything that may separate you from fully preparing yourself for Christ? The thoughts, words, or actions do not have to be what some consider "sin" in the conventional sense, but rather anything that could prevent you from dwelling in the closest proximity possible to Jesus.

Follow the Spirit

What God wants me to do:

_____

_____

_____

_____

Remember Your Thoughts

Special insights I have learned:

_____

_____

_____

_____

More Light on the Text
Revelation 22:12–21

The context of the last chapter of the last book of Scripture brings a close to human history. Like ultimate bookends of humanity's story, our beginning and end are contrasted and captured by authors Moses and John. In Genesis, the serpent tempts the first Adam; he falls, and paradise is lost. In Revelation, the serpent is destroyed, the second Adam is victorious, and paradise is restored. The significant elements of the garden paradise were two people, the tree of life, and a river that watered the garden (Genesis 2:9–10). In the New Jerusalem, the fountain of life flows from the throne of God (Revelation 22:1–2, 4:6), and lining both sides of the river are many trees of life (22:14) that are not only freely accessible but ever fruitful for the enjoyment and healing of many nations (Psalm 46:4). In Eden, one tree was forbidden; in the New Jerusalem,

nothing is forbidden. This succinct picture of our final paradise supersedes the original, particularly because of the absence of temptation, death, and evil.

12 And, behold, I come quickly; and my reward is with me, to give every man according as his work shall be.

Although "quickly" is the standard interpretation of the Greek *tachus* (**tah-KOOS**), the more literal rendering is "suddenly." Both intend for the Church, the bride of Christ, to prepare herself and be ready at any time for the return of her beloved Bridegroom. This is because no one really knows when it will happen. The main point, repeated over and over in Scripture, is to be ready for Christ's return whenever it happens.

It is misguided thinking to take this verse out of context and try to say we are justified by works; too many other Scriptures clarify this issue (Ephesians 2:8–9; James 2:20). Paul clarified that it is God's grace alone that saves us (Galatians 2:16; Ephesians 2:8–9), and Jesus declared that the Law and the Prophets rest on a single commandment to love God and neighbor (Matthew 22:37–30; cf. Deuteronomy 6:5; Leviticus 19:18). In other places like Revelation 22, the Scriptures declare that our deeds are important (Matthew 16:27; James 2:20). Read together, all these verses remind us that as humans, we always fall short of perfection, so we can never save ourselves by our deeds alone. We will always need God's grace for salvation. However, passages such as Matthew 16, James 2 and Revelation 22 also remind us that we cannot expect to get away with corrupt behavior, mistreating one another intentionally. Hollow or shallow faith that does not lead to growth is not enough. A positive take on the verse is that Jesus will come with "rewards" (Gk. *misthos*, **mis-THOS**), like wages or payment for services, for those who have been faithful. While no one is saved by works, those who are saved will be rewarded according to their works (Gk. *ergon*, **ER-gon**, employment or labor).

13 I am Alpha and Omega, the beginning and the end, the first and the last.

Alpha is the first of twenty-four letters in the Greek alphabet and Omega is the last, thus making the connection between the beginning and the end, the first and the last. Psalm 90:2 says God is from "everlasting to everlasting," and He is the same "yesterday, and today, and forever" (Hebrews 13:8). If Genesis and Revelation are the bookends of human history, Jesus is the holder of the bookends both pre-existing and post-existing our temporal time frame. This is true not only in the sense of existence, but also in character and holiness, without beginning or end, and without change (Malachi 3:6). Alpha and Omega, moreover, is one of many self-proclaimed images of Christ found in Scripture. The same names are applied to God (cf. Isaiah 41:4, 44:6; Revelation 1:8, 21:6) and here specifically applied to Christ (cf. Revelation 1:17, 2:8), giving another insurmountable argument for His deity.

14 Blessed are they that do his commandments, that they may have right to the tree of life, and may enter in through the gates into the city. 15 For without are dogs, and sorcerers, and whoremongers, and murderers, and idolaters, and whosoever loveth and maketh a lie.

Jesus gives His blessing to those who obey God's commandments; this is their qualification for entering the gates of the heavenly city, the New Jerusalem. These people have a right (*exousia*, **ek-ZOO-see-ah**) or authority to eat from the tree of life. Adam and Eve were banished from the garden and they were not able to eat from its tree (Genesis 3:22–24). Now the tree is available to all who follow Jesus and obey God's commandments.

The people outside the city are those who do not keep God's commandments. Since the whole city is God's temple, then those who would defile it are kept outside. These people have disobeyed God to the point that their disobedience has become their identity. This list is very similar to the list in Revelation 21:8, with the addition of the category of dogs. Dogs were considered unclean animals in Judaism because they would eat carrion (Leviticus 11:27; Deuteronomy 14:7), and by extension in Greco-Roman and Jewish culture, dogs sometimes represented immorality, including at times sexual immorality (Deuteronomy 23:18; Matthew 7:6; Philip 3:2). The phrase "whosoever loveth and maketh a lie" is more than likely a further description of idolaters.

16 I Jesus have sent mine angel to testify unto you these things in the churches. I am the root and the offspring of David, and the bright and morning star.

Jesus places His stamp of approval on the testimony of the message of Revelation to the Church (the word "you" in the Greek is plural), which includes our present age. No mortal could be both root (the Creator) and offspring (Isaiah 11:1); Jesus is both the Lord of David and the son of David (Matthew 22:42–45). The fallen angel Lucifer, once called a morning star (Isaiah 14:12; also day star in some versions), has from the beginning lied to mankind and falsely presented himself as an angel of light (2 Corinthians 11:14). Jesus affirms that He alone is the true Morning Star. Here three words associated with light are used to describe Jesus: star (Gk. *aster*, **ah-STAIR**; star, flame), bright (Gk. *lampros*, **lam-PROS**; white, radiant) and morning (Gk. *orthinos*, **or-thin-OS**; what is to the right, correct). Morning is associated with the re-introduction of light to the world. After a period of darkness, the star of the morning will appear, shining brightly.

17 And the Spirit and the bride say, Come. And let him that heareth say, Come. And let him that is athirst come. And whosoever will, let him take the water of life freely.

The Spirit of God and the bride of Christ invites everyone who has yet to decide for Christ to come to the water of life! We, along with the Spirit, wait expectantly, but we also serve as a testimony that the human heart is satisfied by coming to Jesus, and any who come to Him may freely drink of the water of life (John 7:37–39; Revelation 22:1), both now and forever.

18 For I testify unto every man that heareth the words of the prophecy of this book, If any man shall add unto these things, God shall add unto him the plagues that are written in this book: 19 And if any man shall take away from the words of the book of this prophecy, God shall take away his part out of the book of life, and out of the holy city, and from the things which are written in this book.

Matthew Henry, a 17th century Bible scholar, observes that the words of warning resemble previous words of protection found in Scripture: "This sanction is like a flaming sword, to guard the canon of the Scripture from profane hands." Henry's words are reminiscent of the angel guarding the tree of life with a flaming sword (Genesis 3:24). God installed similar sanctions for the protection of the Law (see Deuteronomy 4:2, 12:32; Proverbs 30:5–6). God will judge offenders appropriately for their violation of His *logos*. The clearly promised curse balances the previous promised blessing offered to the faithful (v. 12) and together retain a familiar blessing/curse theme

from the Old Testament as the New Testament closes.

20 He which testifieth these things saith, Surely I come quickly. Amen. Even so, come, Lord Jesus.

Christ's parting words are filled with mercy and hope. When Jesus ascended after His resurrection, He promised to be with them by His Spirit; now He promises He will soon return. His coming will be fulfilled as completely as the fulfillment of sending the Holy Spirit, the Comforter and Teacher of the church. The Greek word for "testify" is *martureo* (**mar-too-REH-oh**), meaning to give or bear witness, just as the apostles were witnesses of the life, death, burial, and resurrection of Christ. Once Christ does return, it will be the end for all who rejected Him. The primary message for the church is to be and remain ready. The book of Revelation started with the Spirit (1:10), the church lives and exists because of the Spirit, and individual believers are raised to newness of life only through being born of the Spirit (John 3:5, 8; Galatians 4:29). The heartbeat of every Christian (the body of Christ) is the Spirit. The Spirit has been our teacher of truth, always leading us toward Christ. All born–again believers will be ready because of the Spirit and will wait expectantly, no matter how long it takes.

21 The grace of our Lord Jesus Christ be with you all. Amen.

It is no coincidence that both the book and the Word end with a word of grace. Christ came to bring us grace. When His work on earth was finished, He left to prepare a place for us, and as surely as He first came according to His promise, He will return as promised for His bride. Until we are perfected in Him, we can find no better comfort, stronger peace, or more enduring hope than the presence of His grace to sustain us until His return.

Say It Correctly

Plagues. **PLAYGZ**.
Testifieth. **TES**-ti-**FEYE**-ith.

Daily Bible Readings

MONDAY
You Will Not Find Me
(John 7:32–36)

TUESDAY
This is the Messiah
(John 7:37–43)

WEDNESDAY
The Lord God, the Almighty
(Revelation 1:4b–8)

THURSDAY
Your First Work Rewarded
(Revelation 2:1–7)

FRIDAY
Worship Without End
(Revelation 7:9–12)

SATURDAY
Promised Redemption Fulfilled
(Isaiah 43:1–7)

SUNDAY
Yes, I am Coming Soon!
(Revelation 22:8–21)

Notes

_____

_____

_____

_____

Creation: A Divine Cycle

With the advent of the Savior by the power of the Holy Spirit, God set in motion the fulfillment of the divine plan of salvation. Luke's Gospel, several psalms, and the epistle to the Galatians explore God's ongoing actions in blessing and reconciling the whole creation.

UNIT 1 • The Savior is Born

The four lessons in this unit are developed from the Gospel of Luke. Lessons 1 and 2 offer a study of how Mary, a virgin, received and joyfully accepted the announcement that she had been highly favored by God to give birth to His Son and the story of her cousin Elisabeth's affirmation of the same. Lesson 3 studies John's mission as the forerunner of the Savior. The Christmas Day lesson deals with the birth of Jesus and the circumstances and events pursuant to it.

Lesson 1: December 4, 2016
God Promises a Savior
Luke 1:26–38

Our actions, decisions, and even well-being are often based on our trust in promises made by others. On whose promises can we ultimately depend? Luke recounts the angel's announcement of the coming birth of Jesus, God's promised Savior.

Lesson 2: December 11, 2016
The Affirmation of the Promise
Luke 1:39–56

Receiving confirmation of pending good fortune is a joyful event. In such moments, how can we respond? Luke tells of Elisabeth's affirmation of God's promise of the Savior and Mary's joyful praise to God for being chosen as the bearer of that divine promise.

Lesson 3: December 18, 2016
The Forerunner of the Savior
Luke 1:8–20

At times we are entrusted with incredible responsibilities beyond anything we might have imagined for ourselves. How might we respond? Luke tells of Zacharias' growing acceptance of his role as father to John, the one called to be the forerunner of the Savior.

Lesson 4: December 25, 2016
The Savior Has Been Born
Luke 2:8–20

People wait with great anticipation for the birth of a new baby. How do they react when at last the child is safely delivered? Luke tells the good news of the promised Savior's birth and the reactions of the angels, shepherds, and Mary to this miraculous event.

UNIT 2 • All Creation Praises God

The five lessons in this unit employ five psalms. Several psalms emphasize praise for God that emanates from creation itself. Others invite us to praise God for creation.

Lesson 5: January 1, 2017
God is Worthy of Praise
Psalm 33:1–9

People praise the achievements of others. What should be the subject of our praise? The psalmist teaches that the Word and work of God the Creator are worthy of our praise.

Lesson 6: January 8, 2017
All Creation Overflows with Praise
Psalm 96:1–6, 10–13

We are awed by the beauty and grandeur of creation. How can we appropriately express these feelings of awe? The psalmist calls all creation to declare the glory of the Lord for His marvelous works.

Lesson 7: January 15, 2017
Praise God for the Provider
Psalm 65:1–2, 9–13

We often take for granted how we get the good things we enjoy. What is the source of our material bounty? The psalmist calls us to praise God for the bounty He provides.

Lesson 8: January 22, 2017
Praise God the Creator
Psalm 104:1–4, 24–30

When we experience the vast diversity of creation, we wonder how it is all held together. What does this complexity tell us about the world we live in? The psalmist praises God for sustaining creation.

Lesson 9: January 29, 2017
All Creation Praises God
Psalm 148

We think that nature exists for our benefit alone. For what purpose was the world created? The psalmist commands every element of creation to join the chorus of praise for all that God has created.

UNIT 3 • The Church is Born

The four lessons in this unit will focus on Galatians, in which God's creative process can be seen through the birthing of a new faith community with Jesus Christ as its foundation. The lessons address the importance of spiritual freedom, cooperation, and righteous living in building and maintaining the community.

Lesson 10: February 5, 2017
Re-Created to Live in Harmony
Galatians 3:26–4:7

Differences of race, class, and gender make it hard for people to get along. How can we live in harmony? Paul tells the Galatians that through Christ we have received the Spirit, making us heirs of God and bringing us into a community of oneness where human differences are no longer divisive.

Lesson 11: February 12, 2017
New Birth Brings Freedom
Galatians 4:8–20

People are tempted to sacrifice freedom in order to gain a sense of security. What are the dangers of this trade-off? Paul rebuked the Galatians for trading the freedom Christ gives for slavery to religious legalism.

Lesson 12: February 19, 2017
Freedom in Christ
Galatians 5:1–17

Rigorous self-discipline is appealing to some because it seems to promise mastery over temptation. What is the key to living a morally acceptable life? Paul urges the Galatians to stand firm in Christian freedom and to live by the Spirit, which leads to greater holiness, not greater self-indulgence.

Lesson 13: February 26, 2017
Christ Creates Holy Living
Galatians 5:18–6:10

Many people reduce their religious obligations to fulfilling a set of legalistic requirements. What are the characteristics of an authentic Christian lifestyle? Paul sharply contrasts a Spirit-filled life with life in the flesh.

Worshiping the Creator God

Have you ever stood at the foot of a mountain? Even the smallest mountain can make us feel like ants in its presence. Looking at them makes us realize we are small and insignificant. Mountains are wondrous to behold. Yet even in all their splendor and majesty, the mountains didn't just appear by chance; they were formed as part of God's creative work. Theologians call this "creatio ex nihilo," a Latin phrase meaning "creation out of nothing." Before these mountains were formed, God was there: Father, Son, and Spirit (see Psalm 90:2), ready to set in motion a series of events that would include humanity's creation, fall, sinful bondage, and redemption through Christ Jesus. Paul later tells believers in Rome that this creation, having been adversely affected by the Fall, has been "groaning" (Romans 8:22, NIV) for the redemption offered through Christ. What a wonderful description!

The same God who formed magnificent mountains (Amos 4:13) was caring enough to form us and create us in His image (Genesis 1:27). And He cared enough for us to send His Son to fulfill the righteous requirement so we may be saved (Romans 8:3–4). The mere fact that the Potter would become the very clay He shaped in the beginning is mind-blowing (John 1:14). We want you to think about God's plan—from beginning to end. In forming the mountains and seas, and crowning His work by forming mankind, evidence of His love is visible around us daily. In doing so, we hope you realize that the Creator of heaven and earth causes "all things to work together for good to them that love God..." (from Romans 8:28, KJV, author's paraphrase). When you realize this, you begin to prioritize your life. The kingdom of God becomes the driving force for everything you do. And that's just the way Jesus wants it (see Matthew 6:33).

Bara is the Hebrew word for "create," used in the Old Testament. *Kitzo* is the Greek word for "create," used in the New Testament. It's no coincidence that the only time the two words are used in Scripture references God. After all, only God can create. Humans have attempted to re-create. We've attempted to duplicate. We've attempted to simulate. Creating is special, but reserved for the Creator. The psalmist declares that God can even create in humans a clean heart (see Psalm 51:10)—a heart that forgives, is slow to anger, isn't easily offended,

that cares for the poor and disenfranchised. Most of all, He can create a heart that becomes the dwelling place of His Spirit. Humans may have perfected the art of heart transplants, but there is One who knows how to create a new heart—from scratch.

Knowing this moves us to worship the Creator God. Everything that exists comes from Him as the source. Every good thing that we enjoy would not be around unless He created it. The psalmists in the Old Testament knew this. They acknowledged their dependence on God. They saw the wonder and beauty of His creation. This moved them to write psalms that spoke of the greatness and glory of God the Creator. As we look at these Scriptures, we too are invited to sense the awe and majesty of creation and be moved to worship the Creator.

Technology in Christian Education

by Virginia Stiths

Technology greatly affects the education of all humankind. The way we live, work, and learn is continuously changing. The needs it has created for our society are different from those of past generations. Increased knowledge has improved our quality of life, and extended life expectancy. Technology expands from new and improved medicines to wireless communications. Computers and health technology have tremendously advanced society. However, the field of Christian education often seems to move at a slower pace, particularly in the African American community. While it is human nature to fear the unknown, the Scriptures encourage us to seek knowledge. Solomon tells us to "cry out for insight, and ask for understanding. Search for them as you would for silver; seek them like hidden treasures" (Proverbs 2:3–4, NLT). Technology influences the learning process of all ages, from preschool to retirement age, from private devotionals to biblical scholarship.

A Christian philosophy of education is the communication of the eternal Word of God as revealed in Scripture and creation. Christian education is not about running or hiding from the world, but rather about embracing and pursuing the mind of Christ. It is founded on the biblical truth that all that can be discovered, studied, fathomed, created, adorned, or enjoyed existed first in the mind of God, and it is sustained by Christ's power and revealed through the Holy Spirit's presence. "The Son is the image of the invisible God, the firstborn over all creation. For in him all things were created: things in heaven and on earth, visible and invisible, whether thrones or powers or rulers or authorities; all things were created through him and for him. He is before all things, and in him all things hold together. And he is the head of the body, the church; he is the beginning and the firstborn from among the dead, so that in everything he might have the supremacy ... For in Christ all the fullness of the Deity lives in bodily form, and in Christ you have been brought to fullness. He is the head over every power and authority" (Colossians 1:15–18, 2:9–10, NIV).

The increased accessibility of the Internet offers a challenge for Christian education. Schools for all ages use the Internet. The question for us should be: How can Christian schools make use of the Internet? They can benefit in the same ways as non-Christian schools. Schools can use the Internet to add to their library resources. They can supplement or replace printed textbooks and handouts with Web sites for each course. It can be used to help students communicate with their instructors, as well as aid in discussion, both among the students themselves and with those outside the school community. E-mail and education forums also allow those associated with Christian education to quickly share ideas and concerns.

While the Internet affects Christian education in many ways, Christian schools have unique needs. Christian schools seek to teach students to view everything in light of the self-attesting Christ of Scripture. They seek to prepare students to live their entire lives in terms of Christ's Great Commission. Unfortunately, Christian schools often have tight budgets as they must operate without state funding, relying on private tuition and donations from charities.

Technology must be placed in context with a curriculum, teachers, and a community to support real learning. On most of today's college campuses, students have the use of wireless networks, laptops, and educational apps for smartphones. They can use video conferencing as a way to study with experts in any field with the use of high-speed connections. The ways in which the Internet is able to contribute to Christian education are many and varied.

Church school teachers increasingly have many aids at their disposal. *Precepts For Living*® Online is an excellent tool that should definitely be used for preparing the lesson. This contains virtually every resource that anyone studying the Scriptures might need. Some educators regrettably fear the computer and all that accompanies it, but we are encouraged by the Apostle Paul to make every effort "to shew [ourselves] approved unto God, a workman that needeth not to be ashamed, rightly dividing the word of truth" (from 2 Timothy 2:15, KJV). Technology can certainly help us do that.

In the future, other applications of technology for Christian education will be discovered. Breakthroughs of this kind have given this field of study great potential and the ability to reach students both far and near. Of course educators must be willing to accept the ever-changing world of technology and its superhighway to knowledge, particularly as it relates to research and mastering inquiry itself, thereby in many instances generating the answer before the question is asked. Technology in Christian education is an enabling tool when used with the guidance of the Holy Spirit in our search for wisdom, which ultimately brings happiness to those who find it.

Sources:
Barbour, Ian G. *Ethics in an Age of Technology: The Gifford Lectures Volume Two.* New York, N.Y.: HarperSanFrancisco, 1992.
Eisner, Elliot W. *The Educational Imagination: On the Design and Evaluation of School Programs.* Indianapolis, IN: Prentice Hall Professional Technical Reference, 1994.

Virginia Stiths is adjunct professor at Piedmont Technical College.

Creation: A Reason to Praise God

by Rev. Ricky A. Woods

President Barack Obama's 2015 visit to the Arctic highlighted the beauty of creation and our need to preserve the gift of creation that God has given us in our world. Where politicians and news talk show hosts debate the reality of climate change and whether our environment needs protecting, the psalmist takes a different approach; he sees the earth as God's creation and a call for all of humanity to praise Him. In Psalms 104 and 148, hymns of praise used in temple worship remind the people of God's presence, provision, and protection through creation.

God was not just seen in the temple and through ritual worship; His presence was everywhere in creation. Each time people looked at the world, they could see some witness of God's goodness in creation. Leslie Allen calls the psalmist's position "a courageous act of faith, persisted in when there was often much in personal experience and competing religions and outlooks, that suggested that such a conviction was false."

"Bless the Lord" and "praise the Lord" are two phrases that begin Psalm 104 and 148, and suggest that the psalmist allows everything that he sees in creation to inform his worship of God. The psalmist is not a scientist trying to define creation, but a worshiper giving God glory for being able to participate in it. God's handiwork is seen in everything: clouds, water, mountains, valleys, birds, and all creatures. Because the psalmist believes he is viewing God's creation, he is moved to praise Him.

We take far too much in our world for granted and sometimes fail to ponder not only the beauty of creation but the God who created it all. To look at snow-capped mountains on a summer day or stand over the Grand Canyon should move us to awe of more than just their beauty, but inspire us to praise the Lord. My favorite time of the year is when the trees begin to change color in the fall. I am always amazed at how trees that all have green leaves can give us so many variations of colors when autumn comes. Looking upon the myriad of colors causes me to know that surely not only science is at work, but also something mysterious and wonderful that can only come from the hand of God.

When we praise God for creation, our relationship to it will change. The earth will no longer be something that exists for humans to dominate and abuse. The natural resources of the earth may be used, but never in ways that rob other parts of creation of their splendor and glory. Corporate profits and human conveniences should not be our primary concern when it comes to our environment. The Bible provides a model of stewardship where we care for and tend to God's creation, and in the process enjoy its benefits.

The psalmist sees not only a beautiful world, but one where God has provided everything needed to live. Creation gives the psalmist not just air to breathe and water to drink, but also meaningful work with the ground to till and livestock to tend. Creation gives him trees to make shelter and the clothes he wears from animals' linen and wool. Creation has even given him all the items to build the temple that serves as his place of worship and where God's Spirit resides.

Creation is a sign of God's faithfulness. Kingdoms may come and go, but as the sun rises and sets and the seasons come and go, the psalmist knows some things can be counted upon not to change.

The psalms often describe and depict God's faithfulness, and one way the psalmists talk about God's faithfulness is through what they have seen in creation. Faithfulness is also a reason to praise God, and His faithfulness is so grand that everything and everyone is called upon to praise Him.

As wonderful as it is to praise God for creation, we have even a greater reason to praise God as believers in Jesus Christ: being new creatures in Him. While all of humanity is part of God's creation, those who have accepted Jesus Christ as Lord know the value and meaning of being a new creation in Him. The old humanity was marred by the Fall that brought sin into the world, but the new humanity is formed by the Holy Spirit, where we are witnesses to the kingdom of God.

Being in Christ opens our eyes to see ourselves, the world, and others differently. It allows us to take on the work of reconciliation, where we are used by God to bring creation and others back into a right relationship with the Creator. J. David Pleins, in his book *The Social Vision of the Hebrew Bible*, says that God has a social vision for creation, based on justice and peace. The Hebrew word *shalom* most accurately captures the notion of justice and peace that points to a particular harmony which will make weapons unnecessary. This vision of shalom makes caring for creation and humanity priorities that help us be the salt and light in the world that Jesus said His followers would be (Matthew 5:13–14).

Being a new creation in Christ moves us away from individual concerns and makes us aware that our world needs the kind of change that can only come from people changed by the power of Christ. The Apostle Paul allowed the power of his changed life to be used by God mightily as he spread the Good News throughout the Roman Empire. Because Paul's life was changed, God used him to change the lives of countless others as he established churches, helped leaders, and trained the next generation of leaders like Timothy, Titus, and Onesimus.

It always takes change to see things properly—the right kind of change, that comes from God. Changed lives know the value of praise. Lives that witness a new day are given the opportunity to make that praise known. "Praise the LORD. Praise the LORD from the heavens; praise him in the heights above. Praise him, all his angels; praise him, all his heavenly hosts" (Psalm 148:1–2, NIV).

Source:
Allen, Leslie. *Word Biblical Commentary*. Psalms 101-150. Waco, TX: Word Publisher, 1983.
Pleins, J. David. *The Social Vision of the Hebrew Bible*. Louisville, KY: Westminster John Knox Press, 2000.
Rogerson, J.W. "The Old Testament View of Nature." *Instruction and Interpretation: Studies in Hebrew Language, Palestinian Archaeology and Biblical Exegesis*. Leiden, the Netherlands: E.J. Brill, 1977.

Rev. Ricky A. Woods is the Senior Pastor of First Baptist Church West, the oldest Black Baptist church in Charlotte, North Carolina.

Kenneth B. Clark

1914-2005

Just as God raised up men and women of promise in the first century to speak for Him, the dark days of American history show that God also had some "called-out ones" during this period as well. In the middle and latter part of the 20th century, as an educator and psychologist, Dr. Kenneth B. Clark definitely walked in these shoes.

Kenneth was born in 1914 in the Panama Canal Zone to middle-class parents. He later moved with his mother to Harlem in New York City, where he attended public schools.

Dr. Kenneth Clark was the first African American to earn a doctorate in psychology at Columbia and to hold a permanent professorship at City College of New York. His wife, Mamie Phipps Clark, was also a first in her field, as the first African American woman and the second African American (after her husband) in Columbia University's history to receive a doctorate of psychology.

As a graduate student at Howard University, Mamie had been studying self-perception in Black children. While she was there, she met, married, and started collaborating with Kenneth. Both did the study showing that Black children preferred to play with White dolls over Black dolls. They concluded that this was because these children had a poor self-image.

Kenneth used this study in 1950 to show that school segregation not only marred the development of Black students, but White students as well. The Supreme Court cited these findings in the famous 1954 case of Brown v. Board of Education, declaring racial segregation in public schools unconstitutional.

At the time, Justice Earl Warren wrote that "separating Black children from White solely because of their race generates a feeling of inferiority as to their status in the community that may affect their hearts and minds in a way unlikely ever to be undone." Many of us still live with the effects of that separation and discrimination.

Kenneth and Mamie excelled in the field of psychology at a time when America was relying on inferior data to support segregation of public education. White psychologists posited that due to the mental inferiority of Black Americans, Black and White children should have "separate but equal education." However, Kenneth and Mamie's research challenged the notion of these mental differences, and their findings were used to knock down segregation laws.

According to Kenneth, American society had birthed, germinated, and enhanced this poor self-image by shutting Black people in ghettos and marginalizing them. Some of Dr. Kenneth Clark's thoughts on segregation and the American society include:

- "White and Blacks should be taught to respect their fellow human beings as an integral part of being educated."
- "A racist system inevitably destroys and damages human beings; it brutalizes and dehumanizes them, Blacks and Whites alike."
- From a 1984 *New York Times* interview: "I believed in the 1950s that a significant percentage of Americans were looking for a way out of the morass of segregation. It was wishful thinking."
- "It took me 10 to 15 years to realize that I seriously underestimated the depth and complexity of Northern racism. ...

In the South, you could use the courts to do away with separate toilets and all that nonsense. We haven't found a way of dealing with discrimination in the North."

Both Kenneth and Mamie felt that education was important in overcoming racism. At one point, Kenneth Clark fought for decentralizing New York City schools, but later deemed it a failure and declared that he had been wrong. Dr. Clark's published books include *Prejudice and Your Child* and *Dark Ghetto*. In 1961, he won the prestigious NAACP Spingarn Medal. He won the Four Freedoms Award in 1985.

Teaching Tips

December 4
Bible Study Guide 1

Words You Should Know

A. Espoused (Luke 1:27) *mnesteuo* (Gk.)—To become betrothed, promised to marry, engaged.

B. Salutation (v. 29) *aspasmos* (Gk.)—A greeting or welcome in person or by letter.

Teacher Preparation

Unifying Principle—Reliable Promises. Our actions, decisions, and even well-being are often based on our trust in the promises made by others. On whose promises can we ultimately depend? Luke recounts the angel's announcement of the coming birth of Jesus, God's promised Savior.

A. Meditate on how a lack of trust in people can affect someone.

B. Pray and ask God for empathy and insight regarding how His promises can heal wounded trust.

C. Complete Lesson 1 in the *Precepts For Living*® Personal Study Guide.

O—Open the Lesson

A. Begin the lesson with prayer.

B. Instruct students to write their opinion about trust and trusting on a sheet of paper to be revisited at the end of the session.

C. Read the Aim for Change and Keep in Mind verse.

D. Ask students to read the In Focus story silently and discuss as a group.

P—Present the Scriptures

A. Read the Scripture text.

B. Utilize the Search the Scripture questions to foster group discussion.

C. Pull out key points from the In Depth and Background sections to aid in the discussion.

E—Explore the Meaning

A. Complete Discuss the Meaning and Lesson in Our Society as a group.

B. Encourage the class to deliberate thoughtfully on the Make It Happen activity, using the written opinions about trust that were composed earlier. Allow adequate time for students to complete the section individually.

N—Next Steps for Application

A. Remind students how an excessive amount of distrust can lead to a hardened heart.

B. Close in prayer by having students silently meditate on the importance of trusting others by ultimately trusting in the promises of God.

Worship Guide

For the Superintendent or Teacher
Theme: God Promises a Savior
Song: "Standing on the Promises"
Devotional Reading: Isaiah 6:1–8

God Promises a Savior

Bible Background • LUKE 1:26–38
Printed Text • LUKE 1:26–38 | Devotional Reading • ISAIAH 6:1–8

—— Aim for Change ——

By the end of this lesson, we will: ACKNOWLEDGE God's faithfulness to Mary and ultimately to all His people; EXPERIENCE the joy of worshiping Jesus as God's promised Savior; and EXPRESS trust in God's promises by affirming His will for our lives.

In Focus

Thomas was a God-fearing man who wanted to have faith in something, but over the years, everything he put his trust in seemed to disappoint him. Thomas loved his first wife without question, but she died shortly after giving birth to their son. Soon afterward, he landed a new job and worked diligently, but after 15 years on the job, his company downsized and let him go. A few short years later, just two weeks before his expected graduation, Thomas' son revealed that he had actually dropped out of college the previous year.

No longer able to stomach the emotional roller coaster of believing in people, Thomas grew into a bitter and callous person. Thomas' second wife understood his heartache and knew that he loved her, but his lack of trust wore on their relationship. After reassuring Thomas of her devotion, she asked him if God had ever made him a promise. He replied, "To never leave me, and after all I've been through, that is the only thing I know to be true." "As long as you still trust in God, we have a fighting chance," responded his wife. "I made us an appointment with a counselor to work through the rest."

How do you deal with broken promises? In today's lesson we learn that when the broken promises of the world deplete us, God's promises will keep us.

—— Keep in Mind ——

"And, behold, thou shalt conceive in thy womb, and bring forth a son, and shalt call his name JESUS" (Luke 1:31).

"And, behold, thou shalt conceive in thy womb, and bring forth a son, and shalt call his name JESUS" (Luke 1:31).

Focal Verses

KJV Luke 1:26 And in the sixth month the angel Gabriel was sent from God unto a city of Galilee, named Nazareth,

27 To a virgin espoused to a man whose name was Joseph, of the house of David; and the virgin's name was Mary.

28 And the angel came in unto her, and said, Hail, thou that art highly favoured, the Lord is with thee: blessed art thou among women.

29 And when she saw him, she was troubled at his saying, and cast in her mind what manner of salutation this should be.

30 And the angel said unto her, Fear not, Mary: for thou hast found favour with God.

31 And, behold, thou shalt conceive in thy womb, and bring forth a son, and shalt call his name JESUS.

32 He shall be great, and shall be called the Son of the Highest: and the Lord God shall give unto him the throne of his father David:

33 And he shall reign over the house of Jacob for ever; and of his kingdom there shall be no end.

34 Then said Mary unto the angel, How shall this be, seeing I know not a man?

35 And the angel answered and said unto her, The Holy Ghost shall come upon thee, and the power of the Highest shall overshadow thee: therefore also that holy thing which shall be born of thee shall be called the Son of God.

36 And, behold, thy cousin Elisabeth, she hath also conceived a son in her old age: and this is the sixth month with her, who was called barren.

37 For with God nothing shall be impossible.

38 And Mary said, Behold the handmaid of the Lord; be it unto me according to thy word. And the angel departed from her.

NLT Luke 1:26 In the sixth month of Elizabeth's pregnancy, God sent the angel Gabriel to Nazareth, a village in Galilee,

27 to a virgin named Mary. She was engaged to be married to a man named Joseph, a descendant of King David.

28 Gabriel appeared to her and said, "Greetings, favored woman! The Lord is with you!"

29 Confused and disturbed, Mary tried to think what the angel could mean.

30 "Don't be afraid, Mary," the angel told her, "for you have found favor with God!

31 You will conceive and give birth to a son, and you will name him Jesus.

32 He will be very great and will be called the Son of the Most High. The Lord God will give him the throne of his ancestor David.

33 And he will reign over Israel forever; his Kingdom will never end!

34 Mary asked the angel, "But how can this happen? I am a virgin."

35 The angel replied, "The Holy Spirit will come upon you, and the power of the Most High will overshadow you. So the baby to be born will be holy, and he will be called the Son of God.

36 What's more, your relative Elizabeth has become pregnant in her old age! People used to say she was barren, but she has conceived a son and is now in her sixth month.

37 For the word of God will never fail."

38 Mary responded, "I am the Lord's servant. May everything you have said about me come true." And then the angel left her.

The People, Places, and Times

Nazareth. The Bible presents Nazareth as a very unimportant town aside from being the birthplace of Jesus. It is often described as a ghetto of sorts. Being located in Lower Galilee, it was not bustling with business, and the inhabitants were not held in high regard. One of Jesus' future disciples raises the question, "Can anything good come from Nazareth?" (John 1:46).

All four Gospels mention Nazareth in different contexts, though only ever in connection with Jesus. Matthew 2:23 highlights Jesus' association with Nazareth only as a fulfillment of prophecy. Luke points out that Joseph and Mary had to travel from Nazareth to Bethlehem, his hometown, to register for a census (2:3–4). Mark (1:9) mentions Nazareth during Jesus' baptism, and John presents Jesus via messianic fulfillment and home of origin (1:45).

Holy Spirit. Throughout the Bible the phrase "Holy Spirit" has a number of connotations and serves a number of purposes. In the Old Testament, the Holy Spirit is associated with God, as well as life and renewal (Psalm 51:11). The New Testament adds to the motif by not only presenting the Spirit or *pneuma* as the co-creator with Jesus Christ, but also as an advocate, helper, and mediator of prophetic gifts (John 14:16; 1 Corinthians 12:1–11). Furthermore, the manifestation of the Holy Spirit can have a variety of effects on a person. We see His presence associated with the ability to act outside of one's own abilities (Acts 2:4).

Background

The promise that Gabriel relayed to Mary on behalf of God is more than it appears at first reading. The promise is about the Davidic Messiah whom the Jews had been waiting for since the division of the Northern and Southern kingdoms—an heir to David's throne. The Old Testament prophets, who had foretold of a king, lived during periods of exile and oppression, and the savior they spoke of was one who would deliver them from their political bondage and physical disenfranchisement. All of them expected a messiah with attributes similar to David: military might, strong love for the Lord, and ability to lead the people. In the first century AD, not all Jews expected the Messiah to be a royal Messiah who would take up an earthly throne like David had, but because of the centrality of the prophetic tradition, many still hoped for such a Messiah who would overturn the corrupt political empire in their midst.

Mary and Joseph went to the Temple and followed the religious customs (Luke 2:21–41). Given the information we know, just by reading Scripture, Mary would have been familiar with Messianic prophecies of the anticipated Savior (Isaiah 7:14, 9:6–7, 11:1–5). Living under Roman occupation, Mary understood the implication of the throne of David being re-established, and according to Gabriel, it would soon be manifested through her womb (Luke 1:32). More than anything, the promise she was given carried not just spiritual implications, but this king was expected to regain control of the land, unify the people, and restore their relationship with God.

At-A-Glance

1. God's Messenger (Luke 1:26–29)
2. Favor (vv. 29–34)
3. What's More (vv. 35–38)

In Depth

1. God's Messenger (Luke 1:26–29)

The name Gabriel means "man of God." Gabriel appears to be a special messenger, and the word "angel" is a transliteration of the Greek *aggelos*, which means messenger. Gabriel appears in both the Old and New Testaments; he explains the vision of the ram and goat to Daniel (Daniel 8:15–27, 9:20–27) and announces the births of John the Baptist and Jesus.

Luke consistently uses angels as God's way of announcing, instructing, guiding and protecting (1:11, 26, 2:8–15; Acts 8:26, 12:7). In the Luke narrative, Gabriel not only delivers the news of the birth but can affirm and reassure Mary despite her doubts and questions. On assignment from God, Gabriel is dispatched with the express purpose of bringing good news. In earlier verses, he informs Zacharias that his prayers have been heard and his wife will give birth (Luke 1:11–20).

2. Favor (vv. 29–34)

Today the word "favor" is overused in Christian speech to denote partiality or preference from God. The biblical definition of favor differs from favoritism. It is not rooted in partiality or exclusivity, but in grace on the part of the giver by way of kindness.

Similar to an award ceremony, God has enough honor and grace for all of His people. Mary was the recipient of what some might consider the greatest honor among women, but it came with great cost. Although today we hold Mary in high esteem, she more than likely experienced a great deal of turmoil and backlash due to her out-of-wedlock pregnancy. We know for certain that she had to travel while pregnant and give birth in an unplanned way.

3. What's More (vv. 35–38)

Elisabeth's pregnancy is a significant revelation for Mary. The news that she will conceive elicits Mary's question: "But how can this happen? I am a virgin." The disclosure of Elisabeth's pregnancy is confirmation of the Holy Spirit's power and ability over the human womb. This revelation substantiates all the angel has said. If Elisabeth, who was old and barren, could conceive, then anything was possible. Elisabeth was familiar to Mary, and her life and hardships were real to her. If the Lord could favor Elisabeth, Mary believed she could receive favor, too.

Mary did not have any more questions once she heard of Elisabeth's pregnancy. She readily conceded and welcomed the will of God into her life. Later, Mary would go to visit her kin until it was near time for Elisabeth to give birth (vv. 39–56).

Search the Scriptures

1. A visit by an angel is most unusual, but it is not impossible. Have you ever thought that you had been visited by an angel?

2. Write the important truth that the angel Gabriel shares with Mary in verse 37. Reflect on how this truth guides your life.

Discuss the Meaning

1. The KJV and NLT have different readings of verse 37. What is the significance of each?

2. How do God's promises strengthen our faith?

Lesson in Our Society

It is important to remember that no matter what we experience in life, God has made fundamental promises to all of us that we can hold on to, such as "I will never leave thee nor forsake thee" (Hebrews 13:5) and "We know that all things work together for good to them that love God, to them who are the called according to his purpose" (Romans 8:28). Regardless, whether or not we have lost everything like Job, are seemingly barren like Elisabeth, or find ourselves in an unbelievable situation like Mary, Jesus is God's promised Savior on whom we can depend.

Make It Happen

Intentionally or not, at some point our trust is betrayed. How we are affected depends on several different factors. Consider your opinion of trust, the In Focus story, and today's lesson. How can we trust after experiencing disappointment so that our hearts do not become hardened, like Thomas' in the In Focus story?

Follow the Spirit

What God wants me to do:

_____

_____

_____

_____

Remember Your Thoughts

Special insights I have learned:

_____

_____

_____

_____

More Light on the Text

Luke 1:26–38

26 And in the sixth month the angel Gabriel was sent from God unto a city of Galilee, named Nazareth, 27 To a virgin espoused to a man whose name was Joseph, of the house of David; and the virgin's name was Mary.

The story of Mary and Joseph begins in the region of Galilee and the town of Nazareth, where Jesus would grow up. In Elisabeth's sixth month of pregnancy, God sent Gabriel to Mary to announce that she would miraculously bear a child who would be Israel's Messiah. Luke calls Nazareth a *polis* (Gk. **POE-lees**), which is often translated as "city," but it was a small "town" (NIV) or "village." Its relatively unimportant size contrasts with Jerusalem, where Gabriel's previous appearance to Zacharias had taken place at the Temple (v. 19). In the eighth century BC, Assyria captured Galilee, causing it to be associated with Gentiles, but as a Roman region in the first century AD, it had strong Jewish and Gentile presences. Due to its small population, it was unlikely that anyone in the Roman Empire, whether Jew or Gentile, expected much from this sleeping town (John 1:46). The city and its citizens were disparaged and the object of deep prejudice by the Jews. Yet God had a vessel, by the name of Mary, in this unlikely place. Here we learn an important lesson: God is not a respecter of persons or places. Therefore, we must refrain from our quickness to judge other places. God sent a message to a virgin (Gk. *parthenos*, **par-THEH-noce**) in Nazareth—Mary—as readily as He did to a priest in Jerusalem (Zacharias).

In the Greek translation of the Old Testament (commonly referred to as the Septuagint or LXX), *parthenos* means "girl," with chastity implied. Several verses stress chastity or virginity, such as Leviticus 21:13–14; Deuteronomy 22:15, 28–29; and 2 Samuel 13:2. It also is used in the New Testament with the same understanding (2 Corinthians 11:2; Revelation 14:4). When used in describing Mary, it meant that she had not yet had sexual relations. Mary's question in verse 34, and the reference in verse 27 to her being "espoused" or pledged to be married, make this clear. Since betrothal often took place soon after puberty, Mary might have been a young teenager. Betrothal was similar to an engagement, but it was legally binding, and to break it off was considered divorce (cf. Matthew 1:19). According to Jewish custom, only divorce or death could sever betrothal; and in the latter event, the girl, though unmarried, would be considered a widow. Mary had already committed to marry Joseph, but she had not had sexual relations with him. In the betrothal period, sexual contact was considered adultery and resulted in stoning.

The phrase "house of David" explains that the child would be born in David's line. David was Israel's greatest king, and God had promised him that his kingdom would be everlasting (2 Samuel 7:16). The everlasting kingdom of David is fulfilled in Jesus.

28 And the angel came in unto her, and said, Hail, thou that art highly favoured, the Lord is with thee: blessed art thou among women. 29 And when she saw him, she was troubled at his saying, and cast in her mind what manner of salutation this should be.

The angel greeted Mary and proclaimed that she was highly favored, or literally "having been much graced." "Highly favoured" translates the Greek word *charitoo* (**kha-ree-TOE-oh**), which has the same root as the words for "greetings" (*chairo*, **KHEYE-roh**, v. 28) and "grace" (*charis*, **KHAR-is**, v. 30). Mary is "highly favoured" because she is the recipient of God's grace. But Mary was troubled by the angel's words. The Greek word *diatarasso* (**dee-ah-tah-RAS-so**) means to be confused or greatly perplexed. In contrast to Zacharias, who doubted the angel's words and required some sign before he could believe, Mary was uncertain but did not express doubt. Her terror at the sudden appearance of the angel—who may have appeared to her as a young man clad in garments of a strange dazzling whiteness (cf. Matthew 28:3; Mark 16:5)—was not unfounded. Her confusion was natural considering the sudden, unexpected appearance of an angel and the weight of the message it conveyed. She did not understand how God could so greatly favor a person like herself. Mary probably never dreamed she was anyone special. How could she, so ordinary and humble, do anything special for God? That is the essence of grace. Mary's favor was only by the grace of God. God reversed the human expectations in Mary's situation, because He was willing to use the lowest in that time to be the bearer of a king. Today God continues to use the poor, powerless, helpless, and weak (2 Corinthians 12:9).

30 And the angel said unto her, Fear not, Mary: for thou hast found favour with God. 31 And, behold, thou shalt conceive in thy womb, and bring forth a son, and shalt call his name JESUS. 32 He shall be great, and shall be called the Son of the Highest: and the Lord God shall give unto him the throne of his father David: 33 And he shall reign over the house of Jacob for ever; and of his kingdom there shall be no end.

The specifics that Gabriel announces concerning the ministries of John the Baptist (Luke 1:13–17) and Jesus provide an interesting contrast. The mighty work God foretold He would do through John the Baptist's ministry would be surpassed by an even greater work through His Son's ministry. Whereas John would be "great in the sight of the Lord" (1:15), Jesus would be great without qualification (v. 32) and "called the Son of God" (v. 35). An even more important tie between the accounts is that the whole significance of John's ministry, as pointed out in verse 17, is found in his preparation for the One coming after him who was more powerful than he (3:16).

34 Then said Mary unto the angel, How shall this be, seeing I know not a man? 35 And the angel answered and said unto her, The Holy Ghost shall come upon thee, and the power of the Highest shall overshadow thee: therefore also that holy thing which

shall be born of thee shall be called the Son of God. 36 And, behold, thy cousin Elisabeth, she hath also conceived a son in her old age: and this is the sixth month with her, who was called barren. 37 For with God nothing shall be impossible.

Mary's question, "How shall this be?" probably arose from puzzlement rather than doubt or distrust. She did not ask for some sign or proof as Zacharias did (1:18), and her request was very different from Zacharias'. Hers stemmed from her faith; Zacharias' question stemmed from his lack of faith. She simply asked for more information. She was single and had never known a man sexually. How could she possibly bear a child? Mary's statement that she had not been with a man reveals the miraculous action of God that took place in Jesus' conception through the Holy Spirit. God's divine actions reveal that nothing is impossible for Him. If a woman can have a child despite not having any sexual relations, God can do anything.

To calm any lingering apprehensions that Mary might have had, the angel informed her of another seemingly impossible situation: Elisabeth's pregnancy in her old age. Elisabeth was in her sixth month of pregnancy, again bearing testimony to the fact that nothing is impossible with God. The actual Greek text says, "For with God no word shall be without power." The word translated as impossible is *adynateo* (**ah-doo-nah-TEH-oh**), which is a combination of *alpha* as a negative participle and *dunatos*, which means power, strength, ability, and, in this case, possibility. The translators of the KJV did not include a translation of the Greek word *rhema* (**RAY-ma**), in the original text. This simply means "word" or "thing" and could refer to the message God has sent as well as the events promised.

38 And Mary said, Behold the handmaid of the Lord; be it unto me according to thy word. And the angel departed from her.

Mary's response to the angel was that she was only a servant of the Lord, which reveals her humility, perhaps a reason she had been chosen to bear the Messiah of Israel. Mary was a servant of God and would follow His words. No one could have asked for, or given, any better response. Her attitude of servanthood recalls that of Hannah, who also calls herself the Lord's *doule* (**DOO-lay**), meaning "servant" (1 Samuel 1:11, LXX). Mary's servanthood consisted of a submission to God that characterizes genuine believers in Scripture and should characterize all believers today (cf. Luke 1:48).

How do we respond to God's words even when they seem impossible? Do we accept them with faith, remembering that we are His humble servants? Or do we reject them as impossible? Mary's trusting submission is a worthy example for believers today.

Say It Correctly

Espoused. eh-**SPOWS**-d.
Salutation. sal-you-**TAY**-shun.

Daily Bible Readings

MONDAY
Here Am I, Send Me
(Isaiah 6:1–8)

TUESDAY
Hannah's Womb Was Closed
(1 Samuel 1:1–11)

WEDNESDAY
I Asked Him of the Lord
(1 Samuel 1:15–20)

THURSDAY
Shall I Indeed Bear a Child?
(Genesis 18:9–15)

FRIDAY
Out of Nazareth
(John 1:43–46)

SATURDAY
A Young Woman Will Bear a Son
(Isaiah 7:10–14)

SUNDAY
Birth of Jesus Foretold
(Luke 1:26–38)

Notes

_____

_____

_____

_____

Teaching Tips

Words You Should Know

A. Soul (Luke 1:46) *psuche* (Gk.)—The self, life; the seat of affections and will.

B. Magnify (v. 46) *megaluno* (Gk.)—To make great or conspicuous; to esteem highly; to extol, laud, or celebrate.

Teacher Preparation

Unifying Principle—Expect Great Blessings. Receiving confirmation of pending good fortune is a joyful event. In such moments, how can we respond? Luke tells of Elisabeth's affirmation of God's promise of the Savior and Mary's joyful praise to God for being chosen as the bearer of that divine promise.

A. Read Luke 1–3 so that you understand today's passage in context.

B. Pray that your students will understand and receive God's Word as you teach.

C. Complete the companion lesson in the *Precepts For Living*® Personal Study Guide.

O—Open the Lesson

A. Open with prayer, thanking God that He blesses those whose hearts are humble before Him.

B. Read the Aim for Change out loud.

C. Ask for a volunteer to read the In Focus story.

P—Present the Scriptures

A. Ask for volunteers to read the Focal Verses and The People, Places, and Times. Discuss.

B. Read and discuss the Background section.

C. Use this information to help the students understand the context of today's lesson. Encourage students to ask questions.

E—Explore the Meaning

A. Review and discuss the Search the Scriptures and Discuss the Meaning questions and the Lesson in Our Society section.

B. Ask for a volunteer to read Make It Happen. Discuss.

N—Next Steps for Application

A. Instruct students to complete the Follow the Spirit and Remember Your Thoughts sections.

B. Remind students to read the Daily Bible Readings in preparation for next week's lesson.

C. Ask if there are any prayer needs, then close in prayer.

Worship Guide

For the Superintendent or Teacher
Theme: The Affirmation of the Promise
Song: "Joy to the World"
Devotional Reading: Psalm 111

The Affirmation of the Promise

Bible Background • LUKE 1:39–56
Printed Text • LUKE 1:39–56 | Devotional Reading • PSALM 111

—— Aim for Change ——

By the end of the lesson, we will: EXPLORE the ways Elisabeth and Mary celebrated God's promise of a Savior; FEEL thankful for the ways God is at work in the world; and creatively EXPRESS our confidence in God's promises.

—— In Focus ——

Carlee was discouraged. She was single and well into her 40s. Still she wanted a child. Carlee's prayer partner, Gina, told her there were children living in foster care who were longing for a family. Carlee wondered whether she would be able to adopt a child even though she was unmarried. She decided to do some research. She spent hours looking at children's pictures and reading about them online. When Carlee saw a picture of two African American boys ages 3 and 5, her heart skipped a beat. They seemed to be looking right into her eyes!

Carlee decided to spend a week praying for these children by name, and she asked God to confirm this desire that she believed He had placed in her heart. Gina prayed, too. At the end of the week, Carlee still was hesitant to contact social services, but when she opened her Bible, she had the answer. "So be strong and courageous! Do not be afraid and do not panic before them. For the LORD your God will personally go ahead of you. He will neither fail you nor abandon you" (Deuteronomy 31:6).

Gina celebrated when Carlee told her she had made the call. Later, she asked Gina about the verse. "Yes!" Gina said. "God promises to always be there to help His children. God promises that if we humbly ask him to forgive all of our sins, He will!" *We can react to God's promises with faith or skepticism, humility or pride. In today's lesson, we will learn about Mary's humble acceptance and joy at the promise of the coming Messiah.*

—— Keep in Mind ——

"And Mary said, My soul doth magnify the Lord, And my spirit hath rejoiced in God my Saviour" (Luke 1:46–47).

"And Mary said, My soul doth magnify the Lord, And my spirit hath rejoiced in God my Saviour" (Luke 1:46–47).

Focal Verses

KJV Luke 1:39 And Mary arose in those days, and went into the hill country with haste, into a city of Juda;

40 And entered into the house of Zacharias, and saluted Elisabeth.

41 And it came to pass, that, when Elisabeth heard the salutation of Mary, the babe leaped in her womb; and Elisabeth was filled with the Holy Ghost:

42 And she spake out with a loud voice, and said, Blessed art thou among women, and blessed is the fruit of thy womb.

43 And whence is this to me, that the mother of my Lord should come to me?

44 For, lo, as soon as the voice of thy salutation sounded in mine ears, the babe leaped in my womb for joy.

45 And blessed is she that believed: for there shall be a performance of those things which were told her from the Lord.

46 And Mary said, My soul doth magnify the Lord,

47 And my spirit hath rejoiced in God my Saviour.

48 For he hath regarded the low estate of his handmaiden: for, behold, from henceforth all generations shall call me blessed.

49 For he that is mighty hath done to me great things; and holy is his name.

50 And his mercy is on them that fear him from generation to generation.

51 He hath shewed strength with his arm; he hath scattered the proud in the imagination of their hearts.

52 He hath put down the mighty from their seats, and exalted them of low degree.

53 He hath filled the hungry with good things; and the rich he hath sent empty away.

54 He hath helped his servant Israel, in remembrance of his mercy;

NLT Luke 1:39 A few days later Mary hurried to the hill country of Judea, to the town

40 where Zechariah lived. She entered the house and greeted Elizabeth.

41 At the sound of Mary's greeting, Elizabeth's child leaped within her, and Elizabeth was filled with the Holy Spirit.

42 Elizabeth gave a glad cry and exclaimed to Mary, "God has blessed you above all women, and your child is blessed.

43 Why am I so honored, that the mother of my Lord should visit me?

44 When I heard your greeting, the baby in my womb jumped for joy.

45 You are blessed because you believed that the Lord would do what he said."

46 Mary responded, "Oh, how my soul praises the Lord.

47 How my spirit rejoices in God my Savior!

48 For he took notice of his lowly servant girl, and from now on all generations will call me blessed.

49 For the Mighty One is holy, and he has done great things for me.

50 He shows mercy from generation to generation to all who fear him.

51 His mighty arm has done tremendous things! He has scattered the proud and haughty ones.

52 He has brought down princes from their thrones and exalted the humble.

53 He has filled the hungry with good things and sent the rich away with empty hands.

54 He has helped his servant Israel and remembered to be merciful.

55 For he made this promise to our ancestors, to Abraham and his children forever."

56 Mary stayed with Elizabeth about three months and then went back to her own home.

55 As he spake to our fathers, to Abraham, and to his seed for ever.

56 And Mary abode with her about three months, and returned to her own house.

The People, Places, and Times

Luke. The authorship of the book of Luke is practically undisputed. While his name does not appear in the book, evidence in the book of Acts suggests that Luke, a physician and companion of the Apostle Paul, was the author of both books. Luke was likely a Gentile by birth and well educated in Greek culture. In his writing, Luke emphasized joy at the announcement of the Good News of the Gospel. He is also known for his concern for the role of women and his interest in the have-nots of his day. Major themes in this book include feeding the hungry and ministering to the poor.

Servanthood. In biblical days, servants did not have any rights. They were expected to do what they were told without any expectation of thanks, promotion, or gratitude. Mary's self-defined "low estate" (Luke 1:48) parallels the servant theme of Jesus that we see illustrated throughout the Gospels, as Jesus constantly took on the role of the humble servant. Mary's song, particularly in vv. 54–55, reflects the servant theology of the Old Testament, especially as seen in the "servant songs" of the prophet Isaiah (see Isaiah 42:1–4, 49:1–6, 50:4–9, 52:13–53:12). Isaiah's four servant songs are prophetic passages that identify the Messiah as the Servant of God, whose life of service is marked by suffering, pain, and humiliation. Jesus' final and ultimate act of servanthood—giving His life for ours—resulted in eternal life for those who believe. He is the fulfillment of the promise referenced in Luke 1:55.

Background

Mary's song in Luke 1:46–55 is known as the *Magnificat*, which is the first word in the Latin translation of the song. This beautiful song has become an enduring hymn of the church, sung by millions of Christians down through the ages to this very day. It is not just a song of thanksgiving, but has deep theological implications, prodding God's people to more fully understand His character. Among the topics addressed by this song are God's divine power (vv. 49, 51–52), holiness (vv. 49, 51–52), mercy (v. 50), and faithfulness (vv. 53–55).

This song was deeply rooted in the Scriptures of the Old Testament. It would not have been unusual for a pious Jew of this time period to have memorized many passages of Scripture, but it reflects well on Mary that she was apparently a pious and devout student of Scripture. The *Magnificat* also seems to be modeled after Hannah's prayer in 1 Samuel 2:1–10. Mary would have known of Hannah's prayer of thanksgiving to God for giving her a long-prayed-for son, Samuel. Both women's songs present God as a champion of the poor, weak, and humble.

Though Mary and Hannah's songs are similar, Mary's song has an added element of Messianic fulfillment. Mary clearly recognized that the child she was to bear was the long-awaited, promised Messiah, though at the time she could not have comprehended what this would mean in its entirety. Her song, which foreshadowed Jesus' ministry as described in the Gospel of Luke, is also prophetic in that it was composed under the inspiration of the Holy Spirit.

At-A-Glance

1. Mary Visits Elisabeth (Luke 1:39–45)
2. Mary's Song of Praise (vv. 46–56)

In Depth

1. Mary Visits Elisabeth (Luke 1:39–45)

Mary, filled with excitement and wonder at the angel's words, now hurried to visit her relative, Elisabeth. Though already related by blood, Mary and Elisabeth were now bound together in a common experience. Both women were to bear sons, but not just any sons—sons who were conceived under miraculous conditions. The births of these sons had been foretold and eagerly anticipated by the Jewish people for centuries!

Earlier, we learned that John was "filled with the Holy Spirit even from birth" (Luke 1:15). John was chosen by God to be the forerunner of Jesus the Messiah. Upon hearing Mary's greeting to Elisabeth, John, still in his mother's womb, leapt for joy at the recognition of Jesus' presence. The Holy Spirit also came upon Elisabeth, revealing to her that Mary was the mother of the long-expected Messiah. Elisabeth began to loudly bless and prophesy over Mary, counting herself unworthy to be in the presence of the mother of her Lord. She pronounced Mary blessed because Mary "believed that the Lord would do what He said" (v. 45).

2. Mary's Song of Praise (vv. 46–56)

In the midst of Mary and Elisabeth's joyous meeting, Mary's joy spilled over into a majestic song of praise. Her song began with glorifying God, then quickly moved to reveal her own state of humble awe. She marveled that God would choose someone in such a humble state and recognized that in the future, she would be blessed and honored because of God's hand in her life. People would recognize her as a common human being, touched by God's grace, and used in His divine plan.

Mary then sings about what we might term as an "upside-down" kind of justice: God scatters the proud in the plans of their hearts; He casts down the mighty and exalts the humble; and though He fills those who are hungry, He sends the haughty and rich away empty-handed. Jesus, Mary's unborn son, would soon bring a whole new outlook on what God desired in His people—humility, compassion for the poor and oppressed. In other words, they would be following and obeying God out of love, not obligation.

Search the Scriptures

1. What two things happened to Elisabeth when she heard Mary's greeting to her (Luke 1:41)? Why?

2. What did God do that was "merciful" and "helped Israel"? What was the "promise" (vv. 54–55)?

Discuss the Meaning

Both Elisabeth and Mary reacted with joy to the news of God's work in their lives. Though joy-filled, Mary's song also touched on challenging topics of social justice. How might believers today worship God with songs of praise while living lives that reflect His justice?

Lesson in Our Society

Even while living lives of thanksgiving for God's fulfillment of His promises in our lives, we sometimes neglect our responsibilities in His kingdom. Mary's song points us to three practical applications of our faith. First, we are to live in great humility. A life lived in total surrender to Christ is the death of pride. Secondly, we can cast aside the world's emphasis on social status. God is at work destroying the social strata of the world, humbling the proud and exalting the humble, so we cannot live by the world's standards. Lastly, Mary's song reminds us that God's economy is not the same as ours. In our society of extreme consumerism and materialism, let us hold our possessions lightly and be generous to others.

Make It Happen

When we are humble, like Mary, God will lift us up and give us a song to sing of His great works in our lives. This week, look for opportunities to praise God publicly for what He has done in your life, your family, or your community. Consciously search for ways you could bring His wonderful, "upside-down" justice into situations you encounter.

Follow the Spirit

What God wants me to do:

_____

_____

_____

_____

Remember Your Thoughts

Special insights I have learned:

_____

_____

_____

_____

More Light on the Text
Luke 1:39–56

The last section leaves us with the young virgin Mary, who was overwhelmed by two strange announcements. First, she would be the mother of the Savior, and second, her old cousin Elisabeth, who had passed the age of childbearing, was already six months pregnant. Because of this latter surprising announcement, Mary rushes to visit her cousin.

1:39 And Mary arose in those days, and went into the hill country with haste, into a city of Judah; 40 And entered into the house of Zacharias, and saluted Elisabeth.

Luke's use of the clause "and Mary arose in those days" seems to indicate that she took her journey immediately after the angel's visitation, probably one or two days later. That Mary took the trip fairly soon is apparent from the fact the angel Gabriel told her that Elisabeth was already six months pregnant (v. 36), and that Mary remained with Elisabeth for three months (v. 56). Mary returned home just before the birth of John (v. 57). The next clause "and went into the hill country with haste" also adds to the journey's urgency and immediacy. The word "haste," *spoude* (Gk. **spoo-DAY**), indicates a "speedy" dispatch and makes clear that she traveled immediately, adding excitement and a wondrous undertone to the story. Some commentators suggest that Mary went to Elisabeth because Joseph was about to put her away privately, or that she was being shunned by the inhabitants of Nazareth. However, this suggestion is baseless since her pregnancy was not evident before her travel, and Joseph and Mary had not started living together. The events recorded by Matthew (1:18–25) took place after her return from Elisabeth. By then, Mary would have been three months pregnant and beginning to show.

However, with excitement mixed with wonder and anxiety, Mary took the journey to see this miracle, which the angel had told her. She traveled from Nazareth in the north to a city in Judea. Some have suggested that the distance from Nazareth to Elisabeth and Zacharias' home was about 70 miles, and others suggest the journey took Mary between three and five days. This information and the city's name do not seem to matter much for Luke here, so he does not mention them. What is important to Luke here is what took place as Mary enters the house of Zacharias and greets Elisabeth.

41 And it came to pass that, when Elisabeth heard the salutation of Mary, the babe leaped in her womb; and Elisabeth was filled with the Holy Ghost

The Greek conjunction *hos* (**HOCE**) indicates a connection in time between two events, either at the same time or one right after the other. The underlying idea here is "as soon as" or "just as" Elisabeth heard Mary's greeting, a strange thing happened in her womb: the child inside "leaped" (Gk. *skirtao*, **skir-TAH-oh**, to jump). The word appears only two other times in the New Testament (v. 44 and 6:23) and is associated with joy. One can argue that it is natural for babies to move in the womb during the sixth month of pregnancy. Indeed, Elisabeth must have been experiencing such movements before now; however, she was able to differentiate this from other movements. This movement was extraordinary. The child, stirred by the power of the Holy Spirit, purposely revealed to Elisabeth the fulfillment of God's blessing and the prophecy of the Messiah. The child's leaping is the result of the "filling of the Holy Spirit." Both events definitely happened simultaneously. The angel told Zacharias that the child born to Elisabeth would be filled with the Holy Spirit from his mother's womb (v. 15). Elisabeth is also filled with the Holy Spirit in the same way that the Spirit of God filled some people in the Old Testament as they prophesied, e.g., King Saul (1 Samuel 11:6), Saul's messengers (1 Samuel 19:20), and David (2 Samuel 23:2). This filling of the Holy Spirit is temporary and for specific purposes. It differs from the outpouring and the filling of the Holy Spirit, which started at Pentecost (Acts 2). Here the Holy Spirit uses Elisabeth to confirm to Mary the angel's prediction to her.

42 And she spake out with a loud voice, and said, Blessed art thou among women, and blessed is the fruit of thy womb.

Filled with the Holy Spirit, Elisabeth responded with great excitement and exclaimed that Mary had been blessed among women, and that the child she carried was equally blessed. That she "spoke out with a loud voice" underlies the excitement. The statement "blessed art thou among women" echoes the angelic blessing from Gabriel (v. 28), and it means that Mary is the most blessed of all women. Her child is also blessed, which also echoes the angel's pronouncement concerning Jesus (vv. 32–33). Elisabeth's declaration through the Holy Spirit's power of blessings to both Mary and "the fruit of (her) womb" confirms to Mary that what God has spoken will surely happen. It also increases her faith and trust in God as the angel told her: "With God nothing is impossible" (v. 37). The added lesson is that God uses different agents to speak to us: the Holy Spirit, angels, and humans.

43 And whence is this to me, that the mother of my Lord should come to me? 44 For, lo, as soon as the voice of thy salutation sounded in mine ears, the babe leaped in my womb for joy.

The Holy Spirit also revealed to Elisabeth that this child born of Mary was the promised Messiah, hence she calls him "Lord." She is overwhelmed with excitement and joy, and she expresses her amazement by rhetorically asking, "Why should this happen to me?" Here Elisabeth recognizes that it was a special privilege to be visited by Mary, the mother of the Redeemer of Israel. She also recognizes that Mary has been conferred with a greater honor than her, and she is happy with her. The tone of her question is that of wonder, humility, and excitement; Elisabeth shows no sign of jealousy whatsoever. Her excitement was so apparent that Mary herself must have wondered what was happening, hence the explanation in verse 44 of the strange thing that happened within her womb.

45 And blessed is she that believed: for there shall be a performance of those things which were told her from the Lord.

Elisabeth praises Mary for her faith. This statement shows that Elisabeth is aware of God's prediction and promise to Mary. We are not told how she knew this. The natural view is that Mary might have told Elisabeth of how the angel had visited and of God's promises to her. However, the supernatural view is that the Holy Spirit, as continuation of His work, probably revealed it to Elisabeth. The word "blessed" is the Greek *makarios* (**mah-KAH-ee-os**), which can also be translated as happy or fortunate, and can be used to pronounce blessing upon a person. Here Elisabeth pronounces blessing on Mary because of Mary's faith in accepting the Word of God (cf. Psalm 1:1–2). Why is Mary happy? What does Elisabeth mean by the statement? We can look at this in three possible ways. The first way is to follow the New International Version translation, which states she is blessed because she believed what God promised to her will be accomplished. The second way is to follow the King James Version translation—that she is blessed because of the assurance that God will definitely accomplish

what He has spoken. Here is the premise for faith, and an urge to trust in God's faithfulness. He does not fail. Mary believed, so she is, and will be, happy. Finally, she is happy and blessed because she does not have to go through the same fate as Zacharias, who doubted God and became mute as a result (v. 20). Any of these three or a combination of all three could explain Elisabeth's pronouncement of blessing on Mary.

46 And Mary said, My soul doth magnify the Lord, 47 And my spirit hath rejoiced in God my Saviour.

Verses 46 to 55 constitute what is generally known as the Magnificat, or Mary's song. After Elisabeth had explained what happened when she heard Mary's greeting and how blessed Mary was, Mary praised God for what He had done. The song can be divided into three strophes (stanzas). The first strophe (vv. 46–49) speaks of God's grace or favor on Mary herself. The second strophe (vv. 50–53) talks about what God has done in the life of the people of Israel. The third strophe (vv. 54–55) is about God's faithfulness in keeping His promise to Abraham by sending the Messiah.

We first notice that Mary praises the Lord after Elisabeth, by the Holy Spirit, confirms what the angel had told her earlier. Overwhelmed with joy and gratitude, and accepting God's promise, Mary reacts spontaneously and glorifies God. These verses indicate a total involvement of the whole self (emotional and spiritual) in praising God. The use of both "soul" and "spirit" underlies this fact. The word "soul" is a translation of the Greek *psuche* (**psoo-KHAY**), which generally means breath or life. It is the center of and makes up the whole being. The soul is the seat of feelings, emotion, desire, and affection. The word "magnify" (Gk. *megaluno*, **meh-gah-LOO-no**) means to make great, extol, or esteem highly.

"Spirit" (Gk. *pneuma*, **PNEW-mah**) oftentimes is synonymous with soul, and also refers to breath of life (that which gives a being existence). Mary employs the totality of her being (the soul and spirit) to glorify God in grateful worship of her Savior.

48 For he hath regarded the low estate of his handmaiden: for, behold, from henceforth all generations shall call me blessed. 49 For he that is mighty hath done to me great things; and holy is his name.

In verses 48–49, Mary gives the reason for her rejoicing and gratitude—God "hath regarded the low estate of his handmaiden." This means that God had looked upon her with respect, showing favor to her who was otherwise insignificant. Mary calls herself God's "handmaiden" (Gk. *doule*, **DOO-lay**), which means female slave—the lowest position one can have in Greco-Roman culture. Women and slaves were regarded as the lowest class in the Ancient Near East, and they were often relegated to the background, the place of dishonor. To be both (woman and slave) makes her place even worse; society has no regard for her. In contrast, God has regard for her. He has looked on her with favor, and given her a place of honor. The magnitude and extent of her elevation is brought to bear in the person who made it possible, the "mighty" and the "holy" (v. 49). Here Mary brings out what systematic theologians call the immutable (i.e., unchangeable) and incommunicable attributes of God— His omnipotence and holiness. Here we see God, who is so mighty and holy on one hand, is able to look upon and have regard for Mary, who, on the other hand, is of the lowest class. Her low estate is not only because of her person, but also her heritage—Nazareth. Nazareth was one of the most insignificant and despised villages in Galilee (cf. John 1:45–46). In spite of these seeming disadvantages, God exalted

and honored Mary. She has been tremendously blessed by God, she says. For "all generations shall call me blessed," which means every generation will acknowledge her as one blessed and most fortunate woman among all women (cf. vv. 28, 42). We have seen that the first strophe deals with God's blessing to Mary. She now turns to sing about what God has done in the life of the people of Israel (vv. 50–53).

50 And his mercy is on them that fear him from generation to generation.

The beginning "and his" connects us to the previous subject and refers us to God respectively. Here Mary brings to bear God's merciful attribute, His consistency, and His faithfulness. Here she celebrates God's mercy on all those who "fear" (Gk. *phobeo*, **foe-BEH-oh**) Him, which are those who venerate or revere Him. The fear of God is verifiable by the people's obedience and keeping His Law. God's mercy is accorded specifically to the people of Israel in keeping with His promises, which started with Abraham (Genesis 17:7, 18:18, 22:17). The display of God's strength and power demonstrates this mercy (vv. 51–53).

51 He hath shewed strength with his arm; he hath scattered the proud in the imagination of their hearts. 52 He hath put down the mighty from their seats, and exalted them of low degree. 53 He hath filled the hungry with good things; and the rich he hath sent empty away.

These two pairs of contrasting parallels are the direct results of God's mighty act in the coming of the Messiah. By His show of strength, God has completely altered the human view of life in general. The "proud" (Gk. *huperephanos*, **hoo-pair-AY-fa-noce**), the haughty, or those who exalt themselves, are scattered. The verb "scattered" (Gk. *diaskorpizo*, **dee-ah-skor-PEED-zo**) is used figuratively here in either a military or agricultural sense. In its military sense, the strong, proud army that relies in its own strength without God is brought to nothing, driven and dispersed by a stronger force. In its agricultural sense, scattering refers to the winnowing process, where the chaff is separated from the wheat and blown away.

Not only are the proud scattered like chaff or put in disarray like an egoistic army, but God has also "put down the mighty from their seats." Here the mighty are synonymous with the proud—the "powers that be," the oppressors of the poor, the self-exalted who look down on and tyrannize others. The mighty are deprived of their self-exalted positions, while those who are truly humble ("them of low degree"), the insignificant, are exalted.

The next pair of parallels starts with the insignificant, "the hungry," which is synonymous with "them of low degree," and associated with poverty. Those who "fear Him" (v. 50) are fed (that is, "filled with good things") and shown mercy (v. 50). On the contrary, those who are "rich," proud, and self-sufficient without God, are sent "away empty." This is revolutionary indeed. It describes the purpose of Christ's coming into the world: to change the human view and principles of living. Christ spells out this principle in His Sermon on the Mount (especially Matthew 5:3–6), and He teaches the same to His disciples (Matthew 23:12; Luke 18:14).

Here Mary praises God's transformation of society, whereby the proud and powerful are brought low, while the lowly are brought up. Not only do Mary and Elisabeth represent the humble who have been exalted, but Nazareth signifies the revolutionary aspect of God's act through the coming of the Messiah. Historically, the Old Testament is full of examples of the proud and mighty whom God, by His infinite power and design, brought down: Pharaoh (Exodus 15:1–11), Haman (Esther 6:6–7:10), Nebuchadnezzar (Daniel 4:24–37), and other proud and haughty people (1 Peter 5:5; James 4:6). Similar examples of the humble being exalted by God are abundant: Joseph (Genesis 41:38–45), David (1 Samuel 18; 2 Samuel 7), Mordecai (Esther 6:6–14), Daniel (Daniel 1:8–21), and all the humble (Matthew 23:12).

54 He hath helped his servant Israel, in remembrance of his mercy; 55 As he spake to our fathers, to Abraham, and to his seed for ever. 56 And Mary abode with her about three months, and returned to her own house.

The third strophe of Mary's hymn reveals God's faithfulness in fulfilling His promises to Abraham by sending the Messiah. Here Mary celebrates God's mercy to Israel. Just as He promised Abraham and his descendants, God helps Israel, not forgetting His promise but remembering His mercy. This act of mercy is an old promise (covenant) God made to Abraham and all his generations after him. It is a living covenant to all humankind that is fulfilled in the incarnation of Jesus Christ—the Son of God.

Through this hymn of praise, Mary reveals the excellent nature of God: His divine power and authority over all things both spiritual and human (vv. 49, 51); His holiness (v. 49); His mercy and justice (v. 50); and His faithfulness and trustworthiness in fulfilling His promises (vv. 54–55). Through the incarnation of Christ, we realize the omnipotence, holiness, mercy, justice, and faithfulness of God. After this, Luke notes that Mary lived with Elisabeth and Zacharias for three more months. This was enough time to witness the birth of John. She remained to see the fulfillment of what God did in Elisabeth's life.

Say It Correctly

Patriarch. **PAY**-tree-ark.
Swaddling. **SWAD**-ling.

Daily Bible Readings

MONDAY
Holy and Awesome Is His Name
(Psalm 111)

TUESDAY
Faithfulness, Righteousness, and Justice
(Psalm 89:1-6, 14)

WEDNESDAY
God's Covenant with Abraham
(Genesis 17:1-8)

THURSDAY
Gideon Responds to God's Call
(Judges 6:12-18)

FRIDAY
Hannah Praises God
(1 Samuel 2:1-10)

SATURDAY
The Promised House for David
(2 Samuel 7:11b-17)

SUNDAY
Mary and Elizabeth Praise God Together
(Luke 1:39-56)

Notes

_____

_____

_____

_____

Teaching Tips

Words You Should Know

A. Great (Luke 1:15) *megas* (Gk.)—Eminent for ability, virtue, authority, power.

B. Season (v. 20) *kairos* (Gk.)—Due measure; a fixed and definite time, the time when things are brought to crisis, the decisive epoch waited for; the right time.

Teacher Preparation

Unifying Principle—Great Expectations. At times we are entrusted with incredible responsibilities beyond anything we might have imagined for ourselves. How might we respond? Luke tells of Zacharias' growing acceptance of his role as father of John, the one called to be the forerunner of the Savior.

A. Read the Bible Background and Devotional Readings.

B. Complete Lesson 3 in the *Precepts For Living®* Personal Study Guide.

O—Open the Lesson

A. Open with prayer, asking God to give your class "great expectations" of what they can learn from God's Word today.

B. Have students read Aim for Change in unison.

C. Ask for a volunteer to read the In Focus story.

P—Present the Scriptures

A. Ask for volunteers to read the Focal Verses and The People, Places, and Times. Discuss.

B. Read and discuss the Background section. Ask if there are questions and give clarification if needed.

E—Explore the Meaning

A. Review and discuss the Search the Scriptures and Discuss the Meaning questions and the Lesson in Our Society section.

B. Ask students to share the most significant point they learned and how to use that point this week in their everyday lives.

N—Next Steps for Application

A. Complete the Follow the Spirit and Remember Your Thoughts sections.

B. Remind students to read the Daily Bible Readings in preparation for next week's lesson.

C. Close in prayer, asking God to speak to those who are listening for His voice.

Worship Guide

For the Superintendent or Teacher
Theme: The Forerunner of the Savior
Song: "My Faith Looks Up to Thee"
Devotional Reading: John 1:19–23

The Forerunner of the Savior

Bible Background • LUKE 1:1–23, 57–66
Printed Text • LUKE 1:8–20 | Devotional Reading • JOHN 1:19–23

—————————— Aim for Change ——————————

By the end of the lesson, we will: REVIEW Zacharias' role in the story of the birth of John; IDENTIFY with Zacharias' feelings of doubt and apprehension; and ACCEPT and FULFILL the tasks to which God has called us.

—————————— In Focus ——————————

On the way home from work, Devon prayed about how he would break the news of his transfer to another state. *I'm not sure how I'm going to tell Brenda this*, he thought. He and Brenda would have to move, or Devon would need to find a new job.

Though Brenda usually dealt with the unexpected gracefully, she was upset at the thought of moving away from family and friends. Moving across the country was not quite what she had had in mind when she prayed that God would use her and her husband!

However, she and Devon prayed about the decision and agreed to put their house up for sale. The housing market wasn't great in their area, but they asked God to show them if it was His will for them to move or to stay. Their house sold in three days, when most houses were taking a month or two to sell. "I think God has given us our answer," Devon said. So in obedience, they prepared to move.

After arriving in their new community, Devon and Brenda began to understand why God had moved them. Because of their backgrounds and skill sets, both of them were immediately able to join together in ministry in ways that were totally unexpected and fulfilling.

In today's lesson, we will learn how God answered Zacharias' prayers in a powerful and unusual way. Have you ever witnessed God answering your prayers in a powerful and unusual way?

—————————— Keep in Mind ——————————

"Thy wife Elisabeth shall bear thee a son, and thou shalt call his name John. And thou shalt have joy and gladness; and many shall rejoice at his birth" (from Luke 1:13–14).

"Thy wife Elisabeth shall bear thee a son, and thou shalt call his name John. And thou shalt have joy and gladness; and many shall rejoice at his birth" (from Luke 1:13–14).

Focal Verses

KJV **Luke 1:8** And it came to pass, that while he executed the priest's office before God in the order of his course,

9 According to the custom of the priest's office, his lot was to burn incense when he went into the temple of the Lord.

10 And the whole multitude of the people were praying without at the time of incense.

11 And there appeared unto him an angel of the Lord standing on the right side of the altar of incense.

12 And when Zacharias saw him, he was troubled, and fear fell upon him.

13 But the angel said unto him, Fear not, Zacharias: for thy prayer is heard; and thy wife Elisabeth shall bear thee a son, and thou shalt call his name John.

14 And thou shalt have joy and gladness; and many shall rejoice at his birth.

15 For he shall be great in the sight of the Lord, and shall drink neither wine nor strong drink; and he shall be filled with the Holy Ghost, even from his mother's womb.

16 And many of the children of Israel shall he turn to the Lord their God.

17 And he shall go before him in the spirit and power of Elias, to turn the hearts of the fathers to the children, and the disobedient to the wisdom of the just; to make ready a people prepared for the Lord.

18 And Zacharias said unto the angel, Whereby shall I know this? for I am an old man, and my wife well stricken in years.

19 And the angel answering said unto him, I am Gabriel, that stand in the presence of God; and am sent to speak unto thee, and to shew thee these glad tidings.

20 And, behold, thou shalt be dumb, and not able to speak, until the day that these things shall be performed, because thou believest

NLT **Luke 1:8** One day Zechariah was serving God in the Temple, for his order was on duty that week.

9 As was the custom of the priests, he was chosen by lot to enter the sanctuary of the Lord and burn incense.

10 While the incense was being burned, a great crowd stood outside, praying.

11 While Zechariah was in the sanctuary, an angel of the Lord appeared to him, standing to the right of the incense altar.

12 Zechariah was shaken and overwhelmed with fear when he saw him.

13 But the angel said, "Don't be afraid, Zechariah! God has heard your prayer. Your wife, Elizabeth, will give you a son, and you are to name him John.

14 You will have great joy and gladness, and many will rejoice at his birth,

15 for he will be great in the eyes of the Lord. He must never touch wine or other alcoholic drinks. He will be filled with the Holy Spirit, even before his birth.

16 And he will turn many Israelites to the Lord their God.

17 He will be a man with the spirit and power of Elijah. He will prepare the people for the coming of the Lord. He will turn the hearts of the fathers to their children, and he will cause those who are rebellious to accept the wisdom of the godly."

18 Zechariah said to the angel, "How can I be sure this will happen? I'm an old man now, and my wife is also well along in years."

19 Then the angel said, "I am Gabriel! I stand in the very presence of God. It was he who sent me to bring you this good news!

20 But now, since you didn't believe what I said, you will be silent and unable to speak until the child is born. For my words will certainly be fulfilled at the proper time."

not my words, which shall be fulfilled in their season.

The People, Places, and Times

Elisabeth. Priests could marry only a woman of pure Jewish lineage, with preference toward descendants of Aaron. Zacharias' wife Elisabeth met both qualifications. Nevertheless, Zacharias and Elisabeth lived in shame because they were unable to have children. In ancient times, to be barren was a tragedy. A childless couple would have no one to support them in their old age, but worse than that, barrenness was often considered a curse or divine judgment for sin. To nullify the idea that their barrenness was a result of God's judgment on Elisabeth, Luke clearly points out that both Zacharias and Elisabeth were "upright" and "blameless" in their relationship with God (Luke 1:6).

The Nazirite Vow. In Numbers 6:1–21, God delineated a special vow called the Nazirite vow. This was a vow of separation to God and involved consecrating oneself for a specific amount of time of special devotion to God. A person under the constraint of a Nazirite vow was prohibited from drinking any wine or other fermented drink. The Nazirite was also prohibited from eating or drinking anything that came from the grapevine—grapes, raisins, grape juice, and even the seeds and skins of grapes.

Nazirites were also prohibited from using a razor (i.e., cutting their hair) for the duration of their vow, and they could not go near a dead body. They were expected to be entirely devoted to God. At the completion of the vow, Nazirites went through a prescribed ceremony where they presented specific offerings to God.

Though taking a Nazirite vow was usually voluntary, the Bible includes instances where people were apparently chosen by God to be Nazirites for life. Among these are Samson (see Judges 13:2–5), Samuel (see 1 Samuel 1:11), and John the Baptist (Luke 1:15).

Background

According to God's instructions, every male who was directly descended from Aaron was automatically a priest (see Exodus 28:1; Leviticus 8). Because of this, there were many more priests than there were jobs for them to do. The priests were divided into 12 divisions according to their lineage. Every priest would serve during the special holy days such as Passover, Pentecost, or the Feast of Tabernacles, but other than that, each division served two periods of one week each. The priests would draw lots to see who would serve each week. Priests who loved God and loved serving Him considered it the highlight of their life to be chosen to serve for a week. Within each division of nearly one thousand priests, the daily duties were also determined by lot. Daily duties included offering the morning or evening sacrifice for the nation of Israel, other assorted offerings of flour and oil, drink offerings, and burning incense. The purpose of burning incense was so that the sacrifices would ascend to God surrounded with a sweet smell that would please Him. Burning incense was an especially desired duty, and many priests were never selected for this duty in their entire lives of service.

The incense would have been burned at the altar of incense (see Exodus 30:1–10) inside the Temple in the Court of Priests, alternately called the Holy Place. Pious Jews would pray outside in an outer court called the Court of the Israelites, watching for the smoke that would symbolize their prayers rising to God. After burning the incense to conclude the evening sacrifice, the priest would traditionally come out and bless the waiting crowd.

At-A-Glance

1. The Chance of a Lifetime (Luke 1:8–10)
2. Visitation from an Angel (vv. 11–20)

In Depth

1. The Chance of a Lifetime (Luke 1:8–10)

Zacharias was a priest of God from the division that had descended from Aaron through the line of Abijah (see 1 Chronicles 24:5–19, esp. v. 10). He had not only been chosen to serve for his division's week, but also chosen to offer the incense! This was a day that any priest would have dreamed of.

Zacharias entered the Holy Place and began to pray near the heated altar of incense. The Bible does not say that Zacharias was praying for his own needs during this time. Perhaps he was praying for the coming of the Messiah, a prayer that was often prayed and the answer longed for. All people of Israel were constantly waiting in eager expectation for their Deliverer to come. Even now, as Zacharias interceded for the Jewish nation, they were outside mingling their prayers with his.

2. Visitation from an Angel (vv. 11–20)

As Zacharias ministered before the Lord, an angel suddenly appeared to him and assured him that his prayers had been heard. God was going to send the Messiah! The personal prayers of Zacharias' heart were answered, too. He would become the father of a son—but not just any son. Zacharias' son would be a prophet, a Nazirite, a forerunner of the Messiah! Zacharias was instructed to name his son John, meaning "God is gracious." This unexpected son, filled with and empowered by the Holy Spirit from birth, was destined to play an enormous role in God's plan of salvation and would bring joy to many.

But Zacharias responded in fear and disbelief. He asked for proof that what the angel said would truly come to pass. Gabriel, the angel, offered him the "proof" that the message was true because it came directly from God. How could it be anything but truth if God said it? Furthermore, because of Zacharias' disbelief, he would not be able to speak at all until the child was born.

Search the Scriptures

1. Why would many people rejoice at John's birth (Luke 1:14–15)?
2. What does it mean that John will "go before [the Lord] in the spirit and power of [Elijah]" (vv. 17)?

Discuss the Meaning

Zacharias' request for proof from the angel contrasts sharply with Mary's request for details. Though as humans we tend toward skepticism, how might we more fully trust God's promises and joyfully express our realization of His activity in our lives?

Lesson in Our Society

No doubt in a daze, Zacharias silently finished his memorable week of service and went home. Elisabeth conceived a child, and Zacharias got the proof he had been seeking. It is noteworthy that Zacharias heard from God while he was in the Temple worshiping and serving God. He had placed himself in a position to hear from God. When we spend time in God's presence, we open up the door of communication. God speaks to those who listen for His voice.

Make It Happen

Despite our limitations, we know that God has the power to do anything He wants to do, whenever He wants to do it—and He sometimes uses extraordinary means to fulfill His purposes. This can be both scary and exciting. This week, put aside your skepticism and fear. Ask God to do whatever He wants to do in and through you. Expect great things!

Follow the Spirit

What God wants me to do:

_____

_____

_____

_____

Remember Your Thoughts

Special insights I have learned:

_____

_____

_____

_____

More Light on the Text

Luke 1:8–20

8 And it came to pass, that while he executed the priest's office before God in the order of his course, 9 According to the custom of the priest's office, his lot was to burn incense when he went into the temple of the Lord 10 And the whole multitude of the people were praying without at the time of incense.

After all his introductions, Luke uses verses 8–10 to describe the setting for the following story. The angel's appearance, Zacharias' response, and the angel's message all happened while "the course of Abia" (the division in which Zacharias served, v. 5) was engaged in its scheduled turn of Temple service.

Fortunately for Zacharias, he was assigned to perform the particular service of burning incense. Given the number of priests serving in each of the twenty-four divisions, and given that only one priest was required to offer incense at the daily sacrifices, this was a once-in-a-lifetime privilege for Zacharias. Moreover, it afforded him the opportunity to go into the Temple sanctuary (v. 9; Gk. *naos*, **nah-OSE**), which was comprised of the Holy Place and the Holy of Holies, as opposed to the entire Temple complex (cf. Luke 2:27, 37, 46; Gk. *hieron*, **hee-eh-RON**). Few priests were ever afforded this privilege. Because of the large number of priests, no ordinary priest was allowed to burn incense more than once in a lifetime. Consequently, this was the high point of Zacharias' priestly career.

11 And there appeared unto him an angel of the Lord standing on the right side of the altar of incense.

The phrase "an angel of the Lord" is used here from its Old Testament context to refer to a special messenger sent by God to announce an important event (Genesis 16, 22, 31; Exodus 3).

Luke further says that the angel was "standing on the right side of the altar of incense." To stand or be placed on the right side of someone or something suggests being favored (e.g., Matthew 25:34). In other words, the right side is the favored side—the side of joy, happiness, and salvation. Here, when the angel of the Lord appeared "on the right side of the altar of incense," he was positioned to announce a blessing and bestow a favor upon the one who witnessed his appearance.

12 And when Zacharias saw him, he was troubled, and fear fell upon him.

When Zacharias saw the angel of the Lord, "he was troubled." Luke uses the Greek word *tarasso* (**tah-RAS-so**), which—when used in reference to people—expresses uneasiness mixed with fear, even to the point of shaking. Thus Luke adds, "and fear fell on him." The New International Version translates this passage as "he was startled and was gripped with fear." Fear like this is the normal reaction of those who experience the supernatural presence of God.

13 But the angel said unto him, Fear not, Zacharias: for thy prayer is heard; and thy wife Elisabeth shall bear thee a son, and thou shalt call his name John.

Throughout the Bible, "fear not" is a common statement of reassurance upon witnessing or experiencing the supernatural activity and presence of God (see Genesis 15:1; Mark 5:36; Luke 1:30; Revelation 1:17).

The basis for the angel's words of reassurance is the good news that Zacharias' prayer has been heard. Exactly what Zacharias had been praying for is not clear. It is likely that he was praying for children. Luke is sure to set up (v. 7) that Zacharias and his wife, Elisabeth, are childless and beyond child-bearing age. It makes the angel's words more easily understood: "Your prayer [to have a baby] is answered: Elisabeth will have a baby."

Zacharias might also have been praying for the salvation of Israel. Thus the angel's declaration and instruction that "Elisabeth shall bear thee a son, and thou shalt call his name John" was enough to let Zacharias know that his son-to-be would, in some way, be involved in Israel's salvation.

In the social culture of Zacharias' day, the customary privilege was for the father to name his son. In this instance, the name John is divinely provided and therefore has significant meaning: "Jehovah has been gracious." Because of the Lord's grace, John's birth will bring heavenly and eternal joy, so the following verse is an affirmation.

14 And thou shalt have joy and gladness; and many shall rejoice at his birth.

This verse points to a special kind of joy that will come to Zacharias and Elisabeth, and then spread to many. Luke uses three words in connection with John's birth to describe this special kind of joy: *chara* (**khah-RAH**), translated "joy"; *agalliasis* (**ah-gall-LEE-ah-sees**), translated "gladness;" and *chairo* (**KHEYE-ro**), which is a verb used for the act of expressing joy. Luke wants his readers to know that God will do a special work through Zacharias and Elisabeth's son, John, that will benefit many in Israel. God will involve John in a plan for saving people.

15 For he shall be great in the sight of the Lord, and shall drink neither wine nor strong drink; and he shall be filled with the Holy Ghost, even from his mother's womb. 16 And many of the children of Israel shall he turn to the Lord their God. 17 And he shall go before him in the spirit and power of Elias, to turn the hearts of the fathers to the children, and the disobedient to the wisdom of the just; to make ready a people prepared for the Lord.

The angel prophesies of John's destiny. He will be a great man; note that he will be great in the sight of the Lord, not necessarily other people. John would also be restricted from drinking wine or any alcohol, similar to the lifelong Nazirite vow of Samson (Judges 13:4–5, 7). He would also be filled with the Holy Spirit from his mother's womb.

This greatness would be the result of his life mission. John would turn many of the Children of Israel to the Lord. Next, the angel paraphrases Malachi 4:5–6 in describing John's mission: he would be the forerunner of the new exodus as prophesied by Isaiah (40:1–5). John's role was to "make ready a people prepared for the Lord." The word for "make ready" (Gk. *het-oimazo*, **heh-toy-MAHD-zoh**) that Luke uses here is only used in the New Testament in an ethical or religious sense. John's life and message would be used to prepare the people spiritually for this new exodus.

18 And Zacharias said unto the angel, Whereby shall I know this? for I am an old man, and my wife well stricken in years. 19 And the angel answering said unto him, I am Gabriel, that stand in the presence of God; and am sent to speak unto thee, and to shew thee these glad tidings. 20 And, behold, thou shalt be dumb, and not able to speak, until the day that these things shall be performed, because thou believest not my words, which shall be fulfilled in their season.

Zacharias does not believe the angel's words. Similar to Abraham before him, he asks for confirmation (Genesis 15:8). The angel gives his qualifications as a messenger of God, but he also delivers some bad news: Zacharias would become mute until the birth of John, a sign that confirms the promise but also rebukes Zacharias' lack of faith.

Say It Correctly

Nazirite. **NA**-zur-ite.
Jehovah. juh-**HOE**-vah.

Daily Bible Readings

MONDAY
Aaron and Sons, a Perpetual Priesthood
(Exodus 40:12–25)

TUESDAY
Tending the Altar of Incense
(Exodus 30:1–10)

WEDNESDAY
Chosen by Lot to Serve
(Acts 1:21–26)

THURSDAY
Zacharias and Elisabeth Are Childless
(Luke 1:5–7)

FRIDAY
His Name is John
(Luke 1:57–66)

SATURDAY
Testimony of John the Baptist
(John 1:19–23)

SUNDAY
Birth of John the Baptist Foretold
(Luke 1:8–20)

Teaching Tips

December 25
Bible Study Guide 4

Words You Should Know

A. The city of David (Luke 2:11) *polis Dauid* (Gk.)—The name frequently given to the part of Jerusalem built on Mount Zion.

B. Swaddling clothes (v. 12) *sparganoo* (Gk.)— To wrap an infant up in pieces of cloth.

Teacher Preparation

Unifying Principle—Joyous News! Everyone looks for reasons to rejoice. But how can we rejoice in the midst of all that life brings? The shepherds, whose lives were hard, received an announcement of God's fulfilled promise of the Messiah and declared their joy to all.

A. Read the Focal Verses and Luke 1–2 to become familiar with the context of this lesson.

B. Read the Daily Bible Readings as part of your daily devotions. Meditate on these verses, allowing God to reveal eternal truths to your heart concerning this week's lesson.

C. Review the information in The People, Places, and Times; Background; and In Depth sections to gain further insight for the lesson.

O—Open the Lesson

A. Open with prayer using the Aim for Change objectives.

B. Share your testimony.

C. Summarize the In Focus story and discuss the importance of sharing the Good News with others.

D. Discuss how Christians are equipped and called to share the Good News.

P—Present the Scriptures

A. Have volunteers read the Focal Verses.

B. Use The People, Places, and Times; Background; At-A-Glance outline; In Depth; and More Light on the Text to clarify the verses.

E—Explore the Meaning

A. Review and discuss Search the Scriptures, the Discuss the Meaning questions, and Lesson in Our Society section.

B. Ask students to share the most significant point they learned and how to use it this week.

N—Next Steps for Application

A. Complete the Make It Happen, Follow the Spirit, and Remember Your Thoughts sections.

B. Remind students to read the Daily Bible Readings in preparation for next week's lesson.

C. Close in prayer, thanking God for His presence in our lives.

Worship Guide

For the Superintendent or Teacher
Theme: The Savior Has Been Born
Song: "Go Tell It on the Mountain"
Devotional Reading: Luke 2:1–7

The Savior Has Been Born

Bible Background • LUKE 2:1–21
Printed Text • LUKE 2:8–20 | Devotional Reading • LUKE 2:1–7

Aim for Change

By the end of this lesson, we will: INVESTIGATE the circumstances around Jesus' birth and people's responses; EXPRESS joy at the Good News of God's fulfilled promise; and TELL someone about the Good News of God's gift of the Messiah.

 In Focus

Sheri and her coworkers were at the lunch table. One of them asked, "Sheri, how do you get the courage to make it every day with four children and no husband?"

Sheri smiled and replied. "Every morning, the first thing I do when I get up is thank God for another day. I have devotions with my children and tell them the Good News of Jesus. We may not have all the luxuries other people have, but there is one thing we do have: faith in knowing God supplies for all our needs."

Her coworkers stared at her in amazement and inquired, "Aren't you afraid of things getting worse?"

Sheri laughed. "Well, some days are better than others, and I remember when things were worse! Five years ago, I was homeless and eating in a soup kitchen. Now, I have a good job, and a beautiful home, and I volunteer my services on the weekends at the soup kitchen. God promised He would take care of me and my family, and He kept His promise! For that, I am forever grateful!"

Her coworkers were touched by her unshakable faith in God. One of them even came and asked her questions about Christ later on that day.

During this season, many people find it hard to rejoice. As Christians, we can be grateful for a God that keeps His promises. Where do you find joy during this Christmas season?

Keep in Mind

"For unto you is born this day in the city of David a Saviour, which is Christ the Lord" (Luke 2:11).

"For unto you is born this day in the city of David a Saviour, which is Christ the Lord" (Luke 2:11).

Focal Verses

KJV **Luke 2:8** And there were in the same country shepherds abiding in the field, keeping watch over their flock by night.

9 And, lo, the angel of the Lord came upon them, and the glory of the Lord shone round about them: and they were sore afraid.

10 And the angel said unto them, Fear not: for, behold, I bring you good tidings of great joy, which shall be to all people.

11 For unto you is born this day in the city of David a Saviour, which is Christ the Lord.

12 And this shall be a sign unto you; Ye shall find the babe wrapped in swaddling clothes, lying in a manger.

13 And suddenly there was with the angel a multitude of the heavenly host praising God, and saying,

14 Glory to God in the highest, and on earth peace, good will toward men.

15 And it came to pass, as the angels were gone away from them into heaven, the shepherds said one to another, Let us now go even unto Bethlehem, and see this thing which is come to pass, which the Lord hath made known unto us.

16 And they came with haste, and found Mary, and Joseph, and the babe lying in a manger.

17 And when they had seen it, they made known abroad the saying which was told them concerning this child.

18 And all they that heard it wondered at those things which were told them by the shepherds.

19 But Mary kept all these things, and pondered them in her heart.

20 And the shepherds returned, glorifying and praising God for all the things that they had heard and seen, as it was told unto them.

NLT **Luke 2:8** That night there were shepherds staying in the fields nearby, guarding their flocks of sheep.

9 Suddenly, an angel of the Lord appeared among them, and the radiance of the Lord's glory surrounded them. They were terrified,

10 but the angel reassured them. "Don't be afraid!" he said. "I bring you good news that will bring great joy to all people.

11 The Savior—yes, the Messiah, the Lord— has been born today in Bethlehem, the city of David!

12 And you will recognize him by this sign: You will find a baby wrapped snugly in strips of cloth, lying in a manger."

13 Suddenly, the angel was joined by a vast host of others—the armies of heaven—praising God and saying,

14 "Glory to God in highest heaven, and peace on earth to those with whom God is pleased."

15 When the angels had returned to heaven, the shepherds said to each other, "Let's go to Bethlehem! Let's see this thing that has happened, which the Lord has told us about."

16 They hurried to the village and found Mary and Joseph. And there was the baby, lying in the manger.

17 After seeing him, the shepherds told everyone what had happened and what the angel had said to them about this child.

18 All who heard the shepherds' story were astonished,

19 but Mary kept all these things in her heart and thought about them often.

20 The shepherds went back to their flocks, glorifying and praising God for all they had heard and seen. It was just as the angel had told them.

The People, Places, and Times

Angel of the Lord. An angelic and spiritual being mentioned in the Bible, more properly translated as "messengers" of God. Angels perform special functions at particular times in the history of Israel. Sometimes the angel of the Lord acts in the Lord's name and is addressed as the Lord. Angels possess greater power than humans. The English word "angel" comes directly from the Greek word for messenger. Some angels appear in human form. In certain passages the angel refers to God delivering His own message (Genesis 18:2–15). Angels appear in the presence of God's people to announce good news (Luke 2:9–11), warn of danger (Genesis 19:15), guard people from evil (Deuteronomy 3:28, 6:22), guide and protect (Exodus 14:19), nourish (Genesis 21:14–20), or instruct (Acts 7:38).

Messiah. The title is derived from the Hebrew word *mashiach*, meaning "an anointed one," though the New Testament writers generally use the Greek word for anointed one (Christos or "Christ") rather than the Hebrew. The New Testament writers describe and affirm Jesus' Messiahship in all four Gospel accounts. Jesus is described as the fulfillment of Israel's long expectation of a King who would deliver them from their oppressors. Jesus instead became the Savior of the world, delivering humankind from sin and reconciling humanity's relationship with God.

Background

Luke's account differs from the story in the Gospel of Matthew, where the magi follow a star to Bethlehem to find the Savior in a manger. Luke's version describes humble local shepherds responding to a sign that a Savior has been born. In ancient days, the occupation of shepherd was despised. Shepherds were not wealthy or educated, so they were not considered an authority on matters outside of their profession. It is hard to imagine this kind of description for shepherds today; now the word conjures positive, pastoral images, because Jesus is associated with such metaphors as the Good Shepherd, protector, defender, and guardian of His sheep (us, the children of God). The shepherds witness the radiance of the heavenly glory. The angels' message announces the Good News to all people that God's Son, the Savior of all humanity, has entered the earthly realm. Our first picture of Jesus, a baby born in a manger, has been an endless story and depicted as a beautiful Christmas scene. However, we cannot leave Jesus as a tiny helpless baby, because He grew up to live an amazing life, He performed miracles, healed the sick, was crucified, died, and rose again. He will return as King of kings to judge the earth.

At-A-Glance

1. The Announcement: Jesus is Born (Luke 2: 8–10)
2. The Fulfillment: Jesus is God (vv. 11–15)
3. The Response: Jesus is Praiseworthy (vv. 16–20)

In Depth

1. The Announcement: Jesus is Born (Luke 2:8–10)

God did not reveal His Son to the rich and powerful, but instead purposely made known our Messiah's arrival to lowly shepherds. Some biblical commentaries suggest these shepherds delivered the lambs for the temple sacrifices performed for the forgiveness of sin. How humbling that God would choose these shepherds to greet His Son, the Majestic Lamb!

Luke describes the presence of the angel in three accounts: "the angel of the Lord came upon them" and "the glory of the Lord shone round about them," and lastly, "they were [greatly] afraid." These images remind us of Old Testament proclamations seen in Isaiah 9:2, when the darkness is sprinkled with the splendor and radiance of God's presence, and those waiting in darkness see this great light. The difference between the humble setting of the birth and the glory of the angelic proclamation could hardly be more dramatic. This incredible event reminds us that God does not enter our lives based on our occupation, educational status, or position in life. Jesus meets us wherever we are! He comes to the plain and ordinary and the rich and famous—anyone who has an open, humble, and receptive heart. So often people feel they have to clean up their lives before accepting Christ. Some believe Jesus is looking for a polished resume with specific qualifications to make them worthy of salvation. God's acceptance is not like the world's; we need no extraordinary credentials for Jesus to accept us, He loves us just as we are! The angels declared the Good News of the Gospel, resonating with joy in the hearts of the listeners. Jesus' birth signifies God's ample grace, and celebration is the only suitable response.

2. The Fulfillment: Jesus is God (vv. 11–15)

Jesus' birth represented a long-awaited sign to the Children of Israel that the Messianic Prophecy had finally arrived. The fulfillment arrived to God's people in the city of David. Some Israelites expected a Savior who would deliver them from Roman oppression. Some hoped to be cured from physical illnesses. They failed to comprehend that Jesus' entrance far exceeded their imagination. When God supernaturally interrupts our day, our first response is fear, until we realize His visitation is a glimpse of His majestic plan for our lives. This story recaps how God invites us to join Him in His plans, not the other way around.

Jesus established God's kingdom on earth, healed humanity's physical impairments, and delivered us from sin. His birth gave humankind a new way to access God. Jesus' ultimate death on the Cross brought peace, everlasting life, hope, and permanent access to God. The story of Jesus' birth is a melody of hope, joy, and love that has enthused musicians for more than 2,000 years. The angel's song is an unparalleled favorite: "Glory to God in the Highest."

3. The Response: Jesus is Praiseworthy (vv. 16–20)

When the shepherds saw the child in the manger, they rejoiced. They recalled the angel's words and gladly shared all they had heard and seen about the child. Can you imagine how Joseph and Mary must have felt hearing such unbelievable revelatory announcements about their child? The only thing Mary could do was treasure these symphonic lyrics in her heart and consider the meaning of these wonderful events. All who heard the angelic announcement were amazed. In these verses, the author repeatedly emphasizes the theme of faithful witness to the Gospel. The shepherds now join the chorus of witnesses because they have seen and heard God's revelation. The result of the whole episode is the response that should arise from all God's people: the shepherds returned to their flocks glorifying and praising Him.

Search the Scriptures

1. How did the shepherds respond to the angel's good news (Luke 2:15)?

2. What was Mary's response to the shepherd's good news (v. 19)?

Discuss the Meaning

Like the shepherds in the field, some "good news" is frightening when not understood. So we must similarly be mindful of how others might receive the Good News of Jesus. How can we calm their fears?

Lesson in Our Society

During the Christmas season, many people get into debt purchasing gifts. In all the hustle and bustle, we forget the real reason for the season. Christmas is more than just gifts under the tree. God has given us His Son, the greatest gift of them all. Jesus is the gift for all seasons, one we should share more readily than any other gift throughout the year. When is the last time you shared the Good News of Christ?

Make It Happen

In the coming week, note all the opportunities that you have to talk with people about Jesus. Make a point each day to tell people about wonderful things that have happened to you. Try to find out some good news about others by asking the question, "What's the good news?" Note any changes in your perspective and share the results with the class next week.

Follow the Spirit

What God wants me to do:

_____

_____

_____

Remember Your Thoughts

Special insights I have learned:

_____

_____

_____

More Light on the Text

Luke 2:8–20

8 And there were in the same country shepherds abiding in the field, keeping watch over their flock by night. 9 And, lo, the angel of the Lord came upon them, and the glory of the Lord shone round about them: and they were sore afraid.

In the following verses, Luke details the strange events that happened after the birth of Christ—the angelic announcement. Luke writes about shepherds living in the same country (or region), who were keeping their flock at night. The angel came to announce the birth of Christ. The fact that the shepherds were grazing their herd in the field by night contradicts the assumption that Christ was born in December. Shepherds never kept flocks outside during the winter months because of the cold. It was customary to send flocks out after the Passover until the first rain in October or November. The actual month and year of Christ's birth is impossible to prove. Throughout the centuries, different Christian sects have given hundreds of suggestions for the date of His birth, but to no avail. However, we do not need to speculate. One thing is certain: He was born of a virgin in Bethlehem of Judea according to Scripture.

As the shepherds watch their flock, the angel suddenly appears to them. The glory of the Lord shines around them. The "glory" (Gk. *doxa*, **DOK-sah**) describes the radiating splendor and majesty of God's presence. In Scripture, glory always symbolizes the presence of God (Exodus 24:16; 1 Kings 8:10; Isaiah 6:1–6), and it can be seen or felt in different forms. To the Israelites in the wilderness, it was seen as a pillar of cloud and fire. Moses saw it as a burning bush. The worshipers at the Tabernacle and the Temple experienced it as a visible cloud and radiant light (2 Chronicles 7:1–13). This same cloud and radiant light would appear to Peter, James, and John on the

c

Mount of Transfiguration. This phenomenon is often associated with the appearance of an angel. Here God's glory appears to be a bright light, since it "shone round about them." The reaction of the shepherds is consistent with Zacharias and Mary's reaction when Gabriel visited them (1:12, 29). They are all overwhelmed by fear and wonder because of the strange supernatural event.

10 And the angel said unto them, Fear not: for, behold, I bring you good tidings of great joy, which shall be to all people. 11 For unto you is born this day in the city of David a Saviour, which is Christ the Lord.

Here again the reassuring words of the angel, "Fear not" (cf. 1:13, 30), are echoed. The angel tells them not to fear and tells them why: he is bearing good news. In Greek, this phrase is a single word, the verb *euaggelizo* (**ew-ang-gheh-LEED-zo**), which means to announce or declare good news. The English verb "evangelize" is a transliteration of the Greek, which can mean to preach, especially the Gospel. Hence, evangelism is the act of preaching, and evangelists are those who preach or proclaim the Good News of the Gospel. In the Greek translation of the Old Testament, *euaggelizo* referred to any type of happy news, but in the New Testament, it is used primarily for the Gospel of salvation. The angel qualifies the Good News that he announces to the shepherds; it will not only bring great joy, but is also for all people. The words "all people" (Gk. *pas laos*, **PAHS lah-OSE**) communicate the idea of all of God's people as a single group, which is then extended to all groups of peoples in 24:47. Therefore, this Gospel is for all nationalities and intended by God to bring joy to all people universally. The angel announces the Good News, that the long-expected Messiah, the hope of Israel, the Savior, is born.

Notice how the angel describes this newborn babe. First, He is a "Saviour" (Gk. *soter*, **so-TARE**), meaning a deliverer, a preserver; this name was given by the ancients to deities, princes, kings, and men who had brought deliverance to their country. It is used repeatedly for both God and His Christ, the medium of His salvation to humankind.

Secondly, He is Christ. The word "Christ" is a direct transliteration of the Greek word *Christos* (**khrees-TOCE**), which means anointed (the anointed one), an equivalent of the Hebrew word Mashiach (ma-SHE-akh, messiah), both of which are descriptors of Jesus. For some Jews in the first century AD, the Messiah would be the king of the Jews, a political leader who would defeat their enemies and bring a golden era of peace and prosperity. In Christian thought, the term Messiah refers to Jesus' role as a spiritual deliverer, setting His people free from sin and death. In Old Testament times, anointing with oil was part of the ritual of commissioning a person for a special task; the phrase "anointed one" was applied to the person in such cases. The word "messiah" is used more than 30 times to describe kings (2 Samuel 1:14, 16), priests (Leviticus 4:3, 5, 16), and the patriarchs (Psalm 105:15). The Persian king Cyrus was referred to as a messiah (Isaiah 45:1). The word is also used for King David, who became the model of the messianic king who would come at the end of the age (2 Samuel 22:51; Psalm 2:2). During the time of Daniel, the word "Messiah" was used as an actual title of the future king (Daniel 9:25–26). Even later, as the Jewish people struggled against their political enemies, the Messiah came to be thought of as a political, military ruler. Because of political and military expectations attached to the Messiah as deliverer, many Jews did not accept Jesus as God's chosen Messiah. In the first and second centuries, those who did accept Jesus became part of the church, and today those who do either join Christian churches or Messianic Judaism.

Thirdly, He is the "Lord." The word is a translation of the Greek *kurios* (**KOO-ree-oce**), meaning master. It signifies ownership, one with supreme authority over another, or a group of people. It is a title of honor expressing respect and reverence by a servant to his or her master. The word was used in reference to princes, chiefs, and the Roman emperor. In the African context, servants, students, or apprentices call their owners, teachers, or instructors "master" as a sign of respect, never using their names. The Igbo call their master *Nna anyi ukwu* ("our big father" or "dad") or *Oga*. To them the owner, teacher, or instructor has the same responsibility and care over them as their real father while under their instruction. As such, they are obligated to respect them just like their birth father or mother. "Lord" is often used in the New Testament for God and the Christ. Here the angel's designation of the newborn babe as the Lord identifies Him as the possessor and supreme owner of all creation. Later in the Bible, the Apostle Peter declares that "God hath made ... Jesus ... both Lord and Christ" (Acts 2:36). While Christ refers to Jesus' humanity, Lord refers to His deity.

Luke's focus on the shepherds during that night carries a number of reasons and theological implications. The main reason is probably for the purpose of identification. Shepherding in the Jewish tradition was a lowly occupation usually reserved for slaves. Shepherds were not only considered poor at the time of Jesus, but also to be uneducated and therefore unlikely to be divine messengers or people of any authority. Like the tax collectors, their work made them ceremonially unclean. The implication, then, is that the Gospel came first to the social outcasts of Jesus' day. This accounts for Luke's recurring emphasis on Jesus' identification with both the poor and societal outcasts of His day.

He ate with "sinners" (Luke 7:37–39, 19:7). He said that He did not have a place to lay His head (Luke 9:58; cf., Matthew 8:20). He declared that He was commissioned to preach and care for the poor, sick, and less privileged in society (Luke 4:18–19). Even in death He was buried in a borrowed grave (Matthew 27:57 ff.). Therefore, the announcement was to identify Christ's humility with that of the shepherds (cf., Philippians 2:7–8). The announcement also identified His mission—caring and protecting. In both the Old and New Testaments, shepherds symbolize those who care for God's people. Christ later identifies Himself in John's Gospel as the "good Shepherd" (John 10:2, 11, 12, 14, 16). The psalmist also writes, "The Lord is my shepherd" (Psalm 23:1). A number of passages in both testaments identify the Lord as the Shepherd of His people (Isaiah 40:11; Jeremiah 23:1–4; Hebrews 13:20; 1 Peter 2:25, 5:2).

12 And this shall be a sign unto you; Ye shall find the babe wrapped in swaddling clothes, lying in a manger. 13 And suddenly there was with the angel a multitude of the heavenly host praising God, and saying, 14 Glory to God in the highest, and on earth peace, good will toward men.

After the announcement, the angel does not instruct the shepherds to go and see the child—he assumes they would. However, he does inform them how they would recognize Him: rather than being surrounded by grandeur and glory, He would be wrapped in swaddling clothes and lying in a manger. This information is necessary because other children were probably born in Bethlehem the same day, but none would be lying in a manger.

As the angel announces the news to the shepherds, he is suddenly joined by "a multitude of the heavenly host praising God." The word "host" (Gk. *stratia*, **strah-tee-AH**) means an army or rank of soldiers. They are probably too many to count; hence Luke uses the adjective "multitude" (Gk. *plethos*, **play-THOS**) to describe them. This is a sign that something amazing is happening and that this child is no ordinary child.

The heavenly host fills the air with praises to God, singing, "Glory to God in the highest, and on earth peace, good will toward men." With the phrase "glory to God in the highest," the angels seem to declare the purpose of the newborn child's birth. First, His birth brings the highest degree of glory to God. Here the angels foresee the ultimate purpose of Christ on earth—to glorify God through His death and resurrection. Second, Christ's birth ushers in peace on earth. This peace is between a holy God and sinful humanity—peace made possible by and purchased through the redemptive blood of Christ. This peace is offered freely to all who come to Him through faith, the perfect peace that starts inwardly and radiates out; it affects others, making it possible for people to live peaceably with one another. Isaiah said centuries before that He shall be called "the Prince of Peace" (Isaiah 9:6). Thirdly, the birth of Christ reveals God's "good will" for His creation. Right from the beginning, God has never willed otherwise. His desires for His children have always been for their good or well-being, and He seeks to convince us of that desire. We can see this through the creation narrative (Genesis 1:26–28). The psalmist says He will not "withhold [any good thing] from them that walk uprightly" (Psalm 84:11). God's wish for humankind is to "have all men saved" (1 Timothy 2:4). Peter writes, "The Lord is not ... willing that any should perish, but that all should come to repentance" (2 Peter 3:9). Here the angels proclaim the wish of God for humankind.

15 And it came to pass, as the angels were gone away from them into heaven, the shepherds said one to another, Let us now go even unto Bethlehem, and see this thing which is come to pass, which the Lord hath made known unto us. 16 And they came with haste, and found Mary, and Joseph, and the babe lying in a manger.

After these spectacular and supernatural events, the shepherds decide to go to Bethlehem to see for themselves what the angels had told them. Their decision to go is not to verify the truth of what they were told—they never questioned or doubted it—but rather to see this strange event that the Lord has revealed to them through the angels. The clause "this thing which is come to pass" confirms the fact that they accepted the angels' message as truth from God. Hence, they hurried with excitement into Bethlehem to visit the newborn child. They find not only what the angel has told them concerning the child (v. 12), but they also find Mary and Joseph with the baby in the manger. What happened to their flocks, whether the shepherds left them by themselves under the protection of God, or under the care of some other people, the Bible does not tell us. How they found the right manger, the Bible does not say. However, the verb used here, "found" (Gk. *aneurisko*, **ah-new-REES-ko**), implies that they searched before they found the child.

17 And when they had seen it, they made known abroad the saying which was told them concerning this child. 18 And all they that heard it wondered at those things which were told them by the shepherds. 19 But Mary kept all these things, and pondered them in her heart.

The shepherds were the first to hear the Good News of the birth of the Savior, and also the first to proclaim it to others. Their message was simple; they declared what the angels told them concerning the child, and what they had seen. Their message left the listeners with wonder and marvel. However, Mary's reaction is more subdued, as she "kept all these things, and pondered them in her heart." "All these things" includes the story the shepherds told—the appearance of the angel and the heavenly host. This story adds to the chain of miraculous events regarding the Christ, which began with the initial visit of Gabriel announcing to Mary that she would be the mother of the Messiah. The word "kept" is the Greek *suntereo* (**soon-tay-REH-oh**), which can mean to preserve or conserve something of great importance. Hence, it is translated as "treasured" by the New American Standard and New International Version. Mary preserved the shepherds' words in her heart with all the strange things that had taken place, and she meditated upon them as future events unfolded.

20 And the shepherds returned, glorifying and praising God for all the things that they had heard and seen, as it was told unto them.

After visiting the newborn, and finding the child as the angels had told them, the shepherds return, glorifying and praising God. The object of their joyful praise is obvious—the long-expected Messiah is born and they have been witnesses. The birth of a Redeemer brings joy and peace to those who accept Him. Here the shepherds accepted the good tidings. Therefore, they praised and worshiped the Lord, and proclaimed to others the wonders of God's dealing with humankind. Like the shepherds, we are called to declare the birth of the Savior and its purpose to the world. Christ was born to bring peace and redemption to the world. This event occurred more than two thousand years ago, but it is as still relevant to us today as it was then. He came that we might have peace, He suffered that we might be healed, and He died that we might live. That is the message of Christmas.

Say It Correctly

Patriarch. **PAY**-tree-ark.
Swaddling. **SWAD**-ling.

Daily Bible Readings

MONDAY
The New Ruler from Bethlehem
(Micah 5:1–5)

TUESDAY
Joseph Takes Mary as His Wife
(Matthew 1:18–25)

WEDNESDAY
The Visit of the Wise Men
(Matthew 2:1–12)

THURSDAY
The Escape to Egypt
(Matthew 2:13–15)

FRIDAY
Journey from Nazareth to Bethlehem
(Luke 2:1–4)

SATURDAY
Mary Delivers Her Firstborn
(Luke 2:5–7)

SUNDAY
The Shepherds and the Angels
(Luke 2:8–20)

Teaching Tips

January 1
Bible Study Guide 5

Words You Should Know

A. Rejoice (Psalm 33:1) *ranan* (Heb.)—To shout for joy, to cry out; a cause to sing with triumph and gladness.

B. Righteousness (v. 5) *tsedaqah* (Heb.)—Honesty, justice, community loyalty.

Teacher Preparation

Unifying Principle—Word and Works. People of faith know that life and the things that sustain it come from a gracious, just, steadfast, and loving God, not by our own methods and works. In the final analysis, who are we? We are God's creation, and He is the Creator of all things.

A. Read the Focal Verses and meditate on all of Psalm 33 to become familiar with the context of this lesson.

B. Read the Daily Bible Readings as part of your daily devotions. Ask God to reveal eternal truths to your heart concerning this week's lesson.

C. Review the information in The People, Places, and Times; Background; and In Depth to gain further insight for the lesson.

O—Open the Lesson

A. Open with prayer using the Aim for Change objectives.

B. Summarize the In Focus story and discuss the importance of praising God, our Creator.

C. Discuss how people of faith understand that God is the object of worship.

P—Present the Scriptures

A. Have volunteers read the Focal Verses.

B. Use The People, Places, and Times; Background; At-A-Glance outline; In Depth; and More Light on the Text to clarify the verses.

E—Explore the Meaning

A. Review and discuss Search the Scriptures, the Discuss the Meaning questions, and the Lesson in Our Society section.

B. Ask students to share the most significant point they learned and how to use that point this week.

N—Next Steps for Application

A. Complete the Make It Happen, Follow the Spirit, and Remember Your Thoughts sections.

B. Remind students to read the Daily Bible Readings in preparation for next week's lesson.

C. Close in prayer, thanking God for His presence in our lives.

Worship Guide

For the Superintendent or Teacher
Theme: God is Worthy of Praise
Song: "To God Be the Glory"
Devotional Reading: Psalm 146

God is Worthy of Praise

Bible Background • PSALM 33:1–9
Printed Text • PSALM 33:1–9 | Devotional Reading • PSALM 146

—————— Aim for Change ——————

By the end of this lesson, we will: EXPLORE God as the Creator of all things; APPRECIATE His provisions and goodness; and COMMIT to making praise of God a major focus in our lives.

————— 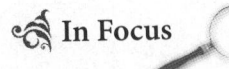 In Focus —————

Ajani and Eric, two recent college graduates, were walking through the city streets. They stopped in a coffee shop and stood in line behind a man who was unkempt and filthy. Eric shook his head and whispered to Ajani, "See, that's why we are blessed. We are educated, hard-working, and will never end up on the streets like this lazy bum." Ajani turned to his friend and asked, "Do you really think his situation is a result of laziness?" Indignantly, Eric responded, "Yes, this dude is lazy and probably on the streets because he refuses to work." Later on that evening, the two young men went to their local church Bible study. Seated in the back of the church was the unkempt gentleman. Eric leaned over to Ajani and both turned to watch the man walk to the front of the church and take the microphone. To their surprise, he was a Christian and former Wall Street investor who had lost his job. He began to tell his story about how he quickly rose to the top and enjoyed many of the finer things in life. He also told about how he just as quickly fell to the bottom. The pastor had invited him to speak to the congregation about praising God through good and hard times.

In this life, many believe that what sustains them comes from their own efforts, education, significant accomplishments, and hard work. We must remember that God is the ultimate Creator and sustainer of life. In what areas do you see God's sustaining power?

————— Keep in Mind —————

"By the word of the LORD were the heavens made; and all the host of them by the breath of his mouth" (Psalm 33:6).

"By the word of the LORD were the heavens made; and all the host of them by the breath of his mouth" (Psalm 33:6).

Focal Verses

KJV **Psalm 33:1** Rejoice in the LORD, O ye righteous: for praise is comely for the upright.

2 Praise the LORD with harp: sing unto him with the psaltery and an instrument of ten strings.

3 Sing unto him a new song; play skillfully with a loud noise.

4 For the word of the LORD is right; and all his works are done in truth.

5 He loveth righteousness and judgment: the earth is full of the goodness of the LORD.

6 By the word of the LORD were the heavens made; and all the host of them by the breath of his mouth.

7 He gathereth the waters of the sea together as an heap: he layeth up the depth in storehouses.

8 Let all the earth fear the LORD: let all the inhabitants of the world stand in awe of him.

9 For he spake, and it was done; he commanded, and it stood fast.

NLT **Psalm 33:1** Let the godly sing for joy to the LORD; it is fitting for the pure to praise him.

2 Praise the LORD with melodies on the lyre; make music for him on the ten-stringed harp.

3 Sing a new song of praise to him; play skillfully on the harp, and sing with joy.

4 For the word of the LORD holds true, and we can trust everything he does.]

5 He loves whatever is just and good; the unfailing love of the LORD fills the earth.

6 The LORD merely spoke, and the heavens were created. He breathed the word, and all the stars were born.

7 He assigned the sea its boundaries and locked the oceans in vast reservoirs.

8 Let the whole world fear the LORD, and let everyone stand in awe of him.

9 For when he spoke, the world began! It appeared at his command.

The People, Places, and Times

Lord. The word "Lord" in English Bibles is the rendering of the Hebrew *adonai* (**ah-doe-NIGH**) or the Greek *kurios* (**CURE-ee-os**). The Hebrew personal name for God, Yahweh, is usually translated "LORD" because God's actual name is not to be pronounced and 'adonai is read instead of Yahweh. God's rule and authority as Lord rests ultimately upon His creation and ownership of all things and people (Psalm 24:1–2). His total supremacy over nature is emphasized by His being called the Lord over earthquakes, wind, and fire (1 Kings 19:10–14), stars (Isaiah 40:26), beasts and sea monsters (Job 40–41), and primeval chaos (Psalm 74:12–14, 89:8–10). The prophets indicated that God is Lord or King of history because He directs the affairs of humans and nations (1 Kings 19:15–18; Isaiah 10:5–9; Amos 9:7), and He is the Lord of universal morality (Ezekiel 25–32; Amos 1:3–2:16). But He is especially the Lord of Israel; His express will represents their civil and religious constitution and demands absolute obedience (Deuteronomy 27:8–9). Israel continued to hope for the future, when a triumphant Day of the Lord would right its wrongs, punish its oppressors, and restore its glory.

Background

At the center of the Bible is the book of Psalms. This book contains an assortment of songs and prayers that express the very heart and soul of humanity. Within the book we find a diversity of human experiences. The writers pour their hearts out to God. The psalmists confess their sins, doubts, and fears, and they ask God for assistance in times of trouble. The writers praise and worship the Lord. In the Psalms, we find individuals crying out to God, exposing their vulnerabilities and fragile hearts. Because of the authors' honesty, people throughout history have come to the book of Psalms again and again for comfort during times of struggle and distress. Additionally, through the psalmists' writings, people in search of hope and comfort discover how to rise from the depths of despair to new heights of joy and praise. Throughout the book of Psalms, people are reassured that the power of God's everlasting love and forgiveness fuels their desire to march forward along this heavenward journey. Psalm 33 reiterates the theme that since God is the Creator, Lord, Savior, and Deliverer, He alone is worthy of our trust and praise. Because God is dependable and faithful, we can rejoice, sing, and give Him thanks that no living creation deserves. The psalmists help us discover a less superficial way to communicate with God, one that guides us to a deeper and genuine relationship with our Lord.

At-A-Glance

1. Rejoice in Praise (Psalm 33:1–3)
2. Reasons for Praise (vv. 4–5)
3. Reverence in Praise (vv. 6–9)

In Depth

1. Rejoice in Praise (Psalm 33:1–3)

This passage of Scripture illustrates how praise is the appropriate response to acknowledge our dependence on God. Praise is essentially offering ourselves to God, including our musical gifts. The first two verses suggest what is important about praise is more the motive and goal than the means. Instrumentation is appropriate, as is the human voice singing or shouting. The motive for praise is recognizing God's reign, and the goal is to offer oneself and one's best gifts to the source of their existence. The singing of a "new song" is also associated elsewhere with the celebration of God's reign (Psalm 96:1, 98:1).

2. Reasons for Praise (vv. 4–5)

As is typical in the songs of praise, the invitation is followed by reasons for praise. God's "word" and "work" are manifestations of His own self. God is elsewhere described as "upright," which suggests that His people derive their identity from Him; in other words, our "godliness" is only a reflection of the characteristic of God, not deriving from our own fleshly goodness. In verse 5, we see the goal of God's speaking and acting in terms associated elsewhere with His character and rule: His righteousness and justice is manifested in His steadfast love for humankind. We must remember human beings are a creation made by a creative genius, God Almighty.

3. Reverence in Praise (vv. 6–9)

God is all-powerful and deserving of our reverence. Our society rarely thinks of personal or political achievements in terms of God's will. We tend to think our successes are a result of our hard work, not any wisdom greater than our own. In fact, we think nations are saved by their great armies and security is achieved through war. Humans fail to recognize the limitations of our mortal capabilities: our limited resources, power, wisdom, and virtue. We forget that God rules the world and we do not. Instead of praising God, our first inclination is to congratulate ourselves on our successes. Humility puts us in position to trust in God rather than human power, virtue, and wisdom. In light of God's sovereignty, the things and people that seem so obviously powerful—politicians, armies, and weapons—are exposed as mere illusions. The real power behind the universe, human history, and personal existence is the steadfast love of God, which fills the earth and is revealed ultimately by His forgiveness of sin.

Search the Scriptures

1. In what ways do you see God's righteousness and justice expressed today (Psalm 33:5)?

2. How do believers demonstrate that they fear God (v. 8)?

Discuss the Meaning

Knowing God is the Creator of all things, how does this change our perspective regarding ourselves, our church, community, one another, and the world as a whole?

Lesson in Our Society

Our society places great emphasis on individualism, self-promotion, and achievement. We are bombarded by media frenzy that models self-entitlement. God desires that we do hard work, remain vigilant, strive for excellence, and acquire some level of success. However, we must remain humble and faithful. So how do we accomplish success without becoming arrogant and ungrateful? What do we need to do to ensure our focus remains centered on our Creator, who is our faithful provider?

Make It Happen

Start tomorrow morning and read Psalm 33. Get a notebook and write a sentence or two and respond to what you read. Make it like a love letter, with your response in words of worship. Think about all the things you are thankful for God doing in your life. If you cannot think of

anything, at least thank Him for saving you. Praise God and share your outcome with the class next week.

Follow the Spirit

What God wants me to do:

_____

_____

_____

_____

Remember Your Thoughts

Special insights I have learned:

_____

_____

_____

_____

More Light on the Text

Psalm 33:1–9

1 Rejoice in the LORD, O ye righteous: for praise is comely for the upright.

The psalmist begins Psalm 33 with a command to rejoice in the Lord. Unlike in some other psalms, this command is not given to all of creation, but specifically to the righteous. The reason for this command is because praise is comely (Heb. *na'veh*, **nah-VEH**), or suitable for the upright (Heb. *yashar*, **yah-SHAR**). The word "upright" literally means to be straight. When used for people, it is used to describe those who are righteous and pleasing in the sight of God.

2 Praise the LORD with harp: sing unto him with the psaltery and an instrument of ten strings.

Next the psalmist points to the instruments and means of praise. The righteous are commanded to praise the Lord with the harp (*kinnor*, **keen-NOR**); the word in Hebrew literally means to twang. This instrument was possibly a zither with a large frame and gave tension to the strings when plucked. The next instrument mentioned is the psaltery, which was a lyre and shaped similar to a vase. They are also commanded to praise Him with the psaltery and an instrument of ten strings, which was an instrument similar to the lyre.

3 Sing unto him a new song; play skillfully with a loud noise.

The people are to use their voices to sing a new song, inspired by the deliverance and mighty acts of God. They are also commanded to play skillfully and with a loud noise. The word "skillfully" (*yatav*, **yah-TAHV**) means to be good and pleasing. The sense used here is to play with high merriment and joy. This would also be accompanied by a loud noise (*teru'ah*, **teh-roo-AH**) or a shout of joy.

4 For the word of the LORD is right; and all his works are done in truth.

Next, the psalmist shifts to point out the underlying reasons for praise. The Word of the Lord is right, which is the same word used to describe the character of those giving praise. He goes on to add that the Lord's works are done in truth (Heb. *'emunah*, **eh-moo-NAH**). The word means more than just accuracy of facts; it means faithfulness. Everything He does is trustworthy and reliable.

5 He loveth righteousness and judgment: the earth is full of the goodness of the LORD.

Two things that the Lord loves is righteousness and judgment. Righteousness (*tsedaqah*, **tse-dah-KAH**) is adherence to a moral standard. Judgment (*mishpat*, **mish-PAHT**) is properly a verdict, here meaning justice or what is right and fair. Both are reasons for praising God, because He is morally pure and has the best in mind for humanity.

The entire earth is full of the goodness (*hesed*, **heh-sed**) or steadfast love of the Lord. This love is covenant love that is tied to God's character and His promises. It is a love that is unfailing and not dependent on the other's love. It is solely based on the covenant. Since the entire earth is in view here, the psalmist must not be referring to the covenant at Sinai, but the previous covenant with Noah, which was directed to the whole earth (Genesis 9:1–17).

6 By the word of the LORD were the heavens made; and all the host of them by the breath of his mouth. 7 He gathereth the waters of the sea together as an heap: he layeth up the depth in storehouses.

The description of the act of creation focuses on the means used. There was nothing and then the Lord spoke—a testimony to His creative power, and another reason to praise Him.

He also gathered the waters of the sea. This is a reference to either separating the waters from the dry land or possibly the Exodus. Either way, it shows that God is sovereign over His creation, including the watery depths. This is significant because in the ancient Near East, the sea was believed to be the home of powerful beings opposed to God and full of chaos. The psalmist refutes this belief; God is sovereign over it all.

8 Let all the earth fear the LORD: let all the inhabitants of the world stand in awe of him. 9 For he spake, and it was done; he commanded, and it stood fast.

The Lord should be feared on a universal level. He is not a territorial God resigned to one province. He should be feared (Heb. *yare'*, **yah-RAY**), or held in reverential awe. All the inhabitants of the world must stand in awe (Heb. *gur*, **GUR**) of Him. The first word for fear is common in the Old Testament to refer to fear, whether the object is a person (Genesis 32:11) or, more frequently, God (Exodus 14:31). The second word only occurs a few times, and here it is used for emphasis. By using two synonyms for fear in conjunction with two synonyms for the world, the psalmist describes the complete awe of God that all of creation should exhibit. This fear is a result of acknowledging the power of God in relation to His Word. When God speaks, it is done. Whatever He commands stands fast. If the Lord has this much power, then He is a God to be feared by the whole earth.

Say It Correctly

Comely. **KUM**-lee.
Psaltery. **SAL**-te-ree.

Daily Bible Readings

MONDAY
Praise, Worship, and Trust
(Psalm 146:1–4)

TUESDAY
Those Whose Help Is the Lord
(Psalm 146:5–10)

WEDNESDAY
The Limits of National Power
(Psalm 33:10–17)

THURSDAY
Hope in God's Steadfast Love
(Psalm 33:18–22)

FRIDAY
Creation a Witness to God's Plan
(Romans 1:16–20)

SATURDAY
Doing Justice and Kindness with Humility
(Micah 6:6–8)

SUNDAY
Hymn of God's Greatness and Goodness
(Psalm 33:1–9)

Notes

_____

_____

_____

_____

Teaching Tips

January 8
Bible Study Guide 6

Words You Should Know

A. Declare (Psalm 96:3) *saphar* (Heb.)—To count, announce, report.

B. Idol (v. 5) *'elil* (Heb.)—An idol or graven image.

Teacher Preparation

Unifying Principle—Sing a New Song. We are awed by the beauty and grandeur of creation. How can we appropriately express these feelings of awe? The psalmist calls all creation to declare the glory of the Lord for His marvelous works.

A. Read the Bible Background and Devotional Readings.

B. Complete Lesson 6 in the *Precepts For Living®* Personal Study Guide.

C. Reread the Focal Verses in a modern translation.

O—Open the Lesson

A. Open with prayer.

B. Have students read the Aim for Change in unison.

C. Ask for a volunteer to read the In Focus story.

D. Discuss various aspects of creation that reflect the beauty and majesty of God.

P—Present the Scriptures

A. Ask for volunteers to read the Focal Verses and The People, Places, and Times. Discuss.

B. Read and discuss the Background section.

C. Encourage students to express praise and worship to God for His great salvation and His marvelous deeds.

E—Explore the Meaning

A. Review and discuss the Search the Scriptures and Discuss the Meaning questions and the Lesson in Our Society section.

B. Ask students to share the most significant point they learned and how to use that point this week.

N—Next Steps for Application

A. Complete the Follow the Spirit and Remember Your Thoughts sections.

B. Remind students to read the Daily Bible Readings in preparation for next week's lesson.

C. Close in prayer, thanking God for His presence in your students' lives.

Worship Guide

For the Superintendent or Teacher
Theme: All Creation Overflows with Praise
Song: "10,000 Reasons (Bless the Lord)"
Devotional Reading: 1 Chronicles 16:23–34

All Creation Overflows with Praise

Bible Background • PSALM 96
Printed Text • PSALM 96:1–6, 10–13 | Devotional Reading • 1 CHRONICLES 16:23–34

Aim for Change

By the end of the lesson, we will: CONTEMPLATE creation's testimony to the majesty of God; EXPERIENCE awe in the presence of God's creation; and PRAISE God wholeheartedly in corporate and individual acts of worship.

In Focus

Karen had a great job that she loved, a lovely family with her husband, Mike, and their three kids, and a great church community. But Karen lived on auto-pilot. Her weekly routine was a continuous cycle of work, home, church, husband, and kids. Everything was routine, and her time with God had become lackluster. Mike suggested that Karen take some time off and go away to a retreat center by the beach for the weekend. Karen was reluctant to go, but she knew that she needed something to recharge and energize her soul. Maybe this retreat would be able to get her out of the routine.

Karen sat on a beach chair on the patio to reflect and watch the sun set. Something inside her stirred. She was taken over by the beauty she saw in all directions. As the bright yellow sun waved goodbye from the horizon, it shifted behind the clouds, and the evening sky changed to vibrant shades of reds and oranges. Karen was overwhelmed. It had been a long time since she stopped to just look at the beauty of nature. She pondered the wonder and awe of God and His creation, and she was mesmerized by the majesty and beauty of what she saw.

In today's lesson, we are encouraged to sing a new song unto the Lord as we remember His salvation, power, and intentional love for each of us. What song would characterize your life in the Lord?

Keep in Mind

"O sing to the Lord a new song; sing to the Lord, all the earth" (Psalm 96:1).

"O sing to the Lord a new song; sing to the Lord, all the earth" (Psalm 96:1).

Focal Verses

KJV **Psalm 96:1** O sing unto the LORD a new song: sing unto the LORD, all the earth.

2 Sing unto the LORD, bless his name; shew forth his salvation from day to day.

3 Declare his glory among the heathen, his wonders among all people.

4 For the LORD is great, and greatly to be praised: he is to be feared above all gods.

5 For all the gods of the nations are idols: but the LORD made the heavens.

6 Honour and majesty are before him: strength and beauty are in his sanctuary.

10 Say among the heathen that the LORD reigneth: the world also shall be established that it shall not be moved: he shall judge the people righteously.

11 Let the heavens rejoice, and let the earth be glad; let the sea roar, and the fulness thereof.

12 Let the field be joyful, and all that is therein: then shall all the trees of the wood rejoice

13 Before the LORD: for he cometh, for he cometh to judge the earth: he shall judge the world with righteousness, and the people with his truth.

NLT **Psalm 96:1** Sing a new song to the LORD! Let the whole earth sing to the LORD!

2 Sing to the LORD; praise his name. Each day proclaim the good news that he saves.

3 Publish his glorious deeds among the nations. Tell everyone about the amazing things he does.

4 Great is the LORD! He is most worthy of praise! He is to be feared above all gods.

5 The gods of other nations are mere idols, but the Lord made the heavens!

6 Honor and majesty surround him; strength and beauty fill his sanctuary.

10 Tell all the nations, "The Lord reigns!" The world stands firm and cannot be shaken. He will judge all peoples fairly.

11 Let the heavens be glad, and the earth rejoice! Let the sea and everything in it shout his praise!

12 Let the fields and their crops burst out with joy! Let the trees of the forest sing for joy

13 before the LORD, for he is coming! He is coming to judge the earth. He will judge the world with justice, and the nations with his truth.

The People, Places, and Times

Tell. The Israelites were expected to always sing the praises of Yahweh and the salvation He brought. The word "tell" comes from the Hebrew word *basar*, which means to bear tidings or to bring news or good tidings. This announcement of good news is both fresh and full, and cheerfully proclaims God's salvation, which brings deliverance and freedom to the captives, and affirms that God rules with power and majesty.

Idols. Israel was commanded to have no other gods but Yahweh, because these other worthless idols cannot be compared to the power and majesty of Israel's God. No crafted image made by human hands can compare with God, enthroned above the earth with power and might (Isaiah 40:22). Other gods are man-made and therefore incapable of creating anything. God is the Creator of everything, and therefore His generative power is unmatched.

Background

This joyful and exuberant psalm parallels Psalms 93 and 95 and is classified as one of the enthronement psalms that celebrate God's sovereignty as King over all creation and all other gods. This psalm is cited in part in 1 Chronicles 16:23–34, which celebrates the Ark of the Covenant's arrival in Jerusalem. The Ark symbolized a covenant agreement established by Yahweh with Israel at Mount Sinai. This hymn therefore celebrates God as both covenant maker and covenant keeper and celebrates His majesty and splendor.

The hymn beckons not only the Israelite audience but all the nations to give homage to Israel's creator God. It describes how Israel, the land, and the nations should respond to Yahweh's kingship, sovereignty, and glory by giving thanks and worshiping the One "majestic in holiness." This hymn of praise for God's strength and wondrous deeds is arranged in a three-part sequence: a call to praise, reflections on why there is a need to praise, and finally climaxing with an acknowledgment that the Lord is King. It celebrates the majesty and splendor of the King and hails the end times hope of the One who will judge the whole world with justice and truth.

At-A-Glance

1. A Call to Praise (Psalm 96:1–3)
2. The Reasons for Praise (vv. 4–6)
3. A Universal Call to Worship (vv. 10–13)

In Depth

1. A Call to Praise (Psalm 96:1–3)

The writer begins the hymn with a direct call to praise through singing a new song. This new song reflects an understanding of a new reality that points toward the transformation found in the Gospel. It speaks of God's greatness to be proclaimed by all nations. This reality is also a hope that contains the future promises that the Lord will fulfill in and through His people (Isaiah 42:10). The call to praise uses six dynamic imperatives—singing (three times), proclaiming, publishing, and telling—to affirm God's name, the Good News of salvation, His works in the world, and all the things that He does. Believers can sing a new hymn articulating their own gratefulness from a heart of thanksgiving and praise.

2. The Reasons for Praise (vv. 4–6)

Praise flows out of the abundance of a grateful and joyful heart. The psalmist articulates the reasons one can praise as confirmation about who God is and why He should be worshiped. First, God should be feared above all other gods (v. 4) because all other deities are mere idols (v. 5) unworthy of value. Yahweh warned Israel (Exodus 20:3) against idol worship; no idol made with human hands could be more powerful than Him.

Secondly, Yahweh created the heavens. His attributes of honor, majesty, strength, and beauty all belong to Him and cannot be attributed to any other god. These attributes reflect the dynamic nature of God, who is beyond our comprehension. However, we often choose cheap substitutes to worship as idols when our hearts stray from the awesomeness of the true and living God.

3. A Universal Call to Worship (vv. 10–13)

The Lord reigns; He is the King! This declaration is the core of the Gospel message, centered in the truth that He is sovereign and has established the world. God is the Creator, Sustainer, and Vindicator of the world. The psalmist has already proclaimed God's reign over the earth, but the climax of this hymn is the call for everything in the universe—all of heaven, earth, the fields, and the sea—to rejoice and glorify its Creator.

But God is also the Judge who will come to arbitrate the world and His people based on the precepts of truth and righteousness. This judgment is the means by which God restores harmony to the universe which has been destroyed by sin and brokenness. Although the earth and God's people have been marred by sin, believers can look forward to the day of redemption when there is a new heaven and a new earth.

Search the Scriptures

1. How can you declare God's glory "among the heathen" (Psalm 96:2)?

2. What does it mean to say the Lord "reigneth" (v. 10)?

Discuss the Meaning

How can we maintain and respond to a consistent and daily awareness of God's majesty and splendor? What offering of worship can we give to God in response to who He is and what He has done (Romans 12:2)?

Lesson in Our Society

Worship is a key component of our daily communion with the Lord. We are reminded that God's sovereignty and glory are still active and present in a world that seems to focus solely on satisfying self. Through worship, we refocus our distracted and wandering hearts that seek after false gods and idols, man-made empty vessels that have no power. Our majestic God made the heavens and the earth, and nothing is out of His reach or control, although the world seeks to convince us otherwise.

Make It Happen

We were created to praise and worship our majestic and powerful God. Ask for revelation about the areas of your life where you neglect to give God honor and majesty, and places where you tend toward shallow idols. Make a commitment to spend time singing a new song of worship to the Lord each day. Finally, think of ways that your entire life could be a song of worship, a testimony of the faithfulness and majesty of your Creator.

Follow the Spirit

What God wants me to do:

_____

_____

_____

_____

Remember Your Thoughts

Special insights I have learned:

_____

_____

_____

_____

More Light on the Text
Psalm 96:1–6, 10–13

Psalm 96 is both a song of praise and more specifically an enthronement psalm, one that celebrates God's divine kingship over the earth. When kings are enthroned, a ritual celebration takes place at the coronation, but unlike human kings, all of creation is involved in God's divine enthronement. This new song for the Lord praises Him for His glory, salvation, and justice.

1 O sing unto the LORD a new song: sing unto the LORD, all the earth.

The psalm begins with a command to sing to the Lord a new song, telling the whole earth to sing. The command to the whole earth includes all of creation, as well as all people. Earth (Heb. *'erets*, **EH-rets**) can refer to creation, but in other contexts, can refer to a group of people joined together in a common identity (i.e., political, religious, familial). Given that the psalm is filled with both creation (vv. 5, 10–13) and clan language (vv. 3, 5, 7, 10, 13), both meanings make sense here. Everyone and everything that God has created must sing a new song to Him.

2 Sing unto the LORD, bless his name; shew forth his salvation from day to day. 3 Declare his glory among the heathen, his wonders among all people.

Verses 2–3 add the contents of the new song: blessings, daily testimonies of His salvation, recollections of His glory and wonders. The date of the psalm's composition is difficult to know because it does not include a superscript or reference to historical people or events, but the psalm commands that God's glory and salvation be proclaimed among the peoples (often "nations"). In other words, His people are to bring this news to everyone, day by day. In the context of the diaspora, where God's people are dispersed among other peoples, this psalm commands the faithful to declare their relationship with the Lord to everyone.

4 For the LORD is great, and greatly to be praised: he is to be feared above all gods. 5 For all the gods of the nations are idols: but the LORD made the heavens. 6 Honour and majesty are before him: strength and beauty are in his sanctuary.

Verses 4–6 may provide both reasons for singing to the Lord and the language for doing so. Both verses 4 and 5 begin with the Hebrew word *ki* (**KEY**), which can mean "because" or introduce a direct quotation, and both meanings fit the context. Why should the whole earth sing to the Lord? Because He is great, powerfully praised, and feared over all gods. At times the Israelites could be tempted to worship other gods, especially if it seemed like those gods were doing good things (cf. Jeremiah 44). The psalmist reminds the people that their God is the Creator of all things. The gods of the peoples are weak, but the Lord made the heavens. The phrase "greatly to be praised" contains a participle in Hebrew that indicates continuous action. In other words, creation constantly praises God because of His greatness and ability to create. Verse 6 intensifies this praise by claiming that everything wonderful is connected to the Lord. The following verses are then a response to the intensity of God's glory and majesty.

10 Say among the heathen that the LORD reigneth: the world also shall be established that it shall not be moved: he shall judge the people righteously.

Building from verses 7–9, the commands to all the clans of the peoples continue here, telling them to tell everyone about the Lord. His continuous rule is a claim that is particularly powerful in the midst of so many imperfect human reigns. What is more, He has established the land, it will never move, and He has judged the peoples with equity. In these claims are both a subtle critique of corrupt human rule and a clear praise of God for being wholly perfect in His rule. The psalm calls us both to praise God for His perfect justice, be aware of earthly injustice, and speak out against it.

11 Let the heavens rejoice, and let the earth be glad; let the sea roar, and the fullness thereof. 12 Let the field be joyful, and

all that is therein: then shall all the trees of the wood rejoice 13 Before the LORD: for he cometh, for he cometh to judge the earth: he shall judge the world with righteousness, and the people with his truth.

After telling the people how to sing this new song to the Lord, the psalm shifts back to creation. The heavens are to rejoice, and the earth is to exult. The sea and its fullness are to roar. Verse 11 mentions three major parts of creation as a way of including everything God has created—the heavens, the earth, and the sea. Then the fields and trees of the forest are added in verse 12. Nothing is left out in this song to the Lord. Moreover, their responses are loud: shouts of joy and exultation, roars like thunder, and cries of rejoicing. No part of creation will miss or be excluded from the song of praise to God.

Verse 13 provides both the location and reason for this new song of praise. It will happen in the Lord's presence, and this is possible because He is coming! When He comes, He will judge the earth with justice and the peoples with faithfulness. The word translated as "righteousness" in the KJV is rendered "justice" in the NLT. Both are viable translations of the Hebrew *tsedek* (**TSEH-dek**). In ancient Israel, there was no distinction between justice and righteousness; both meant to do what was right. God will judge rightly. The word rendered "truth" in both translations (*'emunah*, **eh-moo-NAH**) means faithfulness, honesty, and truth. In Hebrew, these ideas were inseparable. To be faithful was to be honest and true to the one you were in a relationship with. God will act rightly and honestly when He comes, and the response of all creation will be to sing a new song. The entire psalm can provide an opportunity for daily reminder of how to respond to God's glory and justice and how to prepare for His coming. God's justice will turn the world right side up, and our proper response is for all of creation to praise Him!

This psalm is sometimes labeled a psalm of God's justice or judgment. The psalm has an end times tone, especially in the final verses, suggesting that the psalm hopes for God's eradication of human corruption as a final end to injustice. This kind of praise and hope should certainly be a regular part of Christian lives as we look forward to Jesus' second coming. At the same time, it is important to remember that God has called us to be ministers of justice in the world, just as Jesus and His first disciples were, until that time. Jesus warns in a final sermon in Matthew that we should not be found lacking in care for those in need when He returns (Matthew 25:34–46). As we read and meditate on this psalm, we should not only let it serve as words of praise to God, but we should also let the Spirit encourage us to be ministers of God's justice until He comes again.

Say It Correctly

Heathen. **HEE**-thin.
Reigneth. **RAY**-nith.

Daily Bible Readings

MONDAY
O Sing to the Lord
(1 Chronicles 16:23–34)

TUESDAY
Ascribe to the Lord, O Families
(Psalm 96:7–9)

WEDNESDAY
Justice Will Be Established
(Isaiah 42:1–4)

THURSDAY
Salvation is for All Peoples
(Isaiah 49:1–7)

FRIDAY
Sing Praises, O Gentiles
(Romans 15:7–13)

SATURDAY
Singing Around the Throne
(Revelation 5:11–14)

SUNDAY
The Lord Reigns Supreme
(Psalm 96:1–6, 10–13)

Notes

_____

_____

_____

_____

Teaching Tips

January 15
Bible Study Guide 7

Words You Should Know

A. Praise (Psalm 65:1) *tehillah* (Heb.)—A song of praise, a hymn of thanksgiving.

B. Visit (v. 9) *paqad* (Heb.)—To attend to, visit, muster, or appoint.

Teacher Preparation

Unifying Principle—Good and Plenty. We often take for granted how we get the good things we enjoy. What is the source of our material bounty? The psalmist calls us to praise God for the bounty He provides.

A. Read the Bible Background and Devotional Readings.

B. Complete Lesson 7 in the *Precepts For Living®* Personal Study Guide.

C. Reread the Focal Verses in a modern translation.

O—Open the Lesson

A. Open with prayer.

B. Have students read Aim for Change in unison.

C. Ask for a volunteer to read the In Focus story.

D. Discuss various aspects of creation that reflect God's beauty and majesty.

P—Present the Scriptures

A. Ask for volunteers to read the Focal Verses and The People, Places, and Times. Discuss.

B. Read and discuss the Background section.

C. Encourage students to write down and offer a song of thanksgiving for God's forgiveness of sin and His abundant provision for the spiritual and physical necessities of life.

E—Explore the Meaning

A. Review and discuss the Search the Scriptures and Discuss the Meaning questions and the Lesson in Our Society section.

B. Ask students to share the most significant point they learned and how to use that point this week.

N—Next Steps for Application

A. Complete the Follow the Spirit and Remember Your Thoughts sections.

B. Remind students to read the Daily Bible Readings in preparation for next week's lesson.

C. Close in prayer, thanking God for His presence in our lives.

Worship Guide

For the Superintendent or Teacher
Theme: Praise God the Provider
Song: "Your Name" by Philips, Craig and Dean
Devotional Reading: Psalm 66:1–5

Praise God the Provider

Bible Background • PSALM 65; 67:6–7
Printed Text • PSALM 65:1–2, 9–13 | Devotional Reading • PSALM 66:1–5

Aim for Change

By the end of the lesson, we will: DISCERN the natural and human factors responsible for our material well-being; FEEL gratitude for the ways God meets our physical needs; and PRAISE the Creator through good stewardship of our material blessings.

In Focus

Margaret loved spending time with her grandchildren. Many days she would just take them along to the store or to run errands. It almost seemed to make her feel young again. One of the things she loved to do was to take them out into the garden on the side of her house. There she planted tomatoes, cucumbers, and greens. It was nothing like what she had seen growing up in the South, but it was her small piece of land. The children were resistant at first, but soon they were excited about playing in the dirt.

What the kids didn't realize is that they were planting seeds that would one day grow into edible food. They didn't realize that food doesn't just magically appear in grocery stores and most of what they ate wasn't truly food, but junk food. Margaret stopped and began to contemplate the intricate way that God had provided for humanity. To think that such a small and tiny thing as a seed could yield so much nourishment. It caused her to lift up her hands and praise God right there. The children wondered what was wrong with their grandmother. But Margaret just kept praising God and used it as a entry point to teach them about their Father in heaven who provides for all His children.

God is faithful to provide for His children. In today's lesson, we are encouraged to praise God for the material blessings He provides for us. In what ways have you seen God provide for you and your family?

Keep in Mind

"By terrible things in righteousness wilt thou answer us, O God of our salvation; who art the confidence of all the ends of the earth, and of them that are afar off upon the sea" (Psalm 65:5).

"By terrible things in righteousness wilt thou answer us, O God of our salvation; who art the confidence of all the ends of the earth, and of them that are afar off upon the sea" (Psalm 65:5).

Focal Verses

KJV **Psalm 65:1** Praise waiteth for thee, O God, in Sion: and unto thee shall the vow be performed.

2 O thou that hearest prayer, unto thee shall all flesh come.

9 Thou visitest the earth, and waterest it: thou greatly enrichest it with the river of God, which is full of water: thou preparest them corn, when thou hast so provided for it.

10 Thou waterest the ridges thereof abundantly: thou settlest the furrows thereof: thou makest it soft with showers: thou blessest the springing thereof.

11 Thou crownest the year with thy goodness; and thy paths drop fatness.

12 They drop upon the pastures of the wilderness: and the little hills rejoice on every side.

13 The pastures are clothed with flocks; the valleys also are covered over with corn; they shout for joy, they also sing.

NLT **Psalm 65:1** What mighty praise, O God, belongs to you in Zion. We will fulfill our vows to you,

2 for you answer our prayers. All of us must come to you.

9 You take care of the earth and water it, making it rich and fertile. The river of God has plenty of water; it provides a bountiful harvest of grain, for you have ordered it so.

10 You drench the plowed ground with rain, melting the clods and leveling the ridges. You soften the earth with showers and bless its abundant crops.

11 You crown the year with a bountiful harvest; even the hard pathways overflow with abundance.

12 The grasslands of the wilderness become a lush pasture, and the hillsides blossom with joy.

13 The meadows are clothed with flocks of sheep, and the valleys are carpeted with grain. They all shout and sing for joy!

The People, Places, and Times

Zion. A mountain in Jerusalem where the Temple stood and where it was believed that God came to dwell with His people. It is often used synonymously for Jerusalem.

Background

This psalm of David might have been sung in the sanctuary of Zion as a liturgical hymn at the time of the great harvest. It is thought to be a thanksgiving psalm for the abundant harvest Israel experienced after a drought when a famine was averted. This confident hymn tells of God's goodness and power that acknowledges His spiritual (atonement for sin) and physical (tangible abundance) blessings on Israel.

The psalm could have been sung during the Feast of Unleavened Bread and also at Rosh Hashanah, both indicating God's blessing year round. However, Rosh Hashanah would more likely be the theme around which the Psalm was written. This festival celebrated the beginning of the year and resonates with the words of verse 11, "Thou crownest the year with thy goodness." The harvest festival was a time when people found forgiveness of their sins and offered a tribute to God in anticipation of the harvest of that year. This hymn of praise acknowledged that God forgives sin, hears and answers Israel's prayers for abundant rain, and provides an abundant harvest and flourishing flocks. It is one of the most uplifting psalms, because it tangibly captures a spirit of celebration and displays Israel's gratitude toward and dependence on God, reminding them that He is sovereign over creation.

At-A-Glance

1. Praise for the Forgiveness of Sins
(Psalm 65:1–2)
2. Praise for the Blessings of the Land
(vv. 9–13)

In Depth

1. Praise for the Forgiveness of Sins (Psalm 65:1–2)

The psalm begins with a promise to fulfill a vow to praise Yahweh, who is Israel's God. The praise is directed to God and is uttered in thanksgiving for His forgiveness of sin. The vow illustrated that people owed Him their praise—they prayed for something and vowed to give Him glory when He answered. God hears and answers the prayers of His people (Psalm 45:10). Praising God, especially by drawing attention to how He has answered the psalmist's prayer, benefits not only the people of Israel, but also draws others to Him. There was a confident expectation that God would provide for the spiritual and physical needs of His people. At the tower of Babel, humanity was scattered and fractured, but a time will come when humanity will be restored and all will come to worship Yahweh at Zion.

2. Praise for the Blessings of the Land (vv. 9–13)

Israel's God cares for the land He loves, so He pours out an abundance of blessing upon it. God's care for the land is described as abundant and overflowing. His provision of life

and the flourishing harvest bring praise and thanksgiving. God is powerful enough to take care of and provide the physical necessities of life. He is the giver of rain, grain and goodness, and in response, the land joins in with singing praise to Him.

God is active in His creation as He "visitest" (v. 9), "crownest" (v. 11), and "clothed" (v. 13) the pastures and valleys of Israel. His divine provision of rain and constant water enabled the crops and livestock to flourish. This water would be a reminder for Israel of the promise of the new earth, which has a river of life (Revelation 22:1–3) that can never run dry and whose abundant provision gives life to everything (Ezekiel 47:1–2).

Search the Scriptures

1. What are some physical and spiritual ways that God has provided for you in your life that demand a song of praise and thanksgiving?

2. God's works are far beyond what we can see in the natural. What are some of the "unseen" ways in which He works that you could praise Him?

Discuss the Meaning

1. What are the dams in your life that prevent the active flow of the river of life?

2. If salvation extends to all nations, how are you participating in the Great Commission (Matthew 28) to make disciples of the nations?

Lesson in Our Society

We often think that God's blessings are exclusive to only His children, but He desires for all humanity to come to know Him and be restored (2 Peter 3:9). His desire is that no one should perish, but instead everyone would come to salvation and forgiveness in Him. He uses creation as a demonstration of His goodness and grace toward us with the hope of drawing men and women to Himself (Matthew

5:45) beyond the "borders" of Israel. Jesus is our Savior and the hope of all the peoples of the earth.

Make It Happen

Jesus is the water of life to quench our thirsty souls. Ask God to saturate your heart with love for your neighbor, in hopes that you can build relationships and witness to Christ's love. Pray for a stirring of your heart toward evangelism and discipleship of those around you as you find ways to share the Gospel.

Follow the Spirit

What God wants me to do:

_____

_____

_____

_____

Remember Your Thoughts

Special insights I have learned:

_____

_____

_____

_____

More Light on the Text

Psalm 65:1–2, 9–13

Psalm 65 is a song of praise, sometimes called a communal song of thanksgiving, indicating the corporate nature of its praise of God. Not only does the psalm move back and forth between singular and plural in reference to the people (I and we), but all of creation is engaged with God as well. Because of the references to the blessings of crops and harvest, it is often associated with harvest time, and in the United States, it is often read at Thanksgiving, which is also a celebration of the abundance of harvest. Regardless of when it is read in worship, devotion, or deeper study, the psalm is a call to reflect on the awesomeness, connectedness, and interdependence of all of God's creation.

1 Praise waiteth for thee, O God, in Sion: and unto thee shall the vow be performed.

The psalm begins with reasons for praising God. The word for praise here (Heb. *tehillah*, **te-heel-LAH**) is a technical word for a song of praise, and the plural form is the name of the psalter in Hebrew (*tehillim*, **te-heel-LEEM**). Along with the song of praise is the fulfillment of a vow to God. The New Living Translation captures the Hebrew more closely here with "fulfillment" because the Hebrew is the verb for completion (*shillam*, **sheel-LAHM**). In other words, God is worthy of a song of praise and a fulfilled vow. The images of the fullness of creation in the psalm point to this worthiness more clearly. If God fulfills His promises by filling the earth with life, we should keep our promises to Him as well.

2 O thou that hearest prayer, unto thee shall all flesh come.

Verses 2–8 provide a number of reasons for God's worthiness, beginning with the fact that He hears prayers. Verse 2 praises the relationship between God and all living things—to God all flesh will come. The Hebrew word for flesh includes all living things, anything with blood and breath (*basar*, **bah-SAR**). The presence of all creatures in the midst of God echoes the heavenly throne room images in Isaiah 6, Ezekiel 1–2, and Revelation 4, each of which reveals all living things praising God at all times. Verses 3–8 continue praising God for hearing prayers and forgiving sins, adding to His greatness the blessings of being in His presence and experiencing His salvation and justice through all the earth.

9 Thou visitest the earth, and waterest it: thou greatly enrichest it with the river of God, which is full of water: thou preparest them corn, when thou hast so provided for it.

After praising God for His justice, righteousness, blessings, holiness, and power over creation, the psalm exults Him for caring for the land with water. Instead of "Thou visitest," the New Living Translation says, "You take care of..." The Hebrew verb here (*paqad*, **pah-QAHD**) has a number of possible meanings, including visit, which conjures up images of a fully present God. It can also mean to set things up in correct order, suggesting that God has designed things appropriately, so that there are water systems that keep the earth nurtured, including a river of God that promises ample water. For those who have easy access to water and relatively few restrictions even during droughts, the power of this promise can be easily lost. In ancient Israel, flowing water supplies such as rivers and wadis were scarce, and the rainy season was vital for both the crops and the people. In addition to providing the necessary water, God also provides "corn," which stands in here for all grain, and was a staple for both humans and animals. These are basic necessities for creation to thrive, and the psalm calls us to reflect on the beauty of God's design and praise Him for providing for all of creation.

10 Thou waterest the ridges thereof abundantly: thou settlest the furrows thereof: thou makest it soft with showers: thou blessest the springing thereof.

Verse 10 continues the crop imagery by focusing on the process of sowing and the need for moist soil. God is so concerned for creation that He makes sure the plowed fields are watered, providing showers for them. The result is that God blesses the crops' growth in their most vulnerable time, when they are just sprouting. The word translated "springing" by the King James Version (Heb. *tsemach*, **TSEH-makh**) is a word for sprout or a branch, and it is related to a verb for growth, indicating that God is involved in the whole process of crop growth from the beginning.

11 Thou crownest the year with thy goodness; and thy paths drop fatness.

The crown symbolizes the highest honor, revealing that God holds creation in the highest esteem. The reference to crowning the year with goodness and God's paths dripping with fatness suggests the harvest season and its celebration. God blesses the entire year, but the culmination of celebration is at the harvest time when the crops He has blessed are ripe and ready to nourish creation. Just as God has given nature the highest honor and makes sure that all of creation is nurtured, so we should do likewise. We have been called to be God's stewards of creation (Genesis 1:28, 2:15), and this verse is a reminder of the importance of all of creation in His eyes.

12 They drop upon the pastures of the wilderness: and the little hills rejoice on every side. 13 The pastures are clothed with flocks; the valleys also are covered over with corn; they shout for joy, they also sing.

Verses 12–13 provide an all-encompassing picture of the extent of God's blessings. Both the wilderness and the hills, as well as the pastures and valleys, rejoice at His blessings. Flocks and grain are abundant, and creation itself shouts for joy and sings. This final verse closes with an image of an abundance of animals and crops, all of which join in the singing of God's praises!

Those of us who are removed from agricultural communities and always have enough clean water and food can too easily forget the extent to which we rely on the ecosystem for our own lives. God has created a global ecosystem that is intricately connected and interdependent, and the commands in Genesis for humans to fill the earth and rule it (1:28) and to tend to the garden (2:15) were intended as commands for us to take care of creation, just as God takes care of it here in this psalm (v. 9). How are we caring for creation? Are we truly thankful for God, creation, and everyone involved in making sure we have clean water and sufficient food? Do we have a tendency to waste resources provided by God for all of creation to thrive? This psalm is not just a call to praise God for providing. It provides images of a creation that is well tended and lush. How can we be those stewards of creation and the garden who make sure that the earth looks like these thriving images in the psalm?

Say It Correctly

Sion. **SIE**-on.
Furrows. **FUR**-ohs.

Daily Bible Readings

MONDAY
Rejoice During the Festival of Booths
(Deuteronomy 16:13–15)

TUESDAY
God Forgives and Saves the People
(Psalm 65:3–4)

WEDNESDAY
God's Awesome Stabilizing Deeds
(Psalm 65:5–8)

THURSDAY
Let All the People Praise God
(Psalm 66:1–5)

FRIDAY
God's Restoration of All Humanity
(Isaiah 66:18–23)

SATURDAY
Sharing in God's New Community
(Acts 2:37–47)

SUNDAY
Thanks to God for Earth's Bounty
(Psalm 65:1–2, 9–13)

Notes

_____

_____

_____

_____

Teaching Tips

Words You Should Know

A. Bless (Psalm 104:1) *barak* (Heb)—To bless, to ascribe special power to somebody.

B. Maketh (v. 4) *'asah* (Heb)—To do, accomplish, complete.

Teacher Preparation

Unifying Principle—Master Designer. When we experience the vast diversity of creation, we wonder how it is all held together. What does this complexity tell us about the world we live in? The psalmist praises God for sustaining creation.

A. Commit to reading the Daily Bible Reading Scriptures each day this week, asking God for a worshipful heart in preparation for the study of Psalm 104.

B. Complete Lesson 8 in the *Precepts For Living*® Personal Study Guide.

C. Read the Bible passage in several translations. Read over More Light on the Text.

O—Open the Lesson

A. Open with the Scripture reading and prayer. Ask for three prayer volunteers. Have one read Psalm 104:1–4 and say a prayer based on those verses. The next two will do the same with Psalm 104:24–36 and Psalm 104:28–30.

B. Have students read Aim for Change and the Keep in Mind verse silently.

C. Ask for a volunteer to read the In Focus story.

D. Ask students to close their eyes and imagine a sunset, a giant wave crashing down in the ocean, a sky full of stars. Discuss how these scenes cause them to praise God.

P—Present the Scriptures

A. Ask each student to read a verse from the Focal Verses and conclude with reading The People, Places, and Times.

B. Read and discuss the Background section and tie it in with The People, Places and Times.

C. Encourage students to keep their thoughts on God, the ruler of creation, rather than debating evolution.

E—Explore the Meaning

A. Review and discuss Search the Scriptures, Discuss the Meaning, and Lesson in Our Society.

B. Challenge students to share one important point God impressed on their hearts. Ask students how they plan to apply it personally this week.

N—Next Steps for Application

A. Complete the Follow the Spirit and Remember Your Thoughts sections.

B. Remind students to read the Daily Bible Readings in preparation for next week's lesson.

C. Close in prayer.

Worship Guide

For the Superintendent or Teacher
Theme: Praise God the Creator
Song: "How Great is Our God" or
"How Great Thou Art"
Devotional Reading: Psalm 8

Praise God the Creator

Bible Background • PSALM 104
Printed Text • PSALM 104:1–4, 24–30 | Devotional Reading • PSALM 8

Aim for Change

By the end of this lesson we will: PONDER the diversity and complexity of God's creation; AFFIRM God's wisdom in ordering the world as He did; and HONOR God by working to preserve the world's magnificent natural diversity.

In Focus

In 2001, God opened an opportunity for Veronica to be a part of a mission team to Africa. Years later, when asked to share her testimony of the trip at church, she still reflected on that event as life-changing. "The moment I stepped off the plane," Veronica recalled, "it was like a bolt of electricity started with my feet and traveled up to my head. Everything I saw and experienced said, 'You're home.' The unique sounds, colors, activities were so different from America. The people carried an air of contentment even though their circumstances were far from satisfactory. The Christian services were in French or Bambara, but it didn't take long to feel the emotion and sincerity of the people."

Veronica closed her eyes and looked up at the ceiling. "One of my most memorable times is being out at night. Our host family had a wide back yard, and I'd go back there at night and lie down and look up at the stars. Unlike in the U.S., you could see so many stars, layer upon layer of brightness in the sky. Where we were in Mali had much less light pollution than here in the U.S., and you can really see the galaxy. I'd lay there in the dark looking up. I'd never seen anything like it. Instantly my heart filled with praise. I needed no Scripture reading or choir singing. The presence of those stars for me represented God as an amazing Creator. I'll never forget those times of thanking God for giving us such an awesome, awesome creation."

What aspect of creation will most often make you praise God?

Keep in Mind

"O Lord, how manifold are your works! In wisdom you have made them all; the earth is full of your creatures" (Psalm 104:24).

"O Lord, how manifold are your works! In wisdom you have made them all; the earth is full of your creatures." (Psalm 104:24).

Focal Verses

KJV **Psalm 104:1** Bless the LORD, O my soul. O LORD my God, thou art very great; thou art clothed with honour and majesty.

2 Who covers thyself with light as with a garment: who stretchest out the heavens like a curtain:

3 Who layeth the beams of his chambers in the waters: who maketh the clouds his chariot: who walketh upon the wings of the wind:

4 Who maketh his angels spirits; his ministers a flaming fire:

24 O LORD, how manifold are thy works! in wisdom hast thou made them all: the earth is full of thy riches.

25 So is this great and wide sea, wherein are things creeping innumerable, both small and great beasts.

26 There go the ships: there is that leviathan, whom thou hast made to play therein.

27 These wait all upon thee; that thou mayest give them their meat in due season.

28 That thou givest them they gather: thou openest thine hand, they are filled with good.

29 Thou hidest thy face, they are troubled: thou takest away their breath, they die, and return to their dust.

30 Thou sendest forth thy spirit, they are created: and thou renewest the face of the earth.

NLT **Psalm 104:1** Let all that I am praise the LORD. O LORD my God, how great you are! You are robed with honor and majesty.

2 You are dressed in a robe of light. You stretch out the starry curtain of the heavens;

3 you lay out the rafters of your home in the rain clouds. You make the clouds your chariot; you ride upon the wings of the wind.

4 The winds are your messengers; flames of fire are your servants.

24 O LORD, what a variety of things you have made! In wisdom you have made them all. The earth is full of your creatures.

25 Here is the ocean, vast and wide, teeming with life of every kind, both large and small.

26 See the ships sailing along, and Leviathan which you made to play in the sea.

27 They all depend on you to give them food as they need it.

28 When you supply it, they gather it. You open your hand to feed them, and they are richly satisfied.

29 But if you turn away from them, they panic. When you take away their breath, they die and turn again to dust.

30 When you give them your breath, life is created, and you renew the face of the earth.

The People, Places, and Times

Psalmist. Some scholars attribute this psalm to David even though it doesn't list a specific title or author. Nothing in the psalm itself indicates its authorship. The psalmist might have written this hymn when David danced before the Ark of the Covenant with the priest as they carried it into the city of David (2 Samuel 6:14–15). This psalm also could have been written during the return from Babylonian exile and the re-dedication of the Temple (Ezra 6:13–22).

Heavens. The firmament is God's palace or residence. It displays the radiance of His power and glory. Every part of the world, however minute, exhibits some glimmer of beauty, so distinct and bright that no one can use ignorance as an excuse to deny God's existence (Psalm 19).

Leviathan. A sea monster referenced in the Old Testament (Job 40:25 or 41:1 depending on chapter divisions and verse numbering). The word is typically used to refer to any large sea creature, often great whales in literature. In modern Hebrew, it simply means "whale." In the Middle Ages, Leviathan was used to depict Satan, who attempted to destroy God's people and His creation; some scholars at the time associated it with the demon of envy. According to Isaiah 27:1, Leviathan will be destroyed during the time of judgment.

Background

The first three chapters of Genesis outlined God creating the earth. Here the psalmist poetically highlights the same information. This psalm focuses on God's handiwork; it reviews the history of creation and magnifies the greatness of God.

This psalm about nature explicitly points to God as the intelligent creator. The psalmist uses vivid imagery to emotionally move the reader, recreating this colorful wonder before their very eyes. Nature stays within its boundaries and does what God created it to do.

At-A-Glance

1. Creation Shows God's Majesty (Psalm 104:1–2)
2. God Creates Light and Heaven (vv. 2–4)
3. God Creates Creatures (vv. 24–27)
4. God Provides for All Animals (vv. 28–30)

In Depth

1. Creation Shows God's Majesty (Psalm 104:1–2)

Initially, the author spoke of himself blessing the Lord. The psalmist does so to express gratitude and respect. The "soul" is the entire being of a person who truly worships God. The personal blessing exalted a God who has robed Himself with glory and grandeur, yet the author acknowledged God personally as "my God." The garment of authority and nobility is expressive of the character of God. Even the elegant array of King Solomon does not compare. The first thing on God's creation agenda was light. Like a garment, God wrapped Himself in the very light He created. It's unapproachable to any earthly living soul (1 Timothy 6:16).

God's second act in creation was the expanse or the heavens. He stretched it out like a canopy or a tent over all the earth under His complete control (Isaiah 40:22, 44:24).

2. God Creates Light and Heaven (vv. 2–4)

The psalmist here imagines God as if building the world like a multi-story building and the waters above as ceiling rafters. He resides in the midst of it all.

Clouds serve as His chariot, which can be a vehicle to ride bringing judgment or grace to His creation (Exodus 13:21; Isaiah 19:1). The idea that God walks "on the wings of the wind" explains the swiftness in which He comes along. These are signs that God is present everywhere and can offer supernatural help.

3. God Creates Creatures (vv. 24–27)

It is impossible to know the number of creatures on earth. The number of living creatures and plants rises and falls daily in a cycle of endless activity. The world is filled with God's handiwork made by Him and for Him (Colossians 1:16).

In the first part of this psalm, the author highlights the heavens and the earth. Now the attention is on the sea. The seas are full of life—some of it small, some as large as even the leviathan. The whales play throughout the waters, yet despite all the activity, humankind is able to sail a ship. God keeps everything under control and working smoothly.

4. God Provides for All Animals (vv. 28–30)

In conclusion, the writer once again points to God as caretaker and provider for the animals, plants, insects, humans—all life. God's hand is filled with good for all. Nothing in this world brought itself into being or sustains itself; all have to wait on God. He breathes life into all things, and He cuts it off. He created out of dust, and when it's time, He sees to it that humankind and other living creatures will die and return to dust.

Repeatedly, God creates, preserves, and restores. It is His responsibility as Creator. As humans watching these phenomena in nature, we should have assurance that in God's hands, everyone is safe and secure. He is more than able to take care of the most difficult situation or circumstance in an individual's life.

Search the Scriptures

1. What does it mean to bless the Lord with all of your soul (Psalm 104:1)?

2. How does the psalmist's description of God guide your daily life (vv. 3–4)?

Discuss the Meaning

In His wisdom, God provided humankind a wonderful universe in which to dwell. It communicates how God is powerful, majestic, creative, and totally in control of all things. What problems in our lives threaten the belief that God is in control?

Lesson in Our Society

We often take for granted what we are given. People help us out of the kindness of their hearts, family and friends support us, and many of us have homes, jobs, and access to heat and running water. But sometimes we dwell on the things we don't have, or spend too much time revisiting old slights or mistakes without appreciating all that has been provided for us.

It's easy to engage in one's usual routine without thanking God for His magnificent design. Ask God to help you daily recognize His benefits of His creation.

Make It Happen

As a church or Sunday School class, locate a community organization that supports neighborhood gardens or educates youth about the earth's ecology. This fosters an appreciation for the wonders of God's creation.

Follow the Spirit

What God wants me to do:

_____

_____

_____

_____

Remember Your Thoughts

Special insights I have learned:

_____

_____

_____

_____

More Light on the Text
Psalm 104:1–4, 24–30

1 Bless the LORD, O my soul. O LORD my God, thou art very great; thou art clothed with honour and majesty.

Starting and ending similar to Psalm 103 (a fact which underscores David's authorship), this psalm gives God the worship He is due. To "bless" (Heb. *barak*, **bah-ROCK**) means to wish good tidings or ascribe particular power (some versions render this word as "praise"). The word "great" in Hebrew is *gadal* (**gah-DOLL**), which means "to be or become great or strong" or "exalted" (see Genesis 12:2; Exodus 2:10). The word "very" in Hebrew is *me'od* (**meh-ODE**), which means "especially" or "exceedingly" (see Genesis 1:31; Psalm 96:4). Such added superlatives are appropriate within the context. Indeed, God is worthy of every superlative and expression of praise and blessing. We can't physically reach God, but by His visible glories we can see Him "darkly" (1 Corinthians 13:12); indeed, we, like Moses, couldn't survive the full brilliance of His person (Exodus 34:29). Thus, in part, because we could not bear His full appearance, God clothes Himself with the "fabric of the world," in the choice words of John Calvin. While earthly kings adorn themselves with royal finery of every kind, none can compare to God's infinitely greater "robes" of exceeding honor and majestic excellence (Psalm 93:1; 1 Timothy 6:16).

2 Who coverest thyself with light as with a garment; who stretchest out the heavens like a curtain:

In the previous verse, God clothed Himself with honor and majesty; in this verse His attire is light itself. If one of the garments in God's wardrobe is "light" (Heb. *'or*, **OR,** meaning daylight or a bright morning sun), one can't help but ask how bright His being is (Habakkuk 3:4).

"The heavens" (Heb. *shamayim*, **shah-MAH-yeem**) implies that either the visible arch in which the clouds move or the larger space where celestial bodies revolve is merely a curtain. The belief in the ancient Near East was that the sky was a dome or canopy that covered the earth like a disc. One can only wonder how grand God's royal pavilion—His heavenly tabernacle—is. Other verses such as Isaiah 40:12, 54:2, and Job 37:18 refer to the heavens in a similar manner. Isaiah 34:4 and Revelation 6:14 refer to the sky (or heavens) being rolled up like a scroll.

3 Who layeth the beams of his chambers in the waters: who maketh the clouds his chariot; who walketh upon the wings of the wind:

God's construction materials are vastly different from ours (Amos 9:6); everything is supported by His awesome power. His "beams" (Heb. *qara'*, **kah-RAH**, meaning something built from wood or having wooden beams) in footings of water are infinitely more stable than our strongest steel and concrete. Our great King doesn't require chariots or limousines to define His royalty; rather, He rides on the "clouds" (Heb. *'av*, **AHV**, meaning a thick cloud), and the "wind" (Heb. *ruakh*, **ROO-akh**, meaning spirit; also, breath or wind) is harnessed for His traveling needs. The sky itself obeys His every whim like a plane obeys its pilot. If the beams of His tabernacle are stabilized in the oceans, the clouds are His equally firm floorboards, and the wind provides His corridors.

4 Who maketh his angels spirits; his ministers a flaming fire:

Both "spirit(s)" and "wind" (v. 3) are translated from the same Hebrew word (*ruakh*). If "angels" (Heb. *mal'ak*, **mal-AHK**, meaning messenger) are made into spirits, they are also made into wind (see also Hebrews 1:7). In some sense, God speaks words or breathes out life (wind), and angels (messengers) take His breath or words of life to deliver them (Psalm 103:20). We must remember the incredible power and importance of all God's countless angels (Matthew 25:31; 2 Thessalonians 1:7; Hebrews 12:22; Revelation 5:11), especially guardian angels (Psalm 91:11), cherubim (Genesis 3:24; Exodus 25:20), seraphim (Isaiah 6:2, 6), and the archangels (1 Thessalonians 4:16; Jude 9).

24 O LORD, how manifold are thy works! in wisdom hast thou made them all: the earth is full of thy riches.

This second portion of our lesson, verses 24–30, focuses on the animals of creation and the sustaining produce of the earth. In verses prior to this portion (vv. 10-18), the psalm writer elaborates on God's intentional inter-connectedness of creation. Water first finds its place and then becomes a resource for all creation. It sustains life and fruitfulness and produces food, seed, or supply for myriads of needs. Then everything is refreshed and replenished by rain. Everything God does—all His many "works" (cf. v. 13) are wonderful, magnificent, and excellent in every way; individually or collectively, they reveal His wisdom, power, creativity, and glory.

25 So is this great and wide sea, wherein are things creeping innumerable, both small and great beasts. 26 There go the ships: there is that leviathan, whom thou hast made to play therein.

From the perspective of ancient writers, both ships on the sea (Proverbs 30:18–19) and the great sea creatures (Job 41:1; Psalm 74:14; Isaiah 27:1) were marvels that particularly revealed to them God's boundless creative ability. This verse uses a literary device called hendiadys, which is when a part is used to

represent the whole (e.g., from homeless box to penthouse suite, representing all residences). So it is that ships on the great sea and beasts of all kinds in the sea represent all of creation.

27 These wait all upon thee; that thou mayest give them their meat in due season. 28 That thou givest them they gather: thou openest thine hand, they are filled with good. 29 Thou hidest thy face, they are troubled: thou takest away their breath, they die, and return to their dust. 30 Thou sendest forth thy spirit, they are created: and thou renewest the face of the earth.

God is the Source and Sustainer; He is the Maker and the Maintainer—everything comes from Him and everything depends on Him, including humankind. All of the living things expect that God will provide them with food when it's necessary. "Wait" here means to expect or hope for something to happen (Heb *siber*, **see-BARE**). The picture is of God as nurturer—opening His very hand to feed.

In Hebrew, "breath" is *ru'ach* (**RU-akh**), and means wind, breath, mind, or spirit. It is the same word used in Genesis 1:2: "The Spirit [*ruach*] of God moved upon the face of the waters." It is also the same word in Genesis 7:22, referring to all the creatures taken aboard the Ark: "All in whose nostrils was the breath [*ruach*] of life." *Ruach* also is used for both man and animals in Ecclesiastes 3:21. A quick look at the verbs in the last four verses (vv. 27–30) gives an overview of all that God does: He gives food to all, He opens His hand and fills creation with good things, He hides His face, He takes away breath/life [*ruach*], He sends His spirit [*ruach*], and He renews everything.

Interestingly, in Genesis 2:7, when God "breathed into his [man's] nostrils the breath of life," the Hebrew uses *neshamah* (**nesh-a-MA**), but it is essentially an interchangeable synonym for *ruach*. In Isaiah 42:5, "He that giveth breath [*neshemah*] unto the people ... and spirit [*ruach*] to them." Also in Job 34:14, both Hebrew words are used side by side to indicate either man's life or death: "If he gather unto himself his spirit [*ruach*] and his breath [*neshamah*]." Both *neshamah* and *ruach* are used for the English "breath of life" in Genesis 7:22. The essence of the passage is that God is both Giver and Sustainer of the very breath and spirit within all living things—He alone gives, sustains, and takes life away.

Say It Correctly

Innumerable. in-oom-er-ah-**BULL**.
Renewest. **REE**-noo-wist.

Daily Bible Readings

MONDAY
God Sets Boundaries on the Earth
(Psalm 104:5–9)

TUESDAY
God Quenches the Thirsty Earth
(Psalm 104:10–18)

WEDNESDAY
God Establishes Times and Seasons
(Psalm 104:19–23)

THURSDAY
Joy and Wish for Perfect Harmony
(Psalm 104:31–35)

FRIDAY
God Gives Humanity Its Dignity
(Psalm 8)

SATURDAY
Do Not Worry, God Will Provide
(Matthew 6:25–34)

SUNDAY
The Lord Our Creator and Provider
(Psalm 104:1–4, 24–30)

Notes

_____

_____

_____

Teaching Tips

Words You Should Know
A. Praise (Psalm 148:1) *halal* (Heb.)—To make boast, celebrate, commend, to bow.

B. Command (v. 5) *tsavah* (Heb.)—To lay charge upon, give charge to, or order.

Teacher Preparation
Unifying Principle—Global Applause. We think that nature exists for our benefit alone. Why was the world created? The psalmist asks every element of creation to join the chorus of praise for all that God has made.

A. Pray as you read Psalm 148 for the students to understand their part in the choir of praise.

B. Complete Lesson 9 in the *Precepts For Living®* Personal Study Guide.

C. Prepare for class by cutting out pictures of things in creation listed in the psalm (oceans, clouds, insects, birds, etc.).

O—Open the Lesson
A. Pass out the creation pictures to each student as they come in the classroom. Up where the entire class can see, list how each item of nature or animal praises God. Ask, "What does that teach us?"

B. Have each student pray a one- or two-sentence prayer based on the previous exercise.

C. Have one student read the Aim for Change and In Focus story. Ask, "How does this change your perspective on praise?"

D. Read the Keep in Mind verse together.

P—Present the Scriptures
A. Go around the room and take turns reading the Focal Verses and The People, Places, and Times. Discuss.

B. Read and discuss the Background section.

C. Stop at various times throughout the lesson and ask a student to say a sentence praise prayer for that part of the lesson.

E—Explore the Meaning
A. Review and discuss the Search the Scriptures and Discuss the Meaning questions and the Lesson in Our Society section.

B. Ask students to share one or two things that spoke to their hearts from the lesson and how they plan to put it into practice.

N—Next Steps for Application
A. Complete the Follow the Spirit and Remember Your Thoughts sections.

B. Remind students to read the Daily Bible Readings in preparation for next week's lesson.

C. Close in prayer, asking God to teach us how to do our part in the universal choir of praise.

Worship Guide

For the Superintendent or Teacher
Theme: All Creation Praises God
Song: "Total Praise"
Devotional Reading: Psalm 150

All Creation Praises God

Bible Background • PSALM 148
Printed Text • PSALM 148 | Devotional Reading • PSALM 150

Aim for Change

By the end of the lesson, we will: ACKNOWLEDGE that creation exists primarily to praise God, not to meet our physical needs; EXULT in the wonders of God's creation; and TREAT the things of nature with greater respect as befits their divine purpose.

In Focus

Derrick struggled with depression for years. He remembered his mom taking him to doctors and counselors as a child because his teachers commented that he always looked so sad. As an adult, he finally found a medication he thought worked well, but after a few years, the depression continued, like a persistent dark cloud.

Derrick's pastor suggested he take a class chronicling the life of David and the book of Psalms to deal with his depression. He had no idea how it would help, but he agreed to try it. As he read over his final paper for the class, he couldn't believe he'd been a Christian for more than 30 years and missed this important truth. As Derrick studied the life of David and the Psalms, he saw David honestly running to God with every positive and negative event of his life. He praised God for His wisdom, guidance, and courage. Derrick realized he had been self-consumed, angry, and living out the wrong purpose in life.

Since the class began, Derrick got up each morning and not only read Scripture and prayed, but also sang praises to the Lord and asked the Lord to teach him how to be a true worshiper like David. His depression didn't disappear overnight, but now he had hope and a way to deal with it beyond the medication.

One co-worker commented, "Derrick, I've been working with you for five years, and I do believe this is the first time I've seen you really smile."

Do you realize your life's purpose is to worship God? What is God teaching you about how to become a true worshiper?

Keep in Mind

"Let them praise the name of the LORD; for he commanded, and they were created" (Psalm 148:5).

"Let them praise the name of the LORD; for he commanded, and they were created" (Psalm 148:5).

Focal Verses

KJV **Psalm 148:1** Praise ye the LORD, Praise ye the LORD from the heavens; praise him in the heights.

2 Praise ye him, all his angels: praise ye him, all his hosts.

3 Praise ye him, sun and moon; praise him, all ye stars of light.

4 Praise him, ye heavens of heavens, and ye waters that are above the heavens

5 Let them praise the name of the LORD; for he commanded, and they were created.

6 He hath also stablished for them forever and ever; he had made a decree which shall not pass.

7 Praise the LORD from the earth, ye dragons, and all deeps;

8 Fire, and hail; snow, and vapor; stormy wind fulfilling his word.

9 Mountains, and all hills; fruitful trees, and all cedars;

10 Beasts, and all cattle; creeping things, and flying fowl:

11 Kings of the earth, and all people; princes, and all judges of the earth:

12 Both young men, and maidens; old men, and children;

13 Let them praise the name of the LORD: for his name alone is excellent; his glory is above the earth and heaven.

14 He also exalteth the horn of his people, the praise of all his saints; even of the children of Israel, a people near unto him. Praise ye the LORD.

NLT **Psalm 148:1** Praise the LORD! Praise the LORD from the heavens! Praise him from the skies!

2 Praise him, all his angels! Praise him, all the armies of heaven!

3 Praise him, sun and moon! Praise him, all you twinkling stars!

4 Praise him, skies above! Praise him, vapors high above the clouds!

5 Let every created thing give praise to the LORD, for he issued his command, and they came into being.

6 He set them in place forever and ever. His decree will never be revoked.

7 Praise the LORD from the earth, you creatures of the ocean depths,

8 Fire and hail, snow and clouds, wind and weather that obey him,

9 mountains and all hills, fruit trees and all cedars,

10 wild animals and all livestock, small scurrying animals and birds,

11 kings of the earth and all people; rulers and judges on the earth,

12 young men and young women, old men and children.

13 Let them all praise the name of the LORD. For his name is very great; His glory towers over the earth and heaven!

14 He has made his people strong, honoring his faithful ones—the people of Israel who are close to him. Praise the LORD!

The People, Places, and Times

Psalmist. The writer of this psalm is unknown, but he definitely had a passionate heart filled with praise for God. The call is for more praise and worship, not merely an individual's expression but a call to the entire universe. The occasion for this psalm is unknown. Some point to peacetime in King David's reign, when he had rest from all enemies and the kingdom of Israel was settled and prospering. Others point to the time during the Temple rebuilding after the Babylonian exile.

Horn. The horn was a symbol of power and strength in ancient times, and the horn of God's people refers to the strength of His people who praise Him.

Background

The Apostle Paul, in the book of Philippians, spoke of the coming season when every knee will bow and every tongue will confess Jesus as Lord (Philippians 2:5–11). In the last days, this time of worship includes the involvement of all creation.

Christ's second coming and the establishment of the new heaven and new earth will be even better than the Garden of Eden, before the Fall. It's a world without disasters and political unrest, with no chance for sin to enter (Revelation 21:4). Satan no longer roams the earth, causing havoc for God's people. Death has no part in the new kingdom.

At this time, a total praise from every inch of this new creation harmoniously goes up to God without any hindrances or interference. An enormous hallelujah chorus in the heavens and earth—here every created thing—sings praise to the Lord. Everything that has life is at its emotional height, shining its brightest. The universe is once again united in harmonious faith in Jesus, who is worthy (Revelation 5:12). The victory won by the Lamb of God is the reason for this great assembly. Blessing, honor, glory, and power are His. This is the moment all of creation has waited for, and their hope is unashamed (Romans 10:11). This psalm foreshadows that day when all of creation will offer praise to God.

At-A-Glance

1. Heavenly Worship (Psalm 148:1–6)
2. Earthly Worship (vv. 7–10)
3. Specific Worship (vv. 11–12)
4. Everyone Worship (vv. 13–14)

In Depth

1. Heavenly Worship (Psalm 148:1–6)

The author placed the theme of the psalm at the very beginning: "Praise the Lord." The worshiping celebration starts with the heavens, the highest region of God's creation. One of the main groups in heaven is the angelic host. Their duty is to praise God continually and be available to do His bidding.

Sun, moon, stars, and all heavenly elements also join in praise to the Father. God designed them to shine and give Him glory every night and day. The clouds carry within themselves an enormous amount of water. God makes sure only a certain amount is released for humanity's needs. This emphasizes His orderly creation.

Why universal praise to God? He spoke, and everything that exists in the world came into being at His command. The song is absolutely correct: "This is My Father's World." Moreover, He also sustains the world. Nothing will expire or run out; what He causes to rise up will stand forever.

2. Earthly Worship (vv. 7–10)

The author petitions the sea creatures to bring forth praise. This probably referred to extinct animals from the past, and everything present in the depths of the oceans. This likewise included the sea itself, pools, waves, tides, and any other water activity. The perfect harmony of these elements points to an intelligent, perfect Creator.

The next set of elements—fire, water, hail, snow, cloud, and wind—fulfill a specific purpose. It's difficult to understand natural disasters resulting in major destruction of property and loss of lives. Yet, God is in control and at those times one must trust in His plans and sovereignty. Fruit trees produce food and cedars contribute to humankind's shelter. From within hills and mountains, mines and minerals help people survive. The provisions result in people praising God.

Both wild and tame animals and birds are supported by God; He supplies their food and drink. He also directs their course and activities, so every one of them moves in harmony, even the smallest insect and snake. He beckons them to join in with those who praise Him.

3. Specific Worship (vv. 11–12)

Kings, princes, judges, and all those in authority are asked to praise God, because He puts men and women in places of government, provides them with precious gifts, and cancels enemies' plots. God deserves acknowledgment from those in places of power.

The psalmist emphasizes the high-ranking officials and then points out ordinary men, women, and children. Youth in their prime of life, full of vigor and energy, looking forward to plenty of life ahead, and the older generation, thankful for their full lives, both offer praise and thanksgiving to God. Even from children who do not have an extensive history with God, He still calls for praise (Matthew 21:15).

4. Everyone Worship (vv. 13–14)

The psalmist concludes by calling everyone and everything from everywhere to come together and praise the Lord, because He is excellent and His glory is above the earth and heaven. He's perfect in all His dealings, good, and generous. However, if God provided nothing, just His name is worth a celebration of praise.

God specifically pointed out Israel at the end of this hymn. Some scholars believe the address to Israel is not the literal nation, but a spiritual Israel, which includes both Jew and Gentile, who looked to the coming Messiah (Romans 2:28–29). God's children realize their punishment for sin should have been eternal damnation, but God sent Jesus as a payment.

Condemnation no longer hangs over their heads. This fact alone produces a humble worship-filled heart.

Search the Scriptures

1. In what way does nature (sun and moon, fire and hail, etc.) praise the Lord (Psalm 148:1–14)?

2. The command to praise the Lord is for all people (v. 11). Is the command to praise the Lord truly for all people on earth or exclusively those who have a relationship with Him?

Discuss the Meaning

What would a harmonious world look like that praises God together? Is that what we are thinking about and what we truly desire when we have praise and worship in our church?

Lesson in Our Society

People become Christians for various reasons. Some want to escape hell and go to heaven. Others want benefits, such as being wealthy or having good health. Still others are hurt people seeking help for personal problems. But as you grow and mature in Christ, understand you were created to be God's vessel of praise and ask Him how to become a daily worshiper. This should become a life priority.

Make It Happen

Fill the pockets of your heart with praise. In the course of the day, we have waiting time, downtime, and do-nothing time. Is it possible for us to fill those pockets of time with a praise, Scripture, or song this week?

Follow the Spirit

What God wants me to do:

_____

_____

_____

_____

Remember Your Thoughts

Special insights I have learned:

_____

_____

_____

More Light on the Text

Psalm 148:1–14

1 Praise ye the Lord. Praise ye the Lord from the heavens: praise him in the heights. 2 Praise ye him, all his angels: praise ye him, all his hosts.

The psalmist gives the command to praise the Lord. In Hebrew, the phrase is "hallelujah," which means to celebrate or praise the Lord (*Yah* in Hebrew is a form of God's title "Lord"). This phrase is often repeated in Psalms 145–150, occurring more than ten times. Here we end with a crescendo of praise that encompasses the whole known world.

Next, the psalmist calls for praise from the inhabitants of heaven (Heb. *shamayim,* **sha-MAH-yeem**); they can praise God in the heights (Heb. *marom,* **mah-ROME**). These two terms designate not just the sky or expanse above the earth, but where the ancient Israelites believed God resided with His angels (Heb. *mal'ak,* **mall-AHK**) or messengers. Many

of these angels, such as the seraphim, existed solely to worship and praise God.

3 Praise ye him, sun and moon: praise him, all ye stars of light. 4 Praise him, ye heavens of heavens, and ye waters that be above the heavens.

Now, the psalmist turns to the celestial bodies in the heavens, personifying the sun, moon, and stars and making them capable of praising God. These celestial bodies were often objects of worship in the ancient Near East. The psalmist reverses what many would see as objects of reverence and puts them in their rightful place—they are made to revere God. They are not literally inanimate objects verbally boasting about God, but signs and evidence of His greatness. By performing their allotted tasks, they point to the power and wisdom of their Creator.

The "heavens of heavens" may refer to the highest or most distant parts unknown to humankind. The expression is superlative—the best part of the heavens—perhaps indicating the part nearest to God. The psalmist here expands the scope of the praise due to God. Praise issues forth to Him from even the farthest reaches. The "waters that be above the heavens" (Genesis 1:7) alludes to the ancient idea of a canopy of water that existed in the sky over the earth. This canopy was thought to be a worldwide blanket of water vapor. Some believe this to be the cause of the worldwide flood in Genesis 7. Although this reference to the canopy or expanse of water is well after the flood, it is well fixed in the mind of the ancient writer as a part of God's creation.

5 Let them praise the name of the LORD: for he commanded, and they were created. 6 He hath also stablished them for ever and ever: he hath made a decree which shall not pass.

The reason for the heavens and their residents to praise God is His inherent power in creating the universe. The psalmist says that he commanded (Heb. *tsavah*, **tsa-VAH**), which means to charge someone to do something. God is sovereign over His creation. He speaks, and creation must obey. Furthermore, He creates *ex nihilo* or "out of nothing." He commanded, and they were created (Heb. *bara'*, **bah-RAH**). The word has the connotation of cutting out or carving out, meaning to be brought into existence. It is limited to the creative work of God alone, indicating the distinction and superiority of God's work. Nothing would exist without the power of the sovereign God. This is the reason for them to praise Him.

To further add to God's greatness, the psalmist tells how creation was just the beginning. The Lord also "stablished them for ever and ever." The word "stablished" (Heb. *'amad*, **ah-MAHD**) means to stand. The stars, sun, moon, and the entire heavens are standing in position and fulfilling the purpose God created them for at the dawn of time. God made a decree (Heb. *choq*, **HOKE**), or a law, which will never pass (Heb. *'avar*, **ah-VAR**), or fade away.

7 Praise the LORD from the earth, ye dragons, and all deeps:

The psalmist began in the heights, but now he descends to the depths. Whereas before he started the call to praise with the angels, supernatural beings of beauty and perfection, in this verse he points to the great sea creatures or dragons (Heb. *tannin*, **ta-NEEN**). These creatures were believed to dwell in the deeps (Heb. *tehom*, **teh-HOME**) or the ocean. These creatures were believed to oppose God and His people, and they were greatly feared. The psalmist says there is nothing to fear because even these creatures were created by God and are capable of praising Him.

Even the deeps or depths of the oceans and seas praise God. In ancient times, the sea was viewed as an unstable place. It was the great unknown, associated with chaos and darkness. As such, these places were to be avoided. The psalmist says that even these places are created by God and called to give Him praise.

8 Fire, and hail; snow, and vapours; stormy wind fulfilling his word: 9 Mountains, and all hills; fruitful trees, and all cedars: 10 Beasts, and all cattle; creeping things, and flying fowl:

Here the psalmist involves the whole span of creation. The Lord is sovereign over the elements; they fulfill (Heb. *'asah*, **ah-SAH**) or accomplish His Word. The sense is that they thoroughly and entirely put into effect the commands that are given. Nothing is outside the range of God and His sovereignty. The mountains, hills, and trees are called to praise Him. The beasts and cattle are called to praise Him. Even the creeping things (Heb. *remes*, **REH-mes**) or animals that crawl, such as reptiles, are called to praise Him.

11 Kings of the earth, and all people; princes, and all judges of the earth: 12 Both young men, and maidens; old men, and children: 13 Let them praise the name of the Lord: for his name alone is excellent; his glory is above the earth and heaven.

Next, the psalmist includes humanity in the chorus of praise, including those of high position such as kings, princes, and judges. The greatness of these rulers is outmatched by the glory of the Lord. He is King over everyone. He also directs the call toward the young men and the maidens. Those who are in the prime of life are called to praise Him. Both male and female, elders and children—in other words, all in the community—are called to praise God.

This is because the Lord's name alone is excellent (Heb. *sagav*, **sah-GAV**), meaning to be high and unattainable. The sense is that the Lord's name is exalted above all other names, and His glory, or *hod* (Heb. **HODE**), is above the heavens. The word for glory can be translated as majesty and has the same sense of weight, referring to the quality of awe or reverence it inspires in others. Clearly, the psalmist believes the Lord has no equal.

14 He also exalteth the horn of his people, the praise of all his saints; even of the children of Israel, a people near unto him. Praise ye the Lord.

The psalmist ends with an addendum to the reason for joining this chorus of praise. Not only is the Lord's name excellent and His glory above the heavens, but He also is praised for what He has done for His people. He "exalteth the horn of his people," which means He has honored His people for their strength. Although the word "horn" (Heb. *qeren*, **KEH-ren**) can simply refer to an animal horn, in poetry it carries with it the connotation of power and strength. The One who deserves all the glory and praise has lifted up His people.

This exalting of the horn also shows God's greatness and glory. This causes His saints (Heb. *chasid*, **kha-SEED**), or faithful and holy ones, to praise Him even more. This horn is the reason for the praise of the Children of Israel, a people who are near to Him. These people have experienced His majesty and power and have the most reason to praise the Lord.

Say It Correctly

Stablisheth. **STA**-bli-shith.
Exalteth. ek-**ZAL**-tith.

Daily Bible Readings

MONDAY
Praise the Lord!
(Psalm 150)

TUESDAY
Heavenly Beings Shout for Joy
(Job 38:1–7)

WEDNESDAY
Wisdom Present at Creation
(Proverbs 8:22–31)

THURSDAY
Angels Praise God
(Luke 2:8–14)

FRIDAY
Humans Continue God's Caring Ways
(Deuteronomy 24:17–22)

SATURDAY
God's Gracious Ways
(Psalm 145:13b–21)

SUNDAY
Let All Creation Praise the Lord!
(Psalm 148)

Teaching Tips

Words You Should Know

A. Baptize (Galatians 3:27) *baptizo* (Gk.)—To wash ceremonially; to dip or plunge into water.

B. Abba (v. 4:6) *abba* (from Aramaic)—Dear father.

Teacher Preparation

Unifying Principle—Recreated to Live in Harmony. Differences of race, class, and gender make it hard for people to get along. How can we live in harmony? Paul tells the Galatians that through Christ we have received the Spirit, making us heirs of God and bringing us into a community of oneness where human differences are no longer divisive.

A. Complete Lesson 10 in the *Precepts For Living*® Personal Study Guide.

B. Reread the Focal Verses in a few other translations.

O—Open the Lesson

A. Open with prayer.

B. Have a student read the Aim for Change.

C. Ask for a volunteer to read the In Focus story.

D. Discuss how Christians can present their bodies as living sacrifices.

P—Present the Scriptures

A. Ask for volunteers to read the Focal Verses and The People, Places, and Times. Discuss.

B. Read and discuss the Background section.

E—Explore the Meaning

A. Review and discuss the Search the Scriptures, Discuss the Meaning questions, and the Lesson in Our Society section.

B. Ask students to share the most significant point they learned and how to use that point this week.

N—Next Steps for Application

A. Complete the Follow the Spirit and Remember Your Thoughts sections.

B. Remind students to read the Daily Bible Readings in preparation for next week's lesson.

C. Close in prayer, thanking God for His presence in our lives.

Worship Guide

For the Superintendent or Teacher
Theme: Re-Created to Live in Harmony
Song: "Blessed Assurance"
Devotional Reading: Colossians 3:12–17

Re-Created to Live in Harmony

Bible Background • GALATIANS 3:26–4:7
Printed Text • GALATIANS 3:26–4:7 | Devotional Reading • COLOSSIANS 3:12–17

Aim for Change

By the end of the lesson, we will: DISCOVER the unity of Christians based on the saving work of Christ and the Holy Spirit; APPRECIATE that, through Christ, we are all one in the church; and EXAMINE ourselves for prejudiced attitudes against other believers.

In Focus

Keith had been working with Edward for a couple of weeks when he noticed Edward in the break room reading his Bible. They began a deep discussion about Christ and enjoyed each other's fellowship. Soon they began to meet once a week at lunch to study the Word together, and Edward invited Keith to his church. Once Keith looked the church up on the Web, he noticed some things he didn't agree with in their statement of faith. It seemed that they approved of practices that he and his pastor looked down on. It wasn't that they were sins, but he knew he disagreed with them. He wondered if he could continue to be friends with Edward and whether Edward was a bad influence on him.

Instead of deciding to not go to Edward's church service, Keith decided to press through. Surprisingly, he enjoyed the service. The people he met at the door were all very pleasant. Worship was very high-tech and included videos and praise dancers. The message was about the greatness of Jesus Christ and the power of the Gospel. Although Keith didn't agree with much that went on in the service, he knew that his fellowship with Edward centered on Christ. They were brothers because of His blood and not because of their particular worship styles.

How do you strive to maintain unity in the body of Christ as you interact with brothers and sisters who think, look, or act differently?

Keep in Mind

"There is neither Jew nor Greek, there is neither bond nor free, there is neither male nor female: for ye are all one in Christ Jesus" (Galatians 3:28).

"There is neither Jew nor Greek, there is neither bond nor free, there is neither male nor female: for ye are all one in Christ Jesus" (Galatians 3:28).

Focal Verses

KJV Galatians 3:26 For ye are all the children of God by faith in Christ Jesus.

27 For as many of you as have been baptized into Christ have put on Christ.

28 There is neither Jew nor Greek, there is neither bond nor free, there is neither male nor female: for ye are all one in Christ Jesus.

29 And if ye be Christ's, then are ye Abraham's seed, and heirs according to the promise.

4:1 Now I say, That the heir, as long as he is a child, differeth nothing from a servant, though he be lord of all;

2 But is under tutors and governors until the time appointed of the father.

3 Even so we, when we were children, were in bondage under the elements of the world:

4 But when the fulness of the time was come, God sent forth his Son, made of a woman, made under the law,

5 To redeem them that were under the law, that we might receive the adoption of sons.

6 And because ye are sons, God hath sent forth the Spirit of his Son into your hearts, crying, Abba, Father.

7 Wherefore thou art no more a servant, but a son; and if a son, then an heir of God through Christ.

NLT Galatians 3:26 For you are all children of God through faith in Christ Jesus.

27 And all who have been united with Christ in baptism have put on the character of Christ, like putting on new clothes.

28 There is no longer Jew or Gentile, slave or free, male and female. For you are all one in Christ Jesus.

29 And now that you belong to Christ, you are the true children of Abraham. You are his heirs, and God's promise to Abraham belongs to you.

4:1 Think of it this way. If a father dies and leaves an inheritance for his young children, those children are not much better off than slaves until they grow up, even though they actually own everything their father had.

2 They have to obey their guardians until they reach whatever age their father set.

3 And that's the way it was with us before Christ came. We were like children; we were slaves to the basic spiritual principles of this world.

4 But when the right time came, God sent his Son, born of a woman, subject to the law.

5 God sent him to buy freedom for us who were slaves to the law, so that he could adopt us as his very own children.

6 And because we are his children, God has sent the Spirit of his Son into our hearts, prompting us to call out, "Abba, Father."

7 Now you are no longer a slave but God's own child. And since you are his child, God has made you his heir.

The People, Places, and Times

Paul. At one time known as Saul (Hebrew name meaning desired), Paul was born around the same time as Jesus Christ in Tarsus, the capital of Cilicia. His father was Jewish but a Roman citizen. There is not much mention of his mother. However, we can read about a sister and nephew and other relatives in Acts and Romans.

As Paul was growing up, he learned to make tents from goats' haircloth, a common trade in Tarsus. After finishing his basic schooling, Saul was sent to school for law when he was about thirteen years old. For some time after the Pentecost, Stephen, who was one of the seven deacons, preached about Jesus, stirring some of the Jewish leaders (because some were following the disciples). Saul and others persecuted Stephen and those that followed Christ. Saul had an encounter with Jesus on the Damascus road and was converted. Taking on the name Paul (Greek for small or little), he spent his life preaching the Gospel to the Gentiles.

Galatia. Located in the central region of Asia Minor, Galatia has been referred to as Gallia of the East. In Roman times, Galatia was an ethnically mixed province due to its location in the empire.

Background

The nation of Israel was known as God's children in the Old Testament. Judaism spoke of being clothed by the Spirit. In Paul's time, occasionally Gentiles would convert to Judaism, which included a ritual baptism and circumcision of males. Followers of Jesus included Jews who followed Torah tradition, as well as Gentiles from other cults of the Roman Empire. Galatians reflects, more strongly than most New Testament texts, on the conflict among followers of Jesus regarding whether Gentiles needed to follow all of the Torah or not, with Paul clearly falling on the side of Gentile freedom from such Torah commands such as circumcision and temple sacrifices.

In addition, some Greco-Roman cults did not honor social divisions because they were expensive, and could exclude everyone but the rich. However, the earlier Christians were resistant to division and formed bridges between the Jews and the Gentiles. The Jewish people were known as Abraham's seed, or offspring, with an inheritance to the promise.

Under the Roman law, minors were considered slaves. A minor had to have a legal guardian. If the minor's father was dead, the guardian was chosen from the father's will. If the will was not available, the responsibility went to the nearest male relative. Galatians were freed from slavery or needed a guardian. God adopted them and made them His children, with a powerful inheritance.

At-A-Glance

1. One in Christ (Galatians 3:26–29)
2. The World in Bondage (4:1–3)
3. God Delivered the World (vv. 4–7)

In Depth

1. One in Christ (Galatians 3:26–29)

Faith in Jesus Christ allows Christians to experience the Gospel's benefits because we are no longer slaves or servants but now God's actual children. Accepting Christ Jesus as Lord and Savior changes the perspective of being compelled to perform certain rituals. We believe in Him by faith for justification and salvation, making us the children of God. Baptism allows us to put on Christ Jesus, an outward expression of an inner change. Just as He died for us and rose again, we must also die to sin.

When we believe and receive Christ, God honors our faith and clothes us with His righteousness. Now that we are clothed with Jesus' purity, God no longer sees us without seeing His Son, and He accepts us. This makes us one in Christ Jesus.

Believers in Christ are also Abraham's seed. Christ is the seed of Abraham, and being a Christian makes a person part of that seed, as well as an heir to the promise of Abraham. We are not just heirs, but also joint heirs to Christ Jesus (Romans 8:15–17)!

2. The World in Bondage (4:1–3)

An heir has to wait for an appointed time to receive an inheritance. He (usually a male) would have the security of knowing that he was freeborn and due to receive his father's inheritance. The heir still has to be submissive to those over him until the set time comes. The comparison is made with us, as Christians. Before Christ, we were just like slaves, being controlled by the dominating forces of this world.

It was previously difficult to approach God before Christ, because knowledge about who God is was very limited. The available knowledge had to be accompanied by the discipline and guidance of the Law. When Christ came, He delivered us from the Law, giving us a parent-child relationship with God. Thus, we are not slaves under the Law anymore but children of God, in Christ Jesus.

3. God Delivered the World (vv. 4–7)

An earthly father can choose when his child is an adult eligible to receive the inheritance set aside for him. God did the same thing; He chose the time to send His Son to fulfill His work. God sent His Son for two reasons. The first was to redeem and set free those under the Law. The second reason was to give believers all rights and privileges of being God's children. By faith, God adopts believers through Christ, making them His children. God did not stop there; He also sent the Spirit of His Son. Every believer has the Spirit inside, bearing witness that they are part of God's holy family. God made it personal for believers, allowing them

to refer to Him as Abba Father, indicating an intimacy with His children.

Paul drew this to a conclusion, proclaiming Galatians were not slaves anymore but now children and heirs. The difference in verses 6 and 7 brings out the personal relationship the believer has with the Father through Christ.

Search the Scriptures

1. Why does God choose faith in Christ Jesus as the means of making us His children (Galatians 3:26)?

2. How would you evaluate whether the Spirit of God was in your heart (4:6)?

Discuss the Meaning

We should celebrate our commonalities when we encounter others in the faith. God has chosen to make us His children by faith, and this is worth celebrating. At the same time, how do we recognize and celebrate our unique ethnic identities?

Lesson in Our Society

Being adopted by God as His child comes with great responsibility. As with the inheritance we receive, we also have a responsibility and commitment to live according to the way our Father has set for us. We are new creatures in Christ, and the way we live our lives should line up accordingly.

Make It Happen

Ask yourself: Do I treat every believer in the faith as my brother and sister in Christ? If I do, how can I express love in a greater way? If not, try to make a conscious effort to ask God for help to see His children the way He does and to treat them as such.

Follow the Spirit

What God wants me to do:

_____

_____

_____

_____

Remember Your Thoughts

Special insights I have learned:

_____

_____

_____

_____

More Light on the Text

Galatians 3:26–4:7

26 For ye are all the children of God by faith in Christ Jesus.

This verse expresses Paul's compassionate and pastoral heart. Though correct in his presentation of the Gospel, he says harsh things about the Galatians' failure to understand and learn the message of justification by faith. This is because some Jewish leaders of the church tried (and succeeded) in getting the Gentile Galatians to circumcise their males, which Paul thought unnecessary for participation in the promise of Christ (see 2:11–21). Paul reminds the Galatians, however, that despite their failings, they are now "the children of God by faith in Christ Jesus." Paul teaches that we are made acceptable to God not because we fully understand the doctrine, but because we believe in the Lord Jesus Christ.

27 For as many of you as have been baptized into Christ have put on Christ.

Although this is Paul's only reference to Christian baptism in this letter to the Galatians, the reference is significant. The phrase "have been baptized into Christ" is Paul's way of calling out those who have accepted God's free grace through faith. The Greek word for "put on" (*enduo*, **en-DOO-oh**) means to be clothed, wear, or dress. Their water baptism, being a symbolic expression of their acceptance of Christ, affirms that they have indeed "clothed" themselves with Christ.

28 There is neither Jew nor Greek, there is neither bond nor free, there is neither male nor female: for ye are all one in Christ Jesus.

Paul uses three couplets to represent inequality. The first being ethnic: Jew/Greek; second, economic: bound/free; and third, gender: male/female. He states that all who, by faith, believe in the Lord Jesus Christ become one with each other. In a culture where Jews were a minority but viewed themselves as the children of God, free-born Gentiles who joined the church were in a precarious position. For non-Jews who had abandoned their official cults, slaves who had no rights, and women who were second-class citizens, Paul's claim of unity is a radical statement. It was good news for the Gentiles, slaves, and women who joined the family of faith.

29 And if ye be Christ's then are ye Abraham's seed, and heirs according to the promise.

With this point, Paul brings the reasoning from the last few verses back to the broader point he has been working through for the whole chapter, explaining how the Gentiles are welcomed into God's family through faith rather than works. Paul wants his Gentile readers to know that their relationship with Christ makes them Abraham's seed and qualifies them to be joint and equal heirs to the blessings outlined in God's promise to Abraham.

4:1 Now I say, That the heir, as long as he is a child, differeth nothing from a servant, though he be lord of all; 2 But is under tutors and governors until the time appointed of the father.

Paul recaps his comments in Galatians 3:23–29, where he presented the Galatians as being "heirs according to the promise." Although the Jews were heirs to the promise, some of them were held captive to the discipline of the Law, and treated like children living under the watchful, caring, and protective eye of a steward. This, Paul contended, was necessary because Jesus Christ had not yet come (Galatians 3:23). But after the coming of Christ (v. 3:25), believers were "no longer under" the Law. After the Incarnation, those who believe in Christ were now "sons of God," free to live their lives "unto God" (v. 2:19), "by the faith of the Son of God, who ... gave himself for" them (v. 2:20).

Paul makes the point that although an heir has certain privileges and rights that a slave does not, as a child, the heir is still under the supervision of guardians and tutors. The heir's subjection to the tutors and governors is only "until the time appointed of the father." In other words, the heir will receive inheritance, but not until the day set by the father. This imagery recalls Paul's comment in 3:23, and anticipates his comment in 4:4. With great literary skill, Paul uses the legal language governing the inheritance law of his day to set the stage for his statements in verses 3–5.

3 Even so we, when we were children, were in bondage under the elements of the world:

In the next three verses, Paul applies the illustration set forth in verses 1–2 to help explain the Galatians' experience. The question persists, however, about who the pronoun "we" refers to. Is this a reference to Jews or Gentiles, or both—including Paul? Given Paul's message of inclusiveness and his conviction that Christ came to rescue all people from enslavement to "the elements of the world" (of which the Law was one enslaving element), it is reasonable to believe that "we" refers to Jews, Gentiles, and Paul.

4 But when the fullness of the time was come, God sent forth his Son, made of a woman, made under the law.

The "fullness of time" recalls the "time appointed of the father" in Paul's illustration about the inheritance in verse 2. This analogy shows that where the Galatians were concerned, their inheritance was in the form of God sending "forth his Son." God's Son was human in that He was "made of a woman" and a Jew in that He was "made under the law." The Greek word for "made" used here is *ginomai* (**GHEE-no-my**), which can also be translated "born" (cf. NLT, NIV, ESV, etc.). In other words, Jesus was born of a woman, and born under the Law. Jesus, God's Son, came into the world like any other Jewish male child. But He came into the world with a mission.

5 To redeem them that were under the law, that we might receive the adoption of sons.

The mission of God's Son was to "redeem" or to emancipate from slavery to the Law those who were heirs to the promise, in order that they might receive the inheritance, namely "the adoption of sons." Paul uses adoption language here as a way of including the Gentiles who were not born Jews, in the inheritance that God has to offer. This brings Paul closer to the conclusion of his analogy. He has one more thing to say.

6 And because ye are sons, God hath sent forth the Spirit of his Son into your hearts, crying Abba, Father.

Before making his concluding statement, Paul reminds the Galatians that receiving their adoption as God's children resulted also in His sending into their hearts "the Spirit of his Son." Not only did the sending of God's Spirit confirm the Galatians' new status and freedom as His children, but it also empowered them to use their freedom responsibly.

7 Wherefore thou art no more a servant, but a son; and if a son, then an heir of God through Christ.

It is obvious from Paul's reasoning that he views each individual Galatian as being in a privileged position. The phrase "thou art" is singular, which indicates that Paul wants to direct his comment to each individual Galatian. It is as if he is saying, "You, you as an individual, are no longer a servant, but a child." The KJV continues, "…and if a son, then an heir of God through Christ." This translation is debatable primarily because the available Greek manuscripts do not all agree. (Some say "through Christ," some say "through God," others have minor variations on the phrasing.) However, the most commonly used Greek New Testament and the earliest manuscripts (one as early as the second century AD) read "through God." This translation makes the Galatians' status as heirs a work of God's grace, which supports Paul's message that salvation is not by works of the Law, but by God's grace freely given through faith in Jesus Christ.

One of the interesting contrasts that Paul makes throughout this section in Galatians is that of son versus servant. The familial language is very significant. The privileges of a son versus those of a servant help to illustrate the difference between having a relationship with God through the efficacious death and resurrection of Jesus Christ and trying to be righteous by obeying the Law. The difference is quite clear. The death of Christ and saving faith brings a believer into the family of God as His adopted children who have an inheritance. As servants, we were not part of the family and did not have any privileges. Why go back to such a system? Through Christ, we are heirs! Through Christ, we cry to God, "Abba, Father."

Say It Correctly

Abba. **AH**-bah.
Differeth. di-**FIR**-ith.

Daily Bible Readings

MONDAY
The Spirit Made You a Believer
(Galatians 3:1–5)

TUESDAY
All Peoples are Blessed Through Abraham
(Genesis 22:15–18)

WEDNESDAY
Jesus Fulfills the Promise to Abraham
(Galatians 3:15–18)

THURSDAY
Baptized into One Body
(1 Corinthians 12:12–18)

FRIDAY
Know that You are Children of God
(1 John 2:28–3:3)

SATURDAY
Serve in the Name of Christ
(Colossians 3:12–17)

SUNDAY
Changed by Christ to Live in Harmony
(Galatians 3:26–4:7)

Notes

Teaching Tips

Words You Should Know

A. Elements (Galatians 4:9) *stoicheion* (Gk.)—Any first thing, from which others belonging to some series or composite whole are composed; a basic or first principle.

B. Zealously affect (v. 17) *zeloo* (Gk.)—To desire earnestly, to strive after, to be focused on a certain thing.

Teacher Preparation

Unifying Principle—No Turning Back. People are tempted to sacrifice freedom in order to gain a sense of security. What are the dangers of this trade-off? Paul rebuked the Galatians for trading the freedom Christ gives for slavery to religious legalism.

A. Reread the Focal Verses in a few other translations.

B. Complete Lesson 11 in the *Precepts For Living*® Personal Study Guide.

O—Open the Lesson

A. Open with prayer.

B. Have a student read the Aim for Change.

C. Ask for a volunteer to read the In Focus story.

P—Present the Scriptures

A. Ask for volunteers to read and discuss the Focal Verses and The People, Places, and Times.

B. Read and discuss the Background section along with the In Depth section.

E—Explore the Meaning

A. Review and discuss the Search the Scriptures section, Discuss the Meaning questions, and the Lesson in Our Society sections.

B. Ask students to share the most significant point they learned and how to use that point this week.

N—Next Steps for Application

A. Review the suggestions for application in the Make It Happen section.

B. Remind students to read the Daily Bible Readings in preparation for next week's lesson.

C. Close in prayer, thanking God for His presence in our life.

Worship Guide

For the Superintendent or Teacher
Theme: New Birth Brings Freedom
Song: "I'm Saved"
Devotional Reading: Romans 8:1–11

New Birth Brings Freedom

Bible Background • GALATIANS 4
Printed Text • GALATIANS 4:8–20 | Devotional Reading • ROMANS 8:1–11

--------- Aim for Change ---------

By the end of this lesson we will: CLASSIFY religious expectations and practices that diminish Christian freedom; EMPATHIZE with those who have been harmed by narrow religiosity; and CHALLENGE unhealthy attitudes toward religious practices or traditions.

--------- In Focus ---------

Every week the preacher would ask if anyone needed to come down the aisle to receive Christ. Every week, Keira would walk down the aisle like it was her first time. She would pray the sinner's prayer fervently. Since it was a large church, no one noticed that she had come up multiple times. Keira had been raised in a church that had a lot of rules and regulations. Many of them had no biblical basis and were based on tradition more than the Word of God. Whenever she violated any of these traditions, Keira began to feel guilty. She knew the Gospel. She knew that Jesus died for her to have a relationship with God, but she still trusted in her behavior to make her right with God.

One day, as she was talking to her friend Regina about what happened over the weekend, Regina noticed the flaw in Keira's thinking. "Keira, you don't have to keep going to the altar and getting saved all over again," Regina said. Keira looked at her like a deer in headlights. "All that means nothing if you don't trust Christ," Regina added. Deep inside something clicked for Keira. It was the start of being free from man-made rules and entering into a deeper relationship with Christ.

In today's lesson, we will explore the religious practices and traditions that can hinder our freedom in Christ. What are some of the unhealthy attitudes and traditions that can distract us from salvation in Christ?

--------- Keep in Mind ---------

"But now, after that ye have known God, or rather are known of God, how turn ye again to the weak and beggarly elements, whereunto ye desire again to be in bondage?" (Galatians 4:9).

"But now, after that ye have known God, or rather are known of God, how turn ye again to the weak and beggarly elements, whereunto ye desire again to be in bondage?" (Galatians 4:9).

Focal Verses

KJV **Galatians 4:8** Howbeit then, when ye knew not God, ye did service unto them which by nature are no gods.

9 But now, after that ye have known God, or rather are known of God, how turn ye again to the weak and beggarly elements, whereunto ye desire again to be in bondage?

10 Ye observe days, and months, and times, and years.

11 I am afraid of you, lest I have bestowed upon you labour in vain.

12 Brethren, I beseech you, be as I am; for I am as ye are: ye have not injured me at all.

13 Ye know how through infirmity of the flesh I preached the gospel unto you at the first.

14 And my temptation which was in my flesh ye despised not, nor rejected; but received me as an angel of God, even as Christ Jesus.

15 Where is then the blessedness ye spake of? for I bear you record, that, if it had been possible, ye would have plucked out your own eyes, and have given them to me.

16 Am I therefore become your enemy, because I tell you the truth?

17 They zealously affect you, but not well; yea, they would exclude you, that ye might affect them.

18 But it is good to be zealously affected always in a good thing, and not only when I am present with you.

19 My little children, of whom I travail in birth again until Christ be formed in you,

20 I desire to be present with you now, and to change my voice; for I stand in doubt of you.

NLT **Galatians 4:8** Before you Gentiles knew God, you were slaves to so-called gods that do not even exist.

9 So now that you know God (or should I say, now that God knows you), why do you want to go back again and become slaves once more to the weak and useless spiritual principles of this world?

10 You are trying to earn favor with God by observing certain days or months or seasons or years.

11 I fear for you. Perhaps all my hard work with you was for nothing.

12 Dear brothers and sisters, I plead with you to live as I do in freedom from these things, for I have become like you Gentiles— free from those laws. You did not mistreat me when I first preached to you.

13 Surely you remember that I was sick when I first brought you the Good News.

14 But even though my condition tempted you to reject me, you did not despise me or turn me away. No, you took me in and cared for me as though I were an angel from God or even Christ Jesus himself.

15 Where is that joyful and grateful spirit you felt then? I am sure you would have taken out your own eyes and given them to me if it had been possible.

16 Have I now become your enemy because I am telling you the truth?

17 Those false teachers are so eager to win your favor, but their intentions are not good. They are trying to shut you off from me so that you will pay attention only to them.

18 If someone is eager to do good things for you, that's all right; but let them do it all the time, not just when I'm with you.

19 Oh, my dear children! I feel as if I'm going through labor pains for you again, and they will continue until Christ is fully developed in your lives.

20 I wish I were with you right now so I could change my tone. But at this distance I don't know how else to help you.

The People, Places, and Times

Judaizers. Throughout the book of Galatians, Paul mounts an unrelenting argument against the Judaizers' beliefs and activities. They were teachers who believed that the way for Gentiles to be right with God was to obey the Law of Moses, including the rite of circumcision. We do not know who the Judaizers were by name, but we do know that they argued and debated with Paul at the Jerusalem Council (Acts 15). The council ruled in favor of Paul and Barnabas and accepted the Gentiles as part of God's people on the basis of their belief in Christ, not circumcision.

Elemental Spirits. In ancient times, many believed in spirits that moved and operated the sun, moon, planets, and stars. These were worshiped as deities and believed to control the fate of individuals. This type of belief system is the origin of astrology, or knowledge of the stars. The astral spirits were associated with special days and rituals. Paul seems to believe that through customs and rituals involving calendar and dates, the Galatians were still in bondage to spiritual powers.

Background

Paul's thoughts in Galatians focus on the truth of the Gospel and the means of justification: Jesus Christ. Throughout the book, he denounces any attempt to justify ourselves through any other means but faith in Jesus. The Judasizers' work had undermined this belief in the Galatian church. Paul lets the Galatians know that what the Judaizers preach is not the Gospel, but in fact anti-gospel leading them back into the same bondage they were in before they believed in Christ. Putting their trust in religion or the Law is just as detrimental as putting their trust in a false deity. They both are idols that cannot save.

For Paul, this matter is of the utmost importance, and he minces no words. He pulls the curtain back and shows how he withstood Peter to his face for behavior in direct opposition to the Gospel (Galatians 2:11–16). In the beginning of the letter, he lets them know that even if an angel from heaven preached another Gospel, let them be accursed. For Paul, the truth of the Gospel is of utmost importance. We can only be justified through our faith in Christ, and can accept no substitutes. Anything less will put us in bondage.

At-A-Glance

1. The Galatians' Deception (Galatians 4:8–11)
2. The Gospel's Reception (vv. 12–15)
3. Paul's Expression (vv. 16–20)

In Depth

1. The Galatians' Deception (Galatians 4:8–11)

Paul lets the Galatians know that they had been set free from serving and worshiping idols. He then presents a rhetorical question to them, asking why they would return to bondage to the "weak and beggarly elements." The Galatians were concerned about special religious days, times, and years. They had been deceived into thinking this was the way to be right with God. These things only served to put them into bondage, while Christ came to set them free.

Paul says that observing these things was expected when they did not know God. However, now that they have heard the Gospel and known God, it is foolish to return to these things. The Galatians were released from the bondage of pagan idolatry, but now the Judaizers were seeking to bring them into religious idolatry. They were using the Jewish religion as a mediator and not trusting in Christ to be their mediator. Paul laments that if this is the case, then he has labored in vain by preaching and teaching them the Gospel.

2. The Gospel's Reception (vv. 12–15)

Next, the apostle appeals to them to become like him. He asks them to do this as a reciprocal action to his becoming like them (i.e., as a Gentile not under the Law). Paul exercised his freedom from the Law in order to contextualize the Gospel message for his Gentile audience in Galatia.

Next, he launches into his past history with the Galatians. He speaks of how he labored and preached the Gospel to them while suffering. Paul speaks of an infirmity of the flesh. We do not know exactly what this infirmity is, but we do know that the Galatians knew about it and Paul endured the pain of it while preaching to them. He also steers the letter toward the Galatians' reception of the Gospel and himself. While he was preaching and suffering, they received him as an angel of God and as Christ Himself. He recalls that if they could have, they would have plucked out their own eyes and given them to him. Paul states this to

remind them of the truth they had committed themselves to previously. Prior to their turning to religion to make themselves righteous, they had received the Gospel that he preached and believed in the sufficiency of Christ and His righteousness. Paul speaks to them to remind them and alert them to the empty path that they are now on.

3. Paul's Expression (vv. 16–20)

Paul is doubtlessly grieved as he asks if he is their enemy for speaking the truth. The Judaizers had influenced the Galatians with false teaching and effectively shut down Paul's influence on the young church. They wanted the Galatians to solely pay attention to them, not Paul. Paul says it is good to go after the right thing. The Judaizers were after the Galatians but for the wrong reasons: to preach strict Torah observance that they claimed would result in exclusion from the faith if transgressed.

Paul ends this section with a metaphor that reveals his true feelings and desire. He says that he travails like a woman in labor until Christ is formed in them. The metaphor here cannot be missed. His emotional state for them is likened to a woman in labor pains. This is how badly he wants to see the Galatians transformed into the image of Christ. This turn toward a false gospel of religion is a move away from that goal. Paul's grief is intense. He states his desire that he would like to be present with the Galatians and change his tone, because now he doubts the authenticity of their faith.

Search the Scriptures

1. How will the "weak and beggarly elements" lead the Galatians into bondage (Galatians 4:8)?

2. How would you evaluate whether a preacher should be received "as an angel of God, even as Christ Jesus" (v. 14)?

Discuss the Meaning

1. The Galatians turned to the weak and beggarly elements that led them into bondage again. As followers of Jesus in the twenty-first century, what "weak and beggarly elements" can potentially lead us into bondage?

2. Paul says that he travails until Christ is formed in the Galatians. How can we develop the same passion to see people transformed into the image of Christ?

Lesson in Our Society

Many people in our society do not know what the Gospel is. They might say it is a style of music or going to church and getting yourself together. These things are not the same as the Gospel of Jesus Christ. We might not have to deal with the "weak and beggarly elements" the Galatians dealt with, but many things can trip us up and distract us from the true Gospel that sets us free. Wealth, power, relationships, and status can be used as a substitute for justification through Christ. Religion and going to church can be used to substitute for the place of Jesus Christ. These things cannot make us right with God or justified in His sight. None of these things can save you or died for you. To turn to these things is to turn toward religious bondage.

Make It Happen

As a believer, you cannot afford to be led into bondage. Here are a few things you can do to help yourself and others to maintain your freedom through the Gospels:

- Take a minute to write down all of the potential "weak and beggarly" things that personally distract you from the Gospel.
- Pray for new believers that Christ would be formed in them and that they would not be led into bondage.
- Write out a definition of the Gospel and share with three people.

Follow the Spirit

What God wants me to do:

_____

_____

_____

_____

Remember Your Thoughts

Special insights I have learned:

_____

_____

_____

_____

More Light on the Text

Galatians 4:8–20

8 Howbeit then, when ye knew not God, ye did service unto them which by nature are no gods. 9 But now, after that ye have known God, or rather are known of God, how turn ye again to the weak and beggarly elements, whereunto ye desire again to be in bondage? 10 Ye observe days, and months, and times, and years. 11 I am afraid of you, lest I have bestowed upon you labour in vain.

This section builds on Paul's argument in Galatians 3:26–4:7. Paul continues his argument that God has sent His Son, Jesus Christ, so that both Jews and Gentiles might be set free and become the children of God. In verse 8, Paul portrays the Galatians' pre-Christian life in very bleak terms. They did not know God, although they falsely believed their masters were gods. They were pagans and, as such, sacrificed to imaginary deities—gods that were not gods. But now, their present condition differs from their former one, because God knows them and they know Him. Their previous ignorance had been replaced by a personal, experiential knowledge of the true God. Paul emphasizes that they owe their salvation to God's initiative and that their knowledge was dependent on Him, not them. What matters most is not that we know God, but that He knows us.

Compared to the true God to whom the Galatians have now surrendered, the "gods" to whom they were turning again were, to say the least, "weak and beggarly." Paul wondered why someone who had been delivered from such evil entities would choose to enter their control again. The Galatians probably did not know better at that time, but now they have no excuse. They knew the slavery they once lived under; in its place they found the liberty as children of God.

They were turning again to the observance of days, months, times, and years. Paul was not suggesting that it is improper to observe special days in the Jewish or Christian calendar, such as Passover, the Day of Atonement, Christmas or Easter. Paul's teaching is that while circumcision itself is neither good nor evil, so too the observance of special days is neither mandatory nor inherently wrong. Paul's concern was that the Galatians might be drawn into a religious system where adherence to certain calendar celebrations was necessary to maintain a good standing with God.

Paul had sacrificed much for Galatia and labored there without reservation. Therefore, in verse 11, he expresses fear that all his labor has been wasted. He knew it was possible for true converts to be so distracted from the Gospel of Christ that all his labors to convert them would be thrown away if they reverted back to Judaism. The case was really distressing. Paul had toiled hard to save them from sin and idolatry. Now, legalists had come among

them, professing to be the true preachers of the Gospel, and persuaded them that they cannot be saved without keeping ordinances. But this distracted their attention from Christ, who alone could save and keep them saved.

Today we must not downplay or ignore the terrible possibility of the kind of loss Paul feared. Some people today believe that rites and rituals, such as weekly or annual confession, and communion are the minimum requirement for being in good standing in the church. How many people today flock to the church in semi-annual pilgrimages at Christmas and Easter, assuming that this is all the Lord requires of them? These holidays are not bad, and they might even strengthen faith if one does not drift into the idea of their essentiality, in which case they become idols and rivals of Christ, fraught with terrible peril to spirituality.

12 Brethren, I beseech you, be as I am; for I am as ye are: ye have not injured me at all. 13 Ye know how through infirmity of the flesh I preached the gospel unto you at the first. 14 And my temptation which was in my flesh ye despised not, nor rejected; but received me as an angel of God, even as Christ Jesus. 15 Where is then the blessedness ye spake of? for I bear you record, that, if it had been possible, ye would have plucked out your own eyes, and have given them to me. 16 Am I therefore become your enemy, because I tell you the truth?

Paul proceeds to make a personal appeal to his Galatian converts. Using affectionate language, he calls the Galatians "brethren," which means "brothers and sisters," and then he pleads with them. Ministers, particularly pastors, must maintain a proper balance between theological teaching and pastoral concern. "Beseech" (Gk. *deomai*, **DEH-oh-my**) can mean to long for, or to beg. Paul was no longer arguing but imploring.

He reminds them that for their sake, he had become a Gentile, cutting away from the traditions he was raised in and becoming what they are. Therefore, his appeal is that they should not seek to become Jews but become like himself. They should adopt an attitude like his own toward ceremonial Jewish law, which was the understanding that it was fine for Jews to continue to observe Torah tradition but unnecessary for Gentiles who wanted to join the church. The Galatians have accepted the Christian faith, and they must not disown it for the Law, which Paul himself set aside in community with Gentiles. They should emulate Paul by remaining loyal to the truth of the Gospel (2:5, 14), by being dead to and not under the Law (2:19, 3:25), and by living out their faith in Christ (2:20, 3:26–29), and thereby not nullifying the grace of God (2:21) but enjoying all the benefits of the Gospel by means of faith in Christ (3:22). Paul concludes his imperative in verse 12 by assuring them that his appeal is not based on some personal grievance or failure, but on his genuine care and concern for them.

Paul follows up this assurance with the reminder of how they treated him while he was with them earlier. He recalls that he was with them due to an unspecified "weakness of the flesh," an "illness," on that first occasion. The exact nature of Paul's illness is undisclosed, but it caused Paul to change his plans and became the opportunity for his preaching the Gospel to the Galatians. They could have rejected Paul and his message on the basis of his illness, out of general superstition (cf. Acts 28:3–6), or as a result of perceiving his illness as caused by demonic activity (cf. 2 Corinthians 12:7). Thus, Paul's sickness was indeed in some sense a "trial" for them, yet in spite of that, the Galatians treated him with high regard and his message, as the truth of God, as though he were "an angel" (Gk. *angelos*, **AHN-ge-los**)

or even Jesus Christ Himself. This affection toward Paul, when the Galatians might have otherwise rejected him and his message makes all the more perplexing their treatment of him now, as they are apparently resisting Paul and his message and following the infiltrators who were preaching "another gospel" among them.

Remembering the kind of welcome he had when he first visited Galatia, Paul could rightly now ask, "Where is then the blessedness ye spake of?" (v. 15). So genuine was their reception, commitment, selflessness, and generosity that Paul said that they would have plucked their own eyes for him (probably a figure of speech to indicate the willingness to meet his needs, rather than an indication that the sickness had to do with Paul's eyes). That affection has now gone. Once considered an angel of God, he is now an enemy because he had preached the true Gospel to them.

17 They zealously affect you, but not well; yea, they would exclude you, that ye might affect them. 18 But it is good to be zealously affected always in a good thing, and not only when I am present with you. 19 My little children, of whom I travail in birth again until Christ be formed in you, 20 I desire to be present with you now, and to change my voice; for I stand in doubt of you.

Paul has more to say about the agitators causing the difficulties in Galatia that distorted the Gospel and damaged the relationship between him and the believers. Paul did not identify them by name, perhaps to not dignify them; he simply referred to them as "they." He accuses this group of earnestly pursuing the Galatians, but not for good reasons. Paul sees them playing a mind game with the Galatians: excluding the Galatians so that the Galatians will earnestly pursue them. Paul concedes that it is good to be zealously affected or have someone concerned about them, but the motive and purpose are important. Paul sees that the Galatians' faith is still young, pointing out that they shouldn't just pursue good things when he is with them. It seems that whoever is with them, whether Paul or this zealous group, can easily influence the Galatians' faith.

Having zeroed on the agitators, Paul now changes his mood and expresses deep concern for the Galatians, in contrast to his opponents' superficial interest. He addresses his hood-winked flock affectionately as "my little children" (v. 19). Although Paul usually addresses his converts as "brothers and sisters," he occasionally refers them as his "children" when he wants to draw attention to the fact that he was instrumental, as their spiritual father, in bringing them to the new birth of faith (1 Corinthians 4:14; Philemon 10). Here, however, the role of the father is not enough to capture his thought. Such is his personal investment that he compares himself to a mother who must go through the pangs of childbirth again for the sake of her children. This image witnesses to the deep personal anguish Paul felt over the defection of his spiritual offspring in Galatia. The graphic language reveals Paul's deep concern. The false teachers' work has put his own work of transformation in jeopardy, and Paul is in deep anguish to get his converts back on track.

There is no doubt about Paul's meaning as he agonizes deeply for the Galatians. He did not want to suffer a spiritual loss, but instead was anxious that Christ be formed in their hearts. Paul concludes his personal appeal by expressing his desire to be with the Galatians in their time of crisis (4:20). A concerned loved one's presence is most important, appreciated, and needed in time of crisis. Written words, although important, can be cold and even misleading. Paul wanted to assure them of his loving concern. He expresses some uncertainty:

"for I stand in doubt of you." His doubt was the uneasiness of being perplexed and baffled.

Say It Correctly

Philemon. **FY**-le-mon.

Daily Bible Readings

MONDAY
Becoming an Heir in God's Family
(Galatians 4:1–7)

TUESDAY
A Faithful Heir Will Succeed
(1 Kings 2:1–4)

WEDNESDAY
Power and Strength through Weakness
(2 Corinthians 12:7b–10)

THURSDAY
The Cost of Being a Disciple
(Luke 9:23-27, 57–62)

FRIDAY
The Spirit Brings Life
(Romans 8:1–11)

SATURDAY
Led by the Spirit of Christ
(Romans 8:12–17)

SUNDAY
Choose Freedom in Christ
(Galatians 4:8–20)

Teaching Tips

Words You Should Know

A. Liberty (Galatians 5:1, 13) *eleutheria* (Gk.)—Freedom, especially from bondage.

B. Flesh (vv. 13, 17) *sarx* (Gk.)—Animal or human skin; the physical body; the mortal part of existence.

Teacher Preparation

Unifying Principle—Celebrate Freedom! Rigorous self-discipline can seem appealing because it appears to promise mastery over temptation. What is the key to living a morally acceptable life? Paul urges the Galatians to stand firm in Christian freedom and live by the Spirit, which leads to greater holiness.

A. Pray for your students and for clarity.

B. Research the conflict in the first-century church over circumcision, starting with Acts 15.

C. Read the whole book of Galatians to understand the context of the lesson.

D. Find various articles on how to succeed in school, business, relationships, etc.

O—Open the Lesson

A. Have one of your students lead the class in prayer.

B. Introduce the lesson title.

C. Share with the class the best four articles you found, stressing all the things people do to be successful in different areas of life and asking them to discuss how all these tasks might affect a person's life.

D. Have the students read the In Focus story and ask them to discuss the similarities between Felicia's story and the articles.

P—Present the Scriptures

A. Have the class read the Focal Verses aloud together and re-read the Keep In Mind verse at the end.

B. Have the students read the People, Places, and Times and Background sections.

C. Using the In Depth and More Light on the Text sections, do an exposition of the lesson text with the students.

D. Facilitate a discussion about the Search the Scriptures section.

E—Explore the Meaning

A. Facilitate a discussion of the Discuss the Meaning and Lesson in Our Society sections.

B. Readdress the Aim for Change and Keep in Mind sections, asking students to determine ways the articles and the overall society are contrary to how God wants believers to live.

N—Next Steps for Application

A. Have the class read the Make It Happen section.

B. Say a prayer for discerning the Holy Spirit's leading.

C. Sing "Sweet, Sweet Spirit" as a class.

D. Say a prayer to close.

Worship Guide

For the Superintendent or Teacher
Theme: Freedom in Christ
Song: "Sweet, Sweet Spirit"
Devotional Reading: Galatians 5:22–26

Freedom in Christ

Bible Background • GALATIANS 5:1–17
Printed Text • GALATIANS 5:1–17 | Devotional Reading • GALATIANS 5:22–26

—————— Aim for Change ——————

By the end of the lesson, we will: REVIEW Paul's teaching about life in the Spirit as foundational for Christian holiness; CELEBRATE the Holy Spirit's presence in their lives; and EMBRACE new ways of creating openness to the Spirit's leading.

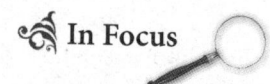 In Focus

"What's wrong with you, Felicia?" Tracy asked as her sister came in and slumped down on the couch.

"I'm tired. Between soup kitchen duty and my usher board meeting, I was helping the night ministry collect clothes for the homeless. It's exhausting serving God's people."

"I suppose," replied Tracy. "You have to pace yourself."

"I think I'm joining the sick-and-shut-in committee next. That would be good, right?"

"Sounds like you have too much on your plate already. You might want to slow down."

"Not if I want to get to heaven. Aren't we supposed to serve one another?" asked Felicia.

"Yes, but we should serve as an outpouring of God's love for us, not to gain points with Him."

"Ouch! Am I that calculating?"

"Hey, I know your intentions are good," Tracy reassured Felicia. "Just understand that God has freely given us His grace, and because of that, we have His favor. So we don't have to figure out what to do when we can seek the Holy Spirit to guide our lives."

In today's text, we learn that Christian freedom offers the opportunity of a Spirit-led life. Why is it so easy for believers to get caught up in the extremes of legalism or catering to their fleshly desires?

—————— Keep in Mind ——————

"For you were called to freedom, brothers and sisters; only do not use your freedom as an opportunity for self-indulgence, but through love become slaves to one another" (Galatians 5:13).

"For you were called to freedom, brothers and sisters; only do not use your freedom as an opportunity for self-indulgence, but through love become slaves to one another" (Galatians 5:13).

Focal Verses

KJV Galatians 5:1 Stand fast therefore in the liberty wherewith Christ hath made us free, and be not entangled again with the yoke of bondage.

2 Behold, I Paul say unto you, that if ye be circumcised, Christ shall profit you nothing.

3 For I testify again to every man that is circumcised, that he is a debtor to do the whole law.

4 Christ is become of no effect unto you, whosoever of you are justified by the law; ye are fallen from grace.

5 For we through the Spirit wait for the hope of righteousness by faith.

6 For in Jesus Christ neither circumcision availeth any thing, nor uncircumcision; but faith which worketh by love.

7 Ye did run well; who did hinder you that ye should not obey the truth?

8 This persuasion cometh not of him that calleth you.

9 A little leaven leaveneth the whole lump.

10 I have confidence in you through the Lord, that ye will be none otherwise minded: but he that troubleth you shall bear his judgment, whosoever he be.

11 And I, brethren, if I yet preach circumcision, why do I yet suffer persecution? then is the offence of the cross ceased.

12 I would they were even cut off which trouble you.

13 For, brethren, ye have been called unto liberty; only use not liberty for an occasion to the flesh, but by love serve one another.

14 For all the law is fulfilled in one word, even in this; Thou shalt love thy neighbour as thyself.

15 But if ye bite and devour one another, take heed that ye be not consumed one of another.

NLT Galatians 5:1 So Christ has truly set us free. Now make sure that you stay free, and don't get tied up again in slavery to the law.

2 Listen! I, Paul, tell you this: If you are counting on circumcision to make you right with God, then Christ will be of no benefit to you.

3 I'll say it again. If you are trying to find favor with God by being circumcised, you must obey every regulation in the whole law of Moses.

4 For if you are trying to make yourselves right with God by keeping the law, you have been cut off from Christ! You have fallen away from God's grace.

5 But we who live by the Spirit eagerly wait to receive by faith the righteousness God has promised to us.

6 For when we place our faith in Christ Jesus, there is no benefit in being circumcised or being uncircumcised. What is important is faith expressing itself in love.

7 You were running the race so well. Who has held you back from following the truth?

8 It certainly isn't God, for he is the one who called you to freedom.

9 This false teaching is like a little yeast that spreads through the whole batch of dough!

10 I am trusting the Lord to keep you from believing false teachings. God will judge that person, whoever he is, who has been confusing you.

11 Dear brothers and sisters, if I were still preaching that you must be circumcised—as some say I do—why am I still being persecuted? If I were no longer preaching salvation through the cross of Christ, no one would be offended.

16 This I say then, Walk in the Spirit, and ye shall not fulfil the lust of the flesh.

17 For the flesh lusteth against the Spirit, and the Spirit against the flesh: and these are contrary the one to the other: so that ye cannot do the things that ye would.

12 I just wish that those troublemakers who want to mutilate you by circumcision would mutilate themselves.

13 For you have been called to live in freedom, my brothers and sisters. But don't use your freedom to satisfy your sinful nature. Instead, use your freedom to serve one another in love.

14 For the whole law can be summed up in this one command: "Love your neighbor as yourself."

15 But if you are always biting and devouring one another, watch out! Beware of destroying one another.

16 So I say, let the Holy Spirit guide your lives. Then you won't be doing what your sinful nature craves.

17 The sinful nature wants to do evil, which is just the opposite of what the Spirit wants. And the Spirit gives us desires that are the opposite of what the sinful nature desires. These two forces are constantly fighting each other, so you are not free to carry out your good intentions.

The People, Places, and Times

Galatia. The Galatia of the New Testament was an area in what is now north central Turkey, where people of many different cultural backgrounds lived together. The Gauls, a Celtic people, had invaded the Asia Minor peninsula by invitation of the king of Bithynia, who enlisted their help in fighting civil wars. They eventually settled in parts of the region formerly known as Cappadocia and Phrygia. The area became a Roman province in 25 BC. Because of Rome's tendency to rezone its provinces, the Galatians Paul addressed in his letter would not have only been inhabitants of Galatia proper, but also citizens of other nearby regions.

Circumcision. Circumcision is a symbol of God's covenant with Abraham (Genesis 17). Every male among Abraham's people (blood relatives and servants) was to be circumcised. Although circumcision was common in ancient societies, the Abrahamic covenant's circumcision was unique in that after the initial group of men was circumcised, the ritual was from then on practiced on eight-day-old infant boys. When circumcision was written down as part of the Law (Leviticus 12:3), Moses shared the procedure's spiritual understanding by "instructing the Israelites to circumcise their hearts" (Deuteronomy 10:16), which meant that in addition to the physical sign, they were also under God's covenant and had to follow His instructions. As Judaism grew, circumcision also became a symbol of Jewish identity, especially in the Greco-Roman Empire, where the dominant culture did not circumcise their males.

Background

At the time Paul wrote this letter to the Galatians, a group of Jewish Christians, known as Judaizers, was teaching that Gentile converts needed to be circumcised both as a sign of their covenant with God and a means of justification or being made right with Him. They also insisted the Gentile Christians also observe other parts of Mosaic Law. Paul and others of like mind found the demand for circumcision was in contradiction to salvation by the grace of Jesus Christ. The debate about circumcision and the Law in the growing Christian community had created such division among believers that it threatened to implode Christianity. In chapter 4, Paul reminds the Galatians that before they knew God, they had been slaves to pagan gods, and he asks them why they would want to be slaves once again now that God knows them (Galatians 4:8–9). Paul tells them they are not the children of bondage, but of freedom (4:31).

At-A-Glance

1. Be Not Entangled (Galatians 5:1–6)
2. Stay on the Right Course (vv. 7–12)
3. Called to Be Free (vv. 13–17)

In Depth

1. Be Not Entangled (Galatians 5:1–6)

Today's text begins in the middle of Paul's efforts to persuade the Galatians to not follow false teachers who want them to be subject to Mosaic Law. Paul urges the Galatians to stand firm in the freedom Christ has set before them. The yoke of bondage, a metaphor for the Law, is meant to illustrate that the Law stands in contrast to the yoke of Christ, which is easy and light (Matthew 11:29–30). Anyone who accepts circumcision must observe the entire Law, "for whosoever shall keep the whole law, and yet offend in one point, he is guilty of all" (James 2:10). In this regard, those under the Law are in constant debt, because keeping all the statutes without fail is impossible. Paul writes that anyone seeking to be right with God through observing the Law has in fact "fallen from grace" (Galatians 5:4). In essence, for those intending to follow the Law, the grace of Jesus Christ is useless to them because they have forsaken the advantages of His free gift of grace. To persuade the Galatians to not be entangled by the Law, Paul explains that the Holy Spirit and faith, not the Law, make their relationships with God right (v. 5). He adds that in Christ, it is of no consequence whether one is circumcised because what matters is faith manifested in love.

2. Stay on the Right Course (vv. 7–12)

In verse 7, Paul reminds the Galatians that when they were new believers, they were striving in the faith. However, false teachers wanted to divert them from truth. These people's plans are not the work of God, and their teachings do not reflect the foundation of Christianity: "by grace are ye saved through faith; and that not of yourselves: it is the gift of God: Not of works, lest any man should boast" (Ephesians 2:8–9). To illustrate the harm these false teachings could cause, Paul compares them to yeast, a fungus which, when a small amount is used, can spread throughout the whole dough. If these teacher's tongues were left unfettered, they could infect the whole church. However,

Paul is confident God will keep the Galatians from believing their erroneous claims. Those trying to confuse them will have to contend with God's judgment for their behavior.

Verse 11 reveals the false teachers were lying by telling the people that Paul had preached that circumcision was necessary to salvation. Paul asks why he is still persecuted by Pharisees at the synagogues (2 Corinthians 11:24) and Jewish Christians who had once been Pharisees (Acts 15), if he had changed his teachings. If he had agreed with them, then the Cross of Christ would no longer be an obstacle for them (1 Corinthians 1:18–25). Probably out of his exasperation, Paul wishes that those insisting upon circumcision would mutilate themselves.

3. Called to Be Free (vv. 13–17)

Today's text ends with Paul again reminding the Galatians that they were called to be free and should not use their freedom as an opportunity to sin, but instead they should serve each other in love. For those still concerned with the Law, Paul writes that the whole Law is summed up in the command "Thou shalt love your neighbor as thyself" (Leviticus 19:18). Engaging in conflict would only destroy their community. Paul beseeches the Galatians to live lives led by the Holy Spirit so they will not give in to their sinful nature. He explains that the desires of the flesh and the Spirit are constantly warring within believers, preventing us from doing what is right (cf. Romans 7:15–24).

Search the Scriptures

1. Why is Paul against the practice of circumcision for believers (Galatians 5:2–4, 6)?

2. How should believers use their liberty (vv. 13, 16)?

Discuss the Meaning

This world believes that to get anything, you must work. It's hard to accept that salvation is free with no task required.

1. What are some ways we try to work for salvation?

2. How can you discern whether you are working for salvation or walking in the Spirit?

Lesson in Our Society

Our society is merit-based, meaning we perform to get rewards. We perform certain duties at work to get a raise. We must meet certain requirements to get A's in school. Some even make grand gestures to win the heart of someone they love. We are enslaved by our own actions. It's a foreign concept that salvation is given by grace, not acts, but this is the gift of Christ.

Make It Happen

It's a blessing to have the Holy Spirit to guide us in the right direction. In your daily devotion, before sharing your petitions, ask God to help you be sensitive to the Holy Spirit's leading. Study scriptural accounts of those who were Spirit-led to understand the ways He speaks to us (Acts 8:26–40, 15:5–29, 16:1–15). As you learn to recognize the urging of the Spirit, commit to following His guidance, even if it means you will be traveling outside of your comfort zone. It will be worth it.

Follow the Spirit

What God wants me to do:

_____

_____

_____

_____

Remember Your Thoughts
Special insights I have learned:

_____

_____

_____

_____

More Light on the Text
Galatians 5:1–17

1 Stand fast therefore in the liberty wherewith Christ hath made us free, and be not entangled again with the yoke of bondage.

This is a connecting verse; it summarizes all that has been said and anticipates what will be said. There is greater clarity of thought when this verse is read as two separate statements. First is a statement emphasizing the purpose of God's saving act in Christ: "For freedom Christ has set us free." Second is a statement of entreaty, a plea or an appeal based upon the purpose of God's saving activity: "Stand firm, therefore, and do not let yourselves be burdened again by a yoke of slavery."

The "yoke of slavery" was more than the "yoke" of the Jewish Law. The Gentile Christians were never under the "yoke" of the Jewish Law, but under paganism. Therefore, Paul uses the phrase "yoke of slavery" to mean "the elements of the world" (4:3) that he calls "weak and beggarly" (4:9). Both the Jewish Law and paganism were included in "the elements of the world" that rob people of their freedom in Christ. Another word to examine is "entangled"; the Greek word for entangled is *enecho* (**en-EH-koh**), meaning to be subject to or loaded down with. Paul says to not be loaded down or subjected again to the yoke of bondage.

2 Behold, I Paul say unto you, that if ye be circumcised, Christ shall profit you nothing.

The translation "if ye be circumcised" does not do justice to the Greek. The form of the Greek verb *peritemno* (**per-ee-TEM-no**) means to cut around or circumcise, and its context in the verse carries the meaning of "if you should let yourselves be circumcised" or "to everyone who has himself circumcised." If they do this on the assumption that circumcision justifies, then "Christ shall profit you nothing." The inference is that the Gentile Christians had not yet been circumcised, but were seriously considering doing so. Paul's aim is to correct their thinking that circumcision justifies without offending the Jews for having been circumcised. It is helpful to read this verse in conjunction with the comments in Romans 7:17–20, where Paul shows that circumcision is not the issue. All that matters in salvation is human sinfulness and divine grace. The issue lies in the mistaken notion that circumcision has value in salvation. The Greek word for "profit" is *opheleo* (**oh-feh-LEH-oh**), which mean benefit, help, use, or aid. Paul states that if we rely on works for salvation, then we benefit nothing from Christ. The benefits we have in Him become void, and we find ourselves back under the Law.

3 For I testify again to every man that is circumcised, that he is a debtor to do the whole law.

Paul has already stated that to consent to circumcision is a confession that Christ's death has no saving value or power for Christian living. Now, he adds that to allow oneself to be circumcised is to make oneself a "debtor" obligated to perform the duty of "the whole law."

4 Christ is become of no effect unto you, whosoever of you are justified by the law; ye are fallen from grace.

Paul has said that to put your trust in the Law means Christ has no benefit for you (v. 2). In this verse, Paul uses a different Greek word, *katargeo* (**kah-tar-GEH-oh**), meaning to make void or powerless or to nullify. He states that if one tries to practice both faith and the Law in order to be saved, they have nullified what Christ has done. To think that obeying the Law justifies us before God is to separate oneself from Christ, tantamount to falling from the grace of God and into legalism. The choice is mutually exclusive: either give up legalism, choose grace, and live in the power of His might; or choose legalism, forfeit grace, and live life on your own. Definite and inevitable consequences follow each choice.

5 For we through the Spirit wait for the hope of righteousness by faith.

Paul identifies with the faithful in Galatia, including himself in the "we" here. A paraphrase of Paul's words here would be, "We wait for the full realization of our salvation in the faith that we already have it." This is implied by Paul's use of the word "hope" from *elpis* (Gk. **el-PIS**), which means an expectation for what has not happened yet. Another image helps to understand the full meaning of verse 5. The word "wait" is translated from *apekdechomai* (Gk. **ahp-ek-DEH-kho-meye**) and carries the meaning of awaiting eagerly. This kind of waiting does not suggest sitting around with our arms folded doing nothing. Rather, it conjures the image of a waiter in a restaurant, who is "on the case" patiently and attentively serving, discharging the expectations of the job. It is also important to note that this waiting is "through the Spirit"; we continue to be on the job, empowered by the Spirit, patiently serving our Lord with pleasure—in anticipation of the day when God "will render to every man according to his deeds" (Romans 2:6). At that time, true

followers of Christ will be declared righteous by their faith, fulfilling their hope.

6 For in Jesus Christ neither circumcision availeth any thing, nor uncircumcision; but faith which worketh by love.

Under the Law, circumcision mattered, but under the freedom that comes through faith in Christ, neither circumcision nor uncircumcision matters. The circumcised Jew and the uncircumcised Gentile share equal footing in the fellowship of those who are "in Jesus Christ" expressing the "faith which worketh by love." Neither circumcision nor uncircumcision has any capability (Gk. *ischuo*, **is-CUE-oh**; to have power or ability) with Christ. Instead, faith works through love. Love is the way that faith accomplishes God's will. As we are told by James, "faith without works is dead" (James 2:26).

7 Ye did run well; who did hinder you that ye should not obey the truth?

Having stated his case, Paul now strings together a series of comments and questions in anticipation of a closing exhortation.

"You were running well; who cut in on you to be keeping you from obeying the truth" is the sense of the Greek. "Obey" here is from the verb *peitho* (Gk. **PAY-tho**), which can also mean to be persuaded, comply with, believe, and rely on. Paul is not simply asking, "Who hindered you from obeying?" but rather, "Who hindered you, who cut in on you and kept you from obeying and relying on the truth by which you have already been persuaded?" The question of "who" is obviously rhetorical in nature; Paul knows it was the Judaizers. They were guilty of "cutting in," a phrase translating the Greek word *anakopto* (**ah-nah-COP-to**). This word is used to refer to runners who come across their prescribed course and throw other participants off the track, too. It was also a military term used to refer to breaking up a road or erecting an obstacle to hinder or prevent the opposing army's progress. The Galatians were familiar with these images and therefore understood Paul's question. Paul anticipates and affirms their answer in the following verse.

8 This persuasion cometh not of him that calleth you.

Paul reminds the Galatians that God calls them and is not the author of their confusion. It is interesting that Paul does not blame Satan for the Galatians' confusion. It appears that Paul wants to keep the focus upon the false brethren who cut in and broke up the road that the Galatians were successfully traveling on.

9 A little leaven leaveneth the whole lump.

This is a proverbial saying used here as a literary technique to call further attention to the corruptive influence of the Judaizers' message. Even if there are only a few of them, they can spoil the whole congregation.

10 I have confidence in you through the Lord, that ye will be none otherwise minded: but he that troubleth you shall bear his judgment, whosoever he be.

Paul speaks now confidently that although the Gentile converts might be considering circumcision, his Galatian letter will hopefully cause them to recommit to faith in Christ alone. Paul's confidence in them is "through the Lord"; he is confident of the Lord's rule and reign in the lives of him and the Galatians. Paul calls out the man "that troubleth you." The Greek word for "troubleth" is *tarasso* (**tah-RAS-so**), meaning to stir up, disturb, or throw into confusion. Paul is not just talking about someone being a pain, but about someone intentionally causing havoc. Probably feeling that his letter will not change his opponents,

he leaves their fate to the divine judgment that their false message will inevitably incur.

11 And I, brethren, if I yet preach circumcision, why do I yet suffer persecution? Then is the offence of the cross ceased.

To say the least, this verse is problematic, primarily because we do not know the context of Paul's statement: "if I yet preach circumcision." It might be that he is parenthetically responding to a specific charge from his opponents. The Judaizers, for example, were not above pointing out Paul's association with Timothy's circumcision (Acts 16:3). They could also reference Paul's being circumcised (Philippians 3:5). Moreover, it could be that Paul preached circumcision during his pre-Christian days. In any event, he refutes the suggestion that he now preaches circumcision. In fact, he adds, to do so would be an "offence" to the Cross of Christ.

12 I would they were even cut off which trouble you.

In this verse, the tone of the Greek is harsh. What Paul says is a terrible thing to wish on anyone: "As for those who are troubling you, O that they would go the whole way and castrate themselves." F. F. Bruce translates it as, "I wish that those who are upsetting you would complete their cutting operation—on themselves." Additionally, Sam K. Williams has called our attention to Deuteronomy 23:1, where "the severing of the penis would … cut a man off from the people of God."

If we assume that the Galatians were familiar with this Scripture, we can also assume that they would have heard Paul's harsh comment as a wish that the Judaizers remove or sever themselves from the Christian community. The harshness of Paul's language helps us understand the depth of his disagreement with the Judaizers' message.

13 For, brethren, ye have been called unto liberty; only use not liberty for an occasion to the flesh, but by love serve one another.

Whereas Paul has been concerned about the threat of the Judaizers, here he is concerned about the threat of the flesh or the Galatians' misuse of their Christian freedom. Paul frames his concern by saying two things about the Galatian Christians: first, that they "have been called," and second, that that calling is "unto liberty." Previously, Paul has spoken about the Galatians' "call" with the emphasis on the "call of God" (Galatians 1:6, 5:8). The meaning is the same here: "you have been called by God unto liberty." The liberty the Galatians have been called to is Christian freedom. In other words, God has called the Galatians to be free from the elements of the world so as to be free to live for Him. This call by God is the essence of Christian freedom and therefore has ethical implications. In other words, Christian freedom, more than being a good end, is really a means for fulfilling God's will and lovingly serving one's neighbor. Christian freedom provides both the opportunity and possibility to serve ethical ends.

The balance of verse 13 gives focus to the ethical implications. As the Galatians are warned not to use their Christian freedom to serve their selfish, corrupt, sinful desires (i.e., the flesh, Gk. *sarx*, **SARKS**), but rather they are to serve the will of God by lovingly serving one another and thus—in the spirit of Jesus—fulfill the Law. Paul seems to make a distinction between doing the Law as required by those "under the law" and fulfilling the Law which is the result of living "in Christ." Those who live in the realm of Christian freedom obey not because the Law commands, but because of the love of Christ. From this perspective, we can understand the verse.

14 For all the law is fulfilled in one word, even in this; Thou shalt love thy neighbor as thyself.

As the parable of the Good Samaritan (Luke 10:25–37) teaches, "thy neighbor" is anyone a Christian comes in contact with—including the person who lives next door.

15 But if ye bite and devour one another, take heed that ye be not consumed one of another.

Here Paul highlights the consequences of failure to make doing God's will and loving others the aim of Christian living. Paul uses a conditional clause, saying that if you do such and such, this might happen. He warns the church not to bite and devour one another. The Greek word for bite here is generally used for snakes. The word for devour is *katesthio* (Gk. **kah-tess-THEE-oh**), meaning to eat up, consume, or tear to pieces; this word is often used for animals. In other words, Paul is warning them that they were fighting like wild animals, and if they did not stop, they would all be consumed—thus the preceding admonition to love one another, fulfilling the Law (v. 14) .

16 This I say then, Walk in the Spirit, and ye shall not fulfil the lust of the flesh. 17 For the flesh lusteth against the Spirit, and the Spirit against the flesh: and these are contrary the one to the other: so that ye cannot do the things that ye would.

Paul concludes by contrasting the Spirit and the flesh. The Galatians should walk in the Spirit so that they do not complete their journey with desires of the flesh. Flesh and Spirit are opposed to one another, and the Galatians have to choose between the two. Because of this, they cannot simply do what they want. (This would lead them to fleshly desires.) Paul has a dim view of human ability to control our desires, and so his advice is simple: walk always in the Spirit. Having connected the Spirit with love (v. 6), and returned at the end to the manifestations of love (vv. 13–14), Paul ties together this section of his argument skillfully. If the Galatians want to take advantage of their freedom in Christ, they should do so not by following their fleshly desires but by loving one another, which is the way of the Spirit.

Say It Correctly

Entangled. in-**TANG**-ild.
Leaveneth. **LE**-vin-ith.

Daily Bible Readings

MONDAY
Christ, the Wisdom of God
(1 Corinthians 1:18–25)

TUESDAY
The Lord is God Alone
(Deuteronomy 6:4–9)

WEDNESDAY
You Shall Love Your Neighbor
(Leviticus 19:13–18)

THURSDAY
Rescued from Death
(Romans 7:15–24)

FRIDAY
Keep Focused and Pure
(1 Corinthians 5:1–2, 6–9)

SATURDAY
Produce the Fruit of the Spirit
(Galatians 5:22–26)

SUNDAY
Choose to Love and Serve One Another
(Galatians 5:1–17)

Notes

_____

_____

_____

_____

Teaching Tips

February 26
Bible Study Guide 13

Words You Should Know

A. Burden (Galatians 6:2) *baros* (Gk.)—A weight, anything pressing on one physically or that makes a demand on one's resources, whether material or spiritual.

B. Burden (v. 5) *phortion* (Gk.)—Something carried, used metaphorically for what will be the result of each believer's work at the judgment seat of Christ.

Teacher Preparation

Unifying Principle—Fruitful Living. Many people reduce their religious obligations to fulfilling a set of legalistic requirements. What are the characteristics of an authentic Christian lifestyle? Paul sharply contrasts a Spirit-filled life with life in the flesh.

A. Pray for your students and for clarity.

B. Review the whole book of Galatians to understand the context of the lesson.

C. Research farming in biblical times and collect pictures of various seeds with the fruit they produce.

O—Open the Lesson

A. Have one of your students lead the class in prayer, which should include the Aim For Change and the Keep in Mind verses.

B. Introduce the lesson title.

C. Show the class at least three of the pictures of fruit seeds and have them try to guess the fruit each produces before you show them.

D. Have the class read and discuss The People, Places, and Times.

P—Present the Scriptures

A. Have the class read the Focal Verses aloud together and re-read the Keep in Mind verse at the end.

B. Using the Background, In Depth, and More Light on the Text sections, do an exposition of the lesson text with the students.

C. Facilitate a discussion of the students' answers to the Search the Scriptures questions.

E—Explore the Meaning

A. Have the students read the In Focus story and ask them how the characters exhibited the fruit of the Spirit.

B. Facilitate a discussion about the Discuss the Meaning and Lesson in Our Society sections.

N—Next Steps for Application

A. Have the class read the Make It Happen section.

B. Say a prayer for discerning the Holy Spirit's leading on how to exhibit the fruit of the Spirit.

Worship Guide

For the Superintendent or Teacher
Theme: Christ Creates Holy Living
Song: "The Bond of Love"
Devotional Reading: Romans 6:1–11

Christ Creates Holy Living

Bible Background • GALATIANS 5:18–6:10
Printed Text • GALATIANS 5:18–6:10 | Devotional Reading • ROMANS 6:1–11

Aim for Change

By the end of the lesson, we will: DEFINE the characteristics Paul lists as the fruit of the Spirit; SENSE the needs of others in the church; and WORK, by the Spirit's empowerment, for the good of all, especially the family of faith.

 **In Focus**

Since the day they met in high school, Cassandra and Lisa had been best friends. At proms, birthdays, and college, they were inseparable. As adults, they started going to church together and became Christians at the same time. Lisa, who had always been more outgoing, immediately started serving in church auxiliaries while Cassandra shied away from getting to know their new church family. Although Lisa was making new friends, she and Cassandra had become even closer because they now shared a deep love for Christ. When Lisa got married and moved away, Cassandra felt so alone and started to isolate herself. She began to feel like God had abandoned her. Lisa could hear the sadness in Cassandra's voice whenever they'd talk on the phone and was deeply concerned. She called her friend Betty at the church and asked her to pray for Cassandra. Betty and a few other women from the church prayed. Then she and the others stopped by Cassandra's home to let her know they'd been thinking about her. To this day, Cassandra, Betty, and the other women still meet weekly for prayer and support. Cassandra's Christian walk is stronger than ever because her fellow believers reached out to her in love.

Today's lesson examines the fruit of the Spirit and how it is manifested in our lives. How can you discern the fruit of the Spirit in your own life?

Keep in Mind

"But the fruit of the Spirit is love, joy, peace, longsuffering, gentleness, goodness, faith, Meekness, temperance: against such there is no law" (Galatians 5:22–23).

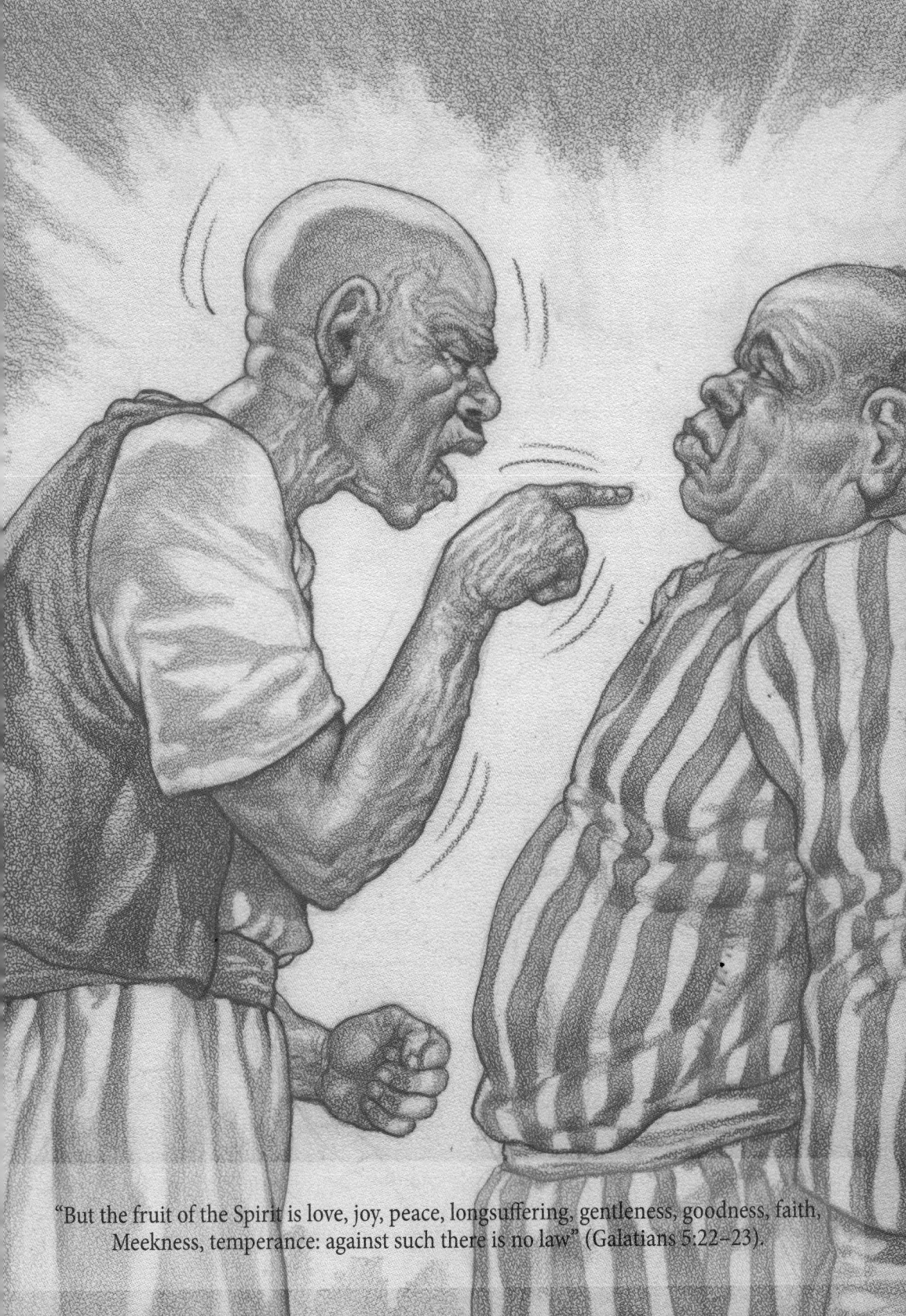

"But the fruit of the Spirit is love, joy, peace, longsuffering, gentleness, goodness, faith, Meekness, temperance: against such there is no law" (Galatians 5:22–23).

Focal Verses

KJV **Galatians 5:18** But if ye be led of the Spirit, ye are not under the law.

19 Now the works of the flesh are manifest, which are these; Adultery, fornication, uncleanness, lasciviousness,

20 Idolatry, witchcraft, hatred, variance, emulations, wrath, strife, seditions, heresies,

21 Envyings, murders, drunkenness, revellings, and such like: of the which I tell you before, as I have also told you in time past, that they which do such things shall not inherit the kingdom of God.

22 But the fruit of the Spirit is love, joy, peace, longsuffering, gentleness, goodness, faith,

23 Meekness, temperance: against such there is no law.

24 And they that are Christ's have crucified the flesh with the affections and lusts.

25 If we live in the Spirit, let us also walk in the Spirit.

26 Let us not be desirous of vain glory, provoking one another, envying one another.

6:1 Brethren, if a man be overtaken in a fault, ye which are spiritual, restore such an one in the spirit of meekness; considering thyself, lest thou also be tempted.

2 Bear ye one another's burdens, and so fulfil the law of Christ.

3 For if a man think himself to be something, when he is nothing, he deceiveth himself.

4 But let every man prove his own work, and then shall he have rejoicing in himself alone, and not in another.

5 For every man shall bear his own burden.

6 Let him that is taught in the word communicate unto him that teacheth in all good things.

7 Be not deceived; God is not mocked: for whatsoever a man soweth, that shall he also reap.

NLT **Galatians 5:18** But when you are directed by the Spirit, you are not under obligation to the law of Moses.

19 When you follow the desires of your sinful nature, the results are very clear: sexual immorality, impurity, lustful pleasures,

20 idolatry, sorcery, hostility, quarreling, jealousy, outbursts of anger, selfish ambition, dissension, division,

21 envy, drunkenness, wild parties, and other sins like these. Let me tell you again, as I have before, that anyone living that sort of life will not inherit the Kingdom of God.

22 But the Holy Spirit produces this kind of fruit in our lives: love, joy, peace, patience, kindness, goodness, faithfulness,

23 gentleness, and self-control. There is no law against these things!

24 Those who belong to Christ Jesus have nailed the passions and desires of their sinful nature to his cross and crucified them there.

25 Since we are living by the Spirit, let us follow the Spirit's leading in every part of our lives.

26 Let us not become conceited, or provoke one another, or be jealous of one another.

6:1 Dear brothers and sisters, if another believer is overcome by some sin, you who are godly should gently and humbly help that person back onto the right path. And be careful not to fall into the same temptation yourself.

2 Share each other's burdens, and in this way obey the law of Christ.

3 If you think you are too important to help someone, you are only fooling yourself. You are not that important.

4 Pay careful attention to your own work, for then you will get the satisfaction of a job well done, and you won't need to compare yourself to anyone else.

8 For he that soweth to his flesh shall of the flesh reap corruption; but he that soweth to the Spirit shall of the Spirit reap life everlasting.

9 And let us not be weary in well doing: for in due season we shall reap, if we faint not.

10 As we have therefore opportunity, let us do good unto all men, especially unto them who are of the household of faith.

5 For we are each responsible for our own conduct.

6 Those who are taught the word of God should provide for their teachers, sharing all good things with them.

7 Don't be misled—you cannot mock the justice of God. You will always harvest what you plant.

8 Those who live only to satisfy their own sinful nature will harvest decay and death from that sinful nature. But those who live to please the Spirit will harvest everlasting life from the Spirit.

9 So let's not get tired of doing what is good. At just the right time we will reap a harvest of blessing if we don't give up.

10 Therefore, whenever we have the opportunity, we should do good to everyone—especially to those in the family of faith.

The People, Places, and Times

Fruit. Most of the time, we cannot recognize a fruit from only its seed. Only after seeds are planted in the ground and start sprouting do we know what type of fruit has been planted. Fruit is used metaphorically in Scripture to illustrate this fact. We do not know the power at work in people's lives until we see the fruit that power produces. In Scripture, fruit (works or deeds) is the sign of God's power moving within a person. Sin produces fruit (works) of the flesh, but the Holy Spirit produces the fruit of the Spirit in the lives of believers.

Sowing and reaping. Agrarian societies, like that of the first-century church, relied on sowing and reaping crops for subsistence. For this reason, agricultural metaphors were often used to illustrate biblical truths. The farming process was grueling. Farmers had to properly till (break up the soil) hard and rocky land to get a healthy harvest. After the seeds were sown, the land had to be watered and the sprouting crops pruned. Watering was not an easy task. Although fields were located near water sources, farmers mostly relied on the rainy season twice a year (fall and spring) to water their crops. While waiting patiently to reap the harvest, farmers had to contend with drought, weeds, and all manner of pests. Because they did not live on farms but in nearby villages, farmers had to worry about thieves stealing crops while they were away. Although the farmer's life was arduous, his or her prize was finally reaping the harvest. The Galatians truly understood the patience it took to "not be weary in well doing for in due season we shall reap if we faint not" (Galatians 6:9).

Background

The Roman government viewed first-century Christianity as merely a sect of Judaism because the church was still searching for its identity , and many in the first-century churches identified as Jewish (Jews who followed Jesus). Many Christians in fact still worshiped in the Jewish synagogues. The first believers did not even call themselves Christians, but "followers of the Way." Antioch was where the term "Christian" was first used (Acts 11:26). As increasing numbers of Gentiles became believers, due largely to Paul's endeavors, the necessity of observing the Mosaic Law came into question. Paul's insistence that our righteousness is based on Christ's righteousness and received as a gift became the foundation of the Christian faith. This marked the separation of Christianity from Judaism. In Paul's letter to the Galatians, he consistently emphasizes the difference between being enslaved by the Law and being free in the Holy Spirit as a means to teach the true Gospel and solidify the church's identity.

At-A-Glance

1. Works of the Flesh (Galatians 5:18–21)
2. The Fruit of the Spirit (vv. 22–26)
3. Carry Another's Burdens (6:1–6)
4. What They Reap, They Will Sow (vv. 7–10)

In Depth

1. Works of the Flesh (Galatians 5:18–21)

Today's lesson begins in the midst of Paul's attempt to convince the Galatians to not become enslaved by the Law, which—unlike the Holy Spirit—was not intended to save, but rather to shed light on sin (Romans 3:20). Paul informs that those led by the Spirit (i.e., those under the continual guidance of and in abiding relationship with the Spirit) are no longer subject to the Law, nor can be condemned by it (Romans 8:1). Paul switches focus to describe the works of the flesh (the sinful state of people). He uses this vice list, a convention of Greco-Roman moral rhetoric, to emphasize that those who continually practice these sins will not inherit the kingdom of God.

2. The Fruit of the Spirit (vv. 22–26)

The works of the flesh contrast the fruit of the Spirit. The word "fruit" denotes an organic growth that stems from the believer's relationship with Christ. The first fruit listed is love. It is also the virtue upon which all the other fruit are based (1 Corinthians 13:1–3). In essence, the operation of the Holy Spirit is love manifested in believers' lives; there is no law against love. Followers of Christ still struggle with sinful human desires, but strive to do good. Paul adds that if believers live by the Spirit, they should walk in the Spirit. In other words, believers should be in one accord in following the Spirit instead of giving in to competition or jealousy.

3. Carry Another's Burdens (6:1–6)

Chapter 6 begins with Paul imploring the spiritually stronger Galatians to help strengthen those among them who are overtaken by sin. Overtaken does not mean continually sinning (Galatians 6:1), but having their guard down. Stronger believers should help meekly, being careful to not also be tempted to sin. Paul then requests they shoulder the burdens of the weak in sin as a way to fulfill the Law of Christ, which is to love one another (Galatians 5:14). Those who try to judge the weaker, thinking themselves above helping others, deceive themselves. They should examine their own work, because all must carry their own burdens. The burden in verse 5 refers to the believer's work, which we will all be held accountable for on Judgment Day. This is different from the burden in verse 2, which refers to daily trials faced by every Christian.

4. What They Reap, They Will Sow (vv. 6–10)

Now that Paul has explained the difference between the flesh and the Spirit and implored them to support one another, he tells the Galatians to not be fooled, because anyone can turn away from God's justice. Whatever they reap, they will sow. If someone pleases their sinful nature, they will perish, but if they please the Spirit, they will have eternal life. Paul says to not get tired of doing right, because if they hold on, they will reap blessings at the appointed time. In the meantime, the Galatians should take advantage of every opportunity to do good for all, especially for fellow believers.

Search the Scriptures

1. Why does Paul compare and contrast the works of the flesh with the fruit of the Spirit (Galatians 5:19–26)?

2. Paul gives abstract concepts for the fruit of the Spirit (i.e., love, joy, peace). What are specific concrete actions that exhibit the fruit of the Spirit (vv. 22–23)?

Discuss the Meaning

We often think that holy living is only a personal endeavor. However, God wants us to live in the Spirit as a community.

1. How do the works of the flesh undermine the Christian community?

2. How does the fruit of the Spirit unify us?

Lesson in Our Society

From the moment we're born, laws govern our lives. Babies must have birth certificates. Children must go to school. Walk on green. Stop on red. Most people try to follow the law to the letter. It's easy for us to look at the fruit of the Spirit as more laws to follow. The Lord desires that our lives reflect the fruit, but not in legalistic ways. Our lives should be an outpouring of our love for Christ and our desire to serve one another.

Make It Happen

We have many opportunities to do good in this world. The question is, what should we do? Create a plan to exhibit at least one fruit of the Spirit each day of the week. Come back and report to the class the challenges and rewards.

Follow the Spirit

What God wants me to do:

_____

_____

_____

_____

Remember Your Thoughts

Special insights I have learned:

_____

_____

_____

_____

More Light on the Text
Galatians 5:18–6:10

18 But if ye be led of the Spirit, ye are not under the law.

Here Paul alerts the Galatians to the possibilities inherent in their new life in Christ. If they let themselves be led by the Spirit, they will not feel obligated to a legal system that can command but is powerless to enforce obedience. By choosing to follow the Spirit's leading, they will be free from the Law and empowered by the Spirit to pursue the things of the Spirit.

The word for "led" in the Greek is *ago* (**AH-go**), used in the passive voice to mean to be brought along or taken along. Therefore, being led by the Spirit means submitting our will to Him, which leads us to do God's will. However, following the Spirit is not passive; the believer is still responsible for performing their obligations. The sense of the original language is that believers must continue to take responsibility and consciously let the Spirit lead them.

19 Now the works of the flesh are manifest, which are these; Adultery, fornication, uncleanness, lasciviousness, 20 idolatry, witchcraft, hatred, variance, emulations, wrath, strife, seditions, heresies. 21 Envyings, murder, drunkenness, revellings, and such like: of the which I tell you before, as I have also told you in time past, that they which do such things shall not inherit the kingdom of God.

These verses clearly define fleshly and improper behavior for Christians called to exercise freedom in Christ. In fact, Paul adds emphatically what he has said on numerous occasions: "they which do such things (i.e., habitually practice such behaviors) shall not (i.e., shall in no way) inherit the kingdom of God." The Greek translates this as a solemn warning.

22 But the fruit of the Spirit is love, joy, peace, longsuffering, gentleness, goodness, faith, 23 meekness, temperance: against such there is no law. 24 And they that are Christ's have crucified the flesh with the affections and lusts.

Paul identifies the qualities evident in those believers who walk in the Spirit. He contrasts the singular fruit of the Spirit with the plural works of the flesh. The singular form of the Greek word *karpos* (**kar-POCE**), meaning

fruit, indicates that the Spirit is capable of producing this fruit in every believer. They are not fruits, but fruit. The Spirit produces character and righteous behavior, which do not need laws and make obedience to the Law obsolete. The "works" produced by the flesh need the Law to keep them in check, so those who try to live by those works (obedience to the Law) always fall short. Those who walk in the Spirit put to death the flesh and its desires, and they allow the Spirit of God to lead them and produce fruit that does not need legislation.

In other words, those who have identified themselves with Christ and belong to Him "have crucified" or put to death everything in opposition to Him, and are free to produce the fruit of the Spirit through their behavior.

25 If we live in the Spirit, let us also walk in the Spirit.

This concisely summarizes what Paul has already said. It states what is true "since we live in the Spirit." It reflects the logical consequence of the reality of living in the Spirit: "let us also walk in the Spirit." Since we live in the Spirit, we must line up with the Spirit. Believers who claim to live in the Spirit must also express behavior resulting from the Spirit's control.

26 Let us not be desirous of vain glory, provoking one another, envying one another.

This verse seems to suggest that Paul does not want his readers to become overconfident about their position in Christ. A person who is in Christ and led by the Spirit will always reflect His spirit and attitude. Sometimes good behavior can provoke and stir up jealousy in others, particularly when done in ways that attract attention.

It is reasonable to think that Paul saw the Galatians arguing among themselves from this vantage point. Those who correctly understood salvation might have acted in ways that provoked others or stirred up envy. Consequently, they conducted themselves worse than those who were wrong. The implication is that believers have an obligation to manage their conduct so as not to tempt others to do wrong.

The attitude that seeks to prove one's rightness at the expense of another's spiritual well-being borders on "vain glory." This does not speak well of the Holy Spirit's leading.

6:1 Brethren, if a man be overtaken in a fault, ye which are spiritual, restore such an one in the spirit of meekness; considering thyself, lest thou also be tempted.

The word "overtaken" (Gk. *prolambano*, **pro-lam-BAH-no**) can mean to be entrapped, taken, caught by surprise, or to take a false step. This gives the meaning that the man "overtaken in a fault" was not intentionally doing wrong, but suddenly became aware that his actions were wrong. In such cases, Paul counsels, believers should have a spirit of meekness and a view toward restoration. They must not satisfy the lust of the flesh by using the situation to gossip, feel superior, or exact overly harsh punishment on those at fault. The antidote to such fleshly behavior is to "consider thyself, lest thou also be tempted." As we correct our fellow Christians, we should keep in mind the famous saying, "There but for the grace of God go I."

2 Bear ye one another's burdens, and so fulfil the law of Christ.

Those led by the Spirit are called to be willing and available to help carry one another's loads. Paul's sense makes this behavior the style of living in Christian fellowship. The verb "bear" is from the Greek word *bastazo* (**bahs-TAHD-zo**), meaning to take up, carry, or endure, suffer, or undergo. The word for "burdens" is *baros* (Gk. **BAH-roce**), meaning weight or, as in this case,

hardship. We should support one another by helping to bear heavy hardship. Bearing each other's burdens should not be occasional, but a way of living and behaving in Christian community. With this behavior, we, like Christ, will have fulfilled the Law.

3 For if a man think himself to be something, when he is nothing, he deceiveth himself.

This verse helps believers understand how vulnerable they are to the influence of the flesh. Every believer is a stone's throw away from thinking too highly of himself or herself. This is particularly true today, when many factors—economic position, racial and ethnic identity, comparing ourselves to others on social media—make it easy to feel better than others. Properly and legitimately estimating our own value is an expression of the Spirit-led life. When verse 2 is connected to verse 3, the message is clear: those who overvalue themselves are unlikely to bear another's burdens.

4 But let every man prove his own work, and then shall he have rejoicing in himself alone, and not in another.

Paul's concern in this verse is that followers compare themselves only to what the Spirit calls them to become. Those led by the Spirit don't need to compare themselves with other believers; self-evaluation comes from proving their work in the light of God's Word. In fact, rejoicing because you think you are better than someone else betrays life in Christ. It is not the way of the Spirit. Given this interpretation of verse 4, verse 5 is a logical restatement.

5 For every man shall bear his own burden.

This might appear to contradict verse 2, where Paul says we should help share each other's burdens. Here he says to bear your own burden. The difference is apparent in the Greek. The Greek word for burden here is *phortion* (**for-TEE-on**). It is different from verse 2; the meaning is better conveyed as "load," referring to everyone "pulling their own weight" in responsibilities. In other words, you should do your work and not expect someone else to do it for you. In this way, the work of ministry is shouldered by everyone and not by a few. We each have a responsibility to carry part of the burden of ministry, such as evangelism, teaching, praising, or showing hospitality. This is quite different from helping someone who is burdened down with problems; in this case we come to their aid to help shoulder their pain. Laziness is not a virtue in Scripture; our Christian responsibility is to carry our own weight and help bear others' misfortunes.

6 Let him that is taught in the word communicate unto him that teacheth in all good things. 7 Be not deceived; God is not mocked: for whatsoever a man soweth, that shall he also reap. 8 For he that soweth to his flesh shall of the flesh reap corruption; but he that soweth to the Spirit shall of the Spirit reap life everlasting.

Paul continues the line of thought that illustrates the interconnectedness of the body of Christ. Those taught in the Word should communicate (Gk. *koinoneo*, **koi-no-NEH-oh**), or share, and partner with those who teach the Word. In other words, those who receive spiritual blessings should share their material blessings with those who labor over them. This is a relationship of mutual reciprocity, and the type of relationship the Lord wants to be maintained between leaders and followers in the church.

Using the metaphor of a farmer who sows and reaps the harvest, Paul says that what a believer sows determines what he or she harvests—our choices determine our consequences. Whether

we choose to live in the Spirit or in the flesh, consequences will follow. Believers are encouraged to sow to the Spirit, and refuse to become discouraged. This explains the need for Paul's note of encouragement in verse 9.

9 And let us not be weary in well doing: for in due season we shall reap if we faint not.

The admonition is to not become "weary" nor "faint." The Greek word for weary is *ekkakeo* (**ek-kah-KEH-oh**), meaning to lose heart or become tired. The word for faint in the Greek is *ekluo* (**ek-LOO-oh**), meaning to faint or give up. These words are synonymous. Paul encourages the Galatians not to give up, because there will be a reward after all is said and done.

10 As we have therefore opportunity, let us do good unto all men, especially unto them who are of the household of faith.

Paul concludes this section with the primary directives for the Christian faith. He points toward the expectation that whenever an opportunity (Gk. *kairos*, **kye-ROCE**) or divine moment presents itself, the believer has already made up his or her mind to act. They must do good, and the scope of their good works includes all people, but especially those of the household (Gk. *oikeios*, **oy-KAY-oce**) of faith. This term was used for everybody who was part of a Roman household—all the people connected to the father or *pater familias*, who was the head of the household. As the people of God, we form the same type of community with Him as our head. In other words, those related to us through faith in Jesus should be the first and foremost recipients of our good deeds.

Say It Correctly

Lasciviousness. lah-**SI**-vee-us-nes.
Variance. **VA**-ree-ens.
Emulations. em-yoo-**LAY**-shuns.

Daily Bible Readings

MONDAY
Walk in Newness of Life
(Romans 6:1–11)

TUESDAY
The Sower and the Seed
(Luke 8:4–15)

WEDNESDAY
Gifts That Lead to Faithfulness
(1 Peter 1:3–9)

THURSDAY
Wholeness by Prayer and Action
(James 5:13–20)

FRIDAY
Practice Mutual Discipline
(Matthew 18:15–20)

SATURDAY
Support Ministers Generously
(1 Corinthians 9:3–12)

SUNDAY
Choose to Love Each Other
(Galatians 5:18–6:10)

Notes

God Loves Us

God's love for us is evident in Scripture from the creation of the first humans through God's constant interactions with individuals and groups of people in their historical circumstances and developments. A survey of select Old and New Testament Scriptures reveals dynamic and encouraging aspects of God's constant love for humankind.

UNIT 1 • GOD'S ETERNAL, PRESERVING, RENEWING LOVE

The four lessons from First John, Ephesians, John, and Joel depict God's love for humans as primary and as the source of all love. The lessons show that God's love overflows, redeems, unites, and renews.

Lesson 1 March 5, 2017
The Source of All Love
1 John 4:7-19

Many search in all the wrong places for a perfect love in which to put their trust. Can other humans be trusted to love without blemish at all times? First John reminds us that God is love and those who abide in love have God's love perfected in them.

Lesson 2: March 12, 2017
God's Overflowing Love
Ephesians 2:1-10

Sometimes those who break the rules become outcasts in the group. Where can those who break rules find acceptance? Out of his great love for us, God saved us by grace through faith and will show the immense richness of this grace in kindness to those who are in Christ Jesus.

Lesson 3: March 19, 2017
God's Love is Manifested
John 15:1-17

In our human condition, we search for that which enables us to love and be loved by others. Where do we find the authentic source of this love? The writer of the Gospel says that God is the source of an all encompassing love, which empowers us to love God and one another.

Lesson 4: March 26, 2017
God's Love Restores
Joel 2:12-13, 18-19, 28-32

The rewards garnered from wholesome relationships may be shattered by unloving and unfaithful actions. How can these relationships be restored to their former glory? John reminds us of a loving, forgiving God who seeks to restore and guarantee eternal life, while Joel recounts the benefits that emanate from a restored relationship with God.

UNIT 2 • GOD'S CARING, SAVING, AND UPHOLDING LOVE

The five lessons drawn from Psalms, John, and Romans reveal God as protector, preserver, healer, comforter, and savior of the people.

Lesson 5: April 2, 2017
God as Our Shepherd
Psalm 23

People face challenges that may seem too difficult to endure. Where can they find the support and reassurance to face these challenges?

The psalmist promises that God's love provides what is necessary to confront any difficulties to live in a fulfilling and intimate relationship with God.

Lesson 6: April 9, 2017
God's Saving Love in Christ
John 3:1-21

A commitment to serve others may require more than what was anticipated. To what extent are we willing to sacrifice for the sake of others? God proved his love for the world through the ultimate sacrifice of God's only Son so that all who believe in Him will have eternal life.

Lesson 7: April 16, 2017
God's Love as Victory Over Death
John 20:1-10

Although we are forewarned, some life events are beyond the realm of our imagination. How do we respond at these times? Even though the disciples were confounded when they entered the empty tomb, they experienced a new birth into a living hope through the Resurrection.

Lesson 8: April 23, 2017
God's Reconciling Love
Romans 5:1-11, 8:31-39

Hardship, distress, and separations of all kinds abound in human life. How can we face these difficulties? Paul is convinced that nothing in all creation is able to separate us from the love of God in Jesus Christ.

Lesson 9: April 30, 2017
God's Preserving Love
John 10:1-15

Everyone is looking for a leader who will solve all the problems of the world. Where can we find the leader we seek? Jesus, as the Good Shepherd, is the leader who shows and imparts God's love to those who follow.

UNIT 3 • GOD'S PERVASIVE AND SUSTAINING LOVE

The four lessons in this unit from the Book of Jonah, which highlight God's unconditional love for humans and the natural world, as well as God's continuing care and concern for individual and group relationships and developments.

Lesson 10: May 7, 2017
God's Sustaining Love
Jonah 1

When calamity comes, people ask, "Why?" Can human behavior cause bad things to happen? In Jonah's case, human behavior did lead to calamity; however, Jonah discovered that God's love still surrounded him.

Lesson 11: May 14, 2017
God's Love Preserved Jonah
Jonah 2

People experience being rescued from dire circumstances and are thankful. Whom do we thank in these circumstances? Jonah acknowledges with thanksgiving that it is God's love that protects and offers deliverance.

Lesson 12: May 21, 2017
God's Love for Nineveh
Jonah 3

Communities today are wracked with separation and violence. What can bring people together to live in wholeness and peace? When the people of Nineveh repented, God brought peace and wholeness through divine love.

Lesson 13: May 28, 2017
God's Pervasive Love
Jonah 4

People become displeased and angry when things do not go their way. How can we gain a larger perspective? Jonah discovers the wide breadth of God's pervasive love.

God Loves Us

The most important thing in the world is to know that you are loved by the Creator of the universe. All the riches and wealth of this world cannot buy this love. No one is beautiful enough to attract this love. It is given solely because of God's free will. The question then becomes, how do we know that God loves us? It is easy for us to measure human love. We see how much someone loves us here on earth by the things they do for us. Children know their parents love them by the countless hours they spend training and rearing them. Husbands and wives know whether their spouse loves them by spending quality time together and sacrificing for each other. So how do we know and understand God's love for us when He is invisible?

One of the ways that we know God loves us is the beautiful world He has provided for us. He has given us the sun's dazzling light and the verdant fields and meadows. The spectacular heights of the Himalayas and the crystal blue tropical waters of the Caribbean are gifts from our Creator. Not to mention all of the delicious foods we eat—we get to experience different flavors from mango to barbecue chicken. There is so much God has given us on this earth to explore and enjoy. Just the experience of life is cause to acknowledge that our Creator loves us.

Still, we also have another way to know that God loves us. We can see that God loves us through reading the pages of His love letter, the Bible. There we see a God who walks faithfully with His people even when they do not walk faithfully with Him. Time after time Israel broke their covenant with God and worshiped idols but that did not break God's covenant love for them. God displayed an unfailing covenant love with Israel and no matter how many times they turned their back on Him, He would not turn His back on them.

Not only that, but God promised them a new covenant. This covenant would wipe away all of their sins and enable Him to write His laws on their hearts. He would give them a new heart and a new spirit. Every covenant is enacted with blood; this covenant would be no different. The only difference is that the blood that enacted this covenant would be His own. He gave His very life to secure a relationship with us. Jesus on the Cross is the sure sign of God's love for us. Every nail and every thorn paid the price for our sins. Every lash of the whip and every bruise was for us.

When we believe in this love, then God sends His Spirit into our hearts and confirms it to be true. God does love us. There is no question of His love when we look at the Cross. It is the ultimate testament of love.

The gift of creation, the pages of the Bible, Jesus' sacrifice on the Cross, and the Spirit living inside of us answer the question of whether God loves us. This is easy to know mentally, but for many it is difficult to experience. Nothing can separate us from this love. All of these things are pledges and tokens of God's immeasurable and unfathomable love for us. It is there for us to experience; all we have to do is rest in knowing the truth of who God is and the power of His love.

Covenant Love

by Jennifer King

A covenant is not simply an agreement between two parties. Covenants are special relationships by which the parties enter into a binding commitment to one another. This committed relationship makes a demand on each party.

In the Bible, we see all types of covenants. Some are made between groups and nations, as is the case where the people of Gibeon covenanted with the Children of Israel (Joshua 9). Throughout the Old Testament, in the covenant between God and the Children of Israel, God offers His love and protection, and in return His people pledge to worship and serve Him alone. Through Jesus Christ, today's Christians are in a covenant relationship with God the Father. This new covenant is expressed throughout the Scripture. God says quite explicitly that "I will give you a new heart and put a new spirit within you; I will take the heart of stone out of your flesh and give you a heart of flesh" (Ezekiel 36:26–27, NKJV). Through Jesus Christ, the righteous Davidic Messiah, God has fulfilled the new covenant. Through His Son's suffering on the Cross, the Resurrection, and the pouring out of the Holy Spirit, God has blessed His people for all eternity. But what of our covenanted obligation to one another?

How often have Christians found themselves ignoring people on the street, frustrated because we are anxious to get to our destination? Perhaps the people around on the highway or train begin to irritate and anger us. We want to shut out the people around us and wish that everyone would leave us alone. Hopefully, we quickly come to our senses and begin to question ourselves, our thoughts, and our hearts. We should then ask ourselves, "What in the world am I saying? Just who are these people I am referring to?" We cannot always understand the people around us—they might speak a language we don't know, struggle with a disability, or be part of a culture we don't understand or approve of. It is easy to forget about people's lived experiences and shared humanity when all we see is the inconvenience they're causing us.

Feeling superior to "others" is an issue that many Christians struggle with. While we will all admit that our reluctance to accept others (those unlike ourselves) is problematic, most of us are far too embarrassed to call it what it really is—discrimination. It is even harder for us to acknowledge that this behavior is completely un-Christian.

The United States has long boasted of being a cultural "melting pot" where the assimilation of various races and cultures is embraced. In truth, most Americans do very little mixing with people of other races and cultures outside of work and classroom situations where diversity is legally mandated. Most of us live in areas where people look like us, and on Sunday mornings, a great majority of Americans worship with people of the same race and cultural background. While diversity might be the popular buzzword, for many Christians it is not a practical reality.

Many Americans harbor resentment toward foreigners in light of the current political climate, particularly in the post-9/11 atmosphere. Television further encourages our discomfort in the company of other ethnic groups, particularly Middle Easterners. Since 9/11, many Americans are openly hostile toward people of Arab descent. While it is only natural that we feel most comfortable in the company of people we identify with racially, culturally, and religiously, the world is filled with people of different ethnicities, cultures, and religions. Loving others does not necessarily mean we agree with each other's teachings, but Christianity demands that we love those who are different. The ultimate expression of our Christianity is our willingness to love others.

Rev. Brian K. Woodson Sr., an Old Testament and Hebrew scholar, speaks at length on the topic of including foreigners by examining the Hebrew word for "stranger," ger (**GARE**). In the Bible, the word is most often used to describe the foreigners or aliens who freely resided among the people of God. Rev. Woodson explained that until the time of Abraham, everyone was a "stranger," since there was no national identity among the Jews yet. The Mosaic Law consistently enforces positive treatment of the ger, or stranger. For example, among a set of laws aimed at distinguishing the Israelites from the surrounding peoples, God instructs: "And if a stranger sojourn with [you] in your land, ye shall not [wrong] him. But the stranger that dwelleth with you shall be unto you as one born among you, and thou shalt love him as thyself; for ye were strangers (gerim) in the land of Egypt" (Leviticus 19:33–34). In this passage, God points out the historical similarity between the Jew and the ger. More importantly, God recognizes that, like His beloved Israelites, the stranger, as an outsider, is vulnerable and in need of His protection.

Many of the Mosaic laws concerning ritual and sacrifice were extended to strangers. They were expected to rest on the Sabbath (Exodus 20:10), observe the Passover (Exodus 12:19), and offer sacrifices (Leviticus 17:8).

Just how inclusive did God intend the relationship to be between His chosen people and the foreigners? Buried in the numerous priestly proscriptions found in Leviticus is a telling account of how God viewed the stranger among His people. Beginning in 24:10, we read that a mixed-race man, the son of an Israelite mother and an Egyptian father, blasphemed the name of God during a fight with an Israelite. The man is brought to Moses, and God tells Moses to take the man outside of the camp and have him publicly stoned. God goes on to tell Moses that laws governing murder and injury are to be equally applied: "Ye shall have one manner of law, as well for the stranger, as for one of your own country: for I am the LORD your God" (Leviticus 24:22). God has already made the stranger safe among His people; He now makes the stranger accountable to Him and His people for his actions.

The interaction between God, His people, and the stranger is chronicled throughout the Old Testament. Ruth, the Moabitess, is a stranger, yet she is included in the lineage of David and Jesus. The interaction with the stranger continues in the New Testament as well. Jesus shows compassion and heals the afflicted daughter of the Syro-Phoenician woman (Matthew 15:21–28; Mark 7:24–30), and later the servant of a Roman centurion (Matthew 8:5–13; Luke 7:2–10). We also see Jesus transcending historical racial hatred between Jews and Samaritans as He witnesses to the Samaritan woman at the well (John 4:1–42).

During Old Testament and New Testament times, strangers were expected to be treated with respect and protection. Jesus responds to the stranger not with hatred and distrust, but with loving compassion. Present-day Christians hoping to emulate our Savior are called to do no less. We must strive, not simply to live, but to live in the new covenant. This means that our love for Christ must motivate us to emulate His love for others. Certainly, we cannot do this on our own. Our flesh is unable to see the "beloved" in those who are not like us. The empowerment of the Holy Spirit will enable us to love others the way that Christ would have us love them: completely and unselfishly. We can love our neighbor only when we recognize, as Jesus did, that whoever is in need is the neighbor we must love. Through Christianity, our hearts are transformed and our former discomforts, suspicions, and prejudices against the stranger are discarded.

Jennifer King is the superintendent of Sunday School at Bay Area Christian Church in Oakland, California.

Love is Not Fondness

by Frederick Thomas

Love is one of the most overused and misunderstood words in the English language. Sports fans love their sports teams, and sweets fans love their desserts and candies. We love our pets and our families. Couples fall in love and often fall out of love. Our music resonates with declarations of love, and the movie industry produces several love stories every year.

The question is: What is love? The dictionary has several different definitions of love, such as a deep and tender feeling of affection and thoughtfulness toward a person; a feeling of intense desire and attraction toward a person with whom one is disposed to make a pair; and the emotion of sex and romance. All of these definitions associate love with feelings and emotions. Maybe that is the reason we really do not understand love at all.

We tend to believe that love is an emotion based upon how we feel. Since emotions fluctuate, love fluctuates also. Relationships end because people no longer feel like they love each other. Many people do not accept God's love because they cannot feel it. Others feel the immediate rush of passion when they first encounter God and then wonder if He still loves them when the passion is gone.

We tend to associate love with powerful emotions and affections. Although many times these emotions and affections are the exciting byproducts of love, they do not accurately describe what true love is. I would guess that the tremendously high divorce rate in this country is an indication that people feel that love is based on their own changing feelings and emotions.

The problem with the emotional concept of love is that it is both selfish and self-serving. It is selfish because it concentrates on what one gets rather than what one gives; and it is self-serving because it is rooted in having one's own needs met by another. Could this possibly be what God meant when He commanded us to love Him with all our being and our neighbor as ourselves? Does God expect us to live our lives feeling constant passion for Him and affection for our neighbors, whom we might not even know?

To find out what love really is, we must turn to the source. In John's first letter, the apostle encourages us, "Beloved, let us love one another; for love is of God, and he who loves is born of God and knows God. He who does not love does not know God; for God is love" (1 John 4:7–8, RSV). The nature of this love is inherent in the very statement John makes: "Love one another."

Love must not be restricted to those who are nice or pleasant to us. Every person is a special creation of God for whom Christ sacrificed His life, and capable of a unique relationship with the Father. That is why we love one another. We are filled with the Spirit of God, and He is love. This love is an interest in and a concern for other people; it seeks what is best for the person and asks nothing in return. It makes no difference if the person is rich or poor, Black or White, old or young, male or female.

This love is demonstrated by God because He is love. The Father does not simply love us; He is love and the source of love. Love is an essential aspect of His nature. In fact, God's creation of humanity is one form of His self-expression. God is love, and He chose to express that love. He began by creating a physical universe so that the object of His love would be constantly reminded of Him (see Romans 1:20). He created plant and animal life so that His beloved would have something to rule over, even as He ruled over all creation. After God saw that everything else was in place, He created a being in His own image. Because humanity is created in His marvelous image, people have both the capacity to love and the free will to choose whether to give love.

Humans are the crowning point of all creation. We are so dear to God that even the way we were formed is unique. God spoke the physical universe and all life into being, but when it came to humanity, He got personal. Rather than speaking man into being, our loving Father scooped up a bit of clay and personally formed it in His gentle, loving hands. Then He lovingly took the lifeless form and intimately blew His holy breath into his nostrils, and man became a living soul. Here, God expressed His love through doing and giving rather than feeling.

When humanity fell into sin and out of relationship with the loving God, He also made the ultimate sacrifice on our behalf. John says that God loved us so much that He offered His own dear Son to pay the cost of our sin and desertion (John 3:16). He did not do this after we repented and returned to Him. Scripture teaches that while we were yet sinners, Christ died for us (Romans 5:8). Again, we see God's love in His giving and doing. That is what love is. It is a decision to give our best on behalf of another. It is an act of will to sacrifice oneself for the good of another. It is not concerned with what a person is like or what she does or how he dresses or how she looks. It sees one thing only: "Here is another person created by God to be loved and for whom Christ died." We recognize others as people like ourselves struggling with the aspirations and frustrations of life. Love sees another person beset with the problems of life and asks, "How can I help?" That is love.

It is no good claiming that you know God if His love is not found in your life. If you cannot treat people objectively and see through the irritating qualities that might offend you—if your reaction to those who offend you is one of opposition, rejection, and instant antagonism—then it is no good saying you belong to Him. If God lives in you, you must be welcoming to all who are in need of love. Rejection is not God's life, nor His love. John's argument is that if the life of God is present in us, then the love of Him will be there also. Doing good for others should not be based on how we feel about the person. In fact, the best expression of love comes from doing good to those toward whom we harbor feelings of resentment (Luke 6:32–35).

The love of God is seen in both creation and our salvation. In both cases, God gave of Himself while demanding nothing in return. Love is an action verb; it is made apparent by what one does, not by feels. If we are to truly love God and one another, we must give our best both to God and to each other. "Greater love hath no man than this, that a man lay down His life for his friends" (John 15:13).

Frederick Thomas is the pastor of Family of Faith Community Church in Chicago, Illinois.

A.G. Gaston

(1892–1996)

When people think of the Civil Rights Movement, the name A.G. Gaston doesn't come to mind. Although not well known to us through history books, Gaston directly and indirectly supported and aided the Civil Rights Movement. In 1892, Gaston was born in poverty as the son of a railroad worker and a cook. After serving in World War I, he found jobs driving a delivery truck for a dry cleaning company, and later as a coal miner. While working as a miner, he concocted the idea to sell his mother's boxed lunches to his co-workers. He then added popcorn and peanuts to his wares and soon earned enough money to become an informal banker, loaning to his co-workers at 25% interest. Gaston soon turned to the insurance business with his Booker T. Washington Burial Society. Soon he took over other parts of the burial process, such as undertaking and casket making.

As Birmingham's largest Black employer, Gaston helped the Civil Rights Movement tremendously. Martin Luther King Jr. and his allies used a motel Gaston owned as a safe refuge to plan their activities. When King was jailed by Bull Connor, Gaston bailed him out with $160,000 from his own pocket. Gaston quietly promoted both financial literacy and voting rights among his customers. He urged Blacks in Birmingham not only to save their money, but register to vote. Gaston's wealth gave him a certain status with the White community. His most effective methods were negotiation, deal making, and private threats. While Gaston was an advocate for civil rights, he also promoted the "Green Power" of Blacks going into business for themselves—something that he not only preached but lived.

Gaston also branched out into other industries besides funeral services. He also owned a construction business and a financial business, CFS Bancshares. The motel that Gaston used as a refuge for civil rights activists is now owned by the city of Birmingham. Plans have been made to annex the building to the Birmingham Civil Rights Institute.

Although A.G. Gaston amassed an unusual amount of wealth, he also had to endure many of the same problems of Black men in the 20th century. After attending a state dinner at the White House with President Kennedy, firebombs were thrown at the Gaston home. At one point, Gaston and his wife were kidnapped and beaten, and Gaston was found tied up in his own car.

Gaston has been quoted as saying, "I never went into anything with the idea to making money ... I thought of doing something and it would come up and make money. I never thought of trying to get rich." These are ironic words from a man who died with a net worth of $130 million. Gaston left behind a construction company, a financial services firm, and an insurance business, as well as a Boys and Girls Club in Birmingham. Most of all, he left behind a legacy of service to the community, and for future generations, the possibilities of being a creative Black entrepreneur.

Teaching Tips

Words You Should Know

A. Propitiation (1 John 4:10) *hilasmos* (Gk.)—Atonement; the benefit of Christ's sacrifice for humanity to bring reconciliation.

B. Made perfect (v. 18) *teleioo* (Gk.)—To complete; to finish; to accomplish one's goal, not wanting.

Teacher Preparation

Unifying Principle—Perfect Love. Many people search in all the wrong places for a perfect love they can trust. Can other humans be trusted to love without fault at all times? John reminds us that God is love and those who abide in love have His love perfected in them.

A. Intercede for your students and ask the Lord to open their hearts to receive His love and forgiveness.

B. Read the lesson and reflect on the culture of your church or ministry to see if it is in alignment with Jesus' brand of love.

O—Open the Lesson

A. Have students read the In Focus story.

B. Briefly overview Dr. Gary Chapman's book *The 5 Love Languages* to help students understand their love language.

C. Discuss why people may be afraid to love.

P—Present the Scriptures

A. Review the life of the Apostle John by using The People, Places, and Times.

B. Read the Focal Verses and have students reflect on the love of God in Christ.

C. Ask students to reflect on times they may have struggled to operate with love as their motive.

E—Explore the Meaning

A. Call out key points in the In Depth section, and ask students if they are open enough to share what God has revealed through this course of study.

B. Ask students to reflect on what would happen if the body of Christ was truly motivated by love. What would change?

N—Next Steps for Application

A. Discuss what can be done to make the love of God contagious in the body of Christ.

B. Ask students for immediate steps to make the love of God visible inside and outside the church.

C. Close with prayer and leave time for personal ministry for those who struggle with giving and receiving love.

Worship Guide

For the Superintendent or Teacher
Theme: The Source of All Love
Song: "No Greater Love"
Devotional Reading: Psalm 40:1–10

The Source of All Love

Bible Background • 1 JOHN 4:7–19
Printed Text • 1 JOHN 4:7–19 | Devotional Reading • PSALM 40:1–10

Aim for Change

By the end of the lesson, we will: CONSIDER differences and similarities between God's love and human love; REFLECT on how His perfect love casts out fear in human life; and DEMONSTRATE what it means to love others the way God loves us.

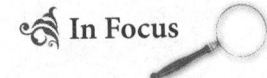 **In Focus**

Steve was always a ladies' man with the ability to charm women. When around his friends, he would brag, "I can't help it if women just love me!" However, deep inside he had a longing that he never expressed to his guy friends for fear of blowing his image. Steve really wanted to settle down with one woman and have a family, but being close to 50, he wondered if his dream had eluded him. Still, he was always afraid of ending up with the "wrong woman" and struggled to remain committed.

Steve was friends with a lot of his ex-girlfriends. Kimberly was his best friend, his "one that got away." Kimberly went through a lot with Steve, and although she still cared deeply for him, she was afraid to let Steve back in her heart romantically. Everyone who knew them could see that the two were made for each other. Neither of them fully trusted God to forget the past and make their relationship new.

Many shy away from giving themselves fully to another, but when we are persuaded of God's love for us, it casts away all fear leaving us free to love. Why is it so difficult to give and receive love?

Keep in Mind

"Beloved, if God so loved us, we ought also to love one another" (1 John 4:11).

"Beloved, if God so loved us, we ought also to love one another" (1 John 4:11).

Focal Verses

KJV **1 John 4:7** Beloved, let us love one another: for love is of God; and every one that loveth is born of God, and knoweth God.

8 He that loveth not knoweth not God; for God is love.

9 In this was manifested the love of God toward us, because that God sent his only begotten Son into the world, that we might live through him.

10 Herein is love, not that we loved God, but that he loved us, and sent his Son to be the propitiation for our sins.

11 Beloved, if God so loved us, we ought also to love one another.

12 No man hath seen God at any time. If we love one another, God dwelleth in us, and his love is perfected in us.

13 Hereby know we that we dwell in him, and he in us, because he hath given us of his Spirit.

14 And we have seen and do testify that the Father sent the Son to be the Saviour of the world.

15 Whosoever shall confess that Jesus is the Son of God, God dwelleth in him, and he in God.

16 And we have known and believed the love that God hath to us. God is love; and he that dwelleth in love dwelleth in God, and God in him.

17 Herein is our love made perfect, that we may have boldness in the day of judgment: because as he is, so are we in this world.

18 There is no fear in love; but perfect love casteth out fear: because fear hath torment. He that feareth is not made perfect in love.

19 We love him, because he first loved us.

NLT **1 John 4:7** Dear friends, let us continue to love one another, for love comes from God. Anyone who loves is a child of God and knows God.

8 But anyone who does not love does not know God, for God is love.

9 God showed how much he loved us by sending his one and only Son into the world so that we might have eternal life through him.

10 This is real love—not that we loved God, but that he loved us and sent his Son as a sacrifice to take away our sins.

11 Dear friends, since God loved us that much, we surely ought to love each other.

12 No one has ever seen God. But if we love each other, God lives in us, and his love is brought to full expression in us.

13 And God has given us his Spirit as proof that we live in him and he in us.

14 Furthermore, we have seen with our own eyes and now testify that the Father sent his Son to be the Savior of the world.

15 All who declare that Jesus is the Son of God have God living in them, and they live in God.

16 We know how much God loves us, and we have put our trust in his love. God is love, and all who live in love live in God, and God lives in them.

17 And as we live in God, our love grows more perfect. So we will not be afraid on the Day of Judgment, but we can face him with confidence because we live like Jesus here in this world.

18 Such love has no fear, because perfect love expels all fear. If we are afraid, it is for fear of punishment, and this shows that we have not fully experienced his perfect love.

19 We love each other because he loved us first.

The People, Places, and Times

John. One of the hand-picked apostles of Jesus, John was in the inner circle and was invited by Jesus to experience His power first-hand. Jesus gave John and his brother James the nickname "Boanerges" or "sons of thunder" (Mark 3:17). The nickname is indicative of their hot tempers and great ambition (Luke 9:51–56; Mark 10:35–41). John's Gospel provides an intimate portrait of God's love in Christ. He refers to himself as "the disciple whom Jesus loved" (John 13:23, 20:2).

Day of Judgment. Early church believers waited with eager anticipation for Christ's return. They knew not the day or the time but were told by Jesus Himself to be ready (Matthew 24:44). At this time, Jesus will set up His kingdom on earth and everyone will stand before the Lord to give an account for their lives in order to receive either their rewards or punishment (cf. 2 Corinthians 5:10; 2 Thessalonians 2:1–8; Revelation 22:12). Also known as the "Day of the Lord" or the "second coming of Christ," it is a day of great joy for those who are in Christ, but to those who do not receive God's redemption through His Son, it is a day of great tribulation.

Background

The Apostle John wrote his epistles (the Johannine letters) to a group of churches in Asia Minor to combat heretical doctrine and false teachings regarding Jesus Christ, most notably about His deity and resurrection, as they awaited His return. Using his authority as an apostle with intimate knowledge and experience with the risen Christ, John wrote his letters to reassure believers of their commitment and to provide moral standards to live by as a reflection of their transformation. John encouraged those challenged in their faith to remain steadfast in their confession of and fidelity to Jesus Christ, and not succumb to the pressures of the world around them (1 John 2:15–27). Writing from Ephesus, John gives explicit instruction in this letter to not entertain false teachings, to stay away from deceptive spirits, and how to recognize an antichrist—one who does not believe that Jesus Christ is the Son of God (1 John 4:1–6).

At-A-Glance

1. God's Command to Love One Another
(1 John 4:7–11)
2. God's Love Perfected in Us (vv. 12–15)
3. God's Love Has No Fear (vv. 16–19)

In Depth

1. God's Command to Love One Another (1 John 4:7–11)

The Apostle John gives hearers and readers of his letter the key indicator of a follower of Jesus Christ—love. Just as God through Moses commanded the Israelites to love Him with all their heart, mind, and strength (Deuteronomy 6:4), and Jesus continued in this vein to love God and one another (Leviticus 19:18; Matthew 22:36–39), John emphasizes what it means to be born of God. Love is the principal thing that identifies someone who knows God. Writing to what is probably a Gentile audience, he appeals to their logic by arguing that the one who does not love does not know God because He is love (v. 8). Of particular note, John expresses that God is the very definition of love, the core of His nature, which runs deeper than believing that God is loving. Love is the very motive behind everything God does. God's love is intense, fervent, and evidenced by redemption through Jesus Christ. John reminds believers of

God's convincing proof of His love for humanity in the Person of Jesus Christ (v. 9).

John further emphasizes God's love through Christ as the propitiation for our sins (v. 10). Even today, many are amazed that God would allow His Son to be the atoning sacrifice for our sins or that Jesus would willingly give His life as a ransom (Mark 10:45). Jesus said Himself that no one took His life, but He laid it down and took it up again at the Father's command (John 10:17–18). The appropriate and righteous response to the great love of God in Christ is that we are driven and motivated to love one another.

2. God's Love Perfected in Us (vv. 12–15)

God's love is perfected in us when we live in community with love as the motive. John reminds us that no one has ever seen God, but we know He is real, especially when we love unselfishly, preferring others over ourselves. We can replicate God in the earth and make Him visible to the world. God's love is "perfected," that is, completed or accomplished, when we trust Him and give love without reservation.

As a mark of a true believer, John says that in confessing our faith in the Lord Jesus Christ, we will bear witness of His Spirit living in us, and the Holy Spirit will testify that sonship has been achieved (John 1:12; Romans 8:14; 1 John 3:1).

3. God's Love Has No Fear (vv. 16–19)

These believers were challenged by philosophical questions about Christ, which caused lots of confusion, particularly about His return. John reminded these believers that they must remain in God and that He is able to complete their love for Him and each other. It was believed that Christ's return would occur at any moment, but John encouraged believers to rest and be confident no matter the day of His return, and that they are eternally secure

as they continue in love. They had no reason to fear judgment or punishment because of the complete love of God in Christ. God's love would drive out any fear or torment.

The same is true for us today. Jesus promises as we abide in Him that the Triune God would dwell with us (John 15:4–10). Because of God's abiding presence with us by our faith in Jesus Christ, we are reassured too.

Search the Scriptures

1. How can you defend the fact that Christians are to always love others regardless of the circumstances according to 1 John 4:7–8?

2 Explain the sinner's role and God's role in propitiation. What did sinners do for God? What did God do for sinners (v. 10)?

Discuss the Meaning

1. What would be different about our community of faith if we truly showed love as the principal mark of true discipleship?

2. If God's love is supposed to compel us to love one another, what gets in the way?

Lesson in Our Society

As Christians we are commanded by God to love, starting first and foremost with our faith community. The early church walked in radical love for God and each other, which caused the church to grow. If God loved us so radically to send His Son to redeem us and repair the breach caused by sin, we must reproduce this love for one another and translate God's love in this age.

Make It Happen

God's love is intense, intentional, believes the best (not the worst), and is not selfish. Pray and ask Him to reveal opportunities to reflect His love in the earth, particularly by how you love in the faith community. If you have to start in your own home, start there. Seek to move outside your comfort zone and reach across barriers to radically love. Make love contagious.

Follow the Spirit

What God wants me to do:

_____

_____

_____

_____

Remember Your Thoughts

Special insights I have learned:

_____

_____

_____

_____

More Light on the Text

1 John 4:7–19

7 Beloved, let us love one another: for love is of God; and every one that loveth is born of God, and knoweth God.

After dealing with the matter of discerning the spirits, John here returns to the discussion on love that he began in chapter 3. He now calls Christians to demonstrate what he identifies as one of the distinguishing marks of a true believer: to love one another, because God is the source of love.

This statement is not meant to stand alone. John is not engaging in deep philosophical and theological discussion. He tells the early church that God is the source of love because he wants to emphasize what it means to be in a true relationship with Him. In other words,

John wants to distinguish between those in a right relationship with God and those who are not. Those who love "have been born of God," John says. They are God's children, and He is their Father. This is why John tells us that God is the source of love, because if we truly love as God loves, we demonstrate that we are His children by manifesting His love toward others.

Expressing love toward one another is one method of demonstrating that we know God. The Greek word for "knoweth," *ginosko* (**ghin-OCE-ko**), denotes knowledge from personal experience. John uses the present tense of the verb here to emphasize that this knowledge is ongoing, not temporary. Thus the person who loves can say that he or she truly knows God and will continue to know Him.

8 He that loveth not knoweth not God; for God is love.

Since love is a distinguishing mark of a true Christian, John says that the one who does not love has not come to know God. He puts this statement in the past tense to indicate that regardless of the orthodoxy of their profession of faith, someone who does not love has never entered into a relationship with God. John's point is not that love must be perfectly demonstrated at all times, but his point is that a believer who claims to be a child of God should show some sign of the practice of true love in their lives.

John reveals God's character by simply stating, "God is love." Just as God is Light (1 John 1:5) or Spirit (John 4:24), so God is love too. Since God is love, claiming that we know God but not expressing love would be inconsistent.

9 In this was manifested the love of God toward us, because that God sent his only begotten Son into the world, that we might live through him.

Next, John turns to the supreme example of God's love—His Son, Jesus Christ. For God, love is more than simply kind words or warm feelings in the heart. True love acts on behalf of and for the sake of another. Love is expressed, intentional action, not mere feelings or emotions.

This is not to say that emotions are exempt, but they are not the primary motivator. John says that the supreme demonstration of love is God sending His only Son into the world to give His life for humankind. Because He loved us so much, God willingly gave up His Son for us. God sent His Son that we might truly live, and by so doing, He demonstrated the reality of His love toward us.

10 Herein is love, not that we loved God, but that he loved us, and sent his Son to be the propitiation for our sins. 11 Beloved, if God so loved us, we ought also to love one another.

God sent His one and only Son into the world to demonstrate His love, so that we who were spiritually dead might have life. John makes it clear that our love for God did not move Him to give up His Son, but rather His love for us. In fact, Scripture tells us that while we were still in our sin, God demonstrated His love toward us by sending His Son to die for us (Romans 5:8).

In verse 10, the word "propitiation" is the Greek word *hilasmos* (**hil-as-MOS**), which is related to removing sin through atonement or sacrifice. There can be little doubt, then, that when John used the term, he emphasized that God sent Jesus Christ to be the atoning sacrifice—to remove the guilt we incurred because of our sins, so that we might have eternal life. Herein lies the supreme example of love. While we were in a state of disobedience toward God because of our sins, God gave up His Son to remove our guilt and called us to Himself to receive eternal life. Now that's love!

In light of this supreme example of love, how can we not love one another? Only by accepting the death of Jesus Christ as our way of salvation can we really experience God's love. Christians ought to become the proverbial "chip off the old block." We must become loving and caring toward others just as God is with us. Christ's sacrifice on the Cross reminds us of God's great love for us. We cannot produce this kind of love in our own strength—it comes from God. When the love that God placed in our hearts is ignited, only then are we able to fulfill His command to love one another.

12 No man hath seen God at any time. If we love one another, God dwelleth in us, and his love is perfected in us.

It is fundamentally true that no one has actually seen God with their natural eyes. Thus the question emerges, "How does one truly see God?" Ultimately, we see God in His Son, but in reference to John's point, we see God in everyday life as we demonstrate true love toward one another. He is the source of love. Therefore, when we show love toward one another, we bear witness to the world of the reality of God's divine presence within us.

The word "perfected" is the Greek verb *teleioo* (**teh-lay-OH-oh**), which means to accomplish, complete, or bring to an end. Therefore, when we love others, we perfect or complete God's command to love as He, through Christ, has loved us.

13 Hereby know we that we dwell in him, and he in us, because he hath given us of his Spirit.

God lives in His people through the Holy Spirit as an assurance of the reality of the relationship we have with Him. The term "dwell" (Gk. *meno*, **MEN-o**) means to abide or remain.

Thus, John affirms that the same Spirit of the living God that taught Jesus also abides within every believer. When couples marry, a ring is used as a symbol of their commitment to one another. Every time the husband or wife looks at his or her ring, it is a reminder of their commitment to abide with one another throughout this life. God has demonstrated His commitment to us by giving us something that is much greater than a ring—the Holy Spirit!

14 And we have seen and do testify that the Father sent the Son to be the Saviour of the world. 15 Whosoever shall confess that Jesus is the Son of God, God dwelleth in him, and he in God.

John notes that eyewitnesses have seen and given testimony that God sent His Son into the world to be our Savior. It is worth mentioning that John's statement should not be taken out of context. At first glance, it would appear that the word "we" refers to the disciples who walked and talked with Jesus (see 1 John 1:1–4). However, some scholars indicate that John is referring to the entire church community because of their abiding faith in God, rather than the original eyewitnesses of Jesus' earthly ministry. Whatever the case, John wants his readers to know that "whosoever" believes can experience God's indwelling. John states that anyone who will "confess" (Gk. *homologeo*, **ho-mo-lo-GEH-oh**, to acknowledge, profess, or agree) that Jesus Christ is the Son of God will dwell with God and He in them.

Loving one another, the presence of the Spirit in us, and our confession of faith that Jesus is the Son of God are all equally important assurances that God abides in us and we in Him. It is not enough to say that we believe in Christ, love the Lord, or have the Spirit. All three together signify the reality of our communion with God and together provide assurance to our hearts that we are rooted in God and He in us.

16 And we have known and believed the love that God hath to us. God is love; and he that dwelleth in love dwelleth in God, and God in him.

John tells us that God is love. This does not mean love is God. Instead it means that love is an inseparable aspect of God's character and God shows us what love is supposed to look like. He restates what he has suggested throughout this passage, that those who "dwelleth" (Gk. *meno*) or abide in God have the benefit of a personal relationship with Him. As a result, those whose lives demonstrate true, Christian love are assured that God will continue to live in them and they in Him.

17 Herein is our love made perfect, that we may have boldness in the day of judgment: because as he is, so are we in this world.

The reality of God's love among believers is a means of confidence on the Day of Judgment. The Greek word used here for "boldness" is *parrhesia* (**par-rhay-SEE-ah**), which means outspokenness, frankness, and confidence, especially among those of high rank. John reintroduces the theme of boldness here, which he mentioned earlier (1 John 2:28, 3:21–22). He reminds readers how God's love is made "perfect" (Gk. *teleioo*) or complete within us. Once we allow God's love to control our lives, it will grow and become complete. As a result, we will be able to come boldly before God's throne of judgment, confident that He will not cast us away.

18 There is no fear in love; but perfect love casteth out fear: because fear hath torment. He that feareth is not made perfect in love.

Having just encouraged the community of believers to have confidence in God's love, John reminds them that true love does not have any fear. In this verse, John shows the disparity between fear (Gk. *phobos*, **FO-bos**), meaning dread or terror, and love (Gk. *agape*, **ah-GAH-pay**), meaning affection, benevolence, or goodwill—the two cannot coexist. The word "torment" is the Greek word *kolasis* (**KO-lah-seese**), which means correction, punishment, or penalty. John says that it is not God's will that any of His children be tormented. When we fear, we are not considering the perfect love God has for us, and the fear in turn prohibits us from demonstrating love toward others (cf. 2 Timothy 1:7).

19 We love him, because he first loved us. 20 If a man say, I love God, and hateth his brother, he is a liar: for he that loveth not his brother whom he hath seen, how can he love God whom he hath not seen?

Expressing love for one another is an outward sign of love for God. We cannot see God, but we can see other human beings around us. In this light, John says that anyone who claims to love God and hates another believer is simply a liar. In short, John is saying it is impossible to have faith in God without showing love toward other people. We might commit loving acts from time to time, but if our motives are false, the deception will not prevail. When we love or fail to love others, we demonstrate whether or not we truly love God.

21 And this commandment have we from him, That he who loveth God love his brother also.

Finally, the apostle returns to a now familiar thought: love one another. God's great love for us ignites our love for Him. The more we understand His great love for us, the more we are motivated to love Him and that love will overflow in love for others. Jesus Himself said, "A new commandment I give to you, that you love one another: just as I have loved you, you also are to love one another. By this all people will know that you are my disciples, if you have love for one another" (John 13:34–35, ESV).

Love is not optional for Christians; love for God and love for one another go hand in hand.

Say It Correctly

Propitiation. pro-pih-she-**AY**-shun.
Dwelleth. **DWEH**-lith.

Daily Bible Readings

MONDAY
Christ Died for Us
(1 John 3:11–17)

TUESDAY
Jesus and the Father's Love
(John 14:18–24)

WEDNESDAY
Believe in Jesus, Love One Another
(1 John 3:18–24)

THURSDAY
The Spirit of God Confesses Jesus
(1 John 4:1–6)

FRIDAY
Loving God and Brothers and Sisters
(1 John 4:20–5:5)

SATURDAY
Thankful for God's Steadfast Love
(Psalm 40:1–10)

SUNDAY
Dwelling in God's Love
(1 John 4:7–19)

Teaching Tips

Words You Should Know

A. Conversation (Ephesians 2:3) *anastrepho* (Gk.)—To live, behave, abide.

B. Saved (vv. 5, 8) *sozo* (Gk.)—To make whole or healthy; to deliver from bondage.

Teacher Preparation

Unifying Principle—Saving Grace. Sometimes those who break the rules become outcasts in the group. Where can those who break rules find acceptance? Out of His great love for us, God saved us by grace through faith and will show the immense richness of this grace in kindness to those who are in Christ Jesus.

A. Pray before studying and ask God for a new revelation, even if this is a familiar text.

B. Read the text in different translations for clarity, highlight key words, and read through The People, Places, and Times; Background; and In Depth sections.

C. Ask the Holy Spirit to guide you through the needs of your students.

O—Open the Lesson

A. Lead the class in prayer and ask for special attention from the Holy Spirit to provide new revelation on this familiar text.

B. Ask volunteers to share their struggles with cultivating their own love walk, and understanding or receiving the love of God.

C. Share the Unifying Principle and, based on the Aim for Change, lead a discussion on the human experience—what does it mean to be human, fallen?

P—Present the Scriptures

A. Read the lesson text and ask students about what is familiar in the text.

B. Have students to review The People, Places, and Times in order to understand the context of the lesson.

C. Call out key points made in the In Depth section and ask students to discuss these in relation to their own life experience.

E—Explore the Meaning

A. Have students make the connection between the Lesson Aim and the text, and have them discuss what Paul expressed in his letter.

B. Review the Discuss the Meaning and Lesson in Our Society sections.

N—Next Steps for Application

A. Have students break up into groups to share ideas for immediate application.

B. Ask students to pair up and hold each other accountable for one of these applications.

C. Have students report back next week on how they used the lesson.

Worship Guide

For the Superintendent or Teacher
Theme: God's Overflowing Love
Song: "If Not for Your Grace"
Devotional Reading: Ephesians 4:1–6

God's Overflowing Love

Bible Background • EPHESIANS 2:1–10 | Printed Text • EPHESIANS 2:1–10
Devotional Reading • EPHESIANS 4:1–6

—————————— Aim for Change ——————————

By the end of the lesson, we will: DISCERN ways in which God's love addresses the separation of sin; GIVE thanks for His grace, which offers new possibilities for living in human community; and DESCRIBE how Christians live out God's love in the world and in our communities.

In Focus

Michelle had a hard time believing her call to ministry. She had strayed from God in her college years because she wanted to experience what she thought was living. Now, in her early thirties, she had returned to Christ and remained rooted in Him. Pastor Morton approached her, sharing what the Lord revealed to him about her assignment—to start a school. Michelle respectfully listened but already made up in her mind that she would focus on her career goals. After the conversation, Michelle went home to cry out to God and asked, "Why do You want me? I'm not worthy to serve You in that capacity. I am afraid that I have let You down too many times to represent You. Besides, I am not going to be able to follow my dreams if I surrender."

The Lord revealed to her in an unexpected way that her call to ministry and her vocation were inextricably connected and that He designed it that way. As well, because of her own young adult experience, God would use her mightily to reach the next generation that was wrestling to understand His nature.

The tapes of our past are replayed in our memories, and it can make it hard for us to receive God's love and forgiveness. Today's lesson shows us the immeasurable love of God to transform us into the image of His Son. In what ways has God's love transformed your life?

—————————— Keep in Mind ——————————

"Even when we were dead in sins, hath quickened us together with Christ, (by grace ye are saved;)" (Ephesians 2:5).

"Even when we were dead in sins, hath quickened us together with Christ, (by grace ye are saved;)" (Ephesians 2:5).

Focal Verses

KJV **Ephesians 2:1** And you hath he quickened, who were dead in trespasses and sins;

2 Wherein in time past ye walked according to the course of this world, according to the prince of the power of the air, the spirit that now worketh in the children of disobedience:

3 Among whom also we all had our conversation in times past in the lusts of our flesh, fulfilling the desires of the flesh and of the mind; and were by nature the children of wrath, even as others.

4 But God, who is rich in mercy, for his great love wherewith he loved us,

5 Even when we were dead in sins, hath quickened us together with Christ, (by grace ye are saved;)

6 And hath raised us up together, and made us sit together in heavenly places in Christ Jesus:

7 That in the ages to come he might shew the exceeding riches of his grace in his kindness toward us through Christ Jesus.

8 For by grace are ye saved through faith; and that not of yourselves: it is the gift of God:

9 Not of works, lest any man should boast.

10 For we are his workmanship, created in Christ Jesus unto good works, which God hath before ordained that we should walk in them.

NLT **Ephesians 2:1** Once you were dead because of your disobedience and your many sins.

2 You used to live in sin, just like the rest of the world, obeying the devil—the commander of the powers in the unseen world. He is the spirit at work in the hearts of those who refuse to obey God.

3 All of us used to live that way, following the passionate desires and inclinations of our sinful nature. By our very nature we were subject to God's anger, just like everyone else.

4 But God is so rich in mercy, and he loved us so much,

5 that even though we were dead because of our sins, he gave us life when he raised Christ from the dead. (It is only by God's grace that you have been saved!)

6 For he raised us from the dead along with Christ and seated us with him in the heavenly realms because we are united with Christ Jesus.

7 So God can point to us in all future ages as examples of the incredible wealth of his grace and kindness toward us, as shown in all he has done for us who are united with Christ Jesus.

8 God saved you by his grace when you believed. And you can't take credit for this; it is a gift from God.

9 Salvation is not a reward for the good things we have done, so none of us can boast about it.

10 For we are God's masterpiece. He has created us anew in Christ Jesus, so we can do the good things he planned for us long ago.

The People, Places, and Times

Paul. Known as the apostle to the Gentiles, Paul was specifically called out by Jesus to a special ministry to bring reconciliation between God and humanity, between Jew and Gentile, bond and free (Acts 9:15, 13:46–47, 20:24; Galatians 3:28). God precisely equipped Paul with the ability to reach all kinds of people for the sake of the Gospel (1 Corinthians 9:21–23). He was born into a rich heritage as a descendant of the tribe of Benjamin, a Pharisee with Roman citizenship, and is believed to be a member of the Sanhedrin. Paul spoke multiple languages and was considered a scholar and suitable carrier of the Gospel to the known world.

Ephesus. A major epicenter of trade in the province of Asia, which is now modern-day Turkey. It was considered one of the major ports for commerce and religion, most notably because of its many temples and marketplace. The temple of Diana (her Roman name; Artemis to the Greeks) was a place of pilgrimage for Greek and Roman deities and generated much trade (Acts 19:29–30). God did extraordinary miracles in Ephesus through Paul to the point that "even handkerchiefs or aprons that had touched his skin were carried away to the sick, and their diseases left them and the evil spirits came out of them" (Acts 19:12).

Background

The book of Ephesians is one of God's masterful works through Paul, rich in theology, designed to form and strengthen faith in God's love and acceptance through Jesus Christ. Paul spent a considerable amount of time in Ephesus, which proved to be a worthy investment, as the church here became one of the leading centers of Christianity. Therefore it was very important for the Lord to use Paul to secure foundational Christian doctrine and unity using Ephesus because of the church's mixed population. It is believed that this letter was not only written to the Ephesians, but also circulated to multiple churches in the region. Major themes of the book of Ephesians include the glorification of Jesus Christ, one's identity in Christ and benefits of being in Christ (the words "in Him" are used often), the importance

of Christian unity, and the responsibility of the faithful to reflect Christian character.

At-A-Glance

1. Dead Before Christ (Ephesians 2:1–3)
2. Made Alive in Christ (vv. 4–7)
3. Created in Christ (vv. 8–10)

In Depth

1. Dead Before Christ (Ephesians 2:1–3)

The Apostle Paul reminds readers of where they came from before they followed Christ. Writing to a Gentile audience, he uses the word "dead" to mean spiritual separation from God. He emphasizes the fallen state of humanity, prone to sin because of the ways of the world. He encourages these Gentile believers that they are no longer bound to their former way of life because they have been "quickened" (made alive) in their spirit, awakened to God's loving presence, raised up and seated in heavenly places with Christ Jesus (Ephesians 2:6). Gentile believers lived under constant pressure to behave counter to their culture, where idolatry followed all kinds of indulgences as people lived by their senses—if it feels good do it; if it seems rational based on the latest philosophy, it is okay. The quickening power of the Holy Spirit gives them power to overcome as they are compelled by God's love to adapt to their new nature that seeks to please Him.

2. Made Alive in Christ (vv. 4–7)

Paul writes that God extends to believers the richness of who He is, merciful and the embodiment of love, as He rescues them from hopelessness. Paul basically tells his readers that prior to Christ, they were not truly living because they were out of fellowship. God in His great love, with all of His fervor and intensity, is stronger than death. When two people are in love, the presence of their significant other brings them to life because that person brings out the very best in them. God, as our first and primary love, does the same for us when we allow ourselves to be caught up in Him.

Paul again emphasizes the believer's identity and position—marked in Christ and seated in heavenly places with Him (v. 6). The church's presence on earth must bear witness to the truth that Jesus lives. The church has a wide impact, as Paul implies when he declares that the whole world would know that immeasurable riches of God's love and grace (i.e., His unmerited favor expressed through Jesus). The only way for the whole world to know this is by the church telling them the Good News. What Paul conveys is so profoundly life-changing that if embraced, it will forever alter how believers live in community. It was important for these Gentile believers to know that they are accepted and that God has lavished His love on them, so they did not revert to their former ways.

3. Created in Christ (vv. 8–10)

This pagan culture believed that followers had to perform favors to receive blessings from their gods. Paul counters this belief with a powerful statement: "For by grace you have been saved through faith. And this is not your own doing; it is the gift of God" (v. 8, NRSV). The pronouncement of the grace of God was radical theology. Grace and salvation are God's design and—out of the counsel of His own will—God in Christ lavishes His love on believers (Ephesians 1:8–10).

Paul makes sure to emphasize that God's love and grace are not the result of works. No one can take credit for making salvation or reconciliation possible. Humility is the key to receiving this grace; the proper response

to God's love is to acknowledge and reciprocate it. Paul tells these Gentile believers and future followers of Christ that they are God's creation, made for good works that He had already designed, predestined, and established to reflect His brilliance. The new life achieved in Christ must become their lifestyle, a life full of love.

Search the Scriptures

1. Create a three- to four-word tagline or phrase that explains "the gift of God." (Ephesians 2:8)?

2. Discuss the relationship between believers who were once separated from Christ (v. 1) and mercy (v. 4).

Discuss the Meaning

1. What does it mean to no longer follow the course of this world? Who is the prince of the power of the air?

2. What is incomprehensible to you about the grace of God?

Lesson in Our Society

God's love for us is extravagant and endless. Out of His great love and mercy, He rescued us through His Son so that we may have life more abundantly in unbroken fellowship. We are compelled to give the love we receive, and we should help people realize they are accepted and loved. We can give thanks to God for His indescribable gift by intentionally loving those who are broken, hurting, and marginalized. They are not forgotten nor forsaken as we express our faith in love.

Make It Happen

Examine your relationship with God. Do you appreciate His grace or take it for granted? This week, pay attention and note God's grace at work in your life. Ask God how you can be an extension of that grace to someone else, especially someone you find hard to love. Radically love someone this week, starting in your own household.

Follow the Spirit

What God wants me to do:

_____

_____

_____

_____

Remember Your Thoughts

Special insights I have learned:

_____

_____

_____

_____

More Light on the Text

Ephesians 2:1–10

1 And you hath he quickened, who were dead in trespasses and sins;

Verse one begins a three-verse segment that lacks a main verb in the Greek. By using an extreme word like "dead," the author emphasizes the helplessness of unbelievers. A dead man can do nothing for himself. He needs a miracle—divine intervention—to live again. And that is what God has done for us.

"Trespasses" (Gk. *paraptoma*, **pah-ROP-toe-mah**) are lapses or deviations from the right way of living. "Sins" (Gk. *hamartia*, **ha-mar-TEE-ah**) are acts in which we "miss the mark"—as an archer sometimes misses their target. These terms overlap and reinforce

each other, to show us the magnitude of the problem of sin.

2 Wherein in time past ye walked according to the course of this world, according to the prince of the power of the air, the spirit that now worketh in the children of disobedience:

"Wherein" is translated "in which" by modern translations. Grammatically, it refers only to the "sins" from verse 1. However, according to the logic of the passage, it also refers to the "trespasses."

Paul now uses familiar imagery: Life is a journey. Every person must travel in one of two directions. Either we walk the broad, easy path that leads to destruction or the difficult, narrow path that leads to life (Matthew 7:13–14).

Instead of "course," the usual translation of the Greek word there is "age" (Gk. *aion*, **eye-ON**), which normally refers to a period of time and retains that meaning here. Before our conversion, we lived not for eternity, but temporary pleasure—the same way everyone else does. We were corrupted by the false beliefs and debased values that permeate this world.

"The prince of the power of the air" is a reference to Satan, who the Bible teaches is real, powerful, and actively trying to subvert God's purposes in this world. The ancients thought of the "air" (Gk. *aer*, **ah-AYR**) as the space between the earth and the moon; the Greeks used this term to refer to the lower, impure air where spirits live. Paul, while not endorsing this pagan view of the spirit world, uses the terminology to make the point that Satan wrongly claims the right to exercise his will in the physical universe. The children of God are characterized by obedience to His will (1 Peter 1:14). Those who disobey, however, reveal themselves to be children of the devil (Matthew 13:38; 1 John 3:10); thus, they are called "children of disobedience."

3 Among whom also we all had our conversation in times past in the lusts of our flesh, fulfilling the desires of the flesh and of the mind; and were by nature the children of wrath, even as others.

In Greek, the phrase "among whom" is nearly identical to the phrase "in which" from verse two, which draws our attention to the way the two verses complement each other. Verse two describes our former life characterized by sinful actions; verse three points out our former alliance with sinful people.

Paul is describing a situation in which we were not only surrounded by sinful people, but we were influenced by them and did the same things. The phrase "had our conversation" does not refer to simply talking together among unbelievers. In the Greek (*anastrepho*, **ah-nah-STRE-foe**), it is a metaphor that means "conducted or behaved ourselves." The desires that dominated us in that previous walk of life were "of the flesh." The "flesh" (Gk. *sarx*, **SARKS**) in Pauline writings refers to the sinful nature that continues to think, speak, and act out of depravity (cf. Galatians 5:19–21). Christians are called to put this nature within them to death by living in the power of the Holy Spirit (Romans 8:13).

"Fulfilling the desires of the flesh and of the mind" intensifies the idea of the previous clause. Apart from Christ, sin not only influenced us, but it dominated our entire being. In Paul's description, we did not choose to repeatedly sin out of free will, but we were bound involuntarily to sin and driven compulsively by it. A tragic destiny awaits those whose lives are held captive by sinful desire. "Children of wrath" speaks to an eternal destiny full of God's just punishment for our rebellion. "Wrath" (Gk. *orge*, **or-GAY**) is anger or indignation; in the Bible, it is also used to mean "judgment" or "punishment."

4 But God, who is rich in mercy, for his great love wherewith he loved us,

The conjunction "but" introduces a stark contrast. Out of gloom and despair comes hope and light. God has seen the plight of His people and decided to do something to deliver them. "Rich" (Gk. *plousios*, **PLOO-see-os**) tells us that He has an abundant supply of what we need. "Mercy" (Gk. *eleos*, **EL-eh-os**) is God's compassion and pity for us in our helpless condition.

"For" is translated "because of" in other English versions and helps the modern reader see Paul's line of reasoning a little bit more clearly. The reason behind God's merciful act of deliverance is His love (affection) for His people. The author intensifies the description of this love with repetition by saying, in essence, that God "loved us with love."

5 Even when we were dead in sins, hath quickened us together with Christ, (by grace ye are saved;)

God's love is magnified when we understand that, after we were already dead in sin, He had mercy on us. The phrase "dead in sins" uses the exact same Greek words as verse 1. Before we or our first parents had even taken their first breath, how could we have been "dead in sin"?

"Quickened together with" (Gk. *suzoopoieo*, **sood-zo-op-oy-EH-o**) is a phrase formed by adding the preposition "with" to the verb "made alive." It is the first of three consecutive "together with" verbs (the other two come in v. 6).

Since the next verb speaks to our resurrection, this word seems to refer mainly to the new condition of spiritual life we currently experience in Christ—the opposite of the spiritual death described earlier in the passage. Since Christ was born and lived without sin, we have this spiritual life when we share in Christ's life. He is our source of spiritual vitality.

"Ye are saved" (Gk. *sozo*, **SODE-zo**) is in the perfect tense, which denotes a past action with continuing consequences—"Ye have been saved" would be a more literal translation. We experience our salvation in the present, but it is rooted in God's real-life intervention in time and eternity past. *Sozo* has a range of possible meanings, all of which illuminate our understanding of what God has done for us in Christ: rescue, liberate, keep from harm, heal, preserve.

6 And hath raised us up together, and made us sit together in heavenly places in Christ Jesus:

This verse strongly echoes 1:20, which uses nearly the exact same words to tell us that God raised Jesus from the dead and set Him at His right hand in heaven. The similarity of both theme and vocabulary is a powerful reinforcement of the "in Christ" motif. What God did for all His children, He did first in Christ. We experience our salvation, through faith, by becoming partakers in Christ's experience.

"Raised up together" (Gk. *sunegeiro*, **soon-eh-GAY-roh**) is a compound word made out of the verb "to raise" and the preposition "with." Other New Testament passages speak of the resurrection of the dead with the verb "to raise." By using "raised with," Paul is emphasizing the fact that our resurrection is a sharing with Christ in His resurrection. Paul even goes so far as to say that if Christ has not been raised, "our preaching is vain, and your faith is also vain" (from 1 Corinthians 15:14). If Jesus had remained in the grave, we would have no hope of life after death. This is why Paul speaks of our resurrection, even though it is in the future, as a past event. Because we can look back in history to the foundational event of Christ's Resurrection, we have the assurance that our resurrection is a certainty. Christ is the "firstfruits" from the grave (1 Corinthians 15:20, 23).

The promises of life and resurrection are not all that we receive in our union with Christ. We also receive the promise of great privilege and responsibility. "Made us sit together with" (Gk. *sugkathizo*, **soon-kah-THEED-zoh**) is the final "together with" verb of the sentence. A compound of "with" and "sit down," the verb can mean "to sit down with" or "to cause to sit down with." Since the subject of the sentence is God and we are the objects of His action, the latter is the obvious meaning here. The "sitting down" together with Christ is a direct reference to Jesus' promise. He promised that His true followers will be seated with Him on thrones as rulers in the eternal kingdom of God (Luke 22:29–30; Revelation 3:20–21).

"Heavenly places" (Gk. *epouranios*, **ep-oo-RAN-ee-os**) is the same phrase used earlier to designate the spiritual realm in which God has blessed His children and in which Christ is currently seated. It is also where we encounter Satan and other spiritual opponents of God's plan of redemption (Ephesians 1:3, 20, 3:10).

Since "with Christ," in verse five, already made it perfectly clear whom we are joined "together with" in these different aspects of our salvation, "in Christ" is repetitive and emphatic. Paul is consumed by his enthusiasm for what Jesus has done for us.

7 That in the ages to come he might shew the exceeding riches of his grace in his kindness toward us through Christ Jesus.

Now, we come to see the reason for God's merciful acts that are described in verses 5 and 6: for all of eternity, God wants to lavish His kindness on His children. An "age" (Gk. *aion*, **eye-OWN**) is an era, duration, or period of time in God's plan of redemption. Paul is not instructing us on the precise number or order of the "ages." This is evident when we consider that in 1:21, he speaks of the present "age" and one (singular) "age to come."

Rather, the author is speaking of eternity as the endless future era, which will begin when Christ returns. The "riches of his grace" describes the means by which God could afford to do all that He has done for His people. The fact that He plans to continue to show us His riches, for all of eternity, reminds us that God is infinitely wealthy—not just in terms of material wealth but in spiritual power. The love He shows to His people is also never-ending (Psalm 103:17).

8 For by grace are ye saved through faith; and that not of yourselves: it is the gift of God: 9 Not of works, lest any man should boast.

Having focused on how our salvation ends in grace, Paul reminds us of the point he made in his verse 5 interjection: our salvation also begins and continues in grace. In verse 5, the exact same statement helped us to see that grace miraculously accomplishes our salvation, in spite of our spiritually dead condition. Here we see that grace generously gives us what we do not deserve.

The words "through faith" do not appear in verse five. "Faith" (Gk. *pistis*, **PIS-tis**) is belief or conviction. True saving faith is that which trusts or relies on what God has done for our salvation. Paul uses the term "works" (Gk. *ergon*, **ER-gon**) to mean "obedience to God's law." Salvation through works, is the opposite of salvation through faith.

Faith relies on Christ's perfect obedience to the law of God. Faith trusts that Christ's sacrifice completely paid for our sin and that His perfect righteousness is fully credited to our account. But those who rely on their own works hope that their obedience earns them God's favor. This is why salvation is a gift. If it were something that we could earn or demand,

it would be a right—a "wage" or a "debt" in the terms of Romans 4:4–5.

Moreover, salvation is a gift in the fullest sense—unrequested, unexpected, and undeserved. The only way in which the recipient of a gift is involved in the giving process is in the receipt or rejection of the gift and expression of either gratitude or contempt toward the giver.

Another aspect of this gift becomes clear when we consider the demonstrative pronoun "that." In the English, it seems to refer most naturally to "faith," which means faith would be the gift of God. However, in the Greek, this is highly unlikely because "faith" is a feminine noun and "that" appears in the neuter. Instead "that" matches with "gift" (also neuter), both of which refer to the first part of verse 8: "by grace are ye saved through faith." God, not humankind, is the source of everything that is necessary for salvation to be accomplished (1 Corinthians 1:30).

This passage challenges our pride. We would like to think that even if we can't take credit for earning our salvation, at least we can take credit for trusting in Christ to save us. When we understand the Gospel, though, we see that no one has any grounds to boast. To "boast" (Gk. *kauchaomai*, **kow-KHAH-oh-meye**) means "to glory in or on account of something." Some Jews (especially some of the Pharisees and Sadducees) boasted that their faithful obedience to the Mosaic Law would earn them righteous standing before God. In fact, Paul himself formerly boasted about such things (Philippians 3:4–6).

10 For we are his workmanship, created in Christ Jesus unto good works, which God hath before ordained that we should walk in them.

This passage ends with a touch of irony. We are not saved by our works, but our salvation means that we are God's workmanship.

"Workmanship" (Gk. *poiema*, **POY-ay-mah**) means "what is made, creation." Elsewhere in Scripture, God uses the metaphor of pottery to help us understand this concept. He is the master potter; we are the clay (Isaiah 64:8; Jeremiah 18:6).

Good works are not optional for Christians. The Scriptures teach us they are not just a calling but also an identifying mark of true faith. James 2:17 warns us that "faith, if it hath not works, is dead." The commands and laws of the Old and New Testaments can't save us, but they help us to tell good works from evil. Good works are those that flow from love for God and love for our fellows (Matthew 22:37–40; Romans 13:8).

Good works are such an integral part of our new identity in Christ that God has "before ordained" them (Gk. *proetoimazo*, **pro-eh-toy-MAD-zo**), meaning He has "prepared (them) beforehand." All that remains for us, is to "walk in them"—to follow the path He has laid out for us. The preparation of our good works includes such blessings as the perfect example of Christ (Ephesians 5:2), the power of the Holy Spirit to live a holy life (Galatians 5:16), the understanding of what God's will is for our life (Romans 12:2), the pouring out of God's own love into our hearts (Romans 5:5), and spiritual gifts that enable us to build up the body of Christ in unique and meaningful ways (1 Corinthians 12:7). Paul was so consumed with living the life the Lord had ordained for him that he said, "It is no longer I who live, but Christ lives in me" (from Galatians 2:20, NLT).

Say It Correctly

Ordained. or-**DAYND**.
Deviation. dee-vee-**AY**-shun.

Daily Bible Readings

MONDAY
God, Be Merciful for Us Sinners
(Luke 18:9–14)

TUESDAY
Justified by Faith
(Romans 3:21–31)

WEDNESDAY
Christ Died for Sinners
(Romans 5:6–11)

THURSDAY
Raised with Christ
(1 Corinthians 15:12–25)

FRIDAY
Know the Love of Christ
(Ephesians 3:14–21)

SATURDAY
Live Worthy of Your Calling
(Ephesians 4:1–6)

SUNDAY
God's Overflowing Love
(Ephesian 2:1–10)

Teaching Tips

Words You Should Know

A. Purgeth (John 15:2) *kathairo* (Gk.)—To prune trees and vines from useless shoots; to cleanse from impurity.

B. Abideth (v. 5) *meno* (Gk.)—To remain; to continue to be present.

Teacher Preparation

Unifying Principle—The Joy of Love. We search for what enables us to love and be loved by others. Where do we find the authentic source of this love? The Apostle John says that God is the source of an all-encompassing love, which empowers us to love God and one another.

A. Pray for your class and wisdom concerning the lesson.

B. Read the Scripture passage in several different translations.

C. Prepare the companion lesson in the *Precepts For Living®* Personal Study Guide.

O—Open the Lesson

A. After receiving prayer requests, ask a volunteer to open the class with prayer including the Aim for Change.

B. Have a volunteer read the In Focus story.

P—Present the Scriptures

A. Ask for a volunteer to read the Focal Verses.

B. Examine the verses, using Words You Should Know; The People, Places, and Times, Background; the At-A-Glance outline; and More Light on the Text sections.

E—Explore the Meaning

A. Answer the Search the Scriptures questions.

B. Summarize the Discuss the Meaning, Lesson in Our Society, and Make It Happen sections.

C. Connect these answers with today's theme.

N—Next Steps for Application

A. Summarize the lesson.

B. Remind students to read and meditate on their Daily Bible Readings.

C. Solicit prayer requests and close in prayer.

Worship Guide

For the Superintendent or Teacher
Theme: God's Love Manifested
Song: "How Deep the Father's Love"
Devotional Reading: 1 John 4:16b–21

God's Love Manifested

Bible Background • JOHN 15:1–17
Printed Text • JOHN 15:1–17 | Devotional Reading • 1 JOHN 4:16b–21

Aim for Change

By the end of the lesson, we will: EXAMINE the role of love in human life and explore how God's love empowers and changes human love; EXPRESS the joy that is found in keeping God's commandments to love others; and REFLECT the love of God in ministries and lifestyles that grow from being called to be disciples.

In Focus

When Kim accepted Jesus Christ as her personal Savior three years earlier, she grew in her newfound faith. She attended church services regularly, Bible study on Wednesday nights, and even Sunday School—all of which helped her understand God's Word. Plus, she had a strong prayer life, seeking God first thing each morning and closing her day in His presence. But deep down Kim knew something was missing. She tried to pray more and attend more worship services. She even began going to conferences, trying to figure out what was missing from her spiritual life.

One day, her neighbor Pam knocked on the door. Kim had never really spoken to her, as she had been so busy with work and her spiritual pursuits. Kim looked down at Pam's two children there with her. Pam had to go to work, but her mom was unable to watch the kids that night. She asked if Kim could take care of them. Kim hesitated but then was reminded of Jesus' command to love her neighbor. She agreed to take care of them. Once she did, she felt closer to God and volunteered to watch them more. Soon her prayer life began to change. She noticed how God would answer. She also noticed God's love flowing through her, encouraging her to help other people.

What can you do today to manifest God's love to the people around you? In this lesson, we will learn how Jesus commanded His disciples to love one another.

Keep in Mind

"This is my commandment, That ye love one another, as I have loved you" (John 15:12).

"This is my commandment, That ye love one another, as I have loved you" (John 15:12).

Focal Verses

KJV John 15:1 "I am the true vine, and my Father is the husbandman.

2 Every branch in me that beareth not fruit he taketh away: and every branch that beareth fruit, he purgeth it, that it may bring forth more fruit.

3 Now ye are clean through the word which I have spoken unto you.

4 Abide in me, and I in you. As the branch cannot bear fruit of itself, except it abide in the vine; no more can ye, except ye abide in me.

5 I am the vine, ye are the branches: He that abideth in me, and I in him, the same bringeth forth much fruit: for without me ye can do nothing.

6 If a man abide not in me, he is cast forth as a branch, and is withered; and men gather them, and cast them into the fire, and they are burned.

7 If ye abide in me, and my words abide in you, ye shall ask what ye will, and it shall be done unto you.

8 Herein is my Father glorified, that ye bear much fruit; so shall ye be my disciples.

9 As the Father hath loved me, so have I loved you: continue ye in my love.

10 If ye keep my commandments, ye shall abide in my love; even as I have kept my Father's commandments, and abide in his love.

11 These things have I spoken unto you, that my joy might remain in you, and that your joy might be full.

12 This is my commandment, That ye love one another, as I have loved you.

13 Greater love hath no man than this, that a man lay down his life for his friends.

14 Ye are my friends, if ye do whatsoever I command you.

15 Henceforth I call you not servants; for the servant knoweth not what his lord doeth: but I have called you friends; for all things that

NLT John 15:1 "I am the true grapevine, and my Father is the gardener.

2 He cuts off every branch of mine that doesn't produce fruit, and he prunes the branches that do bear fruit so they will produce even more.

3 You have already been pruned and purified by the message I have given you.

4 Remain in me, and I will remain in you. For a branch cannot produce fruit if it is severed from the vine, and you cannot be fruitful unless you remain in me.

5 Yes, I am the vine; you are the branches. Those who remain in me, and I in them, will produce much fruit. For apart from me you can do nothing.

6 Anyone who does not remain in me is thrown away like a useless branch and withers. Such branches are gathered into a pile to be burned.

7 But if you remain in me and my words remain in you, you may ask for anything you want, and it will be granted!

8 When you produce much fruit, you are my true disciples. This brings great glory to my Father.

9 I have loved you even as the Father has loved me. Remain in my love.

10 When you obey my commandments, you remain in my love, just as I obey my Father's commandments and remain in his love.

11 I have told you these things so that you will be filled with my joy. Yes, your joy will overflow!

12 This is my commandment: Love each other in the same way I have loved you.

13 There is no greater love than to lay down one's life for one's friends.

14 You are my friends if you do what I command.

I have heard of my Father I have made known unto you.

16 Ye have not chosen me, but I have chosen you, and ordained you, that ye should go and bring forth fruit, and that your fruit should remain: that whatsoever ye shall ask of the Father in my name, he may give it you.

17 These things I command you, that ye love one another.

15 I no longer call you slaves, because a master doesn't confide in his slaves. Now you are my friends, since I have told you everything the Father told me.

16 You didn't choose me. I chose you. I appointed you to go and produce lasting fruit, so that the Father will give you whatever you ask for, using my name.

17 This is my command: Love each other.

The People, Places, and Times

Vine. A plant used for the cultivation of grapes. The vine is often used in the Bible literally and figuratively. The vine is a symbol of prosperity, as the cultivation of grapes was primarily for wine. It is also a symbol of a sedentary life (1 Kings 4:25), which was the ideal for the once nomadic nation of Israel. The vine was used by Jesus and others as a picture of God's people (John 15:2; Psalm 80:8; Isaiah 5:2).

Husbandman. A general term for farmer. In the case of John 15, the word specifically refers to those who cultivate vineyards, or vinedressers. The husbandman or vinedresser would tend to the plants by pruning and repositioning branches to bear more fruit. The vinedresser would also remove dried-up branches that hinder the health of the vine.

Background

Jesus is just a few hours away from the Cross, and He and His disciples are walking through a vineyard. He shares a profound message with them in parallelism: the Father is the vinedresser (the owner of the vineyard); Jesus is the vine (the trunk of the grapevine); and believers are the branches (the part that produces fruit). The branches cannot live or produce unless connected to the vine. The vinedresser sees that the branches are taken care of and produce fruit. Similarly, the vinedresser prunes the branches that bear fruit so that they will produce even more.

At-A-Glance

1. Jesus, the Vine (John 15:1–3)
2. Conditions for Fruit-Bearing (vv. 4–8)
3. Abiding in Love (vv. 9–11)
4. I Am a Friend of God (vv. 12–17)

In Depth

1. Jesus, the Vine (John 15:1–3)

In this discourse, John uses the metaphor of the vine and its branches to show the interconnection between the disciples and Jesus, as well as their connection with one another. As the "husbandman," the Father exercises just as much care for the branches as He does the vine.

The fruitful branches are synonymous with true believers who, by their living union with Christ, are tenderly and lovingly cared for to produce more fruit. But sometimes a branch yields no fruit at all. As a result, the Father cuts off every branch that is unproductive. Likewise, one's spiritual life can become barren and unfruitful, causing disconnection from the vine (Jesus), by not studying God's Word, not witnessing, or an undeveloped prayer life (2 Peter 1:8). When this happens, the husbandman (God) will remove the unproductive branch, which is an ineffective witness. But those branches (believers) that have been pruned (allowed the Word of God to shape them) become more productive (fruitful) Christians, and Jesus promises to abide with them.

2. Conditions for Fruit-Bearing (vv. 4–8)

A branch cannot produce fruit unless it is connected to the root. Just as Jesus depends on His Father, believers need to abide or remain in Him (Jesus) to stay connected to the root. Abiding, for the disciples and for all believers today, means to make a constant, moment-by-moment decision to depend on Christ. And we must not be passive—believers can't just sit and "remain" until they die. Instead, we must be active by producing fruit.

A vine that produces much fruit glorifies God. True disciples, then, do more than just believe what Jesus says; they let His words abide in them. When a believer abides in Christ and holds His Word inside, their prayers will be answered (v. 7). This does not mean that all prayers are granted. In order to pray and get results, a person must remain in Christ. When we remain in Him, our thoughts and desires conform to His, and we can pray "in Jesus' name," knowing that our requests please God.

3. Abiding in Love (vv. 9–11)

We learn that the basis for "abiding" with Jesus is the love that God and Jesus share with each other. Jesus, then, likens His love for the disciples to the type of love He has for His Father. The highest expression of Jesus' love was expressed on the Cross: He loved us enough to give His life for us. Although we have not been called to die for one another, we must learn to love each other sacrificially as Jesus loved us.

In verse 10, Jesus comes to the essence of His message to the disciples: the only way the disciples (or any believer) will continue to abide in God's love is if they, like Him, practice obedience and keep His Father's commandments. Jesus is delighted to do the will of the Father. He tells us that the basis of Christian joy can be found only in Christ.

4. I Am a Friend of God (vv. 12–17)

Jesus called the disciples His friends. However, becoming His friend was not without a condition: they had to obey His commandments. Jesus told the disciples everything He had heard from His Father. He expected them to lay down their lives if necessary (v. 14). If they followed this command, they would no longer be servants, but friends of God. What an awesome thing to be chosen as a friend of God!

Once again we see Jesus referring to His unselfish sacrifice of dying on the Cross (John 3:16). By calling the disciples His friends, Jesus showed that He trusted them, and that He expected them to spread the Gospel and produce fruit for God's kingdom. Jesus chose and ordained the disciples. He chose them for a mission, and His Father would answer their requests to accomplish that mission. Still today, the Lord chooses every believer to be a branch on the vine—a branch that bears fruit that will last.

Search the Scriptures

1. How does Jesus distinguish between productive and nonproductive followers (John 15:2)?

2. What does Jesus promise us when we live in Him (v. 11)?

Discuss the Meaning

1. Discuss the meaning of bearing "much fruit" (v. 8). Reflect on the importance of living a fruitful life in Christ.

2. How does knowing God's plan for His people change your life?

Lesson in Our Society

In today's society, many Christians believe that obeying God begins and ends with going to church once a week. While God commands us to meet with the "body," He expects us to continue to walk in His light daily. A part of that walk should include spreading the Gospel so that nonbelievers may be saved and weak Christians may be strengthened. We must be actively sharing, reaching out, and building godly relationships that glorify our Father and bear fruit for God's kingdom.

Make It Happen

Think about your own fruitfulness. Pray that God would fill you with the Holy Spirit and enable you to do His will. Then go out and share God's command to love one another with at least three people this week. Explain to them that loving one another comes in many forms: helping, listening, encouraging, and giving. Next week, be prepared to share your efforts with the class.

Follow the Spirit

What God wants me to do:

_____

_____

_____

_____

Remember Your Thoughts

Special insights I have learned:

_____

_____

_____

_____

More Light on the Text

John 15:1–17

1 I am the true vine, and my Father is the husbandman.

This is the seventh of Jesus' self-referenced "I am" statements, the complete list of which is found only in John's Gospel. It is interesting to note that Jesus chose the word "true" in tandem with "vine" in speaking to people intimately familiar with farming language and imagery. The odd language clearly implies that "true" is in contrast to all that is false or untrue. Jesus is the only "true vine" in a world of false or untrue vines. Indeed, the Word often warns of false prophets and teachers (Matthew 7:15; Mark 13:22; 1 John 4:1).

Various translations of Scripture use synonyms for "husbandman," including "vine-dresser," "gardener," and "farmer" (cf. 2 Timothy 2:6; James 5:7). All are correct interpretations of the Greek word *georgos* (**gheh-ore-GOS**), which can also mean "tiller of the soil." Christ is saying that when God is the Gardener, the garden could not be in better hands or better tended. Also implied is that the Master Gardener will create the ultimate garden with infinite variety and delicacy of fruit, all of which is produced through and because of His only Son, the one true vine.

2 Every branch in me that beareth not fruit he taketh away: and every branch that beareth fruit, he purgeth it, that it may bring forth more fruit.

Some controversy exists in the interpretation of "taketh away" (Gk. *airo*, **EYE-roh**), and also of "purgeth" (Gk. *kathairo*, **kath-AH-ee-ro**). The two words are similar enough to constitute a play on words or a rhyme, lost in translation. The latter word, from which we get the word "catharsis," is used only twice in the New Testament (Hebrews 10:2). One of the possible meanings of *airo* is "to raise up, elevate, or lift up," as in raising up a fish when catching it. The "taketh away" interpretation is also legitimate, as in "to take off from something attached, remove, or carry away." In context with the entire vine/branch/fruit metaphor, "lifting up" is acceptable in the sense that an unproductive branch might be lifted and cleaned to enhance its productivity (grapevines are tied up). However, when combined with the syntax of the rest of the verse, the sense of "removing" seems stronger.

The husbandman lifts and cleans the vine (washing with the Word, see verse 3; see also Ephesians 5:26) of all that is unproductive (impure, sinful), removing those parts so the good parts (fruit-bearing branches) that remain will have maximum nourishment and become even more productive. Especially in light of later verses that speak of judgment and unproductive branches being cut off, this seems a more contextually faithful rendering. If anything, a gentle, loving but thorough cleansing rather than a harsh, bloody pruning emerges.

3 Now ye are clean through the word which I have spoken unto you.

If "purgeth" doesn't capture the cleansing sense of the Greek word *kathairo*, the more explicit phrase "clean through the word" used immediately afterward should steer the interpreter toward it. Following a thorough scrubbing that removes unproductiveness and impurities, "now ye are clean," a spiritual cleansing that comes only through the Word—the result of which is now being more productive. This is also more in line with reality, rather than straining to make every literal aspect of a metaphor fit human life.

4 Abide in me, and I in you. As the branch cannot bear fruit of itself, except it abide in the vine; no more can ye, except ye abide in me.

To "abide" (Gk. *meno*, **MEN-oh**, meaning "to remain" or "to not depart") is the heart of the entire metaphor and the main point of the entire passage. While it seems obvious, Christians struggle with abiding versus not abiding—and how critical it is to their very survival in Christ. Even when Christ draws an explicit parallel with a physical branch and repeats Himself numerous times on the importance of abiding, how many have yet to transfer the weight of the metaphor to their lives? Just as a branch on a fruit vine doesn't exist just to be a branch but to produce fruit, so we exist not for ourselves, but to produce God's fruit. This is possible only with His nourishment, which we receive only when we abide in Him.

5 I am the vine, ye are the branches: He that abideth in me, and I in him, the same bringeth forth much fruit: for without me ye can do nothing.

Jesus points over and over to the reality of true nourishment from the True Vine, which alone produces true branches, which again in turn produce true fruit. This type of branch comes from the Greek word *klema* (**KLAY-mah**), which specifically refers to a young, tender branch, especially the flexible branch of a vine or a vine sprout, or a young branch that needs a steady supply of nourishment. There is no other source for true fruit and no other chain of supply, though the world tries in vain to imitate Christian fruit.

It is this vital connection to the True Vine to which every believer must attend and that he or she must continually monitor and strengthen. It is also this vital connection that we share with all other believers. No vine produces only one branch, but many; thus, our relationship to other branches is communal or familial.

6 If a man abide not in me, he is cast forth as a branch, and is withered; and men gather them, and cast them into the fire, and they are burned.

Some in the body of Christ question whether or not this verse is a proof text for being able to lose one's salvation. The context informs us that a branch becomes fruitless only when it is no longer connected to the vine; branches that abide continue to receive nourishment and effortlessly produce fruit because that is their sole purpose and design.

Therefore, any fruitless branch is a disconnected branch. If a branch cannot be pruned, cleansed, and restored so it will become fruitful again, it will be cut off and destroyed. One cannot lose one's salvation, but Scripture is clear that all branches (believers) will have a separate judgment (Revelation 20). This coming judgment reinforces the removal aspect of *kathairo* in verse 2, since the Master Gardener wouldn't allow anything to remain that was worthless or in danger of judgment. At the same time, it seems virtually impossible that any genuinely born-again Christian would receive zero nourishment, produce zero fruit for his or her entire life, and then be cut off at the roots and burned wholesale. What is unmistakable is that abiding in Christ should not be seen as an "option" by Christians.

7 If ye abide in me, and my words abide in you, ye shall ask what ye will, and it shall be done unto you.

A vine shares a genuinely symbiotic relationship with its branches. The vine can't produce its own fruit without branches, and the branches can't provide their own nourishment in order to produce fruit. When we abide in Christ, when we are attached to the Vine, His nourishment flows into us, just as in reality His Spirit indwells us (John 14:7; Romans 8:11), we receive His Word into our hearts, and we are predictably fruitful (Luke 8:15). In Psalm 119:11, David says, "Thy word have I hid in mine heart, that I might not sin against thee."

Only in this context—as connected, fruitful believers infused with the Spirit and the Word—will we be able to pray in faith and receive that for which we ask. We receive because our will is conformed to Christ's. We are warned in James 4:2–3 not to "ask amiss," but we are also admonished that we have not because we ask not. The qualifications are steep, but the rewards, freedom, and resulting power are immeasurable.

8 Herein is my Father glorified, that ye bear much fruit; so shall ye be my disciples. 9 As the Father hath loved me, so have I loved you: continue ye in my love.

While the primary meaning of "fruit" is that of the vine or tree, the word also refers to works (Gk. *karpos*, **kar-POS**). Just as a grape does the grapevine no personal good, our fruit is not for ourselves but for others and the glory of God (Philippians 1:11).

Jesus zeroes in on what has been called the ultimate fruit—love. Repeatedly, we are told of God's love for His Son, such as in 2 Peter 1:17, which recalls the pronouncement at Jesus' baptism: "This is my beloved Son, in whom I am well pleased." Jesus loved His disciples with His Father's love, even though, unlike them (and us), He alone was worthy of such great love. Notably, no other versions (not even the NKJV) except the KJV interpret *meno* (**MEN-oh**) here as "continue," while most use "abide" or "remain," in keeping with the theme of the passage. Christ used the word *meno* over and over again in this section of Scripture, and all references are rendered "abide" except this one, which seems strange. The whole thrust of "abide" has been so well established that when the word is read here (and in the next verse) the syntax is restored and the vine image continued.

10 If ye keep my commandments, ye shall abide in my love; even as I have kept my Father's commandments, and abide in his love. 11 These things have I spoken unto you, that my joy might remain in you, and that your joy might be full.

We are never asked to do what Christ would not do. In the book of John, it is well established that Christ proved His love for His Father by His obedience to Him (John 8:29, 12:49, 14:31, 17:4). Following suit, the disciples proved their love by their obedience, and we, in turn, prove our love for Christ by our obedience to Him, and receive His promise of abiding in Him.

It was only because of the joy that lay ahead of Him that Jesus was able to endure the Cross (Hebrews 12:2). James writes that we should consider trials as pure joy (James 1:2), and Nehemiah tells the believers that the joy of the Lord is their strength (Nehemiah 8:10). When we do all that Jesus commands (especially love others), our reward both on earth and in heaven is His great joy, a gift truly beyond compare and priceless above all precious things.

12 This is my commandment, That ye love one another, as I have loved you.

At first, it must have seemed more an exhortation, until the point when Jesus' discourse changed to a commandment. Commandments were familiar to Jesus' disciples, and it must have given them pause to hear Him talk about loving one another as a commandment. At the same time, a commandment coming from Jesus couldn't be compared to the commandments they had grown up with under Mosaic Law. While Jesus had taught this previously (Matthew 22:39), considering the many other things the disciples had failed to grasp at first, one wonders if He sensed their lack of understanding and thus felt the need to repeat Himself three times in a single teaching. Only in God's kingdom is such profound simplicity: to obey His command to love one another is to love as He Himself loved us in obedience to His Father. Indeed, it is the greatest commandment.

13 Greater love hath no man than this, that a man lay down his life for his friends.

Teachers and coaches understand that when a bar is set too low, there is no challenge and consequently no improvement. When the bar is set higher, we have to work to reach the goal, and the challenge makes us grow.

The higher the bar, the greater the required effort, so Jesus here sets the bar at the highest point possible: that of actually sacrificing one's life in order to attain the highest imitation of His love. Many through the ages have been put to this very test, and it makes us question whether we would have what it takes if that terrible day would ever present itself to us. It is a worthy goal to practice loving unto death as Christ loves, in order to be prepared for the ultimate test of showing the greatest love of all.

14 Ye are my friends, if ye do whatsoever I command you. 15 Henceforth I call you not servants; for the servant knoweth not what his lord doeth: but I have called you friends;

for all things that I have heard of my Father I have made known unto you.

In Christ, we are much more than servants; we are sons and daughters (2 Corinthians 6:18). Here, we are called friends (for whom He would lay down His life). This speaks volumes to us about all that Christ means as a friend and brother, but it also speaks eloquently of His perfect love—He who offers so much to those who once were enemies. In fact, Christ laid down His life while we were still enemies (Romans 5:8, 10; Colossians 1:21). When Jesus told us to love our enemies, He spoke from personal experience (Matthew 5:44).

Jesus called the disciples "friends" because of the revelation He disclosed to them. It made them close to Jesus. It wasn't the Father's will that everything that could be known should be made known, but everything that God wanted known was communicated through Christ (Matthew 11:27, 24:36). While servants were common in first-century Israel—and still are in some parts of the world—it is easier for most of us to relate to the concept of employees. Bosses don't confide everything to their employees as a rule, but life would certainly be different in corporate America if CEOs suddenly started calling their employees friends and began a policy of total information disclosure.

16 Ye have not chosen me, but I have chosen you, and ordained you, that ye should go and bring forth fruit, and that your fruit should remain: that whatsoever ye shall ask of the Father in my name, he may give it you.

Christ reminds His disciples (His friends) that He chose them and has given them a task. As with them, when we abide in Christ, we receive His nourishment, we are fruitful, we fulfill our purpose as branches, we please the Gardener, we feed and nourish others, we produce seeds for planting, and we become eligible for pruning (cleansing) so that we will become even more productive. This is fruit and work that endures (John 6:27), and such a believer has fulfilled the qualifications for prayers being answered, just as God answered His people's prayers in times past: "He answered their prayers because they trusted in him" (from 1 Chronicles 5:20, NIV).

17 These things I command you, that ye love one another.

According to 2 Peter 1:5–7, we start with faith and add the various fruits of the Spirit, finally adding love, as if it were the highest attainment of the faith that the Master intended from the beginning. It is almost as though all the other fruit is easier to acquire or produce; indeed, this is possible, since, in the New Testament, so much emphasis is placed on exhorting believers to love, to learn to love, to seek love, to become love. Because it is the highest, it is the hardest; because it most closely resembles Christ, it requires greater surrender and sacrifice. Yet we are virtually surrounded with Scriptures that exhort us to make love our highest priority, to pursue love, and to let love transform us into the very image of Christ, who is love (Romans 12:2; 1 Timothy 6:11; 2 Corinthians 3:18; 2 Timothy 2:22).

Say It Correctly

Purgeth. per-**JITH**.
Abide. uh-**BYDE**.

Daily Bible Readings

MONDAY
Restore Your Vine, O Lord
(Psalm 80:8–19)

TUESDAY
Love, a New Commandment
(John 13:31–35)

WEDNESDAY
Self-Discipline for Holy Living
(1 Peter 1:13–21)

THURSDAY
Walking in Truth and Love
(2 John 4–11)

FRIDAY
Becoming One in Christ
(Ephesians 2:11–21)

SATURDAY
Abiding in God's Love
(1 John 4:16b–19)

SUNDAY
Love One Another and Bear Fruit
(John 15:1–17)

Notes

_____

_____

_____

_____

Teaching Tips

Words You Should Know

A. Gracious (Joel 2:13) *channun* (Heb.)—Disposed to bestow favor and blessings, especially those with less power of authority

B. Pity (v. 18) *khamal* (Heb.)—To spare, to show leniency.

Teacher Preparation

Unifying Principle—Restoring Relationships. The rewards of wholesome relationships may be shattered by unloving and unfaithful actions. How can these relationships be restored to their former glory? Joel recounts the benefits that emanate from a restored relationship with God.

A. Read the Bible Background and Devotional Readings.

B. Complete Lesson 4 in the *Precepts For Living®* Personal Study Guide.

C. Reread the Focal Verses in several translations.

O—Open the Lesson

A. Open with prayer.

B. Have students read the Aim for Change in unison.

C. Ask for a volunteer to read the In Focus story.

D. Discuss the ways that the Lord cares for His people.

P—Present the Scriptures

A. Ask for volunteers to read the Focal Verses and The People, Places, and Times. Discuss.

B. Read and discuss the Background section.

C. Encourage students to praise God for how He has preserved them and thank Him for His unending faithfulness.

E—Explore the Meaning

A. Review and discuss the Search the Scriptures and Discuss the Meaning questions and the Lesson in Our Society section.

B. Ask students to share the most significant point they learned and how to use that point this week.

N—Next Steps for Application

A. Complete the Follow the Spirit and Remember Your Thoughts sections.

B. Remind students to read the Daily Bible Readings in preparation for next week's lesson.

C. Close in prayer, thanking God for His care and provision.

Worship Guide

For the Superintendent or Teacher
Theme: God's Love Restores
Song: "The Lord Keeps Blessing
Me Right Now"
Devotional Reading: 2 Peter 3:1–10

God's Love Restores

Bible Background • JOEL 2
Printed Text • JOEL 2:12–13, 18–19, 28–32 | Devotional Reading • 2 PETER 3:1–10

Aim for Change

By the end of the lesson, we will: EXPLORE what motivates people to repent and seek restoration; APPRECIATE the love of God that enables prophecy, dreams, and visions; and SEEK restored relationships in personal and community life.

In Focus

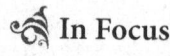

Darlique had her beau, James, wrapped around her finger. He would give her money when she couldn't quite pay her rent, but then she would spend that on a night with her girls. And James would still give her more money to actually pay the bill.

When this sort of thing happened, Darlique would make a big show of being sorry for not spending the money the way James intended. She would be extra sweet to him, make him his favorite dinner, and tell him how much she depended on him. Darlique began to count on James—and his pocketbook—being around to bail her out.

The fourth time this happened James knew he had to do something about it. He sat down with Darlique and told her, "Baby, you can't keep treating me this way. You keep on saying you're sorry for using up my gifts, but then you do the exact same thing the next month. If you were really sorry, you'd at least try to change your spending habits so you could actually pay your own rent or at least not waste the money I give you to help. I can't stay with a woman who acts like this."

Without James to help her, Darlique ended up back in her parents' house. As she sat on her bed, staring at the stickers her teenage self had put on the ceiling, she knew she would do anything to get him back—even live on a budget.

How does God take us from being selfish and sinful to turning toward Him for restoration?

Keep in Mind

"And rend your heart, and not your garments, and turn unto the LORD your God: for He is gracious and merciful, slow to anger, and of great kindness, and repenteth him of the evil" (Joel 2:13).

"And rend your heart, and not your garments, and turn unto the LORD your God: for He is gracious and merciful, slow to anger, and of great kindness, and repenteth him of the evil" (Joel 2:13).

Focal Verses

KJV Joel 2:12 Therefore also now, saith the LORD, turn ye even to me with all your heart, and with fasting, and with weeping, and with mourning:

13 And rend your heart, and not your garments, and turn unto the LORD your God: for He is gracious and merciful, slow to anger, and of great kindness, and repenteth him of the evil.

18 Then will the LORD be jealous for his land, and pity his people.

19 Yea, the LORD will answer and say unto his people, Behold, I will send you corn, and wine, and oil, and ye shall be satisfied therewith: and I will no more make you a reproach among the heathen:

28 And it shall come to pass afterward, that I will pour out my spirit upon all flesh; and your sons and your daughters shall prophesy, your old men shall dream dreams, your young men shall see visions:

29 And also upon the servants and upon the handmaids in those days will I pour out my spirit.

30 And I will shew wonders in the heavens and in the earth, blood, and fire, and pillars of smoke.

31 The sun shall be turned into darkness, and the moon into blood, before the great and terrible day of the Lord come.

32 And it shall come to pass, that whosoever shall call on the name of the LORD shall be delivered: for in mount Zion and in Jerusalem shall be deliverance, as the LORD hath said, and in the remnant whom the LORD shall call.

NLT Joel 2:12 That is why the LORD says, "Turn to me now, while there is time. Give me your hearts. Come with fasting, weeping, and mourning.

13 Don't tear your clothing in your grief, but tear your hearts instead." Return to the LORD your God, for he is merciful and compassionate, slow to get angry and filled with unfailing love. He is eager to relent and not punish.

18 Then the LORD will pity his people and jealously guard the honor of his land.

19 The LORD will reply, "Look! I am sending you grain and new wine and olive oil enough to satisfy your needs. You will no longer be an object of mockery among the surrounding nations.

28 Then, after doing all those things, I will pour out my Spirit upon all people. Your sons and daughters will prophesy. Your old men will dream dreams, and your young men will see visions.

29 In those days I will pour out my Spirit even on servants—men and women alike.

30 And I will cause wonders in the heavens and on the earth—blood and fire and columns of smoke.

31 The sun will become dark, and the moon will turn blood red before that great and terrible day of the LORD arrives.

32 But everyone who calls on the name of the LORD will be saved, for some on Mount Zion in Jerusalem will escape, just as the LORD has said. These will be among the survivors whom the LORD has called.

The People, Places, and Times

Joel. Joel's name means "whose God is Jehovah." Little is known of Joel except that he was the son of a man named Pethuel. It is believed that Joel wrote the book named after him during the time of Judah's return from exile. Others believe that it was written right before the death of King Josiah, just one generation before the exile.

Remnant. In the Scriptures, "remnant" refers to those who survived a disaster or judgment. This remnant would continue the population of humankind or the people of God. They would be holy and devoted to God and constitute the faithful. This concept is found throughout the Old and New Testaments (1 Kings 19:15–18, Amos 5:15, Romans 11:5). A remnant is a sign of God's grace to humanity in light of His stern judgment on unrepentant sin.

Background

Yehud (formerly Judah) was a small province under the power of the Babylonian Empire. During a prior period of unification, Judah was the Southern Kingdom, composed of two of the twelve tribes of Israel with its capital at Jerusalem (1 Kings 12–2 Kings 25). Joel's message comes to Judah as a matter of urgency. It will mean the life or death of Judah, and all future generations.

For Christians, the prophecy of Joel extends to us and to Christ's church even today. The Apostle Peter, speaking to the newly born church on the day of Pentecost, delivers a sermon with the exact prophetic words of this passage from Joel (Joel 2:28–32; Acts 2:17–21). Prophecy functions to teach us God's desires for our lives. It is a warning, a teaching, and a call to action. The prophet must deliver the message to the people, notwithstanding any of their own internal conflicts and hesitations. The prophet should receive no personal gain or recognition. All of the attention resulting from a prophecy should be focused upon God. The responsibility of the hearer of the prophecy is to take heed, transform their lives, and spread the word to those who are unaware of it.

Inner repentance, moral control, and faithfulness to God are of utmost importance as the primary goal of humanity according to God's purposes. Our ultimate path away from God's wrath is through our repentance and faith (Joel 2:12–17). Our capacity to have faith and our ability to interpret the will of God is made possible by the outpouring of His Spirit on all people. God's merciful offering of the Holy Spirit to us is for a purpose: to spread His Word as His witnesses to all the earth.

At-A-Glance

1. God's People Turn Back to Him
(Joel 2:12–13)
2. God Turns Back to His People (vv. 18–19)
3. Whoever Turns to God Will Be Saved
(vv. 28–32)

In Depth

1. God's People Turn Back to Him (Joel 2:12–13)

The prophet Joel describes Judah being devastated by locusts and scorching heat—the judgment Yahweh inflicts upon the people. The prophet answers the question of who will be able to endure this judgment by the Lord when it happens. The only way someone can expect to endure it is to repent, which simply means to turn to God and away from evil. God only wants His people to repent, but this repentance must be a move in the heart. To repent is to turn toward God with all of your heart and away from your current direction of sin.

The prophet leaves an opening for the possibility that as their hearts change, our Lord has the capacity to relent from inflicting horrific consequences on us because of His compassionate heart. Joel asks the question, "Who knows whether God will change from the pronounced judgment?" God is sovereign, with the infinite ability to do whatever He wishes.

When God pronounces goodwill to us, we can count on His stable, strong word. That is the compassion of God, the ability to suffer with His people and feel sorrow for them that He has shown repeatedly in Israel's history. God will relent from punishing us. We have upon us the requirement to relent, repent, and change to move our hearts into His direction.

2. God Turns Back to His People (vv. 18–19)

Joel next lets the people know the results of their repentance. The Lord would be "jealous for his land" (v. 18). He would take special concern for His land and His people as they are His possession and in His care. He would have pity on His people. God's heart would be turned to His people and He would look on them with compassion. He would remember their limitations and weakness. He would see their hearts turned toward Him.

The Lord's care for His people would be represented by provision. His blessing would be seen in their harvest. Prosperity would come to Judah. Their barns and vats would be full of produce. This wouldn't be their own doing, but a result of their relationship with God and His mercy on them.

3. Whoever Turns to God Will Be Saved (vv. 28–32)

Here, we see the benefit of being God's people—the outpouring of His Spirit "in those days," meaning after the day of the coming of the Lord. This gift is from God, but it is not limited to a select few privileged by some materialistic stratification. The lowly are included and will receive God's Spirit (v. 29). These handmaids and servants represent the women and men who are the poor, downtrodden, common, and oppressed. Truly, the last shall be first.

In the midst of catastrophic judgment, a promise is given. Those who call on the Lord will be saved. Their repentance and dependence on God would be a refuge from His wrath. The sun, moon, and heavens would be affected as signs of the coming day of the Lord. Darkness would sweep over the earth, and the moon would turn red like blood. This judgment would not affect God's people who turn to Him in faith.

Search the Scriptures

1. What does it mean for Judah to tear their hearts instead of their clothing (Joel 2:13)?

2. The Lord has poured out His Spirit on all flesh. What is the reason He hasn't darkened the sun and turned the moon to blood (vv. 28–31)?

Discuss the Meaning

1. How can we as believers today to turn to the Lord in repentance?

2. What are the implications of the Spirit of God being poured out on the lowly and downtrodden?

Lesson in Our Society

God is a God of second chances. Many people don't turn to Him for a variety of reasons. Some are too proud, while others see themselves as unworthy and their lives as unredeemable. These are all lies. The truth is that God longs to hear the cries of those who repent. With this repentance comes restoration. God desires to restore His people to a right relationship with Him. As they turn to Him, they can be assured of His love and mercy to meet them where they are. A humble and broken heart of repentance is the key to restoration.

Make It Happen

Read Joel 2:1–2, 12–13. Do you constantly witness the sin, disobedience, and lack of care for humanity and God in our world? Permit the prophecy given to Joel by God for repentance to infuse your thoughts. Can you see how God's Word can be made manifest in your own life and the disobedient world around you? Share with your class members the ways that specific groups and individuals can advance God's kingdom by making a change in their direction and their ways.

Follow the Spirit

What God wants me to do:

_____

_____

_____

_____

Remember Your Thoughts

Special insights I have learned:

_____

_____

_____

_____

More Light on the Text

Joel 2:12–13, 18–19, 28–32

12 Therefore also now, saith the LORD, turn ye even to me with all your heart, and with fasting, and with weeping, and with mourning:

God, Jehovah, is the self-existent or eternal Jehovah, or an Israelite national name of God. It is this Lord that sends this enemy from the north (2:20; Jeremiah 1:14, 4:6, 6:1), causing all of the city dwellers, the Judeans, and everyone else to finally turn toward God with their hearts. To repent is to turn to the direction of God, "turning around" completely with all of your "heart" to the opposite direction. Thus a person lives his or her life totally different than before.

This army sent by God threatens to destroy His enemies (Amos 5:18–20, 9:1; Zephaniah 1:18). Ultimately, the seriousness of the people and the dedication of their hearts in fasting, weeping, and mourning will anticipate the day of God's final judgment of the world in which the Son of Man will return to set up His kingdom on earth. God is faithful to give the people an opportunity to repent and return to Him. Marking the sincere repentance and adherence to God, Joel directs the people to remorseful fasting for His mercy.

13 And rend your heart, and not your garments, and turn unto the LORD your God: for he is gracious and merciful, slow to anger, and of great kindness, and repenteth him of the evil.

God calls upon the Judeans to turn to Him, to worship with all their hearts, and to rend (Heb. *kara'*, **kah-RAH**, to split, tear, or rip) their hearts. God specifically instructs the people not to tear their garments, an expression of grief in the presence of misfortune (Genesis 37:29, 34; Numbers 14:6; 2 Samuel 3:31; 1 Kings 21:27; Ezra 9:3). To tear one's garments was a sign that one's life was in turmoil and was frequently followed by wearing sackcloth, which carried absolutely no status with it (compared to one's every day clothing, which indicated royalty, gender, etc.). This mourning rite signified the mourner's acknowledgment of his or her low state of existence.

Repentance must be in Judah's heart. The "heart" in Hebrew idiom symbolizes the human will and intellect. God is gracious (Heb. *khannun*, **kha-NOON**), giving the total goodwill of a superior to an inferior. He is also merciful (Heb. *rakhum*, **ra-KHOOM**), imparting the kind of love as a parent for his or her child. God is slow to anger in that He does not immediately punish, but rather He always patiently provides an opportunity for people to repent and turn back to Him. God is patient, forgiving, gracious, and merciful, because of His steadfast love (Heb. *khesed*, **KHE-sed**) and the loving faithfulness to the covenant promise with His people.

18 Then will the Lord be jealous for his land, and pity his people. 19 Yea, the Lord will answer and say unto his people, Behold, I will send you corn, and wine, and oil, and ye shall be satisfied therewith: and I will no more make you a reproach among the heathen:

The Lord responds to His people's repentance. He desires to be in relationship with them, expressed in the word "jealous" (Heb. *qanne'*, **kah-NAY**), which denotes desire for exclusivity in relationship. The Lord wants Judah to be His people exclusively and not tied to another. This jealousy is a key part of God's identity (cf. Exodus 20:5). He also will take pity (Heb. *khamal*, **chah-MAL**) on His people. The word means to spare or show leniency. These are not just compassionate feelings, they are backed by compassionate action.

Next, Joel speaks to the totality of God's merciful response. Not only would He spare them from judgment, but He would send wine, oil, and corn (which is better translated "grain"). These are symbols of a rich agricultural harvest and a sign of prosperity. The Lord would cause them to prosper, and they would be filled with satisfaction as their reproach would be removed. They would no longer be a shame and disgrace to the surrounding nations. This language can be used as argument for the book of Joel being written in the post-exilic period,

as this was the time for Judah's disgrace as they are taken into captivity among the nations.

28 And it shall come to pass afterward, that I will pour out my spirit upon all flesh; and your sons and your daughters shall prophesy, your old men shall dream dreams, your young men shall see visions: 29 And also upon the servants and upon the handmaids in those days will I pour out my spirit.

The manifestation of certain powerful signs of the fulfillment of God's promise is evident. God will pour out the Spirit on "all flesh," much like one pours out a fluid. The action to "pour out" is the Hebrew *shafak* (**shah-FAWK**) to spill forth. Figuratively, it also means to expend life, sprawl, or gush out. The Spirit of God is always depicted as a gift of power, given to enable the recipient to fulfill a specific role for God (Exodus 31:2–5; Judges 6:34; Micah 3:8; Haggai 1:14). The parallel for this text in Joel is found in the New Testament, Acts 2:16-21. There the newly appointed Apostle Peter declares that the outpouring of the Spirit upon the disciples is the fulfillment of Joel's prophecy.

God promises the gift of the Spirit extends to all flesh. Both men and women, both young and old, and even servants will receive this gift. The lowliest person in God's household would be a candidate for Him to pour out His Spirit on.

30 And I will shew wonders in the heavens and in the earth, blood, and fire, and pillars of smoke. 31 The sun shall be turned into darkness, and the moon into blood, before the great and terrible day of the Lord come.

These days would be accompanied by wonders (Heb. *mopet*, **MO-feth**), nonverbal actions or gestures that encode a message. Given the context, they are better interpreted as signs. These signs are the sun turning to darkness and the moon turning to blood. These cosmic events would signal the coming of the day of the Lord. The first wonders are blood, fire, and pillars of smoke, which are all signs of death and destruction. Then the Lord promises the sun will be turned into darkness and the moon into blood. The word for "turned" in Hebrew in fact indicates a 180-degree change, or overturning (Heb *haphak*, **hah-FAWK**). What were created as sources of light according to Genesis (1:14–18), are now sources of doom and destruction (darkness and blood). The juxtaposition of darkness and light, as in the creation account in Genesis, should not be missed. The Day of the Lord will bring a complete overturning of the normal patterns of life and growth that God established in the beginning. It will be great and terrible.

32 And it shall come to pass, that whosoever shall call on the name of the Lord shall be delivered: for in mount Zion and in Jerusalem shall be deliverance, as the Lord hath said, and in the remnant whom the Lord shall call.

It is during these days that calling on the Lord's name will be the means of salvation. For the Hebrew mind, this would not be just in a spiritual sense but a real, literal saving from harm and danger. The word for "delivered" (Heb. *malat*, **mah-LAT**) is always used in the Old Testament for escape or rescue from physical harm and danger.

It is on Mount Zion and in Jerusalem, the royal city, that deliverance would come. Jerusalem and Mt. Zion came to be understood as the eschatological site of God's renewal of His covenant with His faithful people. In addition, this is possibly an allusion to the death of Christ as He was crucified just outside of Jerusalem. It is through Him that the Lord would provide a remnant (Heb. *sarid*, **sa-REED**) or survivors. The word is often used for those who have escaped from a great slaughter. All those who call on the name of the Lord will escape His great and terrible judgment.

Say It Correctly

Reproach. ree-**PROCH**.
Repenteth. ree-**PEN**-tith.

Daily Bible Readings

MONDAY
The Prophesied Day of the Lord
(Joel 2:1–11)

TUESDAY
The People Called to Repent
(Joel 2:15–17)

WEDNESDAY
God Restores Land and People
(Joel 2:20–27)

THURSDAY
Day of the Lord at Pentecost
(Acts 2:14–21)

FRIDAY
The Final Day of the Lord
(2 Peter 3:1–10)

SATURDAY
God Judges Nations, Proclaims Judah's Future
(Joel 3:1–3, 18–21)

SUNDAY
Our Gracious and Merciful God
(Joel 2:12–13, 18–19, 28–32)

Teaching Tips

April 2
Bible Study Guide 5

Words You Should Know

A. Anoint (Psalm 23:5) *dashen* (Heb.)—The custom of pouring or smearing oil on a person or object.

B. Mercy (v. 6) *chesed* (Heb.)—Loyalty, faithfulness, goodness, kindness.

Teacher Preparation

Unifying Principle—I've Got Your Back! People face challenges that can seem too difficult to endure. Where can they find the support and reassurance to face these challenges? The psalmist promises that God's love provides what is necessary to confront any difficulties and live in a fulfilling and intimate relationship with Him.

A. Read the Bible Background and Devotional Readings.

B. Complete Lesson 5 in the *Precepts for Living*® Personal Study Guide.

C. Reread the Focal Verses in several translations.

O—Open the Lesson

A. Open with prayer.

B. Have students read Aim for Change in unison.

C. Ask for a volunteer to read the In Focus story.

D. Discuss the ways that the Lord cares for His people.

P—Present the Scriptures

A. Ask for volunteers to read the Focal Verses and The People, Places, and Times. Discuss.

B. Read and discuss the Background section.

C. Encourage students to praise God for how He has preserved them and thank Him for His unending faithfulness.

E—Explore the Meaning

A. Review and discuss the Search the Scriptures and Discuss the Meaning questions and the Lesson in Our Society section.

B. Ask students to share the most significant point they learned and how to use that point this week.

N—Next Steps for Application

A. Complete the Follow the Spirit and Remember Your Thoughts sections.

B. Remind students to read the Daily Bible Readings in preparation for next week's lesson.

C. Close in prayer, thanking God for His care and provision.

Worship Guide

For the Superintendent or Teacher
Theme: God as Our Shepherd
Song: "Great is Thy Faithfulness"
Devotional Reading: John 10:11–18

God as Our Shepherd

Bible Background • PSALM 23
Printed Text • PSALM 23 | Devotional Reading • JOHN 10:11–18

Aim for Change

By the end of the lesson, we will: EXPLORE Psalm 23's use of the metaphor of shepherding for trusting in God; APPRECIATE ways that God's love provides goodness and mercy to people when they face challenges; and CHOOSE to trust God's leading, which transforms challenges and difficulties.

In Focus

Tanya stepped outside for some air but found herself crying. It was happening again. Doug, her supervisor, was making sexual advances toward her, and she felt afraid and embarrassed. Carol came outside after her. She knew what was happening with Doug. "Are you okay?" Tanya nodded, but Carrie knew better. "No, you're not."

"I just feel trapped. I hate what he is doing, but I have no options. If I keep refusing him or go to Human Resources, I'm afraid I'll lose my job."

"You have to do something. I doubt that he will stop on his own." Carol hugged Tanya. "The Lord's gonna take care of this whole situation girl. He'll lead you in what to do and what to say. Trying times like this are why we need God. I believe you should go to the authorities and have them investigate and take action against Doug. Have no fear of retaliation. The Lord'll protect you and fight your battles for you"

"I'm not sure that He will do that for me."

"Girl, He longs to do this for you. God's got your back." Carol prayed for the Lord's comfort, guidance, and protection for Tanya.

The Lord cares for His people and provides for all their needs. He comforts and protects. We are dependent on Him like sheep are dependent on their shepherd. In what ways has God been a shepherd to you?

Keep in Mind

"The LORD is my shepherd, I shall not want" (Psalm 23:1).

"The LORD is my shepherd, I shall not want" (Psalm 23:1).

Focal Verses

KJV **Psalm 23:1** The LORD is my shepherd; I shall not want.

2 He maketh me to lie down in green pastures: He leadeth me beside the still waters.

3 He restoreth my soul: He leadeth me in the paths of righteousness for his name's sake.

4 Yea, though I walk through the valley of the shadow of death, I will fear no evil: for thou art with me; Thy rod and thy staff they comfort me.

5 Thou preparest a table before me in the presence of mine enemies: Thou anointest my head with oil; my cup runneth over.

6 Surely goodness and mercy shall follow me all the days of my life: And I will dwell in the house of the LORD for ever.

NLT **Psalm 23:1** The LORD is my shepherd; I have all that I need.

2 He lets me rest in green meadows; he leads me beside peaceful streams.

3 He renews my strength. He guides me along right paths, bringing honor to his name.

4 Even when I walk through the darkest valley, I will not be afraid, for you are close beside me. Your rod and your staff protect and comfort me.

5 You prepare a feast for me in the presence of my enemies. You honor me by anointing my head with oil. My cup overflows with blessings.

6 Surely your goodness and unfailing love will pursue me all the days of my life, and I will live in the house of the LORD forever.

The People, Places, and Times

David. David was the youngest son of Jesse of the tribe of Judah, and the second king of Israel. David is also the author of many hymns, including Psalm 23. He was brought up to be a shepherd, and in this occupation he learned the courage he would later demonstrate in battle.

Shepherd. The shepherd is charged with caring for the sheep. He must find food and water, protect the sheep from predators, and return any that have strayed.

Background

The role of shepherd goes back to the days of Abel. Psalm 23 is a psalm of David, who was raised in that very occupation. As a shepherd, he fought with lions and bears to protect his sheep (1 Samuel 17:34–35). He was well acquainted with all the responsibilities of a shepherd. David uses his experience as a shepherd to illustrate the love and care of God.

In ancient Middle Eastern culture, sheep were prized symbols of wealth. Their wool was used to make yarn. Also, sheep were a common animal for sacrifice or food, which made them especially precious.

At-A-Glance

1. God as Shepherd (Psalm 23:1–4)
2. Guests in God's House (vv. 5–6)

In Depth

1. God as Shepherd (Psalm 23:1–4)

Psalm 23 presents Yahweh as the Shepherd who loves and cares for His sheep. Sheep are unable to survive on their own, so they depend completely on the shepherd. Psalm 23 elaborates on God's providential care as He cares for, guides, and gives refreshment to His people.

David opens by affirming the Lord as his shepherd, and that he has everything he needs. First, he delights in God's care, providing everything he needed. As his shepherd, the Lord also guided him. He led David beside the still waters, which may be interpreted as a resting place. Like a shepherd who knows the right paths to lead the sheep home, the Lord led David down the right path to bring glory to His name.

David next describes God's protection. With God as his shepherd, David had no reason to fear evil. The shepherd protected his sheep. He fought off wild animals that might attack them. The shepherd used his rod and staff to protect the flock. At night the shepherd would lay in the only doorway to the sheep pen, using his body to bar anyone who might try to steal the sheep. David experienced God's presence and protection.

The Lord is also the shepherd for believers today. We have the same intimate, lifelong fellowship with Him. We experience God's love and peace when facing stressful situations. Jesus describes Himself as the Good Shepherd (Matthew 10:14). As our Leader, He provides all our needs, restores us, and guides us to safety and paths pleasing to Him, bringing glory to His name. Like David, we need not fear the deep, dark valley. The believers are always under the Lord's watchful eye, and He never forsakes His sheep.

2. Guests in God's House (vv. 5–6)

The psalm shifts to God as gracious host and provider. God offers safety and protection, even spreading a table of lavish hospitality. Even in the presence of David's enemies, the Lord made provision for him. God's abundant care can be symbolized by the anointing with oil and the overflowing cup. The psalm ends with David affirming that God gives him victory over death and that he will spend eternity with Him.

As in Psalm 23, God graciously protects and provides for believers today. Believers have enemies and experience stressful and dangerous situations, just like David did. He offers us sanctuary in times of difficulty. God can transform our situations and our lives. As with David, God's blessing is always on His people. We can dwell with the Lord and experience full communion with Him forever.

Search the Scriptures

1. How does David describe his relationship with God (Psalm 23:1)?

2. How does David describe his ongoing fellowship with God (v. 6)?

Discuss the Meaning

1. God still seeks to lead, protect, and provide for His people. As believers, we must submit to His leading as sheep to their shepherd. How do you relate to God as your shepherd?

2. Even believers have problems. We have enemies. We can experience periods of darkness in our lives as David did. How has the Lord protected you or comforted you during trying times?

Lesson in Our Society

Adults face difficult situations. We face danger, anxiety, and fear as we journey through life. We can turn to God as our shepherd to lead, protect, and provide for us. We must understand that He is our shepherd and leader, and must submit to His leadership. We must trust Him as our provider, asking and thanking Him for making provision for our needs. We must run to Him as our refuge in times of trouble. Finally, we must maintain a vital union with God for life.

Make It Happen

Meditate on God's Word and reflect on the Lord as your shepherd. Ask Him to lead you as a shepherd leads and cares for his sheep. Rest in the truth that the Lord will protect and provide for you. Finally, thank Him for His love and providential care in your life.

Follow the Spirit

What God wants me to do:

_____

_____

_____

_____

Remember Your Thoughts

Special insights I have learned:

_____

_____

_____

_____

More Light on the Text

Psalm 23:1–6

This famous psalm (Psalm 23) identifies God as the faithful Shepherd. For the reader, the psalm provides a deep sense of trust and confidence in God. The first four verses describe how our Divine Shepherd watches over His flock. The final two verses speak of the future thanksgiving in God's house. Biblical scholars believe that Psalm 23 utilizes the shepherd metaphor to remember God's help during the Exodus. Most believe King David to be the author. However, regardless of who authored this passage, it still remains one of the best known and loved psalms.

1 The LORD is my shepherd; I shall not want.

Immediately, verse 1 affirms Yahweh as Shepherd. This concept originated in the early life of the Israelites, particularly during the time of Jacob. The traditions of Israel's time in the desert seem to have given rise to the thought of God as their Shepherd. This concept became a favorite idiom throughout Israelite history. Several biblical passages highlight God as Shepherd and Protector (Genesis 49:24; Jeremiah 13:17; Micah 7:14).

Traditionally, the shepherd theme is interpreted communally. The shepherd has a relationship with his flock. The pronoun "my" makes this portion of the psalm distinct in that it speaks of one individual's personal relationship with the shepherd. The speaker confirms that a relationship with the shepherd brings about wonderful results. The needs of the sheep are met and God (the Shepherd) becomes the ultimate source of provision. This verse establishes that God is loyal and devoted to each individual sheep.

2 He maketh me to lie down in green pastures: he leadeth me beside the still waters. 3 He restoreth my soul: he leadeth me in the paths of righteousness for his name's sake.

The verses extend the metaphor of a loving and devoted shepherd, illustrating the nature of the shepherd's guidance and provision. The psalmist speaks of God guiding him through the ups and downs of life. Green pastures and still waters are significant elements in the beginning of the psalm. Grassy pastures indicate tender grass, young herbage, and abundance. God puts the psalmist in the midst of plenty to enjoy it with ease and comfort. The shepherd leading the sheep by still waters portrays the Lord showing the psalmist to a resting place where he could be refreshed safely.

This not only confirms the duties of the shepherd, but also affirms that he is prepared to keep the sheep nourished in every way. It is important to note that it was the shepherd's job to supply the sheep with water either at a running stream or at troughs attached to the wells (Genesis 29:7, 30:38; Exodus 2:16).

4 Yea, though I walk through the valley of the shadow of death, I will fear no evil: for thou art with me; thy rod and thy staff they comfort me.

This verse uses several metaphors to specify the relationship between the Shepherd and His sheep. First, the phrase "valley of shadow of death" might have a few different meanings. The term might refer to the hill country of Judah, which consisted of narrow valleys that were often dark, gloomy, and difficult to climb. Also, the valleys had deep caves where wild beasts and robbers resided. This made the journey for the pilgrim extremely dangerous as he passed through the hill country. Literally, the peril of death could occur in the valleys of the hill country. Second, the phrase might also be used figuratively. The author could be comparing the deep shadow of death's valley to Egyptian slavery or the Israelites' long time in the wilderness.

The Great Shepherd protects His people during their exodus and wandering in the wilderness. Triumphantly, the Good Shepherd leads the sheep out of the wilderness into the Promised Land (Jeremiah 2:6). Such language could also be used as a tool of encouragement to the exiled Israelites later. Certainly God, who led the ancestors out of bondage, will liberate these captives. Whatever the psalmist's intent, he emphasizes that there is divine protection in the midst of danger or death.

In keeping with the image of God as Shepherd, the psalmist highlights a rod and a staff. Shepherds used rods to count the sheep, care for the sheep, and check the condition of the sheep. It was also a symbol of power and authority. Staffs were used to aid the shepherd in climbing hills and beating away bushes and reptiles in the area. These symbols imply that the shepherd is capable of protecting his flock as well as leading them.

5 Thou preparest a table before me in the presence of mine enemies: thou anoinest my head with oil; my cup runneth over. 6 Surely goodness and mercy shall follow me all the days of my life: and I will dwell in the house of the LORD forever.

Here, the image changes from a shepherd to a host. The intimate relationship between God and His people are like that of a host and his guests. God as the gracious host protects the guests from any enemy. In the ancient East, the host would customarily protect the guest from his enemies at all costs. A man pursued by enemies could seek another man's tent for refuge. The owner of that tent would be obligated to protect his guest from the enemy. Additionally, the host would sprinkle the guests with perfume as a way of welcoming them into his fellowship.

Such a loving and gracious host gives pure satisfaction and security to the guests ("my cup overflows"). These images provide us with more detail about God's nature. God is a gracious host who protects His guests from all enemies. He is our shield and protector. Our enemies stand outside the tent door glaring, but they are not allowed to destroy us. Their plans are frustrated while our God makes a statement. He is truly a friend.

God also prepares a great banquet and longs for our fellowship. Feasting in His presence nourishes our souls and prepares us for greatness. The psalm ends with some future expectation. A relationship with the Divine Shepherd or the Gracious Host will result in goodness, mercy, and God's everlasting presence. The psalmist is convinced that God's wise guidance will lead to a promising future.

Say It Correctly

Pastures. **PAS**-chers.
Anointest. ah-**NOYNT**-ist.

Daily Bible Readings

MONDAY
God's People Seek a Resting Place
(Numbers 10:29–36)

TUESDAY
God the True Shepherd
(Ezekiel 34:11–16)

WEDNESDAY
The Lord Brings the People Home
(Jeremiah 23:1–8)

THURSDAY
Jesus Sacrifices for the Flock
(John 10:11–18)

FRIDAY
Shepherds in God's Household Today
(Hebrews 13:17, 20–21)

SATURDAY
Tending the Flock of God
(1 Peter 5:1–11)

SUNDAY
A Caring Shepherd and Gracious Host
(Psalm 23)

Notes

Teaching Tips

Words You Should Know

A. Love (John 3:16) *agapao* (Gk.)—To love or hold someone in high regard.

B. Life (v. 16) *zoe* (Gk.)—Vitality or life, especially eternal life.

Teacher Preparation

Unifying Principle—What Is This Love? A commitment to serve others may require more than anticipated. To what extent are we willing to sacrifice for the sake of others? God proved His love for the world through the ultimate sacrifice of His only Son, so that all who believe in Him will have eternal life.

A. Read the Bible Background and Devotional Readings.

B. Complete Lesson 6 in the *Precepts For Living®* Personal Study Guide.

C. Read the Focal Verses in several translations.

O—Open the Lesson

A. Open with prayer.

B. Have students read the Aim for Change in unison.

C. Ask for a volunteer to read the In Focus story.

D. Discuss the ways that the Lord shows His unfailing love toward His people.

P—Present the Scriptures

A. Ask for volunteers to read the Focal Verses and The People, Places, and Times. Discuss.

B. Read and discuss the Background section.

C. Encourage students to praise God for His love and for access to eternal life through Jesus.

E—Explore the Meaning

A. Review and discuss the Search the Scriptures and Discuss the Meaning questions and the Lesson in Our Society section.

B. Ask students to share the most significant point they learned and how they plan to use that point this week.

N—Next Steps for Application

A. Complete the Follow the Spirit and Remember Your Thoughts sections.

B. Remind students to read the Daily Bible Readings in preparation for next week's lesson.

C. Close in prayer, thanking God for His unfailing love.

Worship Guide

For the Superintendent or Teacher
Theme: God's Saving Love in Christ
Song: "Lift Him Up"
Devotional Reading: Titus 3:1–7

God's Saving Love in Christ

Bible Background • JOHN 3:1–21
Printed Text • JOHN 3:1–16 | Devotional Reading • TITUS 3:1–7

———————————— **Aim for Change** ————————————

By the end of the lesson, we will: EXPLORE the story of Nicodemus who learned from Jesus what it means "to be born from above"; APPRECIATE how God's love offers salvation rather than condemnation; and SEEK to live as spiritually reborn people who know and respond to God's love.

———————————— **In Focus** ————————————

Jeff waited until his coworkers filed out of the break room before he approached Marcus. Marcus had been sharing his testimony, and Jeff had more questions.

"I don't understand," Jeff said. "It seems like everything changed when you became a Christian."

"That's about right. That's what we mean when we say we've been born again or that we have a new life."

Jeff hung his head. "I'd like a new life. I seem to have messed this one up pretty bad."

"We've all done things we're not proud of," Marcus told him. "Jesus offers a fresh start if you accept Him, and He gives eternal life. You can have that today."

"I'm not sure."

"Let me pray for you. I want you to see the truth of God's Word, and only the Holy Spirit can illuminate that for you. Jesus wants you to believe in Him and have everlasting life."

Marcus prayed that the Holy Spirit would continue working in Jeff's heart and that Jeff would continue to seek the truth.

Jesus offers new birth and eternal life to those who believe. How did you experience the new birth?

———————————— **Keep in Mind** ————————————

"For God so loved the world, that he gave his only begotten Son, that whosoever believeth in him should not perish, but have everlasting life" (John 3:16).

"For God so loved the world, that he gave his only begotten Son, that whosoever believeth in him should not perish, but have everlasting life" (John 3:16).

Focal Verses

KJV **John 3:1** There was a man of the Pharisees, named Nicodemus, a ruler of the Jews:

2 The same came to Jesus by night, and said unto him, Rabbi, we know that thou art a teacher come from God: for no man can do these miracles that thou doest, except God be with him.

3 Jesus answered and said unto him, Verily, verily, I say unto thee, Except a man be born again, he cannot see the kingdom of God.

4 Nicodemus saith unto him, How can a man be born when he is old? can he enter the second time into his mother's womb, and be born?

5 Jesus answered, Verily, verily, I say unto thee, Except a man be born of water and of the Spirit, he cannot enter into the kingdom of God.

6 That which is born of the flesh is flesh; and that which is born of the Spirit is spirit.

7 Marvel not that I said unto thee, Ye must be born again.

8 The wind bloweth where it listeth, and thou hearest the sound thereof, but canst not tell whence it cometh, and whither it goeth: so is every one that is born of the Spirit.

9 Nicodemus answered and said unto him, How can these things be?

10 Jesus answered and said unto him, Art thou a master of Israel, and knowest not these things?

11 Verily, verily, I say unto thee, We speak that we do know, and testify that we have seen; and ye receive not our witness.

12 If I have told you earthly things, and ye believe not, how shall ye believe, if I tell you of heavenly things?

13 And no man hath ascended up to heaven, but he that came down from heaven, even the Son of man which is in heaven.

NLT **John 3:1** There was a man named Nicodemus, a Jewish religious leader who was a Pharisee.

2 After dark one evening, he came to speak with Jesus. "Rabbi," he said, "we all know that God has sent you to teach us. Your miraculous signs are evidence that God is with you."

3 Jesus replied, "I tell you the truth, unless you are born again, you cannot see the Kingdom of God."

4 "What do you mean?" exclaimed Nicodemus. "How can an old man go back into his mother's womb and be born again?"

5 Jesus replied, "I assure you, no one can enter the Kingdom of God without being born of water and the Spirit.

6 Humans can reproduce only human life, but the Holy Spirit gives birth to spiritual life.

7 So don't be surprised when I say, 'You must be born again.'

8 The wind blows wherever it wants. Just as you can hear the wind but can't tell where it comes from or where it is going, so you can't explain how people are born of the Spirit."

9 "How are these things possible?" Nicodemus asked.

10 Jesus replied, "You are a respected Jewish teacher, and yet you don't understand these things?

11 I assure you, we tell you what we know and have seen, and yet you won't believe our testimony.

12 But if you don't believe me when I tell you about earthly things, how can you possibly believe if I tell you about heavenly things?

13 No one has ever gone to heaven and returned. But the Son of Man has come down from heaven.

14 And as Moses lifted up the bronze snake on a pole in the wilderness, so the Son of Man must be lifted up,

14 And as Moses lifted up the serpent in the wilderness, even so must the Son of man be lifted up:

15 That whosoever believeth in him should not perish, but have eternal life.

16 For God so loved the world, that he gave his only begotten Son, that whosoever believeth in him should not perish, but have everlasting life.

15 so that everyone who believes in him will have eternal life.

16 For this is how God loved the world: He gave his one and only Son, so that everyone who believes in him will not perish but have eternal life."

The People, Places, and Times

Nicodemus. A religious leader of the Pharisees and member of the Sanhedrin, Nicodemus was both a religious and political leader. He came to Jesus by night; one reason might be because he was afraid to let the other Pharisees know about his interest in Jesus' teachings.

Background

Jesus encounters Nicodemus near the Passover. He had recently cleared out the Temple, which caused some commotion. The religious leaders demanded to know what authority Jesus had to do these things, and they demanded to see a sign. He told them that He would destroy this Temple and raise it again in three days. The religious leaders were furious.

At the same time, John tells us that Jesus performed many miracles during the Passover celebration and that many believed in Him because of them (John 2:23). Word about Jesus began to spread.

Among those who heard about Jesus was Nicodemus, a Pharisee very educated in the Scriptures. He comes to Jesus personally to learn from Him. He recognizes that God is empowering Jesus to perform miracles, and some of the other religious leaders do, too (John 3:2). Not everyone agreed, though. There were differing opinions about Jesus, His

identity, and His power to do such mighty acts. Nicodemus decides to go to Jesus for himself.

At-A-Glance

1. Jesus is from God (John 3:1–2)
2. Born of the Spirit (vv. 3–9)
3. Believing in the Son of Man (vv. 10–15)
4. Jesus Came to Save (v. 16)

In Depth

1. Jesus Is from God (John 3:1–2)

Nicodemus was a member of the Sanhedrin, the highest court of the Jews. He came to Jesus one night to speak to Him. Nicodemus had seen the miracles that Jesus had done and recognized God's work in them. Though he was usually concerned with matters of law, Nicodemus' visit indicates that he was sensitive spiritually.

The reason for the timing of Nicodemus' visit is uncertain. Some scholars suggest that Nicodemus came to Jesus by night because he was fearful. Others scholars have suggested that he came at night because he desired privacy, as Jesus was usually engaged in public ministry during the day. Whatever his reasoning,

Nicodemus recognized that Jesus was from God, and he wanted to hear more from Jesus.

2. Born of the Spirit (vv. 3–9)

Jesus begins to teach Nicodemus. He explains that one must be born again to enter the kingdom of God. Nicodemus was thinking only of a natural birth, but Jesus says that one must be born again, or born "from above," to enter the kingdom of God. The idea of being born again signified conversion, and Nicodemus would have seen no need for this.

This would have puzzled Nicodemus. The prevailing belief was that people were in God's kingdom because they were born from Abraham. "How are these things possible?" he asked. Nicodemus' reaction demonstrates how startled he was by the idea that people would need to enter God's kingdom by other means.

Jesus explains that the physical realm is different from the spiritual realm, and that natural birth could not regenerate the spirit. He acknowledges that this cannot be explained (v. 8). Like the wind, God's Spirit is invisible, unexplainable, and powerful.

3. Believing in the Son of Man (vv. 10–15)

Jesus is surprised that as a religious leader, Nicodemus does not understand about the Spirit. The Old Testament prophets foresaw a time when people would be regenerated by the Spirit. As a religious leader and skilled interpreter of the Law, Nicodemus should have understood about God's Spirit and His work in the lives of believers. If Nicodemus didn't believe the prophets' testimony, would he believe Jesus' testimony? Jesus challenged Nicodemus to do just that.

Jesus indicated that although Nicodemus is a respected religious leader, he had some trouble with spiritual matters. If Nicodemus had difficulty understanding spiritual truths that Jesus had explained in earthly terms, Jesus asked, how would he be able to understand the more abstract spiritual truths?

Jesus affirms that He is indeed from heaven, and like the Israelites, who had but to look up to Moses' bronze serpent (Numbers 21:4–9), those seeking forgiveness and entry into God's kingdom need only to look to Jesus for salvation. He was "raised up" in His crucifixion, and through His death and resurrection, He brought eternal life.

4. Jesus Came to Save (v. 16)

This verse presents the Gospel in short. God, motivated by love, gave His Son to bring salvation. His love was not just for a certain people group, but the whole world. Through His death, Jesus brought sinners, enemies of God, into His family and eternal life. Faith in Jesus takes us from condemnation to salvation and from death to life. Eternal life does not refer to length alone, but also a quality of life in the kingdom of God. God, in love, sent Jesus to make this new life possible.

Search the Scriptures

1. Why does Nicodemus believe that God is with Jesus (John 3:2)?

2. How does one enter the kingdom of God (vv. 3, 5)?

Discuss the Meaning

1. It is easy to be consumed with the legal aspects of the Scriptures. It is even possible to be so focused on the Law that we miss the work of the Spirit. How can we maintain our commitment to the Scriptures and yet be sensitive to the Spirit?

2. God responded to human sin and rebellion in love. How can we accept His love, walk in it, and invite others to experience His love?

Lesson in Our Society

We might not be Jewish or have ancestral ties to Abraham, but the idea of being born into the kingdom of God is just as prevalent in our society. When asked about their faith, people will often remark that their mother is a Christian or that a grandparent is a pastor. We may be born into families that believe in Jesus, but each person, like Nicodemus, must approach Jesus for themselves.

Make It Happen

Often, people are unsure of how to approach Jesus and have faith in Him. Like Nicodemus, we need to seek Jesus and seek to learn from Him. Some things may be difficult to understand, but we must be open to the leading and instruction of the Spirit as we seek to know Jesus more.

Follow the Spirit

What God wants me to do:

_____

_____

_____

_____

Remember Your Thoughts

Special insights I have learned:

_____

_____

_____

_____

More Light on the Text

John 3:1–16

1 There was a man of the Pharisees, named Nicodemus, a ruler of the Jews.

The Pharisees were regarded as the most devout keepers of the Law among the Jews. Thus they sought to guard the standards and judge the actions of the Jewish community. By the first century AD, the Pharisees were the most popular of the three main Jewish sects. The other two sects were the Essenes and the Sadducees. Although Pharisees were extremely detailed in all matters of the Law, their religion was often an outward show based on self-righteousness. Throughout Jesus' ministry, the Pharisees were bitter enemies of our Lord, and they sought to destroy His influence among the people.

The phrase "ruler of the Jews" means that Nicodemus also served on the Sanhedrin Council, which was composed of seventy priests, elders, scribes, and the high priest. Thus Nicodemus was a very powerful and educated man.

2 The same came to Jesus by night, and said unto him, Rabbi, we know that thou art a teacher come from God: for no man can do these miracles that thou doest, except God be with him.

Under the cover of darkness, this man of religious authority sought Jesus out. He addressed Jesus as "Rabbi," a title of honor used by the Jews to address doctors of the Law and distinguished religious teachers. By using this title, Nicodemus was giving honor and recognition to the divine authority of Jesus' teachings and signs that He was performing.

The "we" that Nicodemus speaks for is unclear. It would appear that he was speaking for the Pharisees and/or the Sanhedrin Council. But the Pharisees' behavior would seem to oppose any notion that they sincerely believed

His work was God-inspired. Nicodemus was more likely referring to a group of Pharisees who were beginning to believe in Jesus. It is difficult to judge the sincerity of his statement.

Some have suggested that this could have been just a method of entrapment, as described by the other Gospel writers when referring to the Pharisees. If so, Nicodemus' heart was melted as he spoke with the Master Teacher.

3 Jesus answered, and said unto him, Verily, verily, I say unto thee, Except a man be born again, he cannot see the kingdom of God.

Verse 3 begins by saying Jesus "answered" (Gk. *apokrinomai*, **ah-poe-KREE-no-my**), which means to answer a question or to speak in response to something that is said or done. Nicodemus had not yet asked a question; however, something caused Jesus to give an answer. It might have been Nicodemus' statement of faith, "we know that thou art a teacher come from God," or it might have been that Jesus understood the true question that was in his heart. In either case, Jesus gives the following answer: "Very truly I tell you, no one can see the kingdom of God unless they are born again" (from v. 3, NIV).

Nicodemus and many Jews of the time conceived of the kingdom of God as the rule of the foretold Messiah who would vanquish the enemies of Israel. John and Jesus use the phrase "kingdom of God" to mean Christ's authority, and rule, and all of the blessings and advantages available to those who are subjects of God's kingdom through faith in Christ.

Many thought that being a Jew by birth was to be born into the kingdom because of God's covenant with Moses and the Children of Israel. But what is born of physical heritage is physical, and what is born of the Spirit is spiritual (cf. v. 6; see also Galatians 3:26–29).

4 Nicodemus saith unto him, How can a man be born when he is old? can he enter the second time into his mother's womb, and be born?

Nicodemus' question was a logical response. Notice that he didn't ask, "How can a man be born again," but "How can a man be born, when he is old?" According to Messianic scholar Dr. Arnold Fruchtenbaum of Ariel Ministries, Pharisaic Judaism had six different ways of being born again: (1) when Gentiles converted to Judaism; (2) when a man was crowned king; (3) when a Jewish boy becomes a bar mitzvah (son of the Law) at age 13; (4) when a Jewish man married; (5) when a Jew was ordained as a rabbi; and (6) when a Jew became the head of a rabbinical school. Except for the first two examples, Nicodemus had experienced all of the other rebirths. He had done everything right, but now Jesus tells Nicodemus that something else is lacking in his life.

5 Jesus answered, Verily, verily, I say unto thee, Except a man be born of water and of the Spirit, he cannot enter into the kingdom of God.

To enter God's kingdom requires a new beginning, which Jesus describes as new birth. The metaphor of birth is used here to signal the beginning of life. Therefore, to be "born again" indicates the beginning of new (eternal) life from above.

To "be born of water" is natural birth. The child's birth is preceded by a rush of water as the amniotic sac, which offered protection from the beginning, bursts open, as happens in all births. To be born of the Spirit was a different matter. This has to come from heaven. But Jesus did not say how this was to be done.

Perhaps one should look back to John's statement in 1:12–13: "to them gave he power to become the sons of God ... which were born, not of blood, ... but of God." By God's power, we can trust in Christ's redemptive work. Our new birth by the Spirit of God gives us membership in His family and entrance to His kingdom.

6 That which is born of the flesh is flesh; and that which is born of the Spirit is spirit.

The Greek word for "flesh" (*sarx*, **SARKS**) denotes both the physical body and fallen human nature apart from divine influence. This word is also translated as "carnal" (Romans 8:7). The Bible teaches that the flesh is prone to sin and selfishness, and it is therefore in opposition to the Spirit of God (Romans 8:5–9). Being "in the flesh" means being unrenewed; to live "according to the flesh" is to live and act sinfully (Romans 7:5; Ephesians 2:3).

Flesh cannot enter into the kingdom of God. It belongs to the kingdom of this world, but the spirit belongs to heaven. Flesh and spirit do not share the same realm. One is temporal and the other eternal (see 1 Corinthians 15:50).

7 Marvel not that I said unto thee, Ye must be born again.

In Psalm 51:5, David acknowledges, "Behold, I was shapen in iniquity; and in sin did my mother conceive me." In verse 10, he asks: "Create in me a clean heart, O God; and renew a right spirit within me." Like David, we each have inherited a sin nature from Adam (cf. Romans 5:12). Similarly, in John 3:7, it is as if Jesus is saying to Nicodemus, "Do not be surprised that something drastic must happen to transform the human nature."

The word "must" (Gk. *dei*, **day-EE**) indicates that the new birth is an absolute necessity. Our God represents holiness in the highest sense (cf. Isaiah 6:3; Revelation 15:4). To enter His kingdom and become His children, we must be radically transformed (see 1 Peter 1:16; Hebrews 12:14)—we, who have been "born of the flesh," must be "born of the Spirit."

8 The wind bloweth where it listeth, and thou hearest the sound thereof, but canst not tell whence it cometh, and whither it goeth: so is every one that is born of the Spirit.

In Greek, as well as in Hebrew, the same word (*pneuma*, **PNEW-ma**) is used for both "spirit" and "wind." The wind cannot be controlled because God directs it. Though the source of the wind is invisible, the effect, or evidence, of its activity is plain. So it is with everyone born of the Spirit. Those who are controlled by the Spirit are controlled by God and their source is invisible although their actions are plain.

9 Nicodemus answered and said unto him, How can these things be?

Perhaps Nicodemus was questioning how one can become born of the Spirit. Jesus did not explain how this might be achieved, only that it is a requirement for entering the kingdom of God. Another possibility is that Nicodemus, as a Pharisee who regulated Israel's worship standards, was concerned about the apparent freedom of those born of the Spirit. How could such freedom be permitted? Unregulated lives and worship practices might endanger the established religious system. After all, their history was full of such apostasies.

10 Jesus answered and said unto him, Art thou a master of Israel, and knowest not these things?

Jesus uses the word "master" (Gk. *didaskalos*, **dee-DAS-ka-lohs**) to describe to Nicodemus as one who is expertly qualified to teach, or who thinks that he is. The NIV renders this question as: "You are Israel's teacher … and do you not understand these things?"

Nicodemus could not teach what he does not understand himself. Thus the people would never find out this crucial truth from teachings of the Pharisees.

11 Verily, verily, I say unto thee, We speak that we do know, and testify that we have seen; and ye receive not our witness.

Nicodemus—a prominent Pharisee, a member of the Sanhedrin Council, a doctor of the Jewish Law, and a spiritual leader—did not know these things. However, Jesus makes it clear that He and His followers know the truth through firsthand experience (John 7:16, 8:38, 1 John 1:3). Yet Nicodemus and the Jewish authorities refused to believe them.

12 If I have told you earthly things, and ye believe not, how shall ye believe, if I tell you of heavenly things?

When He talks about "earthly things" (Gk. *epigeios*, **eh-PEE-gay-oce**), meaning the things that occur on earth, Jesus is likely speaking of His analogies related to birth, wind, and water. The phrase "heavenly things" (Gk. *epouranios*, **ep-oo-RAH-nee-os**) refers to things that exist or take place in heaven.

The word "believe" (Gk. *pisteuo*, **peas-TEW-oh**) means to think or be persuaded that something is true; to place confidence, conviction, and trust in something or someone. This word is used in John 3:12, 15–16 to identify a critical requirement. If Nicodemus would not believe or trust Jesus' explanation of mere earthly things, how could he possibly believe or trust the truth about the more important heavenly things associated with the kingdom of God?

13 And no man hath ascended up to heaven, but he that came down from heaven, even the Son of man which is in heaven.

Jesus is more than qualified to reveal the truth about heavenly things because He alone came down from heaven, has ascended into heaven, and is currently in heaven (see John 6:38; Mark 16:19; Ephesians 4:10).

The phrase "Son of man" appears in the Old Testament primarily to specify a member of humanity (cf. Psalm 8:4). It was also used to refer to the prophet in the book of Ezekiel (e.g., Ezekiel 2:1). Later in the apocalyptic book of Daniel, one sees a new development in the use of the phrase (Daniel 7:13). The "Son of man" takes on the character of a divine agent who will carry out judgment and deliverance.

14 And as Moses lifted up the serpent in the wilderness, even so must the Son of man be lifted up: 15 That whosoever believeth in him should not perish, but have eternal life.

In the wilderness when the Israelites murmured against God, He sent fiery (i.e., poisonous) serpents among the people to bite them, and many Israelites died. When the people repented, the Lord told Moses to make a bronze serpent, and set it upon a pole. Then if anyone who was bitten would look at that bronze serpent, they would live (Numbers 21). Our just and merciful God provided a means of salvation for a disobedient people, so that they might survive divine judgment.

The phrase "lifted up" is translated from the Greek word *hupsoo* (**hoop-so'-o**), which means to lift up on high or to exalt; both definitions apply in this verse. Nicodemus might have been among the first to learn that Jesus would be lifted up physically on the Cross of Calvary to become the source of salvation for all who will look to Him in faith. In addition, Jesus Christ should be exalted as Savior and Lord in the heart and life of every believer, and He will ultimately be exalted in all the earth (Philippians 2:8–11). The One who suffered death for us is the source of life for all who believe.

16 For God so loved the world, that he gave his only begotten Son, that whosoever

believeth in him should not perish, but have everlasting life.

John 3:16 is one of the most beloved verses in all of Scripture. However, in this study, we must also remember that it is found in the context of a conversation between Jesus and Nicodemus.

Out of the darkness of night, under the shadow of uncertainty, Nicodemus came to Jesus, the Light of the world. It is in John 3:16 that Nicodemus (and each of us) finds the answer: God takes away our sins and grants us new birth, or "everlasting life," because of His unmerited love for us, which is manifested by the sacrifice of His Son and our Savior Jesus Christ.

Say It Correctly

Nicodemus. ni-co-**DEE**-mus.
Listeth. lis-**TITH**.

Daily Bible Readings

MONDAY
God's Salvation is for the World
(John 3:17–21)

TUESDAY
Don't Love the World's Things
(1 John 2:15–17)

WEDNESDAY
Nicodemus Pleads "Give Jesus a Hearing"
(John 7:45–52)

THURSDAY
The Serpent in the Wilderness
(Numbers 21:4–9)

FRIDAY
Nicodemus Brings Spices for Burial
(John 19:38–42)

SATURDAY
Rebirth and Renewal by Water and Spirit
(Titus 3:1–7)

SUNDAY
God's Saving Love in Christ
(John 3:1–16)

Notes

_____

_____

_____

_____

Teaching Tips

April 16
Bible Study Guide 7

Words You Should Know

A. Sepulchre (John 20:1ff.) *mnemeion* (Gk.)—A visible object used to recall the memory of a person or thing, tomb, monument.

B. Napkin (v. 7) *soudarion* (Gk.)—A cloth used for wiping sweat from the face; also used for covering the head of a corpse.

Teacher Preparation

Unifying Principle—Incredible! Although we are forewarned, some life events are beyond the realm of our imagination. How do we respond at these times? Even though the disciples were confounded when they entered the empty tomb, they experienced a new birth into a living hope through the Resurrection.

A. Read the Focal Verses, using a least one other translation.

B. Read The People, Places, and Times and the Background sections for more insight on the verses.

C. Collect magazine pictures that show what Easter has become (families dressed up, colored eggs, baskets, and bunnies).

O—Open the Lesson

A. Begin the lesson with prayer. Because of the holiday, many may be in Sunday School for this time only. Be mindful of them and pray for those who might need salvation, but don't be condemning.

B. Have a student read the In Focus story. Pass out the magazine pictures and have students comment on the pictures and the story.

Ask if anyone can identify with Kayla. Are her attitude and actions unrealistic or on point?

P—Present the Scriptures

A. Write the At-A-Glance outline where the whole class can see it.

B. Break the class into three groups and have each group read the In Depth section and fill in the blanks in the Search the Scripture section.

E—Explore the Meaning

A. Discus the pastor's comments in Lesson in Our Society. Why do you agree or disagree?

B. Have the students ponder this question: What will the pastor at your funeral have to say about you?

N—Next Steps for Application

A. Reflect as a class on the Lesson in Our Society.

B. Have the class break into groups of three or four. Each person in the group should pray a sentence prayer about the information presented in the lesson.

Worship Guide

For the Superintendent or Teacher
Theme: God's Love as Victory Over Death
Song: "Up from the Grave He Arose"
Devotional Reading: Luke 24:1–12

God's Love as Victory Over Death

Bible Background • JOHN 19:38–42, 20:1–10; 1 PETER 1:3–9
Printed Text • JOHN 20:1–10 | Devotional Reading • LUKE 24:1–12

Aim for Change

By the end of the lesson, we will: REMEMBER in the events of the Resurrection the power of God's love to overcome death; CELEBRATE the saving power of new life offered in the Resurrection; and SHARE with others the power of God's love found in the Good News of the Resurrection.

 In Focus

Albert looked at the suit his wife, Kayla, laid out on the bed for him and heard the click of her white, patent heels coming down the hall. He knew what was coming: "These shoes, or red ones? Or maybe a different dress…" Albert eyed his wife from head to toe, but his thoughts were a thousand miles away.

After almost 10 years of marriage, Kayla also knew what was coming. "Kayla, this is my umpteenth Easter Sunday morning. But I just can't stomach another Easter parade, the auditorium filled with people who only come once a year."

Kayla had had enough arguments in the past with her husband on this issue, and this time she decided to take a quiet moment and ask God for wisdom as to what to say.

"Albert, you're right; Easter has become something I don't think God intended. And if you decide you don't want to go, I'm not going to say another word. But, if you don't mind, I'm going on. I know the resurrection power is still working and active in all this craziness. I'm going to pray for people as they come in and believe God will touch someone's heart with the truth of what Jesus' resurrection is really all about."

Albert sat without a comment, so Kayla got up and continued to put on her makeup in the bathroom. She could hear her husband starting to put on his suit. "Thank You, Jesus," she uttered quietly and then did a little holy dance on the bathroom rug.

How do your church and your personal life show the resurrection power of Jesus?

Keep in Mind

"Then went in also that other disciple, which came first to the sepulchre, and he saw, and believed" (John 20:8).

"Then went in also that other disciple, which came first to the sepulchre, and he saw, and believed" (John 20:8).

Focal Verses

KJV John 20:1 The first day of the week cometh Mary Magdalene early, when it was yet dark, unto the sepulchre, and seeth the stone taken away from the sepulchre.

2 Then she runneth, and cometh to Simon Peter, and to the other disciple, whom Jesus loved, and saith unto them, They have taken away the LORD out of the sepulchre, and we know not where they have laid him.

3 Peter therefore went forth, and that other disciple, and came to the sepulchre.

4 So they ran both together: and the other disciple did outrun Peter, and came first to the sepulchre.

5 And he stooping down, and looking in, saw the linen clothes lying; yet went he not in.

6 Then cometh Simon Peter following him, and went into the sepulchre, and seeth the linen clothes lie,

7 And the napkin, that was about his head, not lying with the linen clothes, but wrapped together in a place by itself.

8 Then went in also that other disciple, which came first to the sepulchre, and he saw, and believed.

9 For as yet they knew not the scripture, that he must rise again from the dead.

10 Then the disciples went away again unto their own home.

NLT John 20:1 Early on Sunday morning, while it was still dark, Mary Magdalene came to the tomb and found that the stone had been rolled away from the entrance.

2 She ran and found Simon Peter and the other disciple, the one whom Jesus loved. She said, "They have taken the Lord's body out of the tomb, and we don't know where they have put him!"

3 Peter and the other disciple started out for the tomb.

4 They were both running, but the other disciple outran Peter and reached the tomb first.

5 He stooped and looked in and saw the linen wrappings lying there, but he didn't go in.

6 Then Simon Peter arrived and went inside. He also noticed the linen wrappings lying there,

7 while the cloth that had covered Jesus' head was folded up and lying apart from the other wrappings.

8 Then the disciple who had reached the tomb first also went in, and he saw and believed—

9 for until then they still hadn't understood the Scriptures that said Jesus must rise from the dead.

10 Then they went home.

The People, Places, and Times

Mary Magdalene. Also called Mary of Mandala, she traveled with Jesus as one of His followers. She witnessed both Jesus' crucifixion and resurrection (Matthew 27:56, 28:1; Mark 15:20, 16:1; John 19:25, 20:1). Jesus cast seven demons out of her (Luke 8:2; Mark 16:9).

Peter. Peter was one of the disciples in Jesus' inner circle. He is perhaps the most outspoken of the Twelve. He often boldly asserts his devotion to Christ with an abundance of zeal, Jesus will then correct him, and Peter will then just as boldly accept his Master's correction. For example, when Jesus washes His disciples' feet before the Last Supper, Peter objects to Christ taking so lowly a role. But when Jesus explains the meaning of the gesture, Peter offers to let Jesus wash all of him. In today's passage, we see Peter running to Jesus' tomb and boldly entering it, in hopes of fully understanding this unique event.

Background

Secular scholars attempt to point to John's account of the Resurrection as the place of contradictions between the Gospels. For example, only Mary is mentioned in John's account, while several women visit the tomb in the other Gospels. But when she speaks to the disciples, she says "We," indicating others were with her. If one reads all four accounts carefully, there is solid evidence of the facts surrounding the empty tomb and Christ's appearances after His crucifixion.

At-A-Glance

1. The Declaration (John 20:1–4)
2. The Confirmation (vv. 5–10)

In Depth

1. The Declaration (John 20:1–4)

On the Sunday morning after Jesus' crucifixion, Mary Magdalene, along with other women, went to Jesus' tomb, bringing aromatics to anoint His body (Matthew 28:1; Mark 16:1). They were confused when they saw the empty tomb, assuming someone had stolen the body. Angels informed the women, "Jesus is not here—He's arisen" (Luke 24:4). Mary ran back to the disciples and reported these events. This is significant because as a woman, Mary would have been disqualified as a credible witness according to the Jewish culture at the time. God chose her and the others to be the first witnesses to the Resurrection, even though society had automatically disqualified them because of their gender.

After Mary's report to the disciples, John (the author of the book, humbly referring to himself as the other disciple) and Peter went to observe the empty tomb for themselves. They immediately "went forth" (v. 3). They had to see it with their own eyes. John outran Peter and made it to the tomb first. Their love and honor for their Rabbi caused them to run to discover the empty tomb. Soon they would discover that He was more than just a Rabbi, but; He was the resurrected Son of God.

2. The Confirmation (vv. 5–10)

The men witnessed that the napkin that was around Christ's head laid in a place by itself and the other wrappings were in another place. A body could not have gotten out of wrappings from head to toe without being cut or unwound. But the wrappings were not cut or in disarray; they were neatly folded. God made sure to highlight these details to offset any lies about a stolen body. If a thief stole a dead body, it's highly unlikely robbers would take the time to unwrap it and fold the wrapping clothes in different places.

Peter and John had heard Jesus talk about His resurrection, but they still did not understand the connection between His teaching, the Old Testament prophecies, and this phenomenal event (e.g., Psalm 16:10). The confused men returned to either their meeting place or their homes. They didn't have all the answers, but they definitely understood something unique and wonderful had taken place.

Search the Scriptures

1. What does Mary report about what has happened to Jesus' body (John 20:2)?

2. What is John's reaction to seeing the empty tomb (v. 8)?

Discuss the Meaning

God's power demonstrated by Christ being raised from the dead should give all believers the hope and assurance that this will also occur at the time of their death. Jesus' resurrection is a showcase of what lies in store for those who have faith in Christ. How does knowing we will partake both in Christ's death and His resurrection (Philippians 3:10–11) affect our daily lives as believers?

Lesson in Our Society

A pastor once said his greatest joy is preaching a funeral of a true believer, a person in which there is no question that his or her heart belonged to Jesus. He or she loved Christ and lived his or her entire life helping others grow in their faith and come to know Him. This same pastor says the saddest time for him in ministry is to preach a funeral when he has no idea whether this person is in heaven. No one knows a person's heart or what might have happened during those last moments before death, but it is a horrible feeling knowing this person blatantly refused to accept any truth about Christ.

Society attempts to paint a pretty picture, saying that a person's good deeds will outweigh the bad ones, or that God would never send anyone to hell. Unfortunately, the Scriptures have never agreed with such ideas.

Make It Happen

It's early; Resurrection Sunday has just begun. Put aside some time and pray about the true meaning of Jesus' resurrection. Ask God to bring to mind anyone—your family, church, group of friends or co-workers—who does not understand salvation in connection to Jesus and the empty tomb. Ask God to give you an opportunity to speak with them about this lesson.

Follow the Spirit

What God wants me to do:

_____

_____

_____

_____

Remember Your Thoughts

Special insights I have learned:

_____

_____

_____

_____

More Light on the Text
John 20:1–10

1 The first day of the week cometh Mary Magdalene early, when it was yet dark, unto the sepulchre, and seeth the stone taken away from the sepulchre.

Mary Magdalene's association with Jesus most likely began when He cured her and other women of demon possession (Luke 8:2) early in His ministry. She is not mentioned before then. Her name indicates that she either came from or was a resident of the town of Magdala, situated on the western shore of the Sea of Galilee. She is often identified as a prostitute, especially by American Catholics and in many western European countries where homes for unwed mothers are routinely named "Magdalene" homes. This notion is, however, unfounded and bears no scriptural evidence to support it.

However, plenty of evidence shows that from the time of her deliverance by Jesus, all of the Gospel writers acknowledge her as a constant presence in His life and ministry. Her miraculous cure by Jesus earned Him her untiring faith and devotion. Mary Magdalene appears to have been a woman of substantial means, as it seems she ministered to the needs of Jesus and the other disciples with her own money (Luke 8:1–3).

Interestingly, the account of the sepulcher visitation differs between the Gospel writers. Matthew reports that Mary Magdalene was accompanied by the "other Mary" (Matthew 28:1). Mark records the presence of three women: Mary Magdalene; Mary, the mother of James; and Salome (Mark 16:1). Luke records the greatest number of women, writing, "It was Mary Magdalene, and Joanna, and Mary the mother of James, and other women that were with them" (from Luke 24:10). John only mentions Mary Magdalene visiting the tomb.

The fact that her name is always mentioned first when listed with a group of women indicates that she was obviously a leader in the female circle of disciples (Matthew 27:56; Mark 16:1; Luke 24:10). The only exception is at the foot of the Cross, when Jesus' female family member's names are listed first (John 19:25).

Faithful to Jesus, even after His death, John presents Mary Magdalene rising early and going to Jesus' tomb to anoint His body with precious ointments and spices, as was the custom of the day. Both Mark (15:47) and Luke (23:55) record that Mary and the other women had watched Jesus' burial and the sealing of the tomb. So, while we are not surprised that Mary could locate the tomb in the dark of the early morning hours, it is not clear how Mary expected to remove the huge stone placed at the entrance of the tomb. Perhaps she expected the Roman soldiers who were guarding the tomb to roll the stone for her. In any case, when Mary Magdalene arrives at the burial site, the giant stone has already been removed.

2 Then she runneth, and cometh to Simon Peter, and to the other disciple, whom Jesus loved, and saith unto them, They have taken away the Lord out of the sepulchre, and we know not where they have laid him. 3 Peter therefore went forth, and that other disciple, and came to the sepulchre.

At this point in John's narrative, Mary Magdalene runs to tell Peter and the other disciples that Jesus' body is missing. John does not tell us that Mary has yet to even enter the tomb. In John's account, Mary does not enter the tomb until after the men leave (20:11–12). Matthew's account tells of a "great earthquake" and has the angel rolling back the stone, making the announcement to the women, and inviting them inside the tomb to see for themselves (28:2–6). The narratives of both Mark and Luke indicate that the women enter the tomb and encounter an angel who announces that Jesus has risen. John's difference does not imply any disharmony in the Gospels, but it suggests a differing view of the more significant points to the account. We must also remember that of the four Gospel writers, only John was actually an eyewitness to this event (Matthew was among the Twelve, but he is not mentioned as going to the tomb). He possibly prioritized the notification of Peter and himself and simply chose to leave out details that occurred before his arrival at the grave site. This is logical in light of the fact that his Gospel is written after the other three; he knows they have already included those details.

Interesting, too, is the fact that John does not name the other disciple, the one "whom Jesus loved." It is undoubtedly the writer of the Gospel, John, the brother of James. John never identifies himself in his own Gospel, choosing instead to refer to himself only as the son of Zebedee or, as he does in this account, the one Jesus loved.

4 So they ran both together: and the other disciple did outrun Peter, and came first to the sepulchre.

Only John's Gospel records that the other disciple outran Peter to the sepulcher. Again, this does not indicate disharmony, but rather the privileging of certain details by the writer, who also happens to be a central character. John is relating the sense of excitement he surely must have felt at that time. He was speculated to be younger than Peter, and certainly would have been able to outdistance the older man as they raced to the tomb.

5 And he stooping down, and looking in, saw the linen clothes lying; yet went he not in.

Although John outruns Peter and arrives at the sepulcher first, he does not go in. Some have argued that perhaps John was afraid to enter the tomb alone. A more likely reason is that he simply defers to the older apostle. Some say it was probably out of respect for Peter's position as leader of the apostles that John allows him to enter the tomb first.

6 Then cometh Simon Peter following him, and went into the sepulchre, and seeth the linen clothes lie, 7 And the napkin, that was about his head, not lying with the linen clothes, but wrapped together in a place by itself.

John seems to emphasize the supernatural implications concerning the burial linens. Also, since Jesus was no longer dead and had conquered death by His resurrection, He no longer had need of burial clothing. The linen grave clothes were for the dead; those who had not risen could not conquer it. Only the Son of the One and Only God could win and seal the victory over sin and death, therefore, securing our own salvation.

8 Then went in also the other disciple, which came first to the sepulchre, and he saw, and believed.

John's Gospel alone records that upon seeing the empty grave and the discarded grave clothes, John "believed." This is understandable since the writer, better than anyone else, would know this to be a fact. It is interesting to note that in Luke's account, Peter, upon seeing the discarded burial clothing, "wonder[ed] in himself at that which was come to pass" (Luke 24:12).

While Peter, the elder statesman, puzzles over the occurrence, the younger disciple believes. John uses the Greek word *pisteuo* (**peas-TEW-oh**), which means to have faith or conviction.

9 For as yet they knew not the scripture, that he must rise again from the dead. 10 Then the disciples went away again unto their own home.

Verse 9 offers a fuller explanation for Peter's puzzlement and John's subsequent belief by emphasizing how unexpected these events were to both of them. Although they were closer to Jesus than any of the other apostles, these events still take these men by surprise. It had only been days earlier when Jesus had spoken to His disciples, telling them "a little while, and ye shall not see me: and again, a little while and ye shall see me" (John 16:19). The apostles were unsure of what Jesus meant. That He would defy the laws of nature and be physically raised from the dead had not occurred to them. Therefore, in verse 10, they simply went to their homes again, pondering all that they had seen and heard.

Say It Correctly

Seeth. **SEE**-ith.
Sepulchre. **SE**-pul-ker.

Daily Bible Readings

MONDAY
Jesus' Side is Pierced
(John 19:31–37)

TUESDAY
The Spirit, Water, and Blood Agree
(1 John 5:6–12)

WEDNESDAY
The Lord Breaks No Bones
(Psalm 34:15–20)

THURSDAY
Soldiers Cast Lots for Jesus' Clothing
(John 19:23–25a)

FRIDAY
Jesus' Final Words to His Mother
(John 19:26–27)

SATURDAY
The Women and Peter Were Amazed
(Luke 24:1–12)

SUNDAY
Victory Over Death
(John 20:1–10)

Notes

_____

_____

_____

_____

Teaching Tips

Words You Should Know

A. Love (Romans 5:8) *agape* (Gk.)—Deep love and affection, as for a family member or friend; divine love that God proffers.

B. Justified (v. 9) *dikaioo* (Gk)—To endorse legally, to show what is right; conformed to a proper standard or upright.

C. Reconcile (v. 10) *katallasso* (Gk)—Two parties changing to the same position; the redemptive sense of a sinner's relationship with the Lord being repaired.

Teacher Preparation

Unifying Principle—Together Forever. Hardship, distress, and separations of all kinds abound in human life. How can we face these difficulties? Paul is convinced that nothing in all creation can separate us from the love of God in Jesus Christ.

A. Read Romans 5 and 8, and then read the Background and The People, Places, and Times sections.

B. Think about some instances in your past when God's love and reconciliation were made very plain to you. Be prepared to share these stories to the class.

C. Pray specifically for each student in your class. If they need to reconcile with God or one another, this lesson should prompt them to take action.

O—Open the Lesson

A. Have a student read the In Focus story. How is Dorothy's experience both filled with love and reconciliation?

B. Briefly share your reconciliation story and give a couple of students time to do the same.

P—Present the Scriptures

A. Read the Focal Verses; Background; and The People, Places, and Times sections as a class.

B. Answer the Search the Scripture and Discuss the Meaning questions.

E—Explore the Meaning

A. Put the words from the Words You Should Know section up where the class can see them.

B. Have several students read the different definitions and add to them or give illustrations.

N—Next Steps for Application

A. Reflect on the Make It Happen section.

B. Have the students write down one thing they plan to do this week as a result of what they have learned or been reminded of in this lesson concerning God's love and reconciliation.

C. Assign the Daily Bible Readings for the upcoming week

Worship Guide

For the Superintendent or Teacher
Theme: God's Reconciling Love
Song: "Oh, How He Loves You and Me"
Devotional Reading: Romans 1:1–15

God's Reconciling Love

Bible Background • ROMANS 5:1–11, 8:31–39
Printed Text • ROMANS 5:6–11, 8:31–39 | Devotional Reading • ROMANS 1:1–15

—————— Aim for Change ——————

By the end of the lesson, we will: EXPLAIN the meaning of justification by faith; EXPERIENCE the joy of God's reconciling love; and LIVE OUT God's reconciling love in the world.

————— 🦋 In Focus 🔍 —————

Dorothy scrolled through various video clips on her computer. For some unknown reason, her eyes landed on a message by a famous preacher titled "God's Love." Something about his facial expression made her want to listen. He began to describe the overwhelming love that God has for us. He went on to state that words failed to accurately describe the love that he experienced from God. Dorothy wanted that love. She had just been down in the dumps about her latest failed relationship. She had thought that Greg was the one. He was kind and smart and very handsome. The only thing was he wanted to move too fast sexually, and Dorothy was committed to abstinence before marriage. Greg didn't want any of that and broke up with her.

Dorothy stopped the speech right there. She could already feel tears spilling over and her heart starting to race. *God, when is the last time I felt that way about You? So overwhelmed by Your love, Your Son dying for me, Your concern over me, and Your presence with me now. God, I confess I've been distracted by so many things that I drifted away from the simple truth of how much You love me.* Dorothy continued to let the tears fall and the prayers tumbling silently from her heart, crying, confessing—completely overwhelmed by God's great and marvelous love.

What are the words that you would use to describe the love that God has for us?

—————— Keep in Mind ——————

"Nor height, nor depth, nor any other creature, shall be able to separate us from the love of God, which is in Christ Jesus our Lord" (Romans 8:39).

"Nor height, nor depth, nor any other creature, shall be able to separate us from the love of God, which is in Christ Jesus our Lord" (Romans 8:39).

Focal Verses

KJV **Romans 5:6** For when we were yet without strength, in due time Christ died for the ungodly.

7 For scarcely for a righteous man will one die: yet adventure for a good man some would even dare to die?

8 But God commendeth his love toward us, in that, while we were yet sinners, Christ died for us.

9 Much more then, being now justified by his blood, we shall be saved from wrath through him.

10 For if, when we were enemies, we were reconciled to God by the death of his Son, much more, being reconciled, we shall be saved by his life.

11 And not only so, but we also joy in God through our Lord Jesus Christ, by whom we have now received the atonement.

8:31 What shall we then say to these things? If God be for us, who can be against us?

32 He that spared not his own Son, but delivered him up for us all, how shall he not with him also freely give us all things?

33 Who shall lay anything to the charge of God's elect? It is God that justifieth.

34 Who is he that condemneth? It is Christ that died, yea rather, that is risen again, who is even at the right hand of God, who also maketh intercession for us.

35 Who shall separate us from the love of Christ? shall tribulation, or distress, or persecution, or famine, or nakedness, or peril, or sword?

36 As it is written, For thy sake we are killed all the day long; we are accounted as sheep for the slaughter.

37 Nay, in all these things we are more than conquerors through him that loved us.

NLT **Romans 5:6** When we were utterly helpless, Christ came at just the right time and died for us sinners.

7 Now, most people would not be willing to die for an upright person, though someone might perhaps be willing to die for a person who is especially good.

8 But God showed his great love for us by sending Christ to die for us while we were still sinners.

9 And since we have been made right in God's sight by the blood of Christ, he will certainly save us from God's condemnation.

10 For since our friendship with God was restored by the death of his Son while we were still his enemies, we will certainly be saved through the life of his Son.

11 So now we can rejoice in our wonderful new relationship with God because our Lord Jesus Christ has made us friends of God.

8:31 What shall we say about such wonderful things as these? If God is for us, who can ever be against us?

32 Since he did not spare even his own Son but gave him up for us all, won't he also give us everything else?

33 Who dares accuse us whom God has chosen for his own? No one—for God himself has given us right standing with himself.

34 Who then will condemn us? No one—for Christ Jesus died for us and was raised to life for us, and he is sitting in the place of honor at God's right hand, pleading for us.

35 Can anything ever separate us from Christ's love? Does it mean he no longer loves us if we have trouble or calamity, or are persecuted, or hungry, or destitute, or in danger, or threatened with death?

36 (As the Scriptures say, "For your sake we are killed every day; we are being slaughtered like sheep.)"

38 For I am persuaded, that neither death, nor life, nor angels, nor principalities, nor powers, nor things present, nor things to come,

39 Nor height, nor depth, nor any other creature, shall be able to separate us from the love of God, which is in Christ Jesus our Lord.

37 No, despite all these things, overwhelming victory is ours through Christ, who loved us.

38 And I am convinced that nothing can ever separate us from God's love. Neither death nor life, neither angels nor demons neither our fears for today nor our worries about tomorrow—not even the powers of hell can separate us from God's love.

39 No power in the sky above or in the earth below—indeed, nothing in all creation will ever be able to separate us from the love of God that is revealed in Christ Jesus our Lord.

The People, Places, and Times

Ungodly. The beginning chapters of Romans point to the sinfulness of people. No one can merit any favor from God at all. The implication is that everyone is ungodly and suffers repulsion in God's eyes—morally weak, unable to figure spiritual things correctly or redeem ourselves. The ungodly are definitely not deserving of the Father's favor. In the context of the letter to the Roman church, which included both Jews and Gentiles, to suggest that everyone is ungodly reveals that we are all equal in God's eyes and is intended to break down divisions in the community.

Due time. Jesus came in a season that was declared and set by the Father. According to God's plan, this was the perfect time for Christ to come into the world (Galatians 4:4). Christians have a great assurance from the fact that God had planned for Christ's redemption and started the process at what He knew was the perfect time for it.

Background

Through Christ, God reconciled the world to Himself. Once a person trusts Christ for their salvation, their sin is no longer counted against

them and their relationship with God has new intimacy. Christ is the instrument God used to unite human beings back into a right relationship with Him (Colossians 1:20–21).

Reconciliation with God is needed because unbelievers' relationship with Him was broken through sin. God is never at fault. Unlike human relationships, where both parties must admit their sin before reconciliation can take place, God never has to admit His incorrect behavior. He is holy, perfect, and blameless. The sinner must admit their sin before God, confessing their inability to save themselves or fix this relationship on their own.

The relationship between God and humankind was so broken that humankind is called God's enemy (Romans 5:10). Humanity—encompassing everyone, because all have sinned (Romans 3:23)—is hostile and angry and it totally does not understand God. In contrast, a person who pursues God and wants to make things right with Him recognizes the great sacrifice made through Christ's death as the way to make peace with God.

When Christ died on the Cross, the war ended. The unbeliever accepted God's terms of peace. The Christian no longer has judgment and wrath hanging over his or her head. Because of Christ, the relationship between God and His followers is no longer adversarial, but friendly (John 15:15).

At-A-Glance

1. Nothing Greater (Romans 5:6–11)
2. Nothing Separating (8:31–39)

In Depth

1. Nothing Greater (Romans 5:6–11)

Paul vividly describes the love of God. The holy, almighty God generously and freely gives His love to those who are ungodly, undeserving, unlovable, and unlovely. When God decided the time was right, He sent Jesus to die on behalf of the people just described—which is everyone (Galatians 4:4). To become a part of God's family, the sinner must admit, "I am all of the above, and Jesus died to save weak and helpless me."

God's love and sacrifice is uniquely different from any earthly compassion. A courageous person might give his or her life for a decent human being or a good cause. It's not uncommon to hear a story about a parent who wrapping themselves around his or her child to save his or her life at the cost of his or her own. But it's unbelievable to think anyone would die for an enemy. To give your own beloved child to die for people who hate and reject you—that's a crazy love. Yet this is exactly what God did to show His love for humankind. There is no greater love!

In addition to this amazing love, Christians are now justified. In other words, believers can be assured that God's planned wrath, anger, and punishment have been placed on Jesus at the Cross. While the ungodly turned their backs to God, Christ died shedding His own innocent blood. Through His own sacrifice Christ took the initiative to reconcile people back to Him.

This personal relationship with God does not begin with death but in the moment one trusts Christ for their salvation. Christ makes all this possible, a wellspring of continual joy in the lives of His followers.

2. Nothing Separating (8:31–39)

In the first part of Romans, Paul recorded several cold, hard facts about the Christian's relationship to God, tackling serious doctrinal issues. In the later chapters, however, Paul reveals more of the softer, loving side of God. Paul begins by asking a question: "If God be for us, who can be against us?" Most think God is in their corner, Christian or not. But one little word indicates some doubt—if. Just because a man thinks God is with him does not make it so. God is only for an individual if that person is reconciled to God through Jesus Christ.

Paul ends this chapter by assuring believers that none of the world's troubles can keep them down for long. Paul listed every extreme he could name, declaring nothing in heaven or on earth can separate God's love from humankind. Many things—Satan, our conscience, and others—constantly accuse us and remind us of past sins and failures, but God won't allow it. He calls us conquerors, victors—secure in God's love.

Search the Scriptures

1. God show His love for us through Christ dying for us (Romans 5:8). How does this inform or influence the way we show love to others?

2. Does the guarantee that God will freely give us all things (8:32) sound too good to be true? Explain why.

Discuss the Meaning

When a person becomes a Christian, he or she now can experience the joy of God's love and reconciliation—making him or herself an example to the world.

The big question is how to live out this truth on a daily basis. How would our lives be different if we truly internalized God's love? Would we love all of our neighbors? Would we be confident in our gifts and abilities? Would we take a stand for biblical truths?

Lesson in Our Society

All over the Internet are articles about how to have a better relationship with your spouse, children, friends, and co-workers. People desire to improve their interpersonal relationships. However, the foundation of that desire is easy to ignore; a good relationship with others starts with God. As His examples and spokespeople to the world, Christians must ensure that their personal walk with God is loving and intimate. Then, with that overflow of love, we can teach the world how to love each other and improve all relationships.

Make It Happen

Find a quiet place for a little personal retreat, just you and the Lord. Spend some time there to review the Scripture and insights in this lesson:

- God loves me!
- God proved His love for me by sending Jesus to die for my sin.
- God wants a close relationship with me; where am I?
- Do I need to confess? (Admit to God what He's showing you.)
- How can I repent? (Examine behaviors and ask God to empower you to go the opposite way you've been going.)

Follow the Spirit

What God wants me to do:

_____

_____

_____

_____

Remember Your Thoughts

Special insights I have learned:

_____

_____

_____

_____

More Light on the Text

Romans 5:6–11, 8:31–39

6 For when we were yet without strength, in due time Christ died for the ungodly.

At the appointed time, Christ offered Himself as our eternal sacrifice "when we were yet without strength"—that is, when we were powerless to save ourselves and thus ready to die. Christ's death reveals three properties of God's love. First, He did this for the "ungodly," those whose character and sinful nature are repulsive in God's eyes. Second, He did this when they were "without strength"—nothing stood between humanity and damnation but divine compassion. Third, He did this "in due time," when it was most appropriate that it should take place. Throughout, Paul uses the language of "we," indicating that he considers himself also to have been without strength, ungodly and a sinner (v. 8).

7 For scarcely for a righteous man will one die: yet peradventure for a good man some would even dare to die. 8 But God commendeth his love toward us, in that, while we were yet sinners, Christ died for us.

The Apostle Paul now proceeds to illustrate God's compassion. Few people would be willing to sacrifice their lives for a "righteous man" of exceptional character. A few more might be willing to die for a person who, besides being exceptional, was also distinguished as a benefactor to society. But God, in glorious contrast to what people might do for each other, displayed His love "while we were yet sinners"— that is, in a state of absolute rebellion. Although most people would not be willing to die to save a wicked or evil person, Christ died for us.

9 Much more then, being now justified by his blood, we shall be saved from wrath through him. 10 For if, when we were enemies, we were reconciled to God by the death of his Son, much more, being reconciled, we shall be saved by his life.

Having been "justified by his blood," we shall be saved from wrath through Christ's sacrifice. Christ's death restored our relationship with God while we were in open rebellion against Him. Since we are now reconciled, "we shall be saved by His life." If Christ's sacrifice was offered for people incapable of the least appreciation for God's love or Christ's labors on their behalf, how much more will He do all that remains to be done? To be "saved from wrath through him" refers to the entire work of salvation—from the moment of justification to the great white throne of judgment (Revelation 20:11–15), when the wrath of God shall be revealed to all who ignore the Gospel of Jesus. The Apostle Jude best described Christ's continuing work of salvation when he said that Christ "is able to keep you from falling, and to present you faultless before the presence of his glory with exceeding joy" (from Jude 24).

11 And not only so, but we also joy in God through our Lord Jesus Christ, by whom we have now received the atonement.

"And not only so" refers to the blessing Paul mentioned previously. We not only find joy in our newfound peace, standing, and salvation, but we rejoice in God Himself. We find joy in our God for what He has done and who He is. Our joy comes from our union with Christ, who brought about our atonement.

"Atonement" (Gk. *katallage*, **kah-tah-lah-GAY**) is the noun form of the verb for "reconcile" in verse 10. It indicates a shift from a negative relationship to a positive one, or a broken relationship to a healthy one. Paul here focuses on the restored relationship provided by Christ's atoning death. This restored relationship with God brings about joy, or more literally boasting (see v. 2, "rejoice").

Atonement is the gracious act by which God restores a relationship of harmony and unity between Himself and believers. The word contains parts that express this great truth in simple but profound terms: "at-one." Through God's atoning grace and forgiveness, we are reinstated to a relationship of being "at one" with God.

8:31 What shall we then say to these things? If God be for us, who can be against us? 32 He that spared not his own Son, but delivered him up for us all, how shall he not with him also freely give us all things?

As a result of this knowledge of divine sovereignty, Paul exults in the comfort of knowing God is for His people. He asks and answers his own question: "If God be for us, who can be against us?" The concept of God being for His people runs throughout the Old Testament (Psalm 56:9, 105:12–15; Isaiah 54:17). What makes Paul's words unique is that now through the lens of Christ, we even see the hard times as under God's control. We face trials and opposition to conform us to Christ's image. God is for us in all things good or bad. With that in mind, Paul says no one is a formidable foe.

Not only that, but God did not spare (Gk. *pheidomai*, **FAY-doh-meye**) His own Son when it came to our good. The word *spare* means to refrain or keep from harm. The sense in this verse is that God did not hold Him back as a treasure. The same word is used in the Septuagint, when Joseph tells his family to "regard not your stuff," or not take their treasured belongings to Egypt (Genesis 45:20). God delivered (Gk. *paradidomi*, **pah-rah-DEE-doh-me**) Him, which means to hand over or give up. The word is often used for betrayal, as in Judas' betrayal of Jesus (Mark 14:10), as well as for the Sanhedrin's giving of Jesus over to Pilate (Mark 15:1), and Pilate's giving of Jesus over to the crowd in Jerusalem (Luke 23:25) and the Roman soldiers for crucifixion. In this sense, Paul is showing that God was sovereignly guiding the entirety of Jesus' death on the Cross. God had ordained that Jesus would be crucified for our good since before the creation of the world (Revelation 13:8).

This understanding of God's gracious act in giving Jesus "for us all" is the grounds by which Paul asks rhetorically, "How shall he not with him also freely give us all things?" The two words "freely give" (Gk. *charizomai*, **khah-REED-zoh-meye**) are actually one word in Greek, meaning to give as a sign of one's goodwill toward another. Paul emphatically states that when we see what God has done in Christ, we can be assured that God has good will toward us.

33 Who shall lay any thing to the charge of God's elect? It is God that justifieth. 34 Who is he that condemneth? It is Christ that died,

yea rather, that is risen again, who is even at the right hand of God, who also maketh intercession for us.

The argument continues as Paul explains the reasons someone could disbelieve God's good will toward His people. He proceeds with legal terminology and asks, "Who shall lay anything to the charge of God's elect?" The phrase "lay anything to the charge" (Gk. *egkaleo*, **eng-kah-LEH-oh**) means to accuse or file a formal legal complaint against someone. For Paul, the answer is obviously no one; God "justifieth" (Gk. *dikaioo*, **dee-kie-OH-oh**), or makes or pronounces one as righteous.

There is no one to condemn (Gk. *katakrino*, **kah-tah-KREE-no**) the believer. The word "condemn" means to pronounce guilt and punishment for a crime in a legal context. Paul's answer to the question of "Who is he that condemneth?" is the work of Christ. This work is not limited to Jesus' death and resurrection, but it also continues with Jesus at the right hand of God, making intercession (Gk. *entugchano*, **en-toon-KHAH-noh**) for us. To make intercession or intercede is to petition an authority on behalf of someone else. Christ speaks to God on behalf of the Christian. Believers' confidence that God hears us and no longer condemns us is assured by Christ's righteousness.

35 Who shall separate us from the love of Christ? shall tribulation, or distress, or persecution, or famine, or nakedness, or peril, or sword? 36 As it is written, For thy sake we are killed all the day long; we are accounted as sheep for the slaughter. 37 Nay, in all these things we are more than conquerors through him that loved us.

Next Paul raises the question of possible separation from Christ's love. The different earthly woes of God's people are listed. Tribulation (Gk. *thlipsis*, **THLEEP-seese**) is the first problem listed; this word comes from *thlibo*, which means to press or squash and metaphorically has the sense of oppression or affliction. The next is distress (Gk. *stenochoria*, **ste-no-kho-REE-ah**), which has the sense of being in constricted conditions, where it seems the world is falling down on someone. The third problem is persecution (Gk. *diogmos*, **dee-og-MOCE**), the systematic hunting down of believers for torture and execution in an effort to destroy the religion. This was a real threat for Paul, who faced much persecution in his lifetime. Famine is the shortage of food, resulting in acute hunger and death. The word for nakedness is *gumnotes* (Gk. **goom-NO-tes**), which in this context means insufficient clothing, not total exposure. Peril (Gk. *kindunos*, **KEEN-doo-noce**) is danger from any circumstance; Paul used this word in reference to his being in danger as an apostle (2 Corinthians 11:26). The believer also faces the reality of the sword (Gk. *machaira*, **MAH-kheye-rah**), which is the word for the small sword as opposed to a large one. This designation causes some to question whether Paul intends the official "sword" of the state. However, this word is also used in Romans 13:4 in connection with the state's authority to punish. Here, Paul may have described official state execution. The general sense is that the believers face death at any moment.

Paul then quotes from Psalm 44:22. This psalm was often quoted by rabbis in the second century A.D. with martyrdom in view, and Paul may have had this in view here. In contrast to this dismal fate, verse 37 has triumph and hope. Although the Christian's life is similar to a sheep prepared for the slaughter, Paul says this is not the whole story. Believers are more than conquerors through Christ. The KJV translates the Greek as "we are more than conquerors" (*hypernikao*, **hoo-per-nee-KAH-oh**). The Greek term is a single word, with the basic verb for conquering with an intensifying prefix that tells the church this will be no normal

victory—it will be the ultimate victory. To think of ultimate victory as persecuted subjects only magnifies God's power to reward the faithful.

38 For I am persuaded, that neither death, nor life, nor angels, nor principalities, nor powers, nor things present, nor things to come, 39 Nor height, nor depth, nor any other creature, shall be able to separate us from the love of God, which is in Christ Jesus our Lord.

Paul is totally convinced. Nothing physical, social, or spiritual can separate us from the love of God in Christ Jesus. Paul speaks of items in the three categories that would have the capacity to separate us from God's love. Paul summarizes these, noting the opposites: life nor death, heights nor depths, things present or things to come with all of their abilities to frighten, paralyze, or make us turn away. None of these can separate us from the love of God.

Say It Correctly

Commendeth. ku-**MEN**-dith.
Peradventure. per-ad-**VEN**-chur.

Daily Bible Readings

MONDAY
Mutually Sharing the Gospel of Christ
(Romans 1:1–15)

TUESDAY
Fruit of Justification by Faith
(Romans 5:1–5)

WEDNESDAY
Grace Abounded through Jesus Christ
(Romans 5:18–21)

THURSDAY
Believers' Present Suffering and Future Glory
(Romans 8:18–25)

FRIDAY
God's Will Shapes Human Direction
(Romans 8:26–30)

SATURDAY
Paul's Faithful Ministry Despite Suffering
(2 Corinthians 11:21b–27)

SUNDAY
God's Love Never Changes
(Romans 5:6–11, 8:31–39)

Notes

Teaching Tips

Words You Should Know

A. Sheep (John 10:1) *probaton* (Gk.)—Any four-footed, tame animal accustomed to grazing, especially sheep and goats.

B. Shepherd (v. 2) *poimen* (Gk.)—A herdsman.

Teacher Preparation

Unifying Principle— True Love. Everyone is looking for a leader who will solve all the problems of the world. Where can we find the leader we seek? Jesus, as the Good Shepherd, is the leader who shows and imparts God's love to those who follow.

A. Pray for your class and wisdom concerning the lesson.

B. Study John 10:1–15. Look in a Bible dictionary or commentary for more information on the role shepherds during this time period.

C. Prepare the companion lesson in the *Precepts For Living®* Personal Study Guide.

D. Write a list composed of the qualities people look for in good leaders.

O—Open the Lesson

A. After receiving prayer requests, ask a volunteer to open the class with prayer and include the Aim for Change.

B. Have a volunteer read the In Focus story. Discuss.

C. Ask the class: "Do you recall a time when a leader betrayed your trust?" "How did you respond? How did it affect your trust of others?" Then say: "There will always be good and bad leaders. We have to be careful in choosing who we will follow. We can look to Jesus as the example because He shows love to all who follow Him."

P—Present the Scriptures

A. Ask for a volunteer to read the Focal Verses.

B. Examine the verses, utilizing Words You Should Know; The People, Places, and Times; Background; the At-A-Glance outline; and More Light on the Text sections.

E—Explore the Meaning

A. Answer the Search the Scriptures questions.

B. Summarize the Discuss the Meaning, Lesson in Our Society, and Make It Happen sections.

C. Connect them with today's theme.

N—Next Steps for Application

A. Summarize the lesson.

B. Remind students to read and meditate on their Daily Bible Readings.

C. Solicit prayer requests and close in prayer.

Worship Guide

For the Superintendent or Teacher
Theme: God's Preserving Love
Song: "Alas! And Did My Savior Bleed"
Devotional Reading: Matthew 18:1–5, 10–14

God's Preserving Love

Bible Background • JOHN 10:1–15
Printed Text • JOHN 10:1–15 | Devotional Reading • MATTHEW 18:1–5, 10–14

Aim for Change

By the end of this lesson, we will: EXPLORE the metaphor of Jesus as the Good Shepherd who opens the gate for the sheep; AFFIRM the love of God expressed in the life and ministry of Jesus, the Good Shepherd; and RESPOND to God's persevering love by loving others.

In Focus

Jasmine sat quietly on the back pew of Emmanuel Methodist Church, like she had for the last three weeks. Her co-worker, Jaylen, insisted she come because her new pastor and his family were genuine, loving Christians. Jasmine did not trust anyone. At the last church she belonged to, the pastor was very vicious toward the members and regularly took money from the offering plates.

As Jasmine listened to Reverend Shepherd preach about the love of God, she felt the power of God begin to take away the pain she had. At the end of the worship service, a woman approached Jasmine. "Hi. My name is Miriam. I'm the pastor's wife. We noticed you have been visiting for the last couple weeks. The pastor wanted me to invite you to go out to dinner with us. We try to invite members and new visitors out at least once or twice a month so we can get to know each other better. Do you think you can come?"

Jasmine hesitated for a moment and then said, "I guess I can come."

"I'm glad. You can meet us in the parking lot."

After spending the afternoon with the pastor and his wife, Jasmine felt Jaylen was right. So far, from what she had observed and experienced, they were leaders who loved and cared about the people.

Good leaders show love toward others. In today's lesson, we will evaluate how the Good Shepherd, Jesus, loves and cares for us. How have you followed Jesus' leadership in your life?

Keep in Mind

"I am the good shepherd, and know my sheep, and am known of mine. As the Father knoweth me, even so know I the Father: and I lay down my life for the sheep" (John 10:14–15).

"I am the good shepherd, and know my sheep, and am known of mine. As the Father knoweth me, even so know I the Father: and I lay down my life for the sheep" (John 10:14–15).

Focal Verses

KJV John 10:1 Verily, verily, I say unto you, He that entereth not by the door into the sheepfold, but climbeth up some other way, the same is a thief and a robber.

2 But he that entereth in by the door is the shepherd of the sheep.

3 To him the porter openeth; and the sheep hear his voice: and he calleth his own sheep by name, and leadeth them out.

4 And when he putteth forth his own sheep, he goeth before them, and the sheep follow him: for they know his voice.

5 And a stranger will they not follow, but will flee from him: for they know not the voice of strangers.

6 This parable spake Jesus unto them: but they understood not what things they were which he spake unto them.

7 Then said Jesus unto them again, Verily, verily, I say unto you, I am the door of the sheep.

8 All that ever came before me are thieves and robbers: but the sheep did not hear them.

9 I am the door: by me if any man enter in, he shall be saved, and shall go in and out, and find pasture.

10 The thief cometh not, but for to steal, and to kill, and to destroy: I am come that they might have life, and that they might have it more abundantly.

11 I am the good shepherd: the good shepherd giveth his life for the sheep.

12 But he that is an hireling, and not the shepherd, whose own the sheep are not, seeth the wolf coming, and leaveth the sheep, and fleeth: and the wolf catcheth them, and scattereth the sheep.

13 The hireling fleeth, because he is an hireling, and careth not for the sheep.

14 I am the good shepherd, and know my sheep, and am known of mine.

NLT John 10:1 "I tell you the truth, anyone who sneaks over the wall of a sheepfold, rather than going through the gate, must surely be a thief and a robber!

2 But the one who enters through the gate is the shepherd of the sheep.

3 The gatekeeper opens the gate for him, and the sheep hear his voice and come to him. He calls his own sheep by name and leads them out.

4 After he has gathered his own flock, he walks ahead of them, and they follow him because they recognize his voice.

5 They won't follow a stranger; they will run from him because they don't recognize his voice."

6 Those who heard Jesus use this illustration didn't understand what he meant,

7 so he explained it to them: "I tell you the truth, I am the gate for the sheep.

8 "All who came before me were thieves and robbers. But the true sheep did not listen to them.

9 Yes, I am the gate. Those who come in through me will be saved. They will come and go freely and will find good pastures.

10 The thief's purpose is to steal and kill and destroy. My purpose is to give life in all its fullness.

11 I am the good shepherd. The good shepherd sacrifices his life for the sheep.

12 A hired hand will run when he sees a wolf coming. He will leave the sheep because they don't belong to him and he isn't their shepherd. And so the wolf attacks them and scatters the flock.

13 The hired hand runs away because he's working only for the money and doesn't really care about the sheep.

14 I am the good shepherd; I know my own sheep, and they know me,

15 As the Father knoweth me, even so know I the Father: and I lay down my life for the sheep.

15 just as my Father knows me and I know the Father. So I sacrifice my life for the sheep."

The People, Places, and Times

Pharisees. The Pharisees were religious leaders who practiced the strict observation of the Mosaic Torah. Their power provided them great influence among the people, especially in the synagogues. They thought it was very important to follow God's will. The Pharisees believed, like Jesus, in the resurrection of the dead. However, they did not believe Jesus was the Messiah because He constantly violated accepted interpretations of the Law of Moses called Oral Torah or Mishnah Torah ("a second Torah," i.e., established Jewish explanations of the meaning of Moses' teachings).

Sabbath. The Sabbath day is considered a time for rest and a day to remember what God had done. It was instituted by God through Moses (Exodus 16:23–29; 20:8–11). It is observed because during creation, God rested on the seventh day from His work. Therefore, it is a holy day. The Israelites' promise to keep the Sabbath throughout all generations symbolized the covenant between them and God (Exodus 31:17).

The Pharisees had established thirty–nine categories of actions forbidden on the Sabbath, based on their own interpretation of God's Law and on Jewish custom. No work was permitted on the Sabbath. They frequently accused Jesus of breaking the Sabbath. Jesus never permitted their interpretation of the Law to hinder Him from His ministry on earth.

Background

Jesus' ministry caused conflict with the religious leaders, especially the Pharisees. John records two times Jesus healed on the Sabbath (5:1–17, 9:1–7). On both occasions the Pharisees accused Him of violating the Law. In John 9, the blind man whom Jesus healed was taken to the Pharisees, who questioned him. He told them Jesus was "a prophet" (9:17). The religious leaders were divided in their understanding of whom Jesus was. However, it had already been predicted that the Messiah would give sight to the blind (Isaiah 29:18, 35:5, 42:7). Jesus had proven once again that He was the Messiah.

The Pharisees even questioned the man's parents, who told them to ask their son what happened. They were afraid of being put out of the synagogue, which meant they could possibly be excommunicated and other Jews would not socialize with them. Their son was not afraid of the consequences and told them his answer was the same as the first time they asked him. The Pharisees threw the man out of the synagogue, and he was ostracized by everyone.

The man's joy of being healed had been transformed into rejection and isolation from others. What happens when we feel lost and alone? The Good Shepherd searches for us.

At-A-Glance

1. The Gatekeeper (John 10:1–10)
2. The Good Shepherd (vv. 11–15)

In Depth

1. The Gatekeeper (John 10:1–10)

Jesus told a parable in 10:1–5 that described Himself as the gatekeeper and Good Shepherd. At night, sheep were gathered into a secure area such as caves, sheds, or open areas surrounded by walls made of stones and branches. The area only had one entrance. The sheep were protected from thieves, bad weather, wild animals, or wandering off. The shepherd remained with them to make sure the sheep were kept secure. Judaism was the religion of the Law, in which God's chosen people were kept and guarded in custody until Christ came.

The Pharisees lacked understanding, so Jesus gave further explanation about the parable. Jesus is now "the gate" through which any person who enters shall be saved (v. 7). All other religious leaders who tell of another way are thieves. Jesus is the only way; "no man cometh unto the Father, but by [Him]" (cf. 14:6). His sheep know not to follow the thieves. Jesus is our protector, provider, and sustainer (vv. 9–10). His interest is in the sheep, but thieves are only interested in themselves and want to destroy lives. Jesus loves us and wants the best for our lives.

2. The Good Shepherd (vv. 11–15)

Jesus declared, "I am the good shepherd" (v. 11; cf. Matthew 18:12–13; Luke 15:4–6). Shepherds often risk dangers to save the sheep, which are loved and worthy of protection. The hired hand is paid to take of the sheep, so when danger comes, he abandons them (vv. 12–13); it is just a job to him. They have no personal interest, just like some religious leaders (Jeremiah 23:1–3; Ezekiel 34:5–10; Zechariah 11:15–17).

The Good Shepherd has an intimate relationship with the sheep, His people (vv. 14–15). They love Him and He loves them. When the sheep turn to Him, the Shepherd offers guidance. Whatever their needs, He provides (Psalm 23). The Shepherd is trustworthy because He proved His love for the sheep by laying down His life (v. 15). Jesus' sacrifice on the Cross was based on His love for the world and His desire to save us. This was pure love.

Search the Scriptures

1. Why do the sheep follow the gatekeeper (John 10:4)?

2. What did Jesus mean when He said, "I lay down my life for the sheep" (v. 15)?

Discuss the Meaning

Jesus said, "The thief cometh not, but for to steal, and to kill, and to destroy: I am come that they might have life, and that they might have it more abundantly" (v. 10). Whom do you identify as "the thief" in today's society? What does an "abundant life" mean?

Lesson in Our Society

We encounter both bad and good leaders in our lifetimes, but we have to ask God for discernment about whom to follow and seek guidance from. Authentic, good leaders will take the time to show love and concern. They do not have hidden motives for their actions, and they are not the first to run when trouble arises. They stay with us as we go through the valleys of life. This is the heart of a genuine leader.

Make It Happen

God's love for us was proven through the sacrifice and death of Jesus Christ. He continues to provide, protect, and guide us each day. Others need to know and experience the love of God. How can that be accomplished? Show interest in others and offer to help. It can be a kind word, a listening ear, an encouraging card, running errands for the sick, babysitting, etc. If they ask, let them know it is the love of God shining through your actions.

Follow the Spirit

What God wants me to do:

_____

_____

_____

_____

Remember Your Thoughts

Special insights I have learned:

_____

_____

_____

_____

More Light on the Text

John 10:1–15

1 Verily, verily, I say unto you, He that entereth not by the door into the sheepfold, but climbeth up some other way, the same is a thief and a robber.

In this discourse, Jesus employs the familiar analogy of a shepherd and his flock to teach an important lesson about Himself and His relationship with believers. Applying the imagery of the shepherd to kings and priests was a common practice in Middle Eastern culture. In the Old Testament, the shepherd was often used to symbolize a royal caretaker of God's people (cf. 2 Samuel 5:2; Isaiah 44:28). God Himself was referred to as the "Shepherd of Israel" (see Genesis 49:24; Psalm 23:1–4, 80:1). The "sheepfold" (Gk. *probaton*, **PRO-bah-tone**) or

herd of sheep were kept in a walled enclosure with one entrance. Usually, a sheepfold would hold several flocks. The "shepherd" (Gk. *poimen*, **poy-MANE**), or gatekeeper, set up sleeping posts near the entrance to ward off wild beasts, thieves, and other intruders.

The parable depicts the shepherd as the only one allowed access to the flock. The shepherd is in stark contrast to a "thief" or a "robber," who must sneak into the fold. Unlike the stranger, from whom the sheep run away, the shepherd has established a relationship with the sheep. The welfare of his sheep is uppermost in his mind.

2 But he that entereth in by the door is the shepherd of the sheep. 3 To him the porter openeth; and the sheep hear his voice: and he calleth his own sheep by name, and leadeth them out.

The shepherd was allowed access to the sheep, as evidenced by the "porter" (Gk. *thuroros*, **thoo-row-ROCE**, meaning "gatekeeper") opening the door for him. The shepherd rose in the mornings to call out his sheep by name. He rightfully entered the fold because the sheep were his, and their best interest was his primary concern. He had no intention of bringing harm to them. Regardless of the number of flocks in the fold, the shepherd called out to his own by name, and they recognized and responded to his familiar "voice" (Gk. *phone*, **fo-NAY**, meaning "sound").

4 And when he putteth forth his own sheep, he goeth before them, and the sheep follow him: for they know his voice.

The shepherd went ahead of the sheep instead of driving them from behind. Their bond was so strong and intimate that the sheep willingly followed him out of the sheepfold as he went ahead of them. They knew the sound of his voice, which reassured them. His presence and his rod and staff brought comfort to the sheep (cf. Psalm 23:4).

5 And a stranger will they not follow, but will flee from him: for they know not the voice of strangers.

Jesus used this parable to teach how the shepherd formed his flock. As in verses 3 and 4, the imagery used in verse 5 communicates a sense of intimacy. Note the role the shepherd's "voice" (Gk. *phone*) plays in this discourse. The sheep followed because they knew the shepherd's voice, but they would never follow a stranger whose voice they did not recognize. The sheep that stayed safe recognized the voice of the shepherd. They came to the shepherd because he called them—the proper response for sheep.

6 This parable spake Jesus unto them: but they understood not what things they were which he spake unto them. 7 Then said Jesus unto them again, Verily, verily, I say unto you, I am the door of the sheep.

Up to this point, Jesus has spoken figuratively about the Pharisees' situation. He realized His audience would certainly understand the analogy of the shepherd/sheep relationship; unfortunately, they missed His intended spiritual lesson. So, Jesus shifts metaphors and declares, "I am the door of the sheep." Again, His hearers would be familiar with the figure of a shepherd as a "door" (Gk. *thura*, **THOO-rah**) of the sheep. Since shepherds habitually lie down across the entrance of the sheepfold with their bodies, forming a barrier to thieves and wild beasts, they speak of themselves as the door to let the flock in or out and to protect it from intruders. Through the door, the flock goes in and out to graze and to rest. If attacked or frightened, the sheep can retreat into the security of the fold.

Several times in the Gospel of John, Jesus describes Himself using the phrase "I am" (Gk. *ego eimi*, **eh-GO ay-ME**; cf. 6:35, 8:12, 9:5, 11:25, 14:6, 15:1, 5). Christ's usage of the phrase in this manner leaves no question about His claim to deity. In fact, to a perceptive Jew who understood the term *ego eimi* as a reference to Exodus 3:14, Jesus was making Himself equal to God (cf. John 10:33).

8 All that ever came before me are thieves and robbers: but the sheep did not hear them.

This verse is not a reference to Old Testament prophets, but to all Messianic pretenders and religious charlatans, like many of the Pharisees and chief priests of the time. Jesus describes them as "thieves" (Gk. *kleptes*) who divest the unwary of their precious possessions, and "robbers" (Gk. *lestes*) who plunder brazenly by violence. They did not care about the spiritual good of the people, only themselves. As a result, the sheep (i.e., those who are faithful) would not heed their voice.

9 I am the door: by me if any man enter in, he shall be saved, and shall go in and out, and find pasture.

Christ claims to be *the* door, not just *a* door. Jesus is explicitly identifying Himself as the means to salvation (cf. Psalm 118:19–21). As the Shepherd, Jesus provides safety and sustenance for His flock. He is the only way of salvation. Through Him, believers find "pasture" (Gk. *nome*, **no-MAY**), or provision for all of their daily needs.

10 The thief cometh not, but for to steal, and to kill, and to destroy: I am come that they might have life, and that they might have it more abundantly.

The thief's motive is diametrically opposed to the shepherd. His interest is selfish. He steals the sheep in order to kill them and feed himself, thus destroying part of the flock. In this description, we see a veiled glimpse into the character of the Pharisees and religious authorities who opposed Jesus. In contrast, Christ is the Life-Giver and Life-Sustainer. His interest is the welfare of the sheep. He enables the sheep to have full and secure lives. The thief takes life, but conversely Christ gives life.

11 I am the good shepherd: the good shepherd giveth his life for the sheep.

The adjective "good" (Gk. *kalos*, **ka-LOCE**) carries the meaning of being a true or a model shepherd. Here, Jesus is referring to the model of a shepherd found in Ezekiel 34:11–16. According to Ezekiel, the good shepherd gathers, feeds, and protects the sheep. A strong bond exists between sheep and shepherd. It was not unusual for Palestinian shepherds to risk their lives for their flocks. Wild beasts, lions, jackals, wolves, and bears were on the prowl. In David's experience as a shepherd, his fights with a lion and a bear over the life of his flock convinced him that God was also able to give Goliath into his hands (1 Samuel 17:34–37). When Jesus says, "I am the good shepherd" (i.e., the true Shepherd), He is expressing how He carries out His mission of salvation.

12 But he that is an hireling, and not the shepherd, whose own the sheep are not, seeth the wolf coming, and leaveth the sheep, and fleeth: and the wolf catcheth them, and scattereth the sheep.

A "hireling" (Gk. *misthotos*, **mees-tho-TOCE**), or hired servant, is someone who is willing to do a specific task for a price. He might not be personally invested in the sheep, but instead he's only willing to do exactly what he is told and not take on additional risks or responsibilities. Therefore, if a wolf shows up, he runs to save his own life, leaving the sheep

to fend for themselves. The result is devastating for the sheep. The hireling's self-interest exposes the flock to fatal danger. Israel had many false religious leaders, selfish kings, and imitation messiahs; as a result, the flock of God suffered constantly from their abuse. This is still the case today, as the church suffers from false teachers and hypocritical leadership.

13 The hireling fleeth, because he is an hireling, and careth not for the sheep. 14 I am the good shepherd, and know my sheep, and am known of mine.

The "hireling" (Gk. *misthotos*) is just that—a hired hand. This reminds one of Israel's selfish kings and false prophets found in the Old Testament. Both here and in the Old Testament, the hired hand's main concern is himself. The sheep are only a means to an end.

By contrast, the "good" (Gk. *kalos*, **kal-OS**, meaning "noble" or "true") shepherd cares for the sheep—so much so that he is willing to lay down his life for them. It is important to note the bond of intimacy between the shepherd and his sheep, as indicated by the phrase "I know" (Gk. *ginosko*, **ghee-NOCE-ko**). The use of the Greek word *ginosko* implies Christ's ownership and watchful oversight of the sheep. The reciprocal point that the sheep know their shepherd identifies the sheep's response to Christ's love and intimate care. Moreover, the use of *ginosko* indicates that this knowledge is of high value to the shepherd.

15 As the Father knoweth me, even so know I the Father: and I lay down my life for the sheep.

The deep mutual knowledge between Christ (the Shepherd) and His sheep is likened to the relationship between the Father and the Son. The "knowing" between God the Father and Jesus, His Son, is a uniquely intimate relationship. The connection between the sheep and the shepherd who knows his sheep and lays down his life for them shows unity of purpose between the Father and the Son. Jesus is more than the Good Shepherd; He is the fulfillment of God's promises to His people. Christ voluntarily laid down His life for us. His death was not an unfortunate accident, but part of the planned purpose of God.

Say It Correctly

Hireling. **HIRE**-leeng.
Fleeth. **FLEE**-ith.

Daily Bible Readings

MONDAY
Why You Don't Understand
(Matthew 13:10–17)

TUESDAY
God Will Rescue the Endangered Sheep
(Ezekiel 34:1–10)

WEDNESDAY
The Shepherd Cares for the Lost
(Matthew 18:1–5, 10–14)

THURSDAY
Pastors Shepherd the Church of God
(Acts 20:25–28)

FRIDAY
Peter, Tend My Sheep
(John 21:15–19)

SATURDAY
The Blind See
(John 9:35–41)

SUNDAY
Jesus the Good Shepherd
(John 10:1–15)

Notes

Teaching Tips

May 7
Bible Study Guide 10

Words You Should Know

A. Evil (Jonah 1:7–8) *ra'* (Heb.)—Distress; misery, injury, calamity.

B. Afraid (v. 10) *yare'* (Heb.)—Fearing; fearful, dreadful; filled with godly fear.

Teacher Preparation

Unifying Principle—When Calamity Comes. When disaster comes, people ask, "Why?" Can human behavior cause bad things to happen? In Jonah's case, human behavior did lead to calamity; however, Jonah discovered that God's love still surrounded him.

A. Pray for your class and wisdom concerning the lesson.

B. Look in a Bible dictionary or commentary for information on Nineveh.

C. Prepare the companion lesson in the *Precepts For Living®* Personal Study Guide.

D. Browse the newspaper and the Internet for current events that involve personal tragedies.

O—Open the Lesson

A. After receiving prayer requests, ask a volunteer to open the class with prayer, including the Aim for Change.

B. Have a volunteer read the In Focus story. Discuss current tragedies in news.

C. Ask the class to recall a time their personal actions caused negative consequences not only for them, but others as well. Did they take full responsibility for their actions? Why or why not? Conclude by saying, "In spite of our misdoings, God still loves us. He will help us through our calamities."

P—Present the Scriptures

A. Ask for a volunteer to read the Focal Verses.

B. Examine the verses, utilizing Words You Should Know; The People, Places, and Times, Background; the At-A-Glance outline; and More Light on the Text sections.

E—Explore the Meaning

A. Answer the Search the Scriptures questions.

B. Summarize the Discuss the Meaning, Lesson in Our Society, and Make It Happen sections.

C. Connect these answers with today's theme.

N—Next Steps for Application

A. Summarize the lesson.

B. Remind students to read and meditate on their Daily Bible Readings.

C. Solicit prayer requests and close in prayer.

Worship Guide

For the Superintendent or Teacher
Theme: God's Sustaining Love
Song: "It Is Well With My Soul"
Devotional Reading: Psalm 139:1–12

God's Sustaining Love

Bible Background • JONAH 1
Printed Text • JONAH 1:7–17 | Devotional Reading • PSALM 139:1–12

—————————— **Aim for Change** ——————————

By the end of the lesson, we will: DISCERN the nature of God's love in the story of Jonah; SENSE how people feel when faced with calamity and how they respond when others think they have caused the calamity; and PRAY for assurance of the presence of God's love in the midst of calamity.

—————————— **In Focus** ——————————

A spring storm had caused major damage throughout the town of Lansdowne. Jumbo's Hoagie Shop had withstood the wind and hail but mysteriously burned down. Mr. Sam was devastated. He and his son, Charles, sat on the curb in tears the next morning. All the residents gathered in disbelief. The store had been in Lansdowne for over 20 years.

The fire chief, Kenneth, asked to speak with Mr. Sam and Charles in the back of the store. "Mr. Sam, I'm so sorry about your store. We figured out what happened. The grill was left on. And when the power went out and then came back on, it caused sparks to fly in the kitchen area. Then flames engulfed the entire building. I'm so sorry." He patted Mr. Sam on the back as he walked away.

"Charles, you were supposed to close up last night. What happened?" Mr. Sam asked.

"Dad, I was talking to Cynthia on the phone. I guess I got distracted and forgot to turn it off. Now, our whole lives are destroyed, and the community will suffer, too." Charles laid his head on his father's shoulder and sobbed." Charles," he hugged his son, "everything will be OK. God will see us through this as we rebuild."

When we make bad choices, others can suffer, too. In today's lesson, we will evaluate how God's love and presence can make a difference in the midst of life's calamities. How has God's presence made a difference when you face the different challenges of life?

—————————— **Keep in Mind** ——————————

"Then were the men exceedingly afraid, and said unto him, Why hast thou done this?"
(Jonah 1:10a).

"Then were the men exceedingly afraid, and said unto him, Why hast thou done this?"
(Jonah 1:10a).

Focal Verses

KJV **Jonah 1:7** And they said every one to his fellow, Come, and let us cast lots, that we may know for whose cause this evil is upon us. So they cast lots, and the lot fell upon Jonah.

8 Then said they unto him, Tell us, we pray thee, for whose cause this evil is upon us; What is thine occupation? and whence comest thou? what is thy country? and of what people art thou?

9 And he said unto them, I am an Hebrew; and I fear the LORD, the God of heaven, which hath made the sea and the dry land.

10 Then were the men exceedingly afraid, and said unto him, Why hast thou done this? For the men knew that he fled from the presence of the LORD, because he had told them.

11 Then said they unto him, What shall we do unto thee, that the sea may be calm unto us? for the sea wrought, and was tempestuous.

12 And he said unto them, Take me up, and cast me forth into the sea; so shall the sea be calm unto you: for I know that for my sake this great tempest is upon you.

13 Nevertheless the men rowed hard to bring it to the land; but they could not: for the sea wrought, and was tempestuous against them.

14 Wherefore they cried unto the LORD, and said, We beseech thee, O LORD, we beseech thee, let us not perish for this man's life, and lay not upon us innocent blood: for thou, O LORD, hast done as it pleased thee.

15 So they took up Jonah, and cast him forth into the sea: and the sea ceased from her raging.

16 Then the men feared the LORD exceedingly, and offered a sacrifice unto the LORD, and made vows.

NLT **Jonah 1:7** Then the crew cast lots to see which of them had offended the gods and caused the terrible storm. When they did this, the lots identified Jonah as the culprit.

8 "Why has this awful storm come down on us?" they demanded. "Who are you? What is your line of work? What country are you from? What is your nationality?"

9 And Jonah answered, "I am a Hebrew, and I worship the LORD, the God of heaven, who made the sea and the land."

10 The sailors were terrified when they heard this, for he had already told them he was running away from the Lord. "Oh, why did you do it?" they groaned.

11 And since the storm was getting worse all the time, they asked him, "What should we do to you to stop this storm?"

12 "Throw me into the sea," Jonah said, "and it will become calm again. I know that this terrible storm is all my fault."

13 Instead, the sailors rowed even harder to get the ship to the land. But the stormy sea was too violent for them, and they couldn't make it.

14 Then they cried out to the LORD, Jonah's God. "O LORD," they pleaded, "don't make us die for this man's sin. And don't hold us responsible for his death. O LORD, you have sent this storm upon him for your own good reasons."

15 Then the sailors picked Jonah up and threw him into the raging sea, and the storm stopped at once!

16 The sailors were awestruck by the LORD's great power, and they offered him a sacrifice and vowed to serve him.

17 Now the Lord had arranged for a great fish to swallow Jonah. And Jonah was inside the fish for three days and three nights.

17 Now the LORD had prepared a great fish to swallow up Jonah. And Jonah was in the belly of the fish three days and three nights.

The People, Places, and Times

Nineveh. Nineveh was a famous ancient city situated on the eastern bank of the Tigris River opposite the modern city of Mosul. It was built by Nimrod and eventually made the capital of Assyria, until its fall in 612 BC. It was more than 500 miles from Jonah's hometown of Gath Hepher in Israel. The prophet Nahum speaks at length about the city's sins, including evil plots against the Lord (Nahum 1:9); prostitution and witchcraft (3:4); and commercial exploitation (3:16).

Background

Jonah's name means "dove." He was the son of Amittai, who came from Gath-hepher, which was three miles northeast of Nazareth. Jonah's prophetic ministry took place before the reign of Jeroboam II (782–753 BC). He predicted the victory over the Syrians and the largest extension of the Israelite border (2 Kings 14:25).

Jonah was commissioned by God to go and prophesy to the people of Nineveh. Like other Israelites, he hated the Assyrians, and so he decided to flee by ship instead. He hopped on board a ship headed to Tarshish in Joppa. That is when the trouble began for all on board. God sent a storm with strong, gusty winds to create havoc. The sailors called on their false gods to calm the sea and nothing happened. They woke up Jonah and implored him to pray to his God for help.

At-A-Glance

1. Jonah's Disobedience Exposed (Jonah 1:7–10)
2. Jonah's Fate (vv. 11–17)

In Depth

1. Jonah's Disobedience Exposed (Jonah 1:7–10)

After the men's prayers did not help to calm the seas, they cast lots. Casting lots was an ancient tradition believed to help determine a matter without influence from others. But this time God intervened. It was determined Jonah was at fault for them being in the midst of a storm. This proved to Jonah he could not run away from God. No matter where we go, He knows (Psalm 139:7–12). So if God calls us to do something, we must be obedient. There is no other way to show we love Him (John 14:15).

Jonah admitted to being a Hebrew who worshiped the God of heaven and creation. The other sailors were angry and afraid. They even confronted Jonah about his disobedience because they were suffering because of him. Sometimes people's actions affect our lives as well. What would they do? People react differently during times of trials and tests. How do you respond when experiencing hardship and calamities?

2. Jonah's Fate (vv. 11–17)

The sailors questioned Jonah about how to calm the seas. Jonah was willing to sacrifice his own life to save the sailors. But he did not want to go to Nineveh to warn them of God's upcoming judgment. Jonah's hatred and prejudices clouded his perception. The sailors were so compassionate that they tried to save Jonah's life by fighting against the storm to get the ship back to land. Their effort was fruitless. We cannot calm God's wrath until we obey His will.

The sailors cried out in prayer to the God of Israel for help. They recognized He was in control. Some who do not follow God or know much about Him will still call on Him in times of hardship and suffering. But once they are delivered, they often turn back to their former ideas. The sailors threw Jonah into the sea, and immediately the storm calmed. They were in awe of God's power and worshiped Him. The Scripture does not state whether the sailors accepted the God of Israel as their God permanently.

Jonah did not die. God had mercy on him, in the form of a big fish that swallowed Him. He remained in the fish's belly for three days and three nights. While in the fish's belly, Jonah called upon God for help. In the midst of our calamities, God wants us to cry out to Him and He will respond. He loves us and will show mercy to any of His children.

Search the Scriptures

1. Is it acceptable for God's people to cast lots(Jonah 1:7)?

2. Do you believe the sailors kept their vow to serve the Lord (v. 16)? Explain why.

Discuss the Meaning

In the story of Jonah, we see God's love in action in the midst of the storm. After Jonah was confronted, he acknowledged his disobedience to God. The sailors he had endangered through his disobedience were angry but still compassionate. Jonah was saved by God's divine actions. What does Jonah's story teach us about God's love?

Lesson in Our Society

God loves all people, even our enemies and those whom we view as different. We have to be obedient to God's commands even if we dislike the task. If we do not, others might be hurt. Repentance is necessary when our words and actions inflict harm on ourselves or others. Prayer is key when we face trials and suffering. God will hear us and have compassion.

Make It Happen

In our lives, we might experience trials and misfortune. It could be our own fault or the fault of others. We might have to acknowledge our wrongdoing to restore relationships and begin the process of healing. We might also have to forgive and show love to those who have caused us harm. No matter what the circumstances, we can be assured that God is present. If we pray and seek God, we will find He is compassionate, loving, and merciful.

Follow the Spirit

What God wants me to do:

_____

_____

_____

_____

_____

Remember Your Thoughts

Special insights I have learned:

_____

_____

_____

_____

More Light on the Text
Jonah 1:7–17

On one hand, the book of Jonah is a story about a personal encounter between Yahweh and His servant Jonah, who tried to avert God's plan. On the other hand, it is also about an encounter for a wicked people to whom He decides to show mercy. These encounters arise from God's call to Jonah to go and preach to the wicked nation—Nineveh—so that they can repent from their evil ways and be saved. The title, "the book of Jonah," tends to suggest that Jonah was the author, but this is misleading; the author is unknown. The book is about Jonah and his encounter with God.

7 And they said every one to his fellow, Come, and let us cast lots, that we may know for whose cause this evil is upon us. So they cast lots, and the lot fell upon Jonah. 8 Then said they unto him, Tell us, we pray thee, for whose cause this evil is upon us; What is thine occupation? and whence comest thou? what is thy country? and of what people art thou?

Casting lots was a common practice in ancient times and was used for decision making. People would throw or pick stones, sticks, or animal bones and used these to determine what steps or course to take next. Even through the casting of lots, God is in control. Jonah thought that he could hide from the Lord, but even now he is exposed as disobedient. The sailors ask him questions to determine the cause of the storm and what part he had to play in bringing it about.

9 And he said unto them, I am an Hebrew; and I fear the LORD, the God of heaven, which hath made the sea and the dry land. 10 Then were the men exceedingly afraid, and said unto him, Why hast thou done this? For the men knew that he fled from

the presence of the LORD, because he had told them.

Jonah begins by stating his nationality and theological beliefs. He fears the God of heaven who created the sea and the dry land. He lets the sailors know that God is the cause of their predicament. The ship's crew are incredulous when they find out that he tried to run away from a God you can't run away from. God made the sea and the dry land, so He has control over all of it. Jonah stands convicted in the presence of those who do not even know the Lord.

11 Then said they unto him, What shall we do unto thee, that the sea may be calm unto us? for the sea wrought and was tempestuous. 12 And he said unto them, Take me up, and cast me forth into the sea; so shall the sea be calm unto you: for I know that for my sake this great tempest is upon you.

The people on the ship ask Jonah what they should do with him to calm the storm, because it was now becoming worse, and the sea was very turbulent. Jonah tells them to throw him overboard in order to pacify the raging sea.

Why does Jonah prefer to die rather than carry out God's instruction? His patriotism and love for his people—because of which he could not comprehend how his God could have mercy on the Ninevites—and (theologically speaking) his ignorance had blinded his spiritual eyes and clouded his mind so that he could not understand God's eternal salvation plan for all peoples (Jonah 4:1–3). Jonah's confession, "I fear the LORD, the God of heaven, which hath made the sea and the dry land," is contradicted by his actions. If he truly feared Yahweh, he would have obeyed Him, rather than trying to die.

Rather than repenting from his sin of disobedience, Jonah decides to give up his life. He tells the people to throw him into the sea, with the idea that he will avert the plan and responsibility God has for him. But God has a different plan for him. His ways are irrevocable; His plans must be fulfilled.

13 Nevertheless the men rowed hard to bring it to the land; but they could not: for the sea wrought, and was tempestuous against them. 14 Wherefore they cried unto the LORD, and said, We beseech thee, O LORD, we beseech thee, let us not perish for this man's life, and lay not upon us innocent blood: for thou, O LORD, hast done as it pleased thee.

Here, the crew decides to return to the port of Joppa so that Jonah can get off the ship alive. By now, they were probably far out to sea and were a great distance from the shore when the storm began. Under normal circumstances, it is suicidal to try to row a boat to shore in a heavy storm like the one described here.

Note that in verse 5, the sailors and everyone in the ship "cried every man unto his god," but now they turn to Yahweh. In their prayer, they acknowledge two facts about the sovereignty of the Lord. First, simply by going ahead with the plan to throw Jonah into the sea, they acknowledge that no human efforts can save them from the fierce storm through which God is exhibiting His authority and anger. Second, they acknowledge that God in His sovereignty does what He pleases. They recognize the hand of God at work.

The clause "lay not upon us innocent blood" indicates their reluctance to carry out Jonah's wish, as does their request that, since they have no other alternative than to throw Jonah overboard, they should not be held accountable for the action they are about to take. They are begging for God's understanding in regards to the crime they are about to commit. There is, however, one positive outcome of the whole situation: the people who hitherto never knew the Lord God of Israel are able to confess Him as the only sovereign God.

15 So they took up Jonah, and cast him forth into the sea: and the sea ceased from her raging.

The verb "took" is the Hebrew word *nasa'* (**nah-SAH**). Jonah goes into the sea, and the sailors' ordeal ends as the storm stops. Here again, as in the previous verses, the sea is personified (vv. 11–12); the reaction of the sea is idiomatically expressed as "the sea ceased from her raging." The word "raging" (Heb. *za'aph*, **ZAH-aff**), i.e., "indignation" or "wrath," is used elsewhere in the Bible to denote emotions attributed to kings and God. The boisterous movement of the sea is restricted, which shows that it is the Lord, the Creator of heaven and earth, the sea and all that is in them, who controls the waves and the sea (cf. Mark 4:37–39).

16 Then the men feared the LORD exceedingly, and offered a sacrifice unto the LORD, and made vows.

The author gives three reactions of the sailors: (1) they "feared the Lord exceedingly," (2) they "offered a sacrifice to the Lord," and (3) they "made vows." Rather than being punished further for what is a potentially murderous act, the sailors receive calm and peace, prompting a different reaction than before. We note that in verse 9 as he confesses to the sailors, Jonah says to them, "I am a Hebrew and I worship the LORD, the God of heaven, who made the sea and the land" (NIV). Although they are terrified by that confession, they do not seem totally convinced by Jonah's word. Now, however, they recognize the Lord's greatness by the instantaneous calm that follows the moment Jonah touches the waters of the sea. They begin to fear the Lord. The verb "fear" (Heb. *yare'*, **yah-RAY**) has a number of connotations, including "to be afraid" or "to be frightened, to be dreadful" as in verse 10, where it is used to describe the reaction of the sailors upon hearing Jonah's confession. It also means "to revere, to be astonished, or to stand in awe." It is a fear that inspires reverence and godly awe, as we see here (v. 16). Jonah's confession in verse 9, "I fear the Lord," is accurately translated "worship" (NIV). Also, *yare* is to be understood in the same light—they stand in reverence and awe and worship the Lord.

Astounded by what they have just experienced, the sailors not only "feared the Lord exceedingly;" they show their reverence for Him by an act of worship: they offer a sacrifice to the Lord followed by vows. We do not know of the type of sacrifice the sailors offered to the Lord from the ship. However, the author's use of both the verb *zabach* (**za-BAKH**, to offer) and its noun derivative *zebach* (**zeh-BAKH**, a sacrifice) suggests that they killed an animal as an offering to the Lord. Therefore, animals were likely on board as part of the ship's cargo, or perhaps reserved for sacrifices to the sailors' gods (a common practice at the time whether at the beginning or end of a journey, or during a crisis). Here, the sailors offer the animal in a legitimate way as a mark of their worship, no more to their own individual gods, but instead to the living God of Israel.

The third thing the author tells us is that the sailors made vows, connoting the act of verbal consecration or promise that is often associated with devotion and service to God. Overwhelmed by the instant quieting of the sea, the sailors make a pledge, not under compulsion or duress, but in appreciation and thanksgiving to the Almighty God. The author is silent, however, about whether the sailors become proselytes and follow the true God later.

17 Now the Lord had prepared a great fish to swallow up Jonah. And Jonah was in the belly of the fish three days and three nights.

As Jonah falls into the sea, the Lord prepares a great fish to swallow him up. The word "now" serves here as both a conjunction and as a transition from where we left Jonah (v. 15) before reading about the sailors' reaction. With this word, the author brings our mind back to the main character and continues the story from there. The statement about God's preparation indicates that even before Jonah touches the sea, even before the sailors throw him overboard, the Lord had already appointed a great fish to swallow him. The verb "prepared" (Heb. *manah*, **ma-NAH**) also means "to appoint, assign, tell, or ordain." We note here that God has control of all His creatures and that He can use anything to serve His purpose.

Say It Correctly

Wrought. **RAWT**.
Tempestuous. tim-**PES**-choo-us.

Daily Bible Readings

MONDAY
Can I Flee from God's Presence?
(Psalm 139:1–12)

TUESDAY
The Lord's Voice in the Storm
(Psalm 29:1–9)

WEDNESDAY
Compassion After Rejection
(Isaiah 54:1–10)

THURSDAY
God's Wrath Against Nineveh
(Nahum 1:1–8)

FRIDAY
Fleeing from God's Call
(Jonah 1:1–5)

SATURDAY
A Stormy Confession
(Jonah 1:6–12)

SUNDAY
God's Sustaining Love Despite Rebellion
(Jonah 1:7–17)

Notes

Teaching Tips

May 14
Bible Study Guide 11

Words You Should Know

A. Hell (Jonah 2:2) *sheol* (Heb.)—The abode of the dead; the underworld.

B. Vanities (v. 8) *hebel* (Heb.)—Vapor, breath; figuratively emptiness and worthlessness, often in reference to idols.

Teacher Preparation

Unifying Principle—Rescued from Danger. People are thankful when they are rescued from dire circumstances. Whom do we thank in these circumstances? Jonah acknowledges with thanksgiving that God's love protects and offers deliverance.

A. Pray before studying the text and ask God to give you understanding

B. Read the text in different translations for clarity and highlight key words. Read through The People, Places, and Times; Background; and In Depth sections.

C. Ask the Holy Spirit to guide you through the needs of your students.

O—Open the Lesson

A. Open class by asking for victories and challenges from the previous week's lesson.

B. Lead the class in prayer and ask for special attention from the Holy Spirit to provide new revelation on this text.

C. Share the Unifying Principle, and based on the Aim for Change, lead a discussion on God's love and deliverance.

P—Present the Scriptures

A. Read the lesson text and ask students what is familiar in the text and what makes it believable.

B. Have students review The People, Places, and Times to understand the context of the lesson.

C. Call out key points made in the In Depth section and ask students to discuss them in relation to their own life experiences.

E—Explore the Meaning

A. Have students discuss what Jonah expressed in his prayer.

B. Review the Discuss the Meaning and Lesson in Our Society sections.

N—Next Steps for Application

A. Have students break up into groups to share ideas for immediate application.

B. Ask students to pair up and hold each other accountable for growth points revealed in the lesson.

C. Have students report back next week on how they used the lesson in their everyday lives.

Worship Guide

For the Superintendent or Teacher
Theme: God's Love Preserved Jonah
Song: "Love Lifted Me"
Devotional Reading: Psalm 116:1–14

God's Love Preserved Jonah

Bible Background • JONAH 2
Printed Text • JONAH 2 | Devotional Reading • PSALM 116:1–14

—— Aim for Change ——

By the end of the lesson, we will: DISCOVER with Jonah that God's love protects and preserves when we make decisions to do His will; FEEL grateful for times God rescued or protected us; and EXPLORE how God's love is expressed when we accept the mission He gives us.

In Focus

Michelle had a chaotic job leading a team of more than fifty people. She was also heavily involved in church activities—volunteering in the youth ministry and singing with the praise team. Along with managing a family of five, Michelle's hectic schedule was taking its toll on her physically and mentally, but most of all spiritually. She knew she needed to spend time in her Bible and to seek God in prayer, but there never was enough time.

Then Michelle started having migraines. She tried to power through them and not let them stop her from all she felt she needed to do, but over time, that only made them worse. Eventually, the migraines got so bad that the only thing that made them subside was lying down in a dark room for a while. "Maybe God's trying to give you a message," Michelle's teen son joked with her one day. "Maybe He just had to make you slow down before you gave yourself a heart attack!"

Michelle wondered at this and started to use these quiet times as opportunities to talk with God. She would rest, pray, and see where God had moved in her life that day. Michelle began to see the ways that God protected and provided for her each day, which helped calm her anxiety about taking care of everything herself. The migraines slowly went away, but she still spent time each day reading and praying in her room as her devotion time.

Has there ever been a time when you experienced God's protection and deliverance?

—— Keep in Mind ——

"But I will sacrifice unto thee with the voice of thanksgiving; I will pay that that I have vowed. Salvation is of the LORD" (Jonah 2:9).

"But I will sacrifice unto thee with the voice of thanksgiving; I will pay that that I have vowed. Salvation is of the LORD" (Jonah 2:9).

Focal Verses

KJV

Jonah 2:1 Then Jonah prayed unto the LORD his God out of the fish's belly,

2 And said, I cried by reason of mine affliction unto the LORD, and he heard me; out of the belly of hell cried I, and thou heardest my voice.

3 For thou hadst cast me into the deep, in the midst of the seas; and the floods compassed me about: all thy billows and thy waves passed over me.

4 Then I said, I am cast out of thy sight; yet I will look again toward thy holy temple.

5 The waters compassed me about, even to the soul: the depth closed me round about, the weeds were wrapped about my head.

6 I went down to the bottoms of the mountains; the earth with her bars was about me for ever: yet hast thou brought up my life from corruption, O LORD my God.

7 When my soul fainted within me I remembered the LORD: and my prayer came in unto thee, into thine holy temple.

8 They that observe lying vanities forsake their own mercy.

9 But I will sacrifice unto thee with the voice of thanksgiving; I will pay that that I have vowed. Salvation is of the LORD.

10 And the LORD spake unto the fish, and it vomited out Jonah upon the dry land.

NLT

Jonah 2:1 Then Jonah prayed to the LORD his God from inside the fish.

2 He said, "I cried out to the LORD in my great trouble, and he answered me. I called to you from the land of the dead, and LORD, you heard me!

3 You threw me into the ocean depths, and I sank down to the heart of the sea. The mighty waters engulfed me; I was buried beneath your wild and stormy waves.

4 Then I said, 'O LORD, you have driven me from your presence. Yet I will look once more toward your holy Temple.'

5 "I sank beneath the waves, and the waters closed over me. Seaweed wrapped itself around my head.

6 I sank down to the very roots of the mountains. I was imprisoned in the earth, whose gates lock shut forever. But you, O LORD my God, snatched me from the jaws of death!

7 As my life was slipping away, I remembered the Lord. And my earnest prayer went out to you in your holy Temple.

8 Those who worship false gods turn their backs on all God's mercies.

9 But I will offer sacrifices to you with songs of praise, and I will fulfill all my vows. For my salvation comes from the LORD alone."

10 Then the LORD ordered the fish to spit Jonah out onto the beach.

The People, Places, and Times

The seas. The seas were known in the ancient world as the realm of chaotic, powerful beings. The sea itself was considered a power in opposition to the gods. Many of the Psalms show that the sea far from being opposed to God, is under His rule. He is in control of it (Psalm 104:7–9) and it gives praise to Him (Psalm 148:7). This is because the Lord created the sea (Genesis 1:9) and declared that it was good.

Vows. Vows were promises and pledges to God to fulfill an obligation. This usually included offering a sacrifice at the end of a vow.

Vows were not mandatory and were done on a volunteer basis. They were usually given in response to God as a form of gratitude (Psalm 56:12), a way to gain the Lord's favor (1 Samuel 1:11, 27–28), or to display total dedication to the Lord (Numbers 6:1–8). The Law provided regulations to making vows, reminding the Israelites that vows were to be taken seriously (Deuteronomy 23:21–23).

Background

In the previous chapter, Jonah disobediently went in the opposite direction from where God had commanded him to go. He did not want to preach to the Assyrian people of Nineveh, so he decided to board a ship headed for Tarshish. The Assyrians were a conquering nation at the time and known for their cruel methods of subjugation. Jonah, instead of hearing and obeying God's voice, gave in to fear and prejudice. As a result, God sent a storm to stop Jonah's ship and a fish to swallow him.

There in the belly of the fish, Jonah discovers repentance for his actions. This seed of repentance is expressed in a prayer for deliverance from this predicament. This prayer is both a request for deliverance and a hymn of praise. Jonah is committed to obeying God and desperately wants to be released from this situation.

At-A-Glance

1. Jonah's Predicament (Jonah 2:1)
2. Jonah's Prayer (vv. 2–8)
3. Jonah's Praise and Preservation (vv. 9–10)

In Depth

1. Jonah's Predicament (Jonah 2:1)

Jonah has gotten himself into a very terrible situation. His disobedience has caused him to be swallowed by a fish. This predicament prompts him to pray. Jonah faces death inside the belly of a fish and has no other option but to cry out to God.

He does not pray from the Temple or the comfort of his home. He prays to God in an impossible and very uncomfortable position. This situation calls for prayer. He is stuck inside a fish and imprisoned. Some would wait out their fate and resign themselves to die, but Jonah has hope in God. He believes that God can hear him no matter where he is and no matter what situation he is in.

2. Jonah's Prayer (vv. 2–8)

Jonah's prayer is a mixture of recounting his immediate circumstances, the horror of what it means to be trapped inside a sea creature, and heartfelt repentance. It is a plea for mercy, but also much more than that—a poetic description of his circumstances. As you read the prayer, you can imagine the seaweed wrapped around his head. You can see the waters overwhelming him. Jonah is intimately familiar with his suffering.

Because of this, Jonah cries out for relief. He wants God's deliverance. He is confident that God will hear his prayer. Although he is trapped in the fish's belly, he believes his prayer has reached God's "holy temple." His hope for deliverance is also contrasted with those who worship idols. They forsake their own hope of salvation from God.

3. Jonah's Praise and Preservation (vv. 9–10)

Jonah is so expectant of God's deliverance that he is already praising Him. His voice of thanksgiving will be his sacrifice to the Lord. He has made a vow to God and will fulfill that vow. This is the attitude of someone fully committed to God no matter what the future holds. Jonah exclaims, "Salvation belongs to the Lord," meaning he will not turn to anyone or anything else for salvation.

The Lord hears Jonah's prayer and speaks to the fish. Jonah was correct to place his complete trust in God. He is sovereign, and even the creatures of the deep obey His voice. The fish obeyed God and vomited Jonah out onto dry land. Jonah's life was preserved because he cried out to God in repentance. Now, he was free to serve the God who saved him.

Search the Scriptures

1. What is the significance of where Jonah chose to look after realizing his distance from God (Jonah 2:4)?

2. What does it mean to forsake your own mercy (v. 8)?

Discuss the Meaning

1. Jonah turned to God in an impossible situation. What popular things do people turn to when they hit rock bottom or their backs are against the wall?

2. Jonah made a vow to God. These were common in the Old Testament. Are we as New Testament believers allowed or expected to make vows?

Lesson in Our Society

Jonah knew where his help came from. So many today do not know where or to whom to turn when things do not turn out well. Many refuse to go to God in hard times, even if their trouble was caused by their disobedience. The Lord is always willing to show us mercy. There is no sin He will not forgive. As long as we have breath in our lungs, we have the opportunity to pray to Him and seek Him out. There are no impossible cases with God.

Make It Happen

List three ways God has come to your aid in an impossible situation, and thank Him. If there is an impossible situation in your life, pray the prayer of Jonah and apply it to your situation, knowing that God will hear your prayer. Tell three people about how God has delivered you after you repented of your sins.

Follow the Spirit

What God wants me to do:

_____

_____

_____

_____

Remember Your Thoughts

Special insights I have learned:

_____

_____

_____

_____

More Light on the Text
Jonah 2:1-10

1 Then Jonah prayed unto the Lord his God out of the fish's belly,

Some argue that Jonah was not miraculously kept alive in the belly of the fish, but rather that he died and was resurrected after three days as a copy of Christ's death, burial, and resurrection (Matthew 12:40). Christ's reference to Jonah here does not indicate that Jonah died or was dead for three days, but that he was in the fish's belly for three days. It signifies that Jonah was alive while in the fish's belly. The reference here therefore should be regarded as a metaphor or analogy of Christ's death, or as a simile used for comparison in the same sense as when Jesus says, "Destroy this temple, and I will raise it again in three days" (from John 2:19). The Matthew passage is clear enough to understand that the emphasis is on "three days and three nights" rather than on death. In the Bible, three days represents a relatively short, divinely-ordained period of time in which something significant and transformative happened (Joshua 3:2; Esther 4:16). God preserved Jonah alive in the belly of the fish, and Jonah was conscious of where he was; thus, he spent three days praying (2:1) and obviously fasting, too. This was also part of God's design to prepare him for the task ahead.

2 And said, I cried by reason of mine affliction unto the LORD, and he heard me; out of the belly of hell cried I, and thou heardest my voice.

Jonah says that he cried "by reason of mine affliction." The word for affliction is taken from a root word meaning enemy or adversary. In other words, Jonah cried to the Lord because of the opposition against him. We do not know whether Jonah referred to the waves while he struggled to survive in the open sea or the wetness and stench in the belly of the fish.

The word translated "hell" (Heb. *she'ol*, **sheh-OLE**) is the Hebrew word for the place of the dead. This is how Jonah describes his brush with death. Sheol was thought to be under the seas, so to be in danger in the sea would be akin to being trapped in the "belly" (Heb. *beten*, **beh-TEN**) or the "depths" of hell.

3 For thou hadst cast me into the deep, in the midst of the seas; and the floods compassed me about: all thy billows and thy waves passed over me.

The language here is similar to language in the Psalms (e.g., 18:4, 42:7, 88:17). Some speculate that this prayer is not really from Jonah but someone else. This might be the case, but Jonah might also be utilizing the language of the hymns and prayers that he knows. Whether using his own words or the words of a familiar prayer/psalm, Jonah's grief is so great that he equates God with the sea itself. God has thrown Jonah into the heart of the sea, and now all of God's breaking and heaping waves are passing over Jonah. The Hebrew for billows (*mishbar*, **mish-BAR**) is from the verb that means to break or even shatter, referring specifically to the moment when waves are most powerful because they are breaking. Likewise, the word for waves (Heb. *gal*, **GALL**) is from the verb meaning to roll over and over, indicating the constant motion of the waves, even as they are breaking all around Jonah. Only the power of God can equate with the power of the sea in this moment.

4 Then I said, I am cast out of thy sight; yet I will look again toward thy holy temple.

Jonah describes his situation. As he is in the belly of the fish, he is cast away from God's sight. The word for "cast out" is *garash* (Heb. **gahr-OSH**), which is often seen in the Scriptures for banishing God's enemies from the Promised Land, as well as divorce in the sense of a husband driving out his divorced wife from his home. This is not a slight to God's omniscience, but a description of Jonah's spiritual state. At this moment, he is out of God's favor and separated from His presence. Contrasted to this, Jonah states that he will "look again toward thy holy temple," confident that he would one day be able to pray in the Temple.

5 The waters compassed me about, even to the soul: the depth closed me round about, the weeds were wrapped about my head. 6 I went down to the bottoms of the mountains; the earth with her bars was about me for

ever: yet hast thou brought up my life from corruption, O LORD my God.

Here Jonah describes his predicament. The waters surrounded him even to his soul (Heb. *nefesh*, **NEH-fesh**). The word for soul in its most basic meaning refers to the throat (where one's very breath fills the lungs and where one accurate cut can kill), as well as to life itself. In other words, the waters were up to his throat and threatening his very life. Jonah was at the brink of death and needed a reversal of fortune.

The phrase "I went down to the bottom of the mountains" also describes Jonah's life-threatening situation. The mountains were thought to be rooted in the depths of the earth. In other words, he was in the deepest parts of the ocean with no hope of help or rescue. As he describes the "earth with her bars," the sense is that there is no turning back. He would drown in the depths of the sea and have no access to the earth.

7 When my soul fainted within me I remembered the LORD: and my prayer came in unto thee, into thine holy temple.

Now, we see a turn in Jonah's prayer. Before, he describes the pain and agony of his predicament. He was in danger and distress. Now, we see a turning point where he knows his prayer has been heard, and can hope for salvation and deliverance. Before he hoped to be in the Temple praying, but now Jonah declares that his prayer reached the Temple where God's presence resided. Although he was far from God and cast out of His sight, his prayer reached His ears.

Being assured that his prayer was heard probably reinforces for Jonah what he recently learned from the storm at sea. He tried to run away from God, fleeing toward Tarshish. When God sent the storm, however, Jonah knew he could not outrun Him. Now in the depths of the sea, Jonah again thought he was beyond God's power, but again finds that he was wrong. God's power stretches across the farthest sea and to the bottom of the deepest ocean.

8 They that observe lying vanities forsake their own mercy. 9 But I will sacrifice unto thee with the voice of thanksgiving; I will pay that that I have vowed. Salvation is of the LORD.

In these two verses, Jonah sets up a contrast. The Hebrew word here translated "observe" (*shamar*, **sha-MAR**) is also translated "keep" or "heed." Jonah contrasts himself with those who heed "vanities" (Heb. *hebel*, **HEH-vel**), a word often used to refer to idols and false gods. Those worshiping false gods will neglect their "mercy" (Heb. *khesed*, **KHE-sed**), which is a key theological idea in the Old Testament, referring to covenant love and faithfulness between God and His children, but also just kindness toward others (cf. Genesis 24:49; Zechariah 7:9). Idolaters forget to be merciful to one another or faithful to their so-called gods. In contrast, Jonah proclaims his faithfulness in sacrifice, thanksgiving, and fulfilling his vows.

Jonah's prayer concludes with a simple yet profound statement: "Salvation is of the Lord." Nowhere does Jonah more directly attest to God's sovereignty. "Salvation" (Heb. *yeshu'ah*, **yeh-SHOO-ah**) can refer to saving one's soul, but more often in the Old Testament it refers to rescuing someone from physical harm. Both are wholly the domain of God. Try as we might to save ourselves, we must surrender to the fact that God is the only One who can save us perfectly from our trials. He can save our bodies from physical harm and our souls from Sheol, as Jonah finally learned.

10 And the LORD spake unto the fish, and it vomited out Jonah upon the dry land.

After three days and three nights, the Lord speaks to the fish (again) and commands it to vomit Jonah onto shore—and it obeys. Once Jonah realizes where his help must come from, he receives it. Jonah does not specifically ask God to save him from the belly of the fish. Instead, he comes to realize that God is the only One who can save him, and that is all the acknowledgment God wants before setting His prophet free to fulfill His will again. It should not be missed that the word for dry land (Heb. *yabashah*, **yah-bah-SHAH**) is the same word Jonah utters in 1:9 when he tells the sailors he worships the Lord "who made the sea and the dry land." Jonah has now experienced both extremes with God, and it is his prayer of confession and salvation that prompts God to remove him from the depths of the sea to the dry land.

If one were to stop reading Jonah here, one would think that Jonah had learned his lesson and obeyed God from then on out. Such a traumatic experience and such a heartfelt prayer could only mean that Jonah's perspective on life was forever changed. Sadly, the tale of Jonah continues and shows instead how so easily people can forget their mountaintop (or in Jonah's case ocean-depth) resolutions.

Say It Correctly

Affliction. uh-**FLICK**-shun.
Corruption. ku-**RUP**-shun.

Daily Bible Readings

MONDAY
Thanks for Deliverance from Death
(Psalm 116:1–14)

TUESDAY
Who Can Be Safe with the Leviathan?
(Job 41:1–11)

WEDNESDAY
The Lord Will Strike, Then Heal
(Isaiah 19:19–22)

THURSDAY
Answer Me, O Lord
(Psalm 69:13–18)

FRIDAY
Something Greater Than Jonah Is Here
(Luke 11:29–32)

SATURDAY
Make Disciples of All Nations
(Matthew 28:16–20)

SUNDAY
Jonah's Song of Thanksgiving
(Jonah 2)

Teaching Tips

May 21
Bible Study Guide 12

Words You Should Know

A. Exceeding (Jonah 3:3) *elohim* (Heb.)—Godlike or very great.

B. Repent (Jonah 3:9–10) *nacham* (Heb.)—Regret, console oneself, be sorry.

Teacher Preparation

Unifying Principle—A Wake-up Call. Communities today are plagued with separation and violence. What can bring people together to live in wholeness and peace? When the people of Nineveh repented, God brought peace and wholeness through divine love.

A. Pray for your class and for wisdom concerning the lesson.

B. Read the Scripture passage in several different translations.

C. Prepare the companion lesson in the *Precepts for Living®* Personal Study Guide.

O—Open the Lesson

A. After receiving prayer requests, ask a volunteer to open the class with prayer, including the Aim for Change.

B. Have a volunteer read the In Focus story.

P—Present the Scriptures

A. Ask for a volunteer to read the Focal Verses.

B. Examine the verses, using Words You Should Know; The People, Places, and Times, Background; the At-A-Glance outline; and More Light on the Text sections.

E—Explore the Meaning

A. Answer the Search the Scriptures questions.

B. Summarize the Discuss the Meaning, Lesson in Our Society, and Make It Happen sections.

C. Connect these answers with today's theme.

N—Next Steps for Application

A. Summarize the lesson.

B. Remind students to read and meditate on their Daily Bible Readings.

C. Solicit prayer requests and close in prayer.

Worship Guide

For the Superintendent or Teacher
Theme: God's Love for Nineveh
Song: "Create in Me a Clean Heart"
Devotional Reading: Acts 11:11–18

God's Love for Nineveh

Bible Background • JONAH 3; NAHUM 1–3
Printed Text • JONAH 3 | Devotional Reading • ACTS 11:11–18

Aim for Change

By the end of the lesson, we will: EXPLORE how repentance is related to God's love; SENSE the joy that comes when we are forgiven a wrong; and SHARE examples of times when wholeness and peace are the result of God's intervening love.

 In Focus

Reverend Johnson was walking through the city slums with his friend Mike, a barber who didn't believe in God. As they took in their depressing surroundings, Mike said to the preacher, "This is why I cannot believe in a God of love. If God were as kind as you say, He would not allow these poor bums to be addicted to dope, alcohol, and other life-destroying habits. No, I cannot believe in a God who permits these things."

The reverend was silent until they met a man who was especially unkempt and filthy. Reverend Johnson said to Mike, "You can't be a very good barber, or you wouldn't permit a man like that to continue living in this neighborhood without a haircut and shave."

Indignantly, Mike answered, "Why blame me for that man's condition? I can't help it that he is like that. He has never come into my shop; there I could fix him up and make him look like a gentleman!"

Giving Mike a penetrating look, the reverend said, "Then don't blame God for allowing the people to continue in their evil ways, when He is constantly inviting them to come into a relationship with Him and be saved. If they did, He would clean up their lives."

In today's lesson, Jonah finally makes his appearance in Nineveh. We will explore God's righteous demand for justice and His desire to show compassion and mercy to all who repent. What types of people is it especially hard to show compassion towards?

Keep in Mind

"And God saw their works, that they turned from their evil way; and God repented of the evil, that he had said that he would do unto them; and he did it not" (Jonah 3:10).

"And God saw their works, that they turned from their evil way; and God repented of the evil, that he had said that he would do unto them; and he did it not" (Jonah 3:10).

KJV Jonah 3:1 And the word of the Lord came unto Jonah the second time, saying,

2 Arise, go unto Nineveh, that great city, and preach unto it the preaching that I bid thee.

3 So Jonah arose, and went unto Nineveh, according to the word of the Lord. Now Nineveh was an exceeding great city of three days' journey.

4 And Jonah began to enter into the city a day's journey, and he cried, and said, Yet forty days, and Nineveh shall be overthrown.

5 So the people of Nineveh believed God, and proclaimed a fast, and put on sackcloth, from the greatest of them even to the least of them.

6 For word came unto the king of Nineveh, and he arose from his throne, and he laid his robe from him, and covered him with sackcloth, and sat in ashes.

7 And he caused it to be proclaimed and published through Nineveh by the decree of the king and his nobles, saying, Let neither man nor beast, herd nor flock, taste any thing: let them not feed, nor drink water:

8 But let man and beast be covered with sackcloth, and cry mightily unto God: yea, let them turn every one from his evil way, and from the violence that is in their hands.

9 Who can tell if God will turn and repent, and turn away from his fierce anger, that we perish not?

10 And God saw their works, that they turned from their evil way; and God repented of the evil, that he had said that he would do unto them; and he did it not.

NLT Jonah 3:1 Then the Lord spoke to Jonah a second time:

2 "Get up and go to the great city of Nineveh, and deliver the message I have given you."

3 This time Jonah obeyed the Lord's command and went to Nineveh, a city so large that it took three days to see it all.

4 On the day Jonah entered the city, he shouted to the crowds: "Forty days from now Nineveh will be destroyed!"

5 The people of Nineveh believed God's message, and from the greatest to the least, they declared a fast and put on burlap to show their sorrow.

6 When the king of Nineveh heard what Jonah was saying, he stepped down from his throne and took off his royal robes. He dressed himself in burlap and sat on a heap of ashes.

7 Then the king and his nobles sent this decree throughout the city: "No one, not even the animals from your herds and flocks, may eat or drink anything at all.

8 People and animals alike must wear garments of mourning, and everyone must pray earnestly to God. They must turn from their evil ways and stop all their violence.

9 Who can tell? Perhaps even yet God will change his mind and hold back his fierce anger from destroying us."

10 When God saw what they had done and how they had put a stop to their evil ways, he changed his mind and did not carry out the destruction he had threatened.

The People, Places, and Times

Fasting. Very little is dictated about fasting in Old Testament law, with only the fast of the Day of Atonement, Yom Kippur, explicitly ordained (Leviticus 16:29–34, 23:27–32). In fact, the Old Testament includes instances of fasting in ancient Israel for purposes such as repentance (Jonah 3:5), petition (2 Samuel 12:16), and mourning (1 Samuel 31:13). Fasting served numerous purposes, but in each case, the individual or community humbled themselves before God by refraining from food and drink.

Sackcloth and ashes. Sackcloth was a coarse garment of poor quality, usually made of goat hair. These garments were worn by those in mourning or by prophets as a sign of their earnestness. Ashes were worn on the head as a sign of mourning as well. They served as a reminder of the fragility of life and that humanity will all go to dust, or the earth.

Background

In last week's lesson, we saw examples of God's grace. Jonah disobeyed God, attempted to run away from His service, and finally was ready to die rather than submit to God's will. In spite of all this, when Jonah's situation appeared hopeless, God prepared a great fish to rescue him.

Jonah was saved from death by grace. God not only saved his life, but He also restored him to his position as prophet. Jonah failed God, but God did not give up on Jonah. God had a job that He wanted Jonah to do, and his failure did not disqualify him for the mission.

God's ultimate purpose was to rid Nineveh of evil. Jonah was sent to warn the people of Nineveh of their impending destruction. God would end the evil of Nineveh through an act of divine judgment or, if they repented, through divine mercy.

At-A-Glance

1. Jonah's Repentance (Jonah 3:1–4)
2. Nineveh's Repentance (vv. 5–9)
3. God's Repentance (v. 10)

In Depth

1. Jonah's Repentance (Jonah 3:1–4)

After his experience on the boat and in the belly of the great fish, Jonah was finally ready to submit to God's will. And God gave the reluctant prophet a second chance. Once again God commanded Jonah to go to Nineveh and announce His judgment against the city. This time Jonah readily obeyed God and made the 500-mile journey to Nineveh. When the prophet arrived in the city, he immediately began to proclaim the message of God's judgment to the inhabitants.

The city of Nineveh itself was about eight miles in circumference. A pace straight through the city would not have taken three days, even starting outside the city itself, but Jonah was expected to spend three days in the city. Jonah walked through the city shouting out God's message, "In forty days Nineveh will be destroyed." The people of Nineveh heard Jonah's words, believed his report, and repented of their sin.

2. Nineveh's Repentance (vv. 5–9)

As an external sign of their repentance, all the people fasted (cf. 1 Samuel 7:6). They clothed themselves in sackcloth (cf. Genesis 37:34). Everyone from the king to the lowest beggar participated in these acts of repentance (Jonah 3:5–6). The people hoped that God would show compassion and turn away from His fierce anger (v. 9). Even the animals were not allowed to eat or drink.

Some have wondered why these pagan people would have responded to an Israelite prophet. Jewish rabbis explain it this way: the Ninevites had heard of Jonah's miraculous deliverance from the fish's belly, and believed that God must be very powerful for His reach to extend so far. This argument is very likely since Jesus said, "For as Jonah was a sign to the Ninevites, so also will the Son of man be to this generation" (Luke 11:30). In the ancient Near Eastern mind, gods ruled over different regions. In the minds of the Ninevites, the God who was worshiped in Israel and still threatened Nineveh was powerful indeed.

3. God's Repentance (v. 10)

When God saw that the people of Nineveh had turned from their evil ways, He turned from destroying the city. The Lord extended His mercy to them by not executing the destruction they so richly deserved. He extended His grace by giving them what they could never deserve: forgiveness. He changed His mind about the judgment they were to receive.

The conversion of Nineveh is the high point of the book of Jonah. The Ninevites not only heard the Word of God, but they also believed. God forgave Nineveh just as He forgave Jonah. He is ready to forgive anyone and everyone who is willing to turn away from their sins and submit to His will.

Search the Scriptures

1. The city of Nineveh is described as a great city, because of the immense size of the city and its surrounding suburbs. What is significant about the size of the city in relation to their need for repentance (v. 3)?

2. Jonah walked through Nineveh proclaiming that in forty days, the city would be destroyed. How do you think Jonah felt while doing this (v. 5)?

Discuss the Meaning

1. Why do you believe that God gave both Jonah and Nineveh a second chance? What does this mean for you personally? What does God's interest in Nineveh convey about God's interest in cities today?

2. The Ninevites were a cruel and very wicked people. What did they do to deserve God's mercy and kindness? What can we do to earn His mercy and kindness?

Lesson in Our Society

Many people find it hard to stop doing something they know is wrong. Whether they are addicted or just stubborn, some people continue to persist in heading in the wrong direction. God's call to repentance is a call to head in the right direction. It is not intended to stop all enjoyment and fun, but to help people experience God's love. This can only happen when we turn from our evil ways.

Make It Happen

God's love is available to all, but not everyone experiences it. Write in your journal the reason you decided to repent and experience God's love. Next, discuss this with another believer. Finally, share with another person how you experienced God's love as a result of turning toward Him.

Follow the Spirit

What God wants me to do:

_____

_____

_____

_____

Remember Your Thoughts

Special insights I have learned:

_____

_____

_____

_____

More Light on the Text
Jonah 3

1 And the word of the LORD came unto Jonah the second time, saying, 2 Arise, go unto Nineveh, that great city, and preach unto it the preaching that I bid thee.

Jonah is returned to dry land by Yahweh's orders to the great fish (Jonah 2:10). The Lord commissions him again to complete the same mission that he had run away from. With the same words, the Lord orders Jonah again as before (1:2), "Arise, go unto Nineveh, that great city, and preach unto it the preaching that I bid thee." Jonah is to go and preach (Heb. *qara'*, **kah-RAH**), which is to proclaim or declare, the Lord's message to the people of Nineveh. The phrase "the preaching that I bid thee" emphasizes the fact that a true preacher speaks not of himself, but the "oracles of God" (cf. 1 Peter 4:11, KJV). That is also true of Christ Jesus (John 3:34), Moses (Exodus 4:10–16), and Jeremiah (Jeremiah 1:6–9). Jonah knows that he must preach the message God gives him. He was disobedient at first. Now, having experienced God's disciplinary hand, Jonah obeys His Word without further argument. However, he goes reluctantly, not enthusiastically.

3 So Jonah arose, and went unto Nineveh, according to the word of the LORD. Now Nineveh was an exceeding great city of three days' journey.

Jonah obeys the Lord and goes to Nineveh as God commissioned him. The author now mentions again that Nineveh was "an exceeding great city of three days' journey," referring to its size. The estimated size of the city of Nineveh measured three miles in length and less than a mile and a half in breadth, and the city wall was about eight miles in length. This does not seem very big; however, when the other surrounding cities that make up the metropolitan area are included, we find that it was an "exceeding great (large) city." The expression "exceedingly great" literally means "great to God" or "great before God" and describes the magnitude of the city in the unique way of expressing a superlative. Nineveh is referred to as "that great city" three other times in the book (1:2, 3:2, 4:11), but only here is Nineveh also described as "great to God"

"Three days' journey" does not mean how long it would take to reach there, but how long it would take to cover the city because of its magnitude. The meaning is probably more figurative than literal, given that Jonah was also in the belly of the great fish for three days and nights (1:17). A normal pace may have taken less time since the city proper was not so large as to require three full days of walking. Perhaps the point is that Jonah was expected to be preaching in Nineveh for as long as he was in the belly of the fish. The repeated mention of the city's size also seems to indicate the enormousness of the task before Jonah.

4 And Jonah began to enter into the city a day's journey, and he cried, and said, Yet forty days, and Nineveh shall be overthrown.

The immense task is soon reduced to a day's journey (or a day's work rather than three), as the inhabitants of the city fall on their knees in repentance as soon as Jonah declares the Lord's message.

The expression "And Jonah began to enter into the city a day's journey" tends to suggest that he entered the city, probably Nineveh proper the first day, and started proclaiming the message of doom awaiting them. The message is simple: "Yet forty days, and Nineveh shall be overthrown." This is the only prophecy in the book and means, "In forty more days, Nineveh will be completely changed" The prophecy here was conditional, and is implicit; the prophecy will be fulfilled if the people do not repent. Had the prophecy been unconditional, they would have received no mercy. God would have overthrown or destroyed the city without warning or notice. It would have been unnecessary to send Jonah or any other messenger to the city to preach to them.

However, it also would have been impossible for the people to repent without the Word of God being preached to them. Paul succinctly put it thus: "Faith cometh by hearing, and hearing by the word of God" (Romans 10:17).

Declaring the importance of preaching and the efficacy of the Word of God earlier, Paul also wrote: "For whosoever shall call upon the name of the Lord shall be saved. How then shall they call on him in whom they have not believed? and how shall they believe in him of whom they have not heard? and how shall they hear without a preacher?"(Romans 10:13–14).

5 So the people of Nineveh believed God, and proclaimed a fast, and put on sackcloth, from the greatest of them even to the least of them. 6 When the king of Nineveh heard what Jonah was saying, he stepped down from his throne and took off his royal robes. He dressed himself in burlap and sat on a heap of ashes. 7 Then the king and his nobles sent this decree throughout the city: "No one, not even the animals from your herds and flocks, may eat or drink anything at all. 8 People and animals alike must wear garments of mourning, and everyone must pray earnestly to God. They must turn from their evil ways and stop all their violence. 9 Who can tell? Perhaps even yet God will change his mind and hold back his fierce anger from destroying us."

Although Jonah did not mention any provision or condition to avert the impending doom awaiting them in 40 days, the people understood very well the purpose of the preaching—repentance. As they heard Jonah's preaching (announcement of doom), they repented and

believed God, and declared a national day of fasting and prayer, asking for forgiveness.

Note the things Nineveh did to obtain mercy. First, they believed God (v. 5), meaning they accepted His verdict against them and trusted Him for salvation. Simply put, they repented of their evil ways and put their trust in God. Second, they declared a fast and "put on sackcloth, from the greatest ... to the least of them," which showed an attitude of sorrow, remorse, and mourning—the marks of genuine repentance for their sin. The king, the nobles, and all the people, including all domestic animals, joined in the national mourning and called on the Lord for forgiveness (vv. 6–9). The people were to turn from their evil ways and from "violence." The Hebrew word for "violence" (*hamas* **ha-MAHS**) actually includes more than physical violence but also any insulting language or negative treatment. The king was saying that the people's repentance had to be complete and involve their disposition as well as their overt actions.

10 And God saw their works, that they turned from their evil way; and God repented of the evil, that he had said that he would do unto them; and he did it not.

Recognizing the genuineness of their repentance from their evil ways, the Lord changes His mind and forgives them. They "turned (Heb. *shub*, **SHOOV**) from their evil," which means that they turned back from what they were doing before, or turned from their evil ways. It carries the idea of changing course and turning back, or changing from one way of life to a new way of life, usually either positive or negative. In this case, the Ninevites' change was positive and pleasing to God. Thus, God "repented" (Heb. *nakham*, **nah-KHAM**), i.e., changed His mind about destroying the city. This has nothing to do with God turning from a wrong. Instead, the word used for repent, *nakham,* carries the idea of having compassion, easing oneself of anger, or being moved to pity. Moved by compassion and by the evidence of sorrow and repentance from the city, the Lord is no longer angry and He spares them the punishment, which He had pronounced on them. Here, we see what we have assumed throughout the book of Jonah: God is merciful. God relents from carrying out His judgments against people who turn to Him with their whole heart in repentance.

The Prophet Joel declares, "Rend your heart and not your garments. Return to the LORD your God, for he is gracious and compassionate, slow to anger and abounding in love, and he relents from sending calamity. Who knows? He may turn and have pity and leave behind a blessing..." (Joel 2:13–14, NIV; see also Jeremiah 18:6–10). However, God does not arbitrarily avert the punishment He has planned to execute against a sinful nation or people without evidence of genuine repentance. The question that faces us is: "Should the Lord have compassion on Nineveh?" Jonah does not think so. This is the core of Jonah's problem.

Say It Correctly

Exceeding. ek-**SEE**-deeng.
Overthrown. oh-vur-**THRONE**.

Daily Bible Readings

MONDAY
Destined to Prophesy to the Nations
(Jeremiah 1:4–10)

TUESDAY
"Return to Me," Says the Lord
(Zechariah 1:1–6)

WEDNESDAY
With Repentance Comes Joy
(Luke 15:8–10)

THURSDAY
Woes to the Unrepentant Communities
(Matthew 11:20–24)

FRIDAY
Proclaiming Repentance, Faith Lives
(Acts 20:18b–24)

SATURDAY
Gentiles Repent and Experience New Life
(Acts 11:11–18)

SUNDAY
Turn from Evil Ways
(Jonah 3)

Teaching Tips

Words You Should Know

A. Anger (Jonah 4:1, 4, 9) *kharah* (Heb.)—Emotional displeasure, ire, vexation caused by wrong, sometimes coupled with plans for revenge.

B. Merciful (v. 2) *racham* (Heb.)—Compassionate (only used of God).

Teacher Preparation

Unifying Principle—Seeing the Big Picture. People become displeased and angry when things do not go their way. How can we gain a larger perspective? Jonah discovers the wide breadth of God's pervasive love.

A. Pray before studying the text that the Holy Spirit will lead you as you teach this lesson.

B. Read the text in different translations for clarity and highlight key words.

C. Complete the accompanying lesson in the *Precepts For Living*® Study Guide.

O—Open the Lesson

A. Open the lesson with prayer.

B. Discuss the concept of self-will: stubborn adherence to one's own will, desires, etc., especially at the expense of others.

C. Ask: "When can ambition be another form of self-will?"

P—Present the Scriptures

A. Have students read the Aim for Change and the Keep In Mind verse together.

B. Connect the Scripture and the In Focus to the concept of self-will.

E—Explore the Meaning

A. Connect the Scripture and the Aim for Change to information presented in the Bible Background and In Depth.

B. Use the questions raised in Search the Scriptures and Discuss the Meaning to encourage the class to examine their beliefs about those with whom they have conflict.

N—Next Steps for Application

A. Begin lesson closure by asking volunteers to state one important word that could summarize today's lesson.

B. Close with prayer.

Worship Guide

For the Superintendent or Teacher
Theme: God's Pervasive and Sustaining Love
Song: "Have Thine Own Way, Lord"
Devotional Reading: Psalm 86:8–13

God's Pervasive Love

Bible Background • JONAH 4
Printed Text • JONAH 4 | Devotional Reading • PSALM 86:8–13

Aim for Change

By the end of the lesson, we will: EXPLAIN God's larger perspective and plan for the salvation of all people; FEEL God's compassion for those who do not know Him; and SHOW compassion to those who are far from God.

In Focus

As Derek watched the screen, his face began to cringe. The story on the news was about terrorists killing and persecuting believers in another country. There on the television he saw images of children with sad faces as they watched their homes being burned down. He saw the dead bodies of people laid out in the streets. Derek couldn't understand why any normal human being would do or approve of this. He exclaimed out loud, "People like that don't deserve to live. I just wish we would just go and bomb them all!" His wife overheard him, walked over to the couch, and put her arms around him. "Sweetheart, you seem to be really worked up about this." "I am," said Derek. "There's no reason why people like that should be allowed to do what they do." "Well," Kelly sighed, "I think you have to look at it with a God's eye view."

"What do you mean?" Derek responded, as he reached out to touch her arm. "Well, God is a God of justice, but he is also a God of compassion," she said. "Maybe He wants them to be touched by the love and the Holy Spirit they witness in the believers that they encounter." "I never thought about it like that," Derek said. "Instead of wanting people to be assassinated, I should be praying that they would be converted."

What makes it hard to love those who are not like us? In this lesson, we learn about the pervasive, all-inclusive love of God.

Keep in Mind

"And should not I spare Nineveh, that great city, wherein are more than sixscore thousand persons that cannot discern between their right hand and their left hand; and also much cattle?" (Jonah 4:11).

"And should not I spare Nineveh, that great city, wherein are more than sixscore thousand persons that cannot discern between their right hand and their left hand; and also much cattle?" (Jonah 4:11).

Focal Verses

KJV **Jonah 4:1** But it displeased Jonah exceedingly, and he was very angry.

2 And he prayed unto the LORD, and said, I pray thee, O LORD, was not this my saying, when I was yet in my country? Therefore I fled before unto Tarshish: for I knew that thou art a gracious God, and merciful, slow to anger, and of great kindness, and repentest thee of the evil.

3 Therefore now, O LORD, take, I beseech thee, my life from me; for it is better for me to die than to live.

4 Then said the LORD, Doest thou well to be angry?

5 So Jonah went out of the city, and sat on the east side of the city, and there made him a booth, and sat under it in the shadow, till he might see what would become of the city.

6 And the LORD God prepared a gourd, and made it to come up over Jonah, that it might be a shadow over his head, to deliver him from his grief. So Jonah was exceeding glad of the gourd.

7 But God prepared a worm when the morning rose the next day, and it smote the gourd that it withered.

8 And it came to pass, when the sun did arise, that God prepared a vehement east wind; and the sun beat upon the head of Jonah, that he fainted, and wished in himself to die, and said, It is better for me to die than to live.

9 And God said to Jonah, Doest thou well to be angry for the gourd? And he said, I do well to be angry, even unto death.

10 Then said the LORD, Thou hast had pity on the gourd, for the which thou hast not laboured, neither madest it grow; which came up in a night, and perished in a night:

11 And should not I spare Nineveh, that great city, wherein are more than sixscore thousand persons that cannot discern between

NLT **Jonah 4:1** This change of plans greatly upset Jonah, and he became very angry.

2 So he complained to the LORD about it: "Didn't I say before I left home that you would do this, LORD? That is why I ran away to Tarshish! I knew that you are a merciful and compassionate God, slow to get angry and filled with unfailing love. You are eager to turn back from destroying people.

3 Just kill me now, LORD! I'd rather be dead than alive if what I predicted will not happen."

4 The LORD replied, "Is it right for you to be angry about this?"

5 Then Jonah went out to the east side of the city and made a shelter to sit under as he waited to see what would happen to the city.

6 And the LORD God arranged for a leafy plant to grow there, and soon it spread its broad leaves over Jonah's head, shading him from the sun. This eased his discomfort, and Jonah was very grateful for the plant.

7 But God also arranged for a worm! The next morning at dawn the worm ate through the stem of the plant so that it withered away.

8 And as the sun grew hot, God arranged for a scorching east wind to blow on Jonah. The sun beat down on his head until he grew faint and wished to die. "Death is certainly better than living like this!" he exclaimed.

9 Then God said to Jonah, "Is it right for you to be angry because the plant died?" "Yes," Jonah retorted, "even angry enough to die!"

10 Then the LORD said, "You feel sorry about the plant, though you did nothing to put it there. It came quickly and died quickly.

11 But Nineveh has more than 120,000 people living in spiritual darkness, not to mention all the animals. Shouldn't I feel sorry for such a great city?"

their right hand and their left hand; and also much cattle?

The People, Places, and Times

Nineveh. Nineveh was located along the eastern bank of the Tigris River. Genesis 10:11 identifies Nimrod, great-grandson of Noah, as the founder of both Nineveh and Babylon. It was the capitol of the Assyrian empire for many years. The inhabitants were described as wealthy, warlike, highly civilized merchants who worshiped Ishtar (Astarte) the fertility goddess. The city was eventually attacked by the Medes and fell around 606 BC.

Assyrians. Assyrians were known for their fierce cruelty. By today's borders, their empire would span the countries of Iraq, Iran, Syria, and Turkey. Isaiah 36 tells us that when the Assyrians were about to attack Jerusalem, they began with a campaign of fear. For example, they sometimes captured their enemies and skinned them alive or cut off their heads and piled them in a pyramid to terrify those still alive in the city.

Background

The king of Israel during Jonah's ministry was Jeroboam II (2 Kings 14:23–29). He ruled for forty-one years. He succeeded Jeroboam, the first king of Israel, an Ephraimite "who had made Israel to sin" by introducing the worship of golden calves at Bethel and Dan. Jeroboam II conquered Hamath, Damascus, and all of the region east of the Jordan down to the Dead Sea. Jonah prophesied this extension of Israel's territory (2 Kings 14:25). Jeroboam II's long reign allowed him to increase his luxury through oppression and vice. Israel prospered while iniquity flourished (Amos 2:6–8; Hosea 4:12–14). Jonah's contemporaries include Hosea (1:1) and Amos (1:1).

After the people of Nineveh repented, Jonah had opportunity to establish a relationship with the Ninevites. Instead, he positioned himself alone, outside the city, under a bush. Jonah's rebellion may have been sparked by self-will or fear. Knowing that God is merciful, he may have been afraid of being labeled a false prophet—someone whose prophecy did not come true.

At-A-Glance

1. Jonah's Complaint (Jonah 4:1–4)
2. Jonah's Gourd (vv. 5–7)
3. Jonah's Rebuke (vv. 9–10)

In Depth

1. Jonah's Complaint (Jonah 4:1–4)

Jonah had just preached to the Ninevites, and the Ninevites were spared the judgment of God. Instead of being happy about God's grace toward the Ninevites, Jonah had his heart in the wrong place as he states his motive for not going to Nineveh the first time. His theological knowledge is right, but it doesn't lead to right practice. He knows God is compassionate and merciful. He just doesn't want God to be compassionate and merciful to the Ninevites.

The extreme hate that Jonah has toward the Assyrian people can be seen in his request for God to kill him. Jonah would rather be dead than for the Ninevites to experience God's grace. God prods Jonah with a question. He asks Jonah if it is right for him to be angry about His grace.

2. Jonah's Gourd (vv. 5–7)

Jonah, fuming in anger, walks outside the city. As he sits in his makeshift shelter, God causes a large, leafy plant to provide shade for Jonah. At this act of kindness, Jonah is thankful to God. The plant provides shade to ease his discomfort. Then God causes the leafy plant to dry up and wither.

Jonah is outraged. He expresses the same kind of anger and frustration as he did when he realized the grace the people of Nineveh experienced. God spared the people of Nineveh, but He wouldn't spare this plant. Jonah actually wants to die after he experiences the heat without the plant's shade.

3. Jonah's Rebuke (vv. 9–10)

God drives the point home with Jonah. First, He questions Jonah's right to be angry. He provokes Jonah to express his emotions over a small thing such as having shade. Jonah retorts that he is right to be angry about this plant. After all, it provided him with shade and allowed him to be comfortable in the heat.

Next, the Lord rebukes Jonah. Jonah feels sorry about the plant but he did nothing to cause it to grow. This plant had a short life span, and Jonah is upset about it. God allows Jonah to see a larger picture when he declares that there are 120,000 in Nineveh who don't know their left from their right and also animals. God wants to show mercy to His creation. He has compassion, and His love ranges wide over humanity.

Search the Scriptures

1. Is Jonah justified in his anger at God (Jonah 4:2)? Explain why.

2. Why do you believe God spared the city (v. 11)?

Discuss the Meaning

1. Jonah did the right actions for the wrong reason. God confronted him about his motives. What does the verbal exchange in this chapter teach us about speaking the truth in love?

2. The book of Jonah concludes with God giving mercy to both Jonah and the inhabitants of Nineveh. What outcomes can Christians expect when extending mercy instead of callousness?

Lesson in Our Society

Opportunities to confront wrong beliefs, in ourselves and in others, present themselves to us daily. Jonah's callous heart prevented him from caring for others. Like Jonah, we may need a fresh love for God's truth to genuinely care for others too. When offended, we can challenge others in love. God's loving challenge is often in the form of blunt questions. For instance, God challenged Jonah to repent by providing for him while pressing him to examine his motives.

Make It Happen

When offended, Christians may respond in anger or frustration. Like Jonah, we may fail to remember God's mercy to us. Our shortsightedness limits our ability to extend mercy to others. This week commit to doing one act of kindness for someone with whom you are having conflict or for a stranger. Pray to see the needs of others as God sees them.

Follow the Spirit

What God wants me to do:

_____

_____

_____

_____

Remember Your Thoughts
Special insights I have learned:

_____

_____

_____

_____

More Light on the Text
Jonah 4

1 But it displeased Jonah exceedingly, and he was very angry.

Rather than being excited over the success of his mission to Nineveh, Jonah is exceedingly displeased with God's action. He is "very angry" that God forgave the inhabitants of the city of Nineveh and spared them the punishment, which He had declared early against them. Here, Jonah explicitly confesses the reason, previously unexplained, for his attempt to escape from the command of God. He does not think that the Ninevites deserved mercy from Yahweh. Consequently, he is extremely angry when the city is spared rather than destroyed. The Hebrew construction and wordplay describing the emotional state of Jonah at this point does not carry over to the English translation. The verb "displeased" is the Hebrew word *ra'a'* (**rah-AH**), immediately linked with its noun *ra'* and modified by the adverb "exceedingly" or "greatly" (Heb. *gadol*, **gah-DOLE**). The word *ra'a'* with the noun *ra'* carries the idea of being evil or wicked, or of being injurious or hurt. Jonah was extremely and greatly hurt, to the extent that he became furious, probably with God: "He was very angry" (Heb. *kharah*, **khah-RAH**). *Kharah* means "to glow, to be hot, or to blaze up." The literal translation of the verse would read something like, "Jonah was greatly displeased with displeasure and he became furious." He was more than upset. He burned with anger. He was enraged and dejected that God's mercy had been extended to the people of Nineveh, the enemy of his people Israel.

2 And he prayed unto the LORD, and said, I pray thee, O LORD, was not this my saying, when I was yet in my country? Therefore I fled before unto Tarshish: for I knew that thou art a gracious God, and merciful, slow to anger and of great kindness, and repentest thee of the evil. 3 Therefore now, O Lord, take, I beseech thee, my life from me; for it is better for me to die than to live.

With anger and frustration, Jonah complains to God, accusing Him of "injustice" for being merciful to the city of Nineveh. He knows who God is and knows His character. He knows that God is gracious, merciful, kind, and compassionate, and that He forgives those who repent of their sin and come to Him. Jonah is aware of the possible outcome of the message that he is called to preach in Nineveh: they would repent and God would forgive them.

Now, that Nineveh has repented, the anger of God against the city is averted and they are spared. Jonah cannot handle this; it was for this very reason he had tried to flee to Tarshish. In his "selfish" prayer, he rhetorically questions God's character by asking, "Was not this my saying, when I was yet in my country?" Is he expecting a positive answer from the Lord? Of course not. His attempt to flee to Tarshish is because of his knowledge of God's unchanging character: "For I knew that thou art a gracious God, and merciful, slow to anger, and of great kindness, and repentest thee of the evil." He cannot reconcile himself with this knowledge.

He therefore begs the Lord to take away his life. The conjunction "therefore now," from the Hebrew word *'attah* (**at-TAH**), reflects the reason Jonah seeks to die. The use of this conjunction here also implies that the time for discussion of the matter is over. There is nothing else to do but to fulfill the request. Jonah seems to say, "Since I know you are a gracious God, and merciful, slow to anger, and of great kindness, and repentest thee of the evil, and I know you cannot change, let me die. It is better for me that way than to see these people forgiven." This statement clearly indicates the extent and degree of his anger and displeasure at what God has done (v. 1). He is so furious that for the second time he would prefer to die (see 1:12).

Here, we see a man who is so patriotic that he puts his love for his people above the will of God and the salvation of 120,000 people of Nineveh. Jonah becomes so angry and enraged at the saving of 120,000 people from destruction—people he converted to God through his preaching—and so angry at the goodness of God that he prefers to die. "It is better for me to die than to live," he says. Is he justified in being so angry?

4 Then said the LORD, Doest thou well to be angry? 5 So Jonah went out of the city, and sat on the east side of the city, and there made him a booth, and sat under it in the shadow, till he might see what would become of the city.

The Lord confronts Jonah in verse 4 and poses the same question to him: "Doest thou well to be angry?" This question can be framed in a variety of ways: "What right have you to be angry?" "Are you right to be angry?" "What justifies your anger?" and so on. In other words, the Lord is, on one hand, asking what gives Jonah authority to question Him or to meddle with His own authority and plan. By questioning Jonah, the Lord implicitly establishes His sovereignty and authority. God alone is the Lord and Creator of all things, and Jonah has no right to question His sovereignty

and authority. What God does with His creation is within His control and power. Jonah seems to have forgotten that the Lord says, "I will… be gracious to whom I will be gracious, and will shew mercy on whom I will shew mercy" (Exodus 33:19). Through this question to Jonah, the Lord implicitly makes it clear that no person merits His grace or His acts of mercy, but that His will is the basis for bestowing His blessings.

God's blessings, grace, and mercy come not because humanity wills them, but because God is essentially good, gracious, and merciful and does all things for humanity of His own free will and for His own pleasure. The question here reminds one of God's encounter with Job, although the encounter with Jonah is not as explicit as that with Job (Job 38).

Of course, just as Job could not answer the Lord's questions, so likewise Jonah cannot answer Him. Rather, still indignant and expecting God to do something (i.e., carry out His threat against Nineveh), Jonah goes out to a solitary place on the east side of the city. There he builds a booth to protect himself from the sun as he awaits God's anger and punishment to come upon the city. He is still hoping that God will destroy the city. He is still so clouded with fury that he finds it difficult to see and understand that God's ways are not humankind's ways, and that God's thoughts differ from the thoughts of humankind.

6 And the LORD God prepared a gourd, and made it to come up over Jonah, that it might be a shadow over his head, to deliver him from his grief. So Jonah was exceeding glad of the gourd.

The Lord caused a plant to grow up over Jonah and give him shade. The word "gourd" is qiqayon (Heb. **ki-kah-YONE**), and most commentators believe this to be the castor oil plant. This plant has an abundance of large leaves as well as small gourds on the branches. It is more than able to give shade to the traveler in the Near East.

Jonah's reaction to the plant is one of joy. Not only is he glad (Heb. *samach*, **sa-MOK**), which means to rejoice and sometimes religiously, but he is exceedingly (Heb. *gadol*) glad, which describes Jonah's strong intensity. This is an unusual amount of emotion for a plant that gives shade.

7 But God prepared a worm when the morning rose the next day, and it smote the gourd that it withered. 8 And it came to pass, when the sun did arise, that God prepared a vehement east wind; and the sun beat upon the head of Jonah, that he fainted, and wished in himself to die, and said, It is better for me to die than to live.

Next, God prepares a worm to eat the plant. This worm is the coccus ilicis. The Hebrew word for this worm (Heb. *tola'*, **toe-LAH**) is also used for the scarlet dye, which was taken from the decayed shell of the female of the species. Throughout the night, the worm smote (Heb. *nakah*, **na-KAH**) the plant. The literal meaning of the word is to kill or wound. The sense here is to blight with disease.

After this, God sends a vehement (Heb. *kha-rishi*, **kha-ree-SHE**) or hot east wind to blow on Jonah. It was intolerable enough for Jonah to become tired and wish that he was dead. It is this same phrase he used in verse 3. This exposes Jonah's twisted emotions as he wrestles with life. He is upset about the plants withering as much as he is upset about the Lord sparing Nineveh.

9 And God said to Jonah, Doest thou well to be angry for the gourd? And he said, I do well to be angry, even unto death. 10 Then said the LORD, Thou hast had pity on the gourd, for the which thou hast not laboured, **neither madest it grow; which came up in a night, and perished in a night:**

Next, the Lord questions Jonah's priorities. Jonah responds with justification for his anger. The Lord says that Jonah had pity (Heb. *khus*, **KHOOS**) on the gourd. The word means "to spare and to have compassion on someone or something." Jonah had not invested any effort in causing the plant to grow. The Lord also points out that the plant had a short life span and shows that Jonah's angry fits are petty.

11 And should not I spare Nineveh, that great city, wherein are more than sixscore thousand persons that cannot discern between their right hand and their left hand; and also much cattle?

The Lord's question stemmed from Jonah's reaction to the withering of the plant (vv. 6–10). How could Jonah be concerned about the death of the gourd but remain unconcerned, and indeed angry, about the well-being of the people of Nineveh? Here again is another rhetorical question. The author emphasizes the contrast between Jonah's relation to the plant and God's relation to the people of Nineveh. The Lord questions Jonah, saying, "If you are so concerned about the well-being of one ordinary plant, do you have any reason I should not have mercy on 120,000 "persons that cannot discern between their right hand and their left hand" and their animals? Why do you wish that they should perish?"

The expression, "persons that cannot discern between their right hand and their left hand" is an idiomatic expression that tends to refer to the ignorance of the people of Nineveh regarding the Law as compared with the Israelites. The expression can also refer to innocent children; in that case, the 120,000 persons do not refer to the entire population of Nineveh at the time, but to the number of children in the city. In either case, the expression directly corresponds in meaning with its Igbo (Nigerian) equivalent. In Igbo, the idiom runs "innocent children who cannot differentiate their left hand from their right," and for children, it has a positive connotation. If used for adults, though, the connotation is negative and expresses ignorance or stupidity. In either case, it also denotes the helplessness of the people in question.

The addition of the phrase "much cattle" signifies the extent of destruction that would have been meted out to the city of Nineveh had they not repented—total destruction of both people and property. However, the ignorance of the people and the helplessness of the animals do not constitute the basis for the exercise of God's mercy; they are mentioned to reveal Jonah's lack of sympathy, his blindness, and his selfishness, which result from his religious exclusiveness, patriotic spirit, and hypocrisy. The book gives no conclusion and leaves us wondering whether or not Jonah's anger is abated and whether he changed his attitude toward Nineveh or not.

However, the story of Jonah does give us an understanding of the Lord's salvation plan and the revelation that in His sovereign mercy and grace, God does not discriminate between peoples—Jews and Gentiles. Quoting the Old Testament passage, Paul writes, "What shall we say then? Is there unrighteousness with God? God forbid. For he saith to Moses, I will have mercy on whom I will have mercy, and I will have compassion on whom I will have compassion" (Romans 9:14–15).

Say It Correctly

Vehement. **VEE**-hi-mint.
Beseech. **bi-SEECH**.

Daily Bible Readings

MONDAY
The Lord's Proclamation
(Exodus 34:4–9)

TUESDAY
The Lord Forgives Iniquity
(Numbers 14:10b–11, 17–20)

WEDNESDAY
The Lord Did Not Forsake
(Nehemiah 9:16–21)

THURSDAY
Bless the Lord, O My Soul
(Psalm 103:1–14)

FRIDAY
A Prayer to the Lord for Help
(Psalm 86:1–7)

SATURDAY
Nations Will Bow Before the Lord
(Psalm 86:8–13)

SUNDAY
God's Compassion Endures
(Jonah 4)

God's Urgent Call

The theme for this quarter reminds us that God continues to speak to us through God's written word. God calls ordinary people from diverse backgrounds to make a difference. From the days of the judges to the prophets to the early church leaders, God called and the faithful answered.

UNIT 1 • CALLED TO BE STRONG

The four lessons in this unit are drawn from the Book of Judges and continue the history of Israel after Joshua's death. God raised up a series of national leaders called judges. Empowered by God, judges delivered the people from their enemies.

Lesson 1: June 4, 2017
Deborah and Barak
Judges 4:1–10
People called to be leaders might doubt their capabilities. How do leaders deal with their doubts? Barak willingly went into battle after the prophetess Deborah agreed to accompany him.

Lesson 2: June 11, 2017
Gideon's Call
Judges 6:11–18
People sometimes view their circumstances as a hindrance to being effective leaders. How do they deal with their doubts? Gideon voiced his doubts and requested a miraculous sign.

Lesson 3: June 18, 2017
Jepthah Answers the Call
Judges 11:4–11, 29–31

People called to be leaders might question the motives of their supporters. How do these leaders know if their supporters' motives are sincere? Jephthah discussed the inconsistencies in the behavior of his supporters and established conditions for his leadership.

Lesson 4: June 25, 2017
Samson's Call
Judges 13:1–7, 24–25
Preparation for leadership may involve life circumstances not of one's own choosing. How do we respond when we find ourselves in such circumstances? Even before birth, Samson's call was assured as shown by the instructions the Lord's angel gave to his mother.

UNIT 2 • CALLING OF THE PROPHETS

The five lessons in this unit focus on how God called various prophets at different times for specific purposes. Included in this unit are the calls and responses of Moses, Isaiah, Jeremiah, Ezekiel, and Amos.

Lesson 5: July 2, 2017
Moses and the Burning Bush
Exodus 3:1–12
People get accustomed to living with the injustices that prevail in society. What does it take to address injustice? God called Moses to address injustice and empowered him with the knowledge of God's identity, purpose, and presence.

Lesson 6: July 9, 2017
Isaiah in the Temple
Isaiah 6:1–8

Unexpected circumstances can lead us into paths we don't anticipate. Where do we gain confidence to undertake these unexpected tasks? Isaiah's confidence came from the unusual and compelling events of his call.

Lesson 7: July 16, 2017
Jeremiah's Call and Commission
Jeremiah 1:4–10

Each of us has some aspect of our lives that might convince us that we have nothing to give others. How do we overcome these perceived shortcomings? Jeremiah's response was based on God's promise to be with Jeremiah as he carried out his calling.

Lesson 8: July 23, 2017
Ezekiel's Call
Ezekiel 3:1–11

Discouragement and doubt can be hindrances to what we hope to achieve. What concrete action can help us get beyond our fears? Ezekiel's call involved eating a scroll that sweetened the bitter taste of his mission and receiving from God extra strength and protection for the challenges that lay ahead.

Lesson 9: July 30, 2017
Amos' Call
Amos 7:10–17

At times we find obeying God's direction to be in direct contrast to what others think we should do. Is it possible to remain determined despite the opposition? Amos committed to serving even in the face of negativity.

UNIT 3 • CALLS IN THE NEW TESTAMENT
The four lessons in this unit focus on how God continued to work through ordinary people. Their witness reminded the early church that God assures the success of those who will answer God's call. The unit highlights the calls of Stephen, Philip, Ananias, and Peter.

Lesson 10: August 6, 2017
Called to Witness
Acts 6:1–8

Recognizing priorities is a continuing challenge. How do we allocate resources in such a way that these priorities are appropriately addressed? The apostles realized that God calls us to make the best use of our specific gifts so that the witness of God can be accomplished.

Lesson 11: August 13, 2017
Called to Break Down Barriers
Acts 8:26–39

People rarely cross cultural boundaries in significant ways. What should motivate us to do so? Acts 8 records a cross–cultural encounter where Philip is called by God to witness to Jesus, the Son of God, as the basis of true meaning and purpose.

Lesson 12: August 20, 2017
Called to Preach
Acts 9:10–20

We often feel urges to act in certain ways. Is it OK to question those urges? Acts 9 describes God's call to Ananias and Saul, Ananias's questioning reaction, and God's firm response.

Lesson 13: August 27, 2017
Called to Be Inclusive
Acts 10:19–33

Traditions and cultural understandings often shape our view of the world and others in ways that limit our interactions. How do we overcome the limitations of such understandings? Through a vision and the Spirit, Peter learned how and why to witness to Cornelius and his household.

Called to the Marketplace

Many Christians long for a role in full time Christian ministry. What many believers don't understand is that we are all called to full time ministry. Ministry equals service, and we are all called to serve in one capacity or another. The only thing that is different is the context to which we are called. Some have been called to give themselves over to the word and prayer (Acts 6:4). While others have been called to wait on tables (Acts 6:2). Still others are called to the marketplace or to labor with their hands so that they can give to others (Ephesians 4:28).

To be called to the marketplace or to a non-church job is not a demotion. It is just a direction. God has blessed us all with gifts and talents and He wants us to use them not just in the four walls of the church building but where most of us rub shoulders with those who do not know Christ. Not only does the Lord want to use our jobs for evangelism, but He also places an intrinsic value on work.

When we work, we obey God's command to subdue the earth and have dominion over it (Genesis 1:28). We tend and keep the "garden" where He placed us (Genesis 2:15). In other words our calling in the marketplace helps us fulfill our identity as being made in the image of God (Genesis 1:27).

That's a different way to look at work. It's about much more than just earning a paycheck. It's about being exactly who God created you to be. It's about fulfilling the calling that God has given each and every one of us. Work was created before marriage. Adam had a job before he had a wife and family. If that is the case, then why do we give work such a bad rap?

One reason is that work in the marketplace is hard. After the Fall, the Lord cursed man's work by cursing the ground from which he would derive food (Genesis 3). As a result many people have a rough climb when it comes to work, no matter what kind it is—whether church related or not. Our efforts to subdue the earth and have dominion over it have led to the earth subduing and having dominion over us in many cases. Just because sometimes it's hard doesn't mean it's not our calling. God has created us for work even though we are challenged by the curse since sin entered the world.

The second reason is faulty theology. Once Christianity was given privilege under Constantine, full time clergy became the norm. This created a worldview that divided everything between secular and sacred. Those who were working in the church full time began to be seen as the ones who were doing God's work. Everyone else had to deal with earthly secular concerns. Because of this, we elevate the sacred over the secular. The truth is everything done to the glory of God is sacred.

Whether you are an artist, an activist, a businesswoman, or a baker, consider looking at your work in a different way. Consider looking at it not as a burden but as a calling. God has called you to your particular work site. God has called you to handle your particular challenges. Managing finances or working with wood is no less important than preaching or praying for the sick. The Lord has called each of us to serve with our unique gifts and talents. The call of God extends beyond the four walls of a church building and into the marketplace.

The Call To Christian Witness in the Book of Acts

by Francis Morkeh

Horatio Hackett in his *Commentary on Acts* writes that the book of Acts furnishes us with the origin, systematic growth, and extension of the church through the work of the apostles, especially Peter and Paul. Conversely, Michael Anthony in *Introducing Christian Education* says it would be "incomplete and reductionism" for one not to mention or emphasize the presence and power of the Holy Spirit to transform the lives of the disciples and guide them as they step out in obedience to The Great Commission (Acts 1:8; Matthew 28:18–20). It is the Holy Spirit who fills and empowers the believer for effective Christian witness.

There are many lessons the modern Christian can learn from these early believers, especially the importance of living in community, praying for healing, bravely facing death, breaking down unjust cultural barriers, and simply studying the Word of God.

Proper Understanding of Christian Witness

It is important to understand the root meaning of the word "witness" from a biblical perspective. Colin Brown states that the word "witness" as used in Acts 1:8 significantly uses the Greek word *martus*, (**MAR-toos**). Here, this word means someone legitimized and authorized to declare the story both of Christ's deeds on earth and His resurrection. Being a witness in this way means to follow a particular way or path of suffering in the process. It is a path that can lead to rejection, suffering, and possibly death for Christ's sake. In summary, it is a path that testifies and identifies with Christ's life and resurrection, even to the point of death. The Christian community is called to be a faithful witness that obeys Christ in all circumstances.

Community and Sharing

Duane Elmer describes two major types of cultures in the world: individualistic cultures in the West and collectivist cultures dominantly found in third world countries. The former centers primarily on the individual's (or simple majority's) feelings, needs, and desires. Many times this emphasis has robbed the Lord's people of having compassion for others within the group. Collectivist cultures, on the other hand, focus on interpersonal relationships, harmony, and community solidarity of the whole society or group. It is, however, important to state here that collectivism as described from the perspective of third world countries may not necessarily be built or founded on a biblical worldview. (It should also not be confused with communism, which is a system imposed by the government rather than naturally followed by the people.) However, there are some basic values and principles commonly found in collectivist cultures that intersect with the basic biblical principles of needing to build and live in a community from a scriptural point of view.

According to the biblical accounts, the disciples were of one mind and heart, and shared all that they had as that given to them by the Lord for their common good. This unified and gracious environment they created helped set the pace to do effective witnessing (Acts 4:33). The key word here is to be intentional in sharing in different ways. It means to care by sharing, love by empathizing, and lift up by supporting each other spiritually, materially, and psychologically in the Christian community.

Let us express our love as individuals, local groups, and the universal church through the sharing of our talents, treasures, and time as people who are living as a healthy Christian community founded on biblical principles. This can be achieved through the empowerment of the Holy Spirit and God's *agape* love in our hearts. It is beyond all human or natural love we have ever experienced or received in this life. Abiding in this kind of love and community will help us be as great witnesses to the Gospel as the apostles in Acts.

Holistic Healing and Miracles

In 1978, in Accra, Ghana, doctors gave up on me because I had a traumatic accident in a soccer training session. African herbalists also could not help me. I was withdrawn from school as a result. After two years of suffering, I was taken to a pastor who prayed for me and I was healed. I went back to continue my education, and today, I have earned my Ph.D. in Educational Studies and my life has become a living witness of God's power. It is important to emphasize that the pastor was not the source of the miracle. He was just a vessel the Holy Spirit used to glorify Christ's name by bringing healing to my life. Jesus Christ still heals people in many ways today through His committed witnesses. The word "healing" or "cure" used many times in the New Testament has the concept of that which is holistic, namely, psychological, emotional, physical, mental, and spiritual. It means people who were diseased are set free from all forms of bondage and uneasiness.

After all, God created humankind not only to develop physically, but also spiritually, socially, emotionally, cognitively, and morally (Wilhoit and Dettoni). The believer, like Peter and John (Acts 3:6), may not have silver and gold. But the power of the Holy Spirit is available to heal people today by faith in Jesus' name. Throughout church history, some individuals or groups have had some reservations and doubts about God's healing power. This may be because some people have abused, misused, and manipulated either the spiritual gifts or the process in itself. Others too have closed themselves up to this topic of divine healing today because of their secularized worldview that dismisses anything supernatural. But Scripture declares: "Jesus Christ is the same yesterday and to day, and for ever" (Hebrews 13:8, KJV). He is the ultimate source for all forms of healing that bring glory to the name of the Lord. Let us not be ashamed or afraid to call on the healing power of God to bear witness to His goodness and strength, just as we see done in Acts.

Boldness and Total Surrender

In the Bible, we read about faithful believers who boldly stood up and died for the sake of the Gospel as the ultimate sacrifice for Christ's sake. One example is Stephen. He was rejected, persecuted, and stoned to death by those who opposed the Gospel because of his unwavering faith in Christ through the empowerment of the Holy Spirit (Acts 6:8, 7:60). God has sometimes called people to stay the course of their faith and conviction, and even die in the process, all for the sake of His purpose. Church history records numerous Christian leaders and followers of Christ who took the path of faithfulness in Christian witness to die for Christ's sake. Many of the early church believers converted because of Polycarp, the great church father who was killed for his faith. In communist countries, millions of believers were killed because they would not give up their Christian witness. As Christians we operate from a biblical worldview. Our Bible teaches us that the only way to be saved is through Christ (Acts 4:12). Stephen's example and lifestyle should make us ready to make an ultimate sacrifice for our faith as we stand as witnesses for the world to see.

Beyond Prejudice and Bias

God commands the believer to proclaim the Gospel to every creature wherever we find ourselves (Mark 16:15–18). However, in human society, there are all forms of social stratification that have the potential of hindering evangelistic outreach. There are structures and systems like tribal and ethnic divisions in Africa, cultural and subcultural differences, caste systems in India, and status and power positions that become major blockers to Christian witness.

While some of these describe negative structures and systems in society, others simply have to do with diversity in God's creation. All these have the potential to create biased and prejudiced mindsets in a believer who wants to reach out to others in their society.

In biblical times, the Jews and Samaritans looked down on one another because of different understandings of God and worship. Yet, Jesus in His earthly ministry went beyond the ugly lines of prejudice to reach out to Samaritans (John 4). He was opposed and rejected in the process but He was determined and courageous, and God confirmed His word with signs and wonders. Similarly, Philip in the power of the Holy Spirit was a witness to the Ethiopian eunuch, a foreigner and an outsider (Acts 8). We should, therefore, not be deterred by social, cultural, or religious systems that have the potential to hinder our witness. Let us go all out for the Lord. The promise of the outpouring of the Holy Spirit, and its fulfillment in Acts 2 on the day of Pentecost, was for all flesh (Joel 2:28–29; Acts 2:38). There is therefore no basis for believers being discriminatory in their evangelistic efforts. There is always an opportunity in our Christian witness for people of all backgrounds and ages to witness for Christ and also receive God's gift of salvation.

God's Word and Effective Witness

Finally, Christian witness becomes effective when the believer studies and grows in God's Word. Studying, understanding, and applying God's Word in the believer's life to shape our actions and understanding of the will of God is a sure foundation for Christian faith and practice. This does not imply that Christians should not read or study other books apart from the Bible that can help them develop a broad and holistic understanding of life and Christian worldview. It is important that we be encouraged to do this. However, these books or materials are not a substitute for God's Word—the Bible.

As believers, we are called to follow Christ, our model and example, and be like Him through the help of the Spirit (2 Corinthians 3:18). The only way to effectively do that is by prayerfully studying the Word of God and living according to its teachings. Philip was able to help the Ethiopian official understand and grow in the Word of God (Acts 8:26–38). We must be encouraged to participate in Bible studies in the church, at home, and in the workplace. Bible study helps us grow emotionally and spiritually, and equips us in our Christian witness. Let us dive deep into God's Word!

Sources:

Anthony, Michael J. *Introducing Christian Education: Foundations for the Twenty-first Century.* Grand Rapids, MI: Baker Academic, 2001.

Brown, Colin, ed. *The International Dictionary of New Testament Theology.* Vol. 3. Grand Rapids, MI: Zondervan, 1986.

Elmer, Duane. *Cross-Cultural Conflict: Building Relationships for Effective Ministry.* Downers Grove, IL: InterVarsity Press, 1993.

Hackett, Horatio. *Commentary on Acts.* Grand Rapids, MI: Kregel Classics, 1992.

Stott, John R.W. *Between Two Worlds: The Art of Preaching in the Twentieth Century.* Grand Rapids, MI: Eerdmans, 1982.

Wilhoit, James C. and John M. Dettoni. *Nurture That Is Christian: Developmental Perspectives on Christian Education.* Grand Rapids, MI: BridgePoint Books, 1998.

Frances Morkeh is an adjunct professor at Christian Life College in Mt. Prospect, IL and holds a Ph.D. in Educational Studies from Chicago State University.

Somebody's Calling My Name

by Rev. Darryl Aaron

Howard Thurman wrote in his classic book *The Inward Journey*, "It is a strange freedom to be adrift in the world of men without a sense of anchor anywhere. Always there is the need of mooring, the need for the firm grip on something that is rooted and will not give. The urge to be accountable to someone, to know that beyond the individual himself there is an answer that must be given, cannot be denied. The deed a man performs must be weighed in a balance held by another's hand." We were not created to be adrift; moreover, we have been claimed by God, which indicates we are being guided and directed by another's power.

To say God calls us or we all have callings is to recognize that humans live under the scrutiny and pull of another. We cannot simply do what we want with our lives; we are to live by the order of the divine. James Baldwin, writer and civil rights activist, tells about his early years of being adrift as a black boy in Harlem in 1950s. Amid pimps and prostitutes, Baldwin asserts he could see that many of his friends were "headed for the Avenue." When Baldwin was asked by a female pastor, "Whose little boy are you?" which were the same words used by the pimps and prostitutes, Baldwin knew he wanted to be somebody's little boy. Having been raised in a Christian home, Baldwin knew something about Paul's admonishment in his letter to the Ephesians when he wrote, "so that we may no longer be children tossed to and fro and carried with every wind of doctrine" (Ephesians 4:14). Deep down we all must know, like James Baldwin, we are somebody's little boy or girl! We have been claimed by God, called by God, and we are God's children.

Once one has accepted that he or she is God's child, then that person can begin to discern what they should do with their lives. Parker Palmer, the renowned Quaker, has purported that we discern our calling by listening to our lives. Many Quakers over a lifetime will hear, "Let your life speak. Let the highest truths and values guide you." Palmer says he had witnessed such heroism in his lifetime and he tried to imitate those heroes. However, at thirty years of age, he discovered that was simply an imitation; it was not his own life. Our callings must be authentic to who we have been created to be. Palmer states that to really let your life speak means: "Before you tell your life what you intend to do with it, listen for what it intends to do with you. Before you tell your life what truths and values you have decided to live up to, let your life tell you what truths you embody, what values you represent." Then Palmer examines the word vocation, which is rooted in the Latin for "voice." With that insight he declares that vocation does not mean a goal that one pursues, rather it is a calling that one hears.

This gets at the heart of our calling from God. There is a voice not merely from without but from within that we must listen to and follow. Too often people get their callings from the wrong place. We cannot let the culture or even our parents dictate what we are going to do with our lives. The old Negro spiritual speaks volumes to this assertion with these words: "Hush, hush, somebody is calling my name... Oh my Lord, oh my Lord, what shall I do?" The song demands that the ego and anything else that tries to speak must be silenced so the authentic calling can be heard.

Once the false voices are silenced and the authentic voice is heard, you find your place to exercise your calling. Our callings manifest themselves in specific seasons and places. In other words our callings are often shaped by our surroundings. At the inauguration of Jesus' ministry He found Himself in Nazareth in the synagogue reading from a scroll of the prophet Isaiah. Jesus found His calling in the prophetic ministry of preaching good news to the poor, proclaiming freedom to the captives, recovery of sight to the blind, and setting the oppressed free (Luke 4:18). Moses was a Hebrew who had to exercise his calling in a land ruled by a tyrant. Esther, a Jewish queen, had to bring to bear her calling when her people were about to be annihilated. Our mission and work are rooted in specific places and times.

Many years after Rosa Parks' courageous act, she was asked why she refused to move to the back of the bus. Legend has it that she didn't say that she sat down to launch a movement; her motives were more basic than that. Rosa said, "I sat down because I was tired." However, she did not mean her feet were tired. She meant that her soul was tired, her heart was tired, and her whole being was tired of playing by the racist rules, of denying her soul's claim to selfhood. Rosa Parks had grown up in the South under the demeaning and degrading hand of Jim Crow laws. She lived out her calling in a place that denied African Americans their God-given rights. It was in Montgomery, Alabama—riding buses where Blacks were demanded by law to stand while Whites sat—that Rosa Parks found her place to answer the question: What shall I do?

"Somebody is calling my name, Oh my Lord, what shall I do," is an ethical echo and the imperative whisper that must be heard and answered by God's people. To answer God's call is to anchor oneself in a windy culture that tosses people to and fro.

Sources:
Baldwin, James. *The Fire Next Time*. Vintage International, New York: 1963.
Palmer, Parker. *Let Your Life Speak*. Jossey-Bass: San Fransisco, CA: 2000.
Thurman, Howard. *The Inward Journey*. Friends United Press, Richmond, IN: 1961.

Rev. Darryl Aaron is the pastor of First Baptist Church in Charlotte, North Carolina. He holds an M.Div. from Samuel Dewitt Proctor Seminary and a D.Min. from Drew University.

MADAM C.J. WALKER

(December 23, 1867–May 25, 1919)

Sarah Breedlove's parents were former slaves who share-cropped in the Louisiana Delta. Orphaned by seven years old, she was shifted from one family to the next until she went to live with her sister Louvina and Louvina's husband, Willie Powell. Willie began abusing her, so she ran away and married Moses McWilliams when she was just 14 years old.

After a few years, Sarah gave birth to Lelia, her only child. Then just a few years later, her husband died. Sarah was almost penniless, so she took her little girl and moved to St. Louis where her four brothers were working as barbers. She worked hard during the days as a laundrywoman so she could provide for her daughter's education. She joined the St. Paul African Methodist Episcopal Church where she sang in the choir. She was greatly influenced by some of the Christian women who were members of that church.

At this time she developed a scalp ailment that caused her to start losing her hair. Sarah began experimenting with various ingredients to create products specifically for the hair of African American women. When her brother died, she moved to Denver, Colorado. When she arrived she had only $2.00 in her pocket, so she worked as a cook in the daytime and then worked on developing her hair product business in the evenings. In Denver she met and married Charles Joseph ("C.J.") Walker and began calling herself and her company Madam C.J. Walker. Mr. Walker was a newspaperman with a talent for marketing. He started placing advertisements for her hair products in African American newspapers throughout the United States. Madam C.J. Walker had a great vision for the growth of her company but Mr. Walker disagreed with her, so they divorced. However, he continued to help as a sales agent. One of his ideas was door-to-door marketing, which was very good for the growth of the business.

By 1906, the company had grown greatly and so she brought on her daughter, who had just graduated from college. Lelia ran the business from the office, while Madam Walker traveled throughout the US, Latin America, and the Caribbean, marketing her products and developing new ones. She also started up a college to train women in how to use and sell the products. By 1910 she had one thousand sales agents, and moved the company to Indianapolis, Indiana. The company continued growing until Madam C.J. Walker was worth a million dollars. After all the suffering, poverty, and hardship she had gone through, she became the first woman, Black or White, who became a millionaire based on her own achievements.

Teaching Tips

Words You Should Know

A. Call (Judges 4:6) *qara* (Heb.)—To address by name; to shout out.

B. Honor (v. 9) *tif'arah* (Heb.)—Beauty, splendor, glory.

Teacher Preparation

Unifying Principle—Without a Doubt. People called to be leaders might doubt their capabilities. How do leaders deal with their doubts? Barak willingly went into battle after the prophetess Deborah agreed to accompany him.

A. Read Judges 4 and Exodus 3. Note how both Barak and Moses lacked confidence. Moses later grows to rely on God (Exodus 15:2). Sometimes leaders doubt their capabilities and hide their insecurities, fearing others might think less of them.

B. Pray that students challenge their fears and grow in reliance on God.

O—Open the Lesson

A. Open with the Keep in Mind verse and prayer.

B. Introduce the summary for the unit on page 418, today's unifying principle, and read the Aim for Change and the Keep in Mind verse together.

C. Read In Focus and have the students share times when they were in a similar situation.

D. Say: "Today we have two models of leadership: Barak and Deborah. From the life of Barak, we learn how to cope with fears. In Deborah, we see an example of strong leadership during challenging times."

P—Present the Scriptures

A. Have volunteers read the Focal Verses.

B. Use The People, Places, and Times, Background; In Depth; and Search the Scriptures sections to clarify the passage.

E—Explore the Meaning

A. Have the students answer the Discuss the Meaning questions.

B. Read the Lesson in Our Society section.

N—Next Steps for Application

A. Summarize the lesson and challenge the students to apply the Make It Happen section to their lives.

B. Close with prayer.

Worship Guide

For the Superintendent or Teacher
Theme: Deborah and Barak
Song: "My Faith Looks Up to Thee"
Devotional Reading: Hebrews 11:29–40

Deborah and Barak

Bible Background • JUDGES 4–5
Printed Text • JUDGES 4:1–10 | Devotional Reading • HEBREWS 11:29–40

Aim for Change

By the end of this lesson, we will: GRASP the changing leadership dynamics during the time of Deborah; EMPATHIZE with Barak's sense of inadequacy and Deborah's sense of confidence; and WELCOME godly counsel and be willing to share such wisdom with others.

In Focus

Placing his dinner on the dinner table, Reggie mechanically mumbled his grace while filling his mouth and checking email. He was feeling pretty beat up after his first week teaching. The kids had given him a run for his money as they challenged his authority and made things hard for the other students. Reggie was beginning to wonder whether he had made the right decision to teach kids in the inner city. Was this his idea or God's? After a day like this, he was beginning to think it was his idea. Maybe he had bitten off more than he could chew. As he looked through his email, he noticed a message from his granddad, with the subject line "Stand and see."

Curious, he opened the mail and read: "You are teaching today's youth like your granddad. I couldn't be more proud of you if I tried. But teaching has changed, and I'm guessing New Bern, North Carolina is very different from the Bronx. I'm sure the last few days in your own classroom has taught you this much (ha ha). Know that I'm praying for you, son. I'm guessing right now you might have some questions and concerns of your own. I'm imagining that you're wondering if you are in God's will. Right?

"Well, I have a word from the Lord— 'Stand still, and see.' That's all, 'Stand, and see.'"

God calls ordinary people to do extraordinary things so that He might receive the glory. When has God challenged you to do something out of your comfort zone?

Keep in Mind

"And she said, I will surely go with thee: notwithstanding the journey that thou takest shall not be for thine honour; for the LORD shall sell Sisera into the hand of a woman" (from Judges 4:9).

"And she said, I will surely go with thee: notwithstanding the journey that thou takest shall not be for thine honour; for the LORD shall sell Sisera into the hand of a woman" (from Judges 4:9).

Focal Verses

KJV **Judges 4:1** And the children of Israel again did evil in the sight of the LORD, when Ehud was dead.

2 And the LORD sold them into the hand of Jabin king of Canaan, that reigned in Hazor; the captain of whose host was Sisera, which dwelt in Harosheth of the Gentiles.

3 And the children of Israel cried unto the LORD: for he had nine hundred chariots of iron; and twenty years he mightily oppressed the children of Israel.

4 And Deborah, a prophetess, the wife of Lapidoth, she judged Israel at that time.

5 And she dwelt under the palm tree of Deborah between Ramah and Bethel in mount Ephraim: and the children of Israel came up to her for judgment.

6 And she sent and called Barak the son of Abinoam out of Kedeshnaphtali, and said unto him, Hath not the LORD God of Israel commanded, saying, Go and draw toward mount Tabor, and take with thee ten thousand men of the children of Naphtali and of the children of Zebulun?

7 And I will draw unto thee to the river Kishon Sisera, the captain of Jabin's army, with his chariots and his multitude; and I will deliver him into thine hand.

8 And Barak said unto her, If thou wilt go with me, then I will go: but if thou wilt not go with me, then I will not go.

9 And she said, I will surely go with thee: notwithstanding the journey that thou takest shall not be for thine honour; for the LORD shall sell Sisera into the hand of a woman. And Deborah arose, and went with Barak to Kedesh.

10 And Barak called Zebulun and Naphtali to Kedesh; and he went up with ten thousand men at his feet: and Deborah went up with him.

NLT **Judges 4:1** After Ehud's death, the Israelites again did evil in the LORD's sight.

2 So the LORD turned them over to King Jabin of Hazor, a Canaanite king. The commander of his army was Sisera, who lived in Harosheth-haggoyim.

3 Sisera, who had 900 iron chariots, ruthlessly oppressed the Israelites for twenty years. Then the people of Israel cried out to the LORD for help.

4 Deborah, the wife of Lappidoth, was a prophet who was judging Israel at that time.

5 She would sit under the Palm of Deborah, between Ramah and Bethel in the hill country of Ephraim, and the Israelites would go to her for judgment.

6 One day she sent for Barak son of Abinoam, who lived in Kedesh in the land of Naphtali. She said to him, "This is what the LORD, the God of Israel, commands you: Call out 10,000 warriors from the tribes of Naphtali and Zebulun at Mount Tabor.

7 And I will call out Sisera, commander of Jabin's army, along with his chariots and warriors, to the Kishon River. There I will give you victory over him."

8 Barak told her, "I will go, but only if you go with me."

9 "Very well," she replied, "I will go with you. But you will receive no honor in this venture, for the LORD's victory over Sisera will be at the hands of a woman." So Deborah went with Barak to Kedesh.

10 At Kedesh, Barak called together the tribes of Zebulun and Naphtali, and 10,000 warriors went up with him. Deborah also went with him.

The People, Places, and Times

Deborah. Deborah, whose name means "honeybee," was a leader, wife, prophetess, and poet. Her responsibilities included settling disputes and offering advice and guidance to leaders like Barak. She was a woman of influence and power, whose decision-making was a marked contrast to that of Jephthah and Samson, who judged Israel after her. Jephthah made a vow in an attempt to manipulate God (Judges 11:29–40); Samson struggled with lust and devoted himself to a prostitute (Judges 16:1). As a woman, Deborah demonstrated fidelity to her husband and to those whom she led. Perhaps she heard disputes under her palm tree because it was inappropriate for a man to visit a woman in her house.

Barak. Barak, whose name means "lightning," initially hesitated to accept his call to fight against Sisera. He later led ten thousand warriors from the tribes of Naphtali and Zebulun into battle against the Canaanites. However, he accepted Deborah's call to battle only after she agreed to accompany him. Regardless, he is listed in Hebrews 11:32 as a hero of faith.

Sisera. Sisera was the general of the Canaanite king Jabin's soldiers. He was possibly a Hurrian, a people known as expert chariot-fighters in the Late Bronze Age. Well-prepared and equipped, he relied on his nine hundred chariots of iron and a host of soldiers.

Background

Israel lived comfortably in peace after Ehud's triumph over Moab (Judges 3:12–30). Then they were forced into survival mode by Canaanite troops. Cities previously destroyed by Joshua had been rebuilt as the Canaanites grew stronger. People previously conquered by the Israelites now ruled and demanded tribute.

Deborah stood to speak for God during challenging times. Without a similar model or mentor, she assumed a role generally filled by men, and rose up to initiate a fight, motivate an army, and encourage a leader.

Barak did not allow Deborah's gender to cloud his response. He answered the call and partnered with Deborah to lead the army.

At-A-Glance

1. Sisera's Oppression (Judges 4:1–3)
2. Deborah's Inspiration (vv. 4–7)
3. Barak's Hesitation (vv. 8-10)

In Depth

1. Sisera's Oppression (Judges 4:1–3)

Once again, after a brief time of peace and safety, the Israelites had gone back to worshiping the gods of their neighbors. This would result in their being oppressed by those same people. God would not tolerate their idolatry and unfaithfulness. They were His people, and He expected them to be loyal to Him.

After Ehud died, the Israelites fell into the hands of Jabin, the king of Canaan. He oppressed the Israelites through his general Sisera, who had nine hundred iron chariots at his command. This definitely placed him at an advantage as the Israelites had no chariots or iron weapons. To go against Sisera would be suicide.

2. Deborah's Inspiration (vv. 4–7)

The Lord would not break His covenant with His people. He raises up an unlikely leader in Deborah. Considering the patriarchal culture of the time, Deborah's leadership as a woman is unusual. She is a prophetess and a judge, speaking God's Word and enforcing His laws and wisdom. Deborah was a formidable leader during this time of oppression and chaos.

Deborah receives inspiration from God, and calls out Barak to lead Israel against Sisera. Not only does she challenge him to fight for Israel's freedom, she also commits to join him in battle, leading Sisera right into Barak's hands.

3. Barak's Hesitation (vv. 8–10)

Barak is not as confident as Deborah. His response shows that he doesn't believe the Lord has really chosen him to lead. He is hesitant to join Deborah in her plan against Sisera. What he doesn't realize is that the plan is not just Deborah's, but God's.

Barak lets Deborah know that he will go only if she does. His faith is not in God, but Deborah's leadership. He doesn't realize that God is the deciding factor; his advantage over Sisera is not Deborah, but that God will be with him. As a result, Deborah informs him that because of his hesitation and fear, the honor of victory will go to a woman, not to him. His personal lack of faith resulted in being dishonored by God and not receiving personal victory.

Search the Scriptures

1. How did having iron chariots help Sisera and his army dominate the Israelites in warfare (Judges 4:3)?

2. What feeling motivated the response Barak gave to Deborah after she challenged him to lead Israel into battle (v. 8)?

Discuss the Meaning

1. What things in our lives can make us feel inadequate to respond to God's call?

2. What are the differences between confidence in God and self-reliance?

Lesson in Our Society

Like the Israelites, Christians engaged in spiritual warfare can sometimes follow a cycle of apostasy, oppression, repentance, and deliverance. The cycle occurs when Christians value their own strength and capabilities over dependence on God. Doubt and over-reliance on something other than God will eventually cause Christians to fall, becoming ensnared in bondage.

Times for courage can be instances where we have to deliver bad news, such as: you did not get the job, you are fired, I'm taking away your cell phone for a week. Focusing on ourselves or the situation rather than God's promises can lead to anxiety, doubt, and even panic. Instead, choose to believe God's message, reach out for fellowship, and accept good advice when it is offered.

Make It Happen

Christian leadership begins with a call—a sense that God has a specific role or task for each Christian to accomplish (Romans 12). God prepared Barak for his battle with Sisera and raised him up to be a general. Similarly, He prepares each believer to accomplish specific tasks. What role has God prepared you for?

The call originates with God, and confidence to accomplish the task begins in us. We grow in confidence by making time to meditate on the Bible's promises, even just by repeating them over and over to ourselves.

Follow the Spirit

What God wants me to do:

_____

_____

_____

Remember Your Thoughts

Special insights I have learned:

_____

_____

_____

_____

More Light on the Text

Judges 4:1–10

1 And the children of Israel again did evil in the sight of the LORD, when Ehud was dead. 2 And the LORD sold them into the hand of Jabin king of Canaan, that reigned in Hazor; the captain whose host was Sisera, which dwelt in the Harosheth of the Gentiles.

God "sold" Israel, or handed Israel over as one would a slave, because of their disobedience. The word translated "sold" (Heb. *makar*, **mah-KAR**) is a common word, also used for selling things like oxen or slaves. Thus the people became merchandise, liable to be sold if no longer useful to their owner. This could also be read to mean that God surrendered them to the enemy, or sent them away from His presence. He sold them "into the hand" of a human being, implying dominion, forced fellowship, or labor joined with pain caused by misuse of power. Note the progression: They left the hand of God, were sold or transferred into a human hand, and were given over into the hands of the nations. In other words, God would allow Jabin and his people to oppress Israel as punishment for sin. This action is the essence of what the Bible means by reaping what you sow (Galatians 6:7–8). Whenever we disobey God, we voluntarily place ourselves outside of His will. Thus, without God's protection, we will suffer from harmful situations as natural consequences or from His punishment (see Hebrews 12:5–7).

The city of Hazor was located within the land of the tribe of Naphtali. Hazor was near the eastern border of the territory of Napthali west of the Jordan River. The land of the tribe of Zebulun was adjacent to the southwest border of Naphtali. Both of these tribal territories were in the northern area of the promised land. Obviously, non-Hebrew people lived on the land which had been captured by Israel under Joshua. Therefore, Sisera's base of operations in Harosheth was located among the northern tribes of Israel, and he could easily reach out to torment them. The king named Jabin in this text is a descendant of another king, also named Jabin, who had previously been defeated by Joshua (see Joshua 11:1, 10). This passage is a continuation of the cycle of rebellion, punishment, and restoration recurring throughout the book of Judges.

3 And the children of Israel cried unto the LORD: for he had nine hundred chariots of iron; and twenty years he mightily oppressed the children of Israel.

Sisera had a great advantage in battle; he commanded many iron chariots. His men could drive through a swarm of Israelite foot soldiers and kill them with swords or trample them with their horses. They also had sharp blades attached to the wheels to injure their enemies. Sisera's men were therefore less vulnerable because of their iron protection. The mismatch in weaponry evidently favored Sisera greatly, because for "twenty years he mightily oppressed the children of Israel."

Seeing their plight, Israel begged the God whom they had rejected to help them. One might wonder if they tacked a familiar refrain onto their plea, something like, "Lord, if You help us out of this jam, we'll never disobey You again." Many Christians have said those words only to repeat the same destructive behavior again and again. Some things never change.

only to repeat the same destructive behavior again and again. Some things never change.

We see the reaction that will become a dominant theme of the book of Judges: "the children of Israel cried unto the LORD." The word "cry" here is more than shedding tears of regret. The Hebrew for "they cried" has as its root the word *tsa'ak* (**tsaw-AK**), which means "to shriek or cry out in pain." The contextual use of this word shows that this kind of proclamation of hurt often calls others' attention. One could read this verse as "they cried out bitterly" or "with a bitter cry."

Note that the reason for the Israelites' mighty cry—this shrieking, deep sobbing, convulsion of the whole body of Israel that shook heaven's door—was the enemy's might (Heb. *khozkah*, **khoze-KAH**), which was grounded in technological superiority. However, their power was not actually due to their technology, but because the Lord had allowed them to prevail over Israel. Israel was so overwhelmed by the war machine of Jabin and Sisera that they had to cry out to the Lord. As the passage suggests, after they had walked out of God's hand into the hand of their enemy, they found themselves without a place to stand.

4 And Deborah, a prophetess, the wife of Lapidoth, she judged Israel at that time. 5 And she dwelt under the palm tree of Deborah between Ramah and Bethel in mount Ephraim: and the children of Israel came up to her for judgment.

Deborah is introduced to us right away as a "prophetess" (Heb. *'ishshah nebi'ah*, **ish-SHAH ne-vee-YAH**), literally "a woman prophet." A prophet spoke on behalf of God to the people (cf. Deuteronomy 18:15–22). Up to this point in Israel's history, Moses was the most eminent of the prophets. Joshua was never referred to as a prophet, since his work was not to reveal new words from the Lord but to lead Israel in

obedience to what the Lord had commanded through Moses. By reading that the Lord is speaking again to His people through a human spokesperson, the reader's hopes are raised that perhaps once again the Lord will do something great to deliver His people, just as when He revealed Himself through Moses.

At the time this story takes place, Deborah was already in a position of leadership. Her work is described as "judging" (Heb. *shafat*, **shah-FOT**), which could include acting as a lawgiver, arbiter, or governor.

Deborah is unique among the judges in that she is identified not as the one whom God chose to be a deliverer, but the messenger to that deliverer (Barak). The reference to Deborah's location under the palm tree could mean several different things. Her home might have been located at that certain spot, or she could have held court outdoors there. The Hebrew word translated "dwelt" (*yashab*, **yah-SHAV**) can mean either "to sit" or "to dwell." Essentially the narrative is saying that she spent a lot of time under that particular tree.

The passage tells us that the Israelites came to Deborah for "judgment" (Heb. *mishpat*, **mish-POT**). The Hebrew wording has led many commentators to assume that Deborah was known as a judge in the legal sense. However, the story emphasizes her role as God's spokesperson by calling her a prophetess and emphasizing the command for Barak that she received from the Lord.

6 And she sent and called Barak, the son of Abinoam out of Kedeshnaphtali, and said unto him, Hath not the LORD God of Israel commanded, saying, Go and draw toward mount Tabor, and take with thee ten thousand men of the children of Naphtali and of the children of Zebulun? 7 And I will draw unto thee to the river Kishon Sisera, the captain of Jabin's army, with his chariots and his

multitude; and I will deliver him into thine hand.

Verse 6 contains all the biographical information we have on Barak. His father is not mentioned in any other context, but we do know that Kedeshnaphtali was in the north of Israel and most likely would have been under the oppression of Jabin.

The word rendered "Hath not" (Heb. *halo*, **ha-LOH**) is probably better understood as "behold" or "indeed." Deborah is not assuming that Barak has already heard from God about what he is supposed to do. By every indication, this is the first time Barak has received this message. Deborah gives him the message, however, in a way that prophets commonly gave messages from God: with words that carry authority and demand a resolute answer.

Mount Tabor rises steeply 1,843 feet above sea level at the northeast corner of the Jezreel Valley, and forces stationed on it could easily control one of the most important crossroads in the region. Tabor also offered the advantage of being a prominent landmark, and the forces Barak summoned would have no confusion about where to make their stand. Essentially, God was telling Barak to use his forces to defiantly take control of the strategic high ground, forcing the enemy to come to him. Note that God provided the leader as well as the strategy.

Naphtali and Zebulun were regions subject to the oppressive rule of Jabin, king of Canaan. Hazor (Jabin's capital city) and Harosheth (Sisera's home city) straddled these two areas—Hazor to the northeast of Naphtali, and Harosheth to the southwest of Zebulun.

God tells Barak that He will draw Sisera and his army to the Kishon River. Evidently, Sisera will hear that the Israelites have taken control of Mount Tabor and move to put down their uprising. The key to Sisera's military power is his possession of 900 iron chariots, something the Israelites had encountered before and found to be intimidating (cf. Joshua 17:16; Judges 1:19). These chariots were seen as so threatening that the Israelites had lived under Jabin's domination for twenty years (4:3). Chariots were state-of-the-art technology at the time, and the thought of opposing a chariot was understandably terrifying to the ordinary infantryman—not that different, perhaps, from an infantryman of our time opposing a tank. A chariot had the advantage in speed, weight, armor, and height.

The Kishon River flows through the Jezreel Valley, a wide plain known for its extremely fertile soil. For most of the year, the Kishon is fed only by springs, and its waters are too minimal to be used for irrigation. During the winter rains, however, the Kishon can become a raging torrent, and large sections of the plain turn to mud.

The Lord not only called Barak to lead the people of Israel against Jabin, but promised to accomplish the task for him—literally, "give" or "deliver" (Heb. *natan*, **nah-TAHN**) him into Barak's hands. Of course, the Lord had already promised to fight for His people if they were faithful to drive out the other peoples living in the Promised Land. Ironically, God had used the same language in His promise to give the enemy over to the Israelites when Joshua had contemplated his assault on Hazor (Joshua 11:8–13). God had been faithful then, and Joshua had completely destroyed Hazor and burned it to the ground.

8 And Barak said unto her, If thou wilt go with me, then I will go: but if thou wilt not go with me, then I will not go.

Barak hesitated at the task given to him. Even with 10,000 men in his army, the Canaanite force was clearly superior. Barak was not the first or last leader God chose for Israel who hesitated to obey: recall Moses (Exodus 3:11) and Gideon (Judges 6:15).

We must not be too quick to judge Barak for his reluctance. Hebrews 11:32–33 includes Barak and Gideon in a list of courageous men and women who acted in great faith, trusting God to do miraculous things to deliver His people. And we must remember that Barak was not asking any ordinary woman to accompany him. As a prophetess, Deborah was a representative of God Himself. Perhaps Barak's request was rooted in his recognition that mere military might would not suffice to win the battle that lay ahead. He knew that victory would require God's direct intervention. In other words, he was willing to step out in faith, but not sign up for a suicide mission.

9 And she said, I will surely go with thee: notwithstanding the journey that thou takest shall not be for thine honour; for the LORD shall sell Sisera into the hand of a woman. And Deborah arose, and went with Barak to Kedesh.

Deborah's promise to go with Barak at this place in the story is astounding because it comes at the point when God normally promises His presence with the leader He is sending (cf. Exodus 3:12; Joshua 1:5; Judges 6:16). It seems best to understand the promise of her presence as the promise of God's presence, given to help Barak in his weakness. God has repeatedly shown that He is willing to accommodate the weakness of His chosen instruments (cf. Deuteronomy 7:7, 9:4–6). Nevertheless, Barak should have known that God had promised to drive out the Canaanites for the Israelites if only they were faithful to continue to fight (cf. Joshua 13:6, 23:5).

Deborah's displeasure with Barak's hesitation is obvious in her prediction that Barak will not gain glory on this mission. In a touch of beautiful irony, since he has refused to go unless a woman accompanies him, a yet unnamed and unknown woman will gain the glory.

10 And Barak called Zebulun and Naphtali to Kedesh; and he went up with ten thousand men at his feet: and Deborah went up with him.

Ten thousand might sound like a large number of troops to the modern reader. By comparison, however, the Canaanite army had 900 chariots, each manned by two soldiers, and most likely an infantry to boot. The implication is that the Canaanite army was vast—several times the size of Barak's force. Indeed, when Joshua first conquered Hazor, its king conscripted troops from the many outlying cities and villages in his realm. He succeeded in assembling an army "like the sand on the seashore" (Joshua 11:1–5). Note also that Gideon was able to muster 32,000 men—three times more than Barak—when he prepared for his attack on the armies of Midian (Judges 7:3). From this we can surmise that more people could have joined in the fight against Sisera, but God made it a point that He only called for a force of 10,000 against a technologically superior force—and He won.

Say It Correctly

Sisera. **SI**-sur-ah.
Harosheth. kha-**ROW**-sheth.
Lapidoth. la-pee-**DOTE**.

Daily Bible Readings

MONDAY
An Angel Rebukes Israel's Faithlessness
(Judges 2:1–5)

TUESDAY
Joshua's Death Ends an Era
(Judges 2:6–10)

WEDNESDAY
The People Lose God's Protection
(Judges 2:16–23)

THURSDAY
Ode to Israel's Faithful Judges
(Hebrews 11:29–40)

FRIDAY
Victory Song of the Divine Warrior
(Judges 5:1–5)

SATURDAY
Jael Defeats the Enemy Leader, Sisera
(Judges 5:24–27)

SUNDAY
Deborah, Prophetess, Judge, and Commander
(Judges 4:1–10)

Notes

_____

_____

_____

_____

Teaching Tips

Words You Should Know

A. Midianites (Judges 6:11ff.) *Midyan* (Heb.)—a nation descended from Abraham and Keturah.

B. Manasseh (v. 15) *Menashsheh* (Heb.)—A half-tribe of Israel, named after Joseph's older son; the tribe to which Gideon belonged.

Teacher Preparation

Unifying Principle—Wrestling with Doubt. People sometimes view their circumstances as an obstacle to being effective leaders. How do they deal with their doubts? Gideon voiced his doubts and requested a miraculous sign.

A. Come up with some personal scenarios where you had doubts about your abilities as a leader. Also consider times when you questioned whether God was with you when you faced difficulties.

B. Pray for students to have open hearts about their fears about obeying God.

O—Open the Lesson

A. Open with an icebreaker where students introduce themselves and name their biggest fear.

B. Using some of the fears participants named, introduce Gideon as someone who struggled with the fear of inadequacy.

C. Ask someone to read the Aim for Change and direct students to read the In Focus story either as a group or individually.

P—Present the Scriptures

A. Read the Scriptures from either the King James Version or the New Living Translation. Then ask a student to read the text from another translation like the Amplified or Message.

B. Use the At-a-Glance outline; The People, Places, and Times; Background; Search the Scriptures; In Depth; and More Light on the Text sections to explicate the verses.

E—Explore the Meaning

A. Read and answer the Discuss the Meaning questions.

B. Have someone read the Lesson in Our Society section.

N—Next Steps for Application

A. Read the Make It Happen section with students and encourage them to apply it to their lives.

B. Close in prayer.

Worship Guide

For the Superintendent or Teacher
Theme: Gideon's Call
Song: "Strong Finish"
Devotional Reading: Psalm 83:1–12, 18

Gideon's Call

Bible Background • JUDGES 6–8
Printed Text • JUDGES 6:11–18 | Devotional Reading • PSALM 83:1–12, 18

——————— Aim for Change ———————

By the end of the lesson, we will: DISTINGUISH God's criteria for choosing leaders from those set by humans; REMEMBER a time of feeling unqualified for a task because of perceived inadequacies; and WRESTLE with doubts about personal capabilities and requesting signs in a twenty-first century context.

—————— 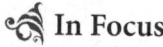 In Focus ——————

After a few years of working as a sales associate at a tech store, James was ready to move toward a new position as a sales manager. With only a few years of experience under his belt, James was up against stiff competition from candidates who already had management experience. Despite this, James was committed to arriving to work on time, and was usually one of the last people to leave work. He strove to show the love of Christ to every customer he encountered throughout the day. His coworkers, however, often scoffed at how happy he'd be to make a "measly sale" on small-ticket items. One day, James mustered up the courage to ask his supervisor for an opportunity to discuss how he could be better prepared for the management position opening up. "James, you're a great associate," she said. "And I think you're ready to move beyond a sales manager position. You're ready to run the entire store."

"Me?" James gasped. James didn't feel like his three years of experience made him qualified enough to run the entire store and manage other people who had more experience than he did.

"Yes, you!" his manager exclaimed. "Apply for the general store manager position next week. I think you have a good chance at being hired."

God doesn't always call the equipped, but He always equips the called. Have you ever faced a task where you felt you were not adequately equipped?

—————— Keep in Mind ——————

"And the angel of the LORD appeared unto him, and said unto him,
The LORD is with thee, thou mighty man of valour" (Judges 6:12).

"And the angel of the LORD appeared unto him, and said unto him,
The LORD is with thee, thou mighty man of valour" (Judges 6:12).

Focal Verses

KJV **Judges 6:11** And there came an angel of the LORD, and sat under an oak which was in Ophrah, that pertained unto Joash the Abiezrite: and his son Gideon threshed wheat by the winepress, to hide it from the Midianites.

12 And the angel of the LORD appeared unto him, and said unto him, The LORD is with thee, thou mighty man of valour.

13 And Gideon said unto him, Oh my Lord, if the LORD be with us, why then is all this befallen us? and where be all his miracles which our fathers told us of, saying, Did not the LORD bring us up from Egypt? but now the LORD hath forsaken us, and delivered us into the hands of the Midianites.

14 And the LORD looked upon him, and said, Go in this thy might, and thou shalt save Israel from the hand of the Midianites: have not I sent thee?

15 And he said unto him, Oh my Lord, wherewith shall I save Israel? behold, my family is poor in Manasseh, and I am the least in my father's house.

16 And the LORD said unto him, Surely I will be with thee, and thou shalt smite the Midianites as one man.

17 And he said unto him, If now I have found grace in thy sight, then shew me a sign that thou talkest with me.

18 Depart not hence, I pray thee, until I come unto thee, and bring forth my present, and set it before thee. And he said, I will tarry until thou come again.

NLT **Judges 6:11** Then the angel of the LORD came and sat beneath the great tree at Ophrah, which belonged to Joash of the clan of Abiezer. Gideon son of Joash was threshing wheat at the bottom of a winepress to hide the grain from the Midianites.

12 The angel of the LORD appeared to him and said, "Mighty hero, the LORD is with you!"

13 "Sir," Gideon replied, "if the LORD is with us, why has all this happened to us? And where are all the miracles our ancestors told us about? Didn't they say, 'The LORD brought us up out of Egypt'? But now the LORD has abandoned us and handed us over to the Midianites."

14 Then the LORD turned to him and said, "Go with the strength you have, and rescue Israel from the Midianites. I am sending you!"

15 "But Lord," Gideon replied, "how can I rescue Israel? My clan is the weakest in the whole tribe of Manasseh, and I am the least in my entire family!"

16 The LORD said to him, "I will be with you. And you will destroy the Midianites as if you were fighting against one man."

17 Gideon replied, "If you are truly going to help me, show me a sign to prove that it is really the LORD speaking to me.

18 Don't go away until I come back and bring my offering to you." He answered, "I will stay here until you return."

The People, Places, and Times

Children of Israel. The book of Judges comes after the Children of Israel entered the Promised Land under Joshua's guidance. When they arrive, the Israelites quickly return to old habits of idol worship, and God calls for judges to "rule" them to create some sense of order there. For many years, the Israelites were at odds with Canaanites and other tribal groups like the Midianites and Amalekites, who eventually challenged Israel's dominance in the Promised Land. The repeated disobedience by the Children of Israel would be a common theme throughout the Old Testament as God looked to establish His people and their leaders in history.

Midianites. The Midianites were a group of people who descended from Abraham's fourth son through his concubine Keturah (1 Chronicles 1:32). The Midianites, who settled in northeast Arabia, would adopt Arabian customs and cultures. Their name pops up in Genesis and Exodus with the stories of Joseph and Moses because of their close proximity to the Israelites. The Midianites were just one of the many nations that would rise against Israel while in the Promised Land.

Background

Israel had become a corrupt nation in God's eyes, worshiping false idols, abandoning the Lord who had delivered them from slavery in Egypt. Throughout the book of Judges, the people of Israel were overtaken by other nations around them. In an effort to guide the Israelites, God appointed judges to help them diplomatically follow His Law, but the Israelites still wanted to follow their own agendas and worship false gods. God desired for the Israelites to remember their ancestors' experiences—traveling through the wilderness so that they would learn how to honor God. But every time God delivered them from their evil ways, the Israelites returned to idolatry. Because of their repeated disobedience, other nations residing in the Promised Land began fighting against the Israelites and testing Israel's faithfulness to God. By the time we get to the calling of Gideon in Judges 6:11–18, the Israelites were severely oppressed by the Midianites and Amalekites, who had taken over every stronghold and resource in the land. Gideon's response to the angel of the Lord is reflective of Israel's long history of remembering what God has done for them—but also questioning His ability to lead a nation with a history of disobedience.

At-A-Glance

1. Doing What You Can (Judges 6:11–12)
2. Remembering the Past (v. 13)
3. Qualifying the Call (vv. 14–16)
4. Worshiping and Waiting (vv. 17–18)

In Depth

1. Doing What You Can (Judges 6:11–12)

When the angel of the Lord visited Gideon, he was threshing wheat at the bottom of a winepress to avoid drawing attention to himself. During biblical times, people would often thresh wheat at the top of the hill so that the chaff of the wheat could be carried away in the wind, leaving only the useful part of the wheat behind. Gideon threshed the wheat in a winepress, usually located in a pit, so that the flying chaff wouldn't give away his location to the Midianites who had taken over the land. By working there, he could hide his produce from those who might try to steal it. Gideon continued doing what he could to live through the oppression. Though Gideon was performing a common task in fear, the angel of the Lord reassures him that God was with him, even before Gideon could verbalize his fears. This reassurance would be the first of many confirmations for Gideon that he would be victorious against the enemy.

2. Remembering the Past (v. 13)

Because Israel had faced many trials in the Promised Land, Gideon was skeptical that God would be with him and the Israelites. First, Gideon expresses these concerns by questioning the angel's words: "If the LORD is with us, why has all this happened to us?" Gideon's expectation for Him to help them doesn't consider Israel's disobedience being the catalyst for what feels like an absent God. Second, Gideon recalls a time when his ancestors spoke of a God who delivered and redeemed them from troubles of the past, questioning whether He would do it for them now. Again, Gideon neglects to reflect on how their troubles are due to the people's disobedience, not to a God who could not deliver them. Sometimes we forget what role we played in a particular situation. Gideon's focus was on God's supposed absence, instead of how Israel's responsibility for their troubles.

3. Qualifying the Call (vv. 14–16)

God responds to Gideon to remind him of his own abilities to do what was necessary to save the Israelites: "Go with the strength you have, and rescue Israel from Midianites. I am sending you!" (v. 14). Gideon questions whether he is qualified to do what God has asked of him because he is the "least" of his tribe. Gideon thought that because he was the smallest in stature or status, he would not be able to defeat the army of Midianites. God qualifies us to do His work. Whenever God calls us to His work, He knows that we are capable. Because God can see the end from the beginning, He already knows we can be successful at whatever He asks us to do—if we do it in His strength.

4. Worshiping and Waiting (vv. 17–18)

God reassures Gideon that He will not only give him a sign, but wait for him to return with a sacrificial meal. This exchange between God and Gideon is the affirmation that Gideon needed to get over his fears and go in obedience—and a sign that Gideon was willing to

go forward in obedience despite his fears. This beautifully demonstrates how God is caring, loving, and concerned about the things we are concerned about; He was willing to wait on Gideon so he could be reassured through this act of worship. God often meets us with the same kind of loving patience. He knows we are prone to worry and fear.

Search the Scriptures

1. Did Gideon give a good reason for not being qualified to rescue the Israelites (Judges 6:15)?

2. Was it wrong for Gideon to ask for reassurance that it was the Lord speaking to him (v. 17)?

Discuss the Meaning

People are always looking for reassurance that they are the right fit for a job, project, or relationship. When we don't measure up, we can often become skeptical that God has called us to something. How can we be reassured that whatever God brings to us, He will also give us the tools to be successful?

Lesson in Our Society

Because we live in a society that emphasizes being "qualified," we can lose sight of what it means to be gifted and called by God, even if we do not meet man-made qualifications. We often miss an opportunity for God to use us because we think we do not have the qualifications to complete what He's asked us to do. Gideon rose to the occasion because he was willing to trust God more than his personal skills and abilities.

Make It Happen

You might be thinking about something God has called you to do, but don't feel capable because you don't have the experience, education, resources, or know-how. Today, write down what God has asked you to do. Then, write down the steps it will take to achieve that goal. Find one thing that you feel you can do to start the process of obedience. Pray for God to continue to give you the courage to obey the plan, even if you feel unequipped to do so.

Follow the Spirit

What God wants me to do:

_____

_____

_____

_____

Remember Your Thoughts

Special insights I have learned:

_____

_____

_____

_____

More Light on the Text

Judges 6:11–18

11 And there came an angel of the LORD, and sat under an oak which was in Ophrah, that pertained unto Joash the Abiezrite: and his son Gideon threshed wheat by the wine-press, to hide it from the Midianites.

After confronting the people and convicting them of their sin, the Lord sends an angel to prepare for them a deliverer. The angel arrives and sits under an oak tree in Ophrah belonging to Joash the Abiezrite. There he meets Gideon, the son of Joash, who is secretly threshing wheat by the wine press, hiding it from the Midianites.

The Israelites were in hiding from their enemies and could not fend for themselves. The Midianites invaded their land, destroyed their farms, and took away all their livestock, leaving them helpless (Judges 6:3–6). Gideon is threshing wheat in a very secluded place, probably for the family to survive on. The fact that Gideon threshed wheat by the winepress expresses the degree of distress and humiliation the people are undergoing. Under normal circumstances, grains were winnowed on a hill or cattle were used to thresh grains on a threshing floor. Gideon is working in an unusual place—in a wine press (Heb. *gath*, **GATH**), which was a circular pit hollowed out of rock—most likely to avoid discovery by the invaders.

Instead of using the winepress for processing wine, Gideon is using it for threshing grain because the Israelites do not have any grapes left to make wine. Their adversaries have taken over all their vineyards. The people were living under great fear.

12 And the angel of the LORD appeared unto him, and said unto him, The LORD is with thee, thou mighty man of valour. 13 And Gideon said unto him, Oh my Lord, if the LORD be with us, why then is all this befallen us? and where be all his miracles which our fathers told us of, saying, Did not the LORD bring us up from Egypt? but now the LORD hath forsaken us, and delivered us into the hands of the Midianites.

As Gideon is working in this secret place, the angel appears to him. We are not told how the angel appears—most likely in a human form. After the angel's disappearance, Gideon realizes he has been talking with the angel of the Lord (vv. 21–22). The angel appears and approaches Gideon and greets him in an unusual manner:

"The LORD is with thee, thou mighty man of valour." Although the greeting is standard for the time, the pronouncement appears to be an ironic mockery because the Lord is not with them (see Deuteronomy 31:17).

The phrase "mighty man of valour" comes from two Hebrew words (*gibbor*, **ghib-BORE**, and *khayil*, **KHAH-yil**) that can be interpreted as "great or powerful warrior; a strong and valiant man." It also can be translated as "man of standing," which is surprising considering Gideon's reasoning in verse 15.

Gideon's reaction is typical. Given the circumstances of the Children of Israel at this time—defeated, subjected to servitude, in hiding, all their belongings confiscated, and living in fear—it sounds strange for someone to say, "The Lord is with you." All this appears contrary to their state of affairs. Even more startling is that a man gripped with fear and hiding from his enemies is referred to as "a mighty man of valour." This does not make sense!

Gideon naturally replies with a series of questions: if God is with us, and in view of what He has done in the past, why are we in such a mess? Why won't He help us like He did when we were in Egypt? Why has God turned us over to our adversaries? The answer to these questions is obvious—sin. Israel has forsaken their God, and He reciprocates by allowing their enemies to conquer and oppress them in accordance with His covenant and warning (Leviticus 26; Deuteronomy 28). He is only fulfilling His part of the covenant just as He has in the past, and on many occasions, He kept the other part of the promise by blessing them when they were obedient to Him.

Through these questions, Gideon is indirectly acknowledging the greatness of the God of Israel and calling to mind stories of His miraculous works in the past. He does not seem to question the validity of these miracles, but is overwhelmed by the magnitude of their suffering, and the absence of God's intervention. He knows and believes what the Lord is capable of doing, but he cannot imagine the extent of His silence.

14 And the LORD looked upon him, and said, Go in this thy might, and thou shalt save Israel from the hand of the Midianites: have not I sent thee?

While Gideon is pondering all his inadequacies and lack of qualifications, and probably doubting his abilities, "the LORD looked upon him" and orders him to go and save his people from the Midianites. We notice that here the angel is referred to as "the LORD," Yahweh Himself speaking. The word "looked" comes from the Hebrew word *panah* (**pah-NAH**), which means "to turn, to face, to look at." That means the Lord turns to look (facing him squarely) and commissions him to action. It is a look of confidence and emphatic assurance.

The Lord tells Gideon to go in the strength he has and rescue the people. In other words, "You have enough power; you don't need more, because the Lord is with you." Here God commissions Gideon in the same way as He did Moses and Joshua (Exodus 3:10, Joshua 1:5). The rhetorical question, "Have not I sent thee?" (Judges 6:14), is another way of reconfirming His calling and certifying the mission. In other words, the Lord says, "I am the One sending you; you need not fear or be afraid, for I am with you." Gideon didn't have to worry about being strong enough, because as Paul says, God's strength is perfected in our weakness (2 Corinthians 12:9–10).

When we depend on ourselves and our own strength or are deterred by our weaknesses, we cannot accomplish the Lord's assignment. But when we faithfully obey and surrender to His will, we can successfully carry out any mission or task the Lord gives to us. When we look at the magnitude of the task, we fail; but when we look at the mightiness of our God, we accomplish all things that come our way. Our success does not depend on us or on who we are, but on whose we are: Almighty God's.

15 And he said unto him, Oh my Lord, wherewith shall I save Israel? behold, my family is poor in Manasseh, and I am the least in my father's house. 16 And the LORD said unto him, Surely I will be with thee, and thou shalt smite the Midianites as one man.

Gideon gives the excuse that his family is poor and he is the least in his father's house. In saying this, he acknowledges that he has no authority. To call soldiers together was the ability of someone of influence. He had no influence over his own family, nor any other families or tribes.

The Lord gives reassurance that He will be with Gideon. He does not reassure Gideon with anything else but His presence. The Israelites will come together to fight under Gideon's leadership and defeat the Midianites. In other words, Gideon will defeat every single one of the Midianites in one fell swoop (as he does).

17 And he said unto him, If now I have found grace in thy sight, then shew me a sign that thou talkest with me. 18 Depart not hence, I pray thee, until I come unto thee, and bring forth my present, and set it before thee. And he said, I will tarry until thou come again.

Gideon wants to confirm this amazing encounter and offer of grace (Heb. *khen*, **KHEN**). This word means a feeling of favorable emotional regard, always given from a person in higher social standing to one of lower rank. Gideon wanted to know for sure whether God would be with him. He asks for a sign, and the angel of the Lord indulges him. He promises to wait for Gideon's present (Heb. *minkhah*, **meen-KHAH**), which is another word for

sacrifice, most often a grain offering. Gideon's desire is to truly confirm that the Lord has sent this messenger by giving a worship offering that only the Lord would receive.

What a great turnaround for Gideon, who must have been contemplating his weaknesses, but now would lead an army. How could he be chosen for the enormous assignment of delivering his people from such a powerful and mean people like the Midianites? He could not fathom being the one to lead his people to face such a mighty army.

But the Lord had other plans. Here we learn that God uses not the famous, the strong, or the most eloquent, but rather ordinary people: the weak and the feeble, the less eloquent, and the seemingly insignificant to carry out His purposes.

Say It Correctly

Abiezrite. ah-bee-**EZ**-rite.
Midianites. **MI**-dee-uh-nites.
Mannasseh. muh-**NA**-suh.

Daily Bible Readings

MONDAY
Oppression Results from Disobedience
(Judges 6:1–10)

TUESDAY
May God Judge Enemies Harshly
(Psalm 83:1–12, 18)

WEDNESDAY
Gideon Sees the Angel of the Lord
(Judges 6:19–24)

THURSDAY
Fleece Confirms Victory Over Midianites
(Judges 6:36–40)

FRIDAY
Midianites Defeated Without Weapons
(Judges 7:19–23)

SATURDAY
Gideon Dies, Israel Forgets God's Ways
(Judges 8:29–35)

SUNDAY
Gideon's Call
(Judges 6:11–18)

Notes

Teaching Tips

Words You Should Know

A. Mizpeh (Judges 11:11) *Mitspah* (Heb.)—Watchtower; a place in Gilead.

B. Vow (v. 30) *neder* (Heb.)—A promise (to God); a thing concretely promised.

Teacher Preparation

Unifying Principle—Building Trust. People called to be leaders may question the motives of their supporters. How do these leaders know if their supporters' motives are sincere? Jephthah discussed the inconsistencies in the behavior of his supporters and established conditions for his leadership.

A. Pray for your students so that their minds and hearts will be open during the study.

B. Think about the vows or promises you've made to people because of something you wanted God to do for you.

C. Research some of the vows other people have taken in the Bible (Jacob, Hannah, etc.).

O—Open the Lesson

A. Open with prayer, including the Aim for Change.

B. Introduce today's lesson and read the Keep in Mind verse together.

C. Ask the students what it means to make a vow. Discuss their different answers.

D. Read the In Focus story as a group or silently.

P—Present the Scriptures

A. Have volunteers read the Focal Verses.

B. Use At-A-Glance outline; The People, Places, and Times; Background; Search the Scriptures; In Depth; and More Light on the Text sections to clarify the verses.

C. Have students act out verses 6–11 as a way of "seeing" why Jephthah responded the way he did to the elders' request. Can students relate to him? Discuss why or why not.

E—Explore the Meaning

A. Form students into groups, and have them answer the Discuss the Meaning questions.

B. Have students read the Lesson in Our Society section.

N—Next Steps for Application

A. Encourage the students to apply the ideas in the Make It Happen section.

B. Close in prayer.

Worship Guide

For the Superintendent or Teacher
Theme: Jephthah Answers the Call
Song: "Order My Steps"
Devotional Reading: Acts 15:6–21

Jephthah Answers the Call

Bible Background • JUDGES 11
Printed Text • JUDGES 11:4–11, 29–31 | Devotional Reading • ACTS 15:6–21

Aim for Change

By the end of the lesson, we will: ACKNOWLEDGE that people who have had disagreements can unite to defeat a common foe; EXPRESS remorse for alienating others; and DISCUSS the importance of reaching "a meeting of the minds" on motives and expected outcome before accepting a leadership role.

In Focus

Growing up in a family of boys, Jesse knew what it was like to have to compete not only to get his parents' attention but have his voice heard. When the four boys all went off to college, Jesse was the son who stayed in touch with his parents through email and phone calls, while his older brothers partied and only called home when they needed money.

One holiday, his father fell sick and the boys tried to make it back to their hometown to see him. Jesse, always responsible and in touch with his parents, was able to make it home. The rest of his brothers, who were irresponsible with not only their money but also their relationship with Jesse and his parents, scrambled trying to make it home. One by one, the brothers reached out to Jesse for help. While Jesse could have left his brothers to fend for themselves, he decided to help them get home, one by one—after discussing how they could all work together to care for their father.

Soon after, their father passed. At the funeral, all of Jesse's brothers chose to follow Jesus. When asked why, they pointed to Jesse's leadership and his example of being there not only for his parents, but also for his brothers when they needed him.

Even in moments of adversity, a leader can rise up to lead those who once worked against him or her. Have you ever experienced a time when God called you to lead those who once rejected or resisted your leadership?

Keep in Mind

"And Jephthah said unto the elders of Gilead, If ye bring me home again to fight against the children of Ammon, and the LORD deliver them before me, shall I be your head?" (Judges 11:9).

"And Jephthah said unto the elders of Gilead, If ye bring me home again to fight against the children of Ammon, and the LORD deliver them before me, shall I be your head?" (Judges 11:9).

Focal Verses

KJV **Judges 11:4** And it came to pass in process of time, that the children of Ammon made war against Israel.

5 And it was so, that when the children of Ammon made war against Israel, the elders of Gilead went to fetch Jephthah out of the land of Tob:

6 And they said unto Jephthah, Come, and be our captain, that we may fight with the children of Ammon.

7 And Jephthah said unto the elders of Gilead, Did not ye hate me, and expel me out of my father's house? and why are ye come unto me now when ye are in distress?

8 And the elders of Gilead said unto Jephthah, Therefore we turn again to thee now, that thou mayest go with us, and fight against the children of Ammon, and be our head over all the inhabitants of Gilead.

9 And Jephthah said unto the elders of Gilead, If ye bring me home again to fight against the children of Ammon, and the LORD deliver them before me, shall I be your head?

10 And the elders of Gilead said unto Jephthah, The LORD be witness between us, if we do not so according to thy words.

11 Then Jephthah went with the elders of Gilead, and the people made him head and captain over them: and Jephthah uttered all his words before the LORD in Mizpeh.

29 Then the Spirit of the LORD came upon Jephthah, and he passed over Gilead, and Manasseh, and passed over Mizpeh of Gilead, and from Mizpeh of Gilead he passed over unto the children of Ammon.

30 And Jephthah vowed a vow unto the LORD, and said, If thou shalt without fail deliver the children of Ammon into mine hands,

31 Then it shall be, that whatsoever cometh forth of the doors of my house to meet me,

NLT **Judges 11:4** At about this time, the Ammonites began their war against Israel.

5 When the Ammonites attacked, the elders of Gilead sent for Jephthah in the land of Tob.

6 The elders said, "Come and be our commander! Help us fight the Ammonites!"

7 But Jephthah said to them, "Aren't you the ones who hated me and drove me from my father's house? Why do you come to me now when you're in trouble?"

8 "Because we need you," the elders replied. "If you lead us in battle against the Ammonites, we will make you ruler over all the people of Gilead."

9 Jephthah said to the elders, "Let me get this straight. If I come with you and if the LORD gives me victory over the Ammonites, will you really make me ruler over all the people?"

10 "The LORD is our witness," the elders replied. "We promise to do whatever you say."

11 So Jephthah went with the elders of Gilead, and the people made him their ruler and commander of the army. At Mizpah, in the presence of the LORD, Jephthah repeated what he had said to the elders.

29 At that time the Spirit of the LORD came upon Jephthah, and he went throughout the land of Gilead and Manasseh, including Mizpah in Gilead, and from there he led an army against the Ammonites.

30 And Jephthah made a vow to the LORD. He said, "If you give me victory over the Ammonites,

31 I will give to the LORD whatever comes out of my house to meet me when I return in triumph. I will sacrifice it as a burnt offering."

when I return in peace from the children of Ammon, shall surely be the LORD's, and I will offer it up for a burnt offering.

The People, Places, and Times

Jephthah. A skilled negotiator and warrior, Jephthah was chosen as a leader to defeat the Ammonites because of his ability to negotiate with both the Israelites and the Ammonite king. Although he was ostracized by his family for being the illegitimate child of his father Gilead and a prostitute, Jephthah rose as a leader to become Israel's judge. Jephthah's history and family line could not change his destiny—God would still use him. He would, however, make a vow that would cost him dearly—and teaches us about the brashness of coming into covenant with God without counting the cost.

Ammonites. The Ammonites were a group of people who descended from Ammon, the son of Lot's younger daughter (Genesis 19:30–38). This is important to note because Ammon was an ally to Moab, another nation conceived through the incestuous relationship between Lot and his daughters. In the time of the judges, the nation of Ammon was at war with Israel. After defeating the tribes of Judah, Benjamin, and Ephraim, Ammon was an impenetrable enemy that Israel had a slim chance of defeating. Defeating them would require uncanny wisdom and much faith in God.

Background

Israel had a longstanding issue with idol-worship and God had grown tired of their disobedience. He allowed Israel to experience increased territorial takeover by other nations. Jephthah was part of a long succession of judges intended to rule and deliver Israel from their distress. The Ammonites, a fortified group from Ammon that ruled over Israel for eighteen years, were allied with Moab in the north. Jephthah was called to defeat the Ammonites to give Israel a reprieve from their troubles. This call came after his family ostracized him for being born of a prostitute. When Jephthah finally settles in Tob, he hears that Israel is under attack and is asked by the elders of Gilead to lead them against the Ammonites.

At-A-Glance

1. Feelings of Rejection (Judges 11:4–8)
2. Seeing the Bigger Picture (vv. 9–11)
4. Making a Vow to the Lord (vv. 29–31)

In Depth

1. Feelings of Rejection (Judges 11:4–8)

Because his brothers and community rejected him, Jephthah entered into a position of leadership with emotional baggage. He carried this resentment with him as he navigated his position as judge and soon-to-be leader of the Israelites. He reminds the elders of Gilead that although they needed his help, they had also been the ones who rejected him. The elders admit their guilt and beg Jephthah to lead them into victory over the Ammonites. But there was something in it for Jephthah as well: not only would he be a judge in the land but also ruler over the people—including his brothers who had rejected him. This kind of power could have gone to Jephthah's head, but he remained focused on his assignment to deliver the people from trouble.

2. Seeing the Bigger Picture (vv. 9–11)

Once Jephthah accepted his position as leader, he had to see the bigger picture: though his family and community had rejected him because of his familial history, he had to take on the role and responsibility of ruler. The city where he accepts this role, Mizpeh, means "lookout" or "watchtower." This is symbolic of Jephthah's role as ruler, as he will "lookout" for the people of Israel and negotiate on their behalf. At Mizpeh, Jephthah repeats to the Lord what the community said to him, as a testimony to what had been proclaimed over him (vv. 9–11). Scholars believe that this process of repeating what was said was a rite of passage in ancient times. There was a bigger implication in Jephthah's acceptance of this role as leader.

3. Making a Vow to the Lord (vv. 29–31)

By accepting the physical responsibility as leader of the people, Jephthah also had to accept the spiritual responsibility of leadership. His vow to God to make a burnt sacrifice of the first thing that greeted him after victory over the Ammonites seemed like a noble vow, but Jephthah had no way to knowing what or who would greet him after the war. For Jephthah, offering a sacrifice to God as a thank you for blessings was a part of the culture. As a leader, Jephthah had to be mindful that being overzealous in his pursuit to reclaim his status did not cause him to promise something he could not fulfill.

Search the Scriptures

1. Why do you believe the elders agreed to let Jephthah rule over them if he was victorious over the Ammonites (Judges 11:9, 11)?

2. How did Jephthah's troubled childhood influence him to make a rash vow?

Discuss the Meaning

Sometimes people who once shunned us will need us to help them carry out their goals in the future. Despite this, God wants us to do what is right for everyone, even if that means joining with people who have wronged you. How can we join unlikely partners to accomplish God's work?

Lesson in Our Society

Have you even been in trouble and said to God, "Lord, if you just get me out of this situation, I promise to (fill in the blank)?" We often make promises to God and each other that are often times impossible to keep, even if we mean well when we make the promise. Scripture reminds us that we should let our "yes" be "yes" and our "no" be "no" (Matthew 5:37), for to promise anything beyond that can lead us down a path of broken promises.

Make It Happen

In a world where we are pulled in many directions to commit ourselves to people and causes, it can be easy to step into roles of leadership that require more of us than we're willing to give. Often, it is our desire to reclaim our position in community. So we take on more responsibilities than we should, making it hard to keep our promises. This week, remember Jephthah's story and find ways to lead others without overpromising.

Follow the Spirit

What God wants me to do:

_____

_____

_____

_____

Remember Your Thoughts

Special insights I have learned:

_____

_____

_____

_____

More Light on the Text

Judges 11:4–11, 29–31

4 And it came to pass in process of time, that the children of Ammon made war against Israel.

The phrase "And it came to pass" introduces a new scene related to the previous scene or event. It can also indicate the passing of time. Another way of saying this is "After a while," implying that some distance has passed between the events that came before the current episode, but that they are related. As such, Judges 11:4 establishes the current state of war with the Ammonites (literally "sons of Ammon" or "children of Ammon") is related to the preceding threat of war by the Ammonites against Israel in Judges 10:17. Up to this point in the story, the Israelites had been under Ammonite subjugation, but now tensions have broken into war between the two nations.

5 And it was so, that when the children of Ammon made war against Israel, the elders of Gilead went to fetch Jephthah out of the land of Tob: 6 And they said unto Jephthah, Come, and be our captain, that we may fight with the children of Ammon.

Gilead was both a personal name and the name of the northern Transjordanian territory occupied by the Israelite tribes of Reuben, Gad, and the half-tribe of Manasseh (Numbers 34:14–15). The Ammonites, who occupied central Transjordan, were on the march to engage Israel in Gilead. The theological justification for the war was that the Israelites were facing the consequences of worshiping foreign gods (Judges 10:6–7, 13). They had rebelled against God, so He allowed them to be oppressed by the Ammonites. When the Israelites could stand their affliction no longer, they cried out to God for deliverance (v. 15), and He took pity on them (v. 16). What usually followed was deliverance in the form of a military "deliverer" raised by God to save the Israelites from their enemies (cf., Judges 3:9, 15). However, as the Ammonites were encroaching on the Gileadites, there was no deliverer for Israel. When the military captains of Gilead realized this, they asked one another who would fight against the Ammonites for them and be their head (Judges 10:18).

Their unlikely hero was Jephthah, a mighty warrior and son of Gilead. The text is ambiguous whether his father's name was Gilead or he was descended from the line of Gilead. Jephthah's story follows a popular motif in the Old Testament narratives of the least becoming the first (e.g., Genesis 25:22–23; Judges 6:15; 1 Samuel 16:13). He was unlikely because his mother was a prostitute (Heb. 'ishsha zonah, **eesh-AH zoh-NAH**; Judges 11:1). It is unclear whether she was a professional sex worker or a woman whose status as an unmarried mother placed her outside social boundaries, since the term used here often refers to a woman having extramarital sex (cf. Hosea 1:2).

One detail that should not be overlooked, in light of the family values rhetoric regarding the myth of the absent Black father, is the fact that despite Gilead's relationship with Jephthah's mother, Jephthah knew his father and was raised within his father's household. Gilead provided for him, including him in his inheritance. The fact that a father is not married to his child's mother does not equate to absenteeism. Nevertheless, his father also had sons from his legal wife, and when they grew older, they forced Jephthah to depart from Gilead to keep him from receiving part of their father's inheritance. Jephthah fled to the land of Tob, where he built a reputation as the leader of a band of outlaws (v. 3). The elders traveled to Tob to bring Jephthah back to Gilead to be their military leader.

7 And Jephthah said unto the elders of Gilead, Did not ye hate me, and expel me out of my father's house? and why are ye come unto me now when ye are in distress? 8 And the elders of Gilead said unto Jephthah, Therefore we turn again to thee now, that thou mayest go with us, and fight against the children of Ammon, and be our head over all the inhabitants of Gilead.

It must have surprised Jephthah when members of the same extended family who had expelled him from Gilead came to bring him back from Tob to lead the military campaign against Ammon. He responded skeptically, reminding them of how they had mistreated him when it suited them. Jephthah accuses the elders of being complicit in his being separated from his family line and inheritance (cf. v. 2). The elders seem to infer that Jephthah will not comply with their request. In response, using a more conciliatory tone, they up the ante; they will make him the head (Heb. *ro'sh*, **ROASH**) of all Gilead. The elders' initial offer was for Jephthah to take the temporary position of military leader or ruler (Heb. *katsin*, **kat-SEEN**). However, now if he would come with them and lead them in battle against the Ammonites, then they would also make him head of the Gileadites, as the military captains had originally planned (Judges 10:18).

9 And Jephthah said unto the elders of Gilead, If ye bring me home again to fight against the children of Ammon, and the LORD deliver them before me, shall I be your head? 10 And the elders of Gilead said unto Jephthah, The LORD be witness between us, if we do not so according to thy words.

Jephthah was likely aware of the captains' offer and feigned reluctance as a negotiating tactic to get the elders to offer to make him both captain and head. The position of military leader was temporary and ceased once the battle was won. However, the offer to make him the head or leader of the Gileadites was a permanent civil position. Jephthah proffered that if God gave him the victory, then they should make him their head. The elders agreed to these terms, reversing Jephthah's fortunes: the cast-out son who was made the least among his brothers would become the first as their ruler.

The formula, "The LORD be witness between us," was used by two or more parties entering into an agreement or covenant to invoke God as a witness to compel the parties to comply with the terms of the agreement (cf. Genesis 31:49). The oath uttered by Laban, "The Lord watch between me and thee, when we are absent one from another," has been turned into a sentimental benediction. However, it was a covenant made between two adversaries, Laban and Jacob, and was a thinly disguised threat from Laban to bring harm to Jacob if he mistreated Laban's daughters, Rachel and Leah.

11 Then Jephthah went with the elders of Gilead, and the people made him head and captain over them: and Jephthah uttered all his words before the LORD in Mizpeh.

The relationship between Jephthah and the elders was not unlike the one between Laban and Jacob. An element of distrust required them to call on God as a witness to their covenant. Jephthah and the elders departed for Mizpeh or Mizpah, where they ratified the agreement to make Jephthah their military and civilian head after the conflict ceased. Mizpeh was a sanctuary located on the border of Gilead between Ephraim and Benjamin. Laban had named it Mizpeh ("watchpost") because it was the place where he invoked God to watch between Jacob and him. Now, after having successfully negotiated the leadership position with the elders, Jephthah was installed as captain and head over all the Gileadites. He concluded the ceremony by affirming his agreement before God.

29 Then the Spirit of the LORD came upon Jephthah, and he passed over Gilead, and Manasseh, and passed over Mizpeh of Gilead, and from Mizpeh of Gilead he passed over unto the children of Ammon.

Despite the circumstances of Jephthah's birth, God raised him up to be the deliverer in Gilead, and He approved the decision by the elders by bestowing His Spirit on Jephthah. Certain judges in the book of Judges were endowed with the Spirit of God, which granted them power and authority to accomplish the task before them, with sometimes mixed results (Judges 3:10; 6:34; 13:25). Endowed with the Spirit, Jephthah goes out to meet the Ammonites. This signals that the focus is less on God delivering the enemy into Jephthah's hand and more on the vow Jephthah made.

30 And Jephthah vowed a vow unto the LORD, and said, If thou shalt without fail deliver the children of Ammon into mine hands, 31 Then it shall be, that whatsoever cometh forth of the doors of my house to meet me, when I return in peace from the children of Ammon, shall surely be the LORD's, and I will offer it up for a burnt offering.

"If…" These two letters can wield such tremendous power. Jephthah makes a vow to God

that included a conditional clause foreboding terrible events to come. Before engaging the Ammonites in war, Jephthah vows that if God gives them into his hand, then whatever came out from his house to meet him, he would offer up to God as a burnt offering. Jephthah's vow interrupts the flow of the narrative. The normal sequence should have been the coming of God's Spirit upon the judge, who goes out to meet the enemy, who is delivered into his hand as a result of the judge being endowed with God's Spirit. However, there is a departure from pattern before the reporting of the battle resumes in v. 32. This signals that the focus is less on God delivering the enemy into Jephthah's hand than on the vow.

When Jephthah returned home, his only child, a daughter, ran to congratulate him with singing and dancing. Jephthah was devastated! Since sacrificing humans is against God's Law (Leviticus 18:21, 20:2–5; Deuteronomy 12:31, 18:10), Jephthah's anxiety to ensure his personal victory meant that his daughter's life would be dedicated to religious service. She would remain a virgin and never marry. She bemoaned her fate by spending two months in the mountains (Judges 11:37–40).

Say It Correctly

Gilead. **GI**-lee-ad.
Ammon. **AH**-moan.
Mizpeh. miz-**PEH**.

Daily Bible Readings

MONDAY
Jephthah, Rejected by His Family, Flees
(Judges 11:1–3)

TUESDAY
Jephthah Resolves a Dispute with Edom
(Judges 11:12–18)

WEDNESDAY
Jephthah Reveals God's Aid of Israel
(Judges 11:19–22)

THURSDAY
Ammonite King Rejects Jephthah's Claims
(Judges 11:23–28)

FRIDAY
Jephthah Sacrifices His Daughter
to Fulfill His Vow
(Judges 11:34–40)

SATURDAY
Leaders Discern the Way Forward
(Acts 15:6–21)

SUNDAY
Jephthah Answers the Call
(Judges 11:4–11)

Notes

_____

_____

_____

_____

Teaching Tips

Words You Should Know

A. Nazarite (Judges 13:5, 7) *nazir* (Heb.)—One who is devoted (set apart, dedicated, consecrated) to God.

B. Strong drink (Judges 13:4, 7) *sheker* (Heb.)—Beer or another alcoholic drink, usually made from barley.

Teacher Preparation

Unifying Principle—Destined for Greatness. Preparation for leadership may involve life circumstances not of one's own choosing. How do we respond when we find ourselves in such circumstances? Even before birth, Samson's call was assured as shown by the instructions the Lord's angel gave to his mother.

A. Pray for your students and for lesson understanding and clarity.

B. Read Judges 1–3 to be familiar with the social context of the Israelites and the world in which Samson was raised.

C. Prepare a brief biography of a leader.

D. Complete the companion lesson in the *Precepts for Living®* Study Guide.

O—Open the Lesson

A. Open with prayer, including the Aim for Change.

B. Introduce today's lesson title.

C. Have your students read the Aim for Change and Keep in Mind verse together. Discuss.

D. Share one story of a leader; with the class, identify and examine his/her strengths and weaknesses. Discuss how his/her story may or may not have shaped the leader he/she has become.

P—Present the Scriptures

A. Have volunteers read the Focal Verses.

B. Use the At-a-Glance outline, People, Places and Times; Background; Search the Scriptures; In Depth; and More Light on the Text sections to clarify the verses.

E—Explore the Meaning

A. Divide the class into groups to discuss the Discuss the Meaning, Lesson in Our Society and Make It Happen sections. Tell students to select a representative to report their responses.

B. Connect these sections to the Aim for Change and Keep in Mind verse.

N—Next Steps for Application

A. Summarize the lesson.

B. Summarize the steps for application, and call students' attention to their answers in Make It Happen.

C. Close in prayer.

Worship Guide

For the Superintendent or Teacher
Theme: Samson's Call
Song: "A Charge to Keep I Have"
Devotional Reading: Judges 13:19–23

Samson's Call

Bible Background • JUDGES 13–16
Printed Text • JUDGES 13:1–7, 24–25 | Devotional Reading • JUDGES 13:19–23

Aim for Change

By the end of this lesson, we will: RECOUNT the details of Samson's birth and calling; EMPATHIZE with the emotions Samson probably experienced regarding lifestyle restrictions imposed on him by others; and LIST some ways that unforeseen circumstances prepare people for leadership roles today.

In Focus

Jasmin and Philip were married for seven years. They tried and tried to have a baby, but each time Jasmin thought she was pregnant, she was not. After the first year of trying, the doctor told them there was a strong possibility that they were experiencing infertility issues. After many months of being poked and prodded for tests, Jasmin and Philip faced the reality that they were, indeed, infertile.

They were a young couple with no money, and in vitro fertilization treatment was too expensive. However, they were a God-fearing couple who believed that God was sovereign. So, they chose to leave their infertility in His hands and trust Him to give them the grace to bear the grief of not having children.

Two years after all the testing, Jasmin was at work one day and began to feel sick. She thought she may have eaten something bad or had a stomach bug. The following day, she started feeling sick again and went to the doctor. The doctor ran tests and shared the good news with Jasmin: she was pregnant! Jasmin ran out of the doctor's office and called Philip as soon as she got in the car. They agreed that this baby was a miracle and that God had a plan for this child.

In today's lesson, we will meet a couple who received a son from God, Samson, whom He set apart for Himself to become one of Israel's judges. Have you ever felt set apart for a specific task?

Keep in Mind

"For, lo, thou shalt conceive, and bear a son; and no razor shall come on his head: for the child shall be a Nazarite unto God from the womb: and he shall begin to deliver Israel out of the hand of the Philistines" (Judges 13:5).

"For, lo, thou shalt conceive, and bear a son; and no razor shall come on his head: for the child shall be a Nazarite unto God from the womb: and he shall begin to deliver Israel out of the hand of the Philistines" (Judges 13:5).

Focal Verses

KJV **Judges 13:1** And the children of Israel did evil again in the sight of the LORD; and the LORD delivered them into the hand of the Philistines forty years.

2 And there was a certain man of Zorah, of the family of the Danites, whose name was Manoah; and his wife was barren, and bare not.

3 And the angel of the LORD appeared unto the woman, and said unto her, Behold now, thou art barren, and bearest not: but thou shalt conceive, and bear a son.

4 Now therefore beware, I pray thee, and drink not wine nor strong drink, and eat not any unclean thing:

5 For, lo, thou shalt conceive, and bear a son; and no razor shall come on his head: for the child shall be a Nazarite unto God from the womb: and he shall begin to deliver Israel out of the hand of the Philistines.

6 Then the woman came and told her husband, saying, A man of God came unto me, and his countenance was like the countenance of an angel of God, very terrible: but I asked him not whence he was, neither told he me his name:

7 But he said unto me, Behold, thou shalt conceive, and bear a son; and now drink no wine nor strong drink, neither eat any unclean thing: for the child shall be a Nazarite to God from the womb to the day of his death.

24 And the woman bare a son, and called his name Samson: and the child grew, and the LORD blessed him.

25 And the Spirit of the LORD began to move him at times in the camp of Dan between Zorah and Eshtaol.

NLT **Judges 13:1** Again the Israelites did evil in the LORD's sight, so the LORD handed them over to the Philistines, who oppressed them for forty years.

2 In those days a man named Manoah from the tribe of Dan lived in the town of Zorah. His wife was unable to become pregnant, and they had no children.

3 The angel of the LORD appeared to Manoah's wife and said, "Even though you have been unable to have children, you will soon become pregnant and give birth to a son.

4 So be careful; you must not drink wine or any other alcoholic drink nor eat any forbidden food.

5 You will become pregnant and give birth to a son, and his hair must never be cut. For he will be dedicated to God as a Nazirite from birth. He will begin to rescue Israel from the Philistines."

6 The woman ran and told her husband, "A man of God appeared to me! He looked like one of God's angels, terrifying to see. I didn't ask where he was from, and he didn't tell me his name.

7 But he told me, 'You will become pregnant and give birth to a son. You must not drink wine or any other alcoholic drink nor eat any forbidden food. For your son will be dedicated to God as a Nazirite from the moment of his birth until the day of his death.'"

24 When her son was born, she named him Samson. And the LORD blessed him as he grew up.

25 And the Spirit of the LORD began to stir him while he lived in Mahaneh-dan, which is located between the towns of Zorah and Eshtaol.

The People, Places, and Times

Philistines. One of the Aegean "Sea Peoples," the Philistines migrated to Palestine in approximately the twelfth century BC and established themselves in five city states called the Philistine Pentapolis: Gaza, Ashkelon, Ashdod, Ekron, and Gath. The Philistines' military superiority, economic strength, and administrative capabilities enabled them to be dominant over the Israelites (Judges 13:1). The Philistine threat to Judah is first seen in the stories of Samson (Judges 13–16).

Nazirite. A Nazirite or Nazarite (KJV) was an Israelite who voluntarily vowed to be consecrated to the Lord (Numbers 6:1–21). In some instances, parents made the Nazirite vow on behalf of their child and promised to set apart their child for God's service (Judges 13:1–7; 1 Samuel 1:1–11). To demonstrate their commitment and devotion to the Lord, the Nazirites abstained from wine and strong drink (an alcoholic drink made from barley), avoided any contact with the dead, and allowed their hair to grow long. These outward signs showed their commitment and devotion to the Lord.

Background

The book of Judges describes a period in Israelite history characterized by idolatry, debauchery, sin, rebellion, and oppression on one hand, and repentance, mercy, grace, and peace on the other. The book spans the period between the death of the Israelite leader Joshua and the chaotic infighting of Israelite tribes before the rise of the monarchy. The Children of Israel did not heed God's instruction and failed to remove the inhabitants completely from the land (Judges 1:19–36, 2:1–2). So, God allowed the Canaanites, Sidonians, Hivites, and Philistines to remain in the land and become snares to the Israelites (Judges 2:3, 3:1–7).

By mixing with the inhabitants of the land, the Israelites assimilated, accommodated, and tolerated the Canaanite lifestyle and worship—idolatry, inter-marriage, rejection of God's Word—that were contrary to the ways and Word of God. So in Israel arose a generation who did not know the Lord (Judges 2:10–13, 3:5–7).

Their apostasy came with a great price because God gave them over to their enemies in the land, and they were oppressed for a time (Judges 2:14–15). The weight and pain of oppression caused the people to cry out in repentance to God; He responded in mercy and delivered them.

The book of Judges contains six periods of oppression that begin with the phrase "Again Israel did evil..." During those times, God raised up people whom He anointed, appointed, and empowered to deliver His people from their oppressors (Judges 2:16–18). When a judge subdued the enemy, the land experienced peace. As soon as the judge died, however, Israel would fall back into sin. They were caught in a cycle of sin (Judges 2:18–23).

At-A-Glance

1. Problem of Sin and Oppression (Judges 13:1)
2. God's Promise of Deliverance (vv. 2–7)
3. Fulfillment of the Promise (vv. 24–25)

In Depth

1. Problem of Sin and Oppression (Judges 13:1)

Judges 13:1 begins another cycle of oppression as God hands Israel over to the Philistines, who would rule over them for forty years. This is the sixth time the phrase "And the children of Israel did evil again ..." is used in the book of Judges (3:7, 12, 4:1, 6:1, 10:6). While the judge-deliverer was alive, the Children of Israel had relative peace. With the judge's death, the Israelites reverted back to their rebellion and rejection of God's commandments. Because of their disobedience and rejection, they were given over to Philistine oppression (Judges 10:6–7, 13:1). In this cycle of oppression, the pattern of repentance was broken: there was no indication that the Children of Israel cried out to God in repentance, as they had done in the past (3:15, 4:3, 6:6, 10:10).

2. God's Promise of Deliverance (vv. 2–7)

The Israelites did not cry out in repentance under the weight of oppression, and God made no announcement that He would raise up a judge-deliverer (2:16, 18, 3:9, 15). Judges 13:2–7 functions as a birth and calling narrative for the final judge, Samson. In Judges 13:2, Manoah is introduced, and his tribal affiliation and geographical location are given. In contrast, his wife is introduced as the unnamed and barren woman. In verse 3, the angel of the Lord appears to the woman and announces to her that she will become pregnant and give birth to a child. Like Sarah, Rachel, and Hannah before her, this woman would bear a son because of the Lord. There is no context for where Manoah's wife was when the angel came to her or whether she had been pleading to God regarding her infertility. However, her barrenness was not unnoticed by God, who is not bound by impossible circumstances. He can and does work in and through what seems impossible in man's eyes to accomplish His purposes.

The boy's conception and birth were God's doing and came with special restrictions (Judges 13:4). The mother was to maintain a strict diet—no wine, no strong alcoholic beverages, and no unclean food—during the time of her pregnancy. The restriction of unclean food was not a new restriction for an Israelite, but given the spiritual state of the people and their rejection of God, this mother had to be reminded about what He required (Leviticus 11; Deuteronomy 14). In verse 5, the restrictions expanded to include postnatal care of the baby: his hair was never to be cut. The reason for the restrictions became evident, as the boy was to be dedicated to God as a Nazirite. He would begin to deliver his people from the Philistines. Numbers 6:1–21 outlines the provisions of the Nazirite vow. Normally, a person would make this vow voluntarily to show his dedication to God for a period of time. In this case, God divinely imposed the vow upon the boy for the duration of his life. The boy had been called by God and was appointed for a specific task.

In response to the angel's announcement, the wife ran to her husband to tell him what had happened (Judges 13:6). Her report first described the angel as a man of God who looked like an angel of God. Only after describing this heavenly visitor did she recount the message she received. She told her husband that they would have a son, and told him about the dietary restrictions. Their son would be dedicated to God as a Nazirite from birth.

3. Fulfillment of the Promise (vv. 24–25)

At the end of chapter 13, the author reiterates that the promise given to the woman was not just a figment of her imagination; it was fulfilled. Manoah's wife did bear a son and she named him Samson. God's call was evident in the boy's life because he grew up and was blessed by the Lord, and the Lord's Spirit began to impel him. God, in His mercy, did not leave His people without deliverance. They did not cry out to Him in repentance nor turn from their wicked ways. Still, God raised up someone whom He would use to begin to deliver His people.

Search the Scriptures

1. Samson was called to be a Nazirite (Judges 13:5, Numbers 6:1–21). Is this particular calling applicable to Christians living in the twenty-first century?

2. The text says that the Spirit of the Lord began to move Samson (v. 25). How do we know when the Spirit of the Lord is moving us?

Discuss the Meaning

1. In what ways should your life as a believer demonstrate that you have been set apart to Christ? List two ways your life might not demonstrate a vibrant relationship with Christ. What steps can you make to change that? Commit to praying and asking the Lord to reveal to you the changes you must make.

Lesson in Our Society

Parents have a huge responsibility as the ones who must teach and lead their children in a growing relationship with Christ. In a culture becoming increasingly non-Christian, parenting has become a huge challenge for those seeking a godly family. Parents must find creative ways to teach their children about who God is and model for them how to have a relationship with Him. Parents are not perfect; neither are kids. We are all flawed. But, God can and will use us when we surrender to Him.

Make It Happen

God uses a variety of things in our lives—our childhood, family situations, personalities, strengths, weaknesses, talents, environments, experiences—for His glory. Nothing that we go through in our lives is wasted, but we must be open to allow the Lord to use these situations to mold and shape us. Prayerfully reflect on your life this week. List three things the Lord might have been doing in your life that you may have overlooked. What are some circumstances He has used to shape you that have influenced your life today?

Follow the Spirit

What God wants me to do:

_____

_____

_____

_____

Remember Your Thoughts

Special insights I have learned:

_____

_____

_____

_____

More Light on the Text

Judges 13:1–7, 24–25

1 And the children of Israel did evil again in the sight of the LORD; and the LORD delivered them into the hand of the Philistines forty years.

Since the Israelites continued to do evil in the sight of God, He punished them—they experienced His wrath, and God used the Philistines to carry out His punishment on His own people. Judges 13:1 tells us that the Israelites chose sin—"evil" (Heb. *ra'*, **RAH**), meaning "wickedness, wrong"—in the sight of the omnipresent (all-present) holy (set apart from sin) Lord. He deemed that their actions were sinful. He "delivered" them (Heb. *natan*, **nah-TAHN**), which means He "gave" them into the hands of their enemies for forty years.

According to biblical scholars, the Philistines were a Gentile people from the area of the Aegean Sea. Eventually they occupied southwest Palestine from about 1200 to 600 BC. The Philistines worshiped many gods, were deeply rooted in pagan cultures of the eastern Mediterranean (especially Greek and Palestinian), and used soothsayers, astrologers, fortune-tellers, and clairvoyants.

In the eleventh century BC, when the Philistines began to attack the Israelites, these enemies possessed superior weapons of iron and were a very formidable adversary. However, the Lord Himself was using these people to punish the Israelites, His own children who were hardheaded, stiff-necked, and disobedient. For forty long years, the Israelites were under the bondage of their foes.

2 And there was a certain man of Zorah, of the family of the Danites, whose name was Manoah; and his wife was barren, and bare not. 3 And the angel of the LORD appeared unto the woman, and said unto her, Behold now, thou art barren, and bearest not: but thou shalt conceive, and bear a son.

Just as the all-powerful, true, and living God was in charge by allowing the Philistines to take the Children of Israel into bondage, He was in charge in delivering them out. God raised up their deliverer through a barren (Heb. *'akar,* **ah-KAR,** sterile, childless, fruitless) woman. This is a clear case of God doing the impossible. The woman's husband whose name was Manoah lived in Zorah, which was a town in Dan. The phrase "a certain man" should also remind us that God uses ordinary—often totally inadequate—people to do His work. Through these people, God can get all the glory and due Him for the outcomes He has caused.

The angel (Heb. *mal'ak,* **mah-LOCK**), which means "messenger," of God brought Manoah and his wife good news of great joy. In spite of her barrenness, Manoah's wife was going to conceive and, not only that, bear Manoah a son—an heir to carry on his name and carry out the will of God.

4 Now therefore beware, I pray thee, and drink not wine nor strong drink, and eat not any unclean thing: 5 For, lo, thou shalt conceive, and bear a son; and no razor shall come on his head: for the child shall be a Nazarite unto God from the womb: and he shall begin to deliver Israel out of the hand of the Philistines.

God's plan to deliver the Israelites from Philistine bondage required Manoah and his wife to obey Him fully. Because of who Samson was to be to God and His people—the role he would play as the last judge who would rule over the Israelites for twenty years—God issued three mandates. Manoah's wife must abstain from alcohol. She is to participate in the Nazirite dietary restrictions while pregnant with the son they are to consecrate. The couple was also to make sure that Samson's hair was not cut because he was going to be a Nazirite (Heb. *nazir,* **nah-ZEER**), which means "consecrated or devoted one." These specifications were essential to set apart this child for service to God. Samson's parents made a vow for him to be a Nazirite for his entire life. This lifelong dedication began even in the womb, as indicated by his mother's observance of a special diet.

6 Then the woman came and told her husband, saying, A man of God came unto me, and his countenance was like the countenance of an angel of God, very terrible: but I asked him not whence he was, neither told he me his name: 7 But he said unto me, Behold, thou shalt conceive, and bear a son; and now drink no wine nor strong drink, neither eat any unclean thing: for the child

shall be a Nazarite to God from the womb to the day of his death.

Manoah's wife brought the good news to her husband and shared the details of what the messenger of God had told her. The word "countenance" is King James English for "appearance." She described the one she recognized as an angel as looking "terrible" (Heb. *yare'*, **yah-RAY**), which means "inspiring fear." At first sight, the messenger probably appeared to be someone she should be afraid of. Indeed, she did not ask him where he came from, and he did not give his name. In the ancient Near East was a widespread belief that to give someone your name was to inform him or her of your character and how to control you. The angel is not allowing them access to his name to avoid being controlled or manipulated. Manoah's wife relays the news simply: A man told her that she would conceive and bear a son, how she must carry him during her pregnancy, and that he "shall be a Nazarite to God" (13:7). In essence, this part of the passage tells us that God can call, consecrate, and anoint us to do His will even before we are born!

24 And the woman bare a son, and called his name Samson: and the child grew, and the LORD blessed him.

There is a song that says, "All God's promises are true." This part of the text demonstrates that God fulfills His promises. Yes, His promises are indeed true! The woman who was barren for so many years gave birth to a son "and called his name Samson" (v. 24). In Hebrew, "Samson" is *Shimshon* (**sheem-SHONE**) and means "like the sun." Samson was also blessed (Heb. *barak*, **bah-ROCK**), which means "saluted, adored"; Samson's blessings flowed from God. In other words, when Samson obeyed God and did His will, his life was blessed.

25 And the Spirit of the LORD began to move him at times in the camp of Dan between Zorah and Eshtaol.

God's Spirit denotes His presence with His people. The word "Spirit" (Heb. *ruakh*, **ROO-akh**) means "wind, breath, mind, spirit," but here it refers to God's presence and power at work in Samson. Ultimately, this is the third Person of the Trinity carrying out the will of God. The one true God was preparing Samson to deliver His people from the hands of their enemies. So God began to prepare Samson for his role as judge of Israel, where he would reign for twenty years. After forty years, the Israelites were going to be set free from the Philistines' bondage, and all that they could do was yield to the power of Almighty God.

Samson's tenure as judge was marked by moments of foolishness and tragedy. Even though Samson sinned terribly and often used poor judgment, God still accomplished much through him. Frail humanity cannot hinder His plans. Whatever He decrees will certainly come to fruition. The bigger picture is that in spite of Samson's behavior—God wanted to free His chosen people from bondage, and He did just that. The destiny of the Children of Israel and God's purpose for their lives were always in His hands. In comparison, Samson was like the nation of Israel: he was called by God to be a judge, and just like how the nation thrived when they obeyed God, Samson thrived as long as he obeyed God. We, too, will thrive as long as we obey God and follow His inerrant Word.

From the book of Judges and this lesson, we should learn that a holy God hates sin and punishes it as well. Sin has dire consequences. The ultimate penalty for sin is death, and God sets before us the way of life and the way of death (Jeremiah 21:8). At the other end of the spectrum is the fact that He also works out miraculous redemption plans and forgives sin;

those who repent (turn from sin and toward God) can be restored to a right relationship with Him.

Say It Correctly

Manoah. ma-**NO**-uh.
Ashkelon. **ASH**-ku-lon.
Ekron. ek-**RAHN**.

Daily Bible Readings

MONDAY
Announcement of Samson's Birth to Manoah
(Judges 13:8–18)

TUESDAY
The Angel Accepts Manoah's Sacrifice
(Judges 13:19–23)

WEDNESDAY
Vow of Separation to the Lord
(Numbers 6:1–8, 13–17)

THURSDAY
Samson Marries a Woman of Timnah
(Judges 14:1–9)

FRIDAY
Samson Conquers the Philistines
(Judges 15:1–8)

SATURDAY
In Death, Samson Defeats the Philistines
(Judges 16:23–31)

SUNDAY
Samson's Call
(Judges 13:1–7, 24–25)

Notes

Teaching Tips

Words You Should Know

A. Holy (Exodus 3:5) *kodesh* (Heb.)—Set apart, sacred, of God.

B. Oppression (v. 9) *lachats* (Heb.)—The state of being kept down by unjust use of authority; a physical pushing down.

Teacher Preparation

Unifying Principle—That's Not Fair. People get accustomed to living with the injustices that prevail in society. What does it take to address injustice? God called Moses to address injustice and empowered him with the knowledge of His identity, purpose, and presence.

A. Pray for your students and for lesson understanding and clarity.

B. Read Exodus 1–3 to become familiar with the context of the passage of study.

C. Complete the companion lesson in the *Precepts For Living®* Study Guide.

O—Open the Lesson

A. Open with prayer, including the Aim for Change.

B. Introduce summary of Unit 2 (page 418) and today's lesson title.

C. Have your students read the Aim for Change and Keep in Mind verse together. Discuss.

D. Read In Focus. Then ask: "Has God ever given you the desire to get involved in some kind of ministry at church or even just to help someone, but you made an excuse not to do it? Why do we do this?" Discuss.

P—Present the Scriptures

A. Have volunteers read the Focal Verses.

B. Use the At-A-Glance outline; The People, Places, and Times; Background; Search the Scriptures; In Depth; and More Light on the Text sections to clarify the verses.

E—Explore the Meaning

A. Divide the class into groups to discuss the Discuss the Meaning, Lesson in Our Society, and Make It Happen sections. Tell the students to select a representative to report responses.

B. Connect these sections to the Aim for Change and Keep in Mind verse.

N—Next Steps for Application

A. Summarize the lesson.

B. Summarize the steps for application, and call students' attention to their answers in the Make It Happen section.

C. Close in prayer.

Worship Guide

For the Superintendent or Teacher
Theme: Moses and the Burning Bush
Song: "I Give Myself Away"
Devotional Reading: 2 Chronicles 19:4–7

Moses and the Burning Bush

Bible Background • EXODUS 3
Printed Text • EXODUS 3:1–12 | Devotional Reading • 2 CHRONICLES 19:4–7

———— Aim for Change ————

By the end of this lesson, we will: EXAMINE the details of how Moses was called and the self-revealed nature of God, who called him; EMPATHIZE with God's awareness of injustice and His desire to correct it; and ADDRESS injustice in ways that honor God's identity, purpose, and presence.

———— In Focus ————

John was a busy salesman who had to travel extensively, driving hours at a time from city to city and sometimes state to state. Although traveling was a job requirement, John made sure he was home every other weekend to be with his family and attend church.

One Sunday at church, the pastor shared with the congregation that he had received multiple complaints from some of the young women in the church, who were being harassed by young men who sat on the corner nearby. "I am aware of the harassment and the fear it has caused. In the past week, one of the girls was attacked," the pastor reported. He asked men in the congregation to reach out to these young men. Through mentoring, the pastor believed they could be helped.

Several weeks later, the pastor approached John and asked him to help. He knew that John had experience with troubled boys, and wanted him to lead the effort. Before the pastor could finish, John objected. He told the pastor that he was not sure he would relate well to the young men, and his work took him away most of the time. The pastor assured John that he would not have to engage the men alone—he and two of the church elders would support him.

In today's lesson, we will examine how God called Moses and used him as an agent in the redemption of His people. Has God ever given you the desire to get involved in some kind of ministry at church or even just to help someone, but you made an excuse not to do it?

———— Keep in Mind ————

"Now therefore, behold, the cry of the children of Israel is come unto me: and I have also seen the oppression wherewith the Egyptians oppress them. Come now therefore, and I will send thee unto Pharaoh, that thou mayest bring forth my people the children of Israel out of Egypt" (Exodus 3:9–10).

"Now therefore, behold, the cry of the children of Israel is come unto me: and I have also seen the oppression wherewith the Egyptians oppress them. Come now therefore, and I will send thee unto Pharaoh, that thou mayest bring forth my people the children of Israel out of Egypt" (Exodus 3:9–10).

Focal Verses

KJV **Exodus 3:1** Now Moses kept the flock of Jethro his father in law, the priest of Midian: and he led the flock to the backside of the desert, and came to the mountain of God, even to Horeb.

2 And the angel of the LORD appeared unto him in a flame of fire out of the midst of a bush: and he looked, and, behold, the bush burned with fire, and the bush was not consumed.

3 And Moses said, I will now turn aside, and see this great sight, why the bush is not burnt.

4 And when the LORD saw that he turned aside to see, God called unto him out of the midst of the bush, and said, Moses, Moses. And he said, Here am I.

5 And he said, Draw not nigh hither: put off thy shoes from off thy feet, for the place whereon thou standest is holy ground.

6 Moreover he said, I am the God of thy father, the God of Abraham, the God of Isaac, and the God of Jacob. And Moses hid his face; for he was afraid to look upon God.

7 And the LORD said, I have surely seen the affliction of my people which are in Egypt, and have heard their cry by reason of their taskmasters; for I know their sorrows;

8 And I am come down to deliver them out of the hand of the Egyptians, and to bring them up out of that land unto a good land and a large, unto a land flowing with milk and honey; unto the place of the Canaanites, and the Hittites, and the Amorites, and the Perizzites, and the Hivites, and the Jebusites.

9 Now therefore, behold, the cry of the children of Israel is come unto me: and I have also seen the oppression wherewith the Egyptians oppress them.

10 Come now therefore, and I will send thee unto Pharaoh, that thou mayest bring forth my people the children of Israel out of Egypt.

NLT **Exodus 3:1** One day Moses was tending the flock of his father-in-law, Jethro, the priest of Midian. He led the flock far into the wilderness and came to Sinai, the mountain of God.

2 There the angel of the LORD appeared to him in a blazing fire from the middle of a bush. Moses stared in amazement. Though the bush was engulfed in flames, it didn't burn up.

3 "This is amazing," Moses said to himself. "Why isn't that bush burning up? I must go see it."

4 When the LORD saw Moses coming to take a closer look, God called to him from the middle of the bush, "Moses! Moses!" "Here I am!" Moses replied.

5 "Do not come any closer," the LORD warned. "Take off your sandals, for you are standing on holy ground.

6 I am the God of your father—the God of Abraham, the God of Isaac, and the God of Jacob." When Moses heard this, he covered his face because he was afraid to look at God.

7 Then the LORD told him, "I have certainly seen the oppression of my people in Egypt. I have heard their cries of distress because of their harsh slave drivers. Yes, I am aware of their suffering.

8 So I have come down to rescue them from the power of the Egyptians and lead them out of Egypt into their own fertile and spacious land. It is a land flowing with milk and honey—the land where the Canaanites, Hittites, Amorites, Perizzites, Hivites, and Jebusites now live.

9 Look! The cry of the people of Israel has reached me, and I have seen how harshly the Egyptians abuse them.

10 Now go, for I am sending you to Pharaoh. You must lead my people Israel out of Egypt."

11 And Moses said unto God, Who am I, that I should go unto Pharaoh, and that I should bring forth the children of Israel out of Egypt?

12 And he said, Certainly I will be with thee; and this shall be a token unto thee, that I have sent thee: When thou hast brought forth the people out of Egypt, ye shall serve God upon this mountain.

11 But Moses protested to God, "Who am I to appear before Pharaoh? Who am I to lead the people of Israel out of Egypt?"

12 God answered, "I will be with you. And this is your sign that I am the one who has sent you: When you have brought the people out of Egypt, you will worship God at this very mountain."

The People, Places, and Times

Mount Sinai. This mountain was a very important landmark for the Israelites. Also called Horeb, it has huge significance in Judaism. Mount Sinai is both the site of Moses receiving his call from God (Exodus 3:1) and the Children of Israel receiving God's Law and covenant (Exodus 19–20). After the Israelites were rescued from Egypt, they crossed the Red Sea into the wilderness; there they camped at the foot of Mt. Sinai while Moses climbed the mountain to enter God's presence. God revealed Himself to Moses and gave to him His law and covenant affirming Israel as His holy nation: they would be one nation under one God, who would be their leader (Exodus 19:3–6).

Theophany. This term does not occur in the Bible, but is used to describe a narrative in which God's presence is made visible to individuals or groups. The word is derived from two Greek words: *theos*, "God," and *phainein*, "to appear." In the Old Testament, God's appearance takes various forms. In Exodus 3:1–12, God appears to Moses as the angel of the Lord in the blazing fire in the bush.

Background

Jacob's family moved to Egypt at the invitation of Joseph, who had been reunited with his family after being raised to a position of prominence in Egypt. Famine was hurting the people, and Joseph had control of Egypt's stores and resources as one of Pharaoh's rulers. Seventy of Jacob's direct descendants moved with him to Egypt. In time, Jacob, Joseph, and Joseph's brothers died; Jacob's descendants grew in number, and the Egyptians began to fear them. The pharaoh who came to power after Joseph's death did not know him or the Israelites' history in Egypt, and became fearful that this growing group of people would one day rise up to conquer his kingdom. So, in an effort to repress the Hebrews, the Egyptians made them slaves and forced them into hard and oppressive labor. God was aware of His people's troubles, because He told Abraham that His people would be strangers in a foreign land and oppressed as slaves for four hundred years. However, He would rescue His people and punish the oppressor (Genesis 15:13–16).

The Egyptians' oppression was fierce: they resorted to genocidal strategies, including killing Hebrew male babies. God in His providence saved Moses in the bushes of the Nile River and allowed him to be raised in Pharaoh's house. When Moses grew older, he saw the oppression of his people and one day, in an attempt to save a Hebrew slave, killed an Egyptian.

His act of murder did not go unnoticed. When Pharaoh ordered Moses' arrest, he escaped to Midian. Moses moved from being a prince in Pharaoh's court to being God's shepherd in the wilderness. In his occupation as a shepherd tending his flock, God calls him, because He had purposed to use Moses as an instrument in the redemption of His people whom He called to Himself.

At-A-Glance

1. God Appears (Exodus 3:1–4)
2. The Presence of God (vv. 5–6)
3. God Engages Moses (vv. 7–10)
4. God Commissions Moses (vv. 11–12)

In Depth

1. God Appears (Exodus 3:1–4)

The lesson text begins by locating Moses in Midian and giving background to demonstrate that his life had changed. Once an Egyptian prince, Moses was now involved in the life of his own people. He was a shepherd, an occupation that he would have thought demeaning as an Egyptian, because Egyptians despised shepherds (Genesis 46:34).

Moses was out tending to his father-in-law's flock, which suggests that he had not accumulated a flock of his own. He was located far away from Midian, because "He led the flock far into the wilderness and came to Sinai, the mountain of God." As a shepherd, he would have traveled to ensure he had good pasture for his flock to graze on. Out in the wilderness, at Sinai, God, in the form of the angel of the Lord, suddenly appears to Moses in a blazing fire from the bush. Moses saw the bush, that it was on fire but did not burn. Through this unusual encounter, God captures Moses' attention and reveals Himself. The Lord also does this in the life of the believer; in the midst of everyday life, He draws us to Himself.

The Lord not only reveals Himself, but also speaks and calls Moses by name, suggesting that this encounter was personal. In ancient Near Eastern culture, repeating the name signified endearment. This encounter must have disarmed Moses, because he immediately answers, "Here I am!" suggesting his readiness to listen.

2. The Presence of God (vv. 5–6)

Without disclosing His identity, God commands Moses not to come any closer, but to remove his sandals. He immediately reveals to Moses the holy nature of His presence. The ground itself was not holy, but became holy because God was there. God is holy, and we cannot enter into His presence lightly or in any way that does not recognize the magnitude of His holiness. In acknowledgment of God's holiness, Moses takes off his sandals. Then, God discloses His identity, saying that He is the God of the patriarchs—Abraham, Isaac, and Jacob. God connects Moses to his heritage. Moses realizes that he is in the presence of God and responds by hiding his face because he was afraid to look at Him. In ancient Near Eastern culture, it was believed that if someone looked at a god, his life was in danger. Moses knew that looking at God could have meant death (Genesis 32:30; Exodus 33:20; Judges 13:22), because he understood that God is holy.

3. God Engages Moses (vv. 7–10)

In Exodus 2:23–25, the Israelites cried out to God for deliverance. He heard their cry, remembered the covenant He made with Abraham, Issac, and Jacob (Genesis 15:4–6, 26:1–5, 35:9–12), and felt deep concern. The interaction between God and Moses continues in verse 7. God tells Moses He has seen, heard, and is aware of the suffering of His people in Egypt. In fact, the Hebrew text emphatically indicates that God certainly had seen His people's affliction. The emphasis in the text implies God's personal interest in His people's suffering. God keeps His promises.

As believers, we must not forget that God is not blind to our suffering nor unconcerned with His people's afflictions (Matthew 10:29–31). We must trust Him in the midst of what we face, knowing that He will deliver in due time.

In verse 8, God shares His rescue plan with Moses: He has come down to deliver His people from their slavery. God was going to do something about their suffering. He would not only remove them from oppression, but lead them to a good land, fertile and spacious but inhabited (Genesis 12:1–3). In verse 9, God reiterates that He has seen their oppression and has heard the cries of His people (Exodus 2:23–25, 3:7).

In verse 10, God tells Moses that He has chosen him to be an instrument in His hand. Moses will go to Pharaoh and will lead the people of Israel out of Egypt. In Exodus 2:11–12, Moses had rescued a Hebrew, killed an Egyptian, and fled. That time, Moses operated in his own strength. This time, his rescue mission was ordained by God.

Sometimes, we move ahead of the Lord, taking on tasks in our own strength rather than waiting to be empowered by the Lord. God called Moses to partner with Him to redeem His people from slavery.

4. God Commissions Moses (vv. 11–12)

Moses, who earlier said "Here I am," now responds to God's call with questions: "Who am I to appear before Pharaoh?" and "Who am I to lead the people of Israel out of Egypt?" God assures Moses that He would be with him. God's call and presence would give Moses the authority and power he would need to stand before Pharaoh and lead the people. God would not only be with Moses but also give him a sign that would prove to him that he fulfilled God's assigned task. The people would successfully leave Egypt, come to Mount Sinai, and worship before their God. The sign would only be seen after Moses was obedient.

No matter how Moses felt about what God had called him to do, what was important was that God empowered him and would be with him to execute His plan. Moses' success was not dependent on who he was or his ability, but his obedience and trust in God. God equips and empowers those whom He calls. For we believers whom God calls to do His work, we too must be obedient to the call and faithful to the tasks He has called us to do, knowing that He will enable us to complete them.

Search the Scriptures

1. Recount the specifics of Moses' call. What was unusual about his experience (Exodus 13:1–6)?

2. What does the account of Moses' call tell about God? What characteristics of God are highlighted in this story (vv. 1–12)?

Discuss the Meaning

1. How do fear or feelings of inadequacy prevent us from serving the way the Lord is showing us?

2. How did God encourage Moses in his assignment? How should that promise propel us to join God in His kingdom work and help those He brings in our path?

Lesson in Our Society

The Israelites were oppressed foreigners in Egypt. Moses understood God's holiness and surrendered to His call to help redeem the Israelites whom God called to Himself. As believers, we have to see injustice through the lens of who God is and get involved. Today, in our country and all over the world, people are being oppressed. Statistics show that approximately 27 million people are in some form of slavery today worldwide. Here in the United States, sex trafficking and other kinds of injustices are apparent in our society. How can the church get involved to help fight against such atrocities? How can you get involved to fight against injustice?

Make It Happen

Commit to pray this week, asking God to reveal to you specifically where and how you can become involved in helping those suffering and in need.

List two ways God may be signaling you to get more involved at church, in the community, or with charity to help those in need.

Partner with your church, and select one place to volunteer for a few hours.

Partner with your church outreach team, and go into the community and share the Gospel of Jesus Christ.

Follow the Spirit

What God wants me to do:

_____

_____

_____

_____

Remember Your Thoughts

Special insights I have learned:

_____

_____

_____

_____

More Light on the Text

Exodus 3:1–12

1 Now Moses kept the flock of Jethro his father in law, the priest of Midian: and he led the flock to the backside of the desert, and came to the mountain of God, even to Horeb.

Moses was carrying out his usual work as a shepherd. The verb translated "kept" is more literally "was shepherding" in the Hebrew (*hayah ro'eh*, **hah-YAH ro-EH**). This participle expresses the continuance of the job; it was his habitual occupation.

Moses had become the shepherd of Jethro, his father-in-law. Jethro, called Reuel (Exodus 2:18–20), is probably a title meaning "eminence" or "highness." The story takes place many years after Moses fled from Egypt to Midian. According to Acts 7:30, it was forty years later.

One day Moses led the sheep as far as Horeb, the mountain of God. Horeb is called the mountain of God (1 Kings 19:8) either because there God would reveal Himself first to Moses and then to the Israelites, or it was already known as a sacred place. Horeb and Sinai are two names for the same mountain or group of mountains (1 Kings 8:9; Nehemiah 9:13). Moses passed through the desert before reaching the pasture land of Horeb. The word "backside" (Heb. *'akhar*, **ah-KHAR**) can be understood as the west side of the desert—in Semitic thought, one faces east when giving compass directions so west is to one's back. Moses did not go to Horeb, the mountain of God, with a religious intention—just to take care of his father-in-law's flock.

2 And the angel of the LORD appeared unto him in a flame of fire out of the midst of a bush: and he looked, and, behold, the bush burned with fire, and the bush was not consumed. 3 And Moses said, I will now turn

aside, and see this great sight, why the bush is not burnt.

Moses was going about his usual business when God appeared to him as an "angel." The term "angel" (Heb. *mal'ak*, **mal-OCK**) literally means "messenger." Here, the angel is not to be thought of as a supernatural messenger of Yahweh, but a direct manifestation of Yahweh Himself. The term is interchangeable with Yahweh (v. 4 speaks of Yahweh Himself calling out of the bush), and is a reverential way of referring to Yahweh as His appearance in patriarchal stories shows (Genesis 16:7, 18:1–2, 22:11; cf. Judges 6:12). At the same time, the angel is described as both Yahweh and yet distinguished from Him. This revelation prepares the reader of the Bible for the fuller revelation in the New Testament of God as three-in-one.

The Lord appeared to Moses as fire coming out of a bush. The term "bush" in Hebrew (Heb. *seneh*, **seh-NEH**) is similar in sound to Sinai (Heb. *sinay*, **si-NEYE**). This bush is referred to again in Deuteronomy 33:16. The Lord is called He "him that dwelt in the bush." Fire in the Bible is often a symbol of God's presence (Exodus 13:21, 19:18); it speaks of His holiness and His anger in relation to sin (32:10). Moses decided to investigate more closely this strange event: the bush was burning, yet not consumed. The Lord used Moses' initial curiosity to attract him to the place.

4 And when the LORD saw that he turned aside to see, God called unto him out of the midst of the bush, and said, Moses, Moses. And he said, Here am I.

The transition from the angel (v. 2) to the Lord (v. 4) proves the identity of the two. This passage uses two names for God interchangeably: "LORD" (Heb. *yahweh*, **YA-way**) and "God" (Heb. *elohim*, **eh-loh-HEEM**, "deities, God"). Emphasizing the sameness of Yahweh (a personal, covenant name of God) and

Elohim excludes the idea of Yahweh being only the God of Israel or merely a national God.

In a personal display, the likes of which hadn't been seen since the patriarchs, the Lord called Moses. He communicated with him personally and called him by name. Moses responded, "Here am I" (cf. Genesis 22:1, 11; 1 Samuel 3:4–8).

5 And he said, Draw not nigh hither: put off thy shoes from off thy feet, for the place whereon thou standest is holy ground.

Moses was told not to come near. The phrase "draw not nigh hither" can be translated in modern language as "stop coming near, as you are doing." Moses did not recognize the presence or nature of God. Later, after his experience with the Lord, he would be ready to draw near Him and intercede for others (see Exodus 32:30).

The Lord commanded Moses to take off his shoes. This practice, still observed in many religions, indicates the presence of God in the sanctuary (but see John 4:21–24; 1 Corinthians 6:19–20; Ephesians 3:14–21). Moses must take off his shoes because he was standing on holy ground, made so by God's presence. Removing shoes was intended to express not merely respect for the place itself, but was also a sign of worship, reverence, and acceptance of a servant's position. It represented removing uncleanness caused by contact with the world, a recognition of Yahweh's holiness.

6 Moreover he said, I am the God of thy father, the God of Abraham, the God of Isaac, and the God of Jacob. And Moses hid his face; for he was afraid to look upon God.

The Lord explained to Moses why He had appeared to him. He was the God of Moses' father. The term "father" (Heb. *av*, **'av**) has a literal and immediate meaning as well as a remote connotation; the phrase could refer to Amram (Moses' biological father) or to all Moses' ancestors (see Genesis 46:3; Exodus 18:4). The Lord identifies Himself as the same God who made the covenant promises to Abraham, Isaac, and Jacob, fathers of Moses and the Israelites. Each father stood out distinctly, as having received the promise of seed directly from God (cf. Genesis 17:16, 26:4, 28:14). Those promises are now to be fulfilled.

Moses was afraid of the sight of the holy God. No sinful man can bear the sight of God (Exodus 33:20; Numbers 4:20; Isaiah 6:2, 5). When fragile, sinful humans encounter the holy God, their initial response is terror and an attempt to hide. However, the encounter is also an event of grace bringing hope and new life (cf. Genesis 32:31; Leviticus 16:2). The same fear struck the witnesses of the glory of Jesus, manifested in His miracles, transfiguration and resurrection (cf. Matthew 17:6; Mark 4:41; Luke 24:5, 37).

7 And the LORD said, I have surely seen the affliction of my people which are in Egypt, and have heard their cry by reason of their taskmasters; for I know their sorrows;

The Lord presents Himself as someone who cares deeply, calling the Israelites "My people." The words "have seen," "have heard," and "know" stress the Lord's almost physical sensitivity toward His people. The emphasis on the pain and suffering that God has seen and heard comes through in the powerful use of Hebrew words related to physical and emotional suffering and oppression. Affliction (Heb. '*oniy*, **oh-NEE**, poverty, oppression) in the literal sense refers to a physical pushing down and can figuratively refer to poverty, slavery, or other oppression. The word for their taskmasters (Heb. *nagas*, **nah-GOS**, money collectors, slave drivers) also connotes a physical pushing down or against something, as if they've been pushed into a position of no escape. In the

midst of this, God knows their sorrows (Heb. *ma'kov*, **mah-KOVE**), referring to pain that is traumatic and perhaps chronic or deadly. He saw their misery; He heard their cries. He knew their sorrows. Now, He is going to do something about it.

8 And I am come down to deliver them out of the hand of the Egyptians, and to bring them up out of that land unto a good land and a large, unto a land flowing with milk and honey; unto the place of the Canaanites, and the Hittites, and the Amorites, and the Perizzites, and the Hivites, and the Jebusites. 9 Now therefore, behold, the cry of the children of Israel is come unto me: and I have also seen the oppression wherewith the Egyptians oppress them.

Yahweh Himself, virtually in bodily form, had come down to deliver His people out the hands of the Egyptians. He would lead them to the land promised to their fathers: a good, large land, flowing with milk and honey. The expression "milk and honey" describes a land with abundant food–a prosperous and fertile land. It is a proverbial description of Canaan symbolizing continuity, stability, and identity—things that only God can give to people.

Calling the land "large" (Heb. *rakhav*, **rah-KHAV**, broad, expansive, spread out) is explained by the listing of the nations occupying the territory at that time (Genesis 10:6, 15–17, 19). Yahweh repeated the fact that the cry of the people had reached Him (see v. 7). He knew of the sinful oppression by the Egyptians and the hardships to which they subjected His people.

10 Come now therefore, and I will send thee unto Pharaoh, that thou mayest bring forth my people the children of Israel out of Egypt.

"Now therefore" draws the conclusion of the Lord's speech: Moses was selected for the work of redemption. God announced that He was going to save His people through Moses, the person chosen to achieve it. Moses was called and sent to Pharaoh to bring the Lord's people out of Egypt. God uses men and women to achieve His purposes. He does not need to do so, but He invites us to share with Him in fulfilling His plans (John 20:21). He normally works through His servants' willing obedience.

11 And Moses said unto God, Who am I, that I should go unto Pharaoh, and that I should bring forth the children of Israel out of Egypt?

Moses would have quickly welcomed the Lord's invitation to free His people years earlier. Indeed, he had once tried to become the liberator of one Israelite from the pharaoh's power (Exodus 2:11–14). The years of hardship and bitterness in the Midian wilderness had changed him. He was no longer bold, impetuous, and impatient, but now timid and hesitant. He had learned his own weaknesses and limitations. This is the first of Moses' four protests against accepting the commission to lead Israel out of Egypt (cf. Exodus 4:1, 10, 13). He expressed his feeling of inadequacy and unworthiness for the task of freeing his people.

12 And he said, Certainly I will be with thee; and this shall be a token unto thee, that I have sent thee: When thou hast brought forth the people out of Egypt, ye shall serve God upon this mountain.

The Lord, in answer to Moses' fear, told him that He Himself would be with him. Where Moses' abilities might fail would be a God of unlimited abilities. What Moses desired was assurance that God had truly sent him.

The Lord offered Moses a sign or token (Heb. *'ot*, **OTE**). The word "sign" covers a variety of events and phenomena in the Bible and should not be restricted to a narrow meaning. A sign is often a natural occurrence or supernatural phenomenon that confirms the truth of what is said by God or a prophet (see 1 Samuel 10:7, 9; 2 Kings 19:29). Here, the sign was that Moses' success in bringing the Israelites out of Egypt would prove the Lord was with him; they would serve God on this same mountain. In other words, the purpose of his mission would be accomplished. Moses received the guarantee that Yahweh was truly the One who sent him. The "I" in "I have sent thee" is emphatic.

The Israelites would serve God on His mountain. "To serve" (Heb. *'avad*, **ah-VAD**) has the meaning of both service and worship. The service offered to God is not a bondage, but rather a joyous, liberating experience. The Israelites, by being free of Pharaoh's yoke, would not enter into a state of anarchy, but use their new freedom to serve God under a covenantal law. They would pass from slavery in service of Pharaoh to the liberty of the service to God—a major theme of the Exodus.

Say It Correctly

Midian. **MI**-dee-an.
Theos. theh-**OCE**.
Phainein. **FEYE**-nane.

Daily Bible Readings

MONDAY
Insist on Justice for All
(Exodus 23:1–9)

TUESDAY
Eternal Cost of Not Offering Justice
(Matthew 25:41–46)

WEDNESDAY
No Perversion of Justice Allowed
(2 Chronicles 19:4–7)

THURSDAY
Persist until Justice is Done
(Luke 18:1–8)

FRIDAY
Deacons Called to Ministry of Justice
(Acts 6:1–7)

SATURDAY
Israelites Meet God at Mount Sinai
(Exodus 19:1–9)

SUNDAY
Moses and the Burning Bush
(Exodus 3:1–12)

Notes

Teaching Tips

July 9
Bible Study Guide 6

Words You Should Know

A. Seraphim (Isaiah 6:2) *saraph* (Heb.)—"The burning ones"; a class of angelic being; a poisonous serpent.

B. Send (v. 8) *shalakh* (Heb.)—Launch, dispatch, send off.

Teacher Preparation

Unifying Principle—Who, Me? Unexpected circumstances can lead us into paths we don't anticipate. Where do we gain confidence to undertake these unexpected tasks? Isaiah's confidence came from the unusual and compelling events of his call.

A. Pray for your students and for lesson clarity.

B. Complete the companion lesson in the *Precepts For Living®* Personal Study Guide.

O—Open the Lesson

A. Open in prayer, including the Aim for Change.

B. Introduce today's lesson title.

C. Have students think of a time when they had to step in for someone and do his or her job or task because that person was unable to do so.

D. Have your students read the Aim for Change and Keep in Mind verse together. Discuss.

P—Present the Scriptures

A. Have volunteers read the Focal Verses.

B. Use the At-A-Glance Outline; The People, Places, and Times; Background; Search the Scriptures; In Depth; and More Light on the Text sections to clarify verses

C. Ask the students questions throughout this portion.

E—Explore the Meaning

A. Divide into groups to respond to the Discuss the Meaning and Lesson in Our Society sections. Tell students to select a representative to report their responses.

B. Connect these sections to the Aim for Change and Keep in Mind verse.

N—Next Steps for Application

A. Summarize the lesson and charge students to follow the suggestions in the Make It Happen section.

B. Close with prayer.

Worship Guide

For the Superintendent or Teacher
Theme: Isaiah in the Temple
Song: "I Give Myself Away"
Devotional Reading: Isaiah 66:18–23

Isaiah in the Temple

Bible Background • ISAIAH 6
Printed Text • ISAIAH 6:1–8 | Devotional Reading • ISAIAH 66:18–23

Aim for Change

By the end of the lesson, we will: EXPLORE the circumstances of Isaiah's call and his reaction to it; ARTICULATE Isaiah's emotions as he reacted to his call; and ANSWER God's call to service.

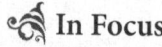 In Focus

A man of few words, Fred was quiet at work. He never went out to lunch with his other coworkers and rarely left his desk. He clocked in at 9 a.m. and clocked out at 5 p.m.

One day, a big meeting was called. Most people thought more layoffs were coming. The meeting was to inform the workers that one of the supervisors was retiring and her position was open. Everyone assumed that the office superstar Corey was going to get the position. Days went by and no word came about who was getting promoted.

The following week, another meeting was called to announce the newest supervisor to the company. To everyone's surprise, including his own, Fred was named the new supervisor. Everyone was shocked! As Fred was announced, he wondered to himself, *Why me? What have I done to receive this promotion?* The CEO stated, "Most of you are probably wondering, why Fred of all people? We chose Fred because of his work ethic and his timeliness. He is very knowledgeable and thorough with his reports. He will be a strong leader."

Some will see potential in us when others or even ourselves do not. In today's lesson, we will learn that God saw the potential in Isaiah to be a leader and called him into service. Has someone ever seen potential in you and challenged you to a specific task?

Keep in Mind

"Also I heard the voice of the Lord, saying, Whom shall I send, and who will go for us? Then said I, Here am I; send me" (Isaiah 6:8).

"Also I heard the voice of the Lord, saying, Whom shall I send, and who will go for us? Then said I, Here am I; send me" (Isaiah 6:8).

Focal Verses

KJV **Isaiah 6:1** In the year that king Uzziah died I saw also the LORD sitting upon a throne, high and lifted up, and his train filled the temple.

2 Above it stood the seraphims: each one had six wings; with twain he covered his face, and with twain he covered his feet, and with twain he did fly.

3 And one cried unto another, and said, Holy, holy, holy, is the LORD of hosts: the whole earth is full of his glory.

4 And the posts of the door moved at the voice of him that cried, and the house was filled with smoke.

5 Then said I, Woe is me! for I am undone; because I am a man of unclean lips, and I dwell in the midst of a people of unclean lips: for mine eyes have seen the King, the LORD of hosts.

6 Then flew one of the seraphims unto me, having a live coal in his hand, which he had taken with the tongs from off the altar:

7 And he laid it upon my mouth, and said, Lo, this hath touched thy lips; and thine iniquity is taken away, and thy sin purged.

8 Also I heard the voice of the Lord, saying, Whom shall I send, and who will go for us? Then said I, Here am I; send me.

NLT **Isaiah 6:1** It was in the year King Uzziah died that I saw the Lord. He was sitting on a lofty throne, and the train of his robe filled the Temple.

2 Attending him were mighty seraphim, each having six wings. With two wings they covered their faces, with two they covered their feet, and with two they flew.

3 They were calling out to each other, "Holy, holy, holy is the LORD of Heaven's Armies! The whole earth is filled with his glory!"

4 Their voices shook the Temple to its foundations, and the entire building was filled with smoke.

5 Then I said, "It's all over! I am doomed, for I am a sinful man. I have filthy lips, and I live among a people with filthy lips. Yet I have seen the King, the LORD of Heaven's Armies."

6 Then one of the seraphim flew to me with a burning coal he had taken from the altar with a pair of tongs.

7 He touched my lips with it and said, "See, this coal has touched your lips. Now your guilt is removed, and your sins are forgiven."

8 Then I heard the Lord asking, "Whom should I send as a messenger to this people? Who will go for us?" I said, "Here I am. Send me."

The People, Places, and Times

Judah and Israel. During the time when Isaiah was called to serve as a prophet (around 740 BC), the nations of Judah and Israel were being disobedient to God, living lives displeasing to Him. These nations worshiped idols and depended on the "power" and abilities of sorcerers and magicians, while turning their back on God and forgetting all He had done for their ancestors. The Lord used warnings of judgment to help lead His people to repentance, salvation, and dependence on Him.

Prophets. God handpicked this unique group of people to be His messengers. Prophets were considered to be God's special representatives. They confronted the leaders during periods of disobedience (cf. 2 Samuel 12—Nathan confronting David) and verbally warned God's people when they were disobedient. Prophets were not the most popular people because of their message, but were respected due to their closeness to God. The prophet's message was used to help God's people get back in line with Him and give them hope for reconciliation.

Background

Throughout biblical history, God's people have been inconsistent in their allegiance to Him. Whether creating golden images for idol worship, taking His love and mercy for granted, or constantly complaining, His people had a history of disobedience to God. During the time when God made Isaiah a prophet, the same pattern continued. In God's eyes, Judah and Israel had broken a covenant agreement with Him. They did this by oppressing the poor, worshiping pagan idols, and turning to sorcerers and magicians. As a result, God sent words of judgment to His people to explain their sins against Him. If they continued to defy God or break their contract with Him, destruction of the two nations would result.

Since God loved His people and continued to have mercy for them, He continued to give hope. God told His people that He would be with them and still deliver them from their enemies if they would repent of their sins. God had so much mercy for His people that He called a person to give these warnings: Isaiah, one of their own. Through the calling of Isaiah as a prophet, God used someone the people could relate to to portray a message of repentance, salvation, and caution. God handpicked Isaiah to give the people a choice of continuing to break their covenant or repairing the breach.

At-A-Glance

1. A God Experience (Isaiah 6:1–4)
2. Isaiah's Response (v. 5)
3. God's Response (vv. 6–7)
4. Isaiah's Commitment (v. 8)

In Depth

1. A God Experience (Isaiah 6:1–4)

Isaiah explains in detail an experience he had with God. Isaiah saw God in His rightful place, sitting on a throne, representing God's position as king and ruler of all. In Isaiah's experience with God, he saw God in fitting attire for his position of ruler: a robe. Isaiah then notices beings called seraphim, which served as helpers for God. Isaiah saw firsthand that God uses others to fulfill His purpose. These seraphim displayed how Isaiah should approach a holy God, covering their face and feet in His presence as a sign of respect and lowliness. The seraphim also approached God with a spirit of worship (v. 3). When in the presence of God, we must worship Him with all we have like the seraphim and not hold anything back. Isaiah's God experience prepared him for his ultimate calling.

2. Isaiah's Response (v. 5)

Once Isaiah has an experience with God, he then does what we should do—respond. His response has several components—fear, confession, and admiration. As followers of God, we should have a healthy fear (reverence or respect) of Him. Isaiah was so in awe with God's presence, that he thought it was the end for him ("Woe is me! for I am undone," Isaiah responds).

Isaiah then confessed himself as a sinful man with filthy or unclean lips. He realized that since he was in God's presence, he should confess and repent for anything displeasing to Him. He responded in admiration for being able to experience God's presence even in his current condition. We must remember to respond when we are in God's presence.

3. God's Response (vv. 6–7)

When Isaiah responded to God by accentuating all his faults, God exhibits to him what

He wants for Israel and Judah: forgiveness. God uses the seraphim (His helpers) to repair Isaiah's condition, using a burning coal to touch the location of his iniquity: his mouth. Through this act, God symbolically prepared Isaiah for his assignment. God will always prepare you for an assignment He gives. In this symbolic preparation, God is transforming Isaiah, and He will transform us so we can be prepared for the task at hand.

As God prepares and transforms Isaiah, He gives Isaiah the experience of forgiveness (v. 7). God removes any guilt Isaiah may feel so he can freely operate in his calling. As God calls us to work for Him, we cannot allow anything to stand in the way, including our own guilt. God will respond to us when we respond to Him.

4. Isaiah's Commitment (v. 8)

After God prepares and forgives Isaiah, He then asks, "Whom shall I send, and who will go for us?" Isaiah now makes a commitment to God to accept His assignment. Isaiah could have easily ignored the question and refused to accept God's call, but he gave of himself for God to use however necessary.

Isaiah remembered his God experience and interaction. He remembered that God forgave him and honored him with His presence. So in return, Isaiah becomes committed to God by accepting His calling. Commitment to God is giving yourself to Him for His use. No matter what God calls us to do—and it won't always be pleasant (cf. Isaiah 6:9–13)—we, like Isaiah, have to say, "Here am I. Send me!"

Search the Scriptures

1. What did the seraphim use to touch Isaiah's lips (Isaiah 6:6)?

2. What did Isaiah say when God was looking for a messenger (v. 8)?

Discuss the Meaning

It is very easy to for us to get so wrapped up in what we believe we cannot do that we ignore God's assignment for our lives. How can we operate in the assignment He gives us?

Lesson in Our Society

Many people say they are ready to go to new levels in different areas of their life. But when given the opportunity to do so, they do not want to go through necessary challenges to get there. When Isaiah faced God, he could have ignored what God asked him to do, but because he responded and made a commitment to God, he was one of the greatest prophets in history.

Make It Happen

Isaiah stepped up to try to help his people avoid destruction. What can you do in your community to step up and make a difference?

Follow the Spirit

What God wants me to do:

_____

_____

_____

Remember Your Thoughts

Special insights I have learned:

_____

_____

_____

_____

More Light on the Text
Isaiah 6:1–8

1 In the year that king Uzziah died I saw also the LORD sitting upon a throne, high and lifted up, and his train filled the temple.

As a nation, Israel turned its back on God and His requirements for His chosen people. The king, having been struck by God with leprosy, was now dead after living in alienation from the people and from God (2 Chronicles 26:18–21). The people were so enmeshed in sin that the nation's prophets had been unable to guide them away. Isaiah must have felt like a failure, fearfully standing alone in the highest heaven awaiting what was sure to be punishment from his holy Father.

For years Israel had traveled a path of its own choosing and was now in spiritual and moral darkness. The king had helped the people's departure from God. Now that leader was dead. A righteous God would be justified in pronouncing the same judgment of death upon the rebellious nation and all of its inhabitants. This was Isaiah's state of mind as he stood observing God upon His "throne" (Heb. *kicce'*, **kis-SAY**), "high" (Heb. *rum*, **ROOM**) and "lifted up" (Heb. *nasa'*, **naw-SAW**). The Holy of Holies in the Temple was considered to be God's throne room. To see God as "high and lifted up" carries the sense that He is exalted. In the ancient Near East, kings' thrones were set atop a series of steps. So it is natural for Isaiah to see God the divine king in the same way. A temple was thought to be the connection between God's heavenly house and earth; in this case, it connects His heavenly throne and earth. As that connection point, some of the throne room spills over to the Temple. But what spills over? Just the "train" (Heb. *shul*, **SHOOL**), which is the long back section of a gown or robe. This is enough to fill up the entire Temple because God is that big and grand.

2 Above it stood the seraphims: each one had six wings; with twain he covered his face, and with twain he covered his feet, and with twain he did fly.

The scene is all the more frightening to Isaiah as he sees the "seraphims" (Heb. *serafim*, **seh-rah-FEEM**, literally "the burning ones") standing in God's presence worshiping and serving Him. The Hebrew word used for God's messengers places an emphasis on the fact that God is utterly holy. The seraphim must appear to Isaiah like living fire, standing above the throne waiting to serve God. With one pair of wings ("twain"), the seraphim cover their eyes lest they peer into the divine, and with another pair, they cover their feet in humble acknowledgment that they stand upon holy ground. Isaiah now sees himself all the more clearly as an unclean creature, dwelling amid unclean and rebellious humanity.

3 And one cried unto another, and said, Holy, holy, holy, is the LORD of hosts: the whole earth is full of his glory. 4 And the posts of the door moved at the voice of him that cried, and the house was filled with smoke.

Every utterance of the seraphs confirms for Isaiah that God is "holy" (Heb. *kadosh*, **kah-DOASH**). God is utterly transcendent, so far above and distinct from His created beings that none is truly worthy to be in His presence. God's holiness is central to His identity. Some scholars argue that it is His primary attribute that permeates all of the others (such as love, sovereignty, omnipotence, etc.). Amid those characteristics of God, His "glory" (Heb. *kavod*, **kah-VODE**) fills the whole earth, making it impossible to escape His presence. The scene must have been overwhelming and frightening, as not only were the seraphim proclaiming God's holiness and glory but also the Temple itself shook. Then there was smoke, which may be analogous to the Shekinah cloud that represented God's presence with the Israelites in the desert (Exodus 40:38). Shekinah is from the Hebrew word for dwelling and refers specifically to the cloud of God's presence that followed the Israelites through the wilderness. The smoke itself is representative of God's presence with the people.

What a predicament for Isaiah, who by this time must have felt that his death was imminent. No explanation was necessary for why he should die. Isaiah's presence, in the midst of such holiness, was sufficient for him to convict himself. As if to confirm Isaiah's sense of God's awesome power and mystery, smoke filled the chamber and once more concealed Him from Isaiah's sight.

5 Then said I, Woe is me! for I am undone; because I am a man of unclean lips, and I dwell in the midst of a people of unclean lips: for mine eyes have seen the King, the LORD of hosts.

Isaiah gives voice to what he was feeling. The word "woe" in Hebrew is 'oy (**O-ee**) and stands for a passionate cry of grief or despair. It's the same as the familiar Jewish expression "oy." Seeing all that transpires around him, Isaiah declares himself and his people guilty before God and prepares for his death. He was "undone" (Heb. *damah*, **dah-MAH**), on the verge of perishing in the face of this revelation of God. Faced with the unfiltered experience of God's holiness, Isaiah recognized his own sinfulness with equal clarity.

6 Then flew one of the seraphims unto me, having a live coal in his hand, which he had taken with the tongs from off the altar: 7 And he laid it upon my mouth, and said, Lo, this hath touched thy lips; and thine iniquity is taken away, and thy sin purged.

A seraph heads in his direction, and like any awestruck human being, Isaiah may have felt that it was about to carry out God's judgment against him. Isaiah still had not realized the depth of God's commitment to His chosen people, Israel. The nation had broken faith with the living God, but He did not break faith with them.

From the midst of the cloud-filled chamber, Isaiah is only able to see a seraph use a pair of tongs and remove a burning coal from the altar. The being then proceeds toward Isaiah with the coal and presses it against his mouth. For the first time, Isaiah realizes what it feels to be fully cleansed of all sin and shame. The text here refers not only to "sin" (Heb. *khatta't*, **khot-TOT**) but also "iniquity" (Heb. *'avon*, **ah-VONE**), which refers to depravity, perversity, and guilt from sin. Rather than the expected punishment, God has pardoned Isaiah. Rather than a deserved death (eternal separation from the living God), Isaiah is given life and begins to experience God's love in a way he has never understood before. He is truly and completely loved.

8 Also I heard the voice of the Lord, saying, Whom shall I send, and who will go for us? Then said I, Here am I; send me.

With the sin and shame removed, Isaiah heard God speak. Isaiah heard God inquire who would be His servant to go and carry out the mission and message He had for His covenant people. Isaiah answered the call. In accepting God's call to be a prophet to the nation, Isaiah understood that he was committing to represent God's holy authority and love on earth. His task would be to guide the people and their leaders into right relationship with God. Isaiah's experience with God and the burning coal from the altar helped the prophet recognize that He was not interested in exacting punishment on His rebellious people, but in purging the nation of the sin that separated God from His people. Isaiah committed himself to the proclamation of this message and would spend the rest of his life in this missionary enterprise.

In embracing this call from God, Isaiah would live the rest of his life set apart from the people he was to serve. The price for accepting God's assignment was loneliness and isolation. From this point on, everything in the prophet's life took a subordinate position to God's mission. Because of the vision of God's glory, Isaiah willingly paid this price.

Say It Correctly

Seraphim. **SAIR**-uh-feem.
Twain. **TWANE**.

Daily Bible Readings

MONDAY
Reign of King Uzziah
(2 Chronicles 26:1–10, 15)

TUESDAY
True Worship in Action
(Isaiah 58:6–12)

WEDNESDAY
Holiness Befits God's House
(Psalm 93)

THURSDAY
Gentiles Will Hear the Good News
(Acts 28:23–29)

FRIDAY
Perfect Your Holiness Living
(2 Corinthians 6:14–7:1)

SATURDAY
Practice Holiness While Waiting
(2 Peter 3:11–16)

SUNDAY
Isaiah in the Temple
(Isaiah 6:1–8)

Notes

_____

_____

_____

_____

Teaching Tips

Words You Should Know

A. Know (Jeremiah 1:5) *yada'* (Heb.)—Have knowledge, be wise; perceive, see, discern.

B. Sanctify (v. 5) *kadash* (Heb.)—Appoint, consecrate, dedicate, be holy.

Teacher Preparation

Unifying Principle—You Can Do It. Each of us has some fear or insecurity that might convince us that we have nothing to give others. How do we overcome these perceived shortcomings? Jeremiah's response was based on God's promise to be with him as he carried out his calling.

A. Pray for your students and for lesson clarity.

B. Complete the companion lesson in the *Precepts For Living®* Personal Study Guide.

O—Open the Lesson

A. Open in prayer, including the Aim for Change.

B. Introduce today's lesson title.

C. Ask students if they have ever felt like God had chosen you to accomplish something. Ask if anyone would like to share with the class.

D. Have your students read the Aim for Change and Keep in Mind verse together. Discuss.

P—Present the Scriptures

A. Have volunteers read the Focal Verses.

B. Use the At-A-Glance Outline; People, Places, and Times; Background; Search the Scriptures; In Depth; and More Light on the Text sections to clarify verses.

C. Ask the students questions throughout this portion.

E—Explore the Meaning

A. Divide into groups to discuss Discuss the Meaning and Lesson in Our Society. Tell students to select a representative to report responses.

B. Connect these sections to the Aim for Change and Keep in Mind verse.

N—Next Steps for Application

A. Summarize the lesson and charge students to follow the suggestion in the Make It Happen section.

B. Close with prayer.

Worship Guide

For the Superintendent or Teacher
Theme: Jeremiah's Call and Commission
Song: "He's Able"
Devotional Reading: Psalm 75

Jeremiah's Call and Commission

Bible Background • JEREMIAH 1
Printed Text • JEREMIAH 1:4–10 | Devotional Reading • PSALM 75

———— Aim for Change ————

By the end of the lesson, we will: RECOUNT the details of the promises God made to Jeremiah; SENSE the intensity of Jeremiah's call and his emotional reaction to it; and RESPOND to a call from God despite feelings of personal inadequacy.

———— In Focus ————

Al loved to play softball for his local team. It was just for fun, but Al really worked the hardest of everyone on the team. Just before the last game of the season, the team captain had to suddenly leave for an emergency. But before he left, he asked Al to coach in his absence. Al was shocked, and replied, "But Cap, there are other players better than me. Why not choose them?" The captain said, "None of them are as diligent and determined as you. You can do it, Al. You have the ability."

Al agreed to coach the team. When the team came to the field, he explained what was going on. Al then created a new batting order. He changed the pitching schedule so the best one would pitch late in the game. The team didn't understand, but they followed Al.

Al's new arrangements worked; his team won the game handily. One player asked, "How did you know to switch the order?" Al said, "We've played against the other team before. I remembered their strengths and weaknesses, and created the order from that information." Al didn't believe in himself at first, but his captain had confidence in his ability. Al stepped up to lead the team because his captain had confidence in him.

In today's lesson, Jeremiah steps up to be a prophet because God called him to do it and believed in him. Is there something God has called you to but you didn't have confidence you would be able to do it?

———— Keep in Mind ————

"Be not afraid of their faces: for I am with thee to deliver thee, saith the LORD"
(Jeremiah 1:8).

"Be not afraid of their faces: for I am with thee to deliver thee, saith the LORD"
(Jeremiah 1:8).

Focal Verses

KJV **Jeremiah 1:4** Then the word of the LORD came unto me, saying,

5 Before I formed thee in the belly I knew thee; and before thou camest forth out of the womb I sanctified thee, and I ordained thee a prophet unto the nations.

6 Then said I, Ah, Lord GOD! behold, I cannot speak: for I am a child.

7 But the LORD said unto me, Say not, I am a child: for thou shalt go to all that I shall send thee, and whatsoever I command thee thou shalt speak.

8 Be not afraid of their faces: for I am with thee to deliver thee, saith the LORD.

9 Then the LORD put forth his hand, and touched my mouth. And the LORD said unto me, Behold, I have put my words in thy mouth.

10 See, I have this day set thee over the nations and over the kingdoms, to root out, and to pull down, and to destroy, and to throw down, to build, and to plant.

NLT **Jeremiah 1:4** The LORD gave me this message:

5 "I knew you before I formed you in your mother's womb. Before you were born I set you apart and appointed you as my prophet to the nations."

6 "O Sovereign LORD," I said, "I can't speak for you! I'm too young!"

7 The LORD replied, "Don't say, 'I'm too young,' for you must go wherever I send you and say whatever I tell you.

8 And don't be afraid of the people, for I will be with you and will protect you. I, the LORD, have spoken!"

9 Then the LORD reached out and touched my mouth and said, "Look, I have put my words in your mouth!

10 Today I appoint you to stand up against nations and kingdoms. Some you must uproot and tear down, destroy and overthrow. Others you must build up and plant."

The People, Places, and Times

Covenant. The relationship between the Lord and His people was based on an agreement. God would continue to protect and be present with His people. In return, His people would follow Him and be obedient to the commandments given to Moses for the people. Unfortunately, while God kept His part of the covenant, His people would blatantly break their promise. This angered God and led to the age of the prophet, who was God's spokesperson.

Judgment. The prophet would give warnings to God's people when they were disobedient. If the people did not heed the warnings, then God would issue a judgment on them. Judgment was a punishment that God would give to the people for disobedience and breaking their covenant. It would only occur after God has given His people multiple chances to repent from their disobedience. The hope was that the people would return to obeying and following God.

Background

The nation of Judah and its capital Jerusalem continued to sin against God. They continued to disobey Him, worship idols, be less faithful to Him, mistreat their neighbor, and disregard everything He had taught them to do. Some of their kings during this time tried to guide these people in the right direction (e.g., King Josiah, 2 Kings 23): following God and being more respectful to Him. It would work briefly, but the people would soon return to old habits. Then God sent another prophet to help guide the people back into covenant with Him.

Jeremiah tried to warn the people what would happen if they continued to break their covenant. He tried to urge the people to repent from their sin and disobedience. Instead of heeding the warnings, they became angry at him. The people of Judah and Jerusalem ignored God's message through Jeremiah. Jeremiah prophesied that they would be in exile for seventy years because of their hardened heart and Jerusalem would be destroyed by their enemy, the Babylonians.

Judah and Jerusalem were completely oblivious to God's anger toward them. They forgot about all the times God had showed them love and support, and focused only on themselves. Unfortunately, some people were innocent victims of their brothers' and sisters' sins, but they too suffered. God gave many chances, but it was up to them to take action.

At-A-Glance

1. Born for This (Jeremiah 1:4–5)
2. Change Focus (v. 6)
3. Equip (vv. 7–9)
4. Commissioned (v. 10)

In Depth

1. Born for This (Jeremiah 1:4–5)

When God called Jeremiah to be a prophet, He wanted to reassure him that he was born to do this. God tells Jeremiah that before he was born, before he was formed in the womb, He knew what Jeremiah was going to do. God had already set him apart to be a prophet. Jeremiah had no need to worry because his path was set. When God sets up something, it will succeed because He can never fail at anything He does. We also learn that God is omniscient, or all-knowing. He already knew that Jeremiah was going to be successful for Him. Whatever God called you to do, you were born to do it also. Jeremiah did not have to be nervous in this new chapter of his life because God created him to be a prophet. He was born for this.

2. Change Focus (v. 6)

Once God shares with Jeremiah that he was created for his calling, Jeremiah loses focus. Instead of focusing on the fact that God was in control, Jeremiah dwells on his inadequacies. He says he is unable to speak because he is too young. Jeremiah feels that he does not have enough experience to do what God called him to do. Jeremiah briefly forgets that when God calls a person to do something, human experience or ability doesn't matter because He gives people the ability to do His work. Though we should always prepare ourselves through education and other avenues, we should not rely on these preparations when it comes to our Heavenly Father's business. When Jeremiah thought the job was too much for him, he focused on himself and not on the One who called him.

3. Equip (vv. 7–9)

As Jeremiah became nervous, God again reassured him by reminding him that age and experience are not factors when it comes to His work. Regardless, Jeremiah had to go wherever God sent him anyway (v. 7). God knew that the task would bring about different challenges, so he tells Jeremiah not to worry about other people harming him because He will be there to protect him. Whatever God calls us to do, His presence will always be with us. He will not abandon us.

God promised to equip Jeremiah with His presence, but then also equips him in the same way He equipped Isaiah: by touching his mouth. God touching Jeremiah's mouth was His way of showing him that He will be talking through him. God equipped Jeremiah with all he needed to operate in his calling.

4. Commissioned (v. 10)

After showing Jeremiah he was born to be a "prophet to the nations" and equipping him, God then commissions him for service (v. 10). He commissions Jeremiah to stand up against nations and kingdoms, and build up those willing to repent. God commissions Jeremiah not only to preach to Jerusalem, but all people. This commissioning means God entrusts Jeremiah to act as an agent for Him. Jeremiah would speak for God, giving people another chance to keep their covenant with Him. Sometimes the words said would tear down and destroy, if Jerusalem did not comply. God's words and actions could also build up, though, for those who come to Him with a repentant heart. God entrusts Jeremiah with the calling of His spokesperson or prophet. God will always give you your assignment when He feels you are ready to accept it.

Search the Scriptures

1. Is there an age limitation when it comes to serving God (Jeremiah 1:6)?

2. How do God's words of reassurance to Jeremiah apply to us (v. 10)?

Discuss the Meaning

When we are given a task that appears too much for us to handle, we sometimes focus on our weaknesses as reasons we can't handle the task. How did God dispel the weaknesses that Jeremiah focused on?

Lesson in Our Society

People tend to only rely on what they can see. It is hard for us to step outside our comfort zone, especially when we allow fear to guide us. God will challenge us to step outside of our comfort zone to see if we are willing to trust Him. Jeremiah was willing to step out of his comfort zone to serve as God's spokesperson because he understood that God was with him.

Make It Happen

Some people refuse to take on new challenges because they are afraid of taking a risk. However, sometimes taking a risk is necessary. Think of someone you know who has a hard time taking on new challenges. How would you help encourage that person to take on a challenge?

Follow the Spirit

What God wants me to do:

_____

_____

_____

_____

Remember Your Thoughts

Special insights I have learned:

_____

_____

_____

_____

More Light on the Text
Jeremiah 1:4–10

4 Then the word of the LORD came unto me, saying, 5 Before I formed thee in the belly I knew thee; and before thou camest forth out of the womb I sanctified thee, and I ordained thee a prophet unto the nations.

Jeremiah 1:4-10 is commonly referred to as the call of Jeremiah. The call narrative here follows the prophetic call formula in the Old Testament: (1) divine confrontation; (2) introductory word; (3) commission; (4) objection; (5) reassurance; (6) sign (Exodus 3:1–4:9, Judges 6:11–24). Jeremiah's call begins with a divine encounter presented here as a dialogue between him and God: "The word of the LORD came unto me" (Jeremiah 1:4). God's appearance is followed by an introductory word that establishes that the choice of Jeremiah as a prophet (Heb. *navi'*, **nah-VEE**) was no arbitrary decision, but that God had set him apart (Heb. *kadash*, **kah-DASH**, consecrate, make holy), before he was even born. A prophet was a spokesperson called by God to serve as an intermediary between Him and the people. God commissioned Jeremiah to preach His Word to the nations (Heb. *goyim*, **goy-EEM**). At this time "nations" still referred especially to a group within a certain territory other than Israel or Judah. However when God's people were under Assyrian, Babylonian, Persian, Greek, and Roman rule, it referred more to a group with non-Jewish ancestral heritage. This word implies His message will be not just for Israel, but for all the world.

6 Then said I, Ah, Lord GOD! behold, I cannot speak: for I am a child. 7 But the LORD said unto me, Say not, I am a child: for thou shalt go to all that I shall send thee, and whatsoever I command thee thou shalt speak.

In classic fashion, Jeremiah protests his call: "I cannot speak: for I am a child" (v. 6; cf. Exodus 4:10). This verse is a favorite among preachers' selections for youth day or other occasions to encourage youth to not let their age limit their ability to do what God has called them to do. This passage conveys that meaning in two ways. The first is the meaning of the word "child." The word translated as "child" (Heb. *na'ar*, **NAH-ar**) in v. 6 has a range of meanings including "lad," "son," "servant," and "member of a professional guild." It has been applied to both infants (Exodus 2:6) and to unmarried people of marriageable age (Genesis 34:19). Solomon replied with a sort of false humility that he is "only a little child" (*na'ar*) when he ascended to the throne of David (1 Kings 3:7). He clearly was not a little child, but a man about twenty years old; however, he was unmarried and had not yet fathered a child, so he had not yet advanced to adulthood in the Israelite life cycle. So this message is relevant for anyone considered a youth, from a toddler to a young adult.

The second challenge in using the call of Jeremiah as a message to youth is conveying the gravity of his vocation as a prophet. God sent him to preach to the nations amid great suffering, death, and destruction in his own home. He experienced derision, death threats, imprisonment, and false accusations for proclaiming God's Word. He was forced to remain single and fatherless as a sign to Judah that this would be its fate.

8 Be not afraid of their faces: for I am with thee to deliver thee, saith the LORD. 9 Then the LORD put forth his hand, and touched my mouth. And the LORD said unto me, Behold, I have put my words in thy mouth.

Despite Jeremiah's doubts about being up to the challenge, and his fears of the opposition he would face, he need not worry because God reassures him. God will accompany him and deliver him from his adversaries. The desire for God to accompany us through dangers and trials and the faith that He will deliver us is our fervent prayer.

At the funeral of Rev. Martin Luther King Jr., the gospel singer Mahalia Jackson sang the words to King's favorite song "Precious Lord":

Precious Lord, take my hand
Lead me on, let me stand

The well-renowned gospel singer and composer Thomas A. Dorsey was inspired to pen the hymn "Precious Lord" upon the death of his wife, who died giving birth to their son, who died shortly after. For both Dorsey and King, the confidence that God would accompany them and lead them on gave them the reassurance to continue delivering God's message to a nation hostile to His Word.

As a sign of His promise, God reached out and touched Jeremiah's mouth. God is ascribed human attributes (such as having arms and hands) to enact this intimate image. He puts His own words in Jeremiah's mouth, which confirms the legitimacy of Jeremiah as a prophet sent by God and authenticates the message as His Word (cf. Deuteronomy 18:18).

10 See, I have this day set thee over the nations and over the kingdoms, to root out, and to pull down, and to destroy, and to throw down, to build, and to plant.

Having assured Jeremiah that God will accompany him and has equipped him for the task, He reiterates the task for which He has commissioned Jeremiah: to be a prophet "over the nations and over the kingdoms" (cf. v. 5). Jeremiah's mission on one hand is to act as a sword: "to root out," "pull down," "destroy," and "throw down." It is no wonder that Jeremiah's messages moved the recipients

to such aggression toward him—he preached a message of doom and destruction to rulers and nations, kings and kingdoms, even his own. On the other hand, he offered a message of hope and renewal: "to build, and to plant." The latter message of reconstruction was harder to receive in the aftermath of the judgment God wrought on the nations and kingdoms.

Say It Correctly

Josiah. jue-**SIGH**-uh.
Commission. co-**MIH**-shun.

Daily Bible Readings

MONDAY
A Prophet like Moses
(Deuteronomy 18:15–22)

TUESDAY
By Almond Branch and Boiling Pot
(Jeremiah 1:11–19)

WEDNESDAY
Assured of the Lord's Deliverance
(Jeremiah 15:10–21)

THURSDAY
Prophetic Message from the Potter
(Jeremiah 18:1–11)

FRIDAY
Egypt Punished; Israel Saved
(Jeremiah 46:25–28)

SATURDAY
Jesus Calls Disciples
(Mark 1:16–20)

SUNDAY
Jeremiah's Call and Commission
(Jeremiah 1:4–10)

Notes

_____

_____

_____

_____

Teaching Tips

July 23
Bible Study Guide 8

Words You Should Know

A. Son of Man (Ezekiel 3:1) *ben 'adam* (Heb.)—A human being; mortal man.

B. Hard-hearted (v. 7) *kasheh* (Heb.)—Hard, cruel, severe, obstinate.

Teacher Preparation

Unifying Principle—Speak the Truth Anyway. Discouragement and doubt can hinder what we hope to achieve. What concrete action can help us get beyond our fears? Ezekiel's call involved eating a scroll that sweetened the bitter taste of his mission and receiving from God extra strength and protection for the challenges that lay ahead.

A. Pray for learners, lesson clarity, and a fruitful harvest of God's Word in unyielding hearts.

B. Find a map showing Israel in Ezekiel's day. Prepare to discuss ways God repeatedly spared Israel from surrounding enemy nations.

C. Complete the companion lesson in the *Precepts For Living®* Personal Study Guide.

O—Open the Lesson

A. Open with prayer, including the Aim for Change.

B. Introduce today's lesson title and read and discuss the In Focus story.

C. Have learners read the Aim for Change and Keep in Mind verse aloud together and discuss.

D. Share the map and discussion points you prepared.

P—Present the Scriptures

A. Have volunteers read the Focal Verses.

B. Use the At-A-Glance outline; The People, Places and Times; Background; Search the Scriptures; In Depth; and More Light on the Text sections to clarify the verses.

E—Explore the Meaning

A. Talk about the Discuss the Meaning, Lesson in Our Society, and Make It Happen sections. Ask learners to think about how God's commandments have been conformed to fit laws written by man; discuss reasons, exceptions, exclusions, injustices, and loopholes.

B. Relate these sections to the Aim for Change and Keep in Mind verse as you share examples of actions you have taken to obey God's call to be His messenger.

N—Next Steps for Application

A. Summarize the lesson.

B. Close with prayer.

Worship Guide

For the Superintendent or Teacher
Theme: Ezekiel's Call
Song: "Maybe God is Trying to Tell You Something"
Devotional Reading: Ezekiel 17:22–24

Ezekiel's Call

Bible Background • EZEKIEL 1–3
Printed Text • EZEKIEL 3:1–11 | Devotional Reading • EZEKIEL 17:22–24

—————— Aim for Change ——————

By the end of the lesson, we will: EXPLORE God's call of Ezekiel; AFFIRM that like Ezekiel, we have an obligation to speak to people who obstinately refuse to listen; and SHARE ways to be "harder than flint" in obeying God's call to be His messengers.

——— In Focus ———

Nathan and his Christian support team held prayer meetings in preparation for their presentation to the board members of their company. The company had been founded with Christian principles in mind, but over time the employees had fallen into selfishness. His coworker prayer team tackled major issues including misuse of company time for outside interests, unfair labor practices, bribing the judicial review board, and fraud in payroll and financial matters. After years of failing to hear warnings, employees were set in their ways and would not listen to the few who wanted to do right to save the company. Nathan had a vision and plan for restoring the company and preventing bankruptcy.

Nathan led the team in prayer. They studied company documents and reports, researched data on similar companies that were successful, and looked at financial forecasts for the future, using this information to build an impressive business plan. Nathan believed the prayer team had an obligation to speak truth even if met with criticism. He prayed that God would help him speak truth with full faith and not waver in the face of criticism and hostility. He was sure that if fellow employees were willing to listen and follow the vision, the company could be saved.

In today's lesson, we will affirm that whether people listen to the Word of God or fail to listen is up to them; however, we are obligated to speak the truth to a rebellious world. Have you ever faced rejection for speaking the truth?

—————— Keep in Mind ——————

"Moreover he said unto me, Son of man, all my words that I shall speak unto thee receive in thine heart, and hear with thine ears. And go, get thee to them of the captivity, unto the children of thy people, and speak unto them, and tell them, Thus saith the Lord GOD; whether they will hear, or whether they will forbear" (Ezekiel 3:10–11).

"Moreover he said unto me, Son of man, all my words that I shall speak unto thee receive in thine heart, and hear with thine ears. And go, get thee to them of the captivity, unto the children of thy people, and speak unto them, and tell them, Thus saith the Lord GOD; whether they will hear, or whether they will forbear" (Ezekiel 3:10–11).

Focal Verses

KJV **Ezekiel 3:1** Moreover he said unto me, Son of man, eat that thou findest; eat this roll, and go speak unto the house of Israel.

2 So I opened my mouth, and he caused me to eat that roll.

3 And he said unto me, Son of man, cause thy belly to eat, and fill thy bowels with this roll that I give thee. Then did I eat it; and it was in my mouth as honey for sweetness.

4 And he said unto me, Son of man, go, get thee unto the house of Israel, and speak with my words unto them.

5 For thou art not sent to a people of a strange speech and of an hard language, but to the house of Israel;

6 Not to many people of a strange speech and of an hard language, whose words thou canst not understand. Surely, had I sent thee to them, they would have hearkened unto thee.

7 But the house of Israel will not hearken unto thee; for they will not hearken unto me: for all the house of Israel are impudent and hardhearted.

8 Behold, I have made thy face strong against their faces, and thy forehead strong against their foreheads.

9 As an adamant harder than flint have I made thy forehead: fear them not, neither be dismayed at their looks, though they be a rebellious house.

10 Moreover he said unto me, Son of man, all my words that I shall speak unto thee receive in thine heart, and hear with thine ears.

11 And go, get thee to them of the captivity, unto the children of thy people, and speak unto them, and tell them, Thus saith the Lord GOD; whether they will hear, or whether they will forbear.

NLT **Ezekiel 3:1** The voice said to me, "Son of man, eat what I am giving you—eat this scroll! Then go and give its message to the people of Israel."

2 So I opened my mouth, and he fed me the scroll.

3 "Fill your stomach with this," he said. And when I ate it, it tasted as sweet as honey in my mouth.

4 Then he said, "Son of man, go to the people of Israel and give them my messages.

5 I am not sending you to a foreign people whose language you cannot understand.

6 No, I am not sending you to people with strange and difficult speech. If I did, they would listen!

7 But the people of Israel won't listen to you any more than they listen to me! For the whole lot of them are hard-hearted and stubborn.

8 But look, I have made you as obstinate and hard-hearted as they are.

9 I have made your forehead as hard as the hardest rock! So don't be afraid of them or fear their angry looks, even though they are rebels."

10 Then he added, "Son of man, let all my words sink deep into your own heart first. Listen to them carefully for yourself.

11 Then go to your people in exile and say to them, 'This is what the Sovereign LORD says!' Do this whether they listen to you or not."

The People, Places, and Times

Ezekiel. The prophet's name meant "God is my strength." He was a Zadokite priest, the son of a priest named Buzi. Ezekiel lived in Jerusalem before being taken captive to Babylon where he lived near the Kebar River during the fifth year of King Jehoiachin's captivity. He was given a message and a vision of God's magnificence and power to fortify him to preach the Word to the first Jewish exiles relocated in Babylon where they would spend seventy years in slavery. He also prophesied warnings of judgment to surrounding enemy nations.

Babylonia. God raised up Babylonia to conquer and punish Assyria for its brutality to Israel. Judah brazenly continued their idolatry and sin after repeated warnings from several prophets and after their relatives in Israel were defeated and enslaved. The Babylonians captured Judah and destroyed the Temple in Jerusalem. Ezekiel's prophecies of judgment, restoration, and a new Temple relate to events before the fall of Judah, 592–587 BC; during the fall, 586 BC; and after the fall, 585–570 BC; over a period of 22 years.

Background

Ezekiel was a priest in Jerusalem at the end of the kingdom of Judah, as well as a contemporary of Jeremiah. Because he had authority, he was exiled to Babylon along with King Jehoiachin in 597 BC at the age of 25. His first vision (Jeremiah 1) is reported to have taken place five years later (592 BC) while in exile along the Chebar Canal, which connected with the Euphrates in the Nippur region. When his beloved wife died suddenly, he focused on his prophetic calling instead of bereavement, demonstrating that God's will over our lives takes precedence over every other duty, including mourning for a loved one, building, city, or past life (Ezekiel 24:15–24). The death of the prophet's wife was a sign of the destruction of Jerusalem by the Chaldeans and the loss of the Temple. God may take all that seems dearest to us, but Ezekiel demonstrates that we should not weep for our afflictions, but yield our broken heart and mourner's prayers as acceptable before God to renew our hope. Ezekiel humbly submitted and followed God's instructions. He could then speak God's Word, and his example generated great respect among the Hebrew exiles and confirmed him as a prophet of God. His message was that the real spiritual temple is in the hearts of God's people; they must be willing to obey, listen, and be broken for a greater eternal hope.

At-A-Glance

1. God's Call to Ezekiel (Ezekiel 3:1)
2. Ezekiel's Response (vv. 2–3)
3. Ezekiel's Mission (vv. 4–9)
4. People's Response (vv. 10–11)

In Depth

1. God's Call to Ezekiel (Ezekiel 3:1)

"Eating the Word of God" is an occurrence found in Ezekiel and in the New Testament book of Revelation, as John is called to eat the book that was in the hands of the angel (Revelation 10:9–10). Those chosen to eat the Word were also chosen because of their faithfulness to deliver God's message no matter the opposition. Several verses use the word "scroll" in Old Testament prophecy (e.g. Jeremiah, Ezekiel, Zechariah) as the conveyance of God's Word. God's instructions are to eat and fully chew on the Word, and experience the sweetness of His Word in preparation to confront the bitter hardness of human hearts.

God's Word must be digested and consumed. We digest His Word with full recognition that we are "sons of man," frail and humble dust without the sustaining Word of God. After the command to eat, Ezekiel was commanded to go and speak. We too are called, like Ezekiel, to eat God's Word, then go and speak truth and light to a dying world.

2. Ezekiel's Response (vv. 2–3)

There is only one acceptable response to a divine message and vision: obedience. Ezekiel did two things: he opened his mouth, and he ate the scroll. Now that Ezekiel proved faithful and allowed the Lord to prepare him, he was given his assignment to speak. His response to obey is immediate; he doesn't hesitate to obey the voice of God.

The scroll Ezekiel is commanded to eat contains "lamentation, mourning, and woe" (2:10). This kind of message might be thought to be bitter or sour, but in Ezekiel's mouth, it is as sweet as honey.

In several passages, written documents have the power to affect the course of human events (2 Samuel 11:14–15; 1 Kings 21:8–9, 11; Esther 8:8, 10). By eating the scroll, Ezekiel becomes one with the words on the scroll. In doing so, he symbolically takes into his inner being the fate of his people. Ezekiel is more than just a messenger detached from his assignment; he has now become the message.

3. Ezekiel's Mission (vv. 4–9)

God's command to Ezekiel requires that he put the sweetness of the Word to urgent use: to go to Judah and tell them now. Right after Ezekiel had eaten the Word of God, tasted its sweetness, been filled with the Spirit, and personally seen God's glory, God commanded him to go right away and tell the people of Judah the consequences of their sin. Ezekiel was able to do this because he had first submitted to the Word of God and yielded his heart; he was equipped to boldly go and tell his fellow Israelites what God said.

Ezekiel is to speak God's words, not his own words. When we evangelize or minister to others, we must be careful to speak God's words, not our opinion or interpretation. Memorize and meditate on His Word, and then you can readily speak His Words in hostile environments and give hope even during trials.

4. People's Response (vv. 10–11)

Ezekiel was called to preach in his own country, to his own people, in his own language— to fellow Israelites, not the Babylonians. God explained that if He had sent him to minister to the Babylonian captors, "they would listen!" In other words, Israel was more hardened than the worst of the nations around them.

Language barriers can be overcome; but a hardened head and heart are another matter. Ezekiel was not to take it personally when his message from God was rejected; Israel's spiritual deafness was acquired over many years of turning away from His Word. Time after time in the Scriptures, we read of Israel choosing to reject God. This is no different. Regardless of their spiritual receptivity, Ezekiel is called to preach to the people of Judah.

Search the Scriptures

1. What did God command Ezekiel to eat? Why (Ezekiel 3:3)?

2. The Lord said the Israelites were hardhearted and stubborn. How did this happen (v. 7)?

Discuss the Meaning

By eating the scroll, Ezekiel takes into his inner being the fate of his people. How does Ezekiel exemplify servanthood and how is his mission symbolic of Jesus' example of servanthood and the sacrifice of His body and blood?

Lesson in Our Society

Many adults remember times when a positive experience "sweetened" their lives in the midst of discouragement and doubt. Many times we doubt our ability to overcome hindrances and feel alone in standing up for what is right. We can easily become discouraged when obstacles prevent us from reaching our goals. God wants us to read, study, memorize, pray, and discuss His Word so that we become bold when we speak before a person or crowd.

Make It Happen

When we reflect on God's unfailing promises and the many examples He has presented in His Word, we should be encouraged to overcome hostile situations. List the different potentially hostile situations you could face personally as a witness for Christ. Ask God to make you hard as flint in order to obey Him when the time comes.

Follow the Spirit

What God wants me to do:

_____

_____

_____

_____

Remember Your Thoughts

Special insights I have learned:

_____

_____

_____

_____

More Light on the Text
Ezekiel 3:1–11

The ministry of Ezekiel, the son of Buzi, extended from 593–571 BC, and mostly took place around Tel Abib, near the Chebar Canal in Babylon (modern-day Iraq), during the Babylonian Captivity (605–538 BC). He was one of approximately 10,000 inhabitants of Judah exiled to Babylon in 597 BC when Nebuchadnezzar invaded Jerusalem. King Jehoiachin and many of his subjects, including warriors, artisans, and many members of the royal and priestly families, were taken away to captivity in Babylon (2 Kings 24:14–16). Five years after this mass deportation, when Ezekiel turned 30, the heavens opened and he saw visions of God (1:1), beginning his prophetic calling.

The first three chapters describe Ezekiel's call and commission. Chapter 1 gives an extravagant account of a fiery vision of God's glory that caught Ezekiel's attention. Chapter 2 begins to tell what Ezekiel heard from the Lord—how he was being sent to speak to the rebellious Israelites. However, before he begins his mission, he must prepare. He must eat the scroll of the Word of God—where chapter 3 begins, continuing the story of Ezekiel's preparation for the ministry of a prophet. The section of chapter 3 in this lesson concludes this discourse with Ezekiel actually eating the scroll. It also repeats the words of encouragement that God gave to Ezekiel in the preceding chapter. Ezekiel certainly needed such encouragement when faced with the daunting task of speaking to hard-headed and hard-hearted people.

1 Moreover he said unto me, Son of man, eat that thou findest; eat this roll, and go speak unto the house of Israel.

God speaks to Ezekiel and calls him "mortal." Most translations have "son of man" (Heb.

ben 'adam, **bin-ah-DAHM**) instead, a term that occurs about ninety times in the book of Ezekiel. This is not the "son of man" that Daniel speaks of in Daniel 7:13, nor the "Son of Man" of the New Testament, used as a title for Jesus Christ. Rather, when God calls Ezekiel the "son of man," it is only to recognize that Ezekiel was a mere human being, regardless of the mighty visions that he sees or his high calling. The title was used to stress the human nature of the agent over the divine source of the message. God would powerfully use this mere human being to rebuke the house of Israel through lofty visions that set him higher than other prophets. This sanctified son of man would often be discouraged and frustrated, just like any other human being. His ministry would be tested by doubt, frustrations, and rejection. In the midst of all this, God would strengthen him, and only as a God-strengthened mortal would he be able to face Israel.

Before he is sent to speak to the rebellious Israelites, God tells Ezekiel to eat the scroll presented to him earlier (Ezekiel 2:8). The order to eat the scroll appears three times (2:8; 3:1, 3). When the scroll first appears, Ezekiel is admonished not to be rebellious, and as if to test him, God tells him to "open your mouth and eat what I give you." Thus, he has no opportunity to make any excuses, and no choice but to obey—both to eat the scroll and then to go speak to Israel.

Before the prophet can speak to the house of Israel, he must devour the Words of God. Ezekiel must admit the Word into his own heart, imprint it onto his mind, and ruminate upon it so that his soul may be nourished and strengthened by it. Similarly, today ministers and preachers of the Gospel must, in their studies and meditations, feed upon that Word of God they will preach to others. In addition, Jeremiah said, "When your words came, I ate them" (Jeremiah 15:16). The Word

must become meat and drink to the minister—heated upon the fire of prayer—before they are shared with God's church.

Ezekiel was told to eat what is offered to him, so he does not have the luxury of choosing what to eat. Whatever God offers, he must eat. Of course, whatever word of God that the Spirit delivers to us, we must receive it without hesitation. What we find on the table set before us in the Scripture, we must eat. God chooses the menu and sets the curriculum. For Ezekiel, words of misery were on the menu. On both sides of Ezekiel's scroll were written many words of lamentation, mourning, and woe (2:10). The circumstances of his ministry needed such a word—he was speaking on behalf of an angry God to an apostate nation receiving its share of judgment. Certainly, more than half the book of Ezekiel is about calamities that would come upon Judah. His general message, thus, reflects the writings on the scroll—essentially a message of judgment followed by one of restoration, based on a covenant relationship between God and Israel. Judgment came because of a double tragedy—the people's rebellion against God's revealed will and their false belief that they enjoyed eternal security.

2 So I opened my mouth, and he caused me to eat that roll. 3 And he said unto me, Son of man, cause thy belly to eat, and fill thy bowels with this roll that I give thee. Then did I eat it; and it was in my mouth as honey for sweetness.

Ezekiel followed the instruction to open his mouth. Only after opening the mouth was he given the scroll. Obeying God is usually a step-by-step journey. God is usually patient, and waits for us to obey the first step before taking us to the second step. Any reluctance to obey on our part only delays the journey, causing

God to repeat instructions until we finally give in.

Again, Ezekiel was told to eat the scroll—the third and final repetition. This time, the request had an extension: "fill thy bowels with this roll that I give thee" Ezekiel had to eat the scroll until it filled his stomach with the Word of God, the bread of heaven. He must fill himself with God's Word until there is no room for his own words.

Here, the Scripture says that Ezekiel finally ate the scroll—and it was sweet. Ezekiel might have expected the scroll to taste bad; after all, gloomy words were written upon it. The Word of the Lord always brings life even when it does not sound appetizing to the mind. Ezekiel obeyed God, and what looked unpalatable became sweet. If we also readily obey even the most difficult of God's commands, we shall find comfort in knowing that He makes all things beautiful in His own time.

Ezekiel's eating of the scroll teaches us a few valuable symbolic lessons. First, the words he spoke would not be his own, but the Word of God. Second, the Word of God is assimilated into the prophet's being to become his very life. Third, the obedient act of eating the scroll indicates Ezekiel's acceptance of the commission God was giving him.

4 And he said unto me, Son of man, go, get thee unto the house of Israel, and speak with my words unto them. 5 For thou art not sent to a people of a strange speech and of an hard language, but to the house of Israel; 6 Not to many people of a strange speech and of an hard language, whose words thou canst not understand. Surely, had I sent thee to them, they would have hearkened unto thee. 7 But the house of Israel will not hearken unto thee; for they will not hearken unto me: for all the house of Israel are impudent and hardhearted.

Finally, the Lord sends Ezekiel to speak to the house of Israel, encouraging him because the task ahead was daunting. He is not sent to a people of "strange speech." The word for "strange" is *ameq* (**ah-MEK**), which means deep and unfathomable. In other words, unintelligible. He is not sent to people of "of an hard language." "Hard" (*kabed*, **kah-BED**) in this context means heavy in the sense of difficult or burdensome to understand. He is sent to the Israelites, to reprove them for their sins. An instruction that Ezekiel had received earlier is also repeated here: "Speak with my words to them" (2:4). Thus, Ezekiel must speak to the Israelites all that God had spoken to him, and only that. However, the people will not listen, not because they do not understand him or his language, but because they are impudent and hard-hearted.

Ezekiel has been prepared well—having eaten the scroll and assimilated its words inside him. Now he must prophesy God's Word to the people. They are his own people, the house of Israel, which makes his task especially difficult. As an exile who understood their situation, Ezekiel hoped that Israel would listen. They had gone through many tribulations together. But on the other hand, the Israelites were intent on not listening to God at all. They had chosen to defy God.

God says that if He had sent Ezekiel to a foreign nation, his message would have been effective. Despite speaking different languages, they would understand God's message. But His own people were too stubborn to listen to Ezekiel. They had turned away from God. They were even worse than the nations around them.

8 Behold, I have made thy face strong against their faces, and thy forehead strong against their foreheads. 9 As an adamant harder than flint have I made thy forehead:

fear them not, neither be dismayed at their looks, though they be a rebellious house.

Ezekiel is sent to a hardheaded and hard-hearted people, who would choose to ignore God's messenger and his message. These people take pride in disrespecting God's messenger and confronting the message. They stubbornly closed their minds and would not even listen. More than that, they fiercely opposed Ezekiel and refused his message. The task before Ezekiel is almost impossible; no matter what he does, the people will not change. However, even if they do not listen, they will know that a prophet has been among them (2:5 and 33:33).

Thus, God made Ezekiel strong-hearted like the Israelites to whom he would be speaking. He needed to be bold, resilient, stubborn, and unyielding in order to cope with his stiff-necked audience. God promises His prophet that He has already imbued him with the firmness and boldness necessary for his cause, making him as unyielding and hardened as his audience. Indeed, God made Ezekiel "adamant" (*shamiyr*, **sha-MEER**), or hard as a diamond. As Ezekiel's name suggests, God strengthened him, and made his heart harder than flint. He had to be hard headed to reach hard-headed Israel.

Our world today demands such hardening for God's servants. Bringing His Word to our society is declaring something very counter-cultural to a people who, like Israel in Ezekiel's day, do not want to listen to God. Most cultures around the world, including the post-Christian cultures of the West, are outright antagonistic to the Christian message of the narrow road and only Savior. Ministers of God in such places must depend on Him for strength. It will take some flintheartedness to speak God's Word today and overcome the many obstacles that come our way. Doubts and fears will attempt to cripple our message. Opposition, both to God's message and God Himself, is to be expected. However, we have good news: those prophets whom God calls and sends, He also equips and strengthens.

10 Moreover he said unto me, Son of man, all my words that I shall speak unto thee receive in thine heart, and hear with thine ears. 11 And go, get thee to them of the captivity, unto the children of thy people, and speak unto them, and tell them, Thus saith the Lord GOD; whether they will hear, or whether they will forbear.

Finally, as we draw toward the end of the commissioning, God admonishes Ezekiel to pay careful attention to everything He says. Ezekiel has to receive what God says with his heart and hear with his ears—he must listen carefully to what God will continue to say. He has to assimilate the Word of God until it becomes a part of him; then he can speak it with confidence and conviction. His mission was to tell the Israelites what the Lord had said and that the Lord had said it. He had to speak to them whether they listened or not—and they would not listen. Judging solely by whether the people listened, it would seem that Ezekiel's ministry failed miserably. However, this is not true; his task was only to speak what God told him. Whether the people changed is not Ezekiel's business; all he had to do was speak the Word.

Say It Correctly

Jehoiachin. juh-**HOY**-uh-kin.
Chaldeans. kal-**DEE**-ens.

Daily Bible Readings

MONDAY
Ezekiel, the Lord's Messenger
(Ezekiel 2:1–7)

TUESDAY
Words of Lamentation, Mourning, and Woe
(Ezekiel 2:8–10)

WEDNESDAY
Eat the Scroll and Prophesy
(Revelation 10:8–11)

THURSDAY
Written Edict Stops Jewish Calamity
(Esther 8:7–10)

FRIDAY
Sentinel Must Convey God's Message
(Ezekiel 3:12–21)

SATURDAY
Israel Exalted at Last
(Ezekiel 17:22–24)

SUNDAY
Ezekiel's Call
(Ezekiel 3:1–11)

Notes

Teaching Tips

Words You Should Know
A. Conspired (Amos 7:10) *kashar* (Heb.)—To be joined with, to tie or bind together.

B. Captive (v. 11, 17) *galah* (Heb.)—To be forced to leave; to deport; to exile or be taken into exile.

Teacher Preparation
Unifying Principle—Facing Hostility. At times we are torn between obeying God's direction and what others think we should do. Is it possible to remain determined despite the opposition? Amos committed to serving even in the face of negativity.

A. Pray for learners and lesson clarity.

B. Recall a time you had to face negativity to fulfill God's calling for you, whether the negativity came from outside or within.

C. Complete the companion lesson in the *Precepts For Living*® Personal Study Guide.

O—Open the Lesson
A. Open with prayer, including the Aim for Change.

B. Introduce today's lesson title, and share your story about facing opposition.

C. Have learners read aloud the Aim for Change and Keep in Mind verse.

P—Present the Scriptures
A. Allow volunteers to read the Focal Verses.

B. Use the At-A-Glance outline; The People, Places, and Times; Background; Search the Scriptures; In Depth; and More Light on the Text sections to clarify the verses.

E—Explore the Meaning
A. Have the class answer the Discuss the Meaning questions.

B. Have volunteers read the Lesson in Our Society.

N—Next Steps for Application
A. Summarize the lesson.

B. Close with prayer.

Worship Guide

For the Superintendent or Teacher
Theme: Amos' Call
Song: "Onward Christian Soldiers"
Devotional Reading: Psalm 119:1–8

Amos' Call

Bible Background • AMOS 7
Printed Text • AMOS 7:10–17 | Devotional Reading • PSALM 119:1–8

—————————— Aim for Change ——————————

By the end of the lesson, we will: EXPLORE the challenges Amaziah and Jeroboam presented to Amos' prophetic ministry; OBSERVE that like Amos, we are called to serve in unfamiliar places and capacities; and SHARE examples of our commitment to serving God in spite of opposition.

In Focus

The veteran teacher at the Seeds of Promise Charter School hurried down the hall to report the new teacher to the principal. Mrs. Priestly enjoyed all the perks of being the senior teacher on staff, plus a strong personal relationship with the principal. She told the principal that the new teacher, Ms. Ashliegh, was having secret meetings with parents, giving them too much information, and bringing them into the school to let them do God knows what.

When the principal talked with Ms. Ashliegh about this report, she explained herself calmly. Ms. Ashliegh was called to work at the school because of her strong Christian beliefs and her reputation for effectively resolving issues. Ashliegh had taken on the most students, all of whom had behavior and learning difficulties and hostile parents. Then she regularly called and e-mailed families to discuss their child's progress. She invited parents to volunteer in the classroom. Ashliegh wanted to educate and engage families in changing the outcomes for their children.

When the principal took no action, Mrs. Priestly felt threatened. She was concerned her year-end report would look poor compared to Ms. Ashliegh's. She began a campaign to turn everyone against Ashliegh with the intent of driving her from the school.

In today's lesson, we will see that the people God calls will often encounter opposition. Have you ever experienced opposition in relation to something God has called you to do?

—————————— Keep in Mind ——————————

"Then answered Amos, and said to Amaziah, I was no prophet, neither was I a prophet's son; but I was an herdman, and a gatherer of sycomore fruit: And the LORD took me as I followed the flock, and the LORD said unto me, Go, prophesy unto my people Israel"
(Amos 7:14–15).

"Then answered Amos, and said to Amaziah, I was no prophet, neither was I a prophet's son; but I was an herdman, and a gatherer of sycomore fruit: And the LORD took me as I followed the flock, and the LORD said unto me, Go, prophesy unto my people Israel" (Amos 7:14–15).

Focal Verses

KJV Amos 7:10 Then Amaziah the priest of Bethel sent to Jeroboam king of Israel, saying, Amos hath conspired against thee in the midst of the house of Israel: the land is not able to bear all his words.

11 For thus Amos saith, Jeroboam shall die by the sword, and Israel shall surely be led away captive out of their own land.

12 Also Amaziah said unto Amos, O thou seer, go, flee thee away into the land of Judah, and there eat bread, and prophesy there:

13 But prophesy not again any more at Bethel: for it is the king's chapel, and it is the king's court.

14 Then answered Amos, and said to Amaziah, I was no prophet, neither was I a prophet's son; but I was an herdman, and a gatherer of sycomore fruit:

15 And the LORD took me as I followed the flock, and the LORD said unto me, Go, prophesy unto my people Israel.

16 Now therefore hear thou the word of the LORD: Thou sayest, Prophesy not against Israel, and drop not thy word against the house of Isaac.

17 Therefore thus saith the LORD; Thy wife shall be an harlot in the city, and thy sons and thy daughters shall fall by the sword, and thy land shall be divided by line; and thou shalt die in a polluted land: and Israel shall surely go into captivity forth of his land.

NLT Amos 7:10 Then Amaziah, the priest of Bethel, sent a message to Jeroboam, king of Israel: "Amos is hatching a plot against you right here on your very doorstep! What he is saying is intolerable.

11 He is saying, 'Jeroboam will soon be killed, and the people of Israel will be sent away into exile.'"

12 Then Amaziah sent orders to Amos: "Get out of here, you prophet! Go on back to the land of Judah, and earn your living by prophesying there!

13 Don't bother us with your prophecies here in Bethel. This is the king's sanctuary and the national place of worship!"

14 But Amos replied, "I'm not a professional prophet, and I was never trained to be one. I'm just a shepherd, and I take care of sycamore-fig trees.

15 But the LORD called me away from my flock and told me, 'Go and prophesy to my people in Israel.'

16 Now then, listen to this message from the LORD: "You say, 'Don't prophesy against Israel. Stop preaching against my people.'

17 But this is what the LORD says: 'Your wife will become a prostitute in this city, and your sons and daughters will be killed. Your land will be divided up and you yourself will die in a foreign land. And the people of Israel will certainly become captives in exile, far from their homeland.'"

The People, Places, and Times

Amos. His personal name means "one who is carried," and he was a prophet from Judah who ministered in Israel around 750 BC. Some might describe the prophet Amos as a "burden bearer." He carried a heavy burden for his people, or rather, his people were a burden he carried. As a prophet, Amos was a primary figure among the series of courageous men known as the minor prophets. They are called "minor" only because their books are far shorter than the major prophets, such as Isaiah, Jeremiah, and Ezekiel. In Judaism, the minor prophets' writings are commonly known as the "Book of the Twelve" because there are twelve of them and they fit onto one scroll (i.e., book).

Priest of Bethel. Once the ten tribes of Israel separated from Judah and Benjamin, they began to worship at Bethel instead of Jerusalem, complete with priests and a temple. But instead of remembering God's commandment not to make any graven images, they worshiped two golden calves. The temple at Bethel was attended to by priests who led people in worshiping these calves. Amaziah was named as the priest of Bethel in the book of Amos.

Background

Amos documented the reasons for God's judgment against Israel, such as legal injustice, economic exploitation, religious hypocrisy, luxurious indulgence, and boastful complacency. The violations resulted in the nation being doomed, but individuals who repented were spared. This did not sit well with those in power. These sins exposed their spiritual state and called them to account. Regardless, Amos continued to show not only the sins of the rich and powerful but also the fate of Israel as the people continued to practice sin and injustice.

Amos was confronted by Amaziah, the priest of Bethel. This confrontation resulted in Amos being charged with conspiracy against the king. Amos had denounced the legitimacy of the shrine at Bethel and the people's worship.

At-A-Glance

1. The Angry Priest (Amos 7:10–13)
2. The Called Prophet (vv. 14–15)
3. The Fateful Prophecy (vv. 16–17)

In Depth

1. The Angry Priest (Amos 7:10–13)

Amaziah was a priest at Bethel who led the people of Israel in idolatry. Bent on keeing his position, he is threatened by Amos' prophecy against the Israelites. Because of this, he tells the king of Israel, Jeroboam, that Amos' message is not good for the kingdom.

Amaziah then tells Amos to leave Israel and go back to Judah. He basically tells Amos that he has no authority there since he is not from Israel but from Judah. Amaziah believes that Amos' prophecy has no place in Israel since it is under Amaziah's and Jeroboam's jurisdiction. The problem is that Amaziah fails to understand the entire universe is under God's jurisdiction, and His Word has the final authority.

2. The Called Prophet (vv. 14–15)

Amos then lets Amaziah know the details of his call. Unlike some who were trained as prophets (perhaps at the school of the prophets mentioned in 1 Samuel 10, 19; 2 Kings 2, 6), Amos was a shepherd and farmer. He had no sights on making a name for himself; he had not planned this or put it into motion. To put it simply, for Amos being a prophet was not a career move.

Amos was content as a shepherd. God had called him away from his flock so that he could speak the truth to God's wayward flock, Israel. Amos was called to prophesy and did not do this out of self-will; God sent him to speak the truth to Israel and call them to repentance.

3. The Fateful Prophecy (vv. 16–17)

Amos' response to Amaziah's message is full of doom and gloom. He not only continues with the message that Amaziah refused to listen to but he also spells out the people's fate in detail. Not only will the Israelites be taken into exile, but also Amaziah's own wife will be a prostitute and his sons and daughters will be killed. Amos' words expound on the message and make it personal for Amaziah.

Because Amaziah refused to listen to Amos' message, he would die in a foreign land. His wife and children would be oppressed and killed by invaders. Their temple of idolatry would not be a sanctuary. Although they believed that Bethel and Israel were under their jurisdiction, the Israelites were mistaken; they were under God's jurisdiction and He would judge them for their sins.

Search the Scriptures

1. Do you think Amaziah gives a good reason for telling Amos to stop prophesying (Amos 7:13)?

2. Why do you think the Lord chose Amos to be a prophet since he was a shepherd and farmer (v. 14)?

Discuss the Meaning

Amos didn't have the training to be a prophet. Do you think it is necessary to have training for preaching the Word? Is seminary or Bible college necessary or helpful? Why or why not?

Lesson in Our Society

God called Amos to prophesy in a land that was not his own. He was called to do something that he was not trained to do. Many times God calls us to situations we have not been in before where we are not properly trained. To get through the backlash and rejection that comes with that, you must be secure in your call. God's call is what qualifies you, not your training. Training is helpful, but the call keeps you going when everyone and everything is against you.

Make It Happen

Have you ever experienced the call of God on your life? Talk to three pastors or missionaries and ask them how they received the call. Also ask them whether it has helped them through tough times to remember God's calling on their life. Bring your answers back to the class to discuss.

Follow the Spirit

What God wants me to do:

_____

_____

_____

_____

Remember Your Thoughts

Special insights I have learned:

_____

_____

_____

_____

More Light on the Text

Amos 7:10–17

10 Then Amaziah the priest of Bethel sent to Jeroboam king of Israel, saying, Amos hath conspired against thee in the midst of the house of Israel: the land is not able to bear all his words.

In this encounter, Amos finds himself in a hostile situation. His prophecies against Israel had earned him enemies in high places—in the sanctuaries and palaces. Amos was a just prophet declaring the Word of the Lord, and because of this, Amaziah accused him of conspiring against Israel. The word for "conspired" (*qashar*, **kah-SHAR**) means to tie or bind together. Amos was being accused of being in league with someone against Israel, which is ironic because his only ally was God Himself. A true prophet will always have enemies because God's Word is never popular, especially among the powerful few benefiting from corruption in the world. Just like Ezekiel, Amos needed a good measure of prophetic flint-headedness to be able to declare that Jeroboam would die by the sword (Ezekiel 3:9; Amos 7:11). A prophet popular among those in power likely compromised God's message. Hostile reactions and false accusations like those leveled against Amos should be expected by all who dare to speak truth to power on behalf of God. The prophet's call is to speak God's truth to the world, which usually involves confronting unjust systems. Prophets do not have to go looking for trouble; more often than not, trouble will find them. Their only crime will be speaking for justice in a corrupt society. Israel's hatred toward the prophets was so intense, many of them were killed.

11 For thus Amos saith, Jeroboam shall die by the sword, and Israel shall surely be led away captive out of their own land.

This is the climax of Amos' message. Jeroboam, king of a thriving kingdom that took pride in its military strength, was to die by the sword in battle. As if this is not enough, all of Israel would be taken captive from their own land. Threats like this are spread throughout the book of Amos (4:2–3; 5:27; 6:7; 7:17; 9:4), but the mention of the sword here takes Amos' prophecies to a higher level. The sword drawn at 7:9 as the Lord rises against the house of Jeroboam shall not return to its sheath until Jeroboam himself (7:11) and the sons and daughters of Amaziah have fallen (7:17). Jeroboam did not deserve to rule over Israel any longer, nor did the idolatrous nation of

Israel deserve any more chances. God's judgment would come without fail.

Delivering such a prophecy is very difficult. A word that threatens the life of the king and the nation can never be taken lightly. Such a word also threatens the life of the prophet. Should he, like Elijah, prophesy and then go into hiding, causing the king to search for him around the country (1 Kings 18:10–15)? Not so with Amos. He prophesied and lingered close to the shrine, well aware that its priest would eventually react. Amaziah had to react, because Amos' prophecy threatened his own livelihood. Amos was clear in his directives: "Seek not Bethel, nor enter into Gilgal, and pass not to Beersheba: for Gilgal shall surely go into captivity, and Bethel shall come to nought" (from Amos 5:5). What would Amaziah do if the people did as Amos directed?

12 Also Amaziah said unto Amos, O thou seer, go, flee thee away into the land of Judah, and there eat bread, and prophesy there: 13 But prophesy not again any more at Bethel: for it is the king's chapel, and it is the king's court.

The Bible does not tell of any response from Jeroboam to Amaziah. He probably paid no attention to the message, thinking it was unworthy of serious consideration. However, Amaziah found it necessary to order Amos to return to the land of Judah: "O thou seer, go, flee thee away into the land of Judah." The Hebrew word khozeh (**kho-ZEH**) is used for "seer" here, meaning "one who has visions." When used elsewhere in the Old Testament, it is a powerful word of respect, but its use here seems contemptuous, in reference to Amos' visions recorded earlier in the chapter.

In a rather patronizing manner, Amaziah attempted to advise Amos to flee for his own safety back to the land of Judah. Of course, if Jeroboam had taken the treason accusations seriously, Amos' life would be in danger, so it would be in his best interests to escape the punishment. Amaziah assumed that, just like himself, Amos was a professional prophet who earned his living like the women mentioned by Ezekiel, who were ready to say whatever pleased their hearers, however false, for "handfuls of barley and pieces of bread" (Ezekiel 13:19). When he said to Amos, "There eat bread, and prophesy," he meant, "You can earn a comfortable livelihood there." He presumed that Amos was in it for the money, so it would make more sense for Amos to go back to safety in Judah, where he would continue to live as a prophet and make better money.

Amaziah did not understand that Amos was inspired and motivated by a different Spirit. It seems safety and earning a livelihood were very important to Amaziah. He probably got his security from his relationship with Jeroboam, which could explain Amaziah's defense of the throne and the shrine, calling it the "king's chapel." He presumed the same of Amos—that he would be safe and able to earn his living back in Judah. The scene of this confrontation, the shrine at Bethel, was both a royal chapel and national cathedral where calf worship took place. It was probably preferred by Jeroboam to Dan and the other shrines because it was nearer to Samaria, the capital. It was also the king's court, where the king's nobles gathered to discuss kingdom business—no place for unknown and uninvited priests and prophets. A place of such significance deserved reverence, and a foreign commoner like Amos was not welcome. His preaching and message near such a place would threaten his own life.

14 Then answered Amos, and said to Amaziah, I was no prophet, neither was I a prophet's son; but I was an herdman, and a gatherer of sycomore fruit: 15 And the LORD took me as I followed the flock, and the LORD said unto me, Go, prophesy unto my people Israel.

In this verse, Amos is forced to defend himself against the charge of being a professional prophet who earns his living through the prophetic ministry. He comes out swinging, asserting that he did not belong to a professional prophetic guild. He was not ordained by any man to be a prophet; he did not study to be a prophet; and he was not born into a prophetic family, nor raised in a prophetic school. He was a sheepbreeder and a caretaker of sycamore trees. He did not need to earn a living from the ministry. He was not in it for the money. He went to Israel to prophesy only because God snatched him from his vocation to send him on a mission. Amaziah's wisdom that Amos would be better off in Judah was contrary to what God had said. God snatched Amos for the sole mission of speaking to Israel, whom He calls "My people." Thus, God still claims Israel as His people, even though they do not follow Him.

Like many other true prophets, Amos laid down his tools to follow God's direction to prophesy against an evil king (with a great military reputation) at the risk of everything he is. His ministry was not intended to provide him with safety and a livelihood. Contrary to expectations of reward, true prophets should expect imprisonment or death from prophesying in Israel, even as the prophets of Baal were maintained at the king's expense (1 Kings 18:19). Nevertheless, when God calls with a Word for His people, the prophet must obey. The risk of earthly oppression will always be there. However, to obey God's bidding is better than to be intimidated by the world's opposition.

16 Now therefore hear thou the word of the LORD: Thou sayest, Prophesy not against Israel, and drop not thy word against the house of Isaac. 17 Therefore thus saith the LORD; Thy wife shall be an harlot in the

city, and thy sons and thy daughters shall fall by the sword, and thy land shall be divided by line; and thou shalt die in a polluted land: and Israel shall surely go into captivity forth of his land.

It would seem that Amaziah had told Amos not to prophesy against Israel and the House of Isaac, invoking the names of their common ancestors as a channel of authority, but Amos turned his attempts against him. He addressed Amaziah regarding his defense of the king and the shrine. Because Amaziah had tried to stop Amos from prophesying against Israel, and also advised him to return to Judah, he too had to be judged. Instead of reducing the force of his words to ease the fire of his condemnation of Amaziah and Israel, or even withdrawing his prophecy, Amos reaffirms them. Amaziah had to hear the true Word of the real Lord whom he contradicted while pretending to serve Him. Indeed, Amaziah had sought to silence Amos, but when his judgment comes, he would be silenced by God's fury. His own family would be destroyed. His wife would be abused and treated as a harlot by the victorious Assyrian army (see Isaiah 13:16; Zechariah 14:2). In addition, his children would be killed by the sword. His land would be divided among the new occupants. Amaziah himself would die in a religiously unclean or polluted (*tame'*, **TAH-meh**) land. To conclude it all, Israel would be taken into exile.

God protects the servants who engage in His work faithfully. The prophet is only required to speak the Word, no matter the circumstance. After that, he must trust and obey, expecting God's next direction.

Say It Correctly

Amaziah. a-mah-**ZEYE**-uh.
Jeroboam. je-ru-**BO**-um.

Daily Bible Readings

MONDAY
The Elect Keep the Commandments
(Deuteronomy 7:7–11)

TUESDAY
Hananiah Opposes the Prophetic Message
(Jeremiah 28:12–16)

WEDNESDAY
Oracle Against Israel
(Amos 1:1–2, 3:12–15)

THURSDAY
Seek Good and Live
(Amos 5:10–15)

FRIDAY
Let Justice Roll Down Like Waters
(Amos 5:18–24)

SATURDAY
David's Kingdom Restored
(Amos 9:11–15)

SUNDAY
Amos' Call
(Amos 7:10–17)

Teaching Tips

Words You Should Know

A. Murmuring (Acts 6:1) *goggusmos* (Gk.)—A murmur or whisper; a quiet, muttered complaint.

B. Proselyte (v. 5) *proselutos* (Gk.)—A person who has recently converted from one religion to another.

Teacher Preparation

Unifying Principle—Meeting Needs. Recognizing priorities is a continuing challenge. How do we allocate resources in such a way that these priorities are appropriately addressed? The apostles realized that God calls us to make the best use of our specific gifts so that the witness of God can be accomplished.

A. Pray for your students and God's guidance as you study this lesson.

B. Complete the companion lesson in the *Precepts For Living®* Personal Study Guide.

C. Make a list of activities you want to accomplish this week. Prioritize those activities. Keep a record of the time you spend on your top priorities.

O—Open the Lesson

A. Open with prayer, including the Aim for Change.

B. Introduce today's lesson title.

C. Share with the class your prioritized list of activities. Discuss how your time and resources aligned with your priorities.

P—Present the Scriptures

A. Have volunteers read the Focal Verses.

B. Use the At-A-Glance outline; The People, Places, and Times; Background; Search the Scriptures; In Depth; and More Light on the Text sections to clarify the verses.

C. Connect these sections to the Aim for Change and the Keep in Mind verse.

E—Explore the Meaning

A. Divide the class into groups to discuss the Lesson in Our Society and Make It Happen sections. Tell the students to select a representative to report their responses.

B. Ask for volunteers to read a Discuss the Meaning question and share their answers.

N—Next Steps for Application

A. Summarize the lesson.

B. Close with prayer.

Worship Guide

For the Superintendent or Teacher
Theme: Called to Witness
Song: "Take My Life and Let It Be"
Devotional Reading: Acts 2:14–28

Called to Witness

Bible Background • ACTS 6–7
Printed Text • ACTS 6:1–7 | Devotional Reading • ACTS 2:14–28

Aim for Change

By the end of the lesson, we will: EXPLAIN the ministry challenges of evangelism and benevolence in the first-century church; DESCRIBE how the church today balances efforts of outreach with other needs; and SHARE some ways to honor your specific ministry call with the needs of your community.

In Focus

"If I have to attend one more meeting this week, I'm going to change professions," Rev. Morrison half-joked to his administrative assistant.

"Yes, there has been more to do since we opened the child care center, the food pantry, and after-school program," replied Vera. "Do you think there's anyone who can help you with these added responsibilities?"

Reverend Morrison had been asking himself that question as well. He realized the importance of caring for the needs of his congregation, but his passion and gift were preaching. He couldn't remember the last time he had prepared a new sermon. Mostly he was recycling messages from a few years back. But what troubled him more was his decision to cancel his annual retreat. Over the past ten years, he had never missed his week of prayer and reflection in that mountain cabin. There in the quiet, his soul was restored and his spirit refreshed. "Vera, call a special meeting of the church board," Rev. Morrison said. "I'm going to get them working on some new staff positions. I need a meeting that will end some of my meetings!" They both laughed, and Vera thanked God for answered prayer.

Prioritizing our time and resources is a continuous challenge. In today's lesson, we'll see how the apostles addressed this concern so that they could make the best use of God's gifts. How do you choose to prioritize your time and resources?

Keep in Mind

"Wherefore, brethren, look ye out among you seven men of honest report, full of the Holy Ghost and wisdom, whom we may appoint over this business" (Acts 6:3).

"Wherefore, brethren, look ye out among you seven men of honest report, full of the Holy Ghost and wisdom, whom we may appoint over this business" (Acts 6:3).

Focal Verses

KJV **Acts 6:1** And in those days, when the number of the disciples was multiplied, there arose a murmuring of the Grecians against the Hebrews, because their widows were neglected in the daily ministration.

2 Then the twelve called the multitude of the disciples unto them, and said, It is not reason that we should leave the word of God, and serve tables.

3 Wherefore, brethren, look ye out among you seven men of honest report, full of the Holy Ghost and wisdom, whom we may appoint over this business.

4 But we will give ourselves continually to prayer, and to the ministry of the word.

5 And the saying pleased the whole multitude: and they chose Stephen, a man full of faith and of the Holy Ghost, and Philip, and Prochorus, and Nicanor, and Timon, and Parmenas, and Nicolas a proselyte of Antioch:

6 Whom they set before the apostles: and when they had prayed, they laid their hands on them.

7 And the word of God increased; and the number of the disciples multiplied in Jerusalem greatly; and a great company of the priests were obedient to the faith.

NLT **Acts 6:1** But as the believers rapidly multiplied, there were rumblings of discontent. The Greek-speaking believers complained about the Hebrew-speaking believers, saying that their widows were being discriminated against in the daily distribution of food.

2 So the Twelve called a meeting of all the believers. They said, "We apostles should spend our time teaching the word of God, not running a food program.

3 And so, brothers, select seven men who are well respected and are full of the Spirit and wisdom. We will give them this responsibility.

4 Then we apostles can spend our time in prayer and teaching the word."

5 Everyone liked this idea, and they chose the following: Stephen (a man full of faith and the Holy Spirit), Philip, Procorus, Nicanor, Timon, Parmenas, and Nicolas of Antioch (an earlier convert to the Jewish faith).

6 These seven were presented to the apostles, who prayed for them as they laid their hands on them.

7 So God's message continued to spread. The number of believers greatly increased in Jerusalem, and many of the Jewish priests were converted, too.

The People, Places, and Times

Palestinian and Hellenistic Jews. The growing number of believers turning to the disciples' teachings were comprised primarily of Palestinian and Hellenistic Jews. This pairing was odd because the two groups' friction with each other was well known. One easily noticeable difference was their languages. Palestinian Jews spoke Aramaic for communication and used Hebrew in worship at the synagogues and Temple, while the Hellenistic Jews, who had dispersed and mixed with cultures along the Mediterranean, were accustomed to Greek. These Greek-speaking Jews were often seen as inferior by Jews in Palestine. The conversion of a large number of Greek-speaking Jews on the day of Pentecost now brought these two groups into community as God drew people from all cultures, backgrounds, ethnic groups, and socioeconomic statuses to Christ.

The Seven. To alleviate any hint of partiality, the apostles allowed the community of believers to select the individuals who would oversee the dispute regarding food distribution. The criteria for selecting these people were their reputation, wisdom, and obedience to the Holy Spirit. The apostles, Jews from the Palestinian area, approved the people's choice even though none of the new administrators was a Palestinian Jew. All seven selected had Greek names. One of the seven, Nicolas, was not even Jewish by birth, but a proselyte, converting from paganism to Judaism and then becoming a believer in Christ. For the apostles, the integrity of the seven was more important than their ethnic or cultural backgrounds.

Background

Although the context was between two different cultures, the first disagreement among believers was about fairness regarding a practical matter. The poor and widows who came from outside Jerusalem felt that they were not receiving an evenhanded share of the daily food distribution. No one likes to be treated unfairly, and grumblings in any organization can quickly tear it apart, especially one in its early development. When the discontent of fellow believers reached the apostles' ears, they took action. They called the entire community together, sharing with them their focus on spreading the Gospel and their concern that everyone be fairly cared for, especially the needy and vulnerable. The apostles offered a solution that the community approved. To manage the daily food distribution, the community would select seven men whom they felt were fair, competent, and obedient to God's Holy Spirit. The apostles affirmed the community's selection by praying for and conferring a blessing on the new administrators. The seven men had different cultural backgrounds from the apostles, but the qualification for service

was not culture, but character. The dispute was successfully resolved. The community had individuals who would establish a system of care for the entire group. The apostles were able to keep preaching and teaching as their priority. And, the community continued to grow and welcome new believers as more people saw God's impartial love in action.

At-A-Glance

1. Problem and Priority (Acts 6:1–2)
2. Solution and Selection (vv. 3–5)
3. Growth and Greatness (vv. 6–7)

In Depth

1. Problem and Priority (Acts 6:1–2)

Starting on the day of Pentecost with Peter's compelling message about a risen Savior, the apostles had been vigilant about sharing the Gospel message. Huge numbers of individuals were identifying themselves as believers and formed a community where they shared their life and possessions. It had to be a wonderful sight to see people of different cultures coming together. To live out true Christianity, people came to realize that their most important identity came from their relationship to Christ, not their nationality. This lesson was taught from a problem that arose in the early church. Jewish believers from outside Jerusalem started to complain about unfair distribution of resources in the community. Such criticism could not be overlooked if the apostles wanted to maintain unity and build bonds of peace among all believers. Yet, the apostles knew that their primary call was to share the Gospel.

2. Solution and Selection (vv. 3–5)

When one has several good things to do, the question turns to the best way to use one's time and resources. The apostles had to make that kind of decision. They chose to continue to spread the Gospel. But they refused to neglect the needs of the growing and diverse body of believers that was forming, many of whom had left family and possessions to follow Christ. They turned to those affected by the problem to find the solution. They realized they couldn't do everything themselves, but could get everything done by recruiting the gifts and talents of those in their community. The members of the community knew the true character of the people among them, and chose seven men whom they trusted to be administrators. The early church community was not without its problems, but its answers were also provided by the community.

3. Growth and Greatness (vv. 6–7)

Through prayer and bestowing blessings, the apostles confirmed the people's selection of the seven administrators. These seven men managed the daily affairs of the community and the apostles preached with unhindered consciences, knowing that any new converts would enter a community prepared to serve them. The community continue to grow; even Jewish priests were converting to the faith. In addition, the seven were not limited by their roles and assigned tasks. God gave Stephen, one of the seven, the ability to perform miracles and signs. His knowledge of Scripture, skill as a debater, and submission to the Holy Spirit were examples for church leaders then and now. Like those who preach and teach, those who hold other positions in ministry have a responsibility to be competent, devoted, and sober-minded servants for Christ.

Search the Scriptures

1. Did it sound harsh for the apostles to say that they were going to spend their time preaching and teaching and others would have to administer the food program (Acts 6:2)? Why or why not?

2. What were some of the outcomes of the apostles maintaining specific priorities (v. 7)?

Discuss the Meaning

1. Are preachers and teachers of the Gospel more important than those who care for the material needs of a congregation?

2. Are there specific moral and spiritual requirements people should meet to serve in ministry today?

Lesson in Our Society

Highly effective people know that they must put first things first to accomplish their tasks. They also know that to live in community, they must not only care about themselves but also consider the needs of others. To do that, they think win-win. They listen with open minds to others' concerns and create safe, creative spaces for people to find workable, mutually beneficial solutions to problems. By incorporating the group's strengths and resources, they accomplish more than they could by themselves. Problems in our homes, at work, or church are often opportunities to learn new skills and develop new relationships, experiences needed for personal and spiritual growth.

Make It Happen

The twentieth-century theologian Howard Thurman once said, "Don't ask yourself what the world needs. Ask yourself what makes you come alive and then go do that. Because what the world needs is people who have come alive." What makes you come alive? What gifts and talents do you enjoy? What are some ways your joyous talents can meet the needs of your community and world?

Follow the Spirit

What God wants me to do:

_____

_____

_____

_____

Remember Your Thoughts

Special insights I have learned:

_____

_____

_____

More Light on the Text

Acts 6:1–7

1 And in those days, when the number of the disciples was multiplied, there arose a murmuring of the Grecians against the Hebrews, because their widows were neglected in the daily ministration.

God caused the church to grow tremendously in the early days of its existence. Such growth was a sign of His presence, power, and truth. The unbelieving world had to admit, if nothing else, that something extraordinary was at work. Of course, believers today understand that the church, and its growth, is fueled by the presence and power of God through the Holy Spirit, and by the truth found in Christ (see 1 Corinthians 12:13; Acts 1:8).

The believers in the church at Jerusalem (v. 7) were called "disciples," which comes from the Greek word for "learners" or "pupils." The early church members were trying to learn about the new way of life they had adopted. They were pupils and students of the ways of God as expressed through Jesus Christ. Modern-day Christians must also become serious "pupils" who learn about God and His Word.

These Greek-speaking disciples began "murmuring" against the Hebrew-speaking (i.e., Aramaic-speaking) disciples, because Greek-speaking widows were not getting their share of the daily distribution of church services, or "ministrations" (*diakonia,* **dee-ah-koe-NEE-ah**). In those days, the church did not just hold a worship service for a couple of hours on Sunday and Wednesday for those who wanted to attend. For the early saints, Christianity was truly an all-encompassing way of life. They were a community that shared property and food (see Acts 2:44–47, 4:32–35). Therefore, the "daily ministration," which was allegedly withheld from Greek-speaking widows, was of serious importance.

The "murmuring" or "grumbling" was a way for Satan to destroy unity and cause a problem within the church. Satan loves to cause problems in relationships. As believers from different languages and cultures squabbled over the treatment of each other's widows, there was fertile ground for a split in the church.

2 Then the twelve called the multitude of the disciples unto them, and said, It is not reason that we should leave the word of God, and serve tables.

Like all good church leadership, "the twelve" got all the followers of Christ together, Greeks and Hebrews, in order to prevent further problems. "The twelve" refers to the original men who followed Jesus during His earthly ministry. They were Jesus' original disciples, with the exception of Judas, who had been replaced by Matthias (Acts 1:23–26).

The twelve leaders suggested to the congregation that it was better for them (the leaders) to spend their time praying and proclaiming the Gospel than on the church's other daily services, such as passing out food (i.e., "serving tables"). This was wise thinking, because at that early point in church history, not many men knew as much about Jesus as those original disciples. So, it was better for them to spend time passing on what they knew, rather than acting as waiters.

Though it might not always be possible for pastors to minister full-time today, a church that can support its pastor and his family puts itself in a better position to get his full devotion to study, prayer, and the delivery of God's Word. Dedicated pastors who are true to the Bible certainly deserve to be supported by those they serve (1 Corinthians 9:7–14). The disciples recognized the importance of a pastor's total dedication to ministry. A wise church today, which is financially able, will do the same.

3 Wherefore, brethren, look ye out among you seven men of honest report, full of the Holy Ghost and wisdom, whom we may appoint over this business.

The twelve then delegated to the congregation the responsibility of selecting seven men to whom they would, in turn, delegate responsibility for the proper distribution of daily church services. The ability to properly delegate responsibility and authority is another hallmark of good leadership. In this case, it served the function of promoting the most efficient use of time by the leaders. One good reason for delegation of duties is to get better results due to expertise in a given area. The Holy Spirit distributes various "spiritual gifts" to everyone in the body of Christ (1 Corinthians 12:4, 11). Thus, some believers are more gifted in certain areas than others. They are the ones who should be given duties in the area of their gift(s).

Delegation also can serve the function of sharing the workload so that leaders are not prematurely burned out. Moses was one of the first Israelite leaders to delegate work to prevent an overload (Exodus 18:17–26).

Finally, the twelve leaders stated the qualifications for the seven men who were to be selected by the congregation. They had to be "of honest report," or have good reputations, so that the people would respect and trust them. Furthermore, they had to be "full of the Holy Ghost" so that they had the proper servant's heart and were led by God's Spirit in their work. Last, they had to be men of "wisdom," so that they had sound judgment and made godly decisions.

4 But we will give ourselves continually to prayer, and to the ministry of the word.

The twelve leaders restated that their primary function was to teach the Word. The root word for give ourselves continually (*proskartereo*, **proce-kar-teh-REH-oh**) means to be devoted to or give unremitting care to something. To gain proper spiritual insight, they had to be "continually [in] prayer," as all good Bible teachers must be. The deep things of God can only be revealed by the Holy Spirit (1 Corinthians 2:10), and an effective teacher of the Word must "pray without ceasing" so that he or she will be guided by the Spirit into God's truth (see John 16:13; 1 Thessalonians 5:17).

5 And the saying pleased the whole multitude: and they chose Stephen, a man full of faith and of the Holy Ghost, and Philip, and Prochorus, and Nicanor, and Timon, and Parmenas, and Nicolas a proselyte of Antioch.

The congregation universally agreed to follow the recommended leadership, bringing everyone on one accord regarding this issue. Not much is said of the seven men who were selected. Evidently, the congregation felt that they fulfilled the qualifications set forth by the leaders. But they are given the honor of being forever recorded in the annals of Scripture.

Two of the men, Nicolas and Stephen, are described more fully in the text. Nicolas was probably of Greek descent and was a "proselyte" (*proselutos,* **pro-SEH-loo-toce**). Now a believer in Christ, he was from the city of Antioch in Syria. The first Gentile church was established there (Acts 11:19–26), and Antioch was where believers were first called "Christians" (Acts 11:26).

Stephen is mentioned first among the seven men and his strong spiritual qualities are emphasized. He was "full of faith and of the Holy Ghost." Both of those qualities were essential for him because he became the first Christian martyr, the first follower of Christ put to death because of his beliefs. He was such a mighty man of God that the Jews hated him and brought him into court on phony charges (Acts 6:9–15). His treatment was reminiscent of the way Jesus was railroaded before His own death (Matthew 26:57–66). The full extent of Stephen's faith and his submission to the Holy Spirit's power and guidance is evidenced by his brilliant testimony concerning God at the rigged "trial" (Acts 7:1–53). Needless to say, he was thereafter condemned to death because of his strong stance upon his faith (Acts 7:54–60).

6 Whom they set before the apostles: and when they had prayed, they laid their hands on them.

The congregation presented the seven men whom they had selected to the Twelve. Those seven men were the forerunners of what now are called "deacons" (see 1 Timothy 3:10–13),

and, "the twelve" here are identified as the first "apostles." At that time, the seven deacons were installed in their office in a ceremony before God. The apostles prayed for them and their new undertaking, and the apostles "laid their hands upon them." This practice was similar to the ordination ceremonies many churches hold now.

The laying on of hands by the apostles was similar to how the Old Testament prophet Samuel anointed Saul and David with oil when God installed them in office as kings (see 1 Samuel 10:1; 16:13). It stems from the Old Testament practice laying hands on an animal to cover sins (see Leviticus 1:4; 3:2, 8, 13; 4:4). The practice symbolized a transfer of one's sins to the sacrificial offering. So, too, the apostles in our study text were anointing the seven deacons for the Lord's service and conducting the flow of God's power into their lives.

7 And the word of God increased; and the number of the disciples multiplied in Jerusalem greatly; and a great company of the priests were obedient to the faith.

Having averted the potential split in the church, everything was in the proper order. As a result of the church at Jerusalem's newfound peace, order, and efficiency, its ministry bore tremendous fruit. Since the apostles were focused only on prayer and preaching, we are told that "the word of God increased." The apostles taught others the Gospel and preached with more power. We have already alluded to the fact that today's pastors can do greater works if they are true to the Bible and able to put in full-time work. The testimony of this Scripture proves the point of such a possibility.

Furthermore, "the number of the disciples multiplied in Jerusalem." The preaching of the Gospel produced many new converts, a phenomenon similar to Jesus' parable wherein He alluded to a sowing of seed which produced "fruit, some an hundredfold, some sixtyfold, some thirtyfold" (Matthew 13:8).

In modern times, we can look around our community and see thousands of people lost and under the heavy yoke of spiritual oppression. We see them on the street corners, in bars and dope houses, and in our jails. As Jesus said, "The harvest truly is plenteous" (from Matthew 9:37). There are enough lost souls in our communities across urban America to bust the seams of every church in sight. But, like the apostles and the early church, we must spread the Gospel message with power. Therefore, we must focus on our mission and devote ourselves to our spiritual gifting, whether that be preaching, teaching, studying, or evangelizing.

Finally, many of the religious leaders who formerly opposed the spread of the Gospel began to accept it. This change of heart shows the awesomeness of God and His Word. The Bible says, "Through the greatness of thy power shall thine enemies submit themselves unto thee" (from Psalm 66:3). Truly the conversion of "a great company of the priests" confirms the truth of Scripture.

Furthermore, the fact that these men were obedient to the faith (see also Romans 16:26) after their conversion speaks volumes about the life-changing power of the Gospel. They decided to conform their ways to what they had previously found offensive to their understanding of the Law.

Say It Correctly

Proselyte. **PRAH**-suh-lite.
Prochorus. prah-**KO**-rus.

Daily Bible Readings

MONDAY
Jesus Commissions Disciples
(Acts 1:1–11)

TUESDAY
Matthias Chosen to Replace Judas
(Acts 1:15–17, 20–26)

WEDNESDAY
The Holy Spirit Descends upon the Disciples
(Acts 2:1–13)

THURSDAY
First Converts Called to the Faith
(Acts 2:37–44)

FRIDAY
Stephen Arrested While Serving
(Acts 6:8–15)

SATURDAY
Stephen Stoned to Death While Praying
(Acts 7:54–81a)

SUNDAY
Called to Witness
(Acts 6:1–8)

Teaching Tips

Words You Should Know

A. Eunuch (Acts 8:27) *eunouchos* (Gk.)— A male who has been castrated; an impotent male; a celibate male; an ancient government title for a man who watched over an official's important possessions.

B. Shearer (v. 32) *keiro* (Gk.)—A person who removes the wool from sheep.

Teacher Preparation

Unifying Principle—Reaching Out. People rarely cross cultural boundaries in significant ways. What should motivate us to do so? Acts 8 records a cross-cultural encounter where Philip is called by God as a witness that Jesus, the Son of God, is the basis of true meaning and purpose.

A. Pray for students and lesson clarity.

B. Complete the companion lesson in the *Precepts For Living*® Personal Study Guide.

O—Open the Lesson

A. Open with prayer.

B. Read the Aim for Change.

C. Tell the class to read the In Focus story silently, then discuss it.

P—Present the Scriptures

A. Have volunteers read or summarize the Focal Verses.

B. Use the At-A-Glance outline; The People, Places, and Times; Background; Search the Scriptures; In Depth; and More Light on the Text sections to clarify the verses.

E—Explore the Meaning

A. Divide the class into groups to discuss the Discuss the Meaning, Lesson in Our Society, and Make It Happen sections. Tell the students to select a representative to share their thoughts with the class.

B. Connect these sections to the Aim for Change and the Keep in Mind verse.

N—Next Steps for Application

A. Give students time to write some takeaway principles under the Follow the Spirit or Remember Your Thoughts section.

B. Close with prayer.

Worship Guide

For the Superintendent or Teacher
Theme: Called to Break Down Barriers
Song: "I Love to Tell the Story"
Devotional Reading: Romans 10:9–15

Called to Break Down Barriers

Bible Background • ACTS 8
Printed Text • ACTS 8:26–39 | Devotional Reading • ROMANS 10:9–15

—————————— Aim for Change ——————————

By the end of the lesson, we will: NOTICE that the encounter between Philip and the Ethiopian represented a cross-cultural recognition of Jesus' identity; APPRECIATE the need for cross-cultural evangelism; and PLAN to participate in cross-cultural outreach.

—————————— In Focus ——————————

"My faith is encouraging me to stay," Latrice daringly replied to Zara as they sat and drank freshly brewed tea in Latrice's kitchen. Zara had been probing Latrice, wanting to know if she'd stay in a neighborhood that was adding new immigrants each day. "This town is changing," Zara noted. "Your friends have moved out; your neighbors now look like me."

Latrice paused for a moment. She had never spoken to Zara about her faith in Christ. She had only visited the family the first day they arrived, bringing freshly baked bread, flowers from her garden, and candy for the children. "God showed His love to me by coming to stay within my heart," Latrice continued. "And I share His love by living with people who I used to see as outsiders. Because of Christ, my life is being enriched by learning to love and know others." Zara didn't understand all that Latrice said, but she had felt Latrice's love from the first time they met. She would have tea with Latrice again and learn more about this love.

Going out of our way to know and help others is perhaps the most powerful witness of God's love we can give. In today's lesson, we see the lengths Philip was willing to go to in order to share the Gospel with one person. What did someone do for you in order to see you come to know Christ?

—————————— Keep in Mind ——————————

"Then Philip opened his mouth, and began at the same scripture, and preached unto him Jesus" (Acts 8:35).

"Then Philip opened his mouth, and began at the same scripture, and preached unto him Jesus" (Acts 8:35).

Focal Verses

KJV **Acts 8:26** And the angel of the Lord spake unto Philip, saying, Arise, and go toward the south unto the way that goeth down from Jerusalem unto Gaza, which is desert.

27 And he arose and went: and, behold, a man of Ethiopia, an eunuch of great authority under Candace queen of the Ethiopians, who had the charge of all her treasure, and had come to Jerusalem for to worship,

28 Was returning, and sitting in his chariot read Esaias the prophet.

29 Then the Spirit said unto Philip, Go near, and join thyself to this chariot.

30 And Philip ran thither to him, and heard him read the prophet Esaias, and said, Understandest thou what thou readest?

31 And he said, How can I, except some man should guide me? And he desired Philip that he would come up and sit with him.

32 The place of the scripture which he read was this, He was led as a sheep to the slaughter; and like a lamb dumb before his shearer, so opened he not his mouth:

33 In his humiliation his judgment was taken away: and who shall declare his generation? for his life is taken from the earth.

34 And the eunuch answered Philip, and said, I pray thee, of whom speaketh the prophet this? of himself, or of some other man?

35 Then Philip opened his mouth, and began at the same scripture, and preached unto him Jesus.

36 And as they went on their way, they came unto a certain water: and the eunuch said, See, here is water; what doth hinder me to be baptized?

37 And Philip said, If thou believest with all thine heart, thou mayest. And he answered and said, I believe that Jesus Christ is the Son of God.

NLT **Acts 8:26** As for Philip, an angel of the Lord said to him, "Go south down the desert road that runs from Jerusalem to Gaza."

27 So he started out, and he met the treasurer of Ethiopia, a eunuch of great authority under the Kandake, the queen of Ethiopia. The eunuch had gone to Jerusalem to worship,

28 and he was now returning. Seated in his carriage, he was reading aloud from the book of the prophet Isaiah.

29 The Holy Spirit said to Philip, "Go over and walk along beside the carriage."

30 Philip ran over and heard the man reading from the prophet Isaiah. Philip asked, "Do you understand what you are reading?"

31 The man replied, "How can I, unless someone instructs me?" And he urged Philip to come up into the carriage and sit with him.

32 The passage of Scripture he had been reading was this: "He was led like a sheep to the slaughter. And as a lamb is silent before the shearers, he did not open his mouth.

33 He was humiliated and received no justice. Who can speak of his descendants? For his life was taken from the earth."

34 The eunuch asked Philip, "Tell me, was the prophet talking about himself or someone else?"

35 So beginning with this same Scripture, Philip told him the Good News about Jesus.

36 As they rode along, they came to some water, and the eunuch said, "Look! There's some water! Why can't I be baptized?"

38 He ordered the carriage to stop, and they went down into the water, and Philip baptized him.

39 When they came up out of the water, the Spirit of the Lord snatched Philip away. The eunuch never saw him again but went on his way rejoicing.

38 And he commanded the chariot to stand still: and they went down both into the water, both Philip and the eunuch; and he baptized him.

39 And when they were come up out of the water, the Spirit of the Lord caught away Philip, that the eunuch saw him no more: and he went on his way rejoicing.

The People, Places, and Times

Philip the Evangelist. The Philip who shares the Gospel with the Ethiopian eunuch is not the Apostle Philip. This Philip was one of the seven men selected in Acts 6 to help ensure that widows and the poor, whether from Hebrew or Greek backgrounds, would be treated fairly. He was chosen because of his integrity and obedience to the guidance of the Holy Spirit. Philip, along with the other six men, are often referred to as the first deacons of the church. They cared for the material needs of the growing group of believers so that the apostles could continue preaching and teaching the Gospel without distraction.

Background

When believers started to be persecuted in Jerusalem, Philip, like many new Christ followers, fled that city. He went to Samaria and began sharing the Gospel of Jesus Christ there. Philip's speaking was accompanied by miraculous signs from God, and people from diverse walks of life turned to Christ because of his words. During this successful evangelistic crusade, Philip responded to a prompting from God to leave the success of the city for a special assignment on a desert road.

At-A-Glance

1. Leaving the Familiar (Acts 8:26–29)
2. Including Others (vv. 30–35)
3. Rejoicing in God's Salvation (vv. 36–39)

In Depth

1. Leaving the Familiar (Acts 8:26–29)

The persecution that caused Philip to leave Jerusalem took him and the Good News of Christ to new people and cultures. In Samaria, his preaching was well received by the crowds there. But he left that success to travel to a desert road leading to Gaza because he felt God's leading. There he met an Ethiopian who was traveling back to his country. Ethiopia, located south of Egypt, was known to Jews from ancient days (Psalm 68:31; Jeremiah 38:7). The man, a eunuch and officer for the queen of Ethiopia, had traveled a long distance to Jerusalem to worship. Still hungry and thirsty to know God, the eunuch was reading the Scriptures, trying to understand their meaning when Philip came alongside his chariot. While Philip's religious upbringing might have dismissed this man from being worthy of God's grace and mercy, Philip acknowledged God's saving work was for all people, even Gentiles and eunuchs (Isaiah 56:3–8), by engaging him in a conversation.

2. Including Others (vv. 30–35)

While in Jerusalem, the eunuch would have been excluded from full participation in Temple worship (Deuteronomy 23:1). If so, the passage he was reading, Isaiah 53:7–8, would have resonated with him because it spoke about a person who was bruised, cut, humiliated, and would have no descendants. The eunuch wanted to know who this person was. Was it Isaiah, the Jewish people, or someone else? Philip used this passage and many others to share the Good News about Jesus Christ and God's redemptive plan of salvation for everyone. For someone who might have felt marginalized and excluded from full access to God's presence, this certainly would have been good news.

3. Rejoicing in God's Salvation (vv. 36–39)

In his discourse, Philip must have shared the importance of baptism in signifying a relationship with Christ and His body, the church. As soon as the Ethiopian saw a body of water, he wanted to be baptized. He confessed his faith in Christ, then went down to the water where Philip baptized him. The Ethiopian continued his journey rejoicing in his newfound salvation. Philip was sent by God to Azotus, an ancient Philistine capital, for another ethnic group that needed to hear the Gospel (v. 40). Philip carried out Jesus' commandment to take the Gospel everywhere and to everyone. His clear understanding of Scripture gave him the ability to share the Gospel with large groups. He also was comfortable sitting with one individual of a different race and stature to explain the love of God. This is a skill that all Christians can seek God's grace to attain. It's a gift worth rejoicing about, then and now.

Search the Scriptures

1. What is meant by the term "angel of the Lord" (Acts 8:26)?

2. What are some similarities between Christ's life and the passage the Ethiopian was reading (vv. 32–33)?

Discuss the Meaning

Sharing the Gospel often starts by listening and learning where others are in their understanding of Scripture, God, or core Bible teachings. List some principles for effective evangelism that Philip used in his encounter with the Ethiopian.

Lesson in Our Society

On our jobs, in our communities, or while shopping at the store, we will meet people from different nations, religions, and socioeconomic backgrounds. Many might dress differently, speak with an accent unlike ours, and have preferences unfamiliar to us. It's easy to ignore those we see as different, missing opportunities to share the Good News. We become Christ's hands and feet when we are willing to cross any boundary for the Gospel's sake.

Make It Happen

Often we are uncomfortable with people who are different from us. Go to a store or restaurant where people speak a different language than yours. Volunteer to teach an English as a Second Language class. Talk to a neighbor of a different ethnicity and ask him or her to tell about his or her country of origin.

Follow the Spirit

What God wants me to do:

_____

_____

_____

Remember Your Thoughts

Special insights I have learned:

_____

_____

_____

_____

More Light on the Text

Acts 8:26–39

26 And the angel of the Lord spake unto Philip, saying, Arise, and go toward the south unto the way that goeth down from Jerusalem unto Gaza, which is desert.

Angels play a critical role in the narrative of Luke and Acts (cf. Luke 1:11–20, 2:9–15; Acts 12:7–10). In this passage, an angel guides Philip away from heavy ministry activity toward the desert. It took an angel's authority to get Philip to leave such a fruitful ministry location in Samaria.

Because Jerusalem was built on a hill, any departure was considered "go[ing] down" from the city. Gaza was one of the five cities occupied by the Philistines in southwest Palestine from approximately 1200-600 BC. At the time Luke writes, it was on a caravan route leading to Egypt that someone traveling from Jerusalem to Ethiopia would naturally take. After Gaza was captured by Nebuchadnezzar and later the Greeks and Romans, it remained an important city of commerce due to its location near the sea.

27 And he arose and went: and, behold, a man of Ethiopia, an eunuch of great authority under Candace queen of the Ethiopians, who had the charge of all her treasure, and had come to Jerusalem for to worship.

Ethiopia bordered Egypt to the south and was known in the Bible as the ancient land of Cush (Genesis 2:13, 10:6; 1 Chronicles 1:8; Isaiah 11:11; Ezekiel 38:5). The Ethiopia referred to in antiquity was not modern Ethiopia, but the region now called Sudan.

Ethiopia was often among the Gentile nations that were named in the Bible as being subject to God's judgment for their corruption (Isaiah 20:3–5, 43:3; Ezekiel 30:1–9; Nahum 3:9; Zephaniah 2:11–12), and its people were among those foreigners who would be converted and acknowledge the true God of Israel. For example, Ethiopia figures prominently in a text of Isaiah concerning the restoration of the people (Isaiah 11:11–12; Zephaniah 3:10).

It was not uncommon for eunuchs to hold positions of importance in royal courts in the region. Some eunuchs were not castrated but simply set apart to serve the government. However, if they were castrated or maimed, this condition meant a rejection of full participation in the Jewish assembly (Deuteronomy 23:1). An emasculated male was physically blemished and in a permanent state of ritual impurity (Leviticus 21:17–21). But Isaiah prophesied that a time would come when "eunuchs [would] keep my sabbaths," "take hold of [his] covenant," and would be given a place in God's house (from Isaiah 56:4–5).

The Ethiopian eunuch held a high position in the Ethiopian government. He was in charge of the entire treasury of the Candace. According to ancient writers such as Pliny the Elder and Callisthenes, Candace, queen of the Ethiopians, was a dynastic rather than personal name; that is, it was used to refer to a royal line of queens over various generations.

The Ethiopian eunuch had come to Jerusalem to worship. The narrative does not indicate whether he was a Jew or a proselyte (i.e., a Gentile who has converted to Judaism). He may have been a God-fearing person (i.e., a non-Jew who, although sympathetic to Judaism, did not submit to circumcision or observe the Torah in its entirety, but did agree with the Jews' ethical monotheism and sometimes attended their synagogue services). If he was a eunuch not only by position but also physically, it would not have been possible for him to participate in worship in the Temple. In this regard, his status was like that of other foreigners who came to the Temple, in spite of being excluded from it.

28 Was returning, and sitting in his chariot read Esaias the prophet. 29 Then the Spirit said unto Philip, Go near, and join thyself to this chariot. 30 And Philip ran thither to him, and heard him read the prophet Esaias, and said, Understandest thou what thou readest?

The angel of the Lord delivered the original message. Here, the Spirit of the Lord further instructs Philip. The point is the same: God is directly guiding Philip. When the Spirit told Philip to go and join up with the chariot, he obeyed. As he came near, he heard the eunuch reading Isaiah. It was customary in the ancient world to read aloud, even when alone. This was especially the case with lengthy scrolls where there was no separation between words; they had to be read syllable by syllable to detect the word divisions. Philip asks the eunuch, "Do you understand what you are reading?" (v. 30). Philip's question derived from the conviction that the prophetic writings contained deeper meaning for the future.

31 And he said, How can I, except some man should guide me? And he desired Philip that he would come up and sit with him.

The eunuch admits he won't be able to understand the text unless someone "guide[s]" him. "Guide" (Gk. *hodegeo*, **ho-day-GEH-oh**) literally means to lead along a road (see Jesus' use of the term "blind leaders" and "blind leading the blind" in Matthew 15:14). Here "guide" gains the transferred sense of "leading" in

righteousness or wisdom similar to its use in passages such as Psalms 5:8, 73:24; John 16:13. Thus, the eunuch invited Philip to get in and sit with him under the assumption that he would be able to explain the passage in Isaiah. Traditionally, the Jews applied the concepts of suffering and humiliation in Isaiah 52:13–53:12 to the nation of Israel or the unrighteous Gentile nations. Thus, the idea of a suffering Messiah was not a common idea among Jews of the time. The deeper meaning of this passage, then, must have been unclear to the eunuch.

32 The place of the scripture which he read was this, He was led as a sheep to the slaughter; and like a lamb dumb before his shearer, so opened he not his mouth. 33 In his humiliation his judgment was taken away: and who shall declare his generation? for his life is taken from the earth.

The passage the eunuch is reading from is Isaiah 53:7–8. The Greek word for "humiliation" (*tapeinosis*, **ta-PAY-no-sees**) provides a possible allusion both to Luke's theme of humbling the haughty and exalting the humble (Luke 1:52, 3:5, 14:11, 18:14), and to the humility of Jesus becoming incarnate and finally His humiliation on the Cross (cf. Philippians 2:7–8).

34 And the eunuch answered Philip, and said, I pray thee, of whom speaketh the prophet this? of himself, or of some other man? 35 Then Philip opened his mouth, and began at the same scripture, and preached unto him Jesus.

The eunuch's question is the pertinent one. The traditional understanding of this passage did not address his deep spiritual hunger. After having been invited into the Ethiopian's chariot, Philip explained the Isaiah passage by beginning with the same text, and showed him that Jesus was the focus of the Scriptures. In a similar scene (Luke 24:13–35), the risen Jesus teaches the two on the road to Emmaus how to understand the Scriptures: "O fools, and slow of heart to believe all that the prophets have spoken: Ought not Christ to have suffered these things, and to enter into his glory? And beginning at Moses and all the prophets, he expounded unto them in all the scriptures the things concerning himself" (from vv. 25–27).

The Scripture passage in Isaiah that the eunuch was reading focused on the humiliation and exaltation of the Messiah. The passage's application to Jesus is clear, to His humiliation and exaltation in particular ("his judgment was taken away," v. 33). This type of interpretation of the prophecy of Isaiah is also seen in other New Testament Scriptures (Romans 10:16, John 12:38), so Isaiah is sometimes called the "fifth Gospel." It outlines many themes which are picked up in the New Testament, such as the coming of the Messiah and the establishment of His kingdom.

36 And as they went on their way, they came unto a certain water: and the eunuch said, See, here is water; what doth hinder me to be baptized? 37 And Philip said, If thou believest with all thine heart, thou mayest. And he answered and said, I believe that Jesus Christ is the Son of God. 38 And he commanded the chariot to stand still: and they went down both into the water, both Philip and the eunuch; and he baptized him.

After hearing the Scripture explained and being shown how it pointed to Jesus, the eunuch asked, "What doth hinder me to be baptized?" "Hinder" (Gk. *koluo*, **ko-LOO-oh**) is also used in Luke 11:52, where Jesus accuses the lawyers of preventing ("hindering") others from entering the kingdom of God. Because there was no reason for his exclusion from full inclusion among the followers of Jesus, the Ethiopian eunuch ordered the chariot to stop;

Philip and the eunuch both went down to the water, and Philip baptized him.

39 And when they were come up out of the water, the Spirit of the Lord caught away Philip, that the eunuch saw him no more: and he went on his way rejoicing.

The Old Testament often portrays the Spirit moving prophets around in this fashion, catching them up and away to another location instantly (cf. 1 Kings 18:12; 2 Kings 2:16; Ezekiel 11:24;).The Greek word used for caught away is *harpazo* (**har-POD-zo**), which also means "to snatch." After his conversion experience, the eunuch continued on his way "rejoicing" (Gk. *chairo*, **KIGH-row**), an appropriate response to salvation. Frequently in the books of Luke and Acts, joy or rejoicing is a noted response to God's work in the world (Luke 1:14, 6:23; Acts 5:41).

Say It Correctly

Eunuch. **YOO**-nik.
Candace. **CAN**-dis.

Daily Bible Readings

MONDAY
Jesus Heals the Canaanite Daughter
(Matthew 15:21–28)

TUESDAY
Good News for All Peoples
(Galatians 3:23–29)

WEDNESDAY
All Who Call Will Be Saved
(Romans 10:9–15)

THURSDAY
Persecution Scatters the Church
(Acts 8:1b–3)

FRIDAY
Converts in Samaria Baptized
(Acts 8:4–13)

SATURDAY
Simon Repents of Selfish Power Grab
(Acts 8:14–25)

SUNDAY
Called to Break Down Barriers
(Acts 8:26–39)

Notes

_____

_____

_____

_____

Teaching Tips

Words You Should Know

A. Vision (Acts 9:12) *horama* (Gk.)—That which is seen.

B. Gentiles (v. 15) *ethnos* (Gk.)— A group of people closely associated, usually by shared government; peoples not from Israel.

Teacher Preparation

Unifying Principle—Speaking Up. What would today's world look like if there were no preachers sharing the Word of Jesus Christ? Preachers in the time of Paul were being persecuted and killed. Christians were given a commission in Mark 16:15, "And he said unto them, Go ye into all the world, and preach the gospel to every creature." Who will answer the call?

A. Pray and ask God to help you encourage those who have been called to preach.

B. Think about how it would feel to be put in prison for preaching the Gospel.

C. Review the plan of salvation this week.

O—Open the Lesson

A. Warmly greet each student individually.

B. Open with prayer and include the Aim for Change.

C. Allow the students to discuss when they accepted Jesus Christ.

D. Have students talk about why we need preachers.

P—Present the Scriptures

A. Have students read the Focal Verses aloud.

B. Instruct students to read the In Focus story silently.

C. Have students use the At-A-Glance outline; The People, Places, and Times; Background; In Depth; and More Light On The Text sections to clarify the verses.

E—Explore the Meaning

A. Have students break up into small groups and discuss what preachers have to face in our society.

B. Have groups come back together and have students discuss what they discovered in their groups.

N—Next Steps for Application

A. Summarize the lesson.

B. Close with prayer and thank God for the role He gave to preachers.

Worship Guide

For the Superintendent or Teacher
Theme: Called to Preach
Song: "Available to You"
Devotional Reading: 1 Timothy 4:6–16

Called to Preach

Bible Background • ACTS 9:1–31
Printed Text • ACTS 9:10–20 | Devotional Reading • 1 TIMOTHY 4:6–16

Aim for Change

At the end of the lesson, we will: GRASP that God calls preachers and others to share His Word; FEEL the love that God has for the world; and ENCOURAGE those called to preach and share His Word.

In Focus

Rasaan didn't know if he should say something in this situation. His friend Benjamin had been going on and on about how he didn't believe in God. Benjamin said that if God were real, then He wouldn't allow all of the bad things in this world to happen. Rasaan had dealt with the same issues about a year before. Benjamin kept talking about God and getting angrier and angrier. Soon their other friends, Tasha and James, came by and began to shake their heads in agreement.

Rasaan didn't know the right words to say, but the night before, he was sure God had spoken to him and said that he was called to preach. So he prayed that the Holy Spirit would guide him. As soon as Benjamin took a breath, Rasaan began to challenge him. "Hold up, B. What about all the good you see in the world? How did all of the good get here?" Benjamin stopped and began to think. His eyebrows were furrowed, and his face looked puzzled.

Rasaan continued, "God created this world and said that it was good. It's us humans who have messed this world up." Tasha and James listened closely. "God even used the evil in this world to create His greatest good for humanity: the love and forgiveness that comes from Jesus Christ." Benjamin looked like he wanted to know more.

In today's lesson, we explore the call to preach. Have you ever experienced a time when God called you to preach, teach, or share His Word?

Keep in Mind

"And straightway he preached Christ in the synagogues, that he is the Son of God" (Acts 9:20).

"And straightway he preached Christ in the synagogues, that he is the Son of God" (Acts 9:20).

Focal Verses

KJV **Acts 9:10** And there was a certain disciple at Damascus, named Ananias; and to him said the Lord in a vision, Ananias. And he said, Behold, I am here, Lord.

11 And the Lord said unto him, Arise, and go into the street which is called Straight, and enquire in the house of Judas for one called Saul, of Tarsus: for, behold, he prayeth,

12 And hath seen in a vision a man named Ananias coming in, and putting his hand on him, that he might receive his sight.

13 Then Ananias answered, Lord, I have heard by many of this man, how much evil he hath done to thy saints at Jerusalem:

14 And here he hath authority from the chief priests to bind all that call on thy name.

15 But the Lord said unto him, Go thy way: for he is a chosen vessel unto me, to bear my name before the Gentiles, and kings, and the children of Israel:

16 For I will shew him how great things he must suffer for my name's sake.

17 And Ananias went his way, and entered into the house; and putting his hands on him said, Brother Saul, the Lord, even Jesus, that appeared unto thee in the way as thou camest, hath sent me, that thou mightest receive thy sight, and be filled with the Holy Ghost.

18 And immediately there fell from his eyes as it had been scales: and he received sight forthwith, and arose, and was baptized.

19 And when he had received meat, he was strengthened. Then was Saul certain days with the disciples which were at Damascus.

20 And straightway he preached Christ in the synagogues, that he is the Son of God.

NLT **Acts 9:10** Now there was a believer in Damascus named Ananias. The Lord spoke to him in a vision, calling, "Ananias!" "Yes, Lord!" he replied.

11 The Lord said, "Go over to Straight Street, to the house of Judas. When you get there, ask for a man from Tarsus named Saul. He is praying to me right now.

12 I have shown him a vision of a man named Ananias coming in and laying his hands on him so that he can see again."

13 "But Lord," exclaimed Ananias, "I've heard many people talk about the terrible things this man has done to the believers in Jerusalem!

14 And he is authorized by the leading priests to arrest everyone who calls upon your name."

15 But the Lord said, "Go, for Saul is my chosen instrument to take my message to the Gentiles and to kings, as well as to the people of Israel.

16 And I will show him how much he must suffer for my name's sake."

17 So Ananias went and found Saul. He laid his hands on him and said, "Brother Saul, the Lord Jesus, who appeared to you on the road, has sent me so that you may get your sight back and be filled with the Holy Spirit."

18 Instantly something like scales fell from Saul's eyes, and he regained his sight. Then he got up and was baptized.

19 Afterward he ate some food and regained his strength. Saul stayed with the believers in Damascus for a few days.

20 And immediately he began preaching about Jesus in the synagogues, saying, "He is indeed the Son of God!"

The People, Places, and Times

Saul/Paul. First known as Saul. His birthplace was Tarsus, the major city in Cilicia. Saul was born a citizen of Rome. Paul was his Roman name and his father was probably a Roman. He also had a Jewish name, "Saul." Saul saw the church in Jerusalem as a threat to the things so dear to him. Saul had an encounter with God on the road to Damascus, which changed his life forever. He became an apostle to the Gentiles.

Damascus. One of the old cities with extensive history of being ruled by many other political powers. Like many cities in the area, it has a turbulent history of being passed from one empire to the next and trying to gain independence. In Roman times, thousands of Jews lived there who worshiped in many synagogues.

Background

Saul showed harsh aggression against the disciples. He went to the high priest, Caiaphas, to obtain written permission giving him power to arrest those of "the Way." Saul was headed to Damascus, a city that had a great number of Jewish Christians. On his way, he saw a great light from heaven and fell to the ground. Then God spoke to him, asking Saul why he was persecuting Him. After his dialogue with Jesus, Saul was both trembling and astonished, and he asked Jesus another question: "What shall I do, Lord?" (Acts 22:10). Jesus told him to get up and go to the city, where he would be told what to do. The men with Saul were speechless because they heard the voice but could not see anyone. They led Saul into Damascus. There he was unable to see, eat, or drink for three days. God was working a mighty change for the church in those three days. Once He had Saul where He wanted him, He called His follower Ananias to do his part.

At-A-Glance

1. Ananias Assigned (Acts 9:10–12)
2. Ananias Answers (vv. 13–16)
3. Ananias Acts (vv. 17–20)

In Depth

1. Ananias Assigned (Acts 9:10–12)

Although Saul came to arrest Christians, he was waylaid on the road to Damascus and told to wait for a man he had never met. Verse 10 tells about a man named Ananias. The Lord speaks to him and gives his assignment: rise and go. Ananias would be the first to show Christian compassion to Saul of Tarsus. God told him what to do—find Saul and lay hands on him—and what would happen—Saul would see again. God will prepare the way for you to minister. In some cases, the Lord will give you assignments and tell you where, what to do, and what to expect. Be ready and say, "I am here, Lord."

2. Ananias Answers (vv. 13–16)

Ananias answered his call from the Lord, but when he heard the assignment, he experienced some apprehension. He told the Lord what he had heard about Saul and his actions against the saints in Jerusalem. He tells the Lord about Saul's authority. The Lord heard what Ananias said, but did not change His mind about the call He had given to him. God knows sometimes you will be fearful. He assures you He has a plan for you (Jeremiah 29:11). So, know that God already knows and cares about your concerns. God had work for Saul to do, and wanted Ananias to assist with the plan. God is calling you to help others get where they need to be. Sometimes it will not be about you, but about others.

3. Ananias Acts (vv. 17–20)

Ananias went to find Saul. Ananias was to lay hands on Saul in order for him to receive his sight. The Lord is looking for people who will act on what He has called them to do. Ananias did not do what he wanted, but instead what God asked him to do. Ananias had to change his attitude about Saul and not see him for what he was, but what he would become. Will you do what the Lord calls you to do? Opening Saul's eyes was not by Ananias' power; he was a vessel the Lord used to do His will. Only the Lord could restore sight to the blind. Now Saul would be able to preach the Word to others.

Search the Scriptures

1. What caused Ananias to obey the Lord's instructions to Him (Acts 9:11–12)?

2. Is Saul's calling to take Jesus' message and suffer for His name applicable to all people (vv. 13–14)?

Discuss the Meaning

Can God pick anyone He wants to work for Him? God has the plan and knows the outcome. Are you ready to submit to God's authority? Will you allow Him to depend on you to work His plan? Why or why not?

Lesson in Our Society

Many people are ready to do whatever it takes to get money and become famous. Some people would kill, steal, lie, or cheat. But where are the Christians today that will do anything to make sure the Gospel is preached? The things that are important to God should also be important to you. Christians need to be ready to give their lives so others can have eternal life.

Make It Happen

Ask God to articulate His calling for you. Be prepared to go beyond your comfort zone to reach those whom God sends to you.

Sometimes people appear mean and nasty, but it is up to you to see what God sees in them. Be the Christian that God can count on to do the hard things.

Follow the Spirit

What God wants me to do:

_____

_____

_____

Remember Your Thoughts

Special insights I have learned:

_____

_____

_____

_____

More Light on the Text
Acts 9:10–20

10 And there was a certain disciple at Damascus, named Ananias; and to him said the Lord in a vision, Ananias. And he said, Behold, I am here, Lord.

Ananias is identified as a "disciple" (Gk. *matthetes*, **mah-they-TASE**), and Paul later describes him as "a devout man according to the law" (Acts 22:12). The pattern of call and response is similar to that of Samuel's (1 Samuel 3:4, 10). Ananias' response contradicts the fear he later experiences.

11 And the Lord said unto him, Arise, and go into the street which is called

Straight, and enquire in the house of Judas for one called Saul, of Tarsus: for, behold, he prayeth, 12 And hath seen in a vision a man named Ananias coming in, and putting his hand on him, that he might receive his sight.

The vivid details in the message—the name of the street, the owner of the house, and the place of Saul's origin—are compatible with reliable historical traditions and good story-telling. We are never told about Saul's vision of Ananias from his own point of view, but only indirectly through the means of another vision.

13 Then Ananias answered, Lord, I have heard by many of this man, how much evil he hath done to thy saints at Jerusalem.

Ananias is allowed not only to voice his (understandable) reluctance to encounter such a dangerous person, but also to help the reader deal with the obvious objections. Human hesitancy is legitimate but can be overturned by the Lord's command. Ananias' version of events gives us a slightly different perspective. Luke uses the term "saints" or "holy ones" (Gk. *hagios*, HAH-gee-ose) with reference to God's people (Acts 9:41, 26:10). Later Paul frequently used this term for the same purpose (Romans 1:7, 15:25; 2 Corinthians 1:1, 8:4; Philippians 1:1).

14 And here he hath authority from the chief priests to bind all that call on thy name. 15 But the Lord said unto him, Go thy way: for he is a chosen vessel unto me, to bear my name before the Gentiles, and kings, and the children of Israel:

Saul is explicitly said to have "authority" (Gk. *exousia*, ek-sue-SEE-ah) from the chief priests. This word implies having both political authority and physical force needed to complete a task. The phrase "all that call on thy name" echoes the statement from Acts 2:21: "[W]hosoever shall call on the name of the Lord shall be saved." It also echoes the

statement of Genesis 4:26 as a foundational principle of what it means to trust in the Lord.

Literally, "a vessel" (*skeuos*, SKEW-oce) can mean any sort of instrument (1 Thessalonians 4:4; Hebrews 9:21), but can be especially used in the context of divine instrumentality (Romans 9:22–23; 2 Timothy 2:20–21). Since God speaks of Saul as His "vessel," Saul appropriately will "bear" the Lord's name, making him a useful instrument for God. The image is remarkably like that used by Paul himself speaking of carrying the glory of God "in earthen vessels" (2 Corinthians 4:7). The designation of Paul as "chosen," in turn, associates him with the description of Jesus as the "chosen of God" (Luke 23:35). This terminology has collectively been applied to all believers, although in this sense it speaks of Saul being chosen for his particular task.

16 For I will shew him how great things he must suffer for my name's sake. 17 And Ananias went his way, and entered into the house; and putting his hands on him said, Brother Saul, the Lord, even Jesus, that appeared unto thee in the way as thou camest, hath sent me, that thou mightest receive thy sight, and be filled with the Holy Ghost.

The use of the phrase "must suffer" places Saul directly and deliberately in the line of suffering prophets like Moses and Jesus (Luke 9:22, 24:26; Hebrews 11:24-26). To suffer for Jesus' name, in turn, means that he does so as Jesus' representative (Luke 6:22, 21:12, 17; Acts 5:41).

The gesture of laying on of hands symbolizes the transfer of power. It appears in sacrificial rites (Exodus 29:10, 19; Leviticus 1:4, 4:15, 16:21) and as part of the ordination of priests (Numbers 8:10). Even more impressive is the formal transfer of authority from Moses to Joshua through this gesture (Numbers 27:18–23). This passage makes clear that the gesture signified that the people should now obey Joshua just as they had Moses. In Luke, the laying on of hands appears as part of Jesus' healings, which Luke clearly understands as a communication of power (Luke 4:40, 13:13). In Acts, the gesture accompanies the bestowal of the Spirit in baptism (8:17, 19, 19:6), healing (28:8), and commissioning for ministry (13:3).

In the present case, the laying on of hands works both as a healing and a bestowal of the Holy Spirit. The use of Saul's name with the title "brother" and the physical gesture of touching recognize Saul's acceptance as a member of God's covenant people.

18 And immediately there fell from his eyes as it had been scales: and he received sight forthwith, and arose, and was baptized. 19 And when he had received meat, he was strengthened. Then was Saul certain days with the disciples which were at Damascus. 20 And straightway he preached Christ in the synagogues, that he is the Son of God.

The composition of what covered Saul's eyes is not clear. The text describes it as something like "scales" that fell from his eyes. This image of scales falling from one's eyes is so iconic that it has become a saying to figuratively describe enlightened understanding or illumination. In the words of the hymn "Amazing Grace," Saul "was blind but now can see." The light that blinded him physically paradoxically relieved him of his spiritual blindness. In Saul's case, his sight was associated with revelation.

After gaining his sight, Saul takes his first step of obedience in undergoing baptism. He now identifies with the Jesus who is worshiped by the believers he once persecuted. There would be no turning back now. He was now part of the body of Christ.

After being baptized, Saul ate and gained strength. Then he connected with the disciples in Damascus. Saul had the opportunity to experience the fellowship of other believers. The same believers whom he had authority to persecute were now welcoming him into their homes. Saul, who is also called Paul, was now a different man and preached that Jesus was the Son of God.

Say It Correctly

Ananias. a-nuh-**NIE**-us.
Tarsus. **TAR**-sus.

Daily Bible Readings

MONDAY
Saul's Mandate to Capture Believers
(Acts 22:1–15)

TUESDAY
A Trustworthy Preacher
(Titus 1:5–9)

WEDNESDAY
Saul Proclaims Jesus in Damascus
(Acts 9:21–25)

THURSDAY
Saul in Tarsus; Jerusalem at Peace
(Acts 9:26–31)

FRIDAY
Paralytic Aeneas Healed in Lydda
(Acts 9:32–35)

SATURDAY
Jesus Calls Saul on Damascus Road
(Acts 9:1–9)

SUNDAY
Called to Preach
(Acts 9:10–20)

Teaching Tips

Words You Should Know

A. Without gainsaying (Acts 10:29) *anantirretos* (Gk.)—Without raising any contradiction, objection, or denial.

B. Alms (v. 31) *eleemosune* (Gk.)—Practice of goodwill, charitable giving.

Teacher Preparation

Unifying Principle—Drawing In. Traditions and cultural understandings often shape our view of the world and other people in ways that limit our interactions. How do we overcome our limited understandings? Through a vision and the Spirit, Peter learned how and why to witness to Cornelius and his household.

A. Pray that your students will be able to interact with other people and cultures.

B. Ask God to give you people to pray for from other backgrounds.

C. Complete the companion lesson in the *Precepts For Living®* Study Guide.

O—Open the Lesson

A. Open by thanking God for people of other backgrounds.

B. Have students discuss other cultures and religions.

C. Share a time you felt like an outcast.

D. Ask about some traditions students or their families hold.

P—Present the Scriptures

A. Have a student read the Focal Verses.

B. Have students discuss the Background section.

C. Allow students time to reflect on the main Scriptures of the lesson.

E—Explore the Meaning

A. Break the class into two groups and have them create a skit about fitting in.

B. Review the students' answers to the Search the Scriptures questions.

N—Next Steps for Application

A. Review the Lesson in Our Society and Make It Happen sections. Commit to putting the lesson into practice in a particular way this week.

B. Summarize the lesson.

C. Close in prayer, thanking God for creating such diversity in the world and for welcoming all into the family of faith.

Worship Guide

For the Superintendent and Teacher
Theme: Called to Be Inclusive
Song: "Oh How He Loves You and Me"
Devotional Reading: Psalm 15

Called to Be Inclusive

Bible Background • ACTS 10
Printed Text • ACTS 10:19–33 | Devotional Reading • PSALM 15

Aim for Change

By the end of this lesson, we will: REVIEW the story of Cornelius' meeting with Peter; APPRECIATE that the Gospel is for everyone and should reach every person; and COMMIT to enhancing the church's cross-cultural mission outreach.

In Focus

Juan was a six-foot-four, three-hundred-pound man and was known as the meanest police officer in his precinct. While at the annual barbecue, he couldn't find Curtis, a retired sergeant from his precinct, who usually came every year. He asked around about Curtis, wondering why his friend would miss the event. One of Juan's co-workers told him that Curtis had recently discovered he had terminal cancer and was currently in the hospital. Juan rushed out of the barbecue to see his friend.

Upon entering the hospital room, Juan struggled for the right words to console Curtis: "Curtis, this is terrible. I didn't realize you were so sick." Curtis pulled on Juan's shirt sleeve and motioned for him to bend down closer so he could hear Curtis speak. In a hushed voice, Curtis said, "Juan, I'm fine. Do you know Christ?" Startled, Juan replied, "What do you mean, man? No, nobody ever told me anything about Christ. You just lie back and relax. Don't get yourself all worked up." But Curtis insisted that Juan listen to what he had to say and began to witness to Juan about Christ. On the ride home, Juan cried out loud. He realized that could be him lying in the hospital near death. The next week Juan accepted Christ as his Savior.

In our lesson today, we will observe how Peter became convinced of his call to share the Gospel with people different from him. Have you ever been challenged to share the Gospel with someone different from you?

Keep in Mind

"And he said unto them, Ye know how that it is an unlawful thing for a man that is a Jew to keep company, or come unto one of another nation; but God hath shewed me that I should not call any man common or unclean" (Acts 10:28).

"And he said unto them, Ye know how that it is an unlawful thing for a man that is a Jew to keep company, or come unto one of another nation; but God hath shewed me that I should not call any man common or unclean" (Acts 10:28).

Focal Verses

KJV **Acts 10:19** While Peter thought on the vision, the Spirit said unto him, Behold, three men seek thee.

20 Arise therefore, and get thee down, and go with them, doubting nothing: for I have sent them.

21 Then Peter went down to the men which were sent unto him from Cornelius; and said, Behold, I am he whom ye seek: what is the cause wherefore ye are come?

22 And they said, Cornelius the centurion, a just man, and one that feareth God, and of good report among all the nation of the Jews, was warned from God by an holy angel to send for thee into his house, and to hear words of thee.

23 Then called he them in, and lodged them. And on the morrow Peter went away with them, and certain brethren from Joppa accompanied him.

24 And the morrow after they entered into Caesarea. And Cornelius waited for them, and he had called together his kinsmen and near friends.

25 And as Peter was coming in, Cornelius met him, and fell down at his feet, and worshipped him.

26 But Peter took him up, saying, Stand up; I myself also am a man.

27 And as he talked with him, he went in, and found many that were come together.

28 And he said unto them, Ye know how that it is an unlawful thing for a man that is a Jew to keep company, or come unto one of another nation; but God hath shewed me that I should not call any man common or unclean.

29 Therefore came I unto you without gainsaying, as soon as I was sent for: I ask therefore for what intent ye have sent for me?

30 And Cornelius said, Four days ago I was fasting until this hour; and at the ninth hour I

NLT **Acts 10:19** Meanwhile, as Peter was puzzling over the vision, the Holy Spirit said to him, "Three men have come looking for you.

20 Get up, go downstairs, and go with them without hesitation. Don't worry, for I have sent them."

21 So Peter went down and said, "I'm the man you are looking for. Why have you come?"

22 They said, "We were sent by Cornelius, a Roman officer. He is a devout and God-fearing man, well respected by all the Jews. A holy angel instructed him to summon you to his house so that he can hear your message."

23 So Peter invited the men to stay for the night. The next day he went with them, accompanied by some of the brothers from Joppa.

24 They arrived in Caesarea the following day. Cornelius was waiting for them and had called together his relatives and close friends.

25 As Peter entered his home, Cornelius fell at his feet and worshiped him.

26 But Peter pulled him up and said, "Stand up! I'm a human being just like you!"

27 So they talked together and went inside, where many others were assembled.

28 Peter told them, "You know it is against our laws for a Jewish man to enter a Gentile home like this or to associate with you. But God has shown me that I should no longer think of anyone as impure or unclean.

29 So I came without objection as soon as I was sent for. Now tell me why you sent for me."

30 Cornelius replied, "Four days ago I was praying in my house about this same time, three o'clock in the afternoon. Suddenly, a man in dazzling clothes was standing in front of me.

31 He told me, 'Cornelius, your prayer has been heard, and your gifts to the poor have been noticed by God!

prayed in my house, and, behold, a man stood before me in bright clothing,

31 And said, Cornelius, thy prayer is heard, and thine alms are had in remembrance in the sight of God.

32 Send therefore to Joppa, and call hither Simon, whose surname is Peter; he is lodged in the house of one Simon a tanner by the sea side: who, when he cometh, shall speak unto thee.

33 Immediately therefore I sent to thee; and thou hast well done that thou art come. Now therefore are we all here present before God, to hear all things that are commanded thee of God.

32 Now send messengers to Joppa, and summon a man named Simon Peter. He is staying in the home of Simon, a tanner who lives near the seashore.'

33 So I sent for you at once, and it was good of you to come. Now we are all here, waiting before God to hear the message the Lord has given you."

The People, Places, and Times

Caesarea. Caesarea, also known as Caesarea Maritima ("of the sea") or Caesarea Augusta, (named after Caesar Augustus) was a port city located twenty five miles north of modern-day Tel Aviv. The city was built by Herod the Great sometime between 22 and 10 BC. Caesarea, known for being a very beautiful city, contained many marble structures. It was also known to contain a large hippodrome, a theater, a sewer system, and a sheltered harbor. Five main roads led into the city which, in addition to the harbor, made transporting people and goods easy.

Tanner. A tanner's job was to clean and prepare animal hides to be used as leather. They employed a process that stripped the remaining hair, fat, and flesh from the animal skins. As one might imagine, it was considered an undesirable job due to the sights and smells it entailed. Furthermore, tanners were considered ceremonially unclean by Jews, because they were in constant contact with dead animals. Tanneries were often required to operate outside of city walls or along the seashore.

Background

Jewish law was very specific about what Jews were to eat and how they were to conduct themselves. The dietary laws that Peter references are found in Leviticus 11. In their original form, these rules were meant to protect the people of Israel and set them apart as God's people. These laws and covenant agreements made it possible for sinful humanity to commune with God. However, through Christ's sacrifice, God had removed the barrier of sin between Himself and His people. Humanity could now commune with God through the acceptance of His Son, Jesus Christ (Romans 3:21–26). This transition from Law to grace through Christ created friction between Jewish Christians who still held to their Jewish culture and the new Gentile believers who hadn't converted to Judaism. Some Jewish believers expected that non-Jewish believers should fully convert to Judaism, taking on all Jewish customs and practices, including circumcision. This tension not only threatened the spread of the Gospel to Gentiles, but also the unity and potency of the Christian church.

Philip's encounter with an Ethiopian eunuch is recorded earlier in Acts 8:26–39. Salvation is given to the Ethiopian man based on his acceptance of Christ, not his cultural background. While this instance occurred in relative isolation, Peter's later interactions with Cornelius would be publicly known. This would represent a deep challenge to the beliefs of Jewish Christians, but it would also be an opportunity for them to finally understand God's will for the Gentiles.

At-A-Glance

1. Seeking (Acts 10:19–23)
2. Expecting (vv. 24–29)
3. Doing (vv. 30–33)

In Depth

1. Seeking (Acts 10:19–23)

Peter thinks about the vision he received from God. He then sees another vision from God as well as guidance about what is specifically going to happen. God tells him exactly how many men are seeking him, and He tells him what to do. The Holy Spirit directs Peter to go with the men and not doubt. Peter has no need to guess what is happening.

The Holy Spirit assures Peter that He sent the men for him. Peter goes with the men and lets them know that he is whom they are seeking. Peter also asks why these men are seeking him. They describe the type of man Cornelius the centurion is. Peter and Cornelius were both seekers. While Cornelius sought God, Peter sought a confirmation from God.

2. Expecting (vv. 24–29)

Peter does not go with the men right away. Because it is too late to take a journey, he invites them to stay at his house. Peter, the men, and others from Joppa travel to Caesarea. Cornelius is expecting Peter. This meeting is clearly important to Cornelius; he has his family and friends there. Cornelius wants to honor Peter, but goes too far by bowing down at his feet. God is the only one who should receive worship, which Peter makes very clear.

Breaking Jewish custom, Peter goes inside the Gentile Cornelius' house. Peter first gives a brief history of the Law and a confession that he believed in the Law. But God shows him that he should not call anything common or unclean. Peter does not deny what God had revealed to him. The reason he comes to Cornelius was the truth God gave to him in a vision. Peter knows now why he had been sought out.

3. Doing (vv. 30–33)

Cornelius begins to describe what took place four days before as he was fasting. He then proceeds to say that at the ninth hour he began to pray, and tells of the vision he saw. What he describes would be the common description of angels, as they appeared in the form of man. Luke, the writer of Acts, does not retell Cornelius' vision because it has already been told. Peter being asked to speak about Christ is a miraculous event. Peter's message is that everyone who believes is forgiven. It is very clear that the Gospel was sent to Israel and also the Gentiles. Peter now sees how God called Him to preach the Gospel to the Gentiles. They are now included in God's family.

Search the Scriptures

1. How did Peter know that it was God speaking to him and not his flesh or Satan (Acts 10:28–29)?

2. Why did Cornelius gather others to hear the message the Lord gave Peter (vv. 32–33)?

Discuss the Meaning

Peter had to be assured of the voice of God in order to embrace the Gentiles. What are the ways that we can be assured when God wants us to do something we thought was inappropriate or out of our comfort zone?

Lesson in Our Society

You are often accepted when you buy the name-brand clothes, the latest phone, and the coolest glasses. If you speak broken English or a language other than English, you might be talked about and feel like an outcast. It is so easy to make people feel like they are outcast or different. What can you do in your community to help those who are outsiders?

Make It Happen

How many people do you know who are not native English speakers and could have a speech barrier in communicating? Do you know people who have come to your church from a different background or culture? Do you see people who struggle to understand why they are not accepted? Remind yourself about when you felt isolated, and make it your goal to help the people you see in these areas.

Follow the Spirit

What God wants me to do:

_____

_____

_____

Remember Your Thoughts

Special insights I have learned:

_____

_____

_____

More Light on the Text

Acts 10:19–33

19 While Peter thought on the vision, the Spirit said unto him, Behold, three men seek thee. 20 Arise therefore, and get thee down, and go with them, doubting nothing: for I have sent them.

The vision was followed by a clear, divine command. Peter was not only addressed by the Spirit, but was also told that God was at work in this affair. The reader understands with Peter that it was not only the human Cornelius who sent the messengers; they were also sent by God.

Peter was commanded to go with the three men who would take him to the home of Cornelius. "Doubting" (Gk. *diakrino*, **dee-ah-KREE-no**) has a double nuance that is important for the development of the story. The Greek verb can mean to doubt or hesitate (James 1:6), but it can also mean to make a discrimination or choose between (James 2:4).

Peter, in effect, is told not to be filled with doubts about the events that will eventually lead him to understand how he is to not discriminate between people (see Acts 15:9).

21 Then Peter went down to the men which were sent unto him from Cornelius; and said, Behold, I am he whom ye seek: what is the cause wherefore ye are come? 22 And they said, Cornelius the centurion, a just man, and one that feareth God, and of good report among all the nation of the Jews, was warned from God by an holy angel

to send for thee into his house, and to hear words of thee.

Peter is expecting the men and is also ready to go with them. He wants to know why they have come. Peter seeks to understand God's intention, while also showing faith by letting them know that he is the one they are looking for. Their description of Cornelius is juxtaposed against his Gentile name. He is described as "one that feareth God" and a "just man." He was "just" (Gk. *dikaios*, **DI-kigh-os**), which means "to be righteous or observing of human and divine laws." He is also of "good report" or reputation among the Jewish people. The messengers here establish Cornelius' credibility as a God-fearer. On top of that, they also tell Peter that God sent an angel to Cornelius to invite Peter to his house.

23 Then called he them in, and lodged them. And on the morrow Peter went away with them, and certain brethren from Joppa accompanied him. 24 And the morrow after they entered into Caesarea. And Cornelius waited for them, and he had called together his kinsmen and near friends.

Peter enters into Caesarea, accompanied by Cornelius' messengers and some disciples from Joppa. This would prove valuable, as they would witness what happened during Peter's preaching. Cornelius, seeing the gravity and importance of the occasion, invites his kinsmen and his close friends into his house.

25 And as Peter was coming in, Cornelius met him, and fell down at his feet, and worshipped him. 26 But Peter took him up, saying, Stand up; I myself also am a man.

Cornelius is struck with awe at Peter's visit. From this, we can infer that Cornelius believed Peter to be a servant of Jesus, thinking that Peter could impart salvation. As a Gentile steeped in paganism, the centurion offers him the required obeisance as a semi-divine son of God who had supernatural powers. Cornelius' reaction is ingrained and reflexive. Peter refuses this worship and tells him to stand up because he was not a god, but a man.

27 And as he talked with him, he went in, and found many that were come together. 28 And he said unto them, Ye know how that it is an unlawful thing for a man that is a Jew to keep company, or come unto one of another nation; but God hath shewed me that I should not call any man common or unclean. 29 Therefore came I unto you without gainsaying, as soon as I was sent for: I ask therefore for what intent ye have sent for me?

Peter talks to Cornelius as they enter the home. When he sees all the people gathered together, he sees an opportunity to express what God has revealed to him. He reminds them of how his presence there is unlawful (Gk. *athemitos*, **ah-THEH-mee-tose**), or contrary to accepted morality or social convention. In the Jewish context, it means forbidden by the Torah. This is in contrast to unrighteous (Gk. *adikaios*, **ah-di-KIGH-os**), which referred to something illegal and wrong.

Peter states that it is contrary to Jewish Law for him to "keep company" with (Gk. *kollao*, **kol-LAH-oh**), or join together with, a Gentile or enter a Gentile's home. Such practices were not prohibited by Jewish Law. Instead, Peter is echoing a common Gentile perception at the time, which developed out of table fellowship issues. Some Jews avoided eating with Gentiles because certain foods were prohibited in the Mosaic Laws. Of particular issue was food or drink that had been offered as sacrifices and libations to Roman or other foreign gods. So, because it was culturally taboo to inquire about these matters, some Jews avoided eating and drinking with Gentiles all together.

Cornelius and his Gentile associates would have been surprised that Peter was willing to enter his home. Peter explains that not only could they fellowship together, but God even told Peter that he should no longer think of anyone or anything as unclean (i.e., unacceptable to God without ritual purification).

Peter says God has "shewed" (Gk. *deiknumi*, **DAKE-new-mi**) him that he should not call any man common or unclean. The word for "shewed" means to establish the validity of something with an explanation or example. Here the explanation or example is the vision Peter received on the rooftop of Simon the tanner (Acts 10:9–16). This vision is the basis for Peter's going to Cornelius' house without gainsaying (Gk. *anantirretos*, **ah-nahn-tee-RAY-tose**), or without objection.

30 And Cornelius said, Four days ago I was fasting until this hour; and at the ninth hour I prayed in my house, and, behold, a man stood before me in bright clothing,

Cornelius was a Roman centurion, or a captain in the army. Although the term *centurion* means "commander of a hundred," this was just a round estimate; centurions actually commanded only eighty men. The Bible says he was a "devout man," meaning he tried to be godly in his ways and gave God due reverence. His godliness was evident by his positive influence over all those in his house, and he gave money to the poor while praying to God "alway" (Acts 10:1–2).

Cornelius recounted to Peter how God had given him a vision to send for Peter. It was around the "ninth hour," which was 3 p.m., when Cornelius had a supernatural encounter. This mention of the ninth hour indicates Cornelius' adherence to the Jewish times of prayer, which corresponded with the morning and evening offerings in the Temple. Because of this Gentile man's efforts to know God, he was blessed with the vision, which would start a series of events leading to his salvation. The

man who wore "bright clothing" was identified as an angel in the actual vision (v. 3). God spoke to Peter and Cornelius in visions leading up to this fateful event to show them both how important and game-changing this encounter was going to be.

31 And said, Cornelius, thy prayer is heard, and thine alms are had in remembrance in the sight of God.

The angel in the vision let Cornelius know that God had been heard his prayer and his alms were remembered (Gk. *mnaomai*, **MNA-oh-my**), or God was mindful of them. The word for "alms" (Gk. *eleemosune*, **eh-leh-ay-mo-SUE-nay**) is literally "compassion or pity." In Judaism in the Roman period, almsgiving was considered comparable to righteousness. Luke intends to show that Cornelius was a righteous, God-fearing man and that God was answering his prayer. These God-fearers were Gentiles who were sympathetic to the Jewish religion, but not full, circumcised converts. They were not fully initiated as Jews but contributed to the synagogue and demonstrated piety.

32 Send therefore to Joppa, and call hither Simon, whose surname is Peter; he is lodged in the house of one Simon a tanner by the sea side: who, when he cometh, shall speak unto thee.

Cornelius recounted his vision to Peter in order to explain why he had sent for him. The angel, and therefore God, had instructed him to do so. The omniscient God knew exactly where Peter was, just as He knows where all of our blessings are. The blessing that God had for Cornelius was that Peter would "speak unto thee"—the gift of the Gospel message.

Peter was lodging with Simon the tanner (Gk. *burseus*, **bur-seh-US**). A tanner was a leatherworker who created leather from hides and skins by treating them with lime and juices and leaves from various plants. This leather was often used for making tents. The Tabernacle coverings were made from the skins of rams or goats and were more than likely created by tanners (Exodus 25:5, 26:14, 35:7, 23, 36:19). Due to the nature of their work, tanners were not regarded highly among Greeks, Romans, or Jews. In Judaism, they were not allowed to go to the Temple during pilgrimage season. They also had their own synagogues, due to the bad odor created by the process of curing the animal hides. The Jewish rabbinical tradition (collected in the Mishnah) even allows that in the case of Levirate marriage, the wife of the deceased brother of a tanner was allowed to remain a widow by saying, "I could endure your brother, but I cannot endure you." Due to the odors, tanners were required to do their work outside the city gates or by the sea side.

33 Immediately therefore I sent to thee; and thou hast well done that thou art come. Now therefore are we all here present before God, to hear all things that are commanded thee of God.

Cornelius tells Peter, "Immediately therefore I sent to thee." Now, he thanks Peter for coming. But what Cornelius did not know was that God gave Peter a vision just before his messengers arrived. And, in Peter's vision, God dealt with Peter's feelings of prejudice toward Gentiles, while telling him to go with Cornelius' messengers (Acts 10:9–20). God's mighty providence works everything out. God can weave a tapestry of people and events in our lives that appear unrelated or totally unknown to us. Then, when the time is right, God will pull all the pieces together so that we are blessed with something He has been preparing for us for some time.

Cornelius showed his love for his household by having everyone gather to hear Peter's words. His example shows that we should not be selfish with God's Word of salvation, but see to it that all of our relatives and friends get to hear it, whether it comes from us or someone else. We owe it to the ones we love to see that they get a chance to hear the Gospel and receive the gift of salvation through Jesus Christ our Lord.

Say It Correctly

Caesarea. seh-sa-**REE**-ah.
Joppa. **JAH**-puh.

Daily Bible Readings

MONDAY
The Servant's Mission to All Nations
(Isaiah 49:1–7)

TUESDAY
Jesus Heals a Centurion's Slave
(Luke 7:1–10)

WEDNESDAY
The Lord Meets Cornelius in a Vision
(Acts 10:1–8)

THURSDAY
People are Neither Unclean Nor Profane
(Acts 10:9–18)

FRIDAY
Gentiles Hear and Accept the Gospel
(Acts 10:34–43)

SATURDAY
Gentiles Included by the Spirit and Water
(Acts 10:44–48)

SUNDAY
Called to Be Inclusive
(Acts 10:19–33)

SEPTEMBER 2016 QUARTER

Aune, David E. *Word Biblical Commentary: Revelation 17-22. Vol 52C.* Nashville, TN: Thomas Nelson Publishers, 1982.

Archaeological Study Bible, New International Version: Imperial Cult. Grand Rapids, MI: Zondervan House Publishers, Inc., 2005. 1651

Archaeological Study Bible, New International Version: Josephus and the Fall of Jerusalem Temple Grand Rapids, MI: Zondervan House Publishers, Inc., 2005. 1606

Archaeological Study Bible, New International Version: Major Events in New Testament History in the First Century A.D. Grand Rapids, MI: Zondervan House Publishers, Inc., 2005. 2068

Archaeological Study Bible, New International Version: Patmos Rapids, MI: Zondervan House Publishers, Inc., 2005. 2046

Aune, David E. *Word Biblical Commentary: Revelation 17-22. Vol 52C.* Nashville, TN: Thomas Nelson Publishers, 1982.

Bromiley, Geoffrey W. *The International Standard Bible Encyclopedia.* Grand Rapids, Michigan: W.B. Eerdmans, 1979.

Hebrew-Greek Key Word Study Bible, King James Version. Chattanooga, TN: AMG Publishers, Inc., 1991.

Holy Bible: Holman Christian Standard Version. Nashville, TN: Holman Bible Publishers, 2010. 1625, 2117.

Holy Bible: Holman Christian Standard Version. Nashville, TN: Holman Bible Publishers, 2010. 2112-2115.

Holy Bible New Living Translation: Carol Streams, IL Tyndale House Foundation Pub. (1996, 2004, 2007)

Keck, Leander E. et al. *The New Interpreters Bible Commentary in Twelve Volumes, Hebrews- Revelation Vol. 12* Nashville, TN: Abingdon Press,1998.

Keener, Craig S., *The IVP Bible Background Commentary: New Testament.* Downers Grove, IL: Intervarsity Press, 1993.

Keener, Craig S., *The IVP Bible Background Commentary: New Testament.* Downers Grove, IL: Intervarsity Press, 1993. 757-763, 815-816.

Keener, Craig S., *The IVP Bible Background Commentary: New Testament.* Downers Grove, IL: Intervarsity Press, 1993.647-650, 678-679.

La Sor, Willian S.; Hubbard, David A; Bush, Frederic Wm. Old Testament Survey: The Message, Form, and Background of the Old Testament, Grand Rapids MI Eerdmans Publishing Co.1982 (Pg 277-312)

Radmacher, Earl D., ed. *Nelson Study Bible, New King James Version.* Nashville, TN: Thomas Nelson Publishers, 1997. 2094-2098.

Radmacher, Earl D., ed. *Nelson Study Bible, New King James Version.* Nashville, TN: Thomas Nelson Publishers, 1997. 2198-2199.

Rendtorff. Rolf, *The Old Testament, An Introduction.* Philadelphia, Fortress Press, 1991, pp. 190-192.

Ryrie, Charles C., *Ryrie Study Bible, New International Version.* Chicago, IL: Moody Press. 1986. 1681-1682.

Ryrie, Charles C., *Ryrie Study Bible, New International Version.* Chicago, IL: Moody Press. 1986. 1744-1745.

Soggin, J. Alberto, *Introduction to the Old Testament From Its Origins to the closing of the Alexandrian Canon.* Louisville, KY, Westminster/John Knox Press, 1987, p. 395.

Unger, Merrill F., *The New Unger's Bible Dictionary.* Chicago, IL: Moody Press, 1988.

Unger, Merrill F., *The New Unger's Bible Dictionary.* Chicago, IL: Moody Press, 1988. 547-548.

Walton, John H. General Ed. *Zondervan Illustrated Bible Background Commentary Vol 4 (Isaiah, Jeremiah, Lamentations, Ezekiel, David)* Grand Rapids, Zondervan Pub 2009 Pg. 56-57

Walvoord, John F., and Roy B. Zuck, eds. The Bible Knowledge Commentary: New Testament. USA: Victor Books, SP Publications, Inc., 1983. 777, 809-810.

Walvoord, John F., and Roy B. Zuck, eds. The Bible Knowledge Commentary: New Testament. USA: Victor Books, SP Publications, Inc., 1983. 925-927, 983-985.

Watson, John H; Matthews, Victor H; Chavalas, Mark W.: *The IVP Bible Background Commentary: Old Testament.* Downers Grove IL (2013)

Young, Edward, J., *The Book of Isaiah: The English Text, with Introduction, Exposition, and Notes (Volume 1 Chapters 1-18).* Grand Rapids, Eerdmans Publishing Company, (1983) pgs. 378-387)

Youngblood, Ronald F., ed. *Nelson's New Illustrated Bible Dictionary.* Nashville, TN: Thomas Nelson Publishers, 1995. 55, 1035-1039, 551-553.

Youngblood, Ronald F., ed. *Nelson's New Illustrated Bible Dictionary.* Nashville, TN: Thomas Nelson Publishers, 1995.

Zodhiates, Spiros, Warren, Baker. *Hebrew-Greek Key Word Study Bible (KJV)* Chattanooga, TN AMG International, Inc Second Revised Edition 1984, 1990, 2008

Zodhiates, Spiros, *Hebrew-Greek Key Word Study Bible (Key Insights into God's Word).* King James Version Second Revised Version. Chattanooga, AMG Publishers, 1984, 1990, 2008

Zondervan Study Bible, New International Version. Grand Rapids, MI: Zondervan Publishers, 2002. 1913-1914.

Zondervan Study Bible, New International Version. Grand Rapids, MI: Zondervan Publishers, 2002. 1988-1989.

DECEMBER 2016 QUARTER

"Lead, Led." *Vines Complete Expository Dictionary of Old and New Testament Words.* Merrill F. Unger and William White, editors. Nashville, TN: Thomas Nelson Publishers, 1996.

Alter, Robert. *The Book of Psalms: A Translation with Commentary.* New York, NY : W.W. Norton & Company., 2007.

Arrington, French L., and Roger Stronstad, eds. *Life in the Spirit New Testament Commentary.* Grand Rapids, MI: Zondervan, 1999. 398-399.

Barclay, William. *The Daily Study Bible Series: The Gospel of Luke.* Philadelphia, PA: The Westminster Press, 1975. 14-16

Brueggemann, Walter. *Psalms.* New York, NY: Cambridge University Press, 2013

Carson, D. A., R. T. France, J. A. Motyer, G. J. Wenham, Eds. *New Bible Commentary* Downer's Grove, IL: Intervarsity Press, 1994.

Craddock, Fred B. *Luke: Interpretation, A Bible Commentary for Preaching and Teaching.* Edited by James Luther Mays, et al. Louisville, KY: John Knox Press, 1990.

Dahood, S. J. *The Anchor Bible: Psalms11.* Garden City, NY : Doubleday & Company., 1968.

Elwell, Walter A. and Comfort, Philip W., *Tyndale Bible Dictionary: Tyndale House Publishers,* Wheaton, IL: 2001, 828

Ferguson, Everett et al. ed. *Encyclopedia of Early Christianity* 2nd ed. New York, NY: Garland Publishing Inc, 1998.

Gaebelein, Frank E., ed. *The Expositor's Bible Commentary Vol. 8*. Grand Rapids, MI: Zondervan, 1984. 835-836

Goldingay, John. Baker *Commentary on the Old Testament. Vol. 3, Psalms 90-150*.Grand Rapids, MI: Baker Academic, 2006.

Guthrie, Donald. *Tyndale New Testament Commentaries: Letter to the Hebrews*. Grand Rapids, MI: Eerdmans, 1983. 216.

Hay, Lewis S. *"Galatians 5: 13 – 26." Interpretation.* 33 no. 1 Jan. 1979, p. 67 – 72.

Hays, Richard B. *"Letter of Paul to the Galatians." The Harper Collins Study Bible*, New Revised Standard Version. Harold W. Attridge, ed. New York, NY.: Harper Collins Publishers, 2006.

Henry, Matthew. *"Galatians 5."* Complete Bible Commentary Online. http://www.biblestudytools.com/commentaries/matthew-henry-complete/galatians/5.html, accessed on 19 June 2015.

Henry, Matthew. *"Galatians 6."* Complete Bible Commentary Online. http://www.biblestudytools.com/commentaries/matthew-henry-complete/galatians/6.html, accessed on 29 June 2015.

Holman Pocket Bible Dictionary. Nashville, TN: Holman Bible Publishers, 2004. 762-764, 773.

Johnson, Luke Timothy. *Hebrews: A Commentary*. The New Testament Library. Louisville, KY: Westminster John Knox Press, 2006. 259.

Keener, Craig S. *The IVP Bible Background Commentary: New Testament*. Downers Grove, IL: InterVarsity Press, 1993.

Keener, Craig S. *The IVP Bible Background Commentary: New Testament*. Downers Grove, IL: InterVarsity Press, 1993. 647-650, 670-671.

Lane, William L. *Hebrews 9-13. Word Biblical Commentary*, Vol. 47B. Dallas, TX: Word Inc., 1991.

Life Application Study Bible, New International Version. Wheaton, IL: Tyndale House Publishers, Inc., 1997. 2154-2155, 2170-2172.

NIV Study Bible, 10th Anniversary Edition, Grand Rapids, Mich.: Zondervan, 1995. 1529-1530.

Padgett, Alan G. *"'Walk in the Spirit': Preaching for Spiritual Growth (Gal. 5: 13 – 6:2." World & World*. Vol. 27, Number 3 Summer 2007, p. 342 – 345.

Painter, John. *"The Fruit of the Spirit is Love: Galatians 5: 22 – 23, an Exegetical Note."* Journal of Theology for Southern Africa. 5 Dec. 1973, p. 57 – 59.

Radmacher, Earl D., ed. *Nelson's New Illustrated Bible Commentary: Spreading the Light of God's Word into Your Life*. Nashville, TN: Thomas Nelson Publishers, 1999. 1648-1653.

Ross, Allen P. *A Commentary on The Psalms. Vol 2* (42-89). Grand Rapids, MI: Kregel Publications, 2013.

Ryken, Leland, ed. *"Farming." Dictionary of Biblical Imagery*. Downers Grove, IL: InterVarsity Press, 2010.

Sakenfield, Katharine Dobb, ed. *New Interpreter's Dictionary of the Bible Me-R Vol. IV.* : Nashville, TN: Abingdon Press, 2009.

Spence, H. D. M., and Joseph S. Exell, eds. *The Pulpit Commentary Vol. 16*. Grand Rapids, MI: Eerdmans Publishing Company, 1980. 22-23

Testament. Grand Rapids, MI: Eerdmans. Reprint, 1988.

The New Interpreter's Bible, General Articles & Introduction, Commentary, & Reflections for each Book of the Bible Including the Apocryphal/Deuterocanonical Books, Volume IV. Nashville, TN: Abingdon Press, 1996, 809-811

Vine, W.E. *"Burden." Vines Complete Expository Dictionary of Old and New Testament Words*. Merrill F. Unger and William White, editors. Nashville, TN: Thomas Nelson Publishers, 1996.

Vine, W.E. *Expository Dictionary of New Testament Words*. Grand Rapids, MI: Zondervan Publishing House, 1981.

Waltner, James H. *Believers Church Bible Commentary* Nelson's. Scottdale, PA: Herald Press, 2006.

Wilson, Gerald H. *The NIV Application Commentary. Psalms Volume 1*. Grand Rapids, MI: Zondervan, 2002.

MARCH 2017 QUARTER

Allen, Leslie C., *The Books of Joel, Obadiah, Jonah and Micah, NICOT*. Grand Rapids: Wm. B. Eerdmans Publishing Co., 1976.

Henry, Matthew. *Matthew Henry's Commentary on the Whole Bible: Complete and Unabridged in One Volume*. Peabody: Hendrickson, 1994.

Jamieson, Robert, A. R. Fausset, and David Brown. *Commentary Critical and Explanatory on the Whole Bible*. Oak Harbor, WA: Logos Research Systems, Inc., 1997.

Knowles, Andrew. *The Bible Guide. 1st Augsburg books ed.* Minneapolis, MN: Augsburg, 2001.

Richards, Larry, and Lawrence O. Richards. *The Teacher's Commentary*. Wheaton, IL: Victor Books, 1987.

Paschall, Franklin H., and Herschel H. Hobbs, eds. *The Teacher's Bible Commentary*. Nashville: Broadman and Holman Publishers, 1972.

Powell, Mark A., *Introducing the New Testament*. Grand Rapids, MI: Baker Academic, 2009. 494-495.

Richards, Lawrence O. *The Bible Reader's Companion. Electronic ed.* Wheaton: Victor Books, 1991.

Walvoord, John F., and Roy B. Zuck, Dallas Theological Seminary. *The Bible Knowledge Commentary: An Exposition of the Scriptures*. Wheaton, IL: Victor Books, 1985.

Wiersbe, Warren W. *The Bible Exposition Commentary*. Wheaton, IL: Victor Books, 1996.

JUNE 2017 QUARTER

Block, Daniel I. *The New American Commentary: Judges, Ruth*. Nashville, TN: B&H Publishing Group, 1999. 391-406, 421-424.

Briggs, Philip. *Ethiopia, Fourth Edition*. Guilford, CT: The Globe Pequot Press, 2005, pp. 26-27.

Bruce, F. F. *The Book of Acts, Revised Edition*. Grand Rapids, MI: Eerdmans. Reprint, 1988, pp. 119-125.

Boling, Robert G. *"The Book of Judges."* In Anchor Bible Dictionary, vol. 3. David Noel Freedman, ed. New York, NY: Doubleday, 1992. 1107-1116.

Cate, Robert L. *Layman's Bible Commentary: Exodus*. Nashville, TN: Broadman Press, 1979. 29-30.

Covey, Stephen R. *Seven Habits of Highly Effective People*. New York, Simon and Schuster. 1989.

Crenshaw, James L. *"Samson." In Anchor Bible Dictionary, Vol. 5*. David Noel Freedman, ed. New York, NY: Doubleday, 1992. 950-954.

Davis, John J. *Moses and the God's of Egypt: Studies in Exodus.* Grand Rapids, MI: Baker Book House, 1986. 67-73.

Drane, John. *Nelson's Illustrated Encyclopedia of the Bible.* Thomas Nelson, Inc. Nashville, TN, 1998. 249

Fensham, F. C. *"In the Old Testament"* In the New Bible Dictionary. *3rd Edition.* Leicester, England; Downers Grove, IL: InterVarsity Press, 1996. 1109.

Jamieson, R., A. R. Fausset, and D. Brown. *Commentary Critical and Explanatory on the Whole Bible.* Oak Harbor, WA: Logos Research Systems, Inc, 1997. 167.

Janzen, J. Gerald. *Exodus.* Louisville, KY: Westminster John Knox, 1997.

Kent, Dan G. *Layman's Bible Book Commentary: Joshua, Judges, Ruth, Vol 4.* Nashville, TN: Broadman Press, 1980.

Lockyer, Herbert. *All the Women of the Bible,* Zondervan Publishing, Grand Rapids, MI, 1988

Montonini, M. D. *"Theophany"* In The Lexham Bible Dictionary. John D. Barry, ed. Bellingham, WA: Lexham Press, 2015.

Niditch, Susan. *Judges: A Commentary.* Louisville, KY: Westminster John Knox Press, 2008.

Radmacher, Earl D., ed. *Nelson's New Illustrated Bible Commentary: Spreading the Light of God's Word into Your Life.* Nashville, TN: Thomas Nelson Publishers, 1999. 1648-1653.

Stuart, Douglas K. *The New American Commentary: Exodus.* Nashville, TN: B&H Publishing, 2006. 108-119.

Wells, Bruce. *"Exodus" In Zondervan Illustrated Bible Background Commentary: Genesis, Exodus, Leviticus, Numbers, Deuteronomy.* John H. Walton, ed. Grand Rapids, MI: Zondervan, 2009. 172-175.

Wright, G. E. *"Book of Exodus" In The Interpreters Dictionary of the Bible: An Illustrated Encyclopedia.* George Arthur Buttrick, ed. New York, NY: Abingdon Press, 1962.

Younger, Lawson K. *The NIV Application Commentary: Judges/Ruth.* Grand Rapids, MI: Zondervan, 2002. 285- 289, 293-295.

A

Abomination: A foul and detestable thing

Affliction: Anguish, burden, persecution, tribulation, or trouble

Angel: A messenger of God, not eternal or all-knowing; specific types include cherubim and seraphim

Ascension: Raising up in authority or physical place. Can especially refer to the event forty days after Jesus' death, burial, and Resurrection, when He went returned to heaven to sit at the right hand of the Father (Acts 1:9–11)

Atone: To propitiate, satisfy the demands of an offended holy God; or reconcile to a holy God after sin

B

Baptize: To dip, immerse, or submerge

Blameless: Irreproachable, faultless, flawless

Blessedness: Happiness, joy, or prosperity, to be well spoken of by God or others

Bless the Lord: To bend the knee in praise to God

Blood of the Lamb: The blood that Jesus shed on the Cross that redeems humanity

Bowels: To ancient Middle Easterners, the place of emotion, distress, or love

C

Called by God: Appointed or commissioned to fulfill a task

Charge: Admonish, order, command

Chosen: To be approved and selected by God

Christ: The Anointed One, The expected Messiah the Jews hoped for and whom Christians believe came as Jesus of Nazareth

Commandments: God's mandates; the entire body of Laws issued by God through Moses for Israel

Conduct: Manner of living

Confess: To acknowledge or fully agree

Consider: To determine or make out

Covenant: An agreement or promise between God and humanity based on God's character, strength, and grace

Crucifixion: A method of Roman execution in which a criminal was hung on a cross

D

Decalogue: From "ten words" in Greek; the Ten Commandments

Desolation: The state of being deserted or uninhabited

Disciples: Learners, students, followers

Dominion: Rule or reign

Dwelling place: A person's refuge or home

E

El: The Hebrew word for "god" or "mighty one"

Evil: Bad, unpleasant, or displeasing things

Evil doer: A malefactor, wrongdoer, criminal, troublemaker

Evil spirits: Messengers and ministers of the devil

Exalt: To raise up to the highest degree possible

Exhortation: Giving someone motivation to change his or her behavior either by rebuke or encouragement

F

Faithfulness: Steadfastness, steadiness

Fear of the Lord: Reverence or awe of who God is resulting in obedience to Him and abstaining from evil

G

Glory: Splendor, unparalleled honor, dignity, or distinction; praise and worship

God's Bride: The church

God's own hand: God's strength, power

Gospel: The Good News of Jesus the Messiah's arrival and founding of His kingdom

Graven image: An idol cut (often from stone, wood, or metal) and worshiped as a god

Great Tribulation: A time of great suffering that has not been experienced since the world began (Matthew 24:21, Revelation 7:14)

H

Hallowed: Consecrated, dedicated, or set apart

Hear: Listen to, yield to, or obey

Hearken: Pay attention to, give attention to

Heart: The figurative place of emotion and passion

Heathens: The Gentiles, all those who are not a part of the people of God

Holy: Anything consecrated and set aside for sacred use; set apart from sin

Honor: To revere or value

Host: An army or vast number

I

Idolatry: The worship of anything other than God

Infidel: One who is unfaithful, unbelieving, and not to be trusted

Iniquity: Perversity, depravity, guilt, sin

J

Just: Righteous, that which is right and fair
Justice: Righteousness in government

K

Kingdom of Christ: The rule and reign of Christ as King both now and in the age to come

L

Law: Either the Mosiac Law or any human law; synonyms include commandments, ordinances, statutes, legal regulations, authoritative instructions, and teachings
Logos (LOG-os): (Gk.) Word; the Word of God, either the Bible or Jesus

M

Manna: Food from heaven baked into a kind of bread, which God miraculously gave to the Israelites in the wilderness
Messiah: The Anointed One
Minister: A servant, an attendant, one who executes the commands of another
Mosiac Law: The law passed down by Moses from God to the Hebrew people at Mt. Sinai

O

Omnipotent: All powerful
Omnipresent: All present, being everywhere
Omniscient: All knowing
Ordained: Established and founded by God; founded, fixed, or appointed

P

Parousia (par-oo-SEE-ah): (Gk.) presence; Christ's Second Coming
Peace: Wholeness, quietness, contentment, health, prosperity; more than an absence of conflict or problems, but every part of life being blessed
Pentateuch: The first five books of the Old Testament
Power: Boldness, might, or strength, especially God's
Prophets: People filled with the Spirit of God and under the authority and command of God, who pleaded His cause and urged humanity to be saved
Profit: To gain or benefit

Prosper: To succeed, especially in spiritual things; to move forward or succeed in one's efforts
Proved: Examined, tested, tried
Psalm: A piece of music or a melody, especially one dedicated to God or a god
Purity: Sinlessness, without blemish spiritually

R

Ransom: To buy back or pay a price for a person, buying their freedom
Redeem: To ransom or purchase
Refuge: A shelter from rain, storm, or danger; stronghold or fortress; a place to run to and be secure when the enemy threatens
Repent: To turn back from sin and turn to God in faith
Righteous: To be declared not guilty
Righteousness: Justness, rightness, especially God's, which He works as a gift in His people; the right way to live as opposed to a lifestyle that treats others unfairly or unjustly

S

Sabbath: From "ceasing (from work)" in Hebrew; the day set aside to worship God
Sanctuary: The holy place, either in the tabernacle or the temple
Salvation: Rescue, safety, or deliverance, especially from eternal punishment
Satan: A fallen angel who is opposed to God and His people
Savior: Defender, rescuer, or deliverer, A term applied to Christ as the rescuer of those who are in bondage to sin and death
Scribes: Secretaries, recorders, men skilled in the Law during Jesus' day
Selah (SEE-lah): (Heb.) A pause in singing to allow for an instrumental musical interlude or silent meditation
Septuagint: "Seventy" in Latin; the Greek translation of the Hebrew Old Testament made by 70 Jewish scholars beginning in the third century BC.
Servant: A slave, subject, or worshiper
Shalom (sha-LOME): (Heb.) Peace, prosperity, blessing
Shekinah Glory: The awesome presence of the Lord; His honor, fame, and reputation
Shofar (sho-FAR): (Heb.) A ram's horn; commonly used in celebration, as well as in signaling armies or large groups of people in

civil assembly

Soul: The immaterial part of a person (what leaves the body after death), or the whole being, the self, one's life

Stiffnecked: Obstinate and difficult

Strengthen: To secure, make firm

Strive: To struggle, to exert oneself

Supplication: Seeking, asking, entreating, pleading, imploring, or petitioning

T

Tabernacle: A tent; the name of the portable temple constructed by Moses and the people of Israel

Tetragrammaton: YHWH; the four consonants of God's name, as the Jews would often write it

Torah: (Heb.) Law, instrument, or direction; the first five books of the Old Testament

Transfiguration: A change or transformation. Often refers to Jesus' transformation while on the Mount of Olives with His disciples Peter, James, and John, when His face shone like the sun and His clothing was white as snow (Matthew 17:2; Mark 9:2; Luke 9:29)

Transgression: Sin, rebellion, breaking God's Law

Try: In the sense of a test: refined or purified

Trumpet: A ram's horn or simple metal tube used in celebration as well as in signaling armies or large groups of people in civil assembly

V

Vanity (vain): A waste, a worthless thing, or simply emptiness

W

Wisdom: Prudence, an understanding of ethics

Woe: Grief or sorrow

Worship: Bow down deeply, show obedience and reverence

Wrath: Burning anger, rage

Y

Yahweh: God's name, often spelled with consonants only (see Tetragrammaton)

Notes

Notes